WITHDR
University
Illinois L
at Urbana-Champaign

D0947278

The person charging this m...
spo...
L...

HUMAN LAW AND HUMAN JUSTICE

This is one of the successor books to the Author's
The Province and Function of Law (1946)
*which was awarded the Royal Society of Arts
and Royal College of Physicians Swiney Prize
for General Jurisprudence for the period
1954-1964*

SU

HUMAN LAW
AND
HUMAN JUSTICE

BY

JULIUS STONE

STANFORD, CALIFORNIA
STANFORD UNIVERSITY PRESS
1965

Published in the United States by Stanford University Press,
of Stanford, California.

Published in Australia by Maitland Publications Pty. Ltd.,
of 65 York Street, Sydney, New South Wales.

Published in Great Britain by Stevens & Sons Limited,
of 11 New Fetter Lane, London, E.C.4.

Published in India by N. M. Tripathi Private Limited,
of Bombay, India.

© BY JULIUS STONE

Set in Times Roman by Northern Line Printing Co. Pty. Ltd., Sydney, Australia.
Registered in Australia for transmission by post as a book.

340.1
St 7h
Cop. 4

To

ZENA SACHS

ACKNOWLEDGMENTS

The major debts arising from this book, as from *Legal System and Lawyers' Reasonings*, are to my Sydney colleague, Dr. Ilmar Tammelo, to my Senior Research Assistant, Mr. Anthony Blackshield, LL.B.(Sydney), and to my Graduate Assistant, Miss Zena Sachs, LL.B.(Sydney).

With her work on this book, Miss Sachs completes a score of years devoted to publications in jurisprudence and international law. During these years, virtually all that came from my pen benefited before publication from her care and judgment. The dedication to her pays tribute to this long record of services to juristic scholarship. Mr. Blackshield provided provocative and fruitful suggestions and materials for the sections on the medieval transmission of notions of justice in Chapter 2, and for a number of sections of Chapters 1, 10 and 11; and he read and criticised the rest of the MS. Dr. Tammelo (along with Professor Jaan Puhvel of the University of California at Berkeley) contributed much on Greek mythology for §2 of Chapter 1. He much enriched (from his knowledge of Radbruch's later years) the account of that great scholar's ideas in Chapter 8, and of the natural law theorisings in the early sections of Chapter 7; and he also read and criticised several other Chapters.

There are other more specific debts. Father P. M. Farrell, S.J., kindly read an earlier draft of Chapter 7 (on Revived Natural Law), and prepared deeply learned criticisms touching my treatment of Aquinas' *Summa Theologica*. This fended off errors, and added insights, contributing thus to our shared intent to reopen secular dialogue with the Thomist tradition. For many useful illustrations from talmudic law I am indebted to Rabbi L. Singer, now of the Bar of New South Wales, and also to my son, Michael Stone, B.A.(Melbourne), Knox Fellow at Harvard University, and Kent Fellow, who read the relevant sections of Chapter 1 and made useful criticisms and suggestions. My former student, David Hodgson, LL.B. (Sydney), offered valuable criticisms of my critique of hedonist utilitarianism. Mr. Bruce McDonald, LL.B.(Sydney), also a former student, prepared some materials for §10 of Chapter 6. Professor Gyan Sharma, Principal of the University Law College, Jaipur, University of Rajasthan, worked with me on the applicability of any "interest" theory of justice to countries like India, relevant to §10 of Chapter 9. Mr. R. C. L. Moffat, M.A., LL.B. (Southern Methodist University), besides assisting Mr. Blackshield in solving residual queries, proposed the brief but important §9 of Chapter 1. Dr. Otto Bondy, Dr.Jur.(Vienna), made helpful criticisms and proposals for revision of the difficult §§1-2 of Chapter 3. Mr. H. E. Strakosch, M.A.(Sydney), contributed valuable materials on post-medieval natural law for Chapter 2. My former Research Assistant, Dr. Giovanni Tarello, of the Faculty of the University of Genoa, prepared valuable preliminary materials, a number of which were used in Chapters 1-2. Chapter 10, in its treatment of linguistic inquiries about justice, owes much to an earlier joint study by Tarello and myself. Discussion of a draft of the concluding Chapter 11, at sessions of the Australian Society of Legal Philosophy, saved me (I am sure) from much unclarity and error. Of course, such criticisms, proposals and materials were not always accepted, or used in the way intended, and I have myself to bear responsibility for what is finally included here.

A number of able graduates of our Faculty at Sydney assisted me in the massive task of scanning for relevant data recent output of major law journals, as well as large compendious works such as Hart-Sacks, *Legal Process*, and Simpson-Stone, *Law and Society*. Debts of this kind are owed to D. G. Hill, B.A., LL.B.(Sydney), LL.M.(Harvard), G. LaPaine, LL.B.(Sydney), E. Solomon, LL.B.(Sydney), LL.M.(Harvard), and J. D. Traill, LL.B.(Sydney). Mr. D. E. Harding, B.A., LL.B.(Sydney), LL.M. (University of California), after taking over duties as my Senior Research Assistant, assisted in the final stages of checking queries and preparing the Index of Subjects.

I am also grateful to Miss Jane Asprey and Miss Dinah Pitt for their faithful and painstaking work in the final stages of typing the manuscript, and their work on the Bibliographical Index and the Indexes of Cases and Statutes.

For their efficiency and helpfulness in bringing to my desk some of the wide range of literature which has been consulted I wish also to express deep appreciation to our acting Law School Librarian, Miss Anne Tobin, B.A., and her assistants.

During the whole span of years since the late 'forties, when work on the present project began, it has benefited from assistance afforded by the Research Committee which advises the Vice-Chancellor of the University of Sydney, from the understanding which the Committee and the Vice-Chancellor have constantly shown of its importance, and from the patience with which they have accepted delays imposed by my desire that the final outcome should be as good as it lay in me to make it.

JULIUS STONE

January, 1965.
Faculty of Law, University of Sydney.

LIST OF ABBREVIATIONS

A.B.A.J.	*American Bar Association Journal*
A.C. (preceded by date)	Law Reports, Appeal Cases, House of Lords since 1890
Am. Anthrop.	*American Anthropologist*
Ambrosetti, *Riforma*	G. Ambrosetti, *Il Diritto Naturale della Riforma Cattolica* (1951)
Am. Ec. Rev.	*American Economic Review*
Am. J. Comp. L.	*American Journal of Comparative Law*
Am. J. Soc.	*American Journal of Sociology*
App. Cas.	Law Reports, Appeal Cases, House of Lords 1875-1890
Arch. de Phil. du Droit	*Archives de Philosophie du Droit* (New Series, 1952-)
Arch. de Phil. et Soc. Jur.	*Archives de Philosophie du Droit et de Sociologie Juridique* (to 1940)
Arch. d'Hist. du Droit	*Archives d'Histoire du Droit*
Arch. Hist. Dr. Oriental	*Archives d'Histoire du Droit Oriental*
Arch. R.- und Sozialph.	*Archiv für Rechts- und Sozialphilosophie*
Arch. R.- und Wirtschaftsph.	*Archiv für Rechts- und Wirtschaftsphilosophie*
Arch. Sozialw. und Sozialph.	*Archiv für Sozialwissenschaften und Sozialphilosophie*
Arch. Sozialw. und Sozial-pol.	*Archiv für Sozialwissenschaft und Sozialpolitik*
Austin, *Lectures*	J. Austin, *Lectures on Jurisprudence* (2 vols., 3 ed. 1863, rev. and ed. R. Campbell, 1869)
Austin, *Province Determined*	*Id., The Province of Jurisprudence Determined* (ed. H. L. A. Hart, 1954)
Aust. J. Psych. Phil.	*Australian Journal of Psychology and Philosophy*
Australian Studies in Legal Philosophy	I. Tammelo, A. Blackshield, and E. Campbell (eds.), *Australian Studies in Legal Philosophy* (1963; published as special *Beiheft* No. 39 of *Das Archiv für Rechts- und Sozialphilosophie*)
Averroes, *Commentary*	E. I. J. Rosenthal (transl. and ed.), *Averroes' Commentary on Plato's Republic* (1956)
Barb.	Barbour's Supreme Court Reports (New York State) U.S. (1847-1876)
Baumgardt, *Bentham*	D. Baumgardt, *Bentham and the Ethics of Today* (1952)
Benn and Peters, *Principles*	S. I. Benn and R. S. Peters, *Social Principles and the Democratic State* (1959, 2 imp. 1961)
Bentham, *Limits*	Jeremy Bentham, *Limits of Jurisprudence Defined* (first publ. 1945, Intro. by C. W. Everett)
Bentham, *Theory*	Jeremy Bentham, *The Theory of Legislation* (Hildreth's transl., 5 ed. 1887, first publ. in French in 1802)
Bentham, *Works*	Jeremy Bentham, *Works* (2 vols., ed. J. Bowring, 1838-43)
Berle, *Capitalist Revolution*	A. A. Berle, *The Twentieth Century Capitalist Revolution* (1955)
Blackshield, *"Pensiero Umano"*	A. R. Blackshield, *"Il Pensiero Umano e la 'Condizione Umana' in Relazione al Diritto e ai Valori"* (1963) 40 *Riv. Int. di Fil. del Dir.* 465-516
Blackstone, *Commentaries*	Sir W. Blackstone, *Commentaries on the Laws of England* (1765)
Braybrooke, "Roscoe Pound"	E. K. Braybrooke, "The Sociological Jurisprudence of Roscoe Pound" (1961) 5 *Univ. of W.A.L.R.* 288-325.
Brebner, *"Laissez Faire"*	J. Brebner, *"Laissez Faire* and State Intervention in 19th Century Britain" (1948) *J. Ec. Hist.* Supp. viii (*The Tasks of Economic History*) 59-73
Brecht, "Relative Justice"	A. Brecht, "Relative and Absolute Justice", in M. D. Forkosch, *The Political Philosophy of Arnold Brecht* (1954) 102
Brecht, "Relativism"	A. Brecht, "The Rise of Relativism in Political and Legal Philosophy" in M. D. Forkosch (ed.), *The Political Philosophy of Arnold Brecht* (1954) 49
Br. Jo. Soc.	*British Journal of Sociology*
Brown, *Modern Legislation*	J. Brown, *The Underlying Principles of Modern Legislation* (1912)

Bryce, *Studies*	Lord Bryce, *Studies in History and Jurisprudence* (2 vols. 1901)
Buch, *"Principes Généraux"*	H. Buch, *"La Nature des Principes Généraux" du Droit*, in *Rapports Belges au VIe Congrès International de Droit Comparé* (1962) 55-70
Bull. Ist. di Dir. Rom.	*Bulletino dell'Istituto di Diritto Romano*
Butterworth's S. Afr. L.R.	*Butterworth's South African Law Review*
B.Y.B.	*British Year Book of International Law*
C.A.	Court of Appeal (England)
Cairns, *Legal Science*	Huntington Cairns, *The Theory of Legal Science* (1941)
Cairns, *Plato to Hegel*	Huntington Cairns, *Legal Philosophy from Plato to Hegel* (1949)
Campbell, *Lives*	Lord Campbell, *Lives of the Chief Justices* (3 ed. 1874) 4 vols.
Can.B.R.	*Canadian Bar Review*
Cardozo, *Growth*	B. N. Cardozo, *The Growth of the Law* (1924)
Cardozo, *Judicial Process*	*Id.*, *Nature of the Judicial Process* (1921)
Cattaneo, *"L'Ultima Fase"*	M. A. Cattaneo, *"L'Ultima Fase del Pensiero di Gustav Radbruch: Dal Relativismo al Giusnaturalismo"* (1959) 50 *Riv. Fil.* 61-80.
Cent.L.J.	*Century Law Journal*
Ch. (with arabic numeral)	Chapter (of this book and its companion works *Legal System and Lawyers' Reasonings* and *Social Dimensions of Law and Justice*; and of the earlier work, *The Province and Function of Law*)
c. (with small roman numeral)	Chapter (of other books)
Ch. (preceded by date)	Law Reports, Chancery Division since 1890 (England)
Ch. App.	Law Reports, Chancery Appeals (England)
C.L.R.	Commonwealth Law Reports (Australia)
Cmd.	Command Papers (U.K.) (1919 to 1956-57)
Cmnd.	The same (1956-57 onwards)
Cogley (ed.), *Natural Law*	J. Cogley (ed.), *Natural Law and Modern Society* (Centre for the Study of Democratic Institutions, 1963)
Cohen, *Ethical Systems*	F. S. Cohen, *Ethical Systems and Legal Ideals* (1933)
Cohen, *Social Order*	M. R. Cohen, *Law and the Social Order* (1933)
Cohn, *"Jewish Law"*	H. Cohn, "Prolegomena to the Theory and History of Jewish Law" in R. A. Newman (ed.), *Essays in Jurisprudence in Honour of Roscoe Pound* (1962, American Society for Legal History)
Co. Litt.	Sir Edward Coke, *A Commentary upon Littleton* (1628)
Columbia L.R.	*Columbia Law Review*
Commr.	Commissioner
Commons, *Capitalism*	J. R. Commons, *Legal Foundations of Capitalism* (1924)
Conn.	Connecticut State Reports (U.S.)
Co. Rep.	Coke's Reports (England)
Crim. L.Q.	*Criminal Law Quarterly*
Curr. L. and S.P.	*Current Law and Social Problems*
Cush.	Cushing's Reports (Massachusetts)
Cwlth.	Commonwealth
Del Vecchio, *Justice*	G. Del Vecchio, *Justice* (transl. Lady Guthrie and ed. A. H. Campbell, 1952)
Dicey, *Law and Opinion*	A. V. Dicey, *Relation between Law and Public Opinion in England in the Nineteenth Century* (1905, 2 ed. 1914)
Dig.	Ulpian, *Digest*
Dowrick, *Justice*	F. E. Dowrick, *Justice According to the English Common Lawyers* (1961)
Duguit, *Droit Objectif*	L. Duguit, *L'Etat, le Droit Objectif et la Loi Positive* (1901)
Duguit, *Droit Privé*	L. Duguit, *Les Transformations Générales du Droit Privé depuis le Code Napoléon* (1912) transl. in *Progress of Continental Law in the Nineteenth Century* 65 (*Continental Legal History Series*, vol. xi)
Duguit, *Droit Public*	L. Duguit, *Les Transformations Générales du Droit Public* (1913)

Duguit Symposium Various articles on the work of Duguit in (1932) 2 *Arch. de Phil. et Soc. Jur.* 1

Ehrenzweig, "Psychoanaly- sis of Justice" A. A. Ehrenzweig, "Toward a Psychoanalysis of Law and Justice: The 'Schools of Jurisprudence' — An End and a Beginning", in the *Festschrift für Karl Olivecrona* (1964) 148-165

Ehrlich, *Sociology* E. Ehrlich, *Fundamental Principles of the Sociology of Law* (1936), being W. L. Moll's transl., with Intro. by R. Pound, of *id.*, *Grundlegung der Soziologie des Rechts* (1913)

F. Federal Reporter (U.S.)
Flückiger, *Geschichte* F. Flückiger, *Geschichte des Naturrechts* (1954)
Freeman, *Ancilla* K. Freeman, *Ancilla to the Pre-Socratic Philosophers* (1952)
Freund, *Supreme Court* P. A. Freund, *The Supreme Court of the United States: Its Business, Purposes and Performance* (1961)
Friedmann, *C h a n g i n g Society* W. Friedmann, *Law in a Changing Society* (1959)
Friedrich, *Philosophy of Law* C. J. Friedrich, *The Philosophy of Law in Historical Perspective* (1958)
Fuller, "Human Purpose" L. L. Fuller, "Human Purpose and Natural Law" (1958) 3 *Nat. L. Forum* 68
Fuller, "Mid-Century" *Id.*, "American Legal Philosophy at Mid-Century" (1954) 6 *J. Leg. Ed.* 457
Fuller, "Positivism" *Id.*, "Positivism and Fidelity to Law" (1958) 71 *H.L.R.* 593
Fuller, "Rejoinder" *Id.*, "A Rejoinder to Professor Nagel" (1958) 3 *Nat. L. Forum* 83

Gaius, *Institutes* *Institutionum Iuris Civilis Commentarii Quattuor* (circa 138-161 A.D.) transl. E. Poste as *Elements of Roman Law by Gaius* (3 ed. 1890)
Garlan, *Legal Realism* E. N. Garlan, *Legal Realism and Justice* (1941)
Gény, *Méthode* F. Gény, *Méthode d'Interprétation et Sources en Droit Privé Positif* (2 vols. 1899, 2 ed. 1919)
Gény, *Science et Technique* *Id.*, *Science et Technique en Droit Privé Positif* (4 vols., 1913-1924)
Gerth-Mills, *From Max Weber* H. H. Gerth and C. W. Mills (eds.), *From Max Weber: Essays in Sociology* (1947)
Ginsberg, *20th Century* M. Ginsberg (ed.), *Law and Opinion in England in the 20th Century* (1959)
Goyder, *Private Enterprise* G. Goyder, *The Future of Private Enterprise* (1951)

Hague Recueil *Recueil des Cours de l'Académie de Droit International*
Haines, *Revival* C. G. Haines, *The Revival of Natural Law Concepts* (1930)
Halévy, *Radicalism* E. Halévy, *The Growth of Philosophical Radicalism* (2 vols. 1900-1903, transl. M. Morris, 1928)
Hart, "Definition" H. L. A. Hart, "Definition and Theory in Jurisprudence" (1954) 70 *L.Q.R.* 37-60 (Inaugural Lecture in the University of Oxford)
Hart, *Law* *Id.*, *The Concept of Law* (1961)
Hart, "Law and Morals" *Id.*, "Positivism and the Separation of Law and Morals" (1958) 71 *H.L.R.* 593
Hartz, *Economic Policy* L. Hartz, *Economic Policy and Democratic Thought (Pennsylvania) 1776-1860* (1948)
Hayek, *Liberty* F. A. Hayek, *The Constitution of Liberty* (1960)
Hayek, *Serfdom* *Id.*, *The Road to Serfdom* (1944)
H.L. House of Lords
H.L.R. *Harvard Law Review*
Hob. Hobart's Reports (England)
Hocking, *Law and Rights* W. E. Hocking, *The Present Status of the Philosophy of Law and of Rights* (1926)
Holmes, "The Path of the Law" O. W. Holmes, Jr., same title (1897) 10 *H.L.R.* 457
Hughes, "Legal System" G. Hughes, "The Existence of a Legal System" (1960) 35 *N.Y.U.L.R.* 1001

Ia. L.R.	*Iowa Law Review*
Ihering, *Geist*	R. von Ihering, *Geist des römischen Rechts auf den verschiedenen Stufen seiner Entwicklung* (1852-65, 4 vols., unfinished)
Ihering, transl.	*Id., Law as a Means to an End* (transl. I. Husik, 1913, from vol. i of *Der Zweck im Recht* (1877), in *Modern Legal Philosophy Series*)
Ihering, *Zweck*	*Id., Der Zweck im Recht* (1877-1883, 2 vols.)
Ill.	Illinois State Reports (U.S.)
Ill. L.R.	*Illinois L.R.*
Ind.	Indiana State Reports
Ind. L.J.	*Indiana L.J.*
Int. Jo. Ethics	*International Journal of Ethics*
Int. Phil. Q.	*International Philosophical Quarterly*
I.S.S.J. Communication	Symposium on "Communication and Information" (1962) 14 *International Social Science Journal* 251-348
Jaipur L.J.	*Jaipur Law Journal*
Jacob-Flink, *Value Decision*	P. E. Jacob and J. J. Flink (with H. L. Shuchman), in (1962) 5 *American Behavioural Scientist* Supplement on "Values and their Function in Decision-Making"
J. Crim. L., Crimin. and Pol. Sc.	*Journal of Criminal Law, Criminology and Police Science*
J. Ec. Hist.	*Journal of Economic History*
J. Hist. Ideas	*Journal of the History of Ideas*
Jennings (ed.), *Theories of Law*	W. I. Jennings (ed.), *Modern Theories of Law* (1933)
Jennings, "Utilitarianism"	W. I. Jennings, "A Plea for Utilitarianism" (1938) 2 *M.L.R.* 22
J. Leg. Ed.	*Journal of Legal Education*
Jolowicz, *Roman Law*	H. F. Jolowicz, *Historical Introduction to the Study of Roman Law* (1932)
Jones, *Theory of Law*	J. W. Jones, *Historical Introduction to the Theory of Law* (1940)
J. Phil.	*Journal of Philosophy*
J. Publ. L.	*Journal of Public Law*
Juridical R.	*Juridical Review*
Kant, *Rechtslehre*	I. Kant, *Metaphysische Anfangsgründe der Rechtslehre* (1791, 2 ed. 1798), transl. W. Hastie as *Philosophy of Law,* 1887. Unless otherwise indicated references are to the translation
K.B. (preceded by date)	Law Reports, King's Bench Division (England)
Keeton *et al., Bentham*	G. W. Keeton and G. Schwarzenberger (eds.), *Jeremy Bentham and the Law* (1948)
Kelsen, *Theory*	H. Kelsen, *General Theory of Law and State* (transl. A. Wedberg, 1945 in *20th Century Legal Philosophy Series*, vol i)
Kohler, *Lehrbuch*	J. Kohler, *Lehrbuch der Rechtsphilosophie* (1908, 3 ed. 1923)
Kohler, transl.	*Id., Lehrbuch* (transl. A. Albrecht as *Philosophy of Law,* 1914, in *Modern Legal Philosophy Series*)
Krabbe, *The State*	H. Krabbe, *The Modern Idea of the State* (1919) (transl. G. H. Sabine and W. J. Shepard, 1922)
Lamont, *Moral Judgment*	W. D. Lamont, *The Principles of Moral Judgment* (1946)
Laski, *Politics*	H. J. Laski, *A Grammar of Politics* (1925; 3 ed. 1938)
Lasswell-Kaplan, *Power*	H. Lasswell and A. Kaplan, *Power and Society* (1950)
Latham, "Commonwealth"	R. T. E. Latham, "The Law and the British Commonwealth", in W. K. Hancock (ed.), *Survey of British Commonwealth Affairs* (2 vols., 1937) vol. i, 510-630
Laun Festschrift	G. C. Hemmarck (ed.), *Festschrift zur Ehren Rudolf Launs* (1947)
Lindsay, *Democratic State*	A. D. Lindsay, *The Modern Democratic State* (1943)
Lindzey (ed.), *Handbook*	G. Lindzey (ed.), *The Handbook of Social Psychology* (2 vols., 1954)
Lloyd, *Jurisprudence*	D. Lloyd, *Introduction to Jurisprudence* (1959)
Louisiana L.R.	*Louisiana Law Review*

Lowie, *Social Org.*	R. H. Lowie, *Social Organisation* (1948)
L.Q.R.	*Law Quarterly Review*
L.R.	Law Reports (England)
L.R. Ch. App.	Law Reports, Chancery Appeals (England)
L.R. Eq.	Law Reports, Equity Cases (England)
MacDermott, *Protection from Power*	Lord MacDermott, *Protection from Power under English Law* (1957)
Macmillan, *Law*	Lord Macmillan, *Law and Other Things* (1937)
Maine, *Institutions*	H. Maine, *Early History of Institutions* (1874)
Marqu. L.R.	*Marquette Law Review*
M. & W.	Meeson and Welsby's Reports (England)
Mass.	Massachusetts State Reports (U.S.)
Mélanges Hauriou	*Mélanges Maurice Hauriou* (1929)
Melb. U.L.R.	*Melbourne University Law Review*
Mich. L.R.	*Michigan Law Review*
Micklem, *Law*	N. Micklem, *Law and the Laws* (1952)
Miller, *Lectures*	W. G. Miller, *Lectures on the Philosophy of Law* (1884)
Minn. L.R.	*Minnesota Law Review*
Mod.	Modern Reports (England)
M.L.R.	*Modern Law Review*
Monatsch. für Krim. und Strafr.	*Monatschrift für Kriminalpsychologie und Strafrechtsreform*
MS. U.C.	Jeremy Bentham, unpublished manuscript collected in University College, London
Myrdal, *Welfare State*	G. Myrdal, *Beyond the Welfare State* (1960)
Nagel, "Fact and Value"	E. Nagel, "On the Fusion of Fact and Value — A Reply to Professor Fuller" (1958) 3 *Nat. L. Forum* 77
Nagel, "Human Purpose"	*Id.*, "Fact, Value and Human Purpose" (1959) 4 *Nat. L. Forum* 26
Nat. L. Forum	*Natural Law Forum*
Nat. L. Inst. Proc.	*University of Notre Dame Natural Law Institute Proceedings*
Nelson, transl.	L. Nelson, *Lectures on the Foundations of Ethics* (vol. i, published as *Critique of Practical Reason* (1917)). Later part published as *System of Ethics and Pedagogics* (1932) transl. as *System of Ethics* by N. Guterman (1956)
Nomos, Justice	*Nomos* (*Yearbook of American Society of Political and Legal Philosophy*), vol. 6 on Justice, C. J. Friedrich and J. W. Chapman (eds.)
Northw. U.L.R.	*Northwestern University Law Review*
N.W.	Northwestern Reporter (U.S.)
N.Y.	New York State Reports (U.S.)
N.Y.U.L.R.	*New York University Law Review* or *New York University Law Quarterly Review*
Olafson, *Social Policy*	F. A. Olafson (ed.), *Justice and Social Policy* (1961)
Orestano, *Diritto Romano*	R. Orestano, *Introduzione allo Studio Storico del Diritto Romano* (1953)
Öst. Z.ö.R.	*Österreichische Zeitschrift für öffentliches Recht*
Pac.	Pacific Reporter (U.S.)
Pa. St.	Pennsylvania State Reports (U.S.)
Pareto	V. Pareto, *The Mind and Society* (1916) ed. and transl. Livingston *et al.*, (4 vols., 1935)
Parsons, *Social Action*	T. Parsons, *The Structure of Social Action* (1937)
Parsons-Shils, *Theory of Action*	T. Parsons and E. Shils (eds.), *Towards a General Theory of Action* (1951)
Patterson, *Jurisprudence*	E. Patterson, *Jurisprudence: Men and Ideas of the Law* (1953)
P.C.	Judicial Committee of the Privy Council
Perelman, "Rationalité"	Ch. Perelman, "*L'Idéal de Rationalité et la Règle de Justice*" (1961) 53 *Bulletin de la Société Française de Philosophie* 1-50
Phil. and Phen. R.	*Philosophy and Phenomenological Research*
Phil. Q.	*Philosophical Quarterly*

Phil. R.   *Philosophical Review*

Pollock, *Essays*   F. Pollock, *Essays in Jurisprudence and Ethics* (1882)

Pol. Sc. Qu.   *Political Science Quarterly*

Popper, "Historicism" (with vol. of *Economica* (N.S.))   K. Popper, "The Poverty of Historicism" (1944) 11 *Economica* (N.S.) 86, 119, (1945), 12 *id.* 69; repr. under same title (1957)

Popper, *Open Society*   *Id., The Open Society and its Enemies* (2 vols., 1945)

Pound Festschrift   R. A. Newman (ed.), *Essays in Jurisprudence in Honour of Roscoe Pound* (1962, American Society for Legal History)

Pound, *Jurisprudence*   Roscoe Pound, *Jurisprudence* (5 vols., 1959)

Pound, *Legal History*   *Id., Interpretations of Legal History* (1922)

Pound, *Outlines*   *Id., Outlines of Lectures on Jurisprudence* (4 ed. 1928, 5 ed. 1943)

Pound, *Philosophy of Law*   *Id., An Introduction to the Philosophy of Law* (1922, rev. ed. 1954 here used)

Pound, *Social Control*   *Id., Social Control Through Law* (1942)

Pound, "Social Interests"   *Id.,* "A Survey of Social Interests" (1943) 57 *H.L.R.* 1-39

Pound-Plucknett, *Readings*   R. Pound and T. F. T. Plucknett, *Readings on the History and System of the Common Law* (3 ed. 1927)

Proc. Am. Soc. Society   *Proceedings of the American Sociological Society*

Proc. Arist. Soc.   *Proceedings of the Aristotelian Society*

Q.B. (preceded by date)   Law Reports, Queen's Bench Division (England)

Radbruch, *Legal Philosophy*   G. Radbruch, *Rechtsphilosophie* (3 ed. 1932, transl. K. Wilk in *Legal Philosophies of Lask, Radbruch and Dabin* (1950) 43-224 (20th Century Legal Philosophy Series (1950)) vol. vi

Radbruch, *Mensch im Recht*   *Id., Der Mensch im Recht* (1951-52)

Radbruch, *Rechts-philosophie*   *Id., Rechtsphilosophie* (3 ed. 1932, transl. by K. Wilk in *Legal Philosophies of Lask, Radbruch and Dabin* (1950)); 4, 5 and 6 (posthumous) eds. by E. Wolf (1950, 1956 and 1963)

Radbruch, "*Sécurité*"   *Id.,* "La Sécurité en Droit d'après la Théorie Anglaise" (1936) 6 (Nos. 3-4) *Arch. de Phil. du Droit* 86-99

Radbruch, *Vorschule*   *Id., Vorschule der Rechtsphilosophie* (1947)

Radzinowicz, *Criminal Law*   L. Radzinowicz, *A History of English Criminal Law and its Administration from 1750* (1956)

Raju, P.T. *et al.* (ed.), *The Concept of Man* (1960)   S. Radhakrishnan and P. T. Raju (eds.), *The Concept of Man* (1960)

Recaséns, *Filosofía del Derecho*   L. Recaséns Siches, *Tratado General de Filosofía del Derecho* (1959)

Rep. Chan.   Reports in Chancery (England) (1615-1710)

R. Hist. Dr. Fr. et Etr.   *Revue Historique du Droit Français et Etranger*

Revue Int. de Phil.   *Revue Internationale de Philosophie*

Rev. Int. T. du Droit   *Revue Internationale de la Théorie du Droit*

Rev. Jur. de B.A.   *Revista Jurídica de Buenos Aires*

Riv. di Dir. Civ.   *Rivista di Diritto Civile*

Riv. Fil.   *Rivista di Filosofia*

Riv. Int. di Fil. del Dir.   *Rivista Internazionale di Filosofia del Diritto*

Rose, *Social Processes*   A. M. Rose (ed.), *Human Behaviour and Social Processes* (1962)

Rosenthal, *Islam*   E. I. J. Rosenthal, *Political Thought in Mediaeval Islam* (1958)

Rutg. L.R.   *Rutgers Law Review*

Sabine-Smith, *Cicero*   G. W. Sabine and S. B. Smith, *Cicero on the Commonwealth* (1929)

Saleilles, "*Ecole Historique*"   R. Saleilles, "L'Ecole Historique et Droit Naturel" (1902) 1 *Revue Trimestrielle de Droit Civil* 80

Sayre (ed.), *Modern Legal Philosophies*   P. Sayre (ed.), *Interpretations of Modern Legal Philosophies* (1947)

S.D.   South Dakota

Simpson-Stone, *Law and Society* — S. P. Simpson and J. Stone, *Law and Society* (1949-1950, 3 vols.)

S.L.T. — Scots Law Times Reports

St. John's L.R. — *St. John's Law Review*

Stammler, *Lehre* — R. Stammler, *Die Lehre von dem richtigen Recht* (1902, 2 ed. 1926)

Stammler, *Theory of Justice* — *Id.*, *Lehre* (transl. 1925, I. Husik as *The Theory of Justice* in *Modern Legal Philosophy Series*, vol. viii)

Stan. L.R. — *Stanford Law Review*

Stone and Tarello, "Justice" — J. Stone and G. Tarello, "Justice, Language and Communication" (1960) 14 *Vanderb. L.R.* 331-381

Stone, *Legal System* — J. Stone, *Legal System and Lawyers' Reasonings* (1964)

Stone, "Pound's Theory of Justice" — *Id.*, "A Critique of Pound's Theory of Justice" (1935) 20 *Ia. L.R.* 53

Stone, *Province* — *Id.*, *The Province and Function of Law* (1946, repr. 1950 and 1961)

Stone, *Social Dimensions* — *Id.*, *Social Dimensions of Law and Justice* (to be published in 1965 under the same imprint as the present work)

Strauss, *Natural Right* — L. Strauss, *Natural Right and History* (1953)

Summa — St. Thomas Aquinas, *Summa Theologica* (1267-)

Swan. — Swanston's Reports (England)

Syd. L.R. — *Sydney Law Review*

Tammelo, "Justice and Doubt" — I. Tammelo, "Justice and Doubt" (1959) 9 *Öst. Z.ö.R.* 308-417

Timasheff, *Sociology of Law* — N. S. Timasheff, *An Introduction to the Sociology of Law* (1939)

Trans. Grotius Soc. — *Transactions of the Grotius Society*

U.C. — University College (London)

U.C.L.A.L.R. — *University of California Los Angeles Law Review*

Univ. of Cin. L.R. — *University of Cincinnati Law Review*

Univ. of Pa. L.R. — *University of Pennsylvania Law Review*

Univ. of W.A.L.R. — *University of Western Australia Law Review*

U.S. — United States Supreme Court Reports

Vanderb. L.R. — *Vanderbilt Law Review*

Viner, "Bentham and Mill" — J. Viner, "Bentham and J. S. Mill: the Utilitarian Background" (1949) 39 *Am. Ec. Rev.* 360

Vinogradoff, *Jurisprudence* — P. Vinogradoff, *Outlines of Historical Jurisprudence* (vol. i, 1920, vol. ii, 1922)

Wall. — Wallace's Reports (U.S. 1863-74)

Welzel, *Naturrecht* — H. Welzel, *Naturrecht und Materiale Gerechtigkeit* (2 ed. 1955)

Wheat. — Wheaton's Reports (U.S. 1816-1827)

Wild, *Plato's Enemies* — J. Wild, *Plato's Modern Enemies and the Theory of Natural Law* (1953)

Wis. — Wisconsin State Reports (U.S.)

W.L.R. — Weekly Law Reports (England)

W.N. (N.S.W.) — New South Wales *Weekly Notes* (Australia)

W. Res. L.R. — *Western Reserve Law Review*

Wright, *Essays* — Lord Wright, *Legal Essays and Addresses* (1939)

Y.B. (with regnal year) — Year Book (England)

Yale L.J. — *Yale Law Journal*

Yerg. Tenn. — Yerger's Tennessee Reports

Z.ö.R. — *Zeitschrift für öffentliches Recht*

ERRATA

P.19   In n.45, add at the end. "As we were on the press, Z. W. Falk, *Hebrew Law in Biblical Times* (1964) appeared, essaying the necessarily problematical task of tracing trends of legal development *within* the Old Testament."

P.43   In n.19, last line, for "1958" read "1957".

P.49   In n.64, 2nd last line, the second "a" in "Maqal" should be accented.

P.51   In n.91, paragraph 1, 3rd last line, for "1953" read "1951".

P.77   In n.249, lines 1-2, for "7 Co. Rep. 4" read "7 Co. Rep. 1".

P.90   In 3rd last line of n.40, for "1923" read "1922".
In n.40, last line, for "883" read "866".

P.91   In n.48, for "Connolly" read "Connelly".

P.92   In n.56, for "Oakley" read "Okely".

P.94   In n.67, line 5, for "1939" read "1941".

Pp. 94, 95, 97. In nn.67, 72 and 84, for "Hotels" read "Hotel".

P.96   In n.78, last line, for "1951" read "1952".
In n.80, line 2, for "1941" read "1942".
In n.81, for "310" read "311".

P.97   In last line of text, the correct spelling of the case-name is "*Nunnemacher*".
In n.84, penultimate line, for "1941" read "1942".

P.99   In n.100, for "435" read "436".

P.108   In n.15, line 1, for "63ff." read "62ff.".

P.111   In n.24, for "Natural Law" read "the Law of Nature".

P.113   In n.34, line 3, for "1758" read "1759".

P.119   In n.58, last line, for "1949" read "1948".

P.140   In 8th line from end of text, for "1872" read "1870".

P.141   In 4th line of text, for "1833" read "1843".

P.147   In n.1, line 2, for "1885" read "1884".

P.160   In n.74, last line, for "640-672" read "641-672".

P.202   In n.52b, line 2, for "209" read "208".

P.209   In n.105, page reference to 1964 article by J. Stone is 145-168.

P.210   In n.108, line 3, for "98-105" read "97-104".

P.277   In n.5, paragraph 2, line 8, for "41" read "11".

P.313   In n.90, line 1, for "1949" read "1947".

TABLE OF CONTENTS

INTRODUCTION

§1. RELATION OF THIS WORK TO THE PROVINCE AND FUNCTION OF LAW. This is the second of three works in which we have sought to survey critically the contemporary problems within the field of jurisprudence. Its purpose is to take stock of that component of legal ordering to which men refer when they speak of justice, *good* order, or its equivalents. It seeks to do this against a background of the changing social contexts within which men's ideas and stances with regard to justice have from time to time arisen, found expression or realised themselves (more or less) in social action. We here attempt, in short, with main emphasis on modern developed societies, to give an analytical, historical and critical account of the growth of human ideals of justice as they bear on human legal orderings, and in their relation to the legal, social and economic contexts in which they have arisen. And not the least important aspect of this is to try and assess the contemporary overall position as to our apprehension of these ideals.

In our earlier work, *Legal System and Lawyers' Reasonings* (1964), we were concerned to examine, against a background of the elements of unity and disunity within a going legal order, the processes of judicial and juristic thought in their resort to logic and to other kinds of reasoning. And we there showed that use of a given kind of reasoning is often in varying degrees dependent on concurrent assumptions (even when these are only made tacitly and unawares) concerning what is a "just" or a "good" solution. To this extent the present work addresses itself to complementary issues. And, indeed, the third of this trilogy of books, *Social Dimensions of Law and Justice* (1965), may also be regarded as similarly complementary to those which will have preceded it. It will seek to illuminate, from the standpoint of the social sciences (embracing the insights of sociological jurisprudence somewhere within these), the full complexity of problems which confront modern democratic government in seeking to use law as an instrument of social control orientated towards the achievement of justice in the time and place.

Nor should we be surprised that these studies are thus mutually complementary, for together they seek to explore the whole ambit of the province and function of legal orderings as we find them in our modern societies. Readers of our work *The Province and Function of Law* will recall that that work also proceeded on such a threefold division of the tasks of jurisprudence. The increasing acceptance of this kind of division, and the vast turnover of thought in each area since that work was first published in 1946, have convinced us that the time has come when each requires for adequate study a separate book to be devoted to it. This present book, like the other two of the trilogy, is designed to be self-contained for those whose concerns lie in only one area, even though all of them are necessary to an all-round *jurisprudential* view of legal ordering.

This work seeks to move forward from the ground covered in the

176 pages of *The Province and Function of Law* devoted to "Law and Justice", a movement only partly indicated by the fact that the present book is more than double that length. Quite apart from review of matters of substance, the former treatment has been much consolidated to make room for later ideas and significant contemporary materials. The wholly new matter is thus even greater than the number of pages indicates. It includes six wholly or virtually new Chapters, described at the end of this Introduction. Nevertheless, we hope that the present treatment may have enhanced the coherence of our earlier positions. The main developments here manifest are probably in level of analysis rather than in conclusions reached, and (we hope) towards a broader, deeper and more historically based analysis. Where necessary, however, as with Benthamite thought in relation to *laissez faire*, we have not shrunk from basic rethinking in the light of studies (in that case historical studies) published after 1946.

§2. NATURE OF THE STUDY OF THEORIES OF JUSTICE. Theories of justice are concerned with the questions—What ought law to do for the men whose conduct it governs? What is the standard or measure or criterion of goodness in law? They are also concerned with criticism of law in its relation to the conditions of a particular time and place, by reference to such standard or measure or criterion. Sometimes these two inquiries are pursued as organically one, leading us, as we are in any case rather likely to be led by the unanswered questions which the theories of justice leave, to the consideration of law in society.[1]

The principal disciplines external to the law which are involved in consideration of these questions are ethical and political philosophy, to which perhaps must now be added "social philosophy".[2] As the title of this work indicates, the discussion of such questions has often been expressly in terms of "theories of *justice*"; that is, it has been squarely devoted to the problem of saying what "justice" is, both in the sense of fixing its axiological (or even ontological) conceptual status as an ethical standard, and in the perhaps more practical sense of saying what are the requirements (or contents) of this standard. But the main *verbal* categories discussed are sometimes quite different, and occasionally the express reference to justice has been altogether lacking. The phrase "theories of justice" as here used will refer to discussions of these kinds also, so long as, whatever their terminology, they are in fact a substantial contribution to the questions referred to in the preceding paragraph.

One *main* head under which these discussions have in the past proceeded is that of "natural law". Here, though the questions involved are similar to those now attributed to theories of justice, and though the *word* "justice" is frequently employed, there are differences of presupposition and conceptual organisation which may conceivably lead to differences not only in presentation of ideas, but in their content. The rather confused interrelations of "natural law" and "justice" will be traced in the opening Chapter to the rather vague intermingling of these ideas in the earliest Greek thought. In

---

[1] On which see Stone, *Social Dimensions*. As to the severability of these matters and their inter-relations see *id.* Ch. 1, §21. And *cf.* Stone, *Legal System*, Intro., §8, as to alternative terminology.

[2] The title of Walter Lippman's *The Public Philosophy* (1954) suggests perhaps a generic title for these. He himself applies the term, however, to a particular *Weltanschauung* rather than a branch of knowledge. As to the term "philosophy of law", here avoided where possible, see Stone, *Legal System*, Intro., §8.

Chapter 2 we shall see that in post-classical antiquity, and particularly in the Middle Ages, the focus for attention came to be almost wholly "natural law". But later Chapters centred on discussions of the last three centuries will show that in modern times, although "natural law" thought is still a force to be reckoned with, attention to the broader ambit of "justice" as such has again come to the fore. And, throughout, there is need for constant awareness of the older bodies of ideas, for these remain more often than not essential anchorages of later thought.

§3. SCOPE AND APPROACHES OF THEORIES OF JUSTICE. Most of the main approaches of the ethical and political philosophers have from time to time been applied by jurists. At times indeed, as with natural law, their speculations have been inextricably interwoven. In modern juristic thought, the link continues. Pound[3] identifies theories of justice such as *metaphysical*,[4] *social utilitarian*,[5] *neo-Kantian*,[6] *neo-Hegelian*,[7] *neo-idealist*,[8] *neo-metaphysical*,[9] *neo-scholastic*,[10] and *positivist*.[11] The present branch of jurisprudence is concerned to study these and other justice theories in relation to legal problems and in the light of the social knowledge available. Like the tasks of ethics and political philosophy themselves, the tasks of the theory of justice will never finally be done. For every change in man and his environment calls for a re-examination of existing values in their application to the new situation, a call more than ever insistent in our mobile democratic type of societies.

Some approaches to this inquiry have sought eternal and unchanging principles of justice valid for all times and places, whether in the form of the natural lawyer's search for universal because self-evident (or intuitively perceived) principles (Chapters 2, 7): or in the search for principles which make possible the exercise of free will by all according to the Kantian universal "law" (Chapter 3). Other approaches, especially in recent times, recognise that criteria of justice cannot be independent of the actual condition of man's social, economic and political life in particular times and places. Instead of pursuing universal principles of justice they seek some method of reaching a just solution in a particular society at a particular time. Within these terms there may still be a wide variation of philosophical origins. Jeremy Bentham (Chapter 4) propounded the test of utility based on a calculus of pleasures and pains in the particular concrete situation—a hedonistic calculus. François Gény[11a] re-asserts medieval belief in reasoned

---

[3] Pound, *Outlines* 197-206.

[4] Deriving from Kant, *Rechtslehre*. He instances *inter alia* J. Lorimer, *Institutes of Law* (1872, 2 ed. 1880); Miller, *Lectures*; *id.*, *Data of Jurisprudence* (1903).

[5] E.g., Ihering, *Zweck*, vol. i, transl. I. Husik as *Law as a Means to an End* (1913) in *Modern Legal Philosophy Series*; to which the writer would add in major gist Cardozo, *Judicial Process*.

[6] E.g., *inter alia*, Stammler, *Lehre*, transl. I. Husik as *Theory of Justice* (1925) in *Modern Legal Philosophy Series*; G. Del Vecchio, *The Formal Bases of Law*, transl. from three works in Italian (1905-1908) by J. Lisle (1914) in the same series, and *id.*, *Philosophy of Law* (transl. T. O. Martin, 1953).

[7] E.g., Kohler, *Lehrbuch*, transl. A. Albrecht as *Philosophy of Law* (1914), also in *Modern Legal Philosophy Series*.

[8] E.g., P. Tourtoulon, *Principes Philosophiques de l' Histoire du Droit* (1908-20), transl. M. Read as "Philosophy in the Development of Law" (1922) in *Modern Legal Philosophy Series*.

[9] E.g., *inter alia* R. Demogue, *Notions Fondamentales du Droit Privé* (1911).

[10] E.g., mainly Gény, *Méthode*; *id.*, *Science et Technique*.

[11] E.g., L. Duguit's works cited *infra* Ch. 5.

[11a] See Stone, *Legal System*, Ch. 6.

intuition, but on a basis of modern social knowledge. Rudolf von Ihering stresses the actual purposes of men and the dominance of "social purposes" (Chapter 5) on the basis, again, of the observed facts. Léon Duguit (Chapter 5) proceeds on a cognate assumption that the facts of social life themselves generate their own criterion of justice. Rudolf Stammler (Chapter 6) derives his method from the Kantian universal maxim. Joseph Kohler (Chapter 6) derives his from Hegel's unfolding "idea", and he locates that "idea" in the complexities of "civilisation". We shall see in Chapter 7 strains of relativism stressed in some modern forms of natural law, and in Chapters 8 and 9 some attempts at systematic statements of relativist positions, notably by Radbruch and Pound. We shall also review in Chapters 10 and 11 the present state of learning in this area, and take our own positions in relation to these and other themes of importance to our own age.

These more recent themes, with the exception perhaps of Stammler's, seem to make explicitly or secretly the assumption that man's actual desires and tendencies in particular times and places are relevant to justice. The pragmatic type of approach goes further. It proposes as a practical test of justice the capacity of the law to achieve the purposes which men demand of it. It points out that the search for an ultimate criterion of justice has already proceeded, without decisive result, for thousands of years, and that as a practical matter jurists cannot wait for agreement on ultimate values. This pragmatist approach is represented in ethics by William James, and has been most fully applied to the law by Roscoe Pound (Chapter 9). For the pragmatist, especially, every sociological inquiry may become simultaneously an inquiry into justice. The severability of the two spheres, however clear or desirable in theory, tends to become impossible in practice. The pragmatist approach, is indeed, in a sense, a meeting-point of sociological jurisprudence and the theory of justice.[12]

§4. SOME TRENDS IN THEORIES OF JUSTICE IN THE MODERN PERIOD. It is widely recognised that over the last two and a half centuries criteria have tended to move from an "individualist" to a "social" direction. The individualist criteria dominant until well into the nineteenth century took roughly three forms. In its early natural law "intuitionist" form, individualism was a weapon in use against medieval universalism and the close-knit social relations of feudalism, as well as of the individual conscience against the authority of the Catholic Church, and the Established Church in England, and against the despotisms of eighteenth century Europe (Chapter 2). The Kantian philosophy reacted against the intuitionism of natural law, but not against its individualism. (See Chapter 3, §§13ff. and Chapter 10, §§17-18.) It sought to demonstrate the validity of the individualist criterion by metaphysics, by laying bare the unchallengeable starting-point of the free will. It may therefore be characterised as metaphysical-individualist. From the more earthy English tradition Bentham stated his individualist criterion in hedonist-utilitarian terms, but, like the Kantians, he also attacked the intuitionism of the natural lawyers. It will later be seen that this criterion is itself thought by many to be a piece of question-begging intuitionism (Chapter 4, §§20-21).

The shift to a stress on "social" (or what Dicey called "collectivist") concerns, which accompanied the processes of industrialisation, urbanisation,

---

[12] See also *infra* Chs. 10 and 11 generally.

and the spread of manhood suffrage, was inspired basically by the changing conditions of industrial society and the problems they raised. Society posed for Bentham and Kant the question—How shall we justify the grant to each man of that maximum sphere of freedom from legal control which is being claimed? Society less than a century later was posing another question—How shall we justify the limitations on the freedom of individuals which we find ourselves compelled to impose?[13] Half a century later still, in 1964, this latter question tends to recede behind still another—On what principles should we grant power (and control the powers we feel compelled to grant) to public officials over the freedom of individuals?

Links of course are clearly visible. The individualist-intuitionism of the natural lawyers became the social intuitionism (often called neo-scholastic) of François Gény.[13a] The metaphysical individualism of Kant was converted into the metaphysical-collectivism (sometimes called "social idealism") of Rudolf Stammler. The hedonist-individualist-utilitarianism of Bentham gave some place to the "social utilitarianism" of Rudolf von Ihering (Chapter 5); and, indeed, was rather ambivalent as between individualism and collectivism in Bentham himself (Chapter 4, §§1, 11, 23). Concurrently, the social implications of the Hegelian dialectic stimulated criteria which stressed the social complex rather than the individual unit, the supposed whole rather than the separate parts.

In its extreme form this tendency away from individualism has produced criteria which may be described as "social solidarist", seeking to resolve the problem of justice by exclusive reference to a supposed inviolable social unity, without adequate regard to the conflicting interests of the individuals and groups of which it is composed.[14] Such solidarist criteria find their most extreme expression in fascist and other totalitarian ideologies. It is to be noted that social solidarism was formulated in the language of political democracy and in a form adapted to democratic states long before the rise of fascism. In the juristic field proper it received expression in the work of the French constitutional lawyer Léon Duguit, for whom "social solidarity" represented the *primum mobile* of the legal order. In the field of political philosophy it received powerful expression in the Anglo-American followers of Hegel who were dominant at the turn of the century.[15] And though it is often thought that natural law thinking is always individualistic in its tenor, "social" versions even of this kind of thinking can be found.[16]

---

[13] Admittedly the answers to the two questions need not be contradictory to each other. That does not alter the fact that the lines of thought promoted by each will be, for a time at any rate, divergent, and that this divergence proceeds from the nature of the problems which press in the contemporary social process. Cf. on this shift Macmillan, *Law* 6-7.

[13a] See Stone, *Legal System*, Ch. 6.

[14] This lack of reference may be concealed by the assumption that by some principle of inherent harmony the unity expresses all interests simultaneously. This assumption being on the present view patently false, this does not invalidate the description in the text.

[15] See, e.g., T. H. Green, *Principles of Political Obligation* (1901).

[16] The "humanist" ("personalist") movement in legal philosophy, notably in Latin America, seems focussed essentially on preserving concern for individual personality as against the tendency for "social" versions to become solidarist ("transpersonalist") in State activity. See, e.g., Recaséns, *Filosofia del Derecho passim*, esp. 511-523, on the history of the ideas involved. Recaséns sees "personalism" ("humanism") and "transpersonalism" as finally irreconcilable, yet also sees no necessary conflict between "individual" and "social" values. Obviously this asks rather than answers questions. See *id.* 538ff. And see on the psychological drives towards submergence of individuality *id.* 500.

§5. THE THEORY OF JUSTICE AS A SUBJECT OF STUDY. The study of the purposes or ideals which men seek to realise through law, sometimes called "the theory of justice", or more ambiguously[17] "legal philosophy", has an important continuous history from the very earliest days of western civilisation, and has been contributed to by many of the greatest minds of successive ages. And at the opening of the nineteenth century it constituted, through the teachings of the natural lawyers, a main preoccupation of both Continental and English lawyers.

The nineteenth century, at least in England, saw a decline in attention to these concerns, which, reinforced no doubt by general scepticism as to absolute ideals or at least as to the possibility of humanly apprehending them, continued into the first half of the present century. Strangely enough, this decline was probably closely related precisely to the dominance of the "natural law" form of this thinking at the time when Bentham and Austin were preparing their systems. Both found themselves impelled to discredit natural law thinking, Bentham mainly because its intuitionism was an obstacle to his utilitarianism, Austin mainly because it was an obstacle to his analytical and imperative delimitation of positive law.[18] So effective were their blows against natural law as a theory of justice that the theory of justice itself was stricken low.[19]

No doubt Bentham did not understand the creative role of natural law during its dominant period in seventeenth and eighteenth century Europe. No doubt, too, that role depended on substantial agreement as to the criteria of good law which later faded. Bentham, indeed, champion as he was of the duty to legislate, and of utility as the criterion of good legislation, can scarcely have intended to oppose a study of the ends of law. Nor can Austin, who rather championed the "science of legislation" and devoted much attention to its basis in the theory of utility.[20]

History, however, is often made more by the effects of words and acts than by the intention of speaker or actor. Bentham's scorn of the "unknown legislator"[21] produced inhibitions against inquiries into the goodness or badness of law which were fully released only by the horrors of a second World War. And Austin's insistence that law is either "positive" or not, and that if not, it is only improperly so called, tended in fact to embed in English legal theory the conviction, even now not entirely dislodged, that law in the stage of becoming is at any rate not the affair of the lawyer.[22]

---

[17] For the reason indicated in Stone, *Legal System*, Intro., §8.

[18] It is, of course, unnecessary to point out that while Austin and Bentham aided and abetted each other in all aspects of their work, still Bentham's utilitarianism is conceptually severable from his analytical and imperative theory of law, and that Austin's analytical and imperative theory is conceptually severable from his adoption of utilitarianism. Historical severability is a different matter. The best account of this matter is still in Maine, *Institutions*, lect. xii, xiii. *Cf.* Jones. *Theory of Law* 90-97.

[19] Even J. Salmond, *Jurisprudence* (8 ed. 1930) 39-54, 139-145, dealt with the theory of justice in a purely formal manner. *Cf.* generally G. Radbruch, "Anglo-American Jurisprudence through Continental Eyes" (1936) 52 *L.Q.R.* 530.

[20] See *infra* Ch. 4, esp. nn. 123, 136, 167, 185.

[21] *Theory of Legislation* (transl. R. Hildreth, 5 ed. 1887) 102.

[22] "The science of jurisprudence . . . is concerned with positive law or with laws strictly so called, as considered without regard to their goodness or badness" (1 *Lectures* 176-77). Traces of this embedded conviction are still seen for instance in *Jacobs* v. *L.C.C.* (1950) A.C. 361, esp. *per* Lord Simonds, e.g., at 368. But for his real ambivalence on the point see *id.* 369: "It is the primary duty of a court of justice to dispense justice to litigants"; though "it is its traditional role to do so by means of an exposition of the relevant law." And see Stone, *Legal System*, Ch. 8, n. 61, and generally §§1-6, *passim*. *Cf.* on the main point Dowrick, *Justice* c. viii.

But in a century of dynamic and even convulsive change and conflict, which has been made repeatedly and violently aware of injustice issuing in both internal discontentment and international horror, and has repeatedly been frustrated and baffled in the intractable tasks of removing such injustices, disclaimers by lawyers of concern with the theory of justice could not continue indefinitely. Their continuance for so long in England, we suggested in 1946, had its substantial foundations in the relative smoothness of English social and economic development, and widespread faith and contentment in contemporary tendencies. That faith and contentment began sooner and lasted longer in England than elsewhere. But even in England a growing confusion and discontent became manifest as collectivist legislation at the turn of the century challenged some of the worst results of *laissez faire*, and even the ideal itself. There was a sense of pain and urgency in Dicey's treatment of collectivism in 1914[23] which was not present when he first published his *Relation between Law and Public Opinion* in 1905.[24] And from the clash between actual social trends and accepted ideas, there arose a new interest in that human striving towards acceptable social adjustment which we may term the search for justice in and through law.

§6. ARRANGEMENT OF THIS WORK AND RELATION TO OUR EARLIER STUDIES OF JUSTICE. The present book, after the preliminary glimpse of the "early horizons of justice", moves in Chapter 2 to an examination of the older natural law ideas which served as the main vessel which bore early criteria of justice into the main stream of western thought, and dominated that thought in the formative seventeenth and eighteenth centuries. Various forms of the individualist criteria which emerged concurrently with the early industrial and political democratic revolutions of the eighteenth and nineteenth centuries are still influential today, and they will be examined in Chapters 3 and 4. We shall then trace in Chapters 5 and 6 the shift to theories which stress the social rather than the autonomous life of the individual unit—often but inadequately termed "social" theories. This shift largely cuts across the age-old polemics between natural lawyer and positivist, and "apriorist", "rationalist", and "empiricist". Chapters 7, 8 and 9 set side by side the three most active streams of contemporary speculation about justice, namely, revived natural law, relativism, and interest-pragmatism, and try to assess their respective adequacy for our actual human situation. The concluding Chapters 10 and 11 seek to take stock of theories of justice in general, in relation to the realities of contemporary social life.

It may be useful, finally, to state in somewhat more detail how this work is related to that part of *The Province and Function of Law* devoted to "Law and Justice". Most of the old Chapters have been substantially enriched; some have also ceased here to be independent, being grouped for treatment within a single Chapter, notably those on Ihering and Duguit (Chapter 5) and Stammler and Kohler (Chapter 6). More than half of the eleven Chapters of the present book are either completely new or have been so substantially reinforced as to amount to new material. We here mention briefly the Chapters thus involved.

The opening Chapter on "Early Horizons of Justice in the West" is

---

[23] See his Intro. (2 ed. 1914) esp. at xxi-liii, lx-lxii.
[24] It is to be remembered that this was itself seven years after the basic approach was settled for the purpose of A. V. Dicey's lectures at Harvard in 1898.

designed, as already indicated, to suggest the main threads which have woven in and out of discourse on justice throughout the western tradition. It also serves to give some impression of the historical relation of these to the Greek and Hebraic traditions from which they first entered the western heritage. There has been a correspondingly radical change of emphasis in the succeeding Chapter on the classical natural law. Chapter 2 now treats of natural law not so much as a specific theory of justice, but rather as the historical bearer at certain epochs of western growth of whatever theories of justice were for the time being current. It thus becomes in effect a continuation into the medieval period of themes of the new opening Chapter on "Early Horizons of Justice in the West". Natural law in the aspect of a modern specific theory of justice now becomes the subject of a wholly new Chapter 7, entitled "Revived Natural Law", which despite its title embraces elements of older thought (notably of Thomism) on which the modernly revived theories build. Chapter 8 on "Relativism in Modern Theories of Justice" is also wholly new, and seeks to give a balanced account of the forms and limitations of relativism in this area. Radbruch's thought, including its deeper vacillations, serves as an excellent frame for this. The Chapter entitled "Theories of Justice and Meaning of Justice" is also in substance new, although most of the concluding Chapter in Part II of the earlier work is absorbed into it. The Chapter seeks to clarify as precisely as possible the main differentiating elements within the theories of justice examined. It also offers an assessment of certain approaches to justice, which have recently had some vogue, through linguistic study, and through an assumedly discoverable common "sense of justice". Finally, the concluding Chapter 11 (though it too draws on the concluding Chapters of Parts II and III of the earlier work) is a substantially new statement of the Author's own position on the search for "absolute", "normative" elements of justice and some of the main such elements offered in the literature; as well as on the descriptive study in actual social contexts of the "elements" there offered.

CHAPTER 1

EARLY HORIZONS OF JUSTICE IN THE WEST

§1. Early Notions of Justice in the Western Heritage. When we look to standards of goodness or badness by which the law may be judged, our primary concern is for our own age. Yet with justice, perhaps more than with any other aspect of law, the mind that seeks understanding is referred back to origins in the beginning of the Western cultural heritage. A full history, to which the present work can obviously not aspire, would have to weave a complicated pattern across space and time, and criss-cross many streams in the history of ideas besides those of the Greek and Judaic traditions; for we are now aware of many contacts and influences between these and a number of other cultures. As a practical matter, however, we are here content to accept as sufficiently correct the generalisation, widely accepted at least since Matthew Arnold,[1] that Hebraism and Hellenism are the main source waters which fed the Western cultural stream. And we should attempt at least to single out those aspects of Greek and Hebraic thought which may help to explain the main contents, or at least the mood and temper, of later Western thought. For this task there is obviously an embarrassment of riches, and we can only select briefly, as well as we may.

We must not, moreover, take too sharply the distinction between Hellenism and Hebraism, nor seek to base any *precise* apportionment of influence upon Arnold's impressionistic contrast between the two. His picture of a Greek world of radiant confidence in man's reason and perfectibility,[2] as opposed to a Zion ever conscious of the obstacles which obstruct man's path to perfection, may well reflect the classical eighteenth century reconstruction of Greece, rather than a Greece that ever existed. The sense of the sinful and fallen state of man was prominent in Orphic religions, and for Plato too the body could be a tomb in which philosophy teaches us how to die and be delivered from the evils of the world and the curse of time.[3] As to the mythology of Greece, indeed, this truth has long been recognised. The fact that its philosophy on the whole subdued its mythology was in broad tendency a massive triumph over irrational elements in the myths. Nor was this triumph of rationality a simple process of philosophy overcoming the myths; for in early Greek notions of justice, for example, the subduing of irrationalism was a process which began *within* the myths, to be continued in philosophy. The triumph, however, was never

---

[1] See Matthew Arnold, *Culture and Anarchy* (1869) 143. *Cf.* A. N. Whitehead, *Adventures of Ideas* (Penguin ed., 1948) 17-18, who attributes to these two influences the origins of the "notions concerning the status of mankind in general and of individual men in particular, and a discipline and direction in the general exercise of mentality", which combined to base "the modern phase of progress within the European races."

[2] See Arnold, *op. cit.* 145ff., esp. at 151-52.

[3] See W. Barrett, *Irrational Man* (1961) 63-64. And *cf.* generally E. R. Dodds, *The Greeks and the Irrational* (1951).

A

absolute, nor the struggle ever fully ended.[4]

§2. DELINEATION OF "JUSTICE" IN GREEK MYTHOLOGY.[5] The attributes of
the mythical Themis, counsellor of Zeus, and Dike, goddess of judgments,
and their relations to each other and to the other gods, allegorise clearly
enough early Greek notions of justice. And however such myths started,
it is clear that genuine ethical insights were steadily joined to their drama
and poetry.

Themis, the daughter of Uranus, god of the firmament, and Gaia, the
goddess of Earth, combined her father's stature with the firmness, form and
depth of her mother. She was a Titan, and her Titanic character came to
dominate the myth,[6] fading, however, as later versions brought out the ethical
and rational import of her role. She was the counsellor of Zeus, king of all
the gods, personifying his rational thought; and she was his foster-mother
and consort too. Later versions make her the counsellor of men in prudence;
and she has the care of oracles, public assemblies, and civilised institutions
generally.

The daughters of Themis and Zeus were Eirene, Eunomia, and Tyche,
the goddesses of peace, good government, and of hidden contingency; and
Dike, the goddess of justice. Justice, then, is the daughter of Power and Good
Counsel, and the sister of Peace, Good Government and Chance, different from
each, but closely related to all. The enemies of justice were the goddesses
Hybris (excess and distortion), Eris (strife), and Dysnomia (disorder),
Lethe (forgetfulness and concealment), and the Amphilogiai (false and
ambiguous words); the last three all daughters of strife (Eris). The other
associates and helpers of Dike were Styx, Nemesis, the Erinyes, and the
Praxidikai, all of them concerned with some aspect of execution of law
or punishment of violation, the last named being assigned to execute the
judgments of Dike herself. These judgments of Dike, by contrast with those
of her mother, Themis, were not always indisputable and inviolable, and
were even open to misunderstanding and argument. While she helped all
who sought their rights, and did so without fear or favour, the final outcome
for the suitors still rested with Tyche, the goddess of chance, who here
paralleled the role of Moira, the Titanic god of inscrutable destiny, mentioned
in the next Section.

When we have discounted all that our modern hindsights have read
into all this, there remains still a composite of insights about justice—of
lawfulness, rightness and reasonableness, of movement from divine origin
into disputation by humans, of continuity and preservation of social balance

---

[4] See F. M. Cornford, *Principium Sapientiae* (1952) *passim. Cf.* on the relation
between philosophy and mythology Strauss, *Natural Right* 82; and Aristotle's distinction
there quoted (*Metaphysics* 981b, 27-29; 982b, 18) between the first philosophers
("men who discoursed on nature") and the mythmakers ("men who discoursed on
gods"). On the early blend of cosmology and mythology see G. S. Kirk and J. E.
Raven, *The Presocratic Philosophers* (2 imp. 1959) 8-72.

[5] For additional references on early Greek thought on justice, see *infra* Ch. 2, n.2.
On the insight from mythology see also W. Jaeger, "Praise of Law" in Sayre (ed.),
Modern Legal Philosophies 352-375.

[6] According to Hesiod, the etymology of "Titan" indicated "straining", or
"vengeance"; see Cornford, *op. cit.* 203. This of course is sheer popular etymology,
but may account for the classification of Themis as a "Titan", which seems to have
been a Hesiodic gloss. It would be apt enough, e.g., for her role in accounts of
the Trojan wars. See generally on the correlation of the developing mythological
picture of Themis with changing social circumstances, H. Vos, *Themis* (1956); J. E.
Harrison, *Themis* (1912). But *cf. infra* n. 10.

emerging from dynamic struggle, the whole in a mood of circumspection and anxious care.[7] Yet the issue of all this, the issue of Dike, is ultimately serenity, for Dike gave virgin birth to one daughter, Hesychia, goddess of "stillness resting in itself".[8]

§3. "JUSTICE" IN EARLY GREEK PHILOSOPHY. We have said that refinement of the insights of the myths largely paralleled the growth of philosophical accounts of justice. And there may well have been moments at which the earlier philosophical accounts still maintained crudities which the mythical tradition had already outgrown. Certainly the philosophical tradition never entirely shook off two features of the early myths. One of these, which continues often into our own day, is the failure or inability to sort out exactly what particular kinds of goodness, of ought-to-be, we call justice; and (even more) to say what it is which makes these kinds of goodness similar to each other and different from other kinds of goodness. The second feature is the visualisation of "justice" on a level quite transcending the regulation of mere human behaviour, and indeed as not directly concerned with it at all.

Cornford has said of the Greek *philosophical* approach to medicine (as distinct from the empirical approach), that it "began with cosmogony, inheriting the traditional problems implied in cosmological myths", and that the consideration of man only entered after a long chain of postulates about how all things began, and about how the order of the universe emerged from this. No less is to be said of the Greek philosophical approach to law, justice and politics.[9] "Justice" first came into view as a kind of metaphysical cosmological principle regulating the operation of the forces of nature on the elements of the universe, securing balance and harmony among all.[10] In the

---

[7] See Tammelo, "Justice and Doubt" 326, esp. 324-26; and in more detail E. Wolf, 1 *Griechisches Rechtsdenken* (1950) 19-69. See also Del Vecchio, *Justice* c. ii; H. Kelsen, *Society and Nature* (1943) 196-199, 356ff.; R. Mondolfo, *Problemi del Mondo Antico* (1936) cc. i, ii; E. Paresce, *La Problematica Storica della Filosofia del Diritto* (1952) c. iv; G. Glotz, *Etudes Sociales et Juridiques sur l'Antiquité Grecque* (1906) c. i.

[8] The above is the basic picture of Dike. We should not, perhaps, indulge further speculation from the fact that while, with Greek sophistication, Themis grew in beauty and ideality, Dike tended rather to diminish in these. Dike grew in power, severity and even cruelty, into a symbol of inexorable vengeance and punishment. Del Vecchio, *Justice* 7, attributes this to the growing authority and secularisation of the State and law.

[9] On the cosmological approach see F. M. Cornford, *supra* n. 4, at 38. As to the impracticality of the *practical* approach to these matters, and the possibility that this very impracticality promoted the philosophical questings here reviewed, see *infra* Ch. 2, n.5. Certainly the moral standards which A. W. Adkins, *Merit and Responsibility* (1960) 201ff. has drawn from Greek *practice* are rather odd-sounding today.

[10] See P. Guérin, *L'Idée de Justice . . . chez les Premiers Philosophes Grecs* (1934). See *infra* §4 as to the similar origin of the idea of "natural law", and *cf.* the discussion of conflicting views on this matter in Patterson, *Jurisprudence* 335. We here substantially agree with Patterson on this point. For a contrary view suggesting that the cosmological principle of justice was an anthropomorphic transference of a social principle already developed in the prephilosophical period see Jaeger, *op. cit. supra* n. 5, 357; and *cf.* (so far as we understand him) H. Wheeler in Cogley (ed.), *Natural Law* 194, at 212-17.

At any rate, the focus on general harmony of all-inclusive ambit is clear. See, e.g., the description in *Odyssey* xix. 108ff., interpreted, however, by Adkins, *op. cit. supra* n. 9, at 66, as foreshadowing the notion of justice as a means to social ends. *Cf.* with this focus the drive to avoid "pollution", and its disastrous consequences (as in the Oedipus legend). See Adkins, *op. cit.* c. v. Both these mystical notions connect no doubt with the continuing idea that justice has among its tasks to "keep right" some kind of regulative balance, and to "set it right" when disturbed. And *cf.* for echoes in Egyptian and Hebrew thought, Cohen, *op. cit. infra* n.71, at 206-207, though as to the latter we question the reliance on *Proverbs* 16. 11.

earliest recorded *philosophical* use of the word "Dike", by Anaximander,[11] all things are said to arise from and to return ultimately to "the Boundless", "for they give justice and make reparation to one another for their injustice, according to the arrangement of time".

For ideas of justice less obscure than this, philosophy had to wait for the Pythagoreans,[12] whose notion of justice as equality has ever since remained in different ways woven into all philosophy about justice. The Pythagorean particular application took the form of retaliation — but in a broad sense requiring both that the reward of good human action equal its degree of goodness, and that punishment of bad action equal its degree of badness. Punishment must fit the crime quantitatively. This human application, however, was but incidental to retaliation in cosmic adjustment generally; and it was further distorted by the mathematical mystique, offered in purported explanation, that "Justice is like a square number: it gives back the same for the same, and thus is the same multiplied by the same."[13]

It was with Plato[14] that Greek philosophy came to make the notion of justice into an ethical principle for human conduct, a specifically human virtue. Yet even then, justice was the virtue of all things, requiring that there

---

[11] *Circa* 560 B.C. See H. Diels, *Die Fragmente der Vorsokratiker* (5 ed. 1934) 89, fragm. 1; and Freeman, *Ancilla* 19, fragm. 1. For interpretations of this *dictum* see W. Jaeger, 1 *Paideia: The Ideals of Greek Culture* (1939) 157ff.; J. Burnet, *Early Greek Philosophy* (4 ed. 1950) 54; R. Mondolfo, *Problemi del Pensiero Antico* (1936) 3-85; G. Vlastos, "Equality and Justice in Early Greek Cosmologies" (1947) 42 *Classical Philology* 156-178, esp. 171ff.; M. Heidegger, *Holzwege* (2 ed. 1950) 296-343; E. Wolf, 1 *Griechisches Rechtsdenken* (1950) 218-234; Kirk and Raven, *op. cit. supra* n. 4, 117-121, 140 (and *cf.* on "the Boundless" *id.* 108-117); and C. H. Kahn, *Anaximander and the Origins of Greek Cosmology* (1960).

[12] Our knowledge of Pythagoras (*flor.* 580-500 B.C.) is derived only from later followers. On his idea of justice see Del Vecchio, *Justice* 42-50; A. Verdross, *Grundlinien der antiken Rechts-und Staatsphilosophie* (2 ed. 1948) 26-29. For Greek criticisms and practical applications of the equality notion see A. H. Jones, *Athenian Democracy* (1957) 45ff. And on the contemporary standing of "equality" as a key to justice see *infra* Ch. 11 §§2-3.

Other pre-Socratic references to justice have survived, including those of Parmenides of Elea (*circa* 475 B.C.: see Freeman, *Ancilla* 43, fragms. 7-8); Damon of Athens (*circa* 460 B.C. reported by Philodemus: see Freeman, *op. cit.* 71, fragm. 4); Democritus of Abdera (*circa* 420 B.C.: see Freeman, *op. cit.* 108, fragm. 174, and 114, fragm. 256). For other *dicta* of Democritus see *infra* nn. 20, 62. Particularly notable here is "To God, all things are beautiful, good and just; but men have assumed some things to be just, others unjust" (Heraclitus of Ephesus, *circa* 500 B.C.: see Freeman, *op. cit.* 31, fragm. 102 and for other sayings of Heraclitus see *infra* §4.) Strauss, *Natural Right* 93-4, sees this as a "crucial" text asserting that "the very distinction between just and unjust is merely a human supposition or a human convention", indicating the emergence of both rationality and relativism closely conjoined. The Greek *locus classicus* of the insight, however, is surely in Protagoras, as to whom see *infra* Ch. 8, §3.

[13] See Aristotle, *Magna Moralia*, i, 1, 1182a, 14, 1194a, 28; *Nichomachean Ethics* v, 8. The first square numbers (4 and 9) were therefore identified with justice: on the apparently quite literal sense in which this identification was intended, see Kirk and Raven, *op. cit supra* n. 4, 248-250. A more interesting contribution of the Greek mathematician-philosophers was that of Archytas of Tarentum (4th century B.C.), who strikingly anticipated the later appeal to "Right Reason" (see *infra* Ch. 2, esp. §11) by appealing to "Right Reckoning". This, he said, "checks civil strife and increases concord; for where it has been achieved, there can be no excess of gain, and equality reigns", whether in business contracts, the distribution of bounty, or the deterring of wrongdoers. And see Freeman, *Ancilla* 80, fragm. 3. No doubt mathematics showed Archytas the way to Right Reckoning; how, we do not know. And *cf. infra* Ch. 2, §12, as to mathematicism in Leibniz and Descartes.

For a comparison with the Hebraic *lex talionis* see Cohen, *infra* n. 71 at 207; and see *infra* §5.

[14] Plato lived 427-347 B.C. On the Platonic idea of justice see J. Hall, "Plato's Legal Philosophy" (1956) 31 *Ind. L.J.* 171; H. Kelsen, *What is Justice?* (1957) 82-109; A. Verdross, *supra* n. 12, 69-126; B. Horvath, *"Die Gerechtigkeitslehre des Sokrates*

shall happen whatever ethically ought to happen, and not one merely characterising human motives and conduct. And Plato's famous formula of justice, that each do what pertains to him, *suum agere*, expresses merely this general idea. Each thing should do or be what it lies in each to do or be; in the modern idiom one should "do oneself justice", and in the social aspect, one should perform one's vocation, pull one's weight, do what is required by one's position.[15] The principle is designed to assign to each action, and to each human virtue, like wisdom, courage and temperance, its proper part in the social and ethical whole. These other virtues have their place in justice; or rather justice is the correct placing of all of them.[16] This remains still finally an identification of "justice" with goodness in general, which theory has ever since struggled to get beyond.[17]

The most influential of the Greek theories of justice was, of course, that of Aristotle. To this subject, as to others, Aristotle brought a capacity for sober, careful, systematic analysis;[18] and though justice retains still, with

---

und des Platon" (1931) 10 *Z.ö.R.* 258-280; A.-H. Chroust, ". . . Plato's Political Philosophy" (1962) 48 *Arch. R.- und Sozialph.* 449-486. The relevant Platonic dialogues are *Politeia* and *Nomoi.* As to traces in his work of the Pythagorean mathematicism discussed *supra* n. 13, see S. Buchanan, in Cogley (ed.), *Natural Law* 82, at 88-90.

[15] See *Republic* 433-434. For a strong attack on this theory of justice as "purely totalitarian and anti-humanitarian", see Popper, 1 *Open Society* c. vi; but see generally on this thesis R. B. Levinson, *In Defense of Plato* (1953), Wild, *Plato's Enemies,* esp. 19ff. On the importance of Plato's social context see Jaeger, essay cited *supra* n. 5, 363-64, and of his intellectual context, Adkins, *op. cit. supra* n. 9, 255ff. Plato's view links with the old view of justice as a principle of cosmological harmony: *cf.* on the analogy between his "justice" as harmony of the parts of the soul, and "health" as harmony of those of the body, *Republic* 444d and Jaeger, *op. cit.* 366. Both these "harmonies" are probably Pythagorean in origin: for "health" see Alcmaeon of Croton (5th century B.C.), discussed Kirk and Raven, *op. cit. supra* n. 4, 234. In modern thought the implications of the analogy with "health" are rather different. See I. Jenkins in *Nomos, Justice* 191 at 218.

On the substantial controversy we permit ourselves to add that when the evils of rigid social stratification come even uninvited, a theory of justice which can easily be misread as a justification of them must have dangerous potentialities in concrete social application. The ideal of the Indian caste system was, no doubt, that each member of society had his own *Dharma,* each class its own proper righteousness, all together doing "the work of the cosmos". (See H. Zimmer, *Philosophies of India* (ed. J. Campbell, 1951; reissued 1956) 162-163). The *Mahabharata* I, 64, 247-248 and *id.,* 68, 2805, looks back to the *Krita* age — a kind of golden age of caste, when this was concretely realised without the evils of caste. *Cf.* Zimmer, *op. cit.* 151. And see Blackshield, *"Pensiero Umano"* 497-98, esp. n.72. But the chances of long survival of such a golden age, if it ever existed, are slight in the Earthly City. And in modern theories of justice the Platonic notion can have, at best, a strictly subsidiary role. See, e.g., Lamont, *Moral Judgment* 157ff., 168ff. And see now Chroust, *cit. supra* last n.

[16] It was indeed a saying of the Greek poets that: "In justice all virtues are gathered together". See, e.g., Theognis 147, Phocylides 17.

[17] Though it still holds important truth in that the need for justice *usually* arises through the presence or absence of some other virtue. Justice tells us to punish (or at least not to reward) *a bad man,* and to reward (or at least not to punish) *a good man.* But this is only *usually*; and indeed in the Anglo-American criminal law it is regarded as basically unjust to allow the character or propensity of the accused to weigh towards conviction of the specific offence charged. See generally on "justice" and "goodness" J. Rawls, in *Nomos, Justice* 98 at 99; C. J. Friedrich, in *id.* 24 at 27; I. Jenkins, in *id.* 191 at 218.

[18] Lived *circa* 384-322 B.C. His influence here is especially based on the *Nichomachean Ethics,* bks. ii, v. And see M. Hamburger, *Morals and Law* (1951) *passim,* esp. 33-110; M. Salomon, *Der Begriff der Gerechtigkeit bei Aristoteles* (1937); Kelsen, *op. cit. supra* n. 14, 110-136; Patterson, *Jurisprudence* 338; B. Horvath, *Die Gerechtigkeitslehre des Aristoteles* (1931); R. McKeon, "Justice and Equality", in *Nomos, Justice* 44, at 54-57.

Aristotle's penchant for "ticketing" and "labelling" perhaps proceeded not only from the above qualities, but from his interest in zoology; just as Pound's similar penchant probably linked with his interest in botany. Most of the much-maligned terminology of the medieval Scholastics (see Ch. 2, §§4-6, and esp. n.117 as to Scotus),

him, primarily a reference comprehending virtue in general, he came to distinguish side by side with this (or perhaps from within it) a narrower concept of justice, nearer to modern thought.[19] In this particular sense justice is equality, when this is thought of as the right proportion, the mean, or middle or equal distance between the extremes of too much and too little.[20] Within this, he further distinguished distributive justice from synallagmatic (or rectificatory or corrective or equalising or bilateral) justice. Distributive justice, he says, is the principle on which wealth and honours are to be distributed to the citizens of the community; here, nearest to the Pythagorean origins, the equality is between what each gets and what he deserves. Synallagmatic justice is the principle governing dealings[21] between one citizen and another; here the equality is to be between what is given and what is received. He also further distinguished natural from conventional justice in a sense shortly to be explained. And he made finally clear that "justice is something that pertains to persons."[22]

§4. GREEK ORIGINS OF "NATURAL LAW". It is clear that the concept of "natural law" emerged in Greek philosophy concurrently and in entanglement with the notions of justice, representing still another expression of the rational endeavour to overcome the irrationalism of early myths. In these myths Moira, who personified inscrutable destiny, allotted to each man a destiny which, be it happy or unhappy, merited or unmerited, he must accept.[23] "Justice" lay first in the inscrutable will of the gods, so that fate impenetrable to the rational understanding took its relentless course. As speculative hope, and then conviction, created a cosmology in which the appearance of chaos and discord were drawn aside to reveal a cosmic order and rationality, so too with human nature and human duties. "Justice" was still fulfilment of the will of the gods, but this was a *rational* will, accessible to human reason. Historically the emergence of the notion of divine law marched with that of the fact of human law, with perhaps some anthro-

---

and many other basic philosophic terms, were derived from Aristotle. *Cf.* on Aristotle's "unrivalled sobriety", Strauss, *Natural Right* 156.

[19] See Salomon, *op. cit. supra* n. 18, 10ff. Even in the comprehensive sense justice is perhaps not so much "the sum of all the virtues" as "the sum of all the social virtues". See *Nichomachean Ethics* v. 1 (1129b, 26); and *cf.* the discussion in *id.* v. II (esp. at 1138a, 19) of whether a man can do injustice to himself.

[20] Though this is still spoken of as "Aristotle's Mean", it had already been somewhat anticipated, e.g., in Democritus of Abdera (in Freeman, *Ancilla* 103, fragm. 102), and perhaps even (in terms of musical harmony) in Pythagoras. See generally for Democritus as the author of "the first rigidly naturalistic ethics in Greek thought", G. Vlastos, "Ethics and Physics in Democritus" (1945) 54 *Phil. R.* 578, (1946) 55 *id.* 53; Kirk and Raven, *op. cit. supra* n. 4, 424-26; and *infra* n.62.

[21] Including both "transactions" in the broadest legal sense, and any other encounters.

[22] *Politics* 1282b; and *cf. Nichomachean Ethics* v, 9 (1137a, 30). This view, with its overtones of individual responsibility for the judgment of justice, would have been impossible before Socrates. *Cf.* the thesis of Adkins, *supra* n. 9, that from the Homeric period onwards the overriding standard and sanction of Greek morality was "what people will say". See the examples given *id.* 48-49, 154-56, esp. *Odyssey* xxi. 323ff. "Until Socrates, no one takes a firm stand and says 'let them mock'." (*id.*, 155-156). *Cf.* Benn and Peters, *Principles* 26.

[23] See Flückiger, 1 *Geschichte* 32. And see *supra* n. 10. *Cf.* Adkins, *op. cit. supra* n. 9, at 17-25, 119, arguing that this presents the world, not as a determined "clockwork", but rather as "a game of celestial snakes and ladders. Most moves are free; but should one alight at the foot of one's own particular ladder, or at the head of one's own personal snake, the next move is determined." (*id.* 19). *Cf.* W. C. Green, *Moira* (1944).

pomorphic transition. The human law was *nomos*, compounded of custom and the exigencies of physical, psychological, political and social conditions. The divine law, *logos*, is made by reason and expresses reason and not mere inscrutable fate.[24]

The notion of law as a cosmic principle is also used quite early to base the individual's placing in the community: the *polis* is seen to rest on *nomos* and *logos*. The fragments of Heraclitus (*circa* 500 B.C.) reveal (for all their obscurity) what are clearly gropings towards self-understanding of man as part of the wider whole of the earthly city, and the order of the universe. Wisdom, said this sage, is "to speak the truth and to act according to nature. . . . If we speak with intelligence, we must base our strength on that which is common to all, as the city on the law (*Nomos*), and even more strongly. For all human laws are nourished by one, which is divine. For it governs as far as it will, and is sufficient for all, and more than enough".[25] Cryptic as are the words, the whole vision is there, of one universal rational law, with which things *in their nature* accord. The law of the State expresses it, and each citizen acting conformably to his nature will find justice in observing it.

If, indeed, the broad vision was thus early achieved, it was not long held steady as state law became secularised and sacred custom came to appear as but custom or habit, or as the statute or decree of human rulers.[26] The breaks in the vision were not due merely to the wide differences between the laws of different peoples. These must have been obvious enough to Heraclitus without preventing him from seeing the universal law *within* the diversity, not beyond it; just as in his whole cosmology it was to be found within the ceaseless flux.[27] It was after all Heraclitus who wrote that "That which is in opposition is in concert, and from things that differ comes the most beautiful harmony."[28] So that it was not a sudden discovery of diversity, but rather a failing of faith, which broke the vision. Or (what seems to be the same thing) it was a more naturalistic philosophical standpoint, from which the divine law, though still accepted, was seen as clearly something *distinct from* and *above* actual human laws. And no doubt, as men exercised their new-found rational access to the divine law, conflict with positive law presented itself as a problem.[29]

---

[24] M. Le Bel, "Natural Law in the Greek Period" (1948) 2 *Nat. L. Inst. Proc.* 3 at 7.

[25] See Freeman, *Ancilla* 32, fragms. 112, 114. See Kirk and Raven, *op. cit. supra* n. 4, 204-05, 212-14. Such *dicta* of Heraclitus were made the basis for the later Stoic philosophy: see *id.* 186.

[26] Friedrich, *Philosophy of Law* 13.

[27] H. A. Rommen, *The Natural Law* (1947) 6; Kirk and Raven, *op. cit.* 187, 192ff. This would be a deeper Heraclitean answer to the challenge of diversity of conceptions of what is right than the more commonplace paradox, *error multiplex veritas una*, that the variety of errors presupposes one truth. Strauss (*Natural Right* 97-100, 124-25) finally refines the commonplace through his account of Socratic "dialectics" almost into the deeper view. But of course neither answer meets the *practical* difficulties which this diversity creates for reliance on "universal" natural law conceptions.

[28] Freeman, *Ancilla* 25, fragm. 8.

[29] For the famous early formulation by Sophocles see *Antigone* 446-470. There should perhaps be more questioning of the assumption that this is *the* origin of natural law, both because great dramatists often give dramatic form to problems currently agitated in society; and because the play presents natural law not only as a revolutionary force (in Antigone's appeal to "the unwritten and unfailing statutes of heaven"), but also as a conservative force which the tyrant Creon invoked. See for perhaps more significant aspects of the *Antigone* as a moving affirmation of humanist faith in the glory of human nature, *id.* 332-375, on which see Le Bel, *supra* n. 24, at 39-41; Jaeger, *supra* n. 5, at 361-62.

There can be no doubt as to either the fact or the importance of the decline of religious faith. The fifth century Sophists departed both from faith and from acceptance of the State *nomos* as such, towards a relativistic, and almost "historical" approach in matters of law and morals.[30] They regarded the latter as determined by circumstances of time and place, and to that extent accidental. Law in their eyes might thus often be contrary to "nature". Envisaging thus the straying of law from "nature", and especially from "human nature", they moved into the position of asserting these latter as the universal criterion of law and all social institutions.[31] Man's nature, or (more briefly) man himself, was for them "the measure of all things",[32] and its fulfilment should be their aim. They formulated the contrast between man-made law and "law according to nature".

A man therefore can best conduct himself in harmony with justice, if when in the company of witnesses he upholds the laws of the city; and when alone without witnesses he upholds the edicts of nature. For the edicts of the laws are imposed artificially, but those of nature are compulsory. And the edicts of the laws are arrived at by consent, not by natural growth, whereas those of nature are not a matter of consent.[33]

In a passage like this, the universal *logos* is in a sense still present. Yet by making man's nature the measure, and (implicitly) man's reason the recorder of its decrees, the Sophists extracted from the humanity-transcending *logos* which man *may* discover, but *must* in any case accept, a way of valuing law, a criterion of its justice, which was to become in the coming millennia the antithetic pole to natural law theorising. In this kind of criterion, justice repudiates the matrix of the universal *logos,* and becomes a value not only discoverable by man, in any case to be obeyed, but even tends to become a value *conferred* by man, man being the measure of all things. And since they often also fixed man's nature by his self-interest and self-preservation, they introduced an *individualistic* version of natural law that was also to set patterns for later times.

The transition from the Sophist man-based natural law to the politico-legal theories of Plato is thought to have been effected by the author of the *Anonymus Iamblichi,* who attacked as the gravest evil the advocacy (which

---

30 Strauss, *Natural Right* 115ff., perhaps goes too far in identifying them with "sophists" in the popular sense. On their later efforts to re-establish a universal obligatory law see Flückiger, 1 *Geschichte* 87. And see generally E. Zeller, 2 *History of Greek Philosophy* (1881) 394ff., esp. at 469-480, 496ff.; M. Untersteiner, *1 Sofisti* (1949); Welzel, *Naturrecht* 12ff.; Vinogradoff, 1 *Jurisprudence* 25; E. García Máynez, *"El Derecho Natural en la Epoca de Socrates"* in *id., Ensayos Filosófico-Jurídicos* (1959) 85ff.

31 The Sophists were thus the first to advance *in so many words* the idea of a "natural law": see Flückiger, 1 *Geschichte* 88 and Verdross, *Abendländische Rechts-philosophie . . .* (1958) 20. Strauss, *Natural Right,* c. iii *passim,* esp. 95, stresses the importance of this emergence, for instance as directing inquiries back to the "original things" which antedate convention, already involved in the mythology. Was this pristine state perfect or imperfect? If imperfect, was it gentleness or savagery? *Cf.* on the importance of such questions A. R. Blackshield, "Empiricist and Rationalist Theories of Justice" (1962) 48 *Arch. R.- und Sozialph.* 25 at 41, and *infra* Ch. 2, §13. And see Cicero, *Pro Sestio* 91-92, and *id., Tusculanarum Quaestionum* v. 5-6.

32 Protagoras, as reported by Plato, *Theaetetus* 152a.

33 Antiphon the Sophist (5th century B.C.). See Freeman, *Ancilla* 147, fragm. 44. Note the whole fragment and *cf.* Strauss, *Natural Right* 102-105. *Cf.* on the *Tetralogies* attributed to Antiphon, interpreting them as an attempt to set up human standards of justice against "the law" identified with the claims of superstition, Adkins, *op. cit. supra* n. 9, 102ff.

he attributed to the Sophists) of the unchecked and ruthless use of one's natural faculties.[34] Plato regarded the moral decay and the reign of power and aggression[35] in the Athens of his day, as the result of the Sophist failure to reestablish the link between justice and law which their scepticism of the *nomos* of the State had undermined.[36] He thought that the question raised by the Sophists whether law (*nomos*) was a mere expression of the positive will of the governors, or was endowed with a "natural" and therefore universal validity, was insoluble unless "nature" was seen to have a wider ontological foundation, that is, a wider ground in reality, than the Sophists admitted.[37] Plato's solution was to elevate "nature" from the sphere of contingent facts to that of supreme and absolute values,[38] assigning "reality" to a world accessible only to the intellect, that of the unchanging archetypes or Forms or Ideas of things. "Natural law" in his sense, then, was the unchanging Idea of law, which being forever the same, readily becomes also the measure and criterion of positive law. And unless the shifting and changing positive laws reflect this true law, this Idea of law, they cannot claim to be law at all. Moreover, said Plato, since only philosophers are freed by disciplined thinking from the illusions of the senses sufficiently to grasp this realm of Ideas, it is philosophers who should make the laws.

Aristotle[39] accepted the view of "nature" which transcended the variability of things as perceived by the senses, but rejected Plato's dichotomy between the essence of things as grasped by the intellect and their factual existence. Or rather he reinterpreted it as the relation between what a thing is perceived to be, on the one hand, and what it is when its potentialities are developed, on the other. "Nature" was an "entelechy". It was teleological, each thing being ordered towards an end, a goal, bearing (as it were) in itself the seed of its full stature. "Reality" was the unfolding of the potentiality, the fulfilment of end, the stature of full growth. "What each thing is when fully developed we call its nature, whether we are speaking of a man, a horse or a family."[40] Applied to man, this concept revealed

---

[34] For diverse and in some respects conflicting interpretations of this work, see Jaeger, essay cited *supra* n. 5, 365-66 (identifying him as "a Sophist who wrote about the end of the Peloponnesian War", and who based a "highly modernistic apology for law" on its "practical usefulness"), and Freeman, *Ancilla* 162.

[35] See the tenor of the Athenian envoys' speech as reported by Thucydides (*Peloponnesian War*, v. 104), which is said finally to have combined Athens' enemies to her ruin. But see for a gentler reading of such speeches in Thucydides, Adkins, *supra* n. 9, 221ff.

[36] Yet, of course, the fading of faith in the old ways and the old gods which had led to all this was an essential part of the rational emancipation of thought. It had begun well before the Sophists (see esp. as to Xenophanes of Colophon (*circa* 570-475 B.C.) Kirk and Raven, *op. cit. supra* n. 4 at 167-172); and was also a *sine qua non* of Plato's own work. *Cf.* the perceptive (even when fanciful) interpretation in Strauss, *Natural Right* 84-85, of the allegorical settings of the Platonic dialogues most relevant to law. The disputants in the *Republic*, for example, are supposed to be watching the traditional torch race honouring the goddess Bendis, and are playing truant as it were in the absence of Cephalus the traditional head of the house.

[37] See A. J. Festugière, *Contemplation et Vie Contemplative selon Platon* (1950) 414. The materialism of Epicurean philosophy met with similar Platonic deprecation (see *Laws* 889b-890); though Plato was himself anxious to show that "the just life" was also the most pleasant life (*id.* 662-63).

[38] *Id.* 136. And see generally on Plato, esp. for a valuable appraisal of practical aspects of his thoughts on law, Cairns, *Plato to Hegel* c. ii; and on his reaction to the Sophists S. Buchanan, in Cogley (ed.), *Natural Law* 82, at 83ff.

[39] As to whom see *id.* c. iii; M. S. Shellens, "Aristotle..." (1959) 4 *Nat. L. Forum* 72; Patterson, *Jurisprudence* 336-341, Wild, *supra* n. 15, c. vi; and other works cited *supra* n. 18. On the brevity of Aristotle's main treatment, in the *Nichomachean Ethics*, see Strauss, *Natural Right* 156, and Shellens, *op. cit.* at 73ff.

[40] Aristotle, *Politics*, i, 2 (Jowett's transl. 28).

his nature as moral, rational and social. For "it is characteristic of man that he alone has any sense of good or evil, of just or unjust; and the association of living beings who have this sense makes a family and a state."[41] And as with man, so with all things. The harmonious ordering of all the phenomena of existence emerged when each of these phenomena was regarded in its fullest development.

This concept, as applied to man in society, yielded Aristotle's famous distinction between natural and conventional justice:[42]

> Of political justice part is natural, that which everywhere has the same force and does not exist by peoples thinking this or that; part is *laid down by law*, that which is originally indifferent, but when it has been laid down is not indifferent. . . . The things which are just by virtue of convention and expediency are like measures: for wine and corn measures are not everywhere equal. . . . Similarly the things which are just not by nature but by human enactment are not everywhere the same . . . though there is but one which is everywhere by nature the best.

For sacral absoluteness and transcendence inaccessible to human understanding Aristotle thus offered to substitute a secular absoluteness and transcendence, based precisely on the potentiality for perfection of all things as seen by man's reason. Man's reason, however, is neither the Sophist reason of each man for himself which negatives both absoluteness and transcendence, nor is it the reason enjoyed by Plato's philosophers. It is the reason of everyman. A particular man's "reason" (as we shall see) might not discover what everyman's discovered; and this was to remain ever a problem for natural law, soothed but never quieted by declaring the particular man's reason corrupt.[43]

At this point the Greek contributions to Western thought about justice merge into the story of natural law as the vessel which bore the ancient ideas of justice to the centre of European juristic and political speculation. And this story is so long and rich and detailed that we have assigned to it a further introductory chapter, Chapter 2. Bearing this in mind, we may devote most of the balance of the present Chapter to the Hebraic stream of influence, especially since this stream is less well-known, and has until very recently been rather neglected in jurisprudential discourse.

§5. HEBREW CONTRIBUTIONS TO "JUSTICE": ORIGINS AND FINAI MEANING OF THE *LEX TALIONIS*. Matthew Arnold was right to detect a sharp difference in interest and in emphasis between Greek and Hebrew

---

[41] Aristotle, *loc. cit.* 29.

[42] Aristotle, *Nichomachean Ethics*, v, 7 (1134b-1135a) (Ross's transl. 1931). We have ventured to substitute the italicised words for Ross's "legal". On the philosophers problem (perhaps self-created) as to Aristotle's assertion, *ibid.*, that what is just i changeable, see Strauss, *Natural Right* 157ff., Shellens, *op. cit.* n.39, at 81ff. And se *id.* 97 for the thesis that Aristotle's "natural law" supplemented his "justice", to cove persons excluded by lack of parity from "the blessings of justice".

[43] Strauss, *Natural Right* 98-99 (and see also *supra* n. 27) admirably restates th problem of the plea of "corruption". In view of the diversity of notions of justice "from society to society or from age to age", the plea implies that only some particular society or societies, or even only one generation therein, would be "normal human beings". The point might be extended to the possibility that only some particular men are "normal". And see *infra* Ch. 2, §24, Ch. 7, §§8ff. Strauss's own position is of course different from the above.

traditions of thought about law and justice. Whether we think of the Torah as transmitted through Moses, or of the prophetic writings, the classical Hebrew teachings were rather precepts for man's daily social conduct, than ideas to prod or satisfy their intellectual questings.[44] Justice and righteousness were to emerge not so much from arguments in the academies, as from living, whether in the home, or at the royal court, on the field of grain, or in the market place, at the gates of the city, or in the wilderness, week in week out, divided only by the sabbatical and jubilee years.

Comparisons of the Mosaic Code with that of Hammurabi show that the latter was more elaborated in its commercial aspects, and obviously designed for a society of more commercial maturity.[45] It is no less clear that the Mosaic code addresses itself with a firm and practical didactic purpose, to correcting the individual and social moralities and customs of its age. This practical drive appears in ordinances of animal sacrifice which seek to adapt existing customs, while abolishing human sacrifice and the worship of idols. It appears no less in its precepts concerning those who lived to a greater or lesser degree at the whim of others. The domestic animal, the slave, the servant, the wife, the child, the orphan, the widow, the people themselves, are the subject no doubt of broad and noble protective proclamations based on the "blessed" nature of all creation. Yet these are but generalisations upon practical minutiae about not seething the kid in its mother's milk, about the sabbath rest and eventual emancipation of the slave, about connubial rights and duties, about leaving for the poor the unreaped corners of the field (and grain dropped in gathering the corn into sheaves, and sheaves forgotten in gathering in the sheaves, and the three-yearly tithe),[46] and about the duties of kingship. The prophetic teachings were addressed centuries later to a people already weaned from the crudest and cruellest customs of the region; for that reason they appear more orientated to principle than to precept. Yet even there the principles will most often be found to be principles of action in human relations rather than cosmological principles, and the precepts, for instance concerning the orphan and the widow, will be found embedded in the poetry and the allegory. And, of course, above all, the Hebrew tradition unlike the Greek appears to have been presented by its authors and redactors as well as by its rabbinic interpreters as a revealed and rather concrete system of regulation.

These and other features can be correctly urged to support the differentiation of the Hebrew from the Greek tradition. But it is all the more necessary not to accept uncritically the characterisation of the distinction usually given. The Hebrew concept, it is sometimes said, is of a retaliatory justice, a justice of vengeance;[47] indeed, the maxim "an eye for an eye and a tooth for a tooth" the *lex talionis,* is often spoken of as if it comprised the essence of "the Mosaic law". Even if this were taken as correct, this differentiation from Greek law would not be very clear; for in

---

[44] *Cf.* K. Kahana Kagan, *Three Great Systems of Jurisprudence* (1955) 128-29.

[45] *Cf.* J. H. Hertz (ed.), *The Pentateuch and Haftorahs* (1950) 405-406. *Cf.* nevertheless, on the greater humaneness of the Mosaic Code, the recent study by the Professor of Near Eastern Studies, Univ. of Michigan, G. Mendenhall, *Law and Covenant in Israel and the Ancient Near East* (1955) 16.

[46] None of these impositions applied to Jewish landholders in foreign countries with other economic systems.

[47] And this is also said to contrast with a guiding principle of love of the New Testament. But see on the ubiquity of both principles in both Testaments, Kelsen, *supra* n. 14, 30-72, and *infra* n.49. See also G. Mendenhall, *op. cit. supra* n. 45, at 17.

Greek thought, too, the retaliatory aspect of justice has been seen to be important.

The truth is that the element of vengeance is a convenient *starting-point* for a study of the Jewish concept of justice, but neither a fruitful nor correct *conclusion*. Undoubtedly Jehovah is seen even by the prophets of the Old Testament as a God of vengeance. *Sometimes* this implied that His people, too, should seek vengeance, not of course for their own wrongs, but for wrongs against the divine law;[48] yet at other times the implication is precisely the contrary, that since vengeance belongs to the Lord it should be *left* to the Lord.[49] In the 19th Chapter of *Leviticus* Moses is told: "Thou shalt not hate thy brother in thine heart. . . . Thou shalt not avenge, nor bear any grudge against the children of thy people, but thou shalt love thy neighbour as thyself".[50] According to the rabbinical interpretation of this commandment, even a criminal remains our neighbour.[51] The precept enjoining men to love each other is independent of any physical, intellectual, or moral attributes of the particular person; it is based on the fact that all men are God's children, made in his image.[52] This concept, if any single one is to be chosen, is the distinctive Jewish contribution to thought about justice.[53] "Love thy neighbour as thyself", said Rabbi Akiba, "is the supreme principle of the Torah. You must not say, since I have been put to shame (by a fellow man), let him be put to shame; since I have been slighted, let him be slighted. . . . If you do so, know whom ye put to shame, for in the likeness of God made He him."[54]

The *lex talionis* itself, be it added, appears not to have been, in any case, the bloodthirsty principle that vulgar usage has conjured up. With gently ironic reflection on the *lex talionis* as somehow setting apart the Mosaic law, the historical meaning of this law best emerges when it is interpreted in the light of Aristotle's mean. What it prescribes is that an injury is to be requited by a reciprocal injury, perhaps no less *and certainly no more*. While syntactically it could be taken as requiring the exaction of the named *talio* it is clear that, historically, enacted in a time-context when private vengeance was uninhibited, it came rather quickly to operate rather as a limit on the exaction. It was an early but far-reaching step to the substitution of self-help authorised but limited by law for unlimited private

---

48 See, e.g., *Jeremiah* 50. 15ff. Mendenhall (*op. cit.* 22, 47) notes that 75% of the occurrences of the term "vengeance" fall between *Jeremiah* and II *Isaiah*, probably due to rediscovery in Josiah's time (see 2 *Kings* 22) of a book of the Mosaic law. This is apart from some questions as to possible ambivalence of the root *nqm* as between "vengeance" and "vindication", also suggested by Mendenhall.

49 The famous "Vengeance is mine; I will repay, saith the Lord", is a later paraphrase by the Apostle Paul (*Romans* 12. 19) of *Deuteronomy* 32. 35 ("To me belongeth vengeance, and recompense").

50 *Leviticus* 19. 17-18.

51 *Pesahim* 75 a.

52 Love — and law — were thus to be extended to all men, foreigners as well. See *Exodus* 12. 49: "One law shall be to him that is homeborn, and unto the stranger that sojourneth among you." And *cf. Exodus* 22. 21, 23. 9; *Leviticus* 19. 33; *Deuteronomy* 1. 16, 10. 18, 23. 7; 24. 14; and M. Radin, *The Life of the People in Biblical Times* (1929) 58. For the importance of this principle in the Western tradition of "equality", see A. Brecht in *Nomos, Justice* 62 at 67.

53 See A. J. Heschel, "The Concept of Man in Jewish Thought", in P. T. Raju (ed.), *The Concept of Man* (1960) 108-157; and Henry George, quoted in J. H. Hertz (ed.), *The Pentateuch and Haftorahs* (1950) 405. On the connection between justice and charity see Kagan, *cit. supra* n. 44, 130ff. The Hebrew terms *zedek* (a righteous or just man) and *zedakah* (an act of charity, and the corresponding abstraction) are of the same root.

54 *Genesis Rabba* 24, 8.

vengeance. Augustine declared the *lex talionis* a law of justice, not of hatred—one eye, not two, for an eye; one tooth, not ten, for a tooth; one life, not a whole family, for a life. And it became a natural lawyers' commonplace that the drive of the *lex talionis* was to establish not only a due relation between crime and punishment, but equality of all persons before the law, since the *lex* requires the injuries of all to be valued according to the same standard. It is interesting to have to add that the literal application of "eye for eye, tooth for tooth" was in fact excluded in rabbinic law; and it seems disputed how far it was literally applied even in earlier Jewish history.[55]

No doubt originally the primitive Jewish tribes shared the hideous blood feuds of most other primitive peoples. Cain's plea to God was: "Everyone that findeth me shall slay me"; and the reply was "Whosoever slayeth Cain, vengeance shall be taken on him sevenfold."[56] So with God's enjoinder to Noah: "Whoso sheddeth man's blood, by man shall his blood be shed".[57] These were, of course, incidents of the period before the Hebrew Patriarchs. The whole tendency in the later precepts, and in the prophets, was to moderate the vengeful drive. The Cities of Refuge of the 19th chapter of *Deuteronomy* were designed to protect accidental or negligent homicides from the blood feud altogether,[58] importing a distinction of such cases from deliberate homicide not at all general in primitive systems. The principle of the human dignity even of the criminal, that "he shall not seem vile unto thee", is expressly asserted in the 25th chapter, as a limitation on punishment.[59] That man is made in the image of God may seem, at the beginning, a reason to pursue vengeance against his brother; before long it is a reason why he must not, but must rather set measure to his wrath. Justice is inevitably central to that measure. Within justice itself retribution and punishment may still be given some role even when vengeance is relegated to the status of an outgrown primitive impulse; but even these were replaced fairly early in Jewish thought by the notions of correction of the offender and social protection against the incorrigible.

---

[55] Contrast Hertz, *loc. cit. supra* n. 45, with Cohn, "Jewish Law" 70-74, citing Philo Judaeus, *De Specialibus Legibus* iii, 181, 182, and *Megillat Taanit* 4, 2. For a doubt whether, indeed, it was "a binding law", see G. Mendenhall, *op. cit. supra* n. 45, at 11, 17.
The lesser emphasis in rabbinic law on even divine vengeance *may* also have a theological foundation, in the introduction after the Babylonian captivity of the concept of Satan. Thus in 2 *Samuel* 24. 1, God in his anger against Israel inspires David to number the people; but in 1 *Chronicles* 21.1 *Satan* moves him to this harmful step. The "Satan" concept is usually credited to Persian theology. See R. Bultmann, *Jesus and the Word* (transl. L. P. Smith and E. H. Lantero, 1934; reissued 1958) 136. The pre-captivity tendency to interpret every adversity as God's judgment for failure to keep His law, also later faded. Jeremiah's words on vengeance, *supra* n. 48, were of course pre-captivity. The attribution of good to God, and evil to Satan would of course also march well with the rabbinic stress on reason in the rabbinic period. See §§7-8 *infra*.
[56] *Genesis* 4. 14-15.
[57] *Genesis* 9. 6, adding as the reason: "for in the image of God made He man." John Locke, *Second Treatise on Government*, sec. 8, quoted the principle as "that great law of nature", but omits the biblical reason.
[58] *Deuteronomy* 19. 1-7. Cf. G. von Rad, *Studies in Deuteronomy* (1953, transl. D. Stalker from German ed. 1948) 22.
[59] *Deuteronomy* 25. 3 (as to flogging). Cf. the rabbinic precept that in capital punishment (made rare by evidentiary rules) the mode of death minimise suffering and humiliation. *Pesahim* 75a. So by neutralising the precepts requiring penal stoning *by the people* (see, e.g., *Leviticus* 20.2, and 24.16) with the precept that the hands of the witnesses should be "first upon him" (*Deuteronomy* 17.7), the talmudists virtually abolished public executions. See Cohn, "Jewish Law" 74-77 discussing *Sanhedrin* 42b, 45a, and J. Makariewicz, *Philosophie des Strafrechts* (1906) 214.

At any rate it is clear that by an astonishing variety of arguments, some as subtle as others were direct and even disingenuous, the talmudic interpreters effectually abolished and prohibited the *talio*, despite the biblical text prescribing it no less than three times.[60] The oral law substituted money damages on a basis not very different from that of the modern common law.[61] And it was to be a fifth-century Greek, and not a fifth-century Jew, who said that "it is the business of intelligence to guard against a threatened injustice, but it is the mark of insensibility not to avenge it when it has happened."[62]

§6. HEBREW DOCTRINES OF "JUSTICE ACCORDING TO LAW". The truth is that what above all divide the idea of justice and the administration of justice from vengeance, are the limits and procedures of law for determining guilt and penalty. And it was the Mosaic law more clearly and completely than ever in Greek tradition, which gave us the notion of "justice-according-to-law". It was in the land of Israel that, for the first time, the ideas of justice and law were inextricably interwoven with each other and even identified.[63] In the Utopias of perfect justice built by Ovid in his *Metamorphoses*,[64] by Marx and Engels in their communist theory of law,[65] and by Isaiah,[66] Ovid and Marx-Engels see justice as perfect when there are neither laws nor judges. But for Isaiah, on the other hand, justice is perfect rather in a perfect judge, and in an understanding and enforcement of laws which guarantee their observance. It was the Old Testament which for the Western world pointed the truth that (with whatever additions or qualifications we please) justice revolves about obedience to law.

This, of course, is true only for law approximating to justice. In the emergence of these Jewish notions, law was justice and justice was law, because both proceeded from God.[67] From the beginning the Jews based themselves on the denial of the separation of powers at the divine level.

---

[60] *Exodus* 21. 24-25; *Leviticus* 24. 20; *Deuteronomy*, 19. 21.

[61] See Stone, *Social Dimensions*, Ch. 3, §§2ff., esp. §3. And see some of the precise arguments with citations to the original authorities in Cohn, "Jewish Law" 70-74. Perhaps the most striking point, among many, is that the rabbinical arguments which turned the meaning of the texts included the argument later used by Shakespeare's Portia to check Shylock. The talionic exaction had to be no more than the *precise* equivalent, and humans were incapable of such precise exaction. The *talio* moved into the background as a divine sanction to support the duty to pay compensation laid down by the rabbinic interpreters. See esp. *Baba Kama* 84a. And see the no less astonishing practical elimination of the *talio* against the perjurer (*Deuteronomy* 19. 16-21) in *Makkot* 5b, Maimonides, *Hikhot Sanhedrin* xii, 4, *Sanhedrin* 46b, discussed Cohn, *op. cit.* 72-73.

[62] Democritus of Abdera (*circa* 420 B.C.). See Freeman, *Ancilla* 110, fragm. 193. See also at 114-15 fragms. 256-262, and esp. 261: "One must punish wrong-doers to the best of one's ability, and not neglect it. Such conduct is just and good, but the neglect of it is unjust and bad."

[63] S. W. Baron, 1 *Social and Religious History of the Jews* (2 ed. 1953) 25, points out that probably one of the oldest parts of the Bible is the so-called Book of the Covenant, containing essentially civil and criminal laws, that most of the Decalogue is concerned with conduct in daily life, and the earliest prophetic writer, Amos, has as his theme justice, especially in controlling the innate powers of the strong. *Cf.* on the central concern for justice in the Covenant Code, as "characteristic above all in Israelite law", G. Mendenhall, *op. cit. supra* n. 45, at 16.

[64] *Metamorphoses* I. 89-93.

[65] See Stone, *Social Dimensions*, Ch. 10.

[66] *Isaiah* 11.

[67] Hence the absence of a distinct concept of natural law or equity, on which see *infra* §7; and also the secondary role of sanctions on which see Kagan, *op. cit.* supra n. 44, at 135. And *cf.* F. H. Knight in *Nomos, Justice* 1-23, at 2n.

"The Lord is our judge; the Lord is our lawgiver; the Lord is our king."[68] And this merger at the divine level carried with it, by dramatic paradox, that on the human level, justice and protection from tyranny[69] require separation of powers. For the minor role of regular royal legislative power, and the absence of any right of the king to be the *final* judge, follow from the king's subjection to God and the law. This kingly subjection which elsewhere was to be a constant centre of spiritual, political and military struggle, was not seriously in question among the Jews,[70] nor was it allowed to be reduced to mere formulae of piety. The prophet Nathan's denunciation of David to his face was a divine judgment based on law that the king could not alter; and the king accepted it as such.[71]

Of course, initial lack of differentiation between the divine and the secular law, and the endowment of law with divine sanction, absoluteness and immutability, are common in early legal orders. It is in what came after, rather than in the beginnings, that the specific Jewish features seemed to emerge. As to what did come after, a full analysis free of apologetics and adequately based both in biblical and talmudic learning, and contemporary knowledge of comparative legal history, is long overdue.[72] Yet even now, certain tentative features can be pointed out. One is the persistence of the divine attribution of the undifferentiated legal order even into the contemporary politics of the State of Israel. This is no doubt explained in part by the remarkable phenomenon of the maintenance of the law of the *Torah*, during nearly 2000 years after the destruction of the State, as a law in some way in force independently of any particular territorial organisation.[73] Yet there is a long period before that to be explained. No doubt in part the explanation is to be found in the powerful charismatic role of the prophets. There is probably to be added the nature of the contents of the *Torah* itself, above all the combined comprehensiveness and detail of its precepts, which left little scope for the secular *invention* of starting-points entirely outside its ambit. Finally, there is the role assumed in the Jewish tradition, not

---

[68] *Isaiah* 33. 22.

[69] *Cf.* generally S. Freehof, "The Natural Law in the Jewish Tradition" (1951) 5 *Nat. L. Inst. Proc.* 15 at 17.

[70] The question did arise at a late stage when, following upon armed intimidation by Herod of the Sanhedrin in connection with the pending trial of one of his servants, a rule was adopted by the Sanhedrin forbidding kings (other than of the House of David) either to sit in judgment or to be brought to judgment. The matter, of course, faded quickly into insignificance with the final downfall of self-government in the ancient kingdom. In other nations where subjection had later to be fought for, Jewish positions already taken were an important base of operations. *Cf.* generally on the later influence of Hebrew thought, Woodrow Wilson, quoted in Hertz, *op. cit. supra* n. 45, at 406; and Friedrich, *Philosophy of Law* at 8-12, esp. (at 9) on the Puritan revolution of the seventeenth century.

[71] Freehof, *cit. supra* n. 69; and *cf.* Kagan, *op. cit. supra* n. 44 at 99, pointing out that in fact "Samuel protested against King Saul, Nathan against King David, Elijah against Ahab, Elisha against Jehoram, Jeremiah against Zedekiah." *Cf. id.* 141, quoting E. R. Bevan, *Jerusalem under the High Priests* (1958) 8. On the royal legislative power see Maimonides, *Hilkhot Melakhim* iii-iv. Cohn, "Jewish Law" 55, speaks of a judicial "usurpation" of royal law-making power; the word may not be apt either in terms of scriptural base, or of chronology. But see G. Mendenhall, *op. cit. supra* n. 45, at 48. And see for examples of rules issuing from particular kings, B. Cohen, *Law and Tradition in Judaism* (1959) 27.

[72] But Cohn, "Jewish Law", which reached us only as this part of the MS. was going to press, manifests so excellent a union of the qualities and mood required, that we may be hopeful that either its author or some other scholar inspired by it will yet fully open this rich area of knowledge to the general world.

[73] On the growth to a degree of multiple local variations in the later dispersed Jewish communities see Cohn, "Jewish Law" 57.

only by priests and prophets, but also and above all by the reason and reasonings of men of learning.

§7. REASON OF THE LEARNED OF EACH GENERATION, AND THE HEBREW JUDICIAL PROCESS. On the one hand, Jewish energies were for the most part not channelled into metaphysical and cosmological speculation. The Greek problem of reconciling human law with divinely ordained law scarcely arose for the Jews, for whom during the formative period of the tradition the two never became separated. On the other hand, within this very unity the Jews were able to accommodate human reason within the system of revealed law. For however comprehensive and detailed the written law (*Torah*), the unwritten law (*Halakha*, or oral tradition) was given a place beside it, being deemed to have been transmitted to Moses by God, also on Mount Sinai, for further transmission from generation to generation throughout time, with all that this implied. The presence of the written law, and the divine origin maintained for it, meant that the unwritten law came into the charge of exegetes, rather than speculative philosophers. For the unwritten law could not be at large, but must respect every revealed precept and word. Yet the scholarly reason was not enslaved by these limits, its product being not seen as proceeding from any mere subsidiary source, nor as at all inferior in divine sanction. The legal fiction involved (if it be one) was all but discarded in the talmudic rationalisation that "Whatever a competent scholar will yet derive from the Law, that was already given to Moses on Mount Sinai".[74]

The discoveries of reason, to rank so high, must of course be anchored to the revealed text, though this might be only by the use of an adjective or a word or syllable variants, or the choice of one of conflicting texts, and that even in most strained interpretation. The standing of what was discovered was measured moreover by reason, and by competence in scholarship.[75] The *Halakha* emergent from individual learning became perfected as it became *Minhag*, that is, accepted among the learned. Of competence in scholarship the fellowship of scholars alone was judge. This fellowship in turn was open

---

[74] *Jerusalem Megillah* IV, 74d; see Freehof, *cit. supra* n. 69, 18-19. And see Cohn, "Jewish Law" 45-48 both on the general point and on the relation of this to the struggle of the Pharisees and Saducees; on the secular nature of the rabbinic techniques of elaboration of the *Halakha* (53-54); on this elaboration as a solution to the problem raised by contradictory rules, both deemed to be divinely supported (48); on the paradox of the immutability of the divine law (including *Halakha*) making *direct* repeal almost impossible, as contrasted with the drastic powers of tacit abrogation by exegesis (55-56); and on the particular rigidity within the *Halakha* of codifications by individual scholars in the eleventh (Yitzhak Alfassi), twelfth (Maimonides), fourteenth (Yaarkov ben Asher), and fifteenth (Yosef Caro) centuries (56-57, 60-61). And see also generally H. L. Strack, *Intro. to Talmud and Midrash* (1931); H. Silving, "Jurisprudence of the Old Testament" (1953) 28 *N.Y.U.L.R.* 1129; and on the contemporary problems in Israel *infra* n. 88.

[75] *Cf.* Cohn, "Jewish Law" 53-54, who observes that in the talmudical period "the judicial and legislative functions . . . were monopolised by scholars"; that the succession to them was by becoming "pupils of the wise"; and that the methods of elaboration were adapted to choosing the most feasible, reasonable and acceptable law, but not necessarily the divinely inspired or willed law.

Competence in scholarship was supplemented or elaborated by other criteria. Thus a certain decisiveness was given (though with unclear priority as between them) to support by a majority of the learned, to later rather than earlier interpretations, and to skill as a judge.

to all the learned as such. Interpreters of this kind, though working with the divine law itself, resembled rather the great Roman jurisconsults, or the great judges of the common law tradition, than the esoteric priestly interpreters common in primitive society. The rabbis resembled the jurisconsults also in receiving no remuneration as such; many distinguished rabbis earned their living as humble manual workers. On this matter, even to the present day, the Jewish tradition has rallied little to the kingly patent or commission of office, even priestly office, as a credential to either scholarship or wisdom.[76] Each generation in turn, this tradition seemed to assume, could receive through its experience and intelligence the eternally expanding word of the Divine Lawgiver.[77] And while the influence of this pattern on medieval scholasticism is obvious,[77a] Jewish tradition was for the most part free of any operative hierarchy of authority, or of organs for declaring dogmas.

A recent penetrating study, available only after this Chapter was written, has sought to formulate the principles (or "methods") on which the learned rabbis, whether in academies or courts, elaborated the rules of the *Halakha*.[78] Lack of space forbids more detailed consideration here, though any reader of Chapters 7 and 8 of our own study *Legal System and Lawyers' Reasonings* will be struck by deep similarities to the modern appellate judicial process, both in the respect for traditional authority and in the adept use of techniques for turning authority to present purposes. The rabbis often reinterpreted the weightiest texts, even neutralised them with each other,[79] gave weight to some particular interpreters but not absolutely,[80] and while attending to earlier precedents left themselves free to cut these down to size in their bearing on contemporary problems. For (they insisted) it was to judges *of their own days*[81] that *Deuteronomy* enjoined men to hearken, and such judges should rather seek counsel from their own teachers and learned colleagues, than simply rely on precedents from even the outstanding rabbis of the past.[82]

The identification of justice with learned reason and of both with law, assumed by these techniques, gave rise to tensions as in other traditions; but these were mostly absorbed in the Jewish tradition within the vast flexibilities of the learned interpretations thus accumulated under the divine sanction. There was thus apparently no major need to express them, as other systems of thought have done, by denying the quality of "law" to

---

[76] According to *Horioth* 13a "a bastard who is learned in the law takes precedence over even a High Priest who is an ignoramus." It should perhaps be added that such doctrines were less socially disturbing than they might have been if the office of High Priest had not already been obsolescent.

[77] Even, says in effect *Brachot* 57a, to the extent of modifying precepts as literally revealed by reference to the purpose of the precept as now understood. Freehof, article cited, 18-19; and see Kagan, *op. cit.* 102-103, 158-160, 177. On the participation of *every* Jew in this process *cf. id.* 158; and see R. T. Herford, *Pharisaism* (1912) 15-16.

[77a] *Cf* J. T. Mooney, *The Scholastic Analysis of Usury* (1957).

[78] Cohn, "Jewish Law", esp. 49-61, provides the rabbinic texts. See further Stone, *Social Dimensions*, Ch. 3, §3.

[79] See *supra* n. 76.

[80] Hillel, Shammai and Akiba were those given most general weight, though differentiated also *inter se*. Rav had special weight on ritual and Shmuel on private law. There were many other general rules; but of course such rules of preeminence usually became flexible in interplay with other methods of interpretation discussed above. See for a suggestive account of the effect of diversity of social and class backgrounds and economic preoccupations among the rabbis on their interpretations of the biblical texts, L. Finkelstein, *Akiba* (1936, repr. 1962) *passim*, esp. 28-51, 177-214.

[81] *Deuteronomy* 17. 8-9. And see Maimonides, *Hilkot Sandhedrin* xx, 8, discussed Cohn, "Jewish Law" 60ff.

[82] Asher (Rosh), *Sanhedrin* iv, 6, quoted and discussed Cohn, "Jewish Law" 60-61.

unjust law of the secular power; nor alternatively by reducing justice to merely what the secular law provides. In short, Jewish learning developed no doctrine of natural law prevailing over positive law, or of equity as against strict law, just as it developed no doctrine of the absolute power of any human lawmaker.[83] Jewish theory of law has some of the marks of natural law, in so far as man, his position, rights and duties are held within a transcending order revealed by the divine word as interpreted by man's reason. But it did not proceed from this to admit that mark of natural law which (as we shall see) consists of the juxtaposition of positive and natural legal orders.

In practice, indeed, it showed signs (as already hinted) of being able to transcend the very transcendence of the divinely given order. The learned might establish rules not merely (as we have seen) in strained reinterpretation of the literal rule by reference to the purpose of the precept as now understood. The exigencies of a new generation and its problems were intruded even more frontally. To justify liberties with the texts the learned cited the fact that Elijah had initiated, despite the prescription of *Deuteronomy* 12, 13-14 that sacrifices be made only in the sanctuary, the contest of sacrifice between the followers of God and those of Baal on the top of Mount Carmel. The principles *Hora'ath Shaah* ("Decisions of the Hour"), validated even some rules contrary to the texts, no doubt so far as they became *Minhag* and were accepted by the learned.[84] This power of derogation, moreover, did not have merely the nature of a temporary emergency measure, for it was agreed that such a derogation once enunciated might come to be accepted permanently, presumably again by the learned.[85]

While it is impossible to assess the exact range of use of this power, the two best-known examples indicate a direction pointing to law reform in its fully secular sense, as an adjustment to contemporary social, economic and psychological conditions. It was used, for example, virtually to abrogate the main survival in the Pentateuch of the magical modes of trial, the "bitter water" test for the suspected adulteress.[86] By the influence of the great Jochanan ben Zakkai,[87] the Sanhedrin at Yavneh put it finally out of use in the first century of the present era, for the revealing (if somewhat ambiguous) reason that it was no longer appropriate "when the adulterers multiply in number". The great Hillel two centuries before introduced the *Prosbul,* virtually abrogating the divinely prescribed cancellation of debts at the sabbatical year. This *Prosbul,* which was rather a regulation than a mere *responsum,* enabled the creditor to preserve the asset by transferring the evidence of debt to the court. The ground taken by Hillel was frankly creative; he said this was necessary *Mipnei Tikkun Haolom,* that is, "in order to right what was wrong with the world". This frank lawmaking was additional to the power regularly taken of correcting the miscarriage of the applicable rule of the Torah in the particular litigation. Here the Jewish courts assumed a residual power, reminiscent of the early interventions of the English

---

[83] See Kagan, *op. cit. supra* n. 44, at 19, 22ff. The unwritten (oral or *Halakhic*) law, despite the divine origin attributed to it, was (as already mentioned in the text) declared by the rabbis to be binding only as it became established as *Minhag,* that is, among the courts and the learned men.

[84] *Deuteronomy* 18. 15 ("Unto him shall ye hearken"), and Psalm 119, v. 126, were also invoked in support. See *Yevamoth* 90b, and on the latter texts *Brachot* 63a.

[85] *Avodah Zarah* 40a, *Gloss of Tosefoth, Mabboth* 23b.

[86] See also *infra* n.92. For other examples see Cohn, "Jewish Law" 69-77.

[87] *Sotah* IX. 9, Sanhedrin at Yavneh.

Chancellor, of declaring ownerless (*Hefker*) the *res litigiosa*, and then disposing of it as they deemed justice to require.[88]

The famous story of the struggle between Rabbi Eliezer as a sole dissenter, and the rest of his colleagues who took the opposite view on the matter before them, has been given diverse interpretations.[89] We ourselves find it most significant in its reflection on the relation between the divine authority of the law and the reasoned consensus of scholarly interpreters. To persuade his colleagues (we are told) Eliezer invoked divine intervention, solemnly causing a tree to uproot itself and move, and water to flow backwards. But the company of scholars declared that "trees were no evidence", nor was water either. Then Eliezer called upon the walls of their assembly place to witness that he spoke the divine truth. And the walls indeed began to topple down, until Rabbi Yehoshua of the majority shouted angrily at them not to interfere ("When scholars debate the *Halakha*, it's none of your business!"); but though they thereupon ceased to topple down, out of respect for him, yet they did not stand quite erect again either, out of respect for Eliezer. Finally Eliezer sought help from the voice of Heaven itself, the *Bath Kol,* and this great voice was indeed heard to declare that the *Halakha* was "always as Eliezer says". But now Yehoshua arose and spoke saying: "The law is not in heaven: the law has been handed down to us on earth from Mount Sinai, and we no longer take notice of heavenly

---

[88] *Yevamoth* 89b. *Cf.* also in its reminiscence of the early Chancellors the procedure, short of declaration of *Hefker,* as against a party whose case lacked merits, though strict proof was not available against him, e.g., of his oral promise. He was summoned before the court which solemnly reminded him in general terms of the certainty of divine vengeance against the unjust, in a declaration which began "He who took vengeance on the generation of Noah..." (*Mi Sheparah*). See *Babba Metzia* 44a, 48b.

The serious and chronic tensions in the modern State of Israel between the rabbinical authorities as interpreters of the *Halakha,* and substantive parts of the population as well as the government and Parliament, thus suggest a failure to maintain (or rather to resume) the classical rabbinical role. See, e.g., recently, the confrontation of rabbinical rulings as to the status of the Bene Israel group of Indian Jews by a virtually unanimous resolution (tactical abstentions apart) of the Knesset. *Cf.* also the crisis arising from refusal of the Chief Rabbinate Council to recognise the jurisdiction of the Supreme Court of Israel in matters involving *Halakhic* interpretation. See the *Jerusalem Post,* August 14 and 21, 1964. This situation and the transformed conditions to which secular and religious institutions must adjust themselves in a modern democracy constitute a great challenge to contemporary leadership in Israel.

[89] *Baba Metziah* 59b, *E'rubin* 7a; *Sanhedrin* 3b; *Hullin* 11a; *Eduyot* I, 5; *Tossefta Brachot* IV, 15, *Brachot* 52a. We are indebted to Cohn's longer account in "Jewish Law" 48-50. See also E. N. Cahn, "Authority and Responsibility" (1951) 51 *Columbia L.R.* 838-851, at 838-39; W. Kaufmann, *Critique of Religion and Philosophy* (1959) 238-241. Cohn uses it to illustrate the weight given to majority opinion without, perhaps, stressing sufficiently that it is the *consensus of the majority reason* which prevailed, as against the voice from Heaven invoked by Eliezer. Cahn uses it as a text on which to hang this thesis that "the path of personal responsibility ... remains the only path anyone has found to wise and righteous judgment" (851). He quotes the striking words of *Ecclesiasticus* 32.23, 37.16, 13-14: "Let reason go before every enterprise and counsel before any action. . . . And let the counsel of thine own heart stand. . . . For a man's mind is sometime wont to tell him more than seven watchmen that sit above in an high tower. . .". This, however, insufficiently stresses that it was for "scholars" (that is the fellowship of the learned), and not merely for his individual heart and reason, that Yehoshua took his stand. Kaufmann, differently again (apart from the sense of humour imputed to the Godhead) sees the story mainly as illustrating the anti-authoritarian element in Judaic thought. He recognises, however, that even this is rather mixed in view of the ban subsequently imposed on Eliezer, adding that according to the sequel of the story the ban was lifted after Eliezer's death many years later even though Eliezer had reaffirmed his defiant view on his death-bed. See *id.* 340.

voices, for the law which we were handed down provides that decisions shall be taken by majority".

And so it was; and we are also told that at that moment the Lord was speaking to Elijah the prophet; and the Lord smiled and said: "My children have defeated me, my children have defeated me."[89a] Not only, in short, did the learned stand their ground even against the divine intervention; the ground on which they chose to stand was that of such reason and wisdom as it had lain in them to find by study and counsel among themselves.

§8. HEBREW NOTIONS OF JUSTICE THROUGH LAW AND RATIONAL PROOF. In general, however, the emphasis of Hebrew practice and of its contribution to Western notions of justice was on the importance of rules of law to the doing of justice, and here again the Hebrew contribution contrasted with that of the Greeks. The Hebrew insight has gone into later thought in the recognition not merely that a rule ensures equality among those caught by it, but also that in so far as we differentiate among people generally because of the requirements of justice, these differentiations too have to be formulated as rules. In these respects Jewish tradition offered an early model of "justice according-to-law".[89b] It is perhaps not unrelated to this, and to the level of practice on which the Jewish tradition moved, that the right of all persons to a hearing and a fair trial is given an importance not less than the observance of the substantive rules of the Torah. This requirement is exalted not merely in terms of the duties of the judge and of witnesses. "Ye shall do no unrighteousness in judgment: thou shalt not respect the person of the poor, nor honour the person of the mighty; but in righteousness shalt thou judge thy neighbour."[90] It is asserted also in terms of the community's duty to provide the arrangements to make trial possible. One purpose of the Cities of Refuge was "that the manslayer die not until he stand before the congregation in judgment";[91] on this and other matters there must be judges who will "thoroughly investigate", "enquire, make search, and ask diligently", "enquire diligently", and the like. The biblical legislator was aware that without fair and fearless application to facts truly found, the fruit even of divine law is not justice, and that the hardest part of this (and therefore the gravest danger of injustice) is in the finding of the concrete facts.

The dependence of judgment on truth was, indeed, of wider application in Jewish thought than merely to justice. Its ambit extended to all ethical

---

[89a] I. Tammelo, reading this in proof, observes on a striking parallel as well as a striking contrast with the Greek Prometheus myth. The parallel is in the assertion of a degree of maturity and independence; the contrast is in the Divine response. The Hebraic God smiles an indulgent ratification; the Greek gods respond with wrath and dire vengeance.

[89b] See *supra* §6. To say that there can be no justice without law is, of course, something quite different from saying (e.g.) that there can be no literary merit without literature, despite the equivalation of these statements by C. Morris, "Law, Justice, and the Public's Aspirations", in *Nomos, Justice* 170. While we agree with I. Jenkins (*id.* 191, at 203) that "the most elemental meaning embedded in the concept of justice is that of the perfect accomplishment of the tasks of law", the point is not that justice is the merit which pertains to good law, but rather that good law is that which achieves justice. "Justice" might well pertain to dispositions of human affairs effected by nothing which we would recognise as law; but in fact "law" is the surest means of achieving regular justice. At 174 Morris seems virtually to concede the point.

[90] *Leviticus* 19. 15. And see *Deuteronomy* 16. 18-20.
[91] *Numbers* 35. 12; *cf. Joshua* 20. 6.

judgment; for whatever be the explanation of our evaluation of facts as good or bad, the facts themselves must first be known. In this emphasis on the search for truth on the practical level of judgment, as distinct from supernatural speculation, the Jewish contribution again differed from that of most other early peoples. It is, indeed, remarkable that a doctrine which identified law with a revelation by direct divine intervention, rarely entertained any regular procedure of judgment of God, or other irrational modes of trial,[92] and that the few instances fell into disuse. For offences generally the Pentateuch requires not only two witnesses, but two *eye*-witnesses;[93] and it deserves to be better known that many of the cruel punishments which it prescribed in the spirit of its early origins were rendered virtually obsolete by similar requirements of proof introduced by reason as part of the unwritten law.[94] The exigencies of finding the true facts were thus used also to mitigate the rigours of the substantive law. When Solomon prayed for "an understanding heart to judge thy people, that I may discern between good and bad", it "pleased the Lord, that Solomon had asked this thing."[95] And when Isaiah denounced the straying of Israel from the ways of justice, the claims of truth, judgment and vengeance, and of the orphan, the widow, the weak and the oppressed were inextricably woven together in his timeless words.

§9. Entry of Hebrew Concepts into the West through Christianity. Although the Hebrew contributions of reason and due process are of unquestioned importance, undoubtedly the most important contribution of the Jewish tradition was the overriding concept of love[96] which was

---

[92] See *Numbers* 5. 11-31 as to the "bitter water" test required to be taken by a woman suspected of adultery. See text *supra* at n. 86. See also *Exodus* 22. 11 as to the oath between bailor and bailee. The former was put into disuse by the Sanhedrin in the time of Jochanan ben Zakkai (see *supra* §8). The two other cases were both of the use of oaths where, because of absence of any evidence, rational determination of the issue was impossible. See *Exodus* 22. 8, 11 (as to claims against a bailee partly admitted by him). G. Mendenhall, *op. cit. supra* n. 45, at 16n. observes that "the very infrequency of references to divine oracle and oath is evidence of the relatively high development of the law."

[93] E.g., in *Deuteronomy* 17. 6.

[94] For example, the judgment of death on a rebellious son was never carried out because of the multitude of requirements, evidentiary and other, attached by rabbinic interpretation. *Tractate Sanhedrin* 71a. We may instance the requirements of proof, of prior admonition of the accused, and of a quorum of 23 judges required for capital trial (as distinct from 3 only in commercial cases). The rabbis added the sophisticated rider that if all the 23 judges were unanimous the accused should be acquitted, since unanimity on so large a bench would indicate bias. Yet in the rare cases where the necessary two eye-witnesses and admonition rules were satisfied the verdict would be rather likely to be unanimous! It is little wonder that it came to be said in the later period that a court which passed the death sentence once in 70 years was "a bloodthirsty court" (*Makkot* 7a). Conversely, the Pentateuchal requirement of two witnesses was relaxed by rabbinic interpretation in commercial matters, "lest the door be locked in face of those who need to borrow". *Tractate Sanhedrin* 3a. Cf. on these technical safeguards T. Spector, ". . . Hebrew Criminal Jurisprudence" (1924) 15 *J.Crim.L., Crimin. and Pol. Sc.* 317. In some cases where conviction failed for such technical reasons the court assumed power (if it decided that the accused was guilty) to have him put under public restraint "until the death of the High Priest".

[95] 1 *Kings* 3. 9-10. The more famous Solomonic judgment concerning parentage of the disputed child (1 *Kings* 3. 24ff.) is not really distinctively Jewish. Cf. F. Thieberger, *King Solomon* (1947) 174.

[96] See *supra* §5. We here speak, of course, of the Judaic and Christian traditions in terms of civilisations bearing certain ethical ideas, not in terms of religious organisation. Yet the distinction is not as sharp as it is sought to be made in Recaséns, *Filosofia del Derecho* 511, to found his "personalist" standpoint.

developed in the rabbinic period and by the post-captivity prophets and expressed in the teaching of Jesus. Through the development and spread of Christianity, this element in thought about justice came to pervade all of Western thinking. It is perhaps paradoxical that this very development of Christianity, particularly as expressed in the Pauline antipathy to legalism,[97] caused a reaction in Jewish circles which led to a more legalistic approach by the rabbis of the first century of the common era than had characterised the general rabbinical teaching up to the time of Jesus.

The anti-legalistic attitude which is commonly characterised as "Christian" is well stated in such sayings as the summing-up of the law by— "Thou shalt love the Lord thy God with all thy heart, and with all thy soul, and with all thy mind, and with all thy strength . . . Love thy neighbour as thyself". Although this is attributed to Jesus in St. Mark's Gospel,[98] it had been anticipated by Rabbi Akiba.[99] In the same fashion the Golden Rule of *Matthew* 7. 12 is only an inversion of the Beth Hillel's "What is hateful to you, do not to your fellow man. That is the entire law; all the rest is commentary."[100] Both these examples tend to support the thesis that Jesus was a rabbi, held by some contemporary Christian theologians.[101] Whether, as Christian thinkers would claim, Jesus added something distinctive to the rabbinical teachings he adopted is irrelevant to our point. What is significant is that the rabbinical teaching of love as pre-eminent was basic to the teaching of Jesus, and came thus to be spread through all the Western world.[101a] This principle—that a man must act within the spirit as well as the letter of the law; that his heart as well as his mind must be right; that his motives and not merely his actions were to be judged—became basic to Western thought. In this way, too, justice became internal to man as well as an external set of criteria of judgment. And the irreducible dignity of each man whether in pronouncing or submitting to judgment became, along with man's infirmity and therefore his need of mercy, a precious thread in the long discourse of justice.

§10. AMBIT OF JUSTICE AS A SOCIAL ETHICAL VALUE. This sampling of historical beginnings suffices to suggest certain further guidelines as to what kind of thing is being discussed in the later theories of justice to be considered in subsequent Chapters. First, even if it be a psychological truth,

---

97 See *infra* Ch. 2, §3. G. Mendenhall, *op. cit. supra* n. 45, at 49, thinks, indeed, that despite Pauline anti-legalism "the basic structure of New Testament religion is actually, as the early church constantly maintained, the continuation of Mosaic religion." The same point was stressed in 19th century Jewish thinking; though the opposite position was also taken. See, e.g., G. G. Montefiore, *Gesù di Nazareth nel Pensiero Ebraico Contemporaneo* (1913).

98 *Mark* 12. 30-31.

99 *Y. Nedarim* 9. 4. See B. Cohen, *op. cit. supra* n. 71, at 224; and see *supra* at n. 54.

100 *Shabbat* 31a. See B. Cohen, *op. cit.* 223. Hillel's statement is a paraphrase of *Leviticus* 19. 18 (*supra* n. 50). See for this and other formulations of the Golden Rule, A. R. Blackshield, "The Meaning and Value of the Golden Rule" (1964) 4 *Jaipur L.J.* 1, §3. The Judaic teaching as to love was thus manifested not only in mercy *after legal judgment*, but within the legal commandments themselves. *Cf.* E. L. Fackenheim, "Kant and Judaism" (1963) 36 *Commentary* 460-467.

101 See, e.g., Bultmann, *op. cit. supra* n. 55, at 57-61.

101a On this teaching in relation to human justice, see Ch. 11, n. 88. And see J. Bowle, *Western Political Thought* (1947) c. vii *passim*; and see *infra* Ch. 2, §3. On the "universality" in rabbinical and Pauline doctrine of the fundamentals of Mosaic and Noachide law, see R. Gordis, "Natural Law and Religion" in Cogley (ed.), *Natural Law* 240, at 262-64. See esp. *Romans* 2. 14-15. But *cf.* as to Gordis' iusnaturalist thesis *infra* Ch. 7, n. 108a.

as some have thought, that men best recognise justice by the absence of it,[102] justice can still only be conceived as a value which men affirmatively seek. Clearly, too, justice is an ethical value, a value by which men judge the conduct of reasonable beings,[103] that is, behaviour directed by the will of the actor.[104] And as we shall see the adjective "just" may be found to characterise either the actor or the conduct or both. Furthermore, though a different view may be taken from a different philosophical standpoint, this work will proceed from the main Aristotelian position that justice is a social value; that is, it pertains to that conduct which takes place in the context of inter-personal relations.[105]

We proceed then on the assumption that justice is a positive ethical social value.[106] There has been considerable discussion also as to whether justice is a "simple" or "primitive" value, not further reducible into component values.[107] The only fruitful way to pursue such a question, in a work of the present kind, is to allow what answer there may be to emerge from whatever else can be said about justice.

§11. ARTICULATES OF THE CONCEPT OF JUSTICE. One of the marks of the natural law approach to justice is that it sees the individual as held within a framework of binding norms not of human creation. Justice in general, the name of which is basically a word of common usage, does not on its face refer us to a set of norms. Men can (and often do) judge things to be just or unjust without formulating any norms attendant on the vague notions which base their judgments; but to explain such judgments, they will always be found to resort to propositions which are tacitly, if not expressly, normative. The sentences "Justice is on A's side", or "A's cause is just", whatever else they mean, amount to statements that—"What A claims, *ought to be* granted". "Values", as Philip Jacob and J. J. Flink have recently ventured, are the "normative standards by which human beings are influenced in their choice among the alternative courses of action which they perceive". And they add, building on related work of Talcott Parsons and others, that "(1) evaluation is an experientially and conceptually distinct component of motivation which includes both affective and cognitive elements, and (2) a value is considered as a yardstick used to measure worth rather

---

[102] See *infra* Ch. 10, §14.

[103] Including putative Beings, allowing us to speak of the justness of God, of angels, of inhabitants of other planets who may be rational but not human, etc.

[104] There are, of course, many problems as to the meaning and scope of will-directable behaviour. At the present stage the common-sense conceptions of will and behaviour must suffice.

[105] Both the *ethical* and *social* characterisations depart from the pre-Socratic conception of justice as a balancing principle of cosmic events. Of course, not all social behaviour is within the ambit of justice: insofar as they are not already excluded by the "ethical" characterisation, we add that (e.g.) matters of language, usage and fashions in dress would not be included. On this point we disagree with Knight, *cit. supra* n. 67, at 11. So, too, behaviour towards non-human animals, and even non-animal natural phenomena, which some modern natural lawyers seek to bring within the ambit of justice (see, e.g., S. Buchanan in Cogley (ed.), *Natural Law* 82, at 140ff.; R. Gordis in *id.* 240 at 266ff.), would here be excluded by the "inter-personal" *proprium*. Its inclusion would, of course, accord with the old cosmological principle discussed *supra* §3. And, of course, kindness to such creatures may contribute content to norms of justice between reasonable beings.

[106] It seems unnecessary to do more than note that values may also be "negative" ("unjust") or "neutral". See on the latter N. Hartmann, *Ethik* (3 ed. 1949) 613-620.

[107] *Cf.* G. E. Moore, *Principia Ethica* (1903) 7, making the point that "good" is a simple notion. And see Tammelo, "Justice and Doubt" 388.

than as worth itself".[107a]

In short, some norm is asserted whenever any value is asserted; so that, indeed, compliance with a value means obedience to the norm or norms which proceed from that value. The "why" of a judgment of value has to be attributed to a norm; the "why" of a norm has to be attributed to the value which it attends. The differences between assertions of justice in general, and natural law assertions, are mainly that in the latter the assertion is always in the form of norms, and that it fixes, independently of the obeying subject, the content of the norms (and of the values which they attend); while none of this is *necessarily* so with assertions of justice in general.[108]

Within the wide notion of judgments of justice, moreover, it may be useful to notice a number of further distinctions, according to whether attention is focussed on the activities out of which a value arises; or on the value itself; or on the human agent who realises the value; or on the thing or state of things in which the value is realised.

In the first place, the human attitudes, tendencies and motives which are relevant to ethical valuation seem to arise from "activities" which are unavoidable or rarely avoidable by human beings, common at least to important groups in the community. Such activities, for instance, are thinking, loving, sharing, knowing, and deciding who is entitled to what; and these may also be stated abstractly as Thought, Love, Mutuality, Knowledge, Justice,[109] abstractions which then tend to be regarded as fundamental "goods".[110] All this can and should be accepted for the present purpose in an entirely unpretentious sense. For obviously that in which men are most active, in the sense of personal commitment will correspond to what they most value. To point out, for example, that "Thought" is a kind of fundamental "good", is only a way of identifying the activities out of which widely acknowledged values such as "Truth" have arisen and become conceptualised. Some such activity, as a "good" out of which the value arises, constitutes one articulate which may be involved in any assertion about a given value such as justice.

The conceptualised value itself which thus arises from the activities, as Truth in relation to Thought and Knowledge, or Well-Being in relation to Life, or Mutuality in relation to Sharing, is a second articulate. It represents an approved kind and level of attainment in the "good" of that activity. Even, however, when these are separated off or not involved, assertions about the value may still be complex. When a freedman of Rome was infamed for ingratitude to his patron, the *infamia* represented neither an activity (non-Sharing), nor a mere negation of a value (non-Mutuality); it referred rather to the quality of a person who defaults in realising this value. So when a man is said to be truthful in the sense that he has realised the value Truth, his "truthfulness" is a quality which

---

107a Jacob-Flink, *Value Decision* 10, 11. See generally Parsons-Shils, *Theory of Action*, and see *infra* Chs. 10-11 and Stone, *Social Dimensions*, Ch. 12.

108 See the fuller discussion *infra* Ch. 10, §§2-4.

109 See Blackshield, *"Pensiero Umano"*, with special reference to the "activity" of "thinking."

110 Ethical values must obviously be anchored to what "goes on" in human life. But not everything that "goes on", even inescapably, is equally relevant. What goes on may be either "activities" (e.g., thinking) or "processes" (e.g., suffering, guilt, experience, or growing old or decaying). It is with the more or less unavoidable *activities* rather than the *processes* that the "goods" seem in fact associated.

is neither the activity nor the value itself. This quality of a person realising the value, is a third possible articulate of assertions about a value. Still a fourth refers to the thing or situation through which a person realises the value. When, for example, we say that though A was truthful, he did not give a "true" picture of the situation, the word "true" refers directly neither to the value "Truth", nor to the quality of a person as measured by it, but rather to a state of affairs ("the situation") as measured by the value.[111]

Any or all of these different elements may be present in a general assertion about a value. With "justice", indeed, we commonly use the very same word to cover all these articulates. Justice is used for the activity from which the value is distilled, as when we speak of "the administration of justice", or of "dispensing justice". It is also used to represent the idealisation of the activity into a "value" as when we speak of the "idea of Justice" here under examination. We also speak of a man as "just", meaning that he always or characteristically "does justice", and this is a measuring of a person against the value. And, finally, when we say that "justice" reigned in the land in Solon's time, this is a measuring of a thing or situation in terms of the value. It might be useful to adopt, as some have suggested,[112] a consistent terminology expressing these distinctions. For example, we might use "justice" to refer to the "good" which is the activity from which in turn the value arises; "the idea of justice" for the value itself; "justness" for the virtue of a man who realises the idea of justice; and "the just" for the quality of a situation or conduct or rule in which the idea of justice is realised.[113] And it is perhaps necessary to add that, of course, the qualities of things or situations in which justice is realised ("the just"), may often (but need not necessarily) coexist with the above quality of persons ("justness") in those responsible for the things or situations. We may also perhaps add as a permissible generality that "values", of which justice is one kind, are usually identifiable by the presence of most or all of a cluster of seven properties. First, values arise from the necessity in all human activities for the exercise of choice among alternative courses of action. This leads to the property of selectivity as among alternatives. Second, values are usually focal centres of concern and debate arising from the conjunction between the variability of these attitudes as adhered to by men, and the claim to universal validity which this adherence imports.[113a] Third, values manifest a high degree of continuity between human generations; and this is only really possible, fourth, because of constant change within them despite this high degree of continuity.[113b] Fifth, values attribute

---

[111] Cf. N. Hartmann, *Grundzüge einer Metaphysik der Erkenntnis* (4 ed. 1949) 427ff.

[112] See, e.g., Tammelo, "Justice and Doubt" 335, 337, 349-351, 387-391, whose terminology is here slightly adapted. Cf. in relation to Aristotle's "broad" and "narrow" senses of justice, Shellens, *supra* n. 39, at 94-95. And see C. J. Friedrich, ". . . The Just Political Act", in *Nomos, Justice* 24 at 26-27; I. Jenkins, "Justice as Ideal . . .", in *id.* 191 at 194.

[113] The personal virtues of persons, and the value-realising qualities of things or situations, because they have no observable physical quality corresponding to them, are sometimes referred to as "tertiary qualities" as distinct from primary qualities (e.g., extension) and secondary qualities (e.g., colours): see, e.g., D. D. Runes, *Dictionary of Philosophy* (1942) 315-16, *sub nom.* "Tertiary Qualities". The testing of values therefore has to be not by observation, but by argument about reasonableness, insight, and the like.

[113a] See *infra passim*, esp. Chs. 2, 7, and Ch. 11, §§4-5.

[113b] See *infra* Ch. 11, §§7-8. See the literature cited in Lindzey, 2 *Handbook* 948.

entitlements and duties, which social scientists are increasingly interpreting in terms of social expectations attached to men's social roles.[113c] Sixth, and seventh, the adherence to values produces self-evaluation by the holder in respect of past attitudes and conduct, and self-inhibition by a process of internalized control, rather than by external coercive sanctions, in respect of future attitudes or conduct. In both cases standards sensed as personal imperatives are operative, whether these be derived from the social inheritance of the group as learned by the individual or from some assumed superhuman authority or innate conscience.[113d]

§12. CRITERIA OF JUSTICE AND "VALIDITY" OF JUDGMENTS CONCERNING JUSTICE. When it is said that the value-ideas or norm-ideas contained in the idea of justice function as criteria for our judgments of justness and the just, what is primarily meant is that they serve as standards in the light of which these judgments can be formulated, and as substantive pre-dispositions from which the content of these judgments is derived. But such criteria are also criteria of the *validity* of value-judgments; that is, they serve as points with reference to which such judgments are said to be valid or invalid. And this function needs to be investigated a little more closely.

It is important to note that "validity" is a relational concept;[114] in other words, assertions of the validity of something must *always* be made in relation to some criterion of validity. This means that various and conflicting validity-assertions are possible, inasmuch as validity may be asserted by recourse to different criteria of valuation. This is merely a logical state of affairs; but neglect of it has led to much unnecessary talking at cross-purposes between natural lawyers of various kinds. To say thus that "validity" is a relational concept does not mean that it would be meaningless to speak of "absolute validity". It does, however, mean that any such "absolute" or "ultimate" validity would simply be validity asserted in reference to *what is contended to be* an absolute or ultimate criterion of valuation. If we conceive of values as hierarchically organised, so that the values *vis-à-vis* each other have higher or lower "axiotic dignity",[115] consistency leads to the idea of a supreme value—which, occupying the "top of the value-pyramid" and there reigning supreme, can censor and even invalidate anything that may be asserted as valid by reference to a lower value. Even here, however, the supposed supreme value is absolute only in relation to its own subordinate values, just as the invalidation is only from the point of view of that supreme value. Validity is still asserted *in relation to* this supreme value, and is as such relational.

Once this is understood, it seems that nothing of substantial significance is affected by recognising the relational nature of the concept of validity. All principal ethical doctrines seem to have this concept implicit in them. Its acceptance does not prejudice any viewpoints held in ethics which offer

---

113c See *supra* n. 15, and on the concept of "social roles" see Stone, *Social Dimensions*, Ch. 1, §§3-6, Ch. 15, §3.

113d We have adopted here with some changes the "operational definition" of values in Jacob-Flink, *Value Decision* 15-16. For these writers' related operational indices see also *infra* Ch. 10, n. 91.

114 *Cf.* W. V. Quine, *Methods of Logic* (2 ed. 1959) 119 for the distinction between relative and absolute terms.

115 On the hierarchical structure of values see Hartmann, *op. cit. supra* n. 106, at 269-278; L. Lavelle, 1 *Traité des Valeurs* (1953) 3ff.

themselves for discussion at all; that is, which do not merely peremptorily demand acceptance. To make it explicit can do no harm, but should, on the contrary, avoid some of the unnecessary misunderstandings and cross-purposes based on ill-thought-out notions of validity.

*   *   *   *   *   *   *

These historical and terminological preliminaries may suffice to introduce the mood and texture of the main theorisings about justice which have played their role in the last three centuries in the intellectual and practical story of Western legal thought. To these theorisings, and such conclusions as may be drawn from them in the concluding Chapters, we shall now turn.

CHAPTER 2

EARLY VOYAGES OF JUSTICE IN THE WEST

THE GOOD VESSEL NATURAL LAW

I. NATURAL LAW TO THE EIGHTEENTH CENTURY[1]

§1. POLARITIES IN THE HISTORICAL ROLES OF NATURAL LAW. The main concern of this Chapter is not with natural law as the claimant to sole lordship of the domain of justice, and with the treason-felony of the modern barons of positivism; nor even with its role as a criterion of justice among other criteria to be considered in later Chapters. Its concern is rather with natural law as the vessel in which the various criteria of justice sailed on to Western horizons,[1a] and with its formative role in Western political thought and action generally.[2] It is from this standpoint,

---

[1] The following selected introductory readings are suggested on conscience, equity, *ius gentium* and *ius naturale*: H. Maine, *Ancient Law* (new ed. 1930) 34 (equity as a later device than fictions); Aristotle, *Ethics*, v, 10 (Browne's transl. 145) (philosophical discussion of the equitable); Aristotle, *Politics*, i, 2, (Jowett's transl. vol. i, 2-5) (the nature of man as his ideal nature); Cicero, *De Republica* (*circa* 55 B.C.) bk. iii, ix, transl. in Sabine-Smith, *Cicero* 206 (influences of Greek speculation in Rome); Gaius, *Institutes* (*ante* 158 A.D.) bk. i, s.i (the Roman law distinction *ius civile, ius gentium*); H. Maine, *op. cit.* 60 (relationship between *ius gentium* and *ius naturale* in Roman law); W. Mitchell, *Essay on the Early History of the Law Merchant* (1904) 113-15 (the law merchant as a separate system in medieval Europe), 1-3, 8-19 (the tendency and claim to universality of the law merchant); Grotius, *De Jure Belli ac Pacis* (1625) *Prolegomena* 7-10 (Whewell's transl. vol. i, xiii) (the social and rational nature of man as the basis of seventeenth century natural law); *id.* bk. i, c.i, 10 (Whewell's transl. vol. i, 10-11) (natural law as a dictate of right reason); and *id. Prolegomena* 40 (Whewell's transl. vol. i, lxvi); R. Pound, "A Comparison of Ideals of Law" (1933) 47 *H.L.R.* 9-12, 14 (natural law as an instrument for criticising authority). The above readings are now collected in Simpson-Stone, 1 *Law and Society* 339-364.

[1a] S. Buchanan's recent thesis (in Cogley (ed.), *Natural Law* 82-153) shows nicely this bearer-role of natural law, esp. at phases of crisis. And see H. Wheeler, in *id.* 194-239, for a hypothesis of the social psychological processes involved, in terms of short-circuiting "the process of proving the necessary implications of a given system of relationships", as magic did with causal enquiries 238). But we beg to doubt this writer's hope that we can attain an analytically verifiable "functionalism" which will dispense with the issues of justice, issues which he rather loosely reduces wholly to natural law terms.

See also on the earlier history of natural law *supra* Ch. 1, *passim*, and on natural law as a specific theory of justice, *infra* Ch. 7, esp. §§8-9.

[2] The following are mentioned for reference: CRITIQUES OF NATURAL LAW FROM REPRESENTATIVE VIEWPOINTS: 1 Pareto, 245-276, §§401-465; J. Bentham, *Anarchical Fallacies*, 2 *Works* (Bowring's ed. 1839-43) 491; D. G. Ritchie, *Natural Rights* (1895); Haines, *Revival*; Cohen, *Ethical Systems* 101ff. and *passim*; E. Barker, Intro. to O. von Gierke, *Natural Law and the Theory of Society 1500-1800* (2 vols., 1913, transl. E. Barker, 1934); I. R. W. and A. J. Carlyle, *History of Medieval Political Theory* (1903) cc. iii-vii.

IN ENGLAND: F. W. Maitland, *Equity* (1913) lect. i, ii; W. S. Holdsworth, "Blackstone's Treatment of Equity" (1929) 43 *H.L.R.* 1; *id., Some Makers of English Law* (1938) 160-175 (on Mansfield); F. Pollock, *Essays in the Law* (1922) 31; *id., Expansion of the Common Law* (1904) 107-136. And see the citations *infra* esp. n.250.

though not explicitly so, that scholarly attention has recently found it more rewarding to study the historical forms and functions of natural law, rather than its mere concept or content.[3]

It may be ventured at the outset that natural law, like the criteria of justice of which it was the historical bearer, was a creature of the rational impulse, and of the practical need for the coercive power of organised society to present itself—and be accepted—as legitimate. And it is a corollary rather than a contradiction of this to add that historically the function of natural law in relation to established seats of power has been two-edged. Its name has been invoked to legitimise existing power, but often also to censor and on occasion even bastardise it. In the eighteenth century American colonies, natural law was invoked as a revolutionary force; within a century it was to become an ideological bulwark of conservative resistance to social legislation which seemed to challenge the existing economic order. This swing between poles of revolutionary and conservative function runs throughout the course of natural law history. While institutions are still stable and not too incongruous with existing demands, natural law tends to be found bolstering up the *status quo*. As the institutional *status quo* becomes increasingly incongruous with the changed social, cultural and economic conditions, this law may become a revolutionary instrument for challenging and demoralising existing institutions.

Other dramatic contrasts have been pointed out within the texture of natural law as historically given. One is a certain restless swinging of its exponents' ideas between recognition, on the one hand, that coercive power is a practical necessity for organised society, so that power must have its legitimacy; and, on the other hand, that such power must ever be questioned, and challenged to legitimise itself before reason. This is related, on the metaphysical and religious level, to the question of Plato's Dialogue

---

COMPARATIVE ACCOUNTS: J. Bryce, "The Law of Nature" in *id.*, 2 *Studies* 112-171; H. Maine, *Ancient Law* (1861), F. Pollock's ed. (1916) cc. iii-iv; and in the modern period Haines, *Revival*; 1 Pareto, 245-277, §§401-465; E. Wolf, *Das Problem der Naturrechtslehre: Versuch einer Orientierung* (2 ed. 1959); Welzel, *Naturrecht*; A. P. d'Entrèves, *Natural Law* (1951).

FOR STANDARD HISTORICAL STUDIES see Flückiger, 1 *Geschichte*; A. Verdross, *Abendländische Rechtsphilosophie ihre Grundlagen und Hauptprobleme in Geschichtlicher Schau* (1958); Friedrich, *Philosophy of Law*. ON THE GREEK ORIGINS see *supra* Ch. 1, and in addition W. Friedmann, *Legal Theory* (4 ed. 1960) c.ii; F. Berolzheimer, *World's Legal Philosophies* (transl. R. S. Jastrow (1912) from his *System der Rechts- und Wirtschaftsphilosophie* (1904-07) vol. ii) c.ii; E. Burle, *Essai sur le ... droit naturel dans l'Antiquité Grecque* (1908); M. Hamburger, *Awakening of Western Legal Thought* (1942); J. Bowle, *Western Political Thought* (1947) cc.iii-v; S. Ranulf, *The Jealousy of the Gods and Criminal Law at Athens* (1933); and F. Battaglia, 1 *Corso di Filosofia del Diritto* (1940) 82-115 (with a further useful bibli.). ROMAN DEVELOPMENT: A. Voigt, *Das Ius Naturale Aequum et Bonum und Ius Gentium der Römer* (1856); W. W. Buckland, *Equity in Roman Law* (1911); Jolowicz, *Roman Law passim*; Sabine-Smith, *Cicero* cc.ii, iii; R. Orestano, *Diritto Romano* App., 255-388. MEDIEVAL EUROPE: C. H. McIlwain, *The Growth of Political Thought in the West* (1932) c.iv; E. Barker, *op. cit. supra*. ROMAN CATHOLIC DOCTRINE: W Friedmann, *op. cit.* cc.vii, xxix; O. Lottin, *Le Droit Naturel chez S. Thomas d'Aquin ... (2 ed. 1931)*; J. Messner, *Das Naturrecht* (1950); H. A. Rommen, *The Natural Law* (1947).

[3] See, e.g., the works of E. Wolf, H. Welzel, and A. P. d'Entrèves, cited *supra* n. 2. A central theme of Wolf is that all legal thought has in it a strain of "iusnaturalism"; and of d'Entrèves that natural law is a kind of durable symbol for what we mean by the ground of "obligation of law". And see A. G. Chloros, "What is Natural Law?" (1958) 21 *M.L.R.* 609-622, esp. 616ff.; A. Ross, "Validity . . . Legal Positivism and Natural Law" (1961) 4 *Rev. Jur. de B.A.* 46. And see as to the latter writer *infra* n.253. Some of the contributions to J. Cogley *et al.*, *Natural Law and Modern Society* (1963) constitute perhaps an exception. See on this symposium *infra* Chs. 10, 11, *passim*.

Euthyphro: Is the just just because it pleases God, or does it please God because it is just? It is also related to the dualism in the history of natural law ideas which is taken as a main theme by Erik Wolf. This is between its voluntaristic strain, in which obligation springs from some transcending will, and which, in the more extreme accounts, seems to exclude natural law altogether; and the rationalistic (or idealistic) strain, in which obligation springs from the reason of the obeying or justifying subject.

Such distinctions among the versions of natural law are obviously not identical with the distinction first-mentioned between the conservative or innovating historical functions of natural law. Rationalistic-idealistic versions of natural law may sometimes be found invoking Reason to bolster as well as to assault fading Authority. Thomist natural law, independently of its inherent value, served the former function in the succeeding centuries of waning Imperial and Papal power; and the natural law of American constitutional decision in the late nineteenth century supported the economic *status quo* against insurgent collectivist ideas pressing through the state legislatures. There are no doubt such moments of hovering social transition in which natural law may go either way, or for that matter both ways, among its exponents for the time being. In general, however, we might expect a certain parallelism between the dominant trends in ideas of natural law for the time being, and what we have called the historical function of natural law in a particular social setting. Voluntaristic theories seem most likely to flourish in conservative phases of natural law, when established authority welcomes its support, as when the Holy Roman Emperors seized on the *Corpus Juris* of Justinian as symbolizing the authoritative will which they aspired to inherit. Rationalistic-idealistic versions of natural law, on the other hand, are more likely to be found playing innovatory creative roles. Such roles themselves, as also the conservative roles, share something of the uniqueness of every historical situation.

Three type-situations may perhaps serve for orientation among the creative roles. There is, first, that of the threatening collapse of authority of an existing power structure, when rationalistic-idealistic versions drive to find or justify some substitute order. So some versions of natural law drove to justify alternative orders to those of Imperial and Papal authority in the Renaissance and Reformation struggles out of which modern Europe emerged. The contemporary crisis of the order of "coordinated" sovereign States, and with it of the classical international law, has also been marked by notable rationalistic-idealistic drives. These have taken various forms such as "revived natural law", or search for the "general principles of law recognised by civilised nations", or for a system of international law based on fundamental human rights. There is, second, the even more dramatic type-situation, as in the French and American revolutions, of the stark confrontation of the authority of an existing power structure by forces of resistance and rebellion. Here the rationalistic-idealistic drive of natural law is a direct weapon used in destroying one legitimacy and substituting another. Equally interesting for the lawyer are, third, the less dramatic functions of technical overhaul of bodies of legal doctrine which have become archaic in new social and economic situations, as with the construction of the *ius gentium-ius naturale* principles in classical Rome, and of equity and natural law in post-medieval England, to replace or supplement the outrun *ius civile* or strict common law.

Whatever insights of these kinds we may try to draw from the two and a half thousand years of the elaboration of natural law in the West, we should guard against illusions of tidy symmetry of distinctions, or of unilinear or rhythmic movement. Where one kind of drive of ideas and functions is dominant, contrasting drives and functions will also be found among the exponents of natural law; and it may often have been less clear to contemporaries than it is to our hindsight which drive was dominant. And the mixture of drives may exist even within the individual minds of particular exponents of natural law. Sharp categorisation and wide generalisation in terms of the above distinctions, must therefore be kept in check. Whatever tendencies of ideas and functions we can distinguish are probably only approximate abstractions from chaotically recurrent movements of action, reaction, interpermeation, cross-fertilisation, reformulation, renewed alienation, rapprochement, and alienation again, in ever-changing contexts of thought and action.

This rich and complex medley of movement is not only between successive generations and peoples, but also within single generations and peoples, and even within the minds of each generation of men in particular societies. The fuller truth may well be that these tendencies in natural law history—the tendencies to explain why power is legitimate as well as necessary, and also why it is illegitimate and must be overthrown; to idealise the actual, and also to actualise the ideal for the undoing of the actual; to support valid law with a sufficiency of power, and to temper power with a "valid law"—these comprehend, if adequately pursued, all the important questions which can be asked about the viability of human societies living under law, and the viability of law within human societies. They embrace much, if not the whole, of the province and function of law as our own work seeks to map it. Natural law, navigating with the charts of Greek and Hebrew explorers, was the vessel which bore these questions on to our horizons. The aim of the present Chapter is but to outline that voyage, learn something of the patterns of thought which the vessel bore, and the fate of the vessel itself as these patterns were disembarked, dispersed and naturalised into the Western State-societies of the modern period.[3a] What remains as the still *specifically identifiable* body of natural law doctrine within the body of contemporary juristic thought will be separately considered in Chapter 7 on "Revived" Natural Law and in Chapters 10 and 11.

§2. ROLE OF NATURAL LAW IN ROMAN LAW. With the Greeks, as we have already seen, natural law remained essentially a philosopher's speculation in an age of unsettled convictions and political disorders, though no doubt occasionally the rhetorician used it in accordance with Aristotle's advice: "If the written law tells against our case, clearly we must appeal to the universal law and insist on its greater equity and justice".[4] At Rome, on the other hand, the problem of whether law was merely an enactment of public authority or founded in nature moved from speculative philosophy into workaday jurisprudence. In part, this was because the Romans were more "law-minded". Greek law scarcely survived as a system because it never found its class of legal specialists, or abandoned its lay administrators

---

　　　[3a] For an attempt (vain, we fear) to reembark on the same vessel several centuries later the full range of contemporary problems not only of justice, but of social and logical analysis, see Micklem, *Law, passim*.
　　　[4] *Rhetorics,* i, 15, 1375a (Ross's Transl.).

or its popular tribunals of grotesque size; while Roman law developed through the efforts of jurisconsults and praetors into a permanent heritage of Western society.[5] In part, it was a response to the challenge of the growth of Roman dominion throughout the Mediterranean world. Dominion made Rome into a great commercial metropolis, in which a legal framework had to be created for relations between Romans and foreigners and amongst foreigners themselves. This could not be provided by Roman civil law, which was still a rather primitive law of a kin-organised society, and by its terms applicable to citizens only. Natural law thought, in this situation, assumed an innovatory role: this role was played through the practical activities of jurisconsults in advising clients and lay judges, of the magistrate charged with the administration of justice in the city, the *praetor urbanus*, and above all in the work of the special praetor for foreigners, the *praetor peregrinus*, charged with the administration of justice where foreigners were involved.

All these activities joined in adapting the old *ius civile* to the needs of the commercial centre of the known world. Protected by the halo of servitors of a superior law of nature, manifesting itself through the *ius gentium*, the rules common to all nations,[6] these officials were able to denude the old civil law of its anomalous tribal and historical features. The theory on which they proceeded was that there were principles common to the legal systems of all peoples. They thus set out to discover (but in fact largely created) a body of principles apt by its simplicity and comprehensiveness to govern transactions among merchants of the various Mediterranean peoples and in particular between Romans and Greeks.[7] They were able, in short, to bridge the gap between obsolete legal institutions and the transformed conditions of Roman civilisation; to adapt the law of a petty tribal agricultural society to the needs of an empire diverse in constituent peoples and great in dominions, wealth and commerce.

In the background of this practical achievement was the naturalisation into Roman intellectual life of Stoic philosophy, as a result of the close contacts with Greek philosophical thought which accompanied the spread of Roman dominion. For the Romans of the Republican era the Greek conception of a law of nature offered support for a legal experience which, completely laicised as it had become, had seemed rather to be suspended in a void. Further, the Greek concept became variously connected with the *"ius divinum"* and served to provide some intellectual connection between the law conceived as being of divine origin and the law of human origin,

---

[5] It is vain for M. Le Bel ("Natural Law in the Greek Period" (1948) 2 *Nat. L. Inst. Proc.* 3 at 6) to kick against these pricks, when he has to concede on the very next page that "Greek jurisprudence and court practice underwent only a slight development from Solon to Aristotle". See also the fuller and more appealing apologia in G. Glotz, *The Greek City and its Institutions* (1929) 232ff., 255, which, however, can scarcely displace Sir E. Barker's generalisation (*Greek Political Theory* . . . (1918) 180) that the Greek genius "was not, like the Roman, specifically legal", but "specifically metaphysical". *Modern* Greek law is of course Roman Byzantine in origin, with modern civilian code elements. See P. J. Zepos, ". . . Greek Civil Code of 1946 . . ." (1962) 36 *Tulane L.R.* 647-662.

[6] *Cf.* the century-old controversy as to the supposed general principles of commercial jurisprudence which under *Swift* v. *Tyson* (1842) 41 U.S. 1 were to be applied by federal courts regardless of state law peculiarities. See Holmes J. (dissenting) in *Black & White Taxi Case* (1928) 276 U.S. 518; Cohen, *Ethical Systems* 104; *Erie* v. *Tompkins* (1938) 304 U.S. 64, esp. 71ff.

[7] See R. Sohm, *Institutionen* (16 ed. 1919) 84; W. Friedmann, *op. cit.* 50; and (for the medieval scholastic use) T. Gilby, *Principality and Polity* (1958) 142ff.

just as in later Greek thinking it had established a link between laws of nature and laws of convention.

Stoic philosophy arose on the threshold of the Greek and Roman worlds, first appearing in Athens about 300 B.C., at a time when the spread of Greek civilisation over the Orient was already creating the ideological foundation for transition from city-state to empire. The Stoics applied the thought of Plato and Aristotle to the new political and cultural dimensions of the emerging *cosmopolis*.[8] This required the further development, for peoples of widely alien cultures, of the seed of universalism planted by the two great philosophers. The Stoic solution, based on the distinction between *lex aeterna, ius naturale,* and *ius humanum,*[9] was to become a central theme of natural law thought in the West.

Lex aeterna is the law of reason of the cosmos, the *logos*, which rules the universe. Human reason, an emanation of cosmic reason,[10] rules the lives of men as *recta ratio*, so that natural law is seen partaking of—though more limited in ambit than—the eternal law. Voluntarily or under invincible compulsion, man must obey this natural law, since it transcends him in every respect.[11] These distinctions moderated the Platonic (and to a degree also the Aristotelian) teaching that full observance of law, since it required understanding of the cosmic order culminating in the vision of God, was possible only for those of highest intellectual attainments. For in the Stoa, the asserted innateness of right reason in all men linked each human person, and not merely Plato's "philosopher-kings", with the cosmic order.

This same Stoic idea of a universally valid moral law also served, of course, to transcend the narrow limits imposed by the *polis* as a model of human society. As Stoic ideas entered into Roman culture this aspect received even clearer formulation in Cicero's famous expressions of it:

> There is in fact a true law, namely right reason, which is in accordance with nature, applies to all men and is unchangeable and eternal. . . .
> It will not lay down one rule at Rome and another at Athens, nor will it be one rule today and another tomorrow. But there will be one

---

8 See Welzel, *Naturrecht* 38.

9 See *id.* 39ff.; R. N. Wilkin, "Cicero and the Law of Nature", in A. L. Harding (ed.), *Origins of the Natural Law Tradition* (1954) 1-25, at 14-16, 22-23; M. Reale, *Politica e Direito em Roma — A Doutrina de Cicero* (1941); *id., Horizontes do Direito e da História* (1956) 55-56. Recent work suggests that the older distinction between *ius humanum* and *ius divinum* first referred to the content rather than authorship of law, the latter kind of law being *concerned with* the gods, not in the general sense of religious or moral precepts, but as regards rites, sacrifices, festivities and so on. See R. Orestano, *"Dal Ius al Fas"* (1939) 46 *Bull. Ist. di Dir. Rom.* 194-273; *id., "Elemento Divino ed Elemento Umano nel Diritto di Roma"* (1941) 21 *Riv. Int. di Fil. del Dir.* 1; *id., Diritto Romano*; P. G. Goidanich, *"Fas e Ius: Concetti ed Etimi"* (1943) 3 *Atti Accademia d'Italia,* fasc. 8; M. Kaser, *Das Altrömische Ius* (1949): and *cf.* on the relation between law, morality and religion in primitive (kin-organised) society, Simpson-Stone, 1 *Law and Society* 28-40. Cicero's use of *ius divinum,* however, comes near to that of the *ius naturale.* (Orestano, *Diritto Romano* 365).

On the *ius gentium* as "a subdivision" of the "vulgar law", the latter developing as part of the rustic and provincial reactions from the refined technicalities of the Roman "city" jurists, see E. Levy, *West Roman Vulgar Law; The Law of Property* (1951) esp. at 6-8.

10 *Cf.* Verdross, *op. cit.* 44-45. Cicero conceived "nature" as being the "beginning" of law, and usually as being human opinion, human conceptions and human creation. (*De Inventione* II, xxii, at 65; *id.* liii, at 161; *cf. De Legibus* I, 13, 35 and *id.* I, 12, 33.) In *Pro Milone* IV, 10, "nature" is contrasted with human creation; but even in that oration *cf. id.* XI, 30.

11 As a dog tied to a cart may choose to run with it, but even if not, it will still be dragged along yelping on its hind legs: see Welzel, *Naturrecht* 30.

B

law eternal and unchangeable binding at all times and upon all peoples.[12] The animal . . . we call man, endowed with foresight and quick intelligence—possessing memory, full of reason and prudence, has been given a certain distinguished status by the supreme God who created him; for he is the only one among so many different kinds and varieties of living beings who have a share in reason and thought, while all the rest are deprived of it. . . .[13] For those creatures who have received the gift of reason from nature have also received right reason and therefore they have also received the gift of law which is right reason applied to command and prohibition.[14]

In one respect Cicero went perhaps beyond the Stoic position. The identification of "right reason" with the existing order brought natural law even more within every man's reach; but by the same token it also made hazardous its role as a censor of the positive prescriptions of the moral and the legal order,[15] as "right reason" (in Cicero's words) "applied to command and prohibition". He himself made the point in the *De Finibus*: "If there were no difference between the things necessary for the conduct of life, and if no decision as to their value could be made between them, the whole of life would become disordered".[16] To provide a basis for such decisions he sought to re-introduce a measure of Platonic idealism, postulating a *ius naturale* not only as the legitimation of the existing order but as the ideal of the more perfect social ordering,[17] towards which the existing order tends for its full development. From this position it was only a short but vital step to reformulating the Platonic and Aristotelian measure of the legitimacy of the power of the state in terms of "*ius*", of a "*ius naturale*" founded on the nature of man and of society, and governing through its universal validity and effectiveness the place of men in the fabric of social life.[18] All this, in its due time, took its place not only among the foundations of the Roman world *imperium*, but in the later conception under the Christian Emperors of the

---

[12] *De Republica* III, 22. *Cf. id.* III, 17; *De Legibus*, II, 4, 8. And see Orestano, *Diritto Romano* 262ff.; J. Gaudemet, ". . . *Droit Naturel à Rome*" (1952) 1 *Arch. . . . Histoire Dr. Oriental* 445-467; G. Galbiati, *De Fontibus M. T. Ciceronis Librorum . . .* (1916); P. W. Kamphuisen, "*L'Influence de la Philosophie . . . chez les Jurisconsultes Romains*" (1932) 11 *R. Hist. Dr. Fr. et Etr.* 389-412. On Cicero's intellectual context see Sabine-Smith, *Cicero* 34-36, with bibli. at 100. Micklem, *Law* 22-29, writing as a Christian theologian, presents Cicero's thought as a kind of prototype of the modern natural law heritage from Greece. On the Greek impact on Cicero and Roman legal thinking, see Orestano, *Diritto Romano* 355ff. (with bibli.), and Cairns, *Plato to Hegel* c. iv. See also F. Schulz, *Roman Legal Science* (1946) 63, 67, 84, 238; S. Riccobono, "*Humanitas*" in 21 *Il Circolo Giuridico* (*N.S.U. of Palermo*, 1950) 146-167; R. N. Wilkin, *Eternal Lawyer: A Legal Biography of Cicero* (1947); *id., cit. supra* n. 9 (esp. on the confluence of philosophical and legal fruitfulness with political crisis); *cf.* J. Bowle, *op. cit. supra* n. 2, 89-103); and Strauss, *Natural Right* 153-55 (esp. on the need for caution in assessing Cicero's contribution). And see S. Buchanan, "Natural Law and Teleology", in Cogley (ed.), *Natural Law* 82, at 93-98, 101-102, 104.

[13] *De Legibus* I, 7 (C. W. Keyes' transl. 1928, 321). Orestano, *Diritto Romano* 366-382, esp. at 366-67, observes that the possibility of relating both *ius divinum* and *ius humanum* (now associated within *ius naturale*) to the human *animus* was also a way of escaping the sense of arbitrariness of law, in a time of enormous legal change, and of the waning of faith in a *ius* directly given by the will of the gods. Cicero was thus bolstering the will to legal observance.

[14] *De Legibus* I, 12, transl. cited 333. On the inconsistencies in Cicero's demonstrations see 1 Pareto 249-250, §§412-16.

[15] *Cf.* Flückiger, 1 *Geschichte* 221-222.

[16] *De Finibus*, III. 15, 50. *Cf.* Welzel, *Naturrecht* 43.

[17] *Cf.* Flückiger, 1 *Geschichte* 221.

[18] Hence Cicero's definition of the state as a "coming together of a considerable number of men who are united by a common agreement about law and rights and by the desire to participate in mutual advantages" (*De Republica*, I, 25; transl. in Sabine-Smith, *Cicero* 129). *Cf.* Flückiger, 1 *Geschichte* 228.

imperial and Christian *oecumene*, the spiritual-cum-political commonness of humanity.[19]

§3. THE BEGINNINGS OF CHRISTIAN NATURAL LAW. The universalism attained in these Graeco-Roman concepts was horizontal across peoples, and did not penetrate vertically down to the subject classes, for instance, of slaves. In due course it was confronted by the Judaeo-Christian universalism, which challenged it by its vertical penetration down to the humblest classes, as well as across peoples. No less vitally, this challenge also affected the assumption that the hierarchy of the mature *Imperium Romanum* was an earthly analogy of the neo-Platonic notion of "order" as an emanation of the divine principle, descending by degrees from its pure expression in God down into the world of material reality. On these philosophic assumptions was based the unquestioned claim of the *imperium* to divine character, and neo-Platonism offered remarkably apt metaphysical support for the whole Roman State hierarchy.[20] Jewish-Christian spirituality was a threat at this sensitive point, quite apart from any overt political opposition. Its God was the creator of the universe, not merely the first principle and source of cosmic order. A God who was Creator and Master was less malleable in human hands than any metaphysical principle; and it also became difficult to associate divinity with a rather unequal succession of Emperors, in a world whose Creator was still its Master.

The divine character of a secular Empire may seem to us not an obviously necessary foundation of order in human society. We must, however, remember that the attributes of the Judaeo-Christian God must also have seemed very strange to the Romans and Greeks, for whom the neo-Platonic philosophy had provided a rational account of cosmic order, emancipated from sacral elements. To the Athenians, whom Paul found "too superstitious",[21] his insistence on God's will as the only source of divine commands[22] must in turn have seemed like a reversion to the superstitious irrationalism of earlier Greek history. Though Paul's Epistles contained traces of the belief that the divine will is accessible to human reason, he rejected the traditional aids to reason in this task,[23] and left the overall impression

---

[19] *Cf.* the "statement of motive" in the law by which Caracalla conferred Roman citizenship on all subjects of the Empire: "that in all languages and to all gods prayers may be said for the duration of the Roman Empire". (In the newly-found Giessen Papyrus No. 40: see E. von Ivànka, *"Humanismus und Latinität"*, in *Soladitas Erasmiana, Roma 20-23 Settembre 1949*.) For the view that Cicero did *not* much influence his contemporary lawyers (as distinct from philosophers) see E. Alberterio, *"Etica e Diritto nel Mondo Classico Latino"* (1932) 12 *Riv. Int. di Fil. del Dir.* 18-35; *id., "Concetto Classico e Definizioni Postclassiche dell'Ius Naturale"* in (1937) 5 *Studi di Diritto Romano* 277-290. But contrast M. Villey, *"Deux Conceptions du Droit Naturel . . ."* (1953) 31 *R. Hist. Dr. Fr. et Etr.* 475; *id., "Sur l'Antique Inclusion du Droit dans la Morale"* (1958) 42 *Arch. R.- und Sozialph.* 15; *id., Leçons d'Histoire de la Philosophie du Droit* (1958); and Orestano, *Diritto Romano.*

[20] In the Christian Byzantine Empire its memory was preserved in the curious fact that the three highest ranks of civil servants were named after the three highest hierarchies of angels in the neo-Platonic system: *illustres, spectabiles,* and *clarissimi.* *Cf.* Flückiger, 1 *Geschichte* 282. And *cf.* generally Buchanan, *cit. supra* n. 12, at 105ff.

[21] *Acts* 17. 22.

[22] See *Acts* 17. 24ff.; *Romans* 2. 14-15, 14. 8; *Colossians* 1. 16ff.; 1 *Corinthians* 4. 20.

[23] The Greek aid, human nature, is something to be overcome: *cf.* the play on different "laws" in *Romans* 7. 23. The Jewish aid, the written law of God, is a preliminary "schoolmaster" now outgrown: see *Galatians* 3. 24-25 and *cf.* passages cited *infra* n. 28.

unmistakable that God's dictates are not to be understood in terms of *human* understanding, and are not rational in terms of *human* reason.[24] Paul believed that the obviously necessary knowledge of the divine will could only be "spiritually discerned",[25] and this only in the sense that God has made it known to us "according to his good pleasure which he hath purposed in himself".[26] As Welzel observes, Paul saw himself finally as an apostle of the will of God, which "has no other ground to will as He wills than that He wills so", and "not in any whatsoever laws binding Him, or eternal truths". So that "what God gives he gives in full freedom, by grace alone".[27]

It fitted well with this that for Paul law as a problem was rather irrelevant. He was, he declared, "dead to the law, that I might live unto God . . .".[28] With only slight exceptions[29] Paul eschewed natural law thinking then current. But his very emphasis on *will* as the source of ethical norms[30] helped to reintroduce voluntarism into the Christian speculations of late antiquity. In one form or another these were all seeking to harmonise the metaphysical positions which saw the absolute in God's will, with that which saw it in his wisdom; to make peace, in short, between Christianity and neo-Platonism.

For St. Augustine (354-430 A.D.) this problem presented itself in the acute contemporary question whether Rome could survive as a Christian state, and whether the denial of its absolute and divine character spelled its imperial doom. He moulded his answer into the Stoic three-tier hierarchy of *lex temporalis*, *lex naturalis* and *lex aeterna*. Temporal law is positive law; changeable according to circumstances of time and place. Even temporal law, however, must be warranted by the unchangeable eternal law,[31] and for Augustine a law which is not just in this sense is not law.[32] His natural law is the transcription of eternal law, inborn in man's soul, reason and heart,[33] through which God speaks to us in our conscience. Eternal law he defined as "the reason *or* will of God (*ratio divina vel voluntas Dei*), which commands us to preserve the natural order and prohibits us to disturb it".[34] As between the voluntarist and the rationalist conceptions of natural law, he thus in terms purported to choose both.

Did this go beyond mere equivocation towards synthesis? Augustine was clearly a "voluntarist", and like Paul denied that the will of God had

---

24 See, e.g., 1 *Corinthians* 1. 19-28, 2. 14, 3. 19; *cf.* 1 *Timothy* 6. 16.
25 1 *Corinthians* 2. 11, 14; *cf.* 2 *Corinthians* 3. 5, *Romans* 1. 20.
26 *Ephesians* 1. 9.
27 Welzel, *Naturrecht* 51. *Cf. Romans* 9. 15-16, 18, 20; 11. 33-34; *Ephesians* 2. 8; 2 *Timothy* 1. 9; *Philippians* 2. 13-14, 3. 12-13. *Cf. Acts* 20. 22ff., 21. 13-14; *Hebrews* 12.
28 *Galatians* 2. 19, 21. *Cf.* also *Romans* 4. 13ff.; *Galatians* 2. 19, 21, 3. 3ff.; 1 *Timothy* 1. 9; *Colossians* 2. 20-22; *Hebrews* 7. 18-19, 8. 13. And see the valuable comment by E. Nobile, "*Il Disdegno della Legge nel Pensiero di Paolo di Tarso*" (1935) 15 *Riv. Int. di Fil. del Dir.* 92-101. This is not to suggest that Paul did not know and claim his own legal rights under both Roman and Jewish law: see *Acts* 22. 25, 23. 3, 25. 10-11.
29 See, e.g., *Romans* 13, asserting the obligation of human law as grounded in divine law. The exceptions seem (with respect) to be blown up into rather too much of a mouthful in G. Quadri, "*Il Fondamento del Diritto di Punire nel Pensiero di S. Paolo*" (1934) 14 *Riv. Int. di Fil. del Dir.* 367-399.
30 See Welzel, *Naturrecht* 50ff. And *cf.* generally on Paul's importance J. Bowle, *op. cit. supra* n. 2, 109-115.
31 *De Libero Arbitrio* I. 6, 14.
32 *Id.* I. 5, 11.
33 *De Diversis Quaestionibus* 53, 2.
34 *Contra Faustum* XXII. 27.

need of grounds, accepting predestination of men as the highest expression of this will.[35] But as he based divine law on both God's Will *and* His Reason as the source of divine law, so he relied on both human faith *and* reason for access to it.[36] He thought the tensions between will and reason were resolved by love as the highest moral principle, as developed by Paul and John. The divine love, while detracting nothing from the absoluteness of God's will, excluded the very possibility of arbitrariness. *"Ama et fac quod vis."* For Cicero's concordant sharing of *laws* among a rational multitude, then, Augustine substituted that of *"the things loved"*, which included justice and therefore implied the rendering to God of what is due to him.[37] Love of God and love of neighbour had become the basis of law in the Augustinian synthesis.[38]

With the collapse, in the generation after Augustine, of government by abstract principles of law and of the Western Empire itself, tribal organisations arose based on fealty to charismatic leaders, that is, men deemed to have a specially close relation to the gods. The Christianisation of the barbarians as they overran the Roman Empire helped to stabilise this system into the feudal archetype of order through a firm social hierarchy. The tolerance of St. Augustine's political philosophy, by finding room within the idea of order for the motif of personal leadership, as a universal principle transcending the mere relations of tribal chief and followers, may well have snatched the idea of government under law from the collapsing ancient world. In new meanings, at any rate, these ideas were to serve the rising socio-political systems of European civilisation.

§4. THE BIRTH OF SCHOLASTICISM. This first synthesis between Christianity and rationalism carried into formative Europe the Graeco-Roman ways of theorising about justice, law and face-to-face power relations. But the tide of history covered over the ruins of the Graeco-Roman exemplarship of the impersonal state and world *imperium*; the small close-knit communities which first arose, based on immediately observable mutual dependence, neither needed nor (for the most part) concerned themselves to intellectualise the principle of *imperium*.[39] Instead the Church provided in its canons an institutional basis for personal fealties, rooted in custom and in universally accepted norms of a moral nature. Hundreds of years were to pass before history demanded also a reconciliation with a now fully Christian environment, of the idea of the state based on a rationally conceivable (natural) law.

Classical theories of the state lived on among scholars. In the twelfth

---

[35] See Welzel, *Naturrecht* 54.

[36] See F. Copleston, 2 *History of Philosophy* (1950) 70. As to whether the role of faith and divine grace makes the concept of "natural law" inapt here, see Flückiger, 1 *Geschichte* 385. We think not, both because of the supposed access to them through reason, and of their function of controlling public power. *Cf.* F. Copleston, 2 *op. cit.* 87-90; J. N. Figgis, *The Political Aspects of St. Augustine's "City of God"* (1921); N. H. Baynes, *The Political Ideas of St. Augustine's De Civitate Dei* (1936, Historical Assoc. Pamphlet No. 104); J. Bowle, *op. cit.* 131-39; S. Cotta, *La Città Politica di Sant'Agostino* (1960).

[37] *De Civitate Dei* XIX. 24; *cf.* Cicero's definition *supra* n. 18. And *cf.* Friedrich, *Philosophy of Law* 36.

[38] See *id.* 37; and *cf.* F. Copleston, 2 *op. cit. supra* n. 36, at 81-83.

[39] See Friedrich, *op. cit.* 43 and *cf.* T. Gilby, *Principality and Polity* (1958) at xviii ff., 90ff.

century the glossators began the revival of Roman law and the attempt to accredit it as the "imperial law"[40] for a Holy Roman Emperor struggling to impose its hierarchy *upon* the feudal substructure and *against* the Catholic Church. As the feudal substructure broke in face of the rivalries of empire and papacy and of the ambitions of feudal magnates, the state leviathan stirred again. It stirred not only in Dante's grandiose dream of a new Empire uniting spiritual and secular power, but in the harsh military and political realities of the English and French conversion of kingship from a coveted prize in the anarchical feudal game into an effective system of governmental power. The rational foundations for the revival of the State were being laid, meanwhile, not only in the cultivation of the Roman law, but in the attempted integration of the classical idea of the *polis* into Christian moral, legal and political thought by the intellectual movement known as scholasticism.

The range of this movement is too vast, and the opinions within it too conflicting and too subtle in their conflicts, to be characterised in a single treatise, let alone in one section of a chapter. Certainly only the Hegels of the world can dismiss it with the phrase "paltry, terribly written and voluminous".[41] We must here limit ourselves to recalling its Christian neo-Platonist and related classical sources, and placing into the context of the present Chapter its revival of the struggle between voluntarism and rationalism, so central to the political function of natural law. In the present Section we deal with the general links with classical thought; in the succeeding Sections with Aquinas and Duns Scotus, as protagonists respectively of reason and will as the foundation of justice, morals, law and the State.

Turning then to the classical links, it must first be noted that while the Platonic tradition remained central in the philosophy of the West after Augustine, the Aristotelian tradition only fully returned to it after centuries of intermediate cultivation by Arab and Jewish philosophers. Aristotle's works were translated into Syrian, and thence into Arabic, in which language they were eagerly studied. The Arab Avicenna (Ibn Sina),[42] for example, born in 980 A.D. into an Islam torn by conflicts which buffeted his

---

40 As received it came to be so known until the 18th century. See L. Enneccerus, 1 *Lehrbuch des bürgerlichen Rechts* (1928) 6.

41 Hegel, 19 *Sämtliche Werke* (ed. H. Glockner, 1928) 149. Among the many more sympathetic accounts of "scholasticism", a most lucid attempt to articulate the spirit of the movement, and the origins and implications of the name, is by D. Knowles, *The Evolution of Medieval Thought* (1962) *passim*, esp. at 71-92. And see J. Pieper, *Scholasticism* (1961). On the notorious scholastic terminology see *supra* Ch. 1, n. 18; *infra* n. 117; and T. Gilby, *op. cit.* 271-73, 278, commenting at 272: "It is strange that an intellectual conviction of the real and not merely symbolical value of the sensible world should have waxed with a decay of style in declaring its beauty." See *id.* 273-74 for a sober assessment of Aquinas' prose style which contrasts strikingly with Gilby's own rhapsodic eulogy at 3.

For the scholastic philosophy in its social and political medieval background, see T. Gilby, *op. cit.*, which however in relating the scholastics to this context occasion-ally understates their dependence on earlier streams of thought, particularly the Platonic. Despite our own stress on the political function of natural law, and on the importance for his thought of the thinker's own social and political context, we tend rather to agree with F. Copleston, 2 *op. cit. supra* n. 36, at 11-12, esp. 310, 412-13 (as to Aquinas). The scholastics' *influence on* their world is, of course, another matter. And see generally the valuable study by J. Bowle, *op. cit. supra* n. 2, bk. ii, esp. cc. iii, iv.

42 "Ibn Sina" is a less corrupted transliteration. So with Averroes (Ibn Rushd), Avempace (Ibn Bajja), Abubacer (Ibn Tufail), and numerous others. See generally on Avicenna, A. M. Goichon, *La Philosophie d'Avicenne* (1944); and F. Copleston, 2 *op. cit. supra* n. 36, 190-95. Knowles, *op. cit.* 194ff., has a valuable account of Aristotle's entry into Arab culture and its effects on both Arab and Western cultures.

personal life, was deeply convinced of Mohammed's prophetic inspiration and authority as Lawgiver of Islam; but he was as strongly attracted to the Greek philosophy of "reason"[43] as he was repelled by the "irrational" bases actually vouched for Islamic doctrine. He therefore set himself *inter alia*[44] to place Islamic doctrine and practices into the frame of Greek, and especially Aristotelian, philosophy.[45]

He saw the human conflict of animal faculty and rational soul[46] as reconcilable and even removable by Aristotle's principle of the mean.[47] "Always the Mean plucks the rational soul from the two extremes",[48] he thought. The soul, endowed as it was with "perfect reason and far-reaching, all-embracing thought", strives to "become as it were an intellectual microcosm, impressed with the form of the All, the order intelligible in the All, and the good pervading the All".[49] In seeking this wholeness of vision, we also seek God, in whom reason is also supreme, and knowledge complete. But God's knowledge is different from man's, since He also created the objects of knowledge and commands them "according to a known order".[50] For this reason God's knowledge does not change, as man's does, with changes in the things known. Moreover, he created first "an abstract substance, namely, the First Intelligence".[51] In short, "the whole world is disposed and pre-determined, known and willed by God".[52]

For human society, declared Avicenna, in terms even closer to those of Plato and Aristotle, God knew and willed the distinctiveness of man, not only in his reason, but in his need of the society and of the help of others. For this mutuality of needs, and to permit cooperation in filling them, society and civic duty exist. And this continuing cooperation "requires a code of law and just regulation, which in their turn call for a lawgiver and regulator".[53] Mohammed was thus ordained and inspired to "prescribe laws for mankind",[54] ensuring the good order of the physical world through political government, and that of the spirit by philosophy.[55]

A second Arab philosopher through whom Aristotle returned to the

---

[43] He records in his autobiography that, fascinated by Aristotle's *Metaphysics,* he read it forty times and knew it by heart, without understanding it. When finally he got the key from another Arab commentary he relates that he "distributed much in alms to the poor in gratitude to Almighty God". See *Avicenna on Theology* (transl. A. J. Arberry, 1951) 12.

[44] He was also a physician, mathematician, theologian, logician, philologist, etc. *Inter alia* he wrote "in about twenty volumes" a work (now lost) entitled *The Import and the Substance* "on jurisprudence, exegesis and asceticism". See *id.* 13.

[45] See A. J. Arberry in *id.,* Intro., esp. at 4-7.

[46] Sometimes this became a triad of animal soul, physical soul, and rational soul: see, e.g., *id.* 51-53.

[47] *Id.* 72.

[48] *Id.* 73.

[49] *Id.* 67; *cf. id.* 53.

[50] *Id.* 36.

[51] *Id.* 35-36, citing the Prophet to like effect.

[52] *Id.* 38.

[53] *Id.* 42ff. And see Rosenthal, *Islam* 145.

[54] With regard to the variation of law with time and place, he took the simple (though question-begging) position that "through it we know the difference between the divine prophecy and all the false pretensions to it." (*Tis'rasa'il* 73ff).

[55] Rosenthal, *Islam* 144. The law of the Prophet came thus to be interposed into the process of human reason as it discovers and obeys the law of divine reason, as a kind of reinforcement and reinsurance. For "men must be bound by one kind of fetter or another — either of the sacred law, or of reason — in order that the order of the world may be maintained in full perfection". (*Op. cit. supra* n. 43, at 41). There is a hint also (*id.* 57) of Maimonides' explanation (*infra* n.85) of the role of habit and training in virtue.

Western world was Averroes (Ibn Rushd)—who flourished in Spain[56] from 1126 to 1198. His original ideas in general philosophy were to have an enormous influence on Western scholasticism, and he reinforced in even more specifically Aristotelian terms[57] Avicenna's version of Aristotle on natural law in its relation to the State. On Aristotle's statement that man is "a political being by nature", Averroes commented that man's life was impossible without the State,[58] that man can attain his natural ends only as part of it,[59] and his highest perfection only in an ideal state with an ideal constitution and law, revealed by a Prophet.[60] For "only the prophetic lawgiver who is also a philosopher" can lay down the right law.[61]

Some variations of law with time and place were explained, he thought, not only by the fact that some peoples were not blessed with a Prophet, but because even what is "ideal" law varies for each people. The Islamic state was ideal for Islam, and Plato's *Republic* for the Greeks.[62] For the prophetic lawgiver is born into a partially developed system of positive and natural law, and his lawgiving must take account not only of elements common to the law of all peoples, and of the particular people's religion, but also of the existing law of the particular people, from which he cannot move too far.[62a] This was a remarkable explanation of how the prophetic statement of the divine will is brought to accord with human reason, as applied to the circumstances of a particular people. It was accompanied by Averroes' assertion that it was to the philosopher, and not the theologian, that we should look for rational interpretation of revelation. This challenge to the priest was as bold[63] as the attempt to base it on

---

[56] He held judicial office in Seville and Cordova, but was also a man of encyclopaedic interests and activities.

[57] See Rosenthal, *Islam* 177, 186. Averroes was of course influenced by Plato as well as Aristotle, and his "ideal state" of the Prophet's revealed law has been thought essentially Platonic. See *id.* 176 and *cf.* Averroes, *Commentary*. Averroes himself praised Aristotle as an "exemplar" of "the final perfection of man", teaching "the supreme truth", and "given to us by divine providence that we might know all there is to be known". (Commentary on Aristotle's *De Anima*, quoted Knowles, *op. cit.* 200.)

[58] See Rosenthal, *Islam* 175.

[59] Averroes, *Commentary* 184.

[60] *Id.* 185.

[61] *Ibid.* The need for the lawgiver to be a Prophet was, however, a matter of perfection rather than of necessity: *id.* 177.

[62] Rosenthal, *Islam* 185. So *cf.* as to variation of ideal religions for different peoples, e.g., as to Judaism for Israel, and Christianity for Rome, *id.* 184, and Averroes, *Commentary* 153. Though he is at this point expounding Plato, Averroes adds disarmingly: "If this is not the opinion of Plato, it is nevertheless the opinion of Aristotle, and is undoubtedly the truth."

[62a] Averroes, *Commentary* 180.

[63] M. Fakhry, *Islamic Occasionalism* (1958) 113, points out that this attack on orthodox theology (or rather defence of philosophy against the attacks of the theologians) was mitigated by Averroes' insistence "that philosophy is the foster-sister of theology; that the truth can never contradict the truth, and therefore no conflict can arise between philosophy and theology". He thinks that finally Averroes did not distinguish the domains of reason and faith, but subordinated theology to reason. *Cf.* F. Copleston, 2 *op. cit. supra* n. 36, 198-99. Rosenthal (179, 292, n.1) thinks that for Averroes finally "there was only one Truth — the truth of revelation at one with the truth of reason", though the "abstract knowledge" in the law is best understood by the philosopher. For a balanced account see D. Knowles, *op. cit. supra* n. 41 at 201. And see on the "orthodox" theory of natural law in the Koran, K. A. Hakim, "The Natural Law in the Moslem Tradition" (1951) 5 *Nat. L. Inst. Proc.* 29.

On Duns Scotus' contrast of philosophy and theology, in some ways thus anticipated by Averroes, see *infra* §6. Generally Avicenna was the greater influence on Scotus.

Aristotle's distinction between the demonstrative and dialectical modes of reasoning was hazardous.[64] But it is clear that Averroes' philosopher has the central function in the Moslem State, as Plato's had in his Republic.[65]

The lines of transmission of Greek thought through Jewish philosophers overlapped with those through Arab philosophers both in time and in mutual inspiration. The Jewish communities of Spain were subjected, after the Mohammedan conquest in the eighth century, to a continuous Arab influence. For Jewish thinkers, as for Arab, the immediate challenge was one of harmonising their own religious law as prophetically revealed[66] with classical philosophy, and the will of God with reason. And the task was complicated by the Christian claim that it was open to God to repeal, abrogate or alter this Divine revealed law.

The first thinker to tackle these problems from squarely Aristotelian bases[67] was Abraham Ibn Daud (*circa* 1110-1180). His solution to the problem of prophecy was essentially that of Avicenna, and need not detain us here.[68] His solution to the problem of change in the revealed law was more interesting.[69] In part, he said, the biblical laws (Torah) were "rational"; and these, accepted by all nations and binding all nations together, were universal, eternal and immutable.[70] As to the traditional or ceremonial parts of the law, if the Torah itself did not lay down their immutability, later laws might change them since "the Lord has a certain purpose in his laws which we do not know, but which is revealed in the new law taking the place of the old".[71] If, however, as is usually the case,[72] the Pentateuch prescribed immutability,[73] then *cadit quaestio*. Ibn Daud further distinguished laws according to their functional importance: as governing belief, or family or social or political life, or (as with many details of sacrifices) as being of function unknown.[74] Regarding belief as the most important function, be pointed out with exquisite paradox that laws whose functions were unknown, and therefore ostensibly unimportant, were also the most important, since they provide a touchstone of belief and unbelief.[75] And he concluded (perhaps with some inconsequence) that all the biblical laws served the needs of human nature as enounced by philosophy,[76] and in

---

[64] As to Aristotle see Stone, *Legal System*, Ch. 8, §7. Averroes thought, briefly, that true knowledge could only be attained by demonstrative argument, and that this was in the command of the philosopher; whereas theologians used dialectical arguments which were inadequate, misleading and dangerous. See *Fasl al-Maqal* 17; M. Fakhry, *op. cit. supra* n. 63, 111ff.

[65] See Rosenthal, *Islam* 178-79, 181.

[66] *Cf.* S. Freehof, "The Natural Law in the Jewish Tradition" (1951) 5 *Nat. L. Inst. Proc.* 15, at 20ff.

[67] See I. Husik, *A History of Mediaeval Jewish Philosophy* (5th impr. 1946) 198-99 (hereafter cited as "Husik").

[68] See *id.* 224ff., following Ibn Daud, *Emunah Ramah* (publ. with German transl. by S. Weil, 1852) 70-75.

[69] See Husik 226ff., following *Emunah Ramah* 75-81.

[70] So, for a different but obvious reason, were laws ordaining events now past.

[71] Husik 227.

[72] As to the special features of withdrawal of promises to Eli and David, see Husik 227.

[73] See, e.g., *Numbers* 10. 8: "and they shall be to you for an ordinance forever throughout your generations". Ibn Daud did not confront the question whether a sovereign could exclude himself from later action.

[74] He cites *Jeremiah* 7. 22: "For I spake not unto your fathers, nor commanded them in the day that I brought them out of the land of Egypt, concerning burnt offerings or sacrifices".

[75] See generally Husik 234-35, following *Emunah Ramah* 98-104. He cited the examples of Moses and Abraham.

[76] See Husik 231-32. "Human nature" comprised vegetative, animal, and rational

fact expressed the virtues involved rather better.[77]

The greatest of the Jewish Aristotelians was Moses Maimonides (1135-1204), a Spanish compatriot and contemporary of Averroes,[78] who followed but overshadowed him in influence on the scholastics. For Maimonides was renowned as a great rabbinical scholar,[79] even apart from his main philosophical work, the *Guide for the Perplexed*. By this eloquent title Maimonides addressed all Jews whose faith in revelation was shaken by philosophy and science. The task, again, was to reconcile the will of God and reason. Maimonides made his main approach, however, by re-expounding the central Judaic doctrine of the absolute unity and non-corporeality of God, rejecting the anthropomorphisms which had arisen in men's minds from the metaphors of the holy writings.[80] God, being an absolute unity, could have no attributes,[81] save such negative ones, as that He is neither dead, nor weak, nor ignorant, nor purposeless in activity like a fire throwing off heat. To say that God is living, powerful, wise and possessed of will, is not to enumerate distinct attributes but merely to state metaphorically these negations concerning his simple unity;[82] and if this were so, then the supposed dichotomy between God's Will and His Reason as the source of divine law could not arise.

God's Will being identical with His Reason, there is a reason in everything He wills, and even the Will of God cannot be arbitrary.[83] For Maimonides, unlike Ibn Daud, there could be no divine laws that had no reason, and he set himself to find a reason for every scriptural law, especially those which Ibn Daud disposed of as mere supreme touchstones of faith. To say that the divine character of such laws can be attested by their irrationality and that it would weaken them to discover their rational purpose, would be to say that while men command only what is of benefit, God commands what is not, and that man is thus superior to God.[84] While therefore Ibn Daud relegated (or elevated) the seemingly reasonless precepts to touchstones of belief, Maimonides attributed them to the comprehensive reason that the purpose of the law is to provide training and inculcate virtuous habits.[85] For virtues and vices[86] are not inborn but acquired by training from childhood, and repeated practice over a long period, until confirmed habits become second nature.

---

faculties. And see *ibid.* on the virtues of each which for him (as for Avicenna) lay in each case in the Aristotelian "mean": in the temperance of the vegetative, in the bravery and gentleness of the animal, and in the justice of the rational. "Justice" also governed the due of the other faculties, and men's relations with family, country, and God.

[77] See Husik 233.

[78] Maimonides, however, lived most of his life outside of Spain, and there is no evidence that he and Averroes had any direct influence on each other.

[79] See Husik 237, 302, 307. For later controversy between Maimonides' adherents and orthodox opponents, see *id.* 307ff; but on his own rejection of Aristotle in favour of Scripture whenever these conflicted, see F. Copleston, 2 *op. cit. supra* n. 36, 203-04.

[80] See *id.* 253-266.

[81] That is, it is not in His nature to have them. See *id.* 265. In the Western tradition this position had been somewhat approached by the Pseudo-Dionysius (*infra* n.97.)

[82] See *id.* 262-265, following Maimonides, *Guide for the Perplexed* (transl. M. Friedlander, 1910) II. 51-58.

[83] See Husik 300.

[84] See *id.* 294, following Maimonides, *op. cit.* III. 26 and 31.

[85] As to the reasons for the Biblical laws, see Husik 294-99, and Maimonides, *op. cit.* III. 27, 29-50, 54.

[86] Both Aristotle's mean (see Husik 283ff.), and his distinction between form and matter, serve to fix these. Sensuous desire, and thus sin and vice, are due to

Virtue being thus not a natural state, but an acquired possession, and man's will being free, it followed for Maimonides that any man can attain any virtue, though some by natural temperament more easily than others. There is thus divine providence for men,[87] but not predestination, for the biblical law would be vain if men were not free to obey or disobey.[88] Since the law of Moses was perfect, Maimonides thought, it could never change; and Moses who received it directly from God was the perfect prophet.[89]

§5. NATURAL LAW AND THOMAS AQUINAS. The Aristotelian heritage re-entered the main stream of Western culture in the twelfth and thirteenth centuries, mainly through translations into Latin of the Arabic texts, and of Jewish and Arabic commentaries.[90] And it was shortly after the first direct translation into Latin of Aristotle's *Politics* (about 1260 A.D.), that it received its great re-interpretation in the light of Christian philosophy in the writings of Aquinas.[91]

matter (living body), the intellectual pursuits and thus virtue and goodness to form (rational soul). His most general ethical precept is therefore that we should have to do with matter only so far as is absolutely necessary. See *id.* 281, Maimonides, *op. cit.* III. 8.

[87] Providence, he thought, is commensurate with the degree of susceptibility to divine influence. It extends to the *species* of plants and animals, but not to *individuals*. Only man enjoys *individual* Providence, and even here it fades as one descends from the prophets, the wise and pious, to the ignorant and disobedient. See Husik 292, and Maimonides, *op. cit.* III. 17-18.

[88] See Husik 286.

[89] See *id.* 280-81. Maimonides gives one of the more exhaustive analyses of prophecy, as of a number of other matters discussed in these centuries. See Husik 276-280, and Maimonides, II. 32-48.

[90] On the difficulties of the process, see J. Pieper, *op. cit. supra* n. 41, at 106; D. Knowles, *op. cit. ibid.,* 189. Recent scholarship shows a flood of translations also direct from the Greek, making the exact contributions of Arab-Jewish writings uncertain. See F. Copleston, 2 *op. cit.* 204-08; D. Knowles, *op. cit.* 185-192. Prior to the 12th century the medieval knowledge of Aristotle in the West was virtually confined to his logic, preserved by Boethius (*circa* 480-525). An early centre of the twelfth-century revival was at Chartres, where John of Salisbury (*circa* 1115-1180) formulated a notable version of natural law, combining Augustinian, Aristotelian, and Roman law elements, and subjecting the "prince" to natural law, on pain of being a mere "tyrant", who might legitimately be overthrown. See further J. Bowle, *op. cit. supra* n. 2, 188-193; C. C. Webb, *John of Salisbury* (1932); F. Copleston, 2 *op. cit. supra* n. 36, 173-74; D. Knowles, *op. cit.* 135-140.

[91] Esp. in the *Summa Theologica* (here cited as "*Summa*"), the *Summa Contra Gentiles,* and the *De Regimine Principum* (of which last all but the first two chapters are probably the work of Ptolemy of Lucca). See F. Copleston, 2 *op. cit.* 305. On Aquinas' thought as a living theory of justice, see *infra* Ch. 7, especially §§3 (at end), 5, 7, 8, 10. Our *present* concern with it (we recall) is as a main part of the natural law vessel bearing earlier thought about justice down into the modern stream. On Aquinas and his teacher Albert the Great in their use of Aristotle, see T. Gilby, *op. cit.* xxiv, 265-271, 274; F. Copleston, 2 *op. cit.* 322-23, 398-400, 423-430. On Aquinas generally see *id.* 302-434, esp. 376-383, 398-422; *id., Aquinas* (1955), esp. c.v; E. Gilson, *The Philosophy of St. Thomas Aquinas* (1924); O. Lottin, *op. cit. supra* n. 2; T. Gilby, *op. cit. supra* n. 39; and Cairns, *Plato to Hegel* 163-204. T. E. Davitt, *The Nature of Law* (1953) c.viii, suffers from the continued estoric use of scholastic terminology and syntax; but see *id.* in A. L. Harding, *op. cit. supra* n. 9, 26-47, esp. on Aquinas' positions as to "nature" and "ordering".

The contemporary bearing of Thomist positions on natural law as a substantive theory of justice is dealt with *infra* Ch. 7, *passim* esp. §§7ff. Aquinas' separate treatment of the Aristotelian notions of distributive and commutative justice (*Summa IIa-IIae,* esp. Qq. 58, 61) hews too close to its Aristotelian original already considered to call for further discussion here. See J. Pieper, *Justice* (1957); D. Granfield, "The Scholastic Dispute on Justice . . ." in *Nomos, Justice* 229, at 234-36.

UNIVERSITY OF
ILLINOIS LIBRARY

At this critical threshold of transition in Europe from feudal local communalism to either Imperial or State dominion, Aquinas (1224-1274) restated in terms of timeless reason Aristotle's differentiation of the *polis* from other groups. Family and other social groups differ from the city-state not only in size but "specifically".[92] The common good, which is the *raison d'être* of the State, is not a mere sum of individual goods, but different in kind, and related to them as the whole is to its parts.[93] For the State alone is a *"communitas perfecta"*,[94] endowed with all the attributes thereof, such as coercive power, law-making capacity, and a *"sufficientia ad omnes necessaria vitae"*, a sufficiency of what is necessary for life for all men.[95] The sovereign possesses his powers only for the good of the whole people; he "represents" and "stands in the place of" the people. "Law" is defined as "an ordinance of reason for the common good, made by him who has care of the community, and promulgated".[95a] And this *communitas perfecta* has come about because (in Aristotle's terms) man is by nature a political animal, that is, one who can fulfil the potentialities of his nature only in society. One who could do this outside society would be either a beast or a god, but not a man. The State is thus founded on the nature of man, without need to postulate an origin in some convention, or "social contract".[96]

The fact that Aquinas was able to take so positive a view of the functions of the State, while avoiding either extreme of individualism and collectivism, is due to the delicately equilibrating combination of ideas with which he rebuilt the classical idea of the State. These included not only the Aristotelian teaching of the openness to reason of the order of the universe, and the Christian faith in the absolute and free will of God as the first transcendent cause of all being, but also the neo-Platonic concept of order. As elaborated by the famous "unknown" author of the fifth century A.D. who called himself Dionysius the Areopagite,[97] this concept had become the principle of the hierarchic order of all being, all things tending towards a fulfilment which lies beyond them in a higher grade of existence.[98] The State, in which the individual was integrated, was itself subject to the higher grade of humanity-wide order, as well as to the will of God. It was endowed with power to make and enforce laws, so that it might help men in preserving and fulfilling their nature; but any claim to immanent absoluteness was kept in check by the fact that this law was to be part of a rational order, ascending to the eternal.

Both Maimonides and Aquinas succeeded in quieting for themselves the struggle between the will of God and reason, between voluntarism and

---

92 See *Aquinas, Selected Political Writings* (ed. with Intro. by A. P. d'Entrèves, 1954) xix. *Cf. Summa IIa-IIae*, Q. 58 art. 7 *ad* 2, and Aristotle, *Politics*, bk. i.
93 See d'Entrèves, *cit. supra* n. 92, xix. On the individualist strain in Aquinas see his *Summa Contra Gentiles* III, 111-15; and T. Gilby, *op. cit.* 237-245.
94 *Id.* xxv.
95 *Summa Ia-IIae*, Q. 90 art. 3; *id.*, Q. 97 art. 3.
95a *Id.*, Q. 90 art. 4, this being (as it were) his "material" definition of law. He has previously offered a definition in "formal" terms, for which see *id.* art. 1: "Law is a rule or measure of action in virtue of which one is led to perform certain actions and restrained from the performance of others." The term law (*lex*) is there also linked etymologically with what is "binding" (root, *ligare*), and materially with "reason" as the measure of human action.
96 *Cf.* W. D. Ross, *Aristotle* (4 ed. 1945) 239, and d'Entrèves, *cit. supra* n. 92, xvi.
97 On the genuineness of his work and its influence on the scholastics, see J. Pieper, *cit. supra* n. 90, 46-54; D. Knowles, *op. cit.* 55-58; F. Copleston, 2 *cit. supra* n. 36, at 91-100.
98 See *Summa I pars*, Q. 94 art. 3; Flückiger, 1 *Geschichte* 446n.

rationalism. But the quiet was only momentary and when the controversy re-opened after Aquinas' death, his natural law seemed unequivocally to side with rationalism.[99] Aquinas, it is true, was not insensitive to the limits of reason, and therefore to the role of "prudence" in reaching conclusions.[100] And he also gave to positive law and its maker their own *raison d'être*,[101] supported and not merely censored by natural law.[102] For the function of law in the social order, as reason prescribes it, cannot be fulfilled without the power of compulsion.[103] Yet all this is within the frame of eternal law, God's law for the universe, which emanates from the divine reason and is promulgated because it is good for His Creation.[104] Natural law is that part of eternal law which man can apprehend with his unaided reason,[105] but can neither create nor change whether by reason or will; for not man, but *God's reason*, is the measure of all that is good. It is true that "divine law", which is that part of eternal law which God makes known through divine revelation, is not to be grasped by *man's* reason but is *given* to man as an Eternal Truth; but even this emanates from the divine reason.[106] In this broad frame, human (or positive) law is created by human reason for the common good, within limits which natural law prescribes,[107] for the

---

[99] See *Summa Ia-IIae*, Q. 90, art. 1; Welzel, *Naturrecht* 57; F. Copleston, 2 *op. cit. supra* n. 36, 382-83.

[100] See his Commentary on Boethius, *De trinitate*, 1, 2 *ad* 1; 1 *ad* 6; *Commentary on the Sentences* 3 d. 1, 1, 3; 3 d. 1, 1, 2; and *Quaestiones Disputatae de Potentia Dei* 7, 5, *ad* 14, where Aquinas says: "This is the extreme of human knowledge of God: to know that we do not know God." *Cf.* F. Copleston, 2 *op. cit.* 395-96. The Absolute still lay for him in a truth inaccessible to discursive reason, and only glimpsed through revelation. He had received not only the rationalism of Aristotle, but the "negative theology" of the Pseudo-Dionysius. See J. Pieper, *The Silence of St. Thomas* (1957). *Cf.* d'Entrèves' denial of Aquinas' "rationalism" in *op. cit.* 45.
So from another direction L. Lachance, *Le Concept de Droit selon Aristote et S. Thomas* (1948) 19, thinks that Aquinas' natural law was as much empirical as rationalist; and this corrective remains important despite the heavy qualifications at 322ff. In testimony of this may be mentioned (1) Aquinas' awareness of the variability and contingency of the *"materia moralis"* (Lachance, *op. cit.* 18); (2) the variability of "human nature" resulting from race, education, culture, religion, soil, climate, etc. (*id.* 145-46, and B. F. Brown, ". . . St. Thomas Aquinas on Jurisprudence" (1957) 3 *The Catholic Lawyer* 356, 364); (3) that Aquinas recognised and (within limits) advocated the kind of judicial creativity discussed in Stone, *Legal System*, Chs. 7-8 (see M. R. MacGuigan, "Positive Law and the Moral Law" (1962) 2 *Curr. L. and S.P.* 89-128). Stress on such examples of the flexibility and "prudence" of Aquinas, stopping him short of extreme rationalism, is a salutary corrective to many caricatures of him. To present him, however, to mystics as a mystic, to sociological jurists as a sociological jurist, to existentialists as an existentialist, and so on, may become as self-defeating an exercise as crying "Wolf!" And see *supra* n. 41. On "prudence" in the Thomist theory of justice see *infra* Ch. 7, §8.

[101] *Cf.* Welzel, *Naturrecht* 59; H. Rommen, *op. cit.* 53; *Summa Ia-IIae*, Q. 91 art. 3. And for the influence of Roman positive law on Aquinas see Lachance, *op. cit.* 27.

[102] *Cf. Summa Ia-IIae*, Q. 95 art. 1. On the importance of the earthly dominion in Aquinas see more generally T. Gilby, *cit. supra* n. 39, esp. at 146-158, 190-202.

[103] See Rommen, *op. cit.* 55.

[104] *Summa Ia-IIae*, Q. 91 art. 1; Q. 93 art. 1. On the relation of Aquinas' philosophy to his theology see *infra* Ch. 7, nn. 115a-116.

[105] *Id.* Q. 91 art. 2. *Lex naturalis* is distinct from *lex naturae*, the latter being physical "laws of nature" governing also non-rational entities. See *Expositio in Libros Ethicorum* . . . (1949) No. 1; Rommen, *op. cit.* 46-47; but *cf.* R. D. Lumb, "The Scholastic Doctrine of Natural Law" (1959) 2 *Melb. U.L.R.* 205 at 207. And see D. Granfield, *cit. supra* n. 91, esp. at 231.

[106] *Summa Ia-IIae*, Q. 91 art. 4.

[107] *Id.* Q. 91 art. 3. Aquinas' precise version of the Augustinian *lex iniusta non est lex* is in Q. 93 art. 3: "Human law has the quality of law only in so far as it proceeds according to right reason: and in this respect it is clear that it derives from the eternal law. In so far as it deviates from reason it is called an unjust law, and has the quality not of law but of violence." Nevertheless, he adds, even an unjust law, as apparently related to the authority of the lawgiver, derives in this respect from

protection and fulfilment of men in the mutuality of needs of their common life.

While eternal law, divine law, and natural law are all unalterable,[108] being all based upon the divine reason, only the precepts of natural law are accessible to man's reason, and this in the sense of immediate, non-discursive, intuitive knowledge, not "darkened by passions and habits of sin".[109] Its primary precept on which all others are based is: "Good is to be done and sought after, and evil is to be avoided",[110] for to do this is equivalent to realising our "essential nature", or acting "according to reason". The secondary principles of natural law are the Ten Commandments and a limited number of other principles establishing duties to preserve life, to propagate, to educate children, to know the truth about God, to live in society, to avoid ignorance and giving offence unnecessarily.[111]

To say that Aquinas' system was rationalist rather than voluntarist, is not to say that Aquinas would always have welcomed the support which rationalism drew from his writings after his death. The point of balance which he had established between Greek rational philosophy and Christian theology was adequate as a resting place for his own final position. Yet it was also too delicately poised to be maintained amid the clash of extreme opinions, especially in a rapidly changing political and intellectual atmosphere.[112] On the practical side—the attempt to buttress the authority of the Church by invoking reason—both the importance and the failure of Thomas' valiant endeavours have been summarized in the observation that "not the Devil, but St. Thomas Aquinas, was the first Whig". For as soon as the Church claimed that reason and natural law supported its authority, it admitted the right of reason and natural law to attack its authority.[113] Here the two-faced role of natural law, adverted to at the

---

the eternal law. And in Q. 95 art. 2, and Q. 96 art. 4, he says that laws "unjust" as detrimental to the established norms of human welfare do not "oblige in conscience" except "to avoid scandal or disorder". Laws "unjust" as contrary to divine goodness (e.g. as enforcing idolatry) are, however, never to be obeyed.

On resistance to tyranny see Q. 95 art. 3, and cf. De Regimine Principum, lib. I Cap. 1, 6; Commentaria in X Libros Ethicorum, lib. vii, Lec. 10; Commentaria in IV Libros Sententiarum Petri Lombardi, lib. II, Dist. 44, Q. 1, a 3. Thomas appears to distinguish two sorts of tyranny, one resting on vice of title (usurpation), the other on vice in ruling regimen). The former kind may with community consensus be slain; the latter must apparently be obeyed if his laws keep within the power licensed by natural law. But this doctrine is far from clear. See P. Tischleder, Ursprung und Träger der Staatsgewalt nach der Lehre des heilige Thomas . . . (1923) 104; Galan y Gutierrez, La Filosofia Politica de Santo Thomas . . . (1945) 206-215; Ambrosetti, Riforma 62-63. And cf. generally A. Verdross, cit. supra n. 2, 77; T. Gilby, cit. supra n. 39, 300ff., esp. 303, 306-310.

[108] See Rommen, op. cit. 51; Copleston, 2 op. cit. supra n. 36, 407-08. Even as to human law the presumption is always that change harms "the public welfare", as diminishing the law's coercive power (Summa Ia-IIae, Q. 97 art. 2).

[109] Id. Q. 94 art. 1; cf. id., I pars, Q. 79 art. 12. And cf. passages cited supra n. 100.

[110] Summa Ia-IIae, Q. 94 art. 2. Cf. Rommen, op. cit. 47-51, and Lumb, op. cit. n.105, 213-16 and passages there cited, for attempts to give significant meaning to this principle. But see infra Ch. 7, §8.

[111] Summa Ia-IIae, Q. 94 art. 2, Q. 100 art. 11. On the contextual limits on the application of these precepts see id. Q. 94 arts. 4, 5; F. C. Copleston, Aquinas (1955) 218-19. On the Ten Commandments see Summa Ia-IIae, QQ. 98-105, 107, esp. Q. 99 art. 2, Q. 100.

[112] The balance lasted, observes J. Pieper, cit. supra n. 41, 11-12, for a "brief, scarcely measurable moment of history". Cf. Copleston, 2 op. cit. supra n. 36, 428-430; and on other unseen dangers of Aquinas' work see T. Gilby, cit. supra n. 39, at 84-86, 211-12, 266. Gilby (xxv, 276) thinks the decline in later use of Aquinas' terms and ideas arose from reduction of man's response to the living God to a set of isolated abstract items "within a system of regulations mechanically adjusted to a hairsbreadth".

[113] 1 Pareto 273, §457, is curiously inadvertent to this aspect. With Aquinas

beginning of this Chapter, is clearly seen. Natural law, as used by Luther and Melanchthon, and by the Protestant jurist-theologians who followed them, like Niels Hemmingsen, became an intellectual weapon against the unity of the Church. And the concepts of State and law which Aquinas helped to warrant by reason, contributed to the essentially secular national State of modern Europe.

The theoretical dangers of Aristotle's rationalism were apparent even during Aquinas' life. The so-called Latin Averroism already erected on Averroes' distinction between philosophers' truth and theologians',[114] seemed capable of bringing rationalism to deny the omnipotence and even the liberty of God.[115] For to be bound by "reason" is still to be bound (unless "reason" be given a sense simply inaccessible to scrutiny, in which case it becomes scarcely distinguishable from "will"). The counter-movement which culminated in 1277 in the condemnation, at Paris and Oxford, of a number of contemporary Aristotelian propositions including some held by Aquinas, was in essence a protest against the concept of a law which would bind God Himself.[116]

§6. NATURAL LAW AND DUNS SCOTUS. This voluntarist counter-movement saw the origin of law in the absolute freedom of God's will alone. The most important representative of the school of uncompromising voluntarists issuing from this counter-movement, was the Franciscan John Duns Scotus, who taught at Oxford about 1300. To the simple aesthetic delight in individuality (in the world of nature generally as well as the world of men) so characteristic of Franciscan thought, Scotus brought a new degree of intellectual intensity and sophistication.[117] Valuing individuality thus most highly,[117a] he exalted free will above reason, reason being but common to all

---

himself, of course, Church authority was still securely based on a religious Absolute. See *supra n.* 100, and *cf.* on the relation between his philosophy and theology *infra* Ch. 7, nn. 115a-116. But within two generations the danger was widespread.

[114] On the exposition by the Parisian doctor Siger of Brabant, see J. Pieper, *op. cit. supra* n. 41, 121-126; and *cf. supra* n. 63 as to the actual inconclusiveness of Averroes' own work as the basis for this later development. And *cf.* E. Renan, *Averroes et l'Averroisme* (3 ed. 1869); Copleston, 2 *op. cit.* 430-32, 435-441.

[115] See E. Gilson, *History of Christian Philosophy in the Middle Ages* (1955) 407. *Cf.* as to denial of the divine dominion over the earthly city, T. Gilby, *op. cit.* 104-05.

[116] On this epoch-making event see *id.* 385; D. Callus, *The Condemnation of St. Thomas at Oxford* (1946); F. van Steenberghen, *Aristotle in the West* (1955).

[117] See Welzel, *Naturrecht* 70. This drive to exalt individuality may well have contributed to the shaping of Scotus' rather distinctive approach to such recurring scholastic conundrums as the "principle of individuation" (see C. R. S. Harris, 2 *Duns Scotus* (1927) 92-103; F. Copleston, 2 *op. cit.* 491-94, 516-17), and the "univocity" or otherwise of Being (see *id.* 501-08). On Scotus' problem of finding a notion of unity to accommodate both that of the individual and that of the species, see E. Gilson, *The Spirit of Mediaeval Philosophy* (1950) 195-97; Harris, 2 *op. cit.* 22ff., 50-51; but *cf.* F. D. Maurice, 1 *Moral and Metaphysical Philosophy* (1872) 646.

[117a] Perhaps incongruous with Scotus' high valuing of beauty was his scholastic love of subtle distinctions expressed with scholastic faults of style and language. See C. R. S. Harris, 1 *op. cit.* 107, following W. G. Tennemann, *Geschichte der Philosophie* (1872) 737. On the other hand, his principle of parsimony for eliminating unnecessary distinctions (*De Rerum Principio*, Q. 11 art. 2, n.8; *Quaestiones super libros Aristotelis de Anima*, Q. 11 n.8-9; and see W. Thorburn, "The Myth of Occam's Razor" (1918) 27 *Mind* 345, 348) is probably the source of the principle known as "Ockham's Razor", William of Ockham being a follower of Scotus and "Ockham's Razor" not being found in his surviving writings. See for its legal use the *Cumberland* and *Reynel*

men, while free will distinguished each from his fellows.[118]

It was man's will, indeed, rather than his intellect, which for Scotus marked off the very species of man. Man differs from other animals precisely because his will is not moved by mere natural necessity,[119] but acts freely,[120] while the intellect is tied to its perception of nature.[121] While recognising, of course, that intellect influences will[122] and that cognition precedes volition,[123] he insisted that neither a universal nor a particular object can force itself on the will.[124] The will remains able in the last resort to act irrationally, or to turn the intellect towards some other object.[125] "Nothing but the will is the total cause of willing."[126]

This philosopher who found in the uniqueness of each created thing a beauty that spoke to him of God,[127] also saw the will as *in itself* something of unique and perfect beauty, man's greatest power, his "most noble perfection".[128] From it, he thought, springs "charity", man's highest virtue,[129] which perfects the will and joins man with God.[130] To love God was

---

Cases, resp. (1610) 8 Co. Rep. 166b at 167a and (1612) 9 Co. Rep. 95a at 95b; and *cf.* Co. Litt. 362b.

More incongruous still was the love Scotus bore to individuality as contrasted with his violent abuse of heretics and Saracens, including even "the cursed Averroes". See *Opus Oxoniense*, prol., Q. 7, comparing also Aquinas, *Summa IIa-IIae*, Q. 11 art. 3.

[118] Following, as often, St. Augustine. See the latter's *De Civitate Dei*, XIV. 6; *Soliloquies*, I. I.

[119] *Quaestiones Quodlibetales* Q. 21, n.14. While Aquinas sometimes takes "free will" as the mark of the "human", he forthwith qualifies this by reference to "rational deliberation" (*Summa Ia-IIae*, Q. 1 art. 1, and *id. ad* 3). And in *Ia-IIae*, Q. 18 art. 5, reason *simpliciter* is the mark of what is "human".

[120] *Quaestiones Quodlibetales* Q. 16, n.3; *cf. Opus Oxoniense*, IV, dist. 49, q.4.

[121] *Quaestiones Quodlibetales* Q. 16, nn.2, 6; *cf. Opus Oxoniense*, IV, dist. 46, q.1, n.10-11, dist. 49, q.4. And see T. E. Davitt, *The Nature of Law* (1951) 25-6; E. Gilson, *op. cit. supra* n. 117, 309-10; C. R. S. Harris, 2 *op. cit. supra* n. 117, 285.

[122] On whether Scotus was irrationalist or anti-rationalist, or merely striving "to grasp more deeply the infinite activity of the Divine Being", see Harris, 1 *op. cit. supra* n. 117, 268; 2 *id.* 59, 61, 74; Copleston, 2 *op. cit.* 540-41. Certainly both Scotus and Aquinas were aware of the limits of reason. See *supra* n. 100. It may well be precisely Scotus' notable contribution to the refinements of stringency in proof, which for him drew in these limits, even while he sought rational knowledge eagerly enough within them. See J. Pieper, *op. cit. supra* n. 41, at 144-45; and *cf.* Harris, 1 *op. cit.* 117-121, and the prayer opening Scotus' *De Rerum Principio*: ". . . Help me, O Lord, to seek out such knowledge of the true being that Thou art as may lie within the power of my natural reason." See E. Gilson, *op. cit. supra* n. 117, 51-52. *Cf.* on the unusual difficulty of stating Scotus' positions, the tensions within them being rather mutually complementary than systematised, P. Delhaye, *Christian Philosophy in the Middle Ages* (transl. S. J. Tester, 1960) 115.

[123] *Opus Oxoniense*, II, dist. 25; dist. 43, q.2, n.2. See Welzel, *Naturrecht* 69.

[124] *Opus Oxoniense*, II, dist. 23, n.8.

[125] *Quaestiones Quodlibetales* Q. 16, n.4; and see Welzel, *Naturrecht* 71; Harris, 2 *op. cit.* 289-290.

[126] *Opus Oxoniense*, II, dist. 25, n.22; dist. 7, n.23; and *id.*, I, dist. 8, q.5, art. 3, n.24. See *Reportata Parisiensia*, II, dist. 25, n.20; and *id.*, IV, dist. 49, q.2, n.6. *Cf. Quaestiones Quodlibetales*, Q. 21, nn.13-17; *Quaestiones Subtilissimae super Libros Metaphysicorum Aristotelis*, IX, Q. 15. *Cf.* Davitt, *op. cit. supra* n.121, at 26; Welzel, *Naturrecht* 69.

[127] On whether his theory of individuals and universals is to be understood as mere analogy or a heretically pantheistic identification of Divine with created being, see, e.g., A. Stöckl, 2 *Geschichte der Philosophie des Mittelalters* (1866) 796ff.; Gilson, *op. cit. supra* n. 117, 256, 264, 266; Harris, 2 *op. cit.* 117-19. And see the *Quaestiones Quodlibetales* Q. 14, n.16-17.

[128] *Reportata Parisiensia*, II dist. 25, n 3, 17.

[129] *Opus Oxoniense*, IV, dist. 25, n.3, 17. Charity, of course, in Paul's sense (I *Corinthians* 13) of love and concern. And *cf.* Augustine, *Enarrationes in Psalmos* 36, serm. 2, n.13.

[130] *Opus Oxoniense*, III, dist. 26, n.18; *cf.* dist. 34, n.17. And see Davitt, *op. cit. supra* n. 121, 25.

thus Scotus' first practical principle,[131] a norm addressed to the will not to the reason. It was so addressed by the "practical science" of "theology", not by philosophy and metaphysics;[132] and to obey it was a free act of the will.[133] (But it is clear that his theology is here rather an ethics of which the single norm is the will of God, as theology seeks to transmit it.)[134] To love God is to obey His will because it is His will. But man's will is free to choose not only between obedience and disobedience, but between obedience for its own sake (which is the perfect good)[135] and obedience because this is naturally conducive to happiness in general[136] (which is not).[137] Insofar as the will is not merely a "natural" faculty, but also free, it will control the natural inclination and act according to justice simply.[138]

Justice, then, is not to be willed as a means to an end (not even when the end is one's own perfection),[139] but solely "in and for itself".[140] What finally distinguishes the will from all other faculties is precisely that it can will a good (even to another) on account of the good itself only.[141] Love of God in Scotus' sense proceeds (as already seen) from free will, not from intellect or reason; it does not therefore proceed, as Aquinas' position rather did, on rational calculation of reciprocal benefit among rational beings.[142] It is with the will's choice of good for its own sake, the *amor amicitiae*, that Scotus associates the will to justice; while "justice" itself is for him what God wills.[143]

---

131 See Davitt, *loc. cit.*; and *Opus Oxoniense*, IV, dist. 46, q.1, n.10.

132 *Opus Oxoniense*, Prol., q.4, n.17, *id.* n.23. And *cf.* Harris, 1 *op. cit. supra* n. 117, 99; *cf. id.* 103. The analogy thus suggested of religious norms to law as both appealing to *rule-making authority* rather than (as in ethical obligation) to the *reasons* for duty, finds contemporary support in H. Kantorowicz, *The Definition of Law* (1958) 34; P. H. Nowell-Smith, *Ethics* (Pelican ed., 1954) 190ff. But it is hazardous for Scotus, for whom the good, God's will, is itself seen as a *reason* for obedience.

133 In love, he thought, freedom meets necessity—not necessity of cause nor of purpose sought, but of immutability. For the act of loving, though free, was (he thought) immutable. Yet the greater the love the greater is the freedom. See *Quaestiones Quodlibetales* Q. 16, n.7; *De Rerum Principio*, Q. 4, art. 2; Copleston, 2 *op. cit.* 532-33.

134 See Harris, 1 *op. cit. supra* n. 117, 78, 101. In this sense his voluntarism seems closer to the *practical* Judaeo-Christian tradition than is Thomist rationalism. *Cf. id.* 112, 170; Copleston, 2 *op. cit.* 495-96. See *supra* Ch. 1, §9.

135 *Reportata Parisiensia*, II, dist. 23; and see Welzel, *Naturrecht* 78. Yet Scotus still identifies moral goodness with "conformity to right reason" (*Opus Oxoniense*, I, dist. 17, n.3, 14) and regards his ethics of the will as merely elucidating what this means. See Copleston, 2 *op. cit.* 545-46. But of course the role of "right reason" is then formal only (if not circular); especially since the *source* of its content is the will of God. On other aspects of Duns' attempt to reconcile absolute freedom of will with necessary natural law see *supra* n. 133, *infra* nn. 148, 153. And see H. H. Milman, 9 *History of Latin Christianity* (1872) 145.

136 *Opus Oxoniense*, IV, dist. 49, q.4, n.6. And see Davitt, *op. cit. supra* n. 121, 27; *cf. Quaestiones Quodlibetales* Q. 18, n.9.

137 *Opus Oxoniense*, III, dist. 26, n.21.

138 *Id.*, II, dist. 6, q.2, nn.8-9; dist. 25, n.23; and see *id.*, III, dist. 17, q.1, n.5; dist. 15, n.37. See Davitt, *cit. supra* n. 121, 29-30; Welzel, *Naturrecht* 76-77, and on Scotus' psychology of the will, Harris, 2 *op. cit. supra* n. 117, 281-230.

139 *Opus Oxoniense*, IV, dist. 28, n.2 to dist. 29, n.2. See Davitt, *op. cit.* 30, contrasting Aquinas, *Summa IIa-IIae*, Q. 26 art. 13 *ad* 3.

140 *Opus Oxoniense*, III, dist. 27, q.1, n.3; *cf. id.*, IV, dist. 49, q.2, n.20 and *Reportata Parisiensia*, III, dist. 29, n.2. And see Harris, 2 *op. cit.* 242-248 (as to divine justice), 320-21 (as to human justice).

141 *Opus Oxoniense*, IV, dist. 49, q.2, n.22; *id.* q.5, n.6.

142 *Per contra* he saw love as expressed rather in sacrifice, or "exposure" to danger. See to this effect, *Opus Oxoniense*, III, dist. 27, q.1, n.17. And *cf.* Welzel, *Naturrecht* 68. And *cf.* on sensual as opposed to spiritual love, in this context, *ibid.*, and *Opus Oxoniense*, IV, dist. 49, q.5, n.3; *id.*, II, dist. 6, q.2, n.3-5.

143 *Ibid.* Welzel's rendering of "*justitia*" in this context not as "*Gerechtigkeit*"

For the subordination of intellect and reason to will holds also for God.[144] Scotus and Aquinas agree that there is only one necessary[145] object of the divine will, namely the divine goodness.[146] But for Aquinas God's will is bound by the norms defining His wisdom;[147] while for Scotus God wills freely, and what He wills is good because He wills it.[148] He does not will it because His intellect judges it good,[149] for "no conceptual necessity can be found in these laws".[150]

Apart from the very goodness of God Himself, then, all other goods receive their value solely from His absolutely free will, and have no inherent value.[151] And it follows from this position of Scotus that, in the sense of the then current philosophical discourse, his natural law theory set its own puzzles. For, first, *lex aeterna* itself being thus a problematical entity,[152] "natural law" could not in any case be found (in Aquinas' sense) as a part of a *lex aeterna*; second, Scotus denied both the role of the divine reason in making the *lex aeterna*, and that of the human reason in gaining access to part of it.

Nor, of course, could Scotus make any simple substitution of "will" for "reason" in the formulae of natural law theory. "Will" according to Scotus, would then be offering only one principle of natural law—"Love God!". This one principle, moreover, would face the difficulty of Scotus' own arguments that love could not be commanded, and, indeed, that if commanded it would not really be love, since not expressing man's free will.[153]

Beyond this cardinal principle of "Love God!", moreover, Scotus' insistence that law proceeds from the divine will itself, not from the divine reason, meant that all other norms for human conduct are mere

---

but as *"Rechtschaffenheit"*, thus emphasising the externality rather than the inner love of justice, seems misleading.

[144] Davitt, *op. cit.* 33, citing *Opus Oxoniense*, IV, dist. 46, q.1, n.10. For another reading as to the divine moving power see Gilson, *cit. supra* n. 117, at 253-254; and *cf.* Harris, 2 *op. cit.* 224. The whole context of Scotus' very complex doctrine of the divine attributes (see 2 *id.* 191-224) is involved. We tend to agree with Harris (*id.* 240) that while "the relative precedence" given by Scotus and Aquinas to the faculties of will and intellect is *as to the divine nature* only a matter of emphasis, the difference becomes very important in the sphere of ethics. And *cf.* as to *human* will and intellect 2 *id.* 298-290; Copleston, 2 *op. cit.* 535-541; and *supra* n. 122.

[145] In the sense indicated *supra* n. 133.

[146] See *Summa I pars*, Q. 19, art. 3.

[147] See *id.* Q. 21, art. 1 *ad* 2.

[148] There are some limits on God's freedom, even for Scotus. He cannot will anything denying His essential goodness (see Welzel, *Naturrecht* 75 and *cf. supra* n.133), nor otherwise self-contradictory; for finally this is nothing. (*Opus Oxoniense*, I dist. 39, q.1, n.22.) God could have beatified Judas; but not a rock (*id.*, dist. 44, q.1, n.4). See also *id.*, IV, dist. 1, q.1, n.26: and Welzel, *Naturrecht* 74. For a lucid *exposé* see Harris, 2 *op. cit.* 214ff. Harris perhaps overstates the role of reason in Scotus' doctrine, though admittedly Scotus stopped well short of the view of Peter Damian (1007-1072), who thought that God's will was unfettered even by the principle of non-contradiction. There remain unsolved problems in Scotus' positions, on which he might well pray in aid Aquinas, *Summa I pars*, Q. 25 arts. 3-4. *Cf.* Copleston, 2 *op. cit.* 530-32, and *supra* n. 144.

[149] See *Opus Oxoniense*, III, dist. 19, q.1, n.7.

[150] *Id.*, I, dist. 44, q.1, n.2. On the anticipation of this "voluntarist" position by Peter Abelard, the great "rationalist", see Knowles, *op. cit. supra* n. 41, at 129.

[151] *Opus Oxoniense*, III, dist. 32, q.1, n.6. On this doctrine see Copleston, 2 *op. cit.* 547-48.

[152] Since what is eternal is not the law, but the lawgiver. See G. de Lagarde, *Secteur Social de la Scolastique* (1942) 314.

[153] *Id.* 77, citing *Opus Oxoniense*, II, dist. 41, q.1, n.4. And see Welzel, *Naturrecht* 71, 80-81. But see *supra* n. 133.

contingent norm-creations of the divine will;[154] their source lies in the absolute divine will from above, not in the rational nature of man from below.[155] They are, therefore, divine law, but divine *positive* law.[156] Within their prescriptions distinctions could be made, as Scotus did make them, between those which have a necessary relation to love of God, as in the first five of the Ten Commandments, and the mere social prescriptions of the others. These latter prescriptions (he thought) could not sensibly be said to be either eternal or natural or even necessary to love of God.[157] "Adultery and murder in themselves would not be sins if God should revoke the precept."[158]

Within this area of "social" rules, which comprehend of course the overwhelming part of what here concerns us, Scotus did seek to set off an area which, by analogy, he might call "natural law". This was the area of precepts which, though not necessarily involved in the duty to "love God", were "consonant" with it.[159] On the level of human law, for instance, private ownership of property might be more "consonant" than communal ownership with the highest end of human law, peaceful coexistence; if so, it would therefore be preferable.[160] But it might also be found (whether in human or natural law) that two or more alternative precepts are equally consonant with the "highest end"; and in such cases if we are to choose rightly we need an authoritative indication of God's will, such as God has given in the last five of the Ten Commandments.[161]

At this point we might have expected some discussion of human positive law and justice and its relation to precepts issuing from the divine will. But of this he has little to say expressly, save to lay down as conditions of justice that such law must have "wisdom" as a correct application of practical reason, and "authority" in the sense of a basis in popular consent.[162] But it is implied that since even precepts of the divine law are ancillary to the primary precept "Love God", the precepts of human law are *a fortiori* so. They are also presumably subject to such precepts of divine law as are "consonant" with the precept "Love God", and even to those not so consonant, so long as God has willed them. Yet of course there are vast areas for manoeuvre within the notion of what is "consonant" with so vague a precept as "Love God". As befits a writer whose constant thought

---

154 *Cf.* Welzel, *Naturrecht* 76, 78, who asserts that once the "universal validity of natural law" is taken seriously, its only precept can be "Do not hate God!". All other norms are "social" merely, and contingent.

155 *Id.* 77; and see generally *id.* 76ff.

156 See Davitt, *op. cit.* 35.

157 Welzel, *Naturrecht* 78, citing *Opus Oxoniense*, III, dist. 37, q.1, n.4-5.

158 *Id.*, IV, dist. 50, q.2, n.10. See Welzel, *Naturrecht* 78-9; Davitt, *op. cit.* 35; Harris, 2 *op. cit.* 327-336. And see *infra* n.163. This question much occupied scholastic natural law.

159 Welzel, *Naturrecht* 79, citing *Opus Oxoniense*, III, dist. 37, q.1, n.8; *id.*, IV, dist. 17, q.1, n.3; dist. 26, q.1, n.7. The notion of "consonance", which remains undeveloped in the literature, might perhaps be pressed further by reference to the rhetor's notion of reasoning under *tópoi*. See Stone, *Legal System*, Ch. 8, §§6-9. And *cf.* Scott Buchanan's notion (article *cit. supra* n. 12, at 136) of natural law "as a body of rules for the making, administration, and adjudication of positive laws. . . . It does not dictate positive law, but it sets the processes of law in operation and directs their activity and influence through dialectic, analogy, and example . . .".

160 Welzel, *Naturrecht* 79, citing *Opus Oxoniense*, III, dist. 37, q.1, n.8.

161 Welzel, *Naturrecht* 81, contrasting *Opus Oxoniense*, IV, dist. 17, q.1, n.3-4, with *id.*, dist. 26, q.1, n. 9, 18.

162 *Opus Oxoniensia*, IV, dist. 15, q.2, n.6-7. See Welzel, *Naturrecht* 79-80; Harris, 2 *op. cit.* 345-48. And *cf. Opus Oxoniense*, III, dist. 34, n.17, distinguishing the justice of the ruler (*presidentia*) from that of the subject ("obedience").

is the unique individual, and the empirical, Duns Scotus' main positions based on the primacy of will led him mostly to less rigid doctrines than the rationalism of Aquinas,[163] both on the level of the precepts of human law and justice, and on that of religion and ethics. And it might not be too fanciful to see the later doctrines of absolute sovereignty of the State entity, both internally and externally, as continuous with Scotus' account of the primacy of the will;[164] just as rationalism was continued in the drives to hold sovereign action within the bounds of reason, and of the natural law to which human reason gave access. But, of course, the transposition of this apotheosis of the untrammelled will of the Divine Being, to the mere foci of temporal power, went beyond anything to which Duns Scotus would have agreed.

§7. NATURAL LAW IN THE GROWTH OF MODERN EUROPEAN LEGAL SYSTEMS. Natural law, as we have seen, may play either a conservative or an innovatory role, according to the circumstances of a given time and place. For, in its usual forms, it is at once constrained to uphold the principle of authority as such, and also to condemn social rigidity and stratification which become unfunctional. At its best, this kind of doctrine becomes by its very inner conflict a factor of balance and flexibility against both anarchy and despotism. Few periods have better displayed these qualities than that of the transition to modern European history from the twelfth century onwards. With the progressive breakdown of the feudal order old principles of cohesion in society had lost their force, and both the Holy Roman Empire and the Church failed in the task of re-integrating personal relations of fealty into a hierarchically graded compact social whole. But the emerging nation-states, which were to embody the new principle of social cohesion based on the concepts of sovereignty and monopoly of governmental power, were

---

[163] Harris, 1 op. cit. 187; and see Welzel, Naturrecht 79. Thus Aquinas admitted no dispensation from any of the Ten Commandments: see Summa I pars, Q. 63 art. 1 ad. 4; De Malo, II, 3. Cf. with Scotus' solution that of Alexander of Hales (circa 1175-1245), also a Franciscan: see Copleston, 2 op. cit. 235-36, id. 548-550.

[164] In such a continuity the reinterpretation of Scotus by William of Ockham (1290-1349) would be crucial. First, the love of individuality was pressed to complete denial of the existence of universals, so that what remained of these were mere names, "flatus vocis". (This nominalism was to base Hobbesian scepticism; see infra §13.) Second, Scotus' emphasis on the potestas Dei absoluta was exaggerated so as virtually to exclude the Thomist potestas Dei ordinaria, through which God governed the world by means of causae secundae and human freedom. These means in a sense set limits on divine power; and insofar as Aquinas held that the world of nature mirrors the reason of God, as precedent to the will of God, the causae secundae were his main resort for explanation. For Ockham will prevailed over knowledge, and revelation tended to exclude the binding character of nature and reason. See A. Dempf, Sacrum Imperium (1929) 504-05; Ambrosetti, Riforma 41. Welzel, Naturrecht 88 (cf. Davitt, op. cit. 39-54) indeed, reduces Ockham's legal philosophy virtually to two points. (1) Natural law is God's will explicit or implicit in the Scriptures; (2) any "law" (including that of the canon) contrary to natural law is not law. This latter obviously opened a wide door to criticism of canon law, by diverse interpretation of scripture. Yet, of course, insofar as interpretation itself proceeds on reason, God's will as manifest among men remains even then somehow moulded by reason. Voluntarism and rationalism seem (as it were) wedded for (man's) life. And see D. Granfield, cit. supra n. 19, at 237-242, esp. 242, quoting Anton Pegis' aphorism ("Concerning William of Ockham" (1944) 2 Traditio 478, at 479) that "Ockhamism is an ideal of a God who has power but not intelligence". We agree with Granfield (id. 241) that Ockham's nominalism strictly interpreted strikes at the very foundations of traditional natural law, and does not merely (as M. Shepard had argued in (1932) 26 Am. Pol. Sc. R. 1015) yield "natural law with a variable content". And see infra §13.

born into complex antinomy. Internal sovereignty was able to subordinate the feudal and customary legal framework of the old social order to the new positive law, issuing as an instrument of the sovereign's will. But the internal legal self-sufficiency of each of the several states also implicitly denied the idea of the Christian *oecumene* among the peoples and states of Europe. Thus state-sovereignty threatened to negate itself by virtue of its potential of anarchy in the international order.

Political philosophy was thus challenged simultaneously to explain the existence of the state as a power-endowed government with a will subject to no higher institution like Church or Holy Roman Empire, and to say what new bases could serve to bring such states into an international order. Further, the very accumulation of law-making power in the state created a need for more detailed guidelines for its exercise, for something approaching a kind of model of law, rather than a mere philosophical justification of it. The response of the natural lawyers to this challenge was impressive.

Side by side with the revived and received Roman law, natural law infiltrated the major states of Europe and transformed the prevailing crude customary law. It did this not only by superimposing the model of a law widely regarded as "written reason", but also by a critical overhaul of the form and content of both this "written reason" and the indigenous local custom.[165] The creative function of the Glossators and their successors paralleled that of the original Roman classical jurisconsults and legislators in their time; though of course the model with which they worked was not the natural law itself, but the Roman law as modified by its doctrines and deemed now still to be in force by the will of the Emperor.[166] In England, too, in alliance with the Chancellor's conscience and the merchant's sense of convenience, natural law contributed from the fifteenth century onwards to the radical transformation of the common law. The great Codes of later centuries, such as Frederick the Great's draft Prussian Code of 1749 and the early drafts of the Austrian Code of 1811, manifest the influence of this model, bringing the received and adapted Roman law,[167] and the indigenous customary law into a more or less stable reconciliation. A similar inspiration has been seen behind the French Civil Code of 1804, and the German Civil Code of 1900.[168]

§8. NATURAL LAW AND THE SPANISH SCHOOL. The Spanish school of natural lawyers of the "golden" sixteenth century were already faced with the problems of the limits on the steadily growing public power at home, and of the legitimacy of its expansion by conquest over the peoples of Central

---

[165] Ehrlich, *Sociology* 421.

[166] See Ehrlich, *Sociology,* c. xviii, esp. 414ff. On the revival of Roman law and its links with the systematic canon law see Knowles, *op. cit.* 155-58, 176-78; Gilby, *op. cit.* 48ff.; and on the environment in which this revival first came to flower at Bologna, see Knowles, *op. cit.* 158-63, 172-73. And see Stone, *Social Dimensions*, Ch. 2, §§3ff. On the subsequent effects on the various national laws see *ibid*; and *cf.* as to Scots law, Viscount Stair, *Institutions of the Law of Scotland* (1682) *passim* and esp. the Dedication. In the emergence of political absolutism in medieval Europe, however, the pressures of Roman law patterns of *imperium* acted rather as a counterforce to the more moderate natural law: see Gilby, *op. cit. supra* n. 39, at 289.

[167] See Stone, *Social Dimensions*, Ch. 2, §§3ff. And see *ibid.* generally on problems of the reception and codification.

[168] See, e.g., Ehrlich, *op. cit.* 420-23.

and South America. The question of inviolability of human rights as such, even of men beyond the Christian *oecumene*, became a centre of attention. In one of the great human documents of all time the Dominican Francisco de Vitoria (*circa* 1483-1546) proclaimed a "natural" community of all mankind, and the universal validity of human rights, even impugning the right of the Spanish monarchy to impose its power on colonies overseas, and rejecting the plea that the suppression of paganism could be a "just" cause of war or of subjection of native peoples.[169]

As natural law thus moved closer to its political functions, the attention to its metaphysical and theological foundations shrank. The process of secularisation was aided by the sharp but endless controversies already adverted to between voluntarism and rationalism, destroying the delicate Thomist compromises, and affecting not only the Catholic but also the new Protestant thinkers. The sixteenth century voluntarists included Fernando Vasquez in Spain[170] and Gabriel Biel in Germany.[171] The former stood squarely in the Catholic tradition; the latter was to have a great influence on Luther. The rationalists included Gabriel Vasquez,[172] a Spanish Jesuit, who taught that the standard of good and evil is neither God's wisdom nor His will, but something which precedes them both, namely the nature of things;[173] and Melanchthon, a Danish Protestant, who enthusiastically took as his central teaching that Roman law was *"ratio scripta"* and conformed to natural law.[174]

---

[169] See G. Stadtmüller, 1 *Geschichte des Völkerrechts* (1951) 107. On Vitoria's humanism (perhaps influenced by his contacts with Erasmus, in Paris) see Ambrosetti, *Riforma* 24-26. The contrary view (also natural law based) that mere primitiveness, idolatry, and pagan practices justified conquest and subjection, was being used by other Spanish thinkers (e.g., Juan Gines de Sepulveda (1490-1573)) to justify military adventures and exploitation in S. America. See generally Vitoria's *Prior de Indis recenter inventis* (1539) nn.4, 6, 19, 24; Ambrosetti, *Riforma* 71. And on the notions of a human community and of international law not as mere "law between states", but as a transformation and transposition to world scale of the medieval conception of *respublica gentium christiana*, see his *De Potestate Civile* (1528) n.21, and Ambrosetti, *op. et loc. cit.* He was obviously centuries ahead of his time, though his anticipation of 20th century democratic notions is perhaps overstated in Ambrosetti, *Riforma* 70ff., and in Galan y Gutierrez, . . . *Poder Politico segun Francisco de Vitoria* (1944) 20ff.

[170] See Welzel, *Naturrecht* 92.

[171] See *id.* 91.

[172] Not to be confused (though he often is) with Fernando Vasquez. See *id.* 92.

[173] *Id.* 96.

[174] See Flückiger, 1 *Geschichte* 236. Melanchthon introduced into Lutheran orthodoxy an element of Thomist rationalism which continued into the 17th century, though *prima facie* it might seem even less likely doctrine for Protestantism than some (e.g., Harris, *loc. cit. supra* n. 134) have thought it to be for a Catholicism in the lineage of Pauline-Augustine stress on will and faith. See Welzel, *Naturrecht* 100; and see the valuable survey in Bowle, *op. cit. supra* n. 2, 270-287. The truth is probably that all generalisations as to Protestant-Catholic alignments of versions of natural law are hazardous. For example, the orthodox Catholic view (e.g., in Ambrosetti, *Riforma* 36) is that Lutheran stress on the corruption of human nature entailed a neglect of natural law conceived as based on reason and man's ideal "nature", and a stress on revelation and a divinely established political authority. Yet this is subject to the comment that it may only be so in terms of concepts *not* common to Catholics and Protestants. Luther himself might subscribe to the formulation (see J. Ficker, 2 *Luthers Vorlesungen über den Römerbrief, 1515-1516* (1908) 143-44, and *cf.* 56 *Martin Luthers Werke* (Wiener ed. 1938) 123ff.), and so perhaps might Calvin (see his *Institution de la Religion Chrétienne*, in 31 *Corpus Reformatorum* (Brunsvigae ed. 1865) Lib. IV, c. xx, §§8-22, 32; and see Bowle, *op. cit.* 277-281). But probably neither of them would understand by the key words, such as "revelation", what Catholics understand by those words. And only with this qualification is such a formulation correct for the "traditional spirit" of Protestantism as now received

A re-integration of warring elements in the moderately rationalist scholastic tradition was attempted by Franciscus Suarez (1548-1617). He maintained that natural law would have the same obligatory force even if (which was impossible) there were no God or if He were unreasonable;[175] but he conceded that what natural law prescribes for different situations must vary, just as medicines vary for different diseases.[176] He thought, for instance, that while natural law provided rules of property for the prevalent system of private ownership, it would equally provide rules for a system of common property, if men decided to adopt this.[177]

While thus avoiding the rigidities of rationalism, he still maintained that law had rational foundations. *Lex aeterna* still provides the outer matrix for all law,[178] and there is still a *lex naturalis* common to all men, and accessible to their reason. As with Aquinas reason and will are co-ordinated;[179] and the state is not only a functioning order directed towards fulfilment in the practical world,[180] but also one which, being committed to the principles of justice, must function within the frame of the *lex aeterna* and *lex naturalis*.[181] From these standpoints Suarez marked out much of the ground which Grotius was to gain for the young law of nations. The unlimited right to wage war for mere *raison d'état* was denied, and legal limits to sovereignty were envisaged. In his practical way Suarez pointed out that even war between states was set in a frame of law, war being a formal business implying both equality of capacity of states, and the existence of some law between them.[182]

(see *infra* Ch. 7, §2). "Natural law and reason" and "witness of the spirit" do not easily marry (or even converse) together.

At the same time, history does seem to show that the delicate Thomist balance of both "nature" and "revelation" as a source of natural law has given durability to his thought, because it did not permit a total severance of individual conscience from at least *the demand* for objective analysis implicit in the notion of "nature". No less clear are the historical facts that, in its time, the Protestant Reformation challenged Catholics to rethink their scholarly, theological and political positions; and that with the lawyers of the "Golden" Spanish school the relation between political and ecclesiastical authority was a main focus of challenge. *Cf.* Ambrosetti, *Riforma* 53. So that the final meaning of the conflicts discussed *supra* n. 169 is as part of a Catholic re-examination of the internal policies of "Catholic" Christendom, and the relations of the temporal to the spiritual power. So *cf.* Vitoria's thesis (*Prior de Potestate Ecclesia*, n. 2) that the spiritual perfection of the Church gives no *direct* authority in the temporal sphere.

175 *De legibus et Deo legislatore* (1612) II, cap. 6, n.3. See Welzel, *Naturrecht* 98.
176 *De legibus*, II, cap. 14, n.12. See J. Kohler, *"Die Spanischen Naturrechtslehrer des 16. und 17. Jahrhunderts"* (1916-17) 10 *Arch. R.- und Wirtschaftsph.* 245.
177 *De Legibus*, II, cap. 16, n.11. He further suggests that in extreme emergencies a natural law of common property emerges, which then prevails over any other law. See L. Legaz y Lacambra, *"Die Rechtsphilosophie des Franciscus Suarez"* (1934) 14 *Z.ö.R.* 272 at 303. Scotus had used similar suggestions to illustrate his idea of "consonance": see citations *supra* n. 160.
178 See Legaz, article cited, at 295.
179 Verdross, *op. cit. supra* n. 2, at 89. Neither label thus strictly fits, though he is often called a voluntarist. See, e.g., Davitt, *op. cit. supra* n. 121, 86ff.; but note *id.* 87ff. on the complexity and development in this aspect of Suarez's thought. For a perhaps too sharp assertion of the swing from Aquinas' rational idealism to Suarez's voluntarism see R. D. Lumb, "The Scholastic Doctrine . . ." (1959) 2 *Melb. U.L.R.* 210-213. And for a theologian's view of the "obscurities" of Suarez's natural law see Micklem, *Law* 31-38.
180 Legaz, *cit. supra* n. 177, at 309.
181 *Id.* 310. In *Defensio Fidei Catholica* . . . (1613) III, 2, he sees political power as derived from a pact with the political community, to be exercised in accordance therewith; but he is (as Aquinas had been) more moderate and cautious than some contemporaries as to when abuse of this power justified rebellion. See Ambrosetti, *Riforma* 62-66, and *supra* n. 107.
182 Legaz, *cit. supra* n. 177, at 313-14.

§9. NATURAL LAW AND INTERNATIONAL LAW. Natural law theory, by its assumed foundation in the reason of all men, must obviously bear on the relations between peoples whether organised in States or not. So that its role in the beginnings of international law is no mere historical coincidence.[183] And if this role seems to contain also elements of magical manipulation, this too must be understood as a response to plain practical necessity. For since the emergent states baulked at any human authority over them, the law to bind them could not be human positive law. Resort to the divine law was also ruled out, both by the prevailing religious conflicts and by its association with institutions of medieval authoritarianism which many of the new states had repudiated. There were left the mellowed and mature versatilities of natural law, which also had the merit of cultural continuity. Natural law, after playing a role in disrupting medieval unity, might serve to base a new framework of community among the fragmented parts.

The *De Jure Belli ac Pacis* of Hugo Grotius (1583-1645), itself published in 1625, has been criticised on several counts. Grotius, on his deathbed, said despairingly that "by undertaking many things I have accomplished little".[184] His self-judgment was too harsh, for despite the continuing disputes as to the shares of credit due to him and his predecessors and contemporaries it remains clear that few influences in humanising international practice and subjecting it to the rule of law have exceeded that of Grotius.[185] In the very laboriousness and confusion of his exposition and documentation he was building a bridge from the Christian *oecumene* of the Middle Ages, across the chasm of the broken Empire and Church, to the hopes of a new kind of legal ordering among the states of modern Europe.

The Thirty Years War, in the midst of which Grotius wrote, vividly and terribly illustrated the consequences of the loss of the Church's guardianship over the moral law of Christendom which had been brought about by the Reformation and the split into hostile camps. *Raison d'état* uninhibited by other standards showed a face of anarchy; and it was Grotius' greatest contribution to retrieve from the ruins of the medieval world elements capable of maintaining a degree of continuing normative restraint, consistently with the altered political framework. He carried into the new age of sovereign States a version of universally valid natural law transcending in obligation and in geographical range any human law, including the law of the sovereign State. Such a version required necessarily an anchorage in speculative philosophy; and yet at the same time it had to bring this legal order down from the empyrean region of speculative principles to provide practical norms for here-and-now existing situations, as to which the new wielders of power might take and even welcome guidance. Grotius did not, of course, solve this problem; but he pointed the way in which the new Europe might live with it, at any rate for three or four centuries.

§10. THEOLOGICAL CONTEXT OF GROTIAN NATURAL LAW. The temper of Grotius' work anticipates the secular mood of later centuries; but he also lived among theological struggles inherited from earlier centuries. Well-born,

---

[183] See J. Stone, "Problems Confronting Sociological Inquiries . . ." (1956) 89 *Hague Recueil* 65 at 69-70.
[184] H. Lauterpacht, "The Grotian Tradition in International Law" (1946) 23 *B.Y.B.* 1, at 2.
[185] *Id.* 15.

precocious enough to graduate at twelve and to become historiographer of
the United Provinces and an accomplished Advocate-General to the States
General in his early twenties, Grotius naturally became involved in contemporary controversies. He was arrested in 1618 and incarcerated until
1621 for his vigorous partisanship in the bitter theological controversies
centred around the teachings of Armenius.[186] Even two generations later
Pufendorf (1632-94), born of Saxon Lutheran stock, was still to be deeply
conscious of the theological context of his speculations when he published
his *De Jure Naturae et Gentium* in 1672.

Aquinas' *Summa*, as we have seen, had given an unrivalled formulation
of the doctrines of the still universal Church in terms of reason, and had
thereby opened the way to less friendly critiques by the light of reason.
In the result, fundamental speculation continued from the twelfth into the
seventeenth century to revolve around the relation of Church and State,
and the relative validity of the legal systems of the Church, the Holy
Roman Empire and the emerging national states. Thus the assault of the
Protestant jurist-theologians like Melanchthon and his pupil Hemmingsen
upon the authority of the Church, involved defining the law of the state so as
to vindicate its validity as against the universalist claims of the Papal and
Imperial authority. And the Spanish School's adumbration of a natural law
governing relations between states, was a part of the Counter-Reformation
movement which arose from the same controversy.[187] By the time of
Grotius the relations of divine law, natural law, and positive law were
thus of deeply political as well as theological import.

Grotius, indeed, turned this entanglement to good advantage. If his
work now seems incumbered by superfluous references to the Scriptures
and the Church Fathers, we must perhaps see this as a presentation of
novel doctrines in a familiar garb which helped to secure acceptance.[188]
These references, long to be echoed by Grotian disciples,[189] appropriated
the authority of the Holy Writings to support the rules which reason drew
from Roman experience. And, of course, revelation added divine testimony
in support; for Grotius accepted the attribution of divine origin to natural
law. It is easy enough, however, from our perspective, to see that the
fires of theological struggle, after kindling those of modern secularism,
were themselves burning down.

§11. SECULAR STRAINS IN GROTIAN NATURAL LAW. Another aspect of this
same tendency is that the main Grotian effort was to translate natural
law from philosophical speculation into a legal ordering by focusing
attention on its practical "middle principles",[190] rather than its philosophical
"first principles". And he approximated these "middle principles" to an
analysis of historical occurrences, as the sources of practical norms of a
going international order. His use of such data culled both from sacred

---

[186] His escape in a chest thanks to his wife's ingenuity is a well-worn tale.
He fled to France where he was first an unpaid pensioner of Louis XIII, and then
Swedish Ambassador at the French Court. It was in France that he wrote his *chef
d'œuvre*, published in 1625.

[187] It is the view of some that the Spanish jurist-theologians anticipated much of
what was significant in the later thinking of Grotius.

[188] *Cf.* 1 Pareto 270-71, §452. H. Lauterpacht, article cited *supra* n. 184.

[189] See, e.g., Rutherforth, *Institutes of Natural Law*, bk. i, c. i, vii (1748, 2 Am. ed.
1832) 13.

[190] Welzel, *Naturrecht* 127.

and secular history, and from the ancient and modern worlds, was well designed to catch the interest of the publicists of his age; just as were his general proofs based on the rational and social nature of man, in which he followed well-known stoic and scholastic lines. His succinct formulation of the quintessence of so much that had gone before was to be the regular currency of publicists for centuries afterwards:

> The law of nature is a dictate of right reason which points out that an act according as it is or is not in conformity with the social and rational nature of man has in it a quality of moral baseness or moral necessity, and that, in consequence, such an act is either forbidden or enjoined by the author of nature, God.[191]

This dictate had for its scope not only "things which are outside the domain of the human will" (as, for instance, the relation between the sexes), but "many things also which result from an act of the human will" (for instance the property relation).[192] And, according to Grotius,[193] this dictate is capable of discovery either *a priori*, by demonstrating the necessary agreement of the rule proposed with a rational nature, or *a posteriori* by ascertaining that the rule proposed is universally accepted among all nations, or among all those who are most advanced in civilization. It was for this reason that Grotius added to his theoretical deductions such a mass of concrete examples from history; and it is here, in this new methodological approach, that he displayed a "new sense of nearness to reality".[194]

It will be noticed that this *a posteriori* method is little more than a generalisation upon the theory of the *ius gentium* worked out by the Roman *praetor peregrinus*. It was a matter of considerable dispute among the followers of Grotius. One line, through Pufendorf, squarely rejected any but the *a priori* method. Another line, through Bynkershoek, abandoned the *a priori* method and began an empirical trend which came to dominate international law first of all, and has spread powerfully in the nineteenth and twentieth centuries in the theory of private law. The interplay of *a priori* and *a posteriori* methods has remained, ever since, a recurrent feature of the theory and practice of international law.[195]

For Grotius as for most natural lawyers, "reason" and "the nature of man" were the points of departure. "Reason" continued for Grotius, as for Aristotle and Cicero and Aquinas, to distinguish man among other

---

[191] *De Jure Belli ac Pacis* (1625) bk. i, c. i, x (transl. Kelsey 38-39, Whewell 10).
[192] *Ibid.*
[193] *Ibid.* bk. i, c. i, xi (transl. Kelsey 42, Whewell 16).
[194] Welzel, *Naturrecht* 128. It is here too, ironically enough, that he is charged with lack of system. But see H. Lauterpacht, article cited *supra* n. 184, esp. 18.
[195] And see R. Pound, *The Formative Era of American Law* (1938) 21-27, for a suggested link (which cannot, however, we submit, be one of direct correlation) of the *a priori* and *a posteriori* methods also with the innovatory and conservative functions of natural law doctrine. Strauss, *Natural Right* 182-83, also offers an over-simple explanation of this Janus-like character of natural law when he suggests that Hobbes originated "an entirely new type of political doctrine", "a shift of emphasis from natural duties to natural rights". It is for this reason (he thinks) that "during the modern period natural law became much more of a revolutionary force than it had been in the past", duties being something to submit to whereas rights are something to fight for. See also *id.* 248 and *cf.* d'Entrèves, *op. cit. supra* n. 2, at 59; Benn and Peters, *Principles* 95. But of course the two faces of natural law are not really susceptible of such a neat historico-logical partition, quite apart from the fact that in juristic analysis "rights" and "duties" are correlatives. See Stone, *Legal System*, 138ff.

creatures, and thus to constitute (along with "sociableness") his "nature" when fully developed, that is, his ideal nature. The application of reason will disclose what conforms or conflicts with man's ideal nature. For, as Pufendorf observed, building on Grotius, man is endowed with "right reason" in the sense that "by reflecting on the nature and constitution of mankind" he can discover the principles, and *demonstrate* the precepts of "living conformably to *the law of nature*".[196]

The objection has been continually made that the natural lawyers assumed that "right reason" was something given, something above and beyond the reason of any particular individual, which every individual was bound to recognise as soon as its dictate was placed before him. This is not literally true since Grotius and Pufendorf did recognise that men might differ in their views of right reason. It is, however, substantially true, since they did deny that divergent reasons of different men might equally claim to be "right". Where different men's reasons reached different conclusions (on matters, of course, not morally indifferent) these writers held that the reason of some must be "depraved".[197] This depravity might be due, in Aquinas' terms, to the fact that reason was "darkened by passions and habits of sin"; or it might arise from "false conclusions drawn from true principles".[198] This latter "depravity", turning ostensibly on faulty logic, raises no great issues between natural lawyers and others.[199] The former, turning on intuitive "discovery", or self-evidence, of "right" principles to serve as premises for moral argument, raises still the greatest issue of all.

Clearly most natural lawyers from the Greeks onward have agreed that the ideal nature of man, on which natural law rests, embraces (in Seneca's words) "those two excellences of reason and society (which) render him the most potent of all creatures who would otherwise be obnoxious to injuries from everything about him".[200] Grotius and Pufendorf continued this agreement in the seventeenth century, adding, however, a more explicit reference to utility. "Natural law," said Grotius, "is reinforced by utility. . . . Utility is the occasion of civil law; for the association or subjection, of which we have just spoken, was at the first instituted for the sake of some utility. And accordingly they who prescribe laws for others, in doing this, aim or ought to aim, at some utility."[201] This "utility"

---

[196] *De Jure Naturae et Gentium* (1672) bk. ii, c. iii, 13, 14 (Kennett's transl. 133, Spavan 139).

[197] *Ibid*. L. Krieger, "History and Law in the Seventeenth Century" (1960) 21 *J. Hist. Ideas* 198, esp. at 209, has penetratingly examined Pufendorf's distinction between "the *relations* among moral actions already committed", subject to universal principles of legal science (embracing history), and "the *processes* of bringing such actions into existence, which was a work of moral freedom flexible in its operation upon different times and circumstances", and unknowable merely through general laws.

[198] It is in their use of logical deductive method, together with the assumption that rules derived through it were in some sense inevitable, that Austin and his followers can be accused of falling unconsciously into the natural law which they attacked.

The aspect of intuitive or self-evident judgment of the good and the just is far more of the essence of natural law thought. It is because of unconscious resort to this aspect that a cryptic natural law is often imputed to Léon Duguit. But, of course, the matter is very complex. See *supra* Ch. 1, §11, *infra* Ch. 7, §§7-12.

[199] Neither the truth of the premises, nor the goodness or badness of the consequences in a social sense, are here involved.

[200] Seneca, *On Benefits*, bk. iv, c. xviii; quoted by Pufendorf, *op. cit.*, bk. ii, v, xv, c. iii.

[201] *Prolegomena* 16.

as an auxiliary criterion of justice was to increase greatly in importance in the eighteenth century and was eventually to provide an important bridge between the natural lawyers and the nineteenth century utilitarians.

The Grotian contribution, however, was not merely to find a continuing basis for binding the action of the new States, but also (and perhaps even more) to frame a comprehensive, coherent and practice-orientated code which might be accepted as binding. And he called upon publicists to transfer some of their attention to the task of detailed elaboration of rules for taxation, administration of justice, proof, and the like.[202] His work marks perhaps a watershed between the "terse" natural law characteristic of the medievals and the "prolific" natural law characteristic of later centuries. His related work for international law had to be not only systematic, but also politically workable.[203] While Grotius recognised the will of sovereign States as a constitutive element in the international order,[204] he still insisted on "the totality of the relations between States as governed by law".[205] So that unlike Machiavelli (and later, Hobbes) he refused to reduce law to the will of the State or its prince, but rather struggled to explain the binding force of State will and consent as itself based on the law of nature.[206] Grotius' unequivocal rejection of *raison d'état* as a just cause for war,[207] and his insistence that even the means and modes of violence in war must be limited by law, struck close to the most urgent problems of his century as well as ours.[208] His genius lay in thus bringing the life and death issues of the new Europe past the road-blocks of religious fanaticism, national pride, and princely ambition, to a point where they could at least be given orderly examination and discussion. By the side of this, the questions whether he was a great systematiser, or an original thinker, are of minor import.

§12. NATURAL LAW AND MATHEMATICISM. Grotius threw a bridge from the medieval world to the modern secular world by a pragmatic selection and reconstruction from among traditional ideas of those capable of bearing modern traffic. In the field of law and justice, the Grotian bridge held, so that (for good or ill) our understanding of international law, and largely of law itself, still refers us back to the whole course of Greek, Roman, Judaic and Christian history. It is interesting to speculate whether matters would have been different if René Descartes' *Discourse on Method* had been published in the generation before Grotius' greatest work, instead of the generation after.[209] In rejecting any doctrine of final causes and insisting

---

[202] *Id.* paras. 30-31.
[203] Lauterpacht, article cited *supra* n. 184, at 17.
[204] *Id.* 10.
[205] *Id.* 19.
[206] *Ibid.*
[207] See *id.* 30ff.
[208] See *id.* 14.
[209] Descartes lived 1596-1650, and the above essay appeared in his *Essais Philosophiques* at Leyden in 1637. It quickly gained influence, esp. in Holland and France, but comparatively little among jurists. See Bowle, *op. cit.* 310ff. Though Leibniz (1646-1716) is to be viewed as still rather in the older, less rigid rationalist position, he too dreamed of a *"mathesis universalis"* with a distinct Cartesian flavour: ". . . the plan I have had for a long time to reduce all human thinking to a calculation, such as we know it in algebra or the *ars combinatoria* . . . so that many arguments could be solved, the certain could be distinguished from the uncertain and even grades of probability could be measured. Then, if two were arguing, they could say to

on strict methods of precise observation and on logical and mathematical calculation, this great French philosopher and scientist gave to the rationalism in the teaching of Aristotle and Aquinas a new intensity and direction. He thereby cut away the possibilities of accommodation between reason and a will postulated as free,[210] which had enabled a traditional body of ideas to be readapted repeatedly to changing situations. Though Aquinas' *Summa* was a book which he constantly consulted, the extreme rationalist drive of his work led to the placing of all of Descartes' work on the *Index* in 1663.

No doubt in the wider history of Western ideas Cartesianism must be seen as representing a cut-off point after which the struggle between rationalism and voluntarism could no longer be, as it had been for so long, a mere bipolar swing interspersed with fruitful pauses of mutual accommodation. It became rather a deep rift in metaphysical thought dividing a hitherto common philosophical heritage into permanently divided camps between which even parleys were difficult.

In juristic speculation and action, however, at least three factors have prevented this more drastic bifurcation. The first is that the impact of Grotian thought preceded that of Descartes and persisted in continuing influence after him. Another was the growingly esoteric nature of the legal field, both in the international and municipal legal orders, which partly immunised it from broader philosophical movements. A third factor lay in the very nature of juristic tasks as soon as these moved out from the sanctum of the theologian and philosopher to approach the specifically legal problems of a given legal order. For the jurist is then confronted in some degree with the public power as an expression of will in positive law; yet that will is rarely sufficiently fully or clearly expressed to dispense the jurist from the effort to place it by the exercise of reason into the wider ordering of which it is a part. Just as he must make his terms with the legislator's will as soon as he leaves the sanctum of the theologian or philosopher, so he must also make his terms with reason as soon as he is out of earshot of the sovereign will, or the sovereign attention has lapsed or the voice fails.

§13. NATURAL LAW AND HOBBESIAN SCEPTICISM. At the other extreme there appeared, long before Descartes, a tendency for Scotus' stress on the individual to move into a denial of the reality of all universal concepts,[211] and to treat the terms in which these purported to be expressed as merely nominal. And this, in turn, led to a scepticism towards universal idealism in general. From this standpoint the use of the term "nature", in the traditional Graeco-Roman and medieval thought, to refer to a putatively perfected or "ideal" nature of man was a deceptive misuse, basing an

---

each other 'Let us calculate' ". (Letter to Protestant pietist, Jacob Spener, July 1687; quoted by R. Meyer, *Leibniz und die europäische Ordnungskrise* (1948) 233.) For a full account of Leibniz' legal philosophy see Cairns, *Plato to Hegel* 295-334. On traces of mathematicism in Hobbes, see Strauss, *Natural Right* 172-73, 199; Bowle, *op. cit.* 317, 319. On its possible influence on Grotius see Benn and Peters, *Principles* 35-36; and on 17th and 18th century natural law generally, *id.* 36-39, 95.

210 For Descartes' own reflections on the will, see *Méditations*, Objection 5, 367-68 and Reply at 441-42 (in C. Adam and P. Tannery (eds.), 7 *Oeuvres de Descartes* (1904) 313-16, 378).

211 On the relation between Scotus, William of Ockham and Hobbes in this regard, see Welzel, *Naturrecht* 113.

ill-founded optimism that the propensity of man was necessarily towards the good. As soon as this view is taken a confusing war of words begins. With Hobbes (1588-1679), as with the Greek sophists,[212] the "nature" of man is not the *ideal* nature *assumed* by traditional natural lawyers, it is rather man in his *assumedly actual* nature, when this is untempered by the controls of social and political authority. And this view of "nature" had its theological parallel in the belief in the total corruption of natural man through original sin.[213]

The linguistic cross-purposes are important, not in themselves, but as a basis for understanding the different kind of "natural law" doctrine propounded by Hobbes. For Hobbes built on the "natural" propensity of man in his sense, that is, the propensity towards unlimited self-assertion and to be *homo homini lupus*, the necessity for an overwhelming public power to preserve individual and social life. This was for him the decisive element in the legal and political order; and this was as different as could be from what reason might draw from the sociable nature of man. In short, the Hobbesian version seems to reject the whole idea of universal and necessary norms of justice based on the ideal nature of man, in favour of the universal and necessary legitimacy of centralised governmental power of the State for protecting men against each other.

Yet insofar as Hobbes also claimed that the common weal was identical with the personal good of the sovereign,[214] he was asserting more than that the will of the State shall prevail because it is the will of the State. He was also asserting that that will should prevail because what it wills is good. This, it has well been said, represented a solid block of rationalism in Hobbes' otherwise voluntarist system.[215] "The proofs of Hobbes," said Leibniz (who maintained a natural law closer to the traditional, though based rather on the freedom and perfectibility of every person) "are valid only for a State in which God is the King to Whom everything may be entrusted."[216]

§14. NATURAL LAW IN THE PERIOD OF ENLIGHTENED ABSOLUTISM. If we

---

[212] *Id.* 115.

[213] *Ibid. Cf.* on Hobbes, W. Friedmann, *Legal Theory* (4 ed. 1960) 70-73; Strauss, *Natural Right* 166-202, esp. 171 on Hobbes' scepticism and Cartesian "radical doubt"; Cairns, *Plato to Hegel* 246-271; Bowle, *op. cit.* 317-332.

[214] *Id.* 119. On Hobbes' "social contract" notion and its variations in Locke and Rousseau, see J. W. Gough, *Social Contract* (2 ed. 1957); Friedmann, *op. cit.* 70-77; Strauss, *Natural Right* 165-294; F. Pollock, *Essays in the Law* (1922) 80-109; Benn and Peters, *Principles* 319-326; Lloyd, *Jurisprudence* 125. On the radically altered notion of "nature" in play in this period see Buchanan, *cit. supra* n. 12, at 115-17, 120-121. *Cf.* the excellent study of Locke by R. H. Cox, "Justice . . . in Locke" in *Nomos, Justice* 243, esp. 256ff.; and *cf.* R. Polin in *id.* 262, at 262, at 266, 283.

For a modern attempt to state with contemporary philosophical cogency a rather different notion of "social contract", see J. Rawls, "Constitutional Liberty . . ." in *id.* 98, esp. 107ff. And see the criticisms by C. Fried in *id.* 126, esp. 129-130, 134-38. There is a parallel reinterpretation of "the public consensus" in J. C. Murray, "The Public Consensus" in Cogley (ed.), *Natural Law* 48.

[215] *Ibid.*

[216] Leibniz, *De jure suprematus*, cap. II, quoted by Welzel, *Naturrecht* 119. In Rousseau's development of Hobbesian theory, the common good and sovereign will are reconciled by making the absolute (and rather mysterious) "General Will" of the whole people "sovereign". For a comparative study of Hobbes and Leibniz, see T. Ascarelli's Intro. to his joint edition (1960) of Hobbes, *Dialogue between a Philosopher and a Student of the Common Laws* . . . and Leibniz, *Specimen Quaestionum Philosophicarum* . . . and other works.

think of Hobbes as a "natural lawyer", then we have to admit that the doctrine of natural law had split into two different universes of discourse. Two doctrines, one of which identifies the "nature" of man with the perfectibility of his specific qualities and the other of which identifies it with his predominant qualities as they are assumed actually to be in his pre-social condition, might be better not called by the same name. In any case, however, it is clear that one central juristic problem of the seventeenth and eighteenth centuries, consequent on the work of both Grotius and Hobbes, emerged with equal urgency from both their different standpoints. This was that of finding some rational *basis* for a law which while transcending the positive law issuing from the will of the state, could yet recognise (as perforce it must) the harsh facts of state power, and the necessity of state power for which Machiavelli and Hobbes had theorised. Leibniz's comment on Hobbes displayed *ad absurdum* any idea of reviving the traditional theological basis of transcendence.[217] And what Grotius offered was, as we have seen, an essentially secular natural law based on a wide use of classical and secular history, but yet not spurning incidental support from holy writ or theology. Grotius poured new wine into old bottles;[218] later thinkers had to struggle with the tasks of devising new bottles and putting new wine into them.[219]

The tasks were not easy. As Grotius himself had envisaged, natural law had to attain to specialised functions, not merely as applied respectively to individuals and nations, but as worked out in distinct branches within each system.[220] In each ramification it was to be founded on self-evident principles. Its range was to be functionally comprehensive and its detailed rules were to be logically coherent with first principles. The political context of this grand design, and of its final failure, was the age of enlightened monarchical absolutism in Europe. After centuries of uneasy struggle with feudal localisms, monarchical power had emerged in Austria, Hungary, France and other countries, with full responsibility of government and monopoly of political power. Even the Royal oath to abide by the funda-

---

217 Quoted on the preceding page, with the citation in n.216. See also Rommen, *op. cit. supra* n.2, at 94, on Pufendorf's somewhat random search for empirical starting-points in place of the old bases.

218 See Grotius' account of his sources in *op. cit.*, *Prolegomena* 42-50, and contrast C. Wolff, *op. cit.* pt. i, c. ii, xli (1772 ed. 22).

219 A few biographical facts may here be noted. J.J. Burlamaqui, author of *Principes du Droit de la Nature et des Gens* (1774) incorporating an earlier work of 1747 on natural law, was a Swiss who lived from 1694-1748 and occupied a Chair at the University of Geneva. His work has indeed been described as "rational utilitarianism" (*Encyclopaedia Britannica* (14 ed.) *sub nom.* "Burlamaqui"). Christian Wolff, author of *Institutiones Iuris Naturae ac Gentium* (1754) in nine volumes, was a disciple of Leibniz, and Dean of the University of Halle. Emeric de Vattel, another Swiss jurist and publicist, also disciple of Leibniz, had a distinguished diplomatic career. His most famous work, *Droit de gens, ou Principes de la Loi Naturelle*, published in 1758, was epoch-making in the history of international law since it bridged the gap between the natural law theory of Grotius and the positivist or conventional theory of the nineteenth and twentieth centuries. In the history of natural law itself his importance was smaller for he was in effect merely a populariser of Wolff's monumental work. T. Rutherforth, Archdeacon of Essex and King's Professor of Divinity at Cambridge, published his *Institutes of Natural Law* "being the substance of a course of lectures on Grotius, *De Jure Belli ac Pacis*" in 1748. His work was the first systematic exposition of natural law by an English author. In most respects it harks back to Grotius' time although it displays such 18th century features as the detailed working out of rules, and the prominence of utilitarianism as a basis.

220 *Cf.* Grotius, *op. cit.*, *Prolegomena* 57. 40, 41, with E. de Vattel, *op. cit.*, *Préface* and *Préliminaires*, 3-6 (1758 ed. 1-2; 1802 ed. iii-iv).

mental laws of the realm was not always accepted as a matter of course.[221] At this stage, however, triumphant absolutism, perhaps to naturalise itself within the traditional structure of European legal and political thought, seemed willing for a time to ally itself with an absolute natural law. For such a law, by the very impersonality of its fully rationalist basis, seemed to avoid any direct demand for concessions of political power. And to a degree, the comparative freedom from arbitrariness of absolute monarchs like Joseph II of Austria or Frederick II of Prussia, can be attributed to acceptance of objective restraints deemed to proceed from the elaborately cultivated natural law of their century.

Yet by the very heroism of the attempt to anchor all significant positive laws fully in a first principle, natural law assumed a rigidity which was also a brittleness, spelling its failure. A typical philosopher of the Cartesian type of rationalistic natural law which arose was Christian Wolff (1679-1754), who began his career as a Professor of Mathematics.[222] His work and that of his colleagues became marked by a pedantry of logical deduction of "rational principles of the common good", which, by their very divorce from the everyday intuitions of justice, dried up the sources of natural law creativeness. As the reign of Joseph II ended, revolt shattered the power of benevolent absolutism, and with it this phase in the career of natural law.

§15. The Crystallisation of Natural Law and the Eighteenth Century Codes. Some of the characteristics and products of eighteenth century natural law merit a closer glance. The differentiation of the branches of natural law is well seen in Vattel's work. In the Preface to his *Droit des Gens*[223] in 1758 he stated his design of avoiding the "mingling" and "confusion" of the "law of nations" with ordinary "natural law", and of rather treating "the natural law of nations" as "a special science".[224] This focus was accompanied by a shift of interest away from the ground of obligation of this law to the formulation of detailed rules:[225] from justification to exposition. Rutherforth in 1754 set himself to trace out the binding rules of natural law, but saw no "great necessity" to enter into the much disputed "cause of our obligation to observe" them.[226] For, he thought, whether the source be an innate moral sense as Aquinas thought, or the relations of things as Montesquieu thought, or the will and appointment of God as Grotius thought, or some combination of these, all sects agreed on the rules which constituted natural law. He felt able on this basis to set out the most detailed rules of natural law, for instance, as to succession.[227]

The converse aspect of this crystallisation was that the ambit of natural

---

[221] So Joseph II of Austria refused to be crowned because he did not want to be bound by the coronation oath.

[222] See Verdross, *op. cit. supra* n. 2, 132.

[223] (1802 ed.) iii-iv. See also *Préliminaires*, c. vi

[224] He criticises on this account Grotius, *op. cit. Prolegomena*, c. xii and Pufendorf, *op. cit.* bk. ii, cc. iii, xxiii.

[225] See, e.g., T. Rutherforth, *op. cit. supra* n. 189, bk. i, cc. i, vi, (1754 ed. 8-9; 1779 ed. 9). As the natural law thus grew in rigidity its creative quality was progressively sapped. See C. Wolff, *op. cit.* pt. i, cc. ii, xl (1754 ed. 21); Blackstone, *Commentaries* (1765) Intro. 27-28; Rutherforth, *op. cit.* bk. i, cc. ii, iii (1754 ed. 26).

[226] *Id.* cc. i, vii.

[227] See the chapter "Of Derivative Acquisition by Act of the Law" in *op. cit.* Of course natural law thinking had been active in this field ever since the Roman *praetor* developed his succession of *cognati*.

law ceased to expand and that it lost its creative drive. The natural law
codes of Prussia and Austria, claiming definite finality, sprang naturally from
such soil. There is an increased stress on its immutability, very parallel with
Lord Eldon's boast that the rules of equity had become as certain and
definite as those of the common law. Wolff, for instance, tells us in 1750 that
since "the nature and essence of man are immutable and necessary, it
follows that natural obligation is also unchangeable", and he deduces that
any rule of natural law, since it contains a natural obligation, is as necessary
and as immutable as the obligation itself.[228]

The codification movement of this century, indeed, expressed well this
phase of natural law in alliance with enlightened absolutism. Local customary
law, which had lived side by side since the fifteenth century with the
received Roman law, tended to be swept away in its course. In France
remnants of the old corporate order, led by the *"parlements"*, managed
partly to frustrate the central codification, which only Napoleon was later
to complete. In Austria, Prussia, Hanover, and other States of the Holy
Roman Empire, codification succeeded, though not easily even there. The
Austrian code was projected in 1713, only begun in 1753, and only completed in 1811. Codification was, of course, a special form of the wider
tendency to detailed crystallisation which showed itself also not only in
natural law writings as such, but in ambitious restatements of positive law
in natural law terms, as with Pothier's work on the French law and
Blackstone's on English law.[229] Lord Mansfield's great judicial work of the
second half of the eighteenth century, because of the opportunities presented
by the long English neglect of commercial law, belongs rather to previous
ages in its creativeness; yet his drive to systematise this branch of law
also shares the spirit of his own age as well.[230]

§16.THE SHIFT TO THE "UTILITY" PRINCIPLE. Finally, there is apparent at
this stage an increased tendency to rest one leg of natural law upon the
human pursuit of utility or happiness. When Bentham launched the utilitarian
theory into jurisprudence it already had its proximate foundations, not only
in English ethical philosophy of the eighteenth century, but in natural law
thought itself.[231] Considerations of utility had, of course, rarely gone quite
unmentioned in natural law writings; but even in the Grotian formulation
quoted above, natural law is merely "reinforced by utility",[232] and what he
goes on to say, in effect, is that insofar as civil law (i.e., positive municipal
law) goes beyond natural law, it "ought to aim at some utility". Like the
just "by convention" in relation to the just "by nature", utility here supplements but is not the foundation of natural law. But eighteenth century

---

[228] *Op. cit.* pt. i, c. ii, xxxviii-xl.
[229] *Cf.* on Blackstone, D. J. Boorstin, *The Mysterious Science of the Law* (1941)
passim.
[230] See the important study of J. Milnes Holden, *The History of Negotiable
Instruments . . .* (1955). On "natural law" as opposed to "moral sense" in Mansfield's
thinking see Dowrick, *Justice* 80-81. The distinction in this context is scarcely a
fruitful subject of debate.
[231] See T. Rutherforth, *op. cit.* bk. i, cc. i, vii (1754 ed. 9-10; 1779 ed. 9-10,
10-11, 12); J. J. Burlamaqui, pt. i, c. v, §4 (1821 ed. 46-47); E. de Vattel, *op. cit.*
(1802 ed.) 8n; S. Pufendorf, *op. cit.* (Spavan's transl.) 178-96; 1 Blackstone, *Commentaries*, 41. And *cf.* Dicey, *Law and Opinion* (1 ed. 1905) 144.
[232] *Op. cit.* 16.

C

writers present the desire for happiness as at least part of the foundation itself.[233]

Indeed, just as the "social nature" of man comes to be stated as an inference from the supreme end of happiness, so we find reason stated by Burlamaqui to be but the means of calculating the happiness-producing tendencies of conduct.

> The desire for happiness is then as essential to man as reason itself: . . . For to reason means to calculate, and to take account, weighing everything, in order to ascertain on which side the advantage lies. It is thus a contradiction to suppose a reasonable being who could be detached from his interests, or be indifferent concerning his own happiness.[234]

The American Declaration of Independence gave epoch-making political importance to this utilitarian infusion of natural law, when it enumerated as "self-evident" truths the propositions that all men are created equal, that they are endowed by their Creator with certain inalienable rights, and that among these are to be found the right to life, liberty and the pursuit of happiness.[235]

On this level natural law presented itself as but one kind of criterion of justice, which had in due course to struggle for its place with other such criteria. The classical stream of natural law as a bearer of all criteria, and of the theory of law itself, continued to be taught as a binding system mainly in the Catholic seminaries and universities. Even now, as will later be seen, this fuller system re-enters the stage from time to time as a recurrent phase of juristic speculation. But it no longer holds the stage alone.

II. NATURAL LAW AS A CENSOR OF THE POSITIVE LEGAL ORDER

§17. The Juxtaposition of Natural and Positive Law. The most biting indictment laid by Bentham and Austin against natural lawyers concerned their supposed "confusion" of law and morals, and their failure to see that positive law might be valid as law, even if it violated natural law. This "confusion", however, was no function of mere muddleheadedness, nor was it a confusion at all, from the standpoint of the ablest natural lawyers.

For Grotius, for example, the positive law of a given society is but one type of voluntary law, and all voluntary law is in one sense to be distinguished from natural law. It derives from the will of particular beings, and is *imposed* upon the persons bound by it. On the other hand, natural law is discovered by the reason of men, including finally the reason of the person bound himself. In one sense, then, natural law was quite distinct

---

233 Rutherforth, *op. cit.*, bk. i, cc. i, vii; Vattel, *op. et loc. cit.* Pareto 262, §441, in commenting on this aspect of Vattel, fails sufficiently to note the generality of the shift of emphasis involved.

234 *Op. cit.* pt. i, c. v, §§4-8, this part being written in 1747. *Cf.* also E. de Vattel, *Introduction* (1758 ed. transl. Fenwick) 5.

235 *Cf.* also Dicey, *Law and Opinion* (1 ed. 1905) 144. "Towards the close of the eighteenth century appeals to the doctrine of utility and appeals to the law of nature were often in reality, though not in words, appeals to one and the same principle. The failure to perceive this led to some strange results . . . ."

from positive law; and Grotius, like Austin himself, criticised his predecessors for not keeping the distinction clear. Natural law cannot, he says, be systematically presented, if positive law is not carefully separated off. "For the principles of the law of nature, since they are always the same, can easily be brought into systematic form": while positive law elements, being contingent on time and place, "are outside the domain of systematic treatment".[236]

§18. THE TESTING OF POSITIVE LAW BY NATURAL LAW. Grotius' distinction, however, does not turn on what for him is the mere artificial question whether the rule is imposed by a certain kind of external authority. The test is whether the rule, whoever laid it down, is a "correct conclusion drawn from the principles of nature".[237] If it is, then it is a rule of natural law. If it is not, then it is positive law merely.

Precisely this distinctiveness gives to natural law its power over positive law. Natural law according to this type of thought is an ideal law to which positive law must conform, and positive law is valid only so far as it declares natural law, or lays down rules on matters which according to natural law are indifferent. For in the Grotian view the validity of positive law derives from a social compact into which the members of the society must be deemed to have entered, yielding power to make positive law. This social compact is binding only by virtue of natural law derived from reason applied to man's nature.[238] It is to be inferred from this that positive law is only valid if it is (so to speak) *intra vires* of the power yielded to the lawmaker in the social compact. It is further to be inferred that the social compact would not have yielded power to make laws flagrantly violating the principles of natural law.

We find these inferences drawn and applied not only by speculative writers but by courts of law, including both English and American courts. The case of *Goshen* v. *Stonington*[239] merits mention here because Hosmer, J. so clearly disclosed his mental processes. The substantial question there was whether a retrospective statute might be held void even though there was no constitutional prohibition. Speaking as late as 1822 that judge found that the question was unsettled.[240] "With those judges who assert the omnipotence of the legislature in all cases where the constitution has not interposed an explicit restraint I cannot agree . . . ". If, for example, a law were made without any cause to deprive a person of his property or to subject him to imprisonment, who would not (Hosmer J. asked) question its illegality, and who would aid in carrying it into effect? For it would be a violation of "the social compact". It could not be supposed, said also a Massachusetts court in 1814,[241] striking down a statute not forbidden by the Constitution, that the people conferred on the legislature so "odious, a power as that of legislation for the benefit of particular persons". And a

---

[236] *Prolegomena,* para. 30.
[237] *Id.* para. 40.
[238] *Id.* paras. 15-16. *Cf.* with this Grotian "social compact" theory the better known versions of Hobbes, Locke, and Rousseau, *supra* n. 214. Some such notion had of course been implicit at least since Aristotle.
[239] (1822) 4 Conn. 209, 225, *per* Hosmer J.
[240] Citing 1 Blackstone, *Commentaries* 27. See now Fullagar J. in *R.* v. *Cwlth. Court of Conciliation* . . . (1950) 81 C.L.R. 229, esp. at 245-46, and in *Maxwell* v. *Murphy* (1957) 96 C.L.R. 261, esp. at 285-290.
[241] *Holden* v. *James* (1814) 11 Mass. 396, 398, 402, 404, 405.

Tennessee court in 1831 cited Coke[242] for a holding that, even apart from constitutional provisions, "there are eternal principles of justice which no government has a right to disregard".[243]

It is characteristic of these confident approaches to justice that they assume its criteria to be self-evident to the reason (that is, the "uncorrupted" reason) of all men. In fact, the criteria applied were increasingly drawn at this time from the customs and emergent demands of the urban middle classes engaged in expanding commerce and industry.[244] It was, indeed, the continuing pressure of these demands from the eighteenth century onwards which also made natural law the forerunner of nineteenth century individualistic theories.[245] Some of these theories would also, in due course, repudiate the paramount censorial power which natural law from the Roman praetors onwards had claimed over the content of positive law. It has been well said, indeed, that the changing content of "natural law" points to the truth that on its ideal side natural law has been "simply a framework for legal ethical thought".[246] Its very assertion, especially in an explosive phase, is a vindication of the claim of an ideal justice to criticise what is laid down by those who wield power. It is a reminder that positive law in the last resort must sustain criticism by other than its own standards, if it is not to degenerate into the commands of naked power.[247]

§19. THE STRIKING DOWN OF POSITIVE LAW BY NATURAL LAW. Natural law is thus distinguished from positive law, to permit it to exert censorial power over the latter. And in natural law theory this power goes beyond merely providing a criterion of the justice embodied in positive law. For insofar as the positive lawmaker acts under authority of the natural law compact, violation of natural law denudes his creation of the quality of law also. Conformity to this justice-standard is for the natural lawyer as necessary a mark of law, as is for Austin the element of sovereign command.

This act of overriding censorship is the final meaning of what is often termed the natural law identification of law and morals. It is also part of the secret of natural law's frequent social effectiveness, even when asserted against the authority of an unlimited sovereign. Blackstone's astonishing proposition on this point is well known.[248] "No human laws are of any validity if contrary to this, and such of them as are valid derive their force and all their authority, mediately or immediately, from this original." It is true that elsewhere Blackstone stresses the absolute unlimited supremacy of the English Parliament, so that his words, and those of the

---

242 In *Bonham's Case*, cited (with relevant literature) *infra* n.249.
243 *State Bank* v. *Cooper* (1831) 2 Yerg. Tenn. 599, 603. The purported ground of decision in the *Holden Case* was that such a law was not a "standing law" within the Constitution, and in the *Cooper Case* that it was not "a law of the land" within the Constitution. But since there was nothing in the respective Constitutions to exclude such laws from these phrases, the actual grounds of decision are rather as the text indicates.
244 See Ehrlich, *Sociology* 421. *Cf.* from the economist's point of view, Commons, *Capitalism* c. vii, esp. 231-35.
245 Ehrlich, *op. cit.* 418-420. S. I. Shuman (*Legal Positivism* (1963) 187-88) suggests that there is a modern "inverted natural law theory" in the Soviet-Marxist insistence that law overrides morals in the service of communism. This, however, may be but a phase of practice or tactics to meet particular situations. See Stone, *Social Dimensions*, Ch. 10, *passim*, Ch. 12, §§8-9.
246 Cohen, *Ethical Systems* 102.
247 See *ibid.*
248 See 1 *Commentaries* (1765, Christian's ed. 1809) 27, 40-43; St. Germain, *Doctor and Student* (*circa* 1518) Dial. i, cc. ii, iv, v (Muchall's ed. 5-14).

judges whom he echoed,[249] may be dismissed as rhetorical usage of a commonplace of their age. Yet the prevalence of such a commonplace is in itself significant.

§20. ENGLISH EQUITY AND THE NATURAL LAW TECHNIQUE.[250] That such assertions were not merely rhetoric, is clear enough from the liberties taken by equity with the common law and even with statutes. Equity showed for centuries a "magisterial" censorship of a natural law kind, by *ad hoc* alleviations of the rigour and formalism of the common law. What else, for instance, was the basis of the Chancellor's confident proposition that the Statute of Frauds may not be made the instrument of fraud? Must it not have been clear to the legislator that insofar as the Statute rendered seriously-made promises unenforceable, it would in fact be availed of for this purpose? How could the purpose of the Statute be fulfilled without its being to some extent an instrument of fraud? The English Chancellor, indeed, elaborated his own techniques, which illustrate the English ability to reach empirically and more or less peacefully results reached by other peoples only by bitter struggles for abstractions.[251]

We have seen that in the last resort the binding force of continental natural law arose from the reason of all human beings, and that the natural

---

[249] *Bonham's Case* (1610) 8 Co. Rep. 114, 118; *Calvin's Case* (1610) 7 Co. Rep. 1, 12b; *Day* v. *Savadge* (1615) Hob. 85, 87, *City of London* v. *Wood* (1701) 12 Mod. 669, 687. *Cf.* earlier, St. Germain, Dialogue 3: "The law of nature of reasonable creatures is called by them that be learned in the law of England the law of reason"; Dialogue 3, c. 2: "some will say that . . . the statutes were against natural reason and not to be observed" (the question being whether tenant for life was liable for damage by Act of God). See *inter alia* on *Bonham's Case*, T. F. T. Plucknett, "Bonham's Case and Judicial Review" (1926) 40 *H.L.R.* 30; C. K. Allen, *Law in the Making* (6 ed. 1958) 432ff.; Haines, *Revival* 32ff.; S. E. Thorne, "Dr. Bonham's Case" (1938) 54 *L.Q.R.* 543. Professor Thorne thinks that Coke's language was a development of an indigenous English doctrine of statutory interpretation (551).

Cf., citing the old authorities in the field of political action, Lord Chatham's speech in 1774 on the competence of the British Parliament to tax the colonists (Debrett, *Parliamentary Debates*, vol. vii, (1792) 12-13); *cf.* Lord Camden, *id.* vol. iv, 354ff.; J. Almon, *A Collection of Tracts* (1773) vol. i, 109-110. And see the discussion in C. K. Allen, *op. cit.* c. vii. Haines, *Revival* 43-44, suggests four main influences of natural law in England: (1) to stabilise and strengthen the "customary" or immemorial rules of the common law during its early growth; (2) to ground the appeal to "fundamental law" in the struggle between King and Barons, and later as against absolutist executive claims; (3) as a basis of subjection of statutory law to "fundamental" common law, identified with natural and divine law; (4) as a source of ideas for judicial reform of the law. *Cf.* generally F. Pollock, *op. cit. supra* n. 2, esp. 53ff., 68ff., 180ff.; and Dowrick, *Justice* 46-72, with which *cf.* however *id.* 79-80.

[250] *Anon.* (1464) Y.B., 4 Edw. IV, 8, 9, Digby's transl. (the separate development of "conscience" and "equity" in Chancery); *Earl of Oxford's Case* (1616) 1 Rep. Chan. 1, 4-11 (as extracted in Pound-Plucknett, *Readings* 205-206) (Lord Ellesmere on the law of God, equity and good conscience as a corrective of the law in Chancery); John Selden, *Table Talk* (ante 1654) Tit. Equity ("roguish" equity); *Gee* v. *Pritchard* (1818) 2 Swan. 402 (Lord Eldon's pain at the reproach of variability); *Lambe* v. *Eames* (1871) L. R. 6 Ch. App. 597 (equity as a system of principles based on precedent); Coke's *Fourth Institute* (1641) c. 8 (Lord Coke's view of the origins of Chancery, executive usurpation); F. W. Maitland, *Lectures on Equity* (1913) 19 (supplementary nature of English equity); *id.* 6-11 (early history of Chancery, trusts and injunctions against actions at law); F. D. MacKinnon, "Origins of Commercial Law" (1936) 52 *L.Q.R.* 30, 32-34 (the law merchant in the Court of Admiralty); Campbell, *Lives* (3 ed.) vol. iii, 274 (Life of Lord Mansfield); (infusion of the law merchant into the common law); H. Maine, *Ancient Law* (new ed. 1930) 69 (limitations on the creativeness of *praetor* and chancellor); Jolowicz, *Roman Law* 380-381 (Roman jurists and common law judges). See most of these materials collected in Simpson-Stone, 1 *Law and Society* 381-402; and on reason and equity in Roman and common law, citations *supra* n.1.

[251] *Cf.* Lord Macmillan, "Two Ways of Thinking" in *Law* 98-101.

lawyers were at some pains to show that there was a quality in the true reason of each human being which set it off from "depraved" reason. In the result natural law in the title of universal reason prescribed a rule for all. The Chancellor's operations, however, were based essentially on the appeal to the particular reason or conscience of the King,[252] and of the Chancellor as its Keeper. Again, this jurisdiction was not pursued, ostensibly at any rate, by promulgating rules binding on all men. At first, both in theory and practice, it was enforced by an appeal to the particular defendant's conscience, he being if necessary detained so as to permit his conscience to operate. Finally, equity in its relation to the common law realised concretely in practice that supremacy which natural law claimed abstractly over the positive law. The theory by which equity left intact the common law rights of the beneficiary of a deed obtained by fraud, and merely made it physically impossible for him to pursue them, was subjecting positive law to the test of morals quite as much as was natural law. The main difference between the Chancellor and the natural lawyer was that the former refrained from formulating in advance the assumptions on which he proceeded.

§21. THE NATURAL RIGHT TO REBEL. It was, of course, in the political field that the full explosive force of natural law was felt. For the very notion that positive law could only be justified by a social compact valid in natural law, though not a necessary or even a general feature of natural law speculation, could and did serve in the field of political action as a persuasive rationalisation of the right to rebellion if the compact were violated. That right, to nineteenth century England, seemed a picturesque survival of an earlier stage of political development. On the continent and in the Americas it was to contribute to the violent French and American revolutions which in their turn perhaps changed the whole course of western civilisation, and were not without influence on the development of democracy in England itself.

And it is well to recall that the American Declaration of Independence, after reciting the "self-evident" fact that men were inalienably endowed with the rights to life, liberty and pursuit of happiness, and that governments are established to secure these rights, declared that whenever any form of government becomes destructive of these rights "it is the Right of the People to alter and abolish it, and to institute new Government, laying its foundation on such principles and organising its powers in such form, as to them shall seem most likely to effect their Safety and Happiness". The Virginian Declaration of Rights was of the same tenor; and this tenor permeates the Bills of Rights of the American federal and state constitutions. In the French Declaration of the Rights of Man of 1789, insurrection against governments violating the rights of man was described as "the most sacred of rights and the most indispensable of duties".

§22. NATURAL LAW AND THE *STATUS QUO*. We shall later examine many

---

[252] On the continued creativeness of this concept for contemporary corporation law see Berle, *Capitalist Revolution* c. iii and *passim*, and Goyder, *Private Enterprise* c. vii and *passim*, which attempts to state *de lege ferenda* a company law based on "the natural order in industry". For an introduction in Italian to the common law-equity relation see M. Rheinstein, under that rubric, in 7 *Enciclopedia del Diritto* (1960), esp. 16-19.

examples of the conservative phase of natural law.[253] The contrast of natural law at a revolutionary stage with natural law at a conservative stage, which has already been described in §1 in terms of the social environment, and its social psychological conditions,[254] may, however, here be stated in terms of doctrine. At a revolutionary stage natural law tends to assimilate actual institutions to a rational ideal of what those institutions ought to be. It is therefore iconoclastic and progressive in tendency. In our own day, for example, natural law (under some name or other) is again being invoked to strengthen international law or otherwise overcome chaos and violence amid the rule of terror in the relations of states. It is also being used to bolster the claims of individuals to respect, dignity and physical integrity against those who exercise power over them, in an age which has seen the gravest recrudescence of cruelty and arbitrariness.

At a conservative stage natural law tends to assimilate the rational ideal of institutions to the social institutions existing at the time. So Aquinas sought to show that reason warranted the existing authority of the Church; so, too, we shall see that the nineteenth century American courts treated as "natural rights" the traditional rights of Englishmen, and even other rights not consecrated by time but which in the conditions of expanding industrialism seemed indispensable to human progress.[255] And we may add that within this conservative phase itself there may be further polarities. As employed by some medieval Catholic philosopher-theologians, for example, natural law was usually conservative in favour of the political *status quo* and its authorities when these were in relative accord with the teachings and requirements of the Church, and conservative in favour of the ecclesiastical *status quo* and its authorities when the political authorities were in disaccord with these (the political authorities then being called "tyrannical").

III. GENERAL OBSERVATIONS ON CLASSICAL NATURAL LAW CRITERIA

§23. INADEQUATE DEMONSTRATIONS OF NATURAL LAW. Natural law thinking became dominant in the modern world at a time when the authoritarianism of medieval Church and Empire were already crumbling. The Reformation in its destructive aspects was already doing its work, and the free inquiry which we associate with the Renaissance had produced a powerful intellec-

---

253 See *infra* Ch. 3, §§4ff. *Cf.* the lively restatement of the present theme, but in over-polemical terms, and based on an over-simple psychology of natural law (e.g., at 227-28, 262-63), in A. Ross, *On Law and Justice* (1958) 227-267, esp. at 263-65. But *cf.* now his own thesis (article cited. *supra* n. 3) that all "validity" theses (including presumably his own in *On Law and Justice*) derive their force from a crypto-iusnaturalist element, in the sense that characterizing a legal order as "valid" involves a concealed implication of ethical justification. To some extent this no doubt proceeds on confusion of the different meanings of "validity" discussed by E. García Máynez, "The Philosophical-Juridical Problem of Validity of Law", in *20th Century Legal Philosophy Series*, vol. iii (1948) 459ff. But *cf. infra* Ch. 10, §§1, 5.
254 See *supra* §1, and *cf.* 1 Pareto §247; R. Gordis, "Natural Law and Religion", in Cogley (ed.), *Natural Law* 240, at 248.
255 *Cf.* in the recent English literature, R. O'Sullivan, "The Bond of Freedom" (1942) 6 *M.L.R.* 177-85. See also *id.*, "A Scale of Values in the Common Law" (1937) 1 *M.L.R.* 27; *id.*, "Natural Law and the Common Law" (1945) 31 *Trans. Grotius Soc.* 117; *id.*, *Christian Philosophy in the Common Law* (1947); *id.*, *The Inheritance of the Common Law* (1950).

tual ferment. In the sphere of law and justice this general ferment manifested itself mainly in the thought and work of the natural lawyers. They were as much children of the Renaissance as was Francis Bacon; and they stand in a comparable relation to modern juristic theory with that which Bacon occupies in relation to scientific theory. As he built his Utopias of science, they built their Utopias of law and society; as he mingled the fancies and prejudices of his age with insights into the discoveries of the future, so did they.[256]

Natural law thinking in whatever age and under whatever form is essentially an assertion of faith in a standard of values, rather than a demonstration. Its dialectical weapons are "right reason; nature, with its appendages, rational nature, state of nature, conformity with nature, sociability and the like; the consensus of all mankind, or of some essential part of mankind; the divine will".[257] The effectiveness of these weapons depends upon the existence of a sufficient number of persons who for one reason or another feel driven to assert the same faith or to accept the assertion made by the intellectual and moral leaders of the time.

It is this central characteristic of natural law thinking which makes difficult a full appreciation of it, and makes easy the ridicule of it in a later age. The most incisive example of such ridicule is still that of Pareto, who finally reduced "natural law" to a mere symbol which stirred emotions also associated in the mind with such symbols as "reason", "perfection", "justice" and the like.[258] Once, in short, the spell of a common intuition is broken the standard appears suspended in mid-air devoid of any apparent basis in reality.

§24. SELF-EVIDENCE IS RELATIVE TO TIME AND PLACE. It is beyond doubt that the justice of particular laws does seem self-evident to many people at particular times and places. The justice of workmen's compensation laws, of income tax, of widows' pensions, or of truck acts, is almost universally recognised today. Yet within the last century many sincere and enlightened men have, as we shall see, opposed the passing of such laws; and judges have been found even to hold them void as arbitrary and unreasonable and contrary to natural justice and reason. In this very twentieth century of ours, conversely, nations that were reckoned as great and civilised have been seen to commit, apparently with some degree of general support and often under forms of law, acts of mass murder and spoliation infinitely more heinous than anything envisaged by Hosmer J.[259] when he spoke of "laws" which no man would recognise or carry into effect.

This is not to palliate such horrors, nor to question that to the vast majority of mankind they are most self-evidently evil. It is rather to point out that, wherever the boundary of the universal and eternally self-evident be drawn, many of the day to day and year to year problems of law and justice fall outside it. Even some most universal and eternally self-evident rules "of natural law" have thus failed from time to time to command recognition among substantial parts of mankind. Further, when we affirm a consensus against sadistic murder and genocide by proclaiming a "natural right to life", it remains still not self-evident what justice requires concerning repro-

---

[256] Cf. Ehrlich, Sociology.
[257] 1 Pareto 245, §403.
[258] Id. 254, §427.
[259] Supra §18.

duction of the imbecile from the imbecile, the merciful despatch of the tortured moribund, or of the newborn child lacking mental or physical capacity for normal survival, or even concerning the taking of life of the murderer. And of course many important day to day and year to year problems are without even *prima facie* guidance from such self-evident rules.

§25. SOCIAL IMPORTANCE IS INDEPENDENT OF DEMONSTRATION. But the mere exposure of the undemonstrated basis of a body of thought does not necessarily destroy either its past influence, or present value and prospects. Natural law, where it has been an effective ideological force in political or legal development, will always be found to have had deep roots in the conditions of the time. No one perhaps, with the exception of Bentham,[260] has lashed more bitterly than Pareto the inadequacy of natural law demonstrations. But Pareto also stated clearly the vital importance of natural law thought.

> But if we disregard forms and consider what it is they hide, we discover inclinations and sentiments that exert a powerful influence in determining the constitution of society and therefore are worthy of the closest study . . . (We must not) stop with the reflection that a certain argument is inconclusive, idiotic, absurd, but ask ourselves whether it may not be expressing sentiments beneficial to society, and expressing them in a manner calculated to persuade many people who would not be at all influenced by the soundest logico-experimental argument.[261]

And even "legal positivists" themselves may acknowledge the relevance of this for social action in certain phases of a society's history.[262]

---

[260] See *infra* Ch. 4, §3.

[261] 1 Pareto 264, §445. For cautions as to this kind of use of the term "logical" see Stone, *Legal System*, Ch. 8, §§1, 6, and n.116; and *id., Social Dimensions*, Ch. 12, §§1ff. On the general problem of "rationality" of action as regards the means "suitable" for attaining a given goal, see Hempel, "Rational Action" 5, esp. 6-7.

[262] See S. I. Shuman, *Legal Positivism* (1963) 208-209.

CHAPTER 3

METAPHYSICAL INDIVIDUALISM

I. THE FREE-WILLING INDIVIDUAL AS A NATURAL LAW IDEAL[1]

§1. THE KANTIAN DOCTRINE OF FREE WILL AND THE CATEGORICAL IMPERATIVE. The individualism emergent in some earlier natural law doctrines was to become prominent in two basic lines of nineteenth century speculation as to justice. One of these was the ethico-juristic teachings of Immanuel Kant, here to be considered; the other was the utilitarianism of Bentham to be considered in the next Chapter. It would here be impossible to attempt any exposition of Kant's system of thought as a whole.[2] His leading ideas as to the end of law are to be found in his *Metaphysische Anfangsgründe der Rechtslehre*,[3] published in 1797. These form part of his moral philosophy which he refers to the sphere of the "ought", known in Kant's system as the sphere of "practical reason".[4]

Kant's central contribution to philosophy is the introduction of what he termed the "transcendental method".[5] This he defined as the systematic use of concepts which refer to our way of knowing objects without reference

---

[1] For a moderately full bibli. see Pound, *Outlines* 14-15, 198-99. The following introductory reading list is here suggested: ON "REASON" AND "WILL". I. Ahrens, 1 *Cours de Droit Naturel* (1837, 1875 ed.) 1, 104, 107; 2 *id.* 17, 20, 21; Miller, *Lectures* 9; J. G. Fichte, *Grundlage des Naturrechts* . . . (1796, 1922 ed.) 11-15; E. Acollas, *L'Idée de Droit* (1886) 13; *id., Intro. à l'Etude de Droit* (1885) 1-2; E. Urman, "*Zur kantischen Rechtsphilosophie*" (1927) 2 *Rev. Int. T. du Droit* 232-34: ON LAW AND MORALS: Kant, *Rechtslehre* 14, 18, 28, 34, 44-46; Ahrens, *op. cit.*, Pref. to 1837 ed.; (1875 ed.) vol. i, xii; vol. ii, 1, 17, 20, 21; J. Lorimer, *Institutes of Law* (1872) 279-283, (2 ed. 1880) 353-54; Miller, *Lectures* 9, 357; Hegel, *Grundlinien der Philosophie des Rechts* (1821) transl. Dyde (1896) as *Hegel's Philosophy of Right*, para. 53; E. Hölsche, 1 *Sittliche Rechtslehre* (1928) 5, 22, entitled "*Die Trennung des Rechts von der sittlichen Ordnung durch Kant und seine Schule*"; A. Poggi, "*Morale e diritto nella dottrina Kantiana*" (1932) 12 *Riv. Int. di Fil. del Dir.* 385-394: ON THE HISTORICAL ASPECT OF METAPHYSICAL THINKING: Hegel, *Philosophy of History*, Sibree's transl. Intro., 1-79 (for atmosphere only, esp. 10-11); Miller, *Lectures* 63, 68-69, 71-72.

References will later be given to the practical operation of metaphysical individualist ideas in §§5ff.

[2] Students may refer for an elementary account of Kant's ethical system to A. C. Field, *Moral Theory* (1921) cc. ii-iv. For a full study see now H. J. Paton, *The Categorical Imperative* (2 ed. 1953), noting esp. the discussion in bks. ii and iv of Kant's preliminaries and presuppositions to the categorical imperative. From the juristic standpoint see W. Friedmann, *Legal Theory* (4 ed. 1960) 106ff.; and the fuller account in Cairns, *Plato to Hegel* 390-463.

[3] Transl. W. Hastie as *Philosophy of Law* (1887), here cited as *"Rechtslehre"*.

[4] Kant is often thought to have exposed the fallacy of the natural lawyers' assumption, which they shared with the eighteenth century "rationalists" generally, that the "dictates of right reason" were something given to all men to see, and see alike, if they would only see aright. We may here accept this view of his relation to the natural lawyers, reserving the right, however, to express later certain doubts as to its significance. See also *infra* Ch. 10, n. 24.

[5] *Kritik der reinen Vernunft* (1781, German ed. by F. Meiner, 1956) 55.

to experience, and therefore discoverable only by *a priori* reasoning. It seems clear that Kant thought that the transcendental method could be applied to the sphere of the "practical reason", including moral and legal philosophy, as well as to that of the "pure reason" which embraced the natural sciences. In its application to the sphere of the practical reason, it is now generally held that Kant was unsuccessful,[6] and the doubt is well raised whether such application is, indeed, at all possible.[7]

Kant's basic tenet in the field of "practical reason" is the "freedom" of human volition. Human volition which to Kant is "free" is for him no mere faculty of desire; but rather the faculty of desire governed by the reason of the subject before the choice is made.[8] This is the sense in which it is "free", and as thus modified it may also be rendered as "free-will". For both ethics and justice are meaningless unless it be supposed that the subject is "free" in the sense of ability to *use his reason* to make one choice rather than another. Kant's argument under this head proceeds as follows:[9]

> The freedom of the act of arbitrary choice is its independence of being determined by sensuous impulses or stimuli; this is the negative expression of its freedom. The positive expression of its freedom is the ability of pure reason to be practical of itself. But this is not possible otherwise than by making the maxim of every action comply with the condition that it be suitable as a universal law.[10]

The concepts of volition and freedom[11] are "pure", that is, not drawn from experience. They are independent of any particular body of moral or legal rules. They are presuppositions of all such rules, valid and necessary for all of them.

It would follow for Kant that any principles drawn from these concepts must be universally valid principles independent of time, place and persons, and their momentary desires. Obviously not all such principles (which Kant calls the "maxims" for human actions) are *supreme* principles. They must all, however, conform to such a supreme principle in order for the human actions to qualify as moral. This supreme principle which (like the concepts of "volition" and "freedom") is established *a priori* without any reference to experience or historical data, Kant calls the categorical imperative. Kant explains the categorical imperative thus:

> The categorical imperative, which is limited to expressing generally what constitutes "obligation", is this: Act according to a maxim which can also claim validity as a universal law. Therefore you must consider your actions in the first place according to the principle with which they comply. Whether this principle is also universally valid can be ascertained only through your reason putting it to the test of whether or not, from the aspect of the role of a universal legislator, it would qualify to form part of a legal system of universal validity. The simplicity

---

[6] Hermann Cohen, *Ethik des reinen Willens* (2 ed. 1907) 227, and Kelsen, *Theory* 445.

[7] See O. Bondy, "The Moral Law Theory . . ." in *Australian Studies in Legal Philosophy* 139-164. *Cf.* as to Stammler, *infra* Ch. 6, §8.

[8] See Kant, *Metaphysics of Morals* (1797) (in T. K. Abbott's transl. of *Kant's Critique of Practical Reason and other Works on the Theory of Ethics*, 4 ed. 1889) 282.

[9] *Rechtslehre* 13. For assistance in revising this and other passages from Kant in this Chapter, I am indebted to my friend Dr. Otto Bondy.

[10] Kant defines "maxim" as the "subjective principle of volition" (*Grundlegung zur Metaphysik der Sitten* (1785); Kant, *Works* (Rosenkrantz and Schubert (1838) ed.), vol. 8, p. 21. It is the principle *according to which the individual acts*.

[11] See *Kritik der reinen Vernunft* (Meiner ed.) 42.

of this principle in comparison with the great and manifold consequences which can be drawn from it . . . must certainly at first appear strange.[12]

§2. "NATURAL LAW" AND "*A PRIORI* CONCEPTS" OF LAW AND JUSTICE. Kant expressed the contrast between such principles as might be derived from the *a priori* concepts on one hand, and positive law on the other, as one between "natural law" and "positive law".[13] The former is based on the *a priori* concepts of volition and freedom, the latter on the empirically found expression of an authoritative will. And we must observe, at the outset, that this use of the term "natural law" should not be identified with uses traditional up to his time.[14] It resembles the traditional kinds of natural law in that it embodies as a criterion of justice. It differs from them in at least two important respects. One is that Kant's "natural law" does not dominate positive law in the sense that positive law is thought invalid *as such* if violative of natural law. Another is that Kant's "natural law" is discovered by his transcendental method, without reference to experience, and not by way of intuition of values deemed immanent in experience.

As to the relations of Kant's natural law to "positive law" it is clear that, since his "natural law" rests on *a priori* concepts while the validity of positive law rests for him on the expression of an authoritative will, the two may coincide, or may conflict without affecting each other's legal validity. Beyond this there are many perplexities. One concerns the precise *a priori* basis. Conceivably Kant might have sought to derive his "natural law" from the categorical imperative established above, though if all that it conveys is (as he suggested) the obligation to act in accordance with a predetermined universal principle, some may think it too void of even potential content to be used for such a purpose.[15] In the *Rechtslehre* Kant rather drew his "natural law" directly from the *a priori* concepts of volition and of freedom.

Law itself, Kant said, is concerned with the external and practical relations of one person to another.[16] These relations, to be ordered at all,

---

[12] *Rechtslehre* 3. (Rosenkrantz ed. 1838, pt. ix, 26.) And see on the problem of ultimate justification and the categorical imperative, H. Prosch, "The Problem of Ultimate Justification" (1961) 71 *Int. Jo. Ethics* 155.

[13] "Obligatory laws for which an external legislation is possible are called generally external laws. Those external laws, the obligatoriness of which can be recognised by reason, *a priori*, even without an external legislation are called natural laws. Those laws again which are not obligatory without actual external legislation are called positive laws." (*Id.* 55.)

[14] And see *supra* Ch. 2; *infra* Ch. 10, §§2ff.

[15] It has been asserted, indeed, (see a good statement by the lamented F. S. Cohen, *Ethical Systems* 222-24) that logically the categorical imperative is meaningless, since it assumes that a particular act can only fall within one universal proposition whereas it may fall equally under innumerable ones. The act of lying may be brought within a principle as to "lies" or one as to lies for various purposes or under various circumstances, as "to save a friend", or "to preserve modesty", or "to spare the hearer's feelings" (white lies), etc. "By a judicious selection of universal principles one can demonstrate on the basis of this theory that anything is good or that anything is bad." At the worst "one can formulate some class of which it is the only member and thus lay down a universal rule applicable to it and free from inconsistency". *Cf.* A. Ross, *On Law and Justice* (1958) 276-77. And see for some concrete manifestations of this alleged fallacy, *infra* §§10ff.

[16] The legality of an action for Kant means its conformity to external law; its moral quality means its conformity to the actor's self-legislated standard. Kant elaborated this distinction (*Rechtslehre* 35, 44-46) as follows: (1). "The conception of (legal) right . . . in the first place has regard only to the external and practical relation of one person to another . . . by their action as facts." (2). It is concerned

involve the ordering of the effects of the *Willkür* (arbitrariness) of each man on others, in the light of the concept of freedom. Kant thus proceeded to combine the *a priori* concepts of freedom and *Willkür* in the definition: "Law is the sum total of conditions under which the arbitrariness of one is compatible with the arbitrariness of others according to a general law of freedom." And though this is stated in terms of "law" *simpliciter*, its significance here is that Kant's ideal of law, or concept of just law, or criterion of justice, in short his "natural law", is embedded in it.

Even then, since the source-concepts of "freedom" and *Willkür* are *a priori* and not derived from experience, this "natural law" of Kant is not in the nature of what has been called a "material value ethics" in the field of law.[17] It is rather a "pure" theory of law such as those later developed in neo-Kantian terms, for example by Stammler and Kelsen in their differently orientated ways. Such writers followed Kant in stipulating the necessity for investigation *a priori* of the concept of law, that is, for investigation in terms of "pure" theory.

Kant himself uses the expression "pure theory of law" only once,[18] and then without prominence. Kelsen, however, introduced it as the ostensibly distinguishing characteristic of his philosophy of law. To both Kant and Kelsen insofar as the investigation of the concept of "law" is *a priori*, the grounds of validity of any *actual* legal order are left open. Indeed, Kant casually remarked at one point that while we may think that laws can exist which are "binding" solely "on the ground of external legislation", this could only be so if a "natural law" were pre-supposed which constitutes the authority of the legislator to impose obligations on others by his own act of will.[19] It is perhaps the driest jest of all legal philosophy that even as Kelsen rests his whole "pure" theory of law on a "basic norm" such as Kant here foreshadowed and called "natural law", he also denounced all natural law ideas. Certainly it is clear that Kant believed that "pure theory of law" could also yield results for the *evaluation of the contents* of legal norms, that is (in our terms) in the search for a criterion of justice. In this respect Stammler followed Kant as decisively as Kelsen repudiated him.[20]

The second contrast between Kant and the natural lawyers, noted above, touched the *a priori* as distinct from intuitive basis of "natural law". For the traditional natural lawyer's natural law was to be discovered by an intuitive response of man's reason to a situation, by recognition of the values immanent in it. With Kant, on the other hand, the theory at any rate was that once his *a priori* concepts were found "the great and manifold

---

with the relation of free action to the free action of others; not to their wishes, as in benevolence; nor (3) is it concerned with the motives of the actor, as is ethical obligation. Finally (4) legal right comprehends the conditions for harmonising voluntary actions according to the "universal law of freedom", and it can determine "what every one shall have as his own with mathematical exactness"; but in ethics the necessary latitude for exceptions prevents this.

[17] See Welzel, *Naturrecht* 7.

[18] *Metaphysische Anfangsgründe der Tugendlehre,* Preface (1797, F. Meiner ed. 1919) 211.

[19] *Id.* 28 (Meiner ed.).

[20] Kelsen's one-sidedness thus places him in a much less acceptable relation to Kant than Austin occupied in relation to Bentham. Austin, while devoting his *main* energy to the analytical questions opened up by Bentham, did not repudiate Bentham's concern with the theory of good law, and indeed shared it. See Stone, *Legal System* 44-45, 86, 90-01, 312-16. As to Stammler see *infra* Ch. 6.

consequences flowing from them"[21] were demonstrated irresistibly. The categorical imperative constitutes the self-legislative human will as a universal moral law. It yields only one "innate right" belonging to everyone by nature, independent of any acts of legislation, the "birthright of freedom"— that is, independent of the arbitrary will of another. "Insofar as this freedom, which is independence from the compelling arbitrariness of another, can co-exist with the freedom of all according to a universal law, it is the one sole original inborn right belonging to every man in virtue of his humanity." All other alleged rights and titles such as equality, justness, common action, so popular with the natural lawyers, were, for Kant, valid only insofar as included in "the principle of Innate Freedom".[22]

§3. NEW METAPHYSICAL INDIVIDUALIST WINES IN NATURAL LAW BOTTLES. Different as was Kant's thinking from that of traditional natural law, the interpretation generally placed on his theories of law and justice came to reinforce the individualist and libertarian trends which natural law had built up successively against medieval Church and Empire, eighteenth century despotism, and the shackles of medieval social, political and economic organisation, increasingly at odds as these were with the growing pressures of the industrial revolution. His teaching, indeed, was quickly put into currency in natural law terms. Johann Gottlieb Fichte published in 1796 his *Grundlage des Naturrechts* which performed admirably the transfer of the new Kantian wine into natural law bottles.[23] Man as a rational being, he said, can only conceive himself as one among others, all living in one world, who are to themselves as he is to himself. Ahrens' *Cours de Droit Naturel*, appearing in 1837, and going through twenty-four editions in many languages, based "rational freedom" on "respect, conservation and development of personality", man being an end in himself, who may not be treated as a thing or a means. The echoings of Kant can scarcely be mistaken.[24]

Within this influence, however, two divergent interpretations of the Kantian criterion of justice were detectable.

---

[21] *Rechtslehre* 35, 44-46.

[22] They "are not really distinguished from it even as dividing members of a higher species of right". *Id.* 55-56. In a sense, of course, Kant's system was still undemonstrated since its categories are arrived at *a priori*. But the Kantian answer to this reproach was clear. Please propose a better one which will be consistent with the nature of matters in the sphere of "obligation", and the "ought".

[23] (1922 ed.) Intro. 11-15. Translations here are the author's. There is a translation by A. E. Kroeger (1889) as "Fichte's Science of Rights", and a valuable account for the lawyer in Cairns, *Plato to Hegel* 464-502. In thus transforming natural law Fichte himself was, of course, well aware of the change, for he criticises the natural lawyers for failure to realise that a criterion of morals must be deduced from the *a priori* nature of obligation itself, and cannot be attained by applying reason directly to the facts. And he summarises the transition in two sentences. "I must necessarily think of myself in the society of people to whom nature has united me . . . . Everyone is bound by the decision of his own will to live in society with others. And if anyone does not wish to restrict his arbitrary will, natural law can only say to him that he must withdraw himself from society".

[24] See the 8th ed. (1892), vol. i, l, 2; vol. ii, 17 and compare with vol. ii, 20. *Cf.* a similar hybrid quality in E. Acollas, *L'Idée du Droit* (1886) and many other works. For Kant's prior formulation see Kant, *Fundamental Principles of the Metaphysic of Ethics* (extracted from the *Critique of Practical Reason*) Abbott's transl. (3 ed. 1907) 56.

§4. Divergencies as to the Role of Law Proceeding from Kant. One trend was an increasing stress on the maximum of individual freedom of action as the end of law, holding in law to that part of ethics which "it is possible to promulgate by external legislation".[25] This, in fact, though not of logical necessity, led to the view that legal restraints should be held in in the name of justice. It tended to relegate law to the function of merely policing, with the minimum of restraint, the allocation of liberty as among men.

The other contrary tendency was to re-interpret "freedom" in terms not merely of absence of restraint but in terms of attainment of individual perfection. This latter trend, which directs attention to *the effect* of the presence or absence of legal restraint rather than condemning restraint as such, foreshadows the shift in the late nineteenth century away from individualist criteria. It pointed out that to make individual freedom the criterion of justice involved for the law not a mere negative restraining role.[26] For "since every negative must be rooted in the validity of a positive, there is behind this negative competence, as its positive organ, the full energy of the ethical".[27] Despite this dissenting trend, the dominant juristic influence from Kant was individualist and *laissez faire*. The Scots philosopher W. G. Miller, writing even after the collectivist "social legislation" in England was well begun, was still convinced in 1884 that the law was abdicating, and ought to abdicate, its governance of human relations, as "the movement for freedom" proceeded.[28] Most current legislation (he thought) was emancipating men from antiquated laws, giving them "the power of self-legislation" by "freedom of contract". The rest was merely supplementary to this "private creation of law".[29] No doubt much of nineteenth century law reform had been of the kind Miller described. But what is interesting is Miller's belief that this manifested the permanent victory of the metaphysical individualist criterion of justice, when its sway was already waning under his very eyes.[30] In due course the confident belief was to turn into a lament for the

---

[25] *Rechtslehre* 43.

[26] F. A. Trendelenburg, *Das Naturrecht auf dem Grunde der Ethik*, (1860) challenged Kant's criterion of justice precisely from this aspect. He urged that the Kantian separation of the legally right from the ethically right is modern, and that there should be a return to Platonic and Aristotelian treatments. He supports the identification by such natural lawyers as Grotius and Pufendorf. He continues (*op. cit.* (2 ed. 1868) 18-22, 83): "Law is a part of the ethical whole of all the general rules as to conduct, from which it appears that the ethical whole and its members support each other and develop further. All law (*Recht*), insofar as it is right and not unright, flows from the urge to maintain an ethical existence". (Our translation.) Fichte's work, *cit. supra* n. 23, and *Der Geschlossene Handelstaat* (1800) gave early signs of these trends. *Cf.* W. Friedmann, *Legal Theory* (4 ed. 1960) 112-13, 121-22.

Cf. also K. C. F. Krause, *Abriss des Systems der Philosophie des Rechts oder des Naturrechts* (1828) and the work of Krause's disciples, K. D. Röder, *Grundzüge der Politik des Rechts* (1837) and I. Ahrens, *Cours de Droit Naturel* (1837). And see the neo-Kantian R. Stammler, *Lehre* c. iv.

[27] F. A. Trendelenburg, *op. et loc. cit. Cf.* Fichte and Ahrens, cited *supra* §3. In this latter form, while the ultimate criterion of justice and of ethics is identical, namely, the attainment of individual perfection, the proximate criterion *of justice* is the maximum of liberty to each, while the proximate as well as the ultimate criterion *of ethics* is perfection of the individual. *Cf.* J. Lorimer, *Institutes of Law* (2 ed. 1880) 353-54.   [28] Miller, *Lectures* 9, 71.

[29] Pp. 72-73. *Cf.* Lord Coleridge's "I have no faith in act of parliament reform". (*Table Talk*, Oxford Classics ed. 190.)

[30] "Contract", Miller also wrote, "is the last product of the perfect idea of personality in the individual, especially when . . . the individuals who enter into the

backslidings of the twentieth century; but the fervour of the vision could still be found.[31]

II. NATURAL RIGHTS AND THE FREE-WILLING INDIVIDUAL

§5. BLACKSTONE AND THE ANGLO-NATURAL RIGHTS OF MAN. The instances of the influence of the ideal of the free-willing individual given in the following pages will fall under four principal heads: (1) The assimilation of the "common law rights" of Englishmen to natural rights, and their injection in this form into the United States Constitution; (2) Freedom of contract as a natural right; (3) Vested property rights and freedom of testamentary disposition as natural rights; and (4) No liability without fault as a dictate of natural law. These will be illustrative merely of what is recognised to be the continuing influence of natural law assumptions. The techniques of judicial law-making in English and American courts, for instance, examined in the closing Chapters of our work on *Legal System and Lawyers' Reasonings*, can perhaps be best understood as proceeding from a judicial belief in the self-evidence of the creative choices made.

Blackstone's *Commentaries* in 1765 ordered and summed up the preceding centuries of legal development. In doing so, it spelled *initium* as well as *finis*, and was a jumping-off point for new development, both in England and America. Its place as a student's book in both countries for almost a century emphasises this prospective importance.[32]

The principal aim of society, said Blackstone, opening his pages in Vattelian fashion,[33] "is to protect individuals in the enjoyment of those absolute rights which were vested in them by the immutable laws of nature. . . ." And he also tells us that "this law of nature being coeval with mankind and dictated by God Himself, is, of course, superior in obligation to any other. . . . No human laws are of any validity if contrary to this".[34] It is often thought that Blackstone, especially in view of his simultaneous stress on the sovereignty of Parliament, wrote such words with his tongue in his cheek. But, as Professor Pound has pointed out, Blackstone was primarily a teacher, formulating the doctrines of his time, and not a philosopher, testing their consistency.[35] And however this be,

---

relation are truly free." His prophecies were, of course, belied, even while he wrote. See Dicey, *Law and Opinion* (1905) lect. vii and viii, and Pref. to 2 ed.; Brown, *Modern Legislation* 59 and *passim*.

[31] See, e.g., R. O'Sullivan, "The Bond of Freedom" (1943) 6 *M.L.R.* at 180ff., who pleads for revival of the common law's emancipation of "Everyman in dignity and status as a free and responsible person living in the fellowship of a free community". See also *infra* §13, as to this writer's consequent attitude to social legislation.

[32] See on this and on the use of Grotius, Pufendorf and Vattel as legal textbooks, R. Pound, *Formative Era of American Law* (1938) 23-26. And see C. Warren, *History of the American Bar* (1911) 177ff. Warren tells us at 187 that the great Chancellor Kent attributed his reputation to the fact that as a student "he had but one book, *Blackstone's Commentaries*, but that one book he mastered". On legal education in England at the time, and on Blackstone's role, see W. S. Holdsworth, *Some Makers of English Law* (1938) 238ff.; and D. J. Boorstin, *The Mysterious Science of the Law* (1941) *passim*, J. W. McKnight, "Blackstone, Quasi-Jurisprudent" (1959) 13 *Southw. L.J.* 399-411.

[33] Bk. i, c. i (Christian's ed. 1809) 124.   [34] *Id.* 27.

[35] Blackstone, indeed, may not have seen any inconsistency between such pro-

it was his words that went forth, not his secret mind. The words quoted may well have contributed some respectable authority to the explosive role of natural law in the break of the colonies from the mother country, an authority the more important because loyalist sentiment was strong among the conservative lawyers.

Moreover, as we shall see, they provided at a later stage excellent slogans for the reactionary use of natural law. For besides sanctifying the natural right of revolution, Blackstone sanctified the *status quo* by identifying the traditional rights or "liberties" of Englishmen with the natural rights of man,[36] "founded on nature and reason . . . coeval with our form of government though subject at times to fluctuation and change". The rights secured by Magna Carta were for him "that residuum of natural liberty . . . not required by the laws of society to be sacrificed to public convenience", which other peoples had lost but which Englishmen preserved. He specified clearly and in detail what were these absolute natural rights enshrined in positive law, enumerating the contents of the rights to life, personal security, personal liberty and private property.[37]

§6. NATURAL RIGHTS IN THE DECLARATION OF INDEPENDENCE AND BILLS OF RIGHTS. When the Declaration of Independence recited as self-evident men's endowment with the rights of life, liberty and the pursuit of happiness, and that the people were entitled to replace any government destructive of these rights, it marked the beginning of a spectacular career of natural law in American constitutional development. In the books,[38] as well as in the Federal and State "Bills of Rights", the doctrine persisted explicitly throughout the century. When its revolutionary phase was over, it still continued to operate, endowing traditional legal rights with the authority of natural rights, and these natural rights in turn with the force and immutability of a rigid constitution.

Of more immediate interest[39] is the manner in which American constitutional decisions imported into the supposedly traditional rights thus sanctified, claims which were merely the expression of nineteenth century individualism, especially of the metaphysical brand.[40] The outstanding

---

positions. His work ushered in the age of what Dicey later called satisfaction with all things English. He might well have said, if pressed, that the superiority of natural law and the supremacy of the English parliament stood well together, since the English parliament would never exercise its sovereignty in a manner violating natural law. See generally on Blackstone's conflicting aims and pre-suppositions, Boorstin, *op. cit. supra* n. 32, esp. c. viii on Blackstone's understanding of "liberty".

[36] *Op. cit.* 1, 127.

[37] *Cf.* the interesting recent example of the interchangeable use of natural rights and traditional common law rights in R. O'Sullivan, *op. cit. supra* n. 31, 176, esp. 182-85.

[38] See, e.g., as late as 1887, E. L. Campbell, *The Science of Law According to the American Theory of Government* 16-20, and the citations in the succeeding sections. The phrases in the Declaration have a history in political as well as juristic writing (e.g., in Locke) into which it has not been thought necessary to enter for present purposes.

[39] On the general creative influence of the natural law in American private law, parallel to its work on the Continent, see R. Pound, *op. cit. supra* n. 32, 3-37; *id., Legal History* 130ff.

[40] See generally on the topics in the following pages: R. Pound, "Liberty of Contract" (1909) 18 *Yale L.J.* 454; F. Frankfurter, "Hours of Labour and Realism" (1916) 29 *H.L.R.* 353; E. Corwin, "The 'Higher' Law Background in American Constitutional Law" (1929) 42 *H.L.R.* 365; and his *The Twilight of the Supreme Court* (1934); W. H. Hamilton, "The Path of Due Process of Law" in C. Read (ed.), *The Constitution Reconsidered* (1938) 167; Commons, *Capitalism* cc. ii, iii; Haines, *Revival; id., The Supreme Court in United States History* (1935); R. E. Cushman, "The

example of this concerns the Fifth Amendment to the United States Constitution, which provided that "no person shall be deprived of life, liberty or property without due process of law",[41] and the corresponding restrictions on the States later imposed by the Fourteenth Amendment in 1868.

All parts of this clause had in 1789 a well settled common law meaning. The liberty sanctified by Magna Carta and its confirmations[42] amounted in effect to personal liberty from physical restraint except according to law and regular legal procedure. It was in this sense that its infringement was complained of in the Petition of Right of 1627, and guarded in the Habeas Corpus Acts. Blackstone, in 1765, after reducing the absolute rights of Englishmen to three—the right of personal security, the right of personal liberty, and the right of private property,[43] made it quite clear that by "liberty" he meant physical liberty.[44]

Yet into this word as shortly afterwards embodied into the Constitution there was to be instilled within a century a sweeping meaning covering liberty to contract, liberty of entry to avocations, and a number of liberties on the borderland of property, for instance, the right to act without being liable except for fault. Less than another century later, as we shall see elsewhere, "liberty" in the Fifth and Fourteenth Amendments had come to embrace a still greater range of interests of personality,[45] while its ambit in terms of contract and property interests had become much constrained. Semantic change must, of course, occur especially in words of common usage, and with words of such emotive quality change is likely to reflect both changing environment and changing ideology. This reflection is precisely our main concern.

Again, the phrase "without due process of law", which up to then had referred merely to regularity and fairness in official procedure, came to mean "arbitrarily and unreasonably". From "due procedure" it came to mean "due purpose" testing the law by "justice". It became for decades a drastic limitation on the power of enacting substantive law, no less real because it was in itself quite indeterminate beyond the procedural

---

Social and Economic Interpretation of the Fourteenth Amendment" (1923) 20 *Mich. L.R.* 737; R.A. Brown, "Police Power and Legislation for Health and Safety" (1929) 42 *H.L.R.* 866; B. Schwartz, *The Supreme Court* (1957) c. v.

[41] On the paternity of the Fifth Amendment see also Waite C.J. in *Munn v Illinois* (1876) 94 U.S. 113, 123-24.

[42] The thirty-ninth article of Magna Carta, of which there had been thirty-two confirming statutes before the Petition of Right (Blackstone, 1 *Commentaries* 128) had provided that: "No freeman shall be taken or imprisoned or disseised or outlawed or banished or any ways destroyed; nor will we pass upon him nor send upon him unless by the legal judgment of his peers, or by the law of the land."

[43] Blackstone, 1 *Commentaries* 129.

[44] *Id.* 134: "This personal liberty consists in the power of locomotion, of changing situation, of moving one's person into whatsoever place one's own inclination may direct, without imprisonment or restraint unless by due course of law. Concerning which we may make the same observation as upon the preceding article (i.e., life) that it is strictly natural, that the laws of England have never abridged it without sufficient cause and that in this kingdom it cannot ever be abridged at the mere discretion of the magistrate without the explicit permission of the law". *Cf.* Cave's *English Liberties* (1721), and see generally C. E. Shattuck, "The True Meaning of 'Liberty' . . . in 'Life, Liberty and Property'" (1891) 4 *H.L.R.* 365; Commons, *Capitalism* 47ff., 331. The term "liberties" itself as used in Magna Carta, c. 29 referred of course to special privileges and powers granted under the prerogative.

[45] See Stone, *Social Dimensions*, Chs. 5, 6. *Cf.* Freund, *Supreme Court* 45-49, who stresses the natural law elements involved also in these mid-twentieth century developments. And see generally R. Pound, *The Development of Constitutional Liberty* (1957); R. A. Rutland, *The Birth of the Bill of Rights 1776-1791* (1955).

field. In the wide range of operation of the due process clause, under which numerous statutes of major importance have been struck down, it is not the clause itself which wholly determines decision. Scholars show wide agreement in the conclusion that such decisions have depended upon content being given to the clause by the social, economic, and political assumptions of the courts and public opinion for the time being.[46] The ideal of the "free-willing individual" here also played its part.

§7. FACTORS FAVOURING THE NEW CONTENT OF LIBERTY AND DUE PROCESS. Liberty in the common law sense was, then, a very much narrower concept than Kant's metaphysical liberty, or the liberty of a Bentham, and it was almost a century before this wider meaning became dominant in American decisions. Nor was this coincidental. We must be ever on guard against the temptation to believe that ideas spring up or extend themselves independently of a social context, or that ideas cause the events of which they are a part. Kantian and Benthamite libertarianism had dominated thought for three-quarters of a century before the new meaning began to be instilled into the Fifth and Fourteenth Amendments.[47] As late as 1876 in *Munn v. Illinois*[48] the Supreme Court declined to accede to arguments based on the extended meaning. In the form of dissents it was, however, making progress.[49] The date is significant. In England, Professor Commons has pointed out, Adam Smith's *Wealth of Nations* appeared in the same year as that in which Watt invented the steam engine. Expanding industrialism came early. The conditions providing the corresponding stimulus only came fully into existence in America after 1870.

The industrial development after the Civil War, going hand in hand with the extension of railroads, led on the one hand to the meagre beginnings of social and labour legislation, and on the other to the appearance of great corporate interests who opposed such legislation. This opposition allied itself with a widespread tendency to exalt "rugged individualism" arising from the pioneering conditions of life during the pushing back of the frontier to the west.[50] Yet it required the skills of the newly specialised corporation lawyers to give intellectual form to these drives

---

[46] See Commons, *Capitalism* 333ff., where the early cases are discussed; Garlan, *Legal Realism* 63-69. For recent usage of "due process" in the old procedural sense see Macmillan, *Law* 16.

[47] It was first applied to the latter.

[48] 94 U.S. 113, but see Field J. at 142. The *Munn Case* was the first of the *Granger Cases*, reported *id.* 113-187, all involving organised protests by farmers against railroad abuses. *Cf. Chicago, etc., R.R. Co. v. Iowa, id.* 155, and the *Peik, Ackley, Blake* and *Stone* cases, resp. at 164, 179, 180, 181. And see also *Bradwell v. The State* (1872) 16 Wall. 130; *Bartemeyer v. Iowa* (1873) 85 U.S. 129; *Hurtado v. California* (1884) 110 U.S. 516; *Barbier v. Connelly* (1884) 113 U.S. 27; *Powell v. Pennsylvania* (1888) 127 U.S. 678, give the development.

[49] Four judges including Field J. dissented in the *Slaughter House Cases* (1872) 16 Wall. 36. *Cf.* also general discussions in this early stage in *U.S. v. Cruikshank* (1875) 92 U.S. 542.

[50] This dual influence is also seen in the background of some of the judges who played a decisive role in the "carnival of unconstitutionality" between 1890 and 1910. On Field see Haines, *Revival* 199ff.; R. Pound, *Spirit of the Common Law* (1921); W. D. Lewis, 7 *Great American Lawyers* (1909) 3; on Harlan and Brewer see Haines, *op. et loc. cit.;* on Bradley, see Lewis, 6 *op. cit.* 347. Field, of Puritan stock and education, had an exciting history in the frontier west when California was opened up. Harlan shared the latter attribute. Bradley was an entirely self-made man, having begun life as a farm-hand and become, prior to his elevation to the bench, the most sought-after corporation lawyer of the day.

and attitudes in the constitutional interpretations urged upon the courts with increasing success in the last quarter of the century.[51]

These, at least, were among the conditions of which Mr. Justice Holmes said in 1897[52] that they had

> led people who no longer hope to control the legislatures to look to the courts as expounders of the Constitution. . . . (In) some courts new principles have been discovered outside the bodies of those instruments, which may be generalised into acceptance of the economic doctrines which prevailed about fifty years ago, and a wholesale prohibition of what a tribunal of lawyers does not think about right. . . .

Though Adam Smith's doctrines were, on occasion, even enshrined in Supreme Court judgments, it seems impossible to separate off their influence from that of Kant's metaphysical individualism, or James Mill's version of Benthamite individualism.[53] The natural law element is also striking and persistent.[54] Cooley, in his standard work on *Constitutional Limitations,* first published in 1868,[55] asserted that definite limitations proceeding from "natural justice" circumscribed the legislative authority, quite apart from express constitutional restraints, and that courts might strike down statutes which violated these unexpressed "principles of natural justice".[56]

§8. LIBERTY OF CONTRACT AS A NATURAL (AND HENCE CONSTITUTIONAL) RIGHT OF THE FREE-WILLING INDIVIDUAL. "It is through contract," wrote Miller in 1884, "that man attains freedom. Although it appears to be the subordination of one man's will to another, the former gains more than he loses".[57] In the *Slaughter House Cases*[58] a majority of the Supreme Court rejected the argument that the Fourteenth Amendment forbade the Louisiana legislature from requiring, on grounds of health, that all cattle within a

---

[51] The corporation lawyers, ironically enough, turned against the public power characteristic arguments of *laissez faire* and natural rights, which had been used earlier in the century against the charter corporations by the alliance of individual and public enterprise: see Hartz, *Economic Policy* 57ff. And see Stone, *Social Dimensions,* Ch. 7, §16.

[52] "Path of the Law" 467-68. For a brief account of this era see B. Russell, *Freedom and Organisation* (1934) cc. xxvi-xxvii.

[53] See *infra* Ch. 4, §§1, 11. *Cf.* on individualist ideologies as an independent factor, Hartz, *Economic Policy* 76-77.

[54] *Cf.* R. Pound, "The Ideal Element in American Judicial Decision" (1931) 45 *H.L.R.* 136; R. Pound, *Formative Era of American Law* (1938) 26-27.

[55] At §iv.

[56] *Constitutional Limitations* (1868). See also his opinion in *Bank of Columbia* v. *Oakley* (1819) 4 Wheat. 235, 244. Cooley's book was followed in the courts on this point. See, e.g., *Millett* v. *The People* (1886) 117 Ill. 294, 301-02.

The question-begging tendencies became particularly patent when courts added to the Kantian formula a reference to "the just exactions and demands of the state" (Andrews J. in *Bertholf* v. *O'Reilly* (1878) 74 N.Y. 509, 515) or to "such restraints as are necessary for the common welfare" (Rapallo J. in *People* v. *Marx* (1885) 99 N.Y. 377, 386). For such a reference substitutes another criterion for that of equal liberty; yet no serious attempt was made to clarify that criterion.

[57] Miller, *Lectures* 71ff.

[58] (1872) 16 Wall. (U.S.) 36. See Commons, *Capitalism* cc. ii, iii, where this and the succeeding cases are seen as a struggle between the two meanings of "property" as "use-value" of physical things, and "exchange value of anything", including "liberty", the latter prevailing eventually. And see in relation to health and other statutes generally R. A. Brown, *op. cit. supra* n. 40.

given area be slaughtered at the premises of a state-organised corporation.[59] It was, however, the minority view which came to prevail in later cases. That view was well expressed by Field J.,[60] who claimed that the Fourteenth Amendment was intended "to make everyone born in this country a freeman, and as such to give him the right to pursue the ordinary avocations of life without other restraint than such as affect all others, and to enjoy equally with them the fruits of his labour". Violation of such right, by barring a man even from one vocation, would place him "in a condition of servitude". The Kantian reference is, indeed, almost explicit in another of Field J.'s dissents, where he insisted that "liberty" in the Amendment means not merely physical freedom, but freedom "to act in such manner not inconsistent with the equal rights of others as his judgment may dictate for the promotion of happiness".[61] The equal liberty thus vindicated, be it noted, was entirely abstract, without regard either to the interests of others vouched to warrant the restraint, or for that matter to the concrete situation of the beneficiary of the liberty himself.

The natural law framework of this thought becomes quite explicit in the reasoning (still minority reasoning though in concurring opinions) of Bradley and Field JJ. in the sequel to those cases.[62] Field J. declared[63] that "certain inherent rights lie at the foundation of all action, and upon a recognition of them alone can free institutions be maintained". He and Bradley J. thought that free choice of vocation was part of the inalienable right to pursue happiness of the Declaration of Independence. Without explaining how this would attract the constitutional guarantees, they nevertheless held any legislative restriction of it to be void. The individualist-natural law assumptions were typically reinforced by resort to the still dominant *laissez faire* economics of Adam Smith's *Wealth of Nations*.[64] In Justice Field's words, such a restraint invaded the poor man's "sacred property" in his strength and dexterity, encroaching thus both on his liberty and on that of those disposed to employ him.

It is not necessary to recount here the history of the struggle between American legislatures and courts and between majority and minority judges on the Supreme Court, which for over two full generations gave full play to the ideas of Field J. and delayed the course of social legislation. The ground is amply covered in the American literature.[65] In his classical article on this subject in 1907[66] Professor Pound was able to enumerate the following types of legislation which had up to that year been held invalid by the American courts as being arbitrary and unreasonable: (1) Acts forbidding interference by employers with their employee's membership in labour unions; (2) Acts prohibiting the imposition of fines on employees; (3) Acts

---

[59] They stressed that the identical provision had been contained in the Fifth Amendment to the federal Constitution and in many state Constitutions without any such extended application.

[60] At 90-91. This came to acceptance first in the *Minnesota Rate Case* (1890) 134 U.S. 418.

[61] In *Munn* v. *Illinois* (1876) 94 U.S. 142, in which the majority held constitutional an Act regulating warehousing and inspection of grain. *Cf.* Rapallo J. in *People* v. *Marx* (1885) 99 N.Y. 377; Andrews J. in *Bertholf* v. *O'Reilly* (1878) 74 N.Y. 509; McReynolds J. in *Meyer* v. *Nebraska* (1923) 262 U.S. 390.

[62] *Butcher's Union Co.* v. *Crescent City Co.* (1883) 111 U.S. 746.

[63] At 756-57; *cf.* Bradley J. at 762.

[64] Bk. i, c. x.

[65] Cited *supra* n. 40.

[66] R. Pound, "Liberty of Contract" (1909) 18 *Yale L.J.* 454.

regulating the mode of weighing coal to determine miners' wages; (4) Truck acts or acts forbidding payment of wages by goods in kind, or in orders on the company stores; (5) Acts regulating hours of labour with certain exceptions, for instance, as to unhealthy, dangerous employment and as to minors. On some of these matters some courts took the opposite view. But even after 1907 the mortality of legislation, including workmen's compensation acts and minimum wage acts, continued high.

It will perhaps suffice to mention the comparatively late case of *Adkins* v. *Children's Hospital*[67] decided in 1922, the direct overruling of which in 1937 marked the bankruptcy of this particular nineteenth century gloss on the due process clause. The Supreme Court, despite considerable evidence as to the evil effects of low wages on women employees, there struck down as violative of liberty of contract a minimum-wage act for women of the District of Columbia. Mr. Justice Sutherland held, for the Court, that liberty of contract was not absolute, but "freedom of contract is nevertheless the general rule and restraint the exception". And by freedom of contract he meant that "the parties have an equal right to obtain from each other the best terms they can as the result of private bargaining".[68] Constitutional lawyers were quick to question the evidence for this supposed "general rule".[69] Mr. Justice Holmes made one of his frequent protesting dissents:

> The earlier decisions upon the same words in the 14th Amendment began within our memory and went no further than an unpretentious assertion of the liberty to follow the ordinary callings. Later that innocuous generality was expanded into the dogma—Liberty of contract. Contract is not specially mentioned in the text which we have to construe. It is merely an example of doing what you want to do embodied in the word "liberty". But pretty much all law consists in forbidding men to do something they want to do, and contract is no more exempt from law than other acts.

Even if it were not historically clear, and even if judges were not always aware of it, the influence of Kantian and *laissez faire* individualism, framed in natural law, stood out in the judicial reasoning.[70] Law, it assumes, is properly only a means of delimiting the liberties of individuals. If then, X and Y both will to do a given thing, what ground can there be for the state to say them nay?

> To sustain the individual freedom of action contemplated by the Constitution is not to strike down the common good but to exalt it, for surely the good of society as a whole cannot be better served than by the preservation, against arbitrary restraint, of the liberties of its constituent members.[71]

---

[67] (1922) 261 U.S. 525. The principal authorities to this date are referred to in the judgments in this case. The *Adkins Case* was overruled in *W. Coast Hotels Co.* v. *Parrish* (1937) 300 U.S. 379, van Devanter, McReynolds, Butler and Sutherland JJ. dissenting at 400. In a parallel field see the overruling of *Ribnik* v. *McBride* (1927) 277 U.S. 350, in *Olsen* v. *Nebraska* (1939) 313 U.S. 236, esp. 244-47. But on the continued use in some state courts see Note, "State Views on Economic Due Process 1937-1953" (1953) 53 *Columbia L.R.* 827-845.

[68] At 546.

[69] Powell inferred that it represented simply Mr. Justice Sutherland's "personal views of desirable governmental policy". See T. R. Powell, "Judiciality of Minimum Wage Legislation" (1924) 37 *H.L.R.* 545, 555.

[70] See esp. the instant case (1922) 261 U.S. 525.

[71] *Id.* 561. *Cf.* Jessel M.R. in *Printing Co.* v. *Sampson* (1875) L.R. 19 Eq. 462, and in one aspect *Roberts* v. *Hopwood* (1925) A.C. 578. *Cf.* the materials collected Simpson-Stone, 1 *Law and Society* 585-606.

§9. UNREAL NATURE OF THE ABSTRACT CONCEPTION OF LIBERTY PRO-
TECTED BY THESE VIEWS. It was the sociological jurists, and in particular
Holmes and Pound,[72] who exposed the unreal nature of the "liberty of
contract" thus guaranteed. But the exposure had long been invited by the
judicial language sanctifying the liberty. In *Godcharles* v. *Wigeman*[73] in
1886, the Pennsylvania Court held that a store order act ("truck" act)
violated the Fourteenth Amendment on the ground that it was "an insulting
attempt to put the labourer under a legislative disability which is not only
degrading to his manhood but subversive of his rights as a citizen of the
United States". Every law which interfered with his selling his labour,
or with his employer's right to sell iron and coal, was unconstitutional,
vicious and void. The fallacy of assimilating a workman, living from daily
labour, to a great corporation bargaining to buy or sell iron or coal is
now well recognised. The rhetorical question: "What is there in the
condition or situation of the labourer in the mine to disqualify him from
contracting in regard to the price of his labour or in regard to the mode
of ascertaining the price?"[74] is answered without difficulty in the common
experience of all modern industrialised nations.

The root fallacies of such reasoning lie in the assumption that economic
relations do not affect political and moral relations.[75] First, this assumption
would only be valid if the parties are equally free to make or refuse a
bargain; that is, have equal choices of alternatives, equal "waiting power"
to hold out in default of agreement, and equal acquaintance with the
market. This is rarely so between employer and individual workman.
Second, it would only be valid if economic relations left the environment
and the distribution of social power unaltered. Moreover, the ways in which
men are organised, whether in production or elsewhere, cannot possibly
be politically or morally irrelevant. And, in final analysis, we are brought
back, interestingly enough, to the two divergent tendencies proceeding from
Kant's concepts of freedom of the will. The extravagant liberty of contract
doctrine saw justice in terms of the tendency to minimise legal restraints.
The criticism which this extravagant doctrine finally provoked was in terms
of fulfilment of individual personality. Jethro Brown, indeed, used precisely
these terms when he insisted that the "real test of liberty is to be
found less in the form of government or in the number of laws . . . than
in the extent to which the citizen is assured of self-realisation . . .". To
overlook this, he insisted was "to confuse liberty in its abstract with liberty
in the concrete sense",[76] and to be blind to the fact that power may be

---

[72] *Cf.* in the British literature Brown, *Modern Legislation*. *Cf.* Taft C.J. dissenting
in the *Adkins Case* (1922) 262 U.S. 525, 562 and the majority in the *W. Coast Hotels
Case* (1937) 300 U.S. 379, 393-400. See also the characterisation of the abstract view
as "fictitious equality" in the *Quong Wing Case* (1911) 223 U.S. 59, 63.

[73] (1886) 113 Pa. St. 431, 435, 437. *Cf.* Rapallo J. in *People* v. *Marx* (1885)
99 N.Y. 377, 386; Andrews J. in *Bertholf* v. *O'Reilly* (1878) 74 N.Y. 509, 515.

[74] Scholfield J. in *Millett* v. *People of State of Illinois* (1886) 117 Ill. 295, 303.
Cf. Brewer J.'s assumption in the *National Waterworks Case* (1894) 62 F. 853, 865
that customers *choose* to connect with the mains of a water monopoly.

[75] *Cf.* Lindsay, *Democratic State* 106ff. *Cf.* R. H. Tawney, *Religion and the
Rise of Capitalism* (1926, Mentor ed.) 11-12, 15ff., on the comparative lateness of
this "divorce", which he dates at the earliest in the late 17th century, with the
Rev. Dr. Tucker, Dean of Gloucester, as the chief exponent before Adam Smith.

[76] *Modern Legislation* 59; *cf.* R. Pound, "Liberty of Contract", *cit. supra* n. 40; R.
Pound, "Do We Need a Philosophy of Law?" (1905) 5 *Columbia L.R.* 339; F.
Frankfurter, "Hours of Labour and Realism", *cit. supra* n. 40.

economic as well as political.[77] And Robert L. Hale has provided more recently an impressive and careful elaboration of the theme that insofar as economic inequalities receive sanctions and even reinforcement from legal compulsion, for example through the law of contract, the law cannot ignore these inequalities.[78]

§10. TRADITIONAL LEGAL RESTRAINTS ON ABSTRACT LIBERTY IN ORDER TO SECURE LIBERTY OF CONTRACT. This abstract ideal is, indeed, at sharp variance with traditional common law ideals. An important and wide-ranging branch of equity devoted itself precisely to interference with liberty of contract in order to protect one of the parties. It relieved against agreed penalties and forfeitures; it created the equity of redemption against the terms agreed; it removed clogs on the equity of redemption though clearly agreed to; it rescinded unfair contracts disposing of sailors' wages or prize money; of interests of heirs and reversioners; and it struck at hard bargains generally. Statutes have long interfered with contract by usury laws, avoidance of infants' contracts, price-fixing statutes and wage-fixing statutes, the latter being commonplace in England and the Colonies even at the time of the revolutionary war.[79] Common law itself, by rules of undue influence, intervened directly to protect a contracting party; and the spacious realm of public policy is above all a series of restraints on liberty of contract dictated in most instances by considerations independent of the expressed will of the parties, and sometimes for their protection.[80] It was well within this tradition that the English Court of Appeal pointed out that there was no absolute doctrine that "an adult man, as to whom undue pressure is not shown to have been exercised, ought to be allowed to enter into any contract he thinks fit affecting his own liberty of action". The court held, in this case, that a contract of loan which purported *inter alia* to assign wages, and among other restraints to prevent the borrower from changing his job or his residence, was against public policy. "No one has a right so to deal with a man's liberty of action as well as his property, and the law says it is contrary to public policy".[81]

[77] See also Stone, *Social Dimensions*, Chs. 6-8 *passim*. However proper such criticism, it might still be preferable not to attempt to use the term "liberty" for what Adam Smith, Kant and Bentham advocated, as well as for what these modern views would substitute for it. With great respect, Professor Laski's use of the term (e.g., *Politics*, 143ff. and *passim*) seems open to the same comment. Economy of language in the fray of political and social life requires admittedly the re-interpretation of basic concepts in every epoch, but it does not seem helpful to carry these ambiguities over into scientific analysis. Of course where the reinterpreted definition is explicit no great harm results. In the second edition (1929) and in his *Liberty in the Modern State* (1930) Laski, reviewing the matter, rather thought that it was mistaken to seek to regard liberty as "more than a negative thing", and best to preserve the notion of absence of restraint on personality. (See Preface to 2 ed.). J. R. Commons' resolution of the concept (*Capitalism* cc. ii, iii) into "powers" and "opportunities" in choosing available alternatives allows the concrete situation to be better seen. And see *id*. c. viii for a concrete analysis of the wage-bargain.

[78] R. L. Hale, *Freedom Through Law* (1953), and (covering the main thesis of this) *id*., "Economic Liberty and the State" (1951) 66 *Pol.Sc.Qu.* 400.

[79] See L. L. Jaffe and M. O. Tobriner, "Legality of Price-Fixing Agreements" (1932) 45 *H.L.R.* 1164-71.

[80] See an excellent survey from the present standpoint by Frankfurter J. dissenting in *U.S.* v. *Bethlehem Steel Corp.* (1941) 315 U.S. 289, 312ff. The whole case is of great interest. And see Stone, *Social Dimensions*, Ch. 4, §8.

[81] Cozens Hardy M.R. in *Horwood* v. *Millar's Timber Co. Ltd.* (1917) 1 K.B. 305, 310. *Cf. Tasman Dry Cleaners Case* (1960) 78 W.N. (N.S.W.) 53.

Here again, though within the narrower ambit of English judicial power, we see the conflicting play of the contradictory trends which in varying social contexts emerged from the libertarian position after Kant.[81a] On the one hand, there is the trend, apparent in the *dictum* of Jessel M.R. in *Printing Co.* v. *Sampson*,[82] that if there is any paramount public policy, it is that adult men of competent understanding shall have the utmost liberty of contracting, and that their contracts shall be enforced. On the other hand, however, is the kind of principle laid down by the House of Lords in the *Nordenfelt Case*,[83] carrying on a long and unbroken line of authority, that "all interference with individual liberty of action in trading and all restraints of trade themselves, if there is nothing more, are contrary to public policy and therefore void". This latter attitude focuses not on the contractual exercise of liberty, but on the effects of its exercise on the residual liberty left if the law enforces the resulting contract.[84] It sees a man's "liberty" as his choice between available alternatives, giving, often, arbitrary power to one party if his range of actual alternatives is excessively wide, or if the other's is excessively narrow.[85]

§11. INVIOLABLE PROPERTY AND INHERITANCE AS A NATURAL RIGHT OF THE FREE-WILLING INDIVIDUAL. Samuel Adams had said in the pre-revolutionary polemics that the demand that there be no taxation without representation was "founded in the eternal law of equity. It is an original right of nature". The British constitution was "copied from nature", and forbade "the supreme power" from taking any man's property without his consent.[86] The combined influence of individualism and natural law also came to rationalise the nineteenth century claim to inviolability of private property. In *Nunemacher* v. *State*[87] a statute imposing a tax graduated according to the

---

81a *Cf.* on tensions as to both property and contract within the natural law tradition itself, e.g., in the Scots law, P. Stein, ". . . Contract and Property" (1963) 8 *Juridical* R.(N.S.) 1-13. And see Ihering's criticism of Mill, *infra* Ch. 5, §§1ff.

82 (1875) L.R. 19 Eq. 462. 465.   83 (1894) A.C. 535, 565.

84 The idea of residual liberty, however, also seems refinable into both abstract and concrete application: see *Wyatt* v. *Kreglinger and Fernau* (1933) 1 K.B. 793, 807. There, the plaintiff, a former employee of the defendant, had been promised in 1923 a pension of £200 on retirement. He was informed at the time that "you are at liberty to undertake any other employment . . . except in the wool trade . . .". The pension was paid until 1932 when it was discontinued because of the depression. Assuming that there was a contract the C.A. held that it was in any case void as in restraint of trade, "the country . . . thereby being deprived without any legitimate justification of the services of a man of sixty years . . . who is quite competent to enter into business". The plaintiff therefore failed. Yet apparently *he* was quite satisfied with the restriction on his liberty: and so far as the community at large was concerned it is not to be supposed that with two million unemployed at the time, his inactivity constituted any grave deprivation. For a late defence of the abstract right of the workman to choose his employer, and thus not to have his week-to-week contract of employment transferred from one company to a statutory amalgamation of companies, see *Nokes* v. *Doncaster Amalgamated Collieries* (1940) A.C. 1014. The concrete disadvantages to the workman of leaving him without contract rights against either the new or the old company was little considered. Contrast the judicial notice by the U.S. Supreme Court in the *W. Coast Hotels Case* (1937) 300 U.S. 379, at 399, of the facts of economic depression. And see Commons, *Capitalism* esp. at 29, 71-72, 303-304, and *cf.* the dissent of Frankfurter J. in *U.S.* v. *Bethlehem Steel Corp.* (1941) 315 U.S. 289, 312ff.

85 Of which so-called "contracts of adhesion" offer many standard examples. See, e.g., F. Kessler, "Contracts of Adhesion—Some Thoughts about Freedom of Contract" (1943) 43 *Columbia L.R.* 629, 643.

86 (1774) in Samuel Adams, *Works*, vol. i, 46, 53.

87 (1906) 129 Wis. 190. *Cf.* also Mason J. in *White* v. *White* (1849) 5 Barb. 474, 484-85 as to married women's property acts; *Noel* v. *Ewing* (1857) 9 Ind. 37, 61.

amount of the inheritance was struck down as unconstitutional, though the Wisconsin constitution did not expressly guarantee property rights. For the court (Winslow J.) found that the statute violated natural rights of property and inheritance "existing in the people prior to the making of any of our constitutions".[88] Reciting the reference to inherent rights to life, liberty and the pursuit of happiness in the Declaration of Independence and the State Constitution, the Court found that "pursuit of happiness" comprehended the desire "planted" in every breast to possess and dispose of property.

Though admitting difficulty of proof, Winslow J. insisted that "the right to take property by inheritance or will" was coeval with civilisation in human memory, making light of the beginnings of English testation of land with 32 Henry VIII, c.1.[89] Of the general absence of testation in kin-organised societies he seemed unaware, as of the restraints on it in Roman law systems.[90] Nor, of course, could he have known of the universal modern trend to limit the power both by taxation, and for the protection of dependants.[91] Inviolate property rights continue to be defended as founded, like freedom, on the rational nature of man.[92] Certainly American constitutional doctrine long displayed a tendency to "enlarge property at the expense of sovereignty".[93] The contemporary problems of the "dual standard" in the application of the Bill of Rights of the United States Constitution, centred on the tendency to reverse this position by granting higher protection to civil rights than to property rights, still echoes the underlying philosophical strife.[94]

§12. No Liability without Fault as a "Natural" Immunity of the Free-Willing Individual. Of equal interest was the claim to a "natural law" immunity from liability without fault. In view of the long period during which the law of torts rested mostly on the writ of trespass, for which fault was not decisive, this doctrine was bold. It was still bolder if we recall that not until Brown v. Kendall[95] in the United States in 1850, and until Stanley v. Powell[96] in England in 1891, did fault seem to become required even for trespass to person.[97] Yet the early workmen's compensation laws

---

The leaning against restraint on the testator's liberty is, of course, still found, but not in natural law terms. See, e.g., Re Makein (1955) Ch. 194, per Harman J.

   [88] At 200.
   [89] At 202.
   [90] Limitations in the form of the part légitime have, of course, long characterised systems deriving from the Roman law. For a general account of inheritance in early and simpler societies see Lowie, Social Org. 136-152.
   [91] As by the family provision and maintenance inheritance acts. See Stone, Social Dimensions, Ch. 5, §§9-10; Ch. 6, §11.
   [92] R. O'Sullivan, cited supra n. 31, at 179n. quoting the well-known passage from Aquinas and the reaffirmation in Leo XIII's encyclical, Rerum Novarum.
   [93] Commons, Capitalism 34-35. Cf. the materials collected in Simpson-Stone, 1 Law and Society 606-619.
   [94] Cf. Freund, Supreme Court cc. i-ii, esp. pp. 45-49; Stone, Social Dimensions, Ch. 5, §§7-8.
   [95] (1850) 6 Cush. 292 (Massachusetts).
   [96] (1891) 1 Q.B. 86, at 94. It was not until 1951 that this much debated holding received decisive approval from a superior court in National Coal Board v. Evans (1951) 2 K.B. 861 although Fowler v. Lanning (1959) 1 Q.B. 426 and Letang v. Cooper (1964) 2 All E.R. 929 have, at least for the time being, finally established its status.
   [97] The exact rule prior to Stanley v. Powell is, of course, still debated. See P. H. Winfield and A. L. Goodhart, "Trespass and Negligence" (1933) 49 L.Q.R.

in the United States were struck down on the ground that they violated this supposed "natural" and therefore constitutional immunity.[98]

As late as 1918, in the *Arizona Employers Liability Cases*,[99] such reasoning still based vigorous dissents. An Arizona statute giving to workmen injured in certain hazardous employments a special action in which negligence need not be proved, was unsuccessfully challenged as violating the Fourteenth Amendment. McKenna J. dissenting said: "It seems to be of the essence of right, of the essence of liberty as it is of morals, to be free from liability if one is free from fault." This principle, he said, was "the sense of the law and the sense of the world".[100] McReynolds J., while not claiming to freeze "law" and "progress", also dissented,[101] on the ground that such liability violated "the natural and inherent principles of natural justice which . . . inspirit our constitution".[102]

McReynolds J. was appealing to principles which he regarded as self-evident, but which were certainly not so in what he called "our traditional jurisprudence". Primitive law generally paid little or no attention to moral blame.[103] The early common law of torts sprang from the writ of trespass of which negligence or evil intent was not the gist. Libel or slander actions will lie and have always lain regardless of the defendant's moral fault. The special liabilities of innkeepers and carriers, which are among the oldest branches of the law of torts, provide many examples of absolute liability.[104] And the vicarious liability of a master for his servants' torts in course of employment is scarcely explicable in terms of moral blame. No doubt, as with trespass to person, some movement to require negligence was apparent. But in view of the complex and shifting patterns of fault, absolute and strict liability, since *Rylands* v. *Fletcher* and continuing today, little can be "self-evident" about this matter in modern legal systems.[105]

§13. PERSISTENCE OF METAPHYSICAL INDIVIDUALIST THOUGHT AT THE PRESENT DAY. Not even today, nor even in British countries, can such modes of thought be neglected. Mr. R. O'Sullivan, K.C., in a paper delivered before the Grotius Society in 1943,[106] pleaded vigorously for a restoration in English law of "the principles of natural law", and its "central conception of *liber et legalis homo*". He conceived these to have been impaired by the Workmen's Compensation Act, which (he said) treats the workman "as a mere unit of earning capacity, and a being who is not fully responsible in

---

359; the excursus of P. A. Landon in F. Pollock, *Law of Torts* (15th ed. 1951) 128-134, and the judgment of Diplock J. in *Fowler* v. *Lanning* (1959) 1 Q.B. 426.

[98] See *Ives* v. *S. Buffalo Rly. Co.* (1911) 201 N.Y. 271, esp. Werner J. at 285, 293. See after the constitutional amendment of 1913, *N.Y.C.R.R.* v. *White* (1917) 243 U.S. 188.

[99] (1918) 250 U.S. 400.

[100] At 435.

[101] At 450. *Cf.* Pitney J. at 422.

[102] He also criticised the statute as dealing with an abstract "employer" regardless of whether he was one man working beside his employees, or a corporation employing thousands. This if, of course, a different point. See *infra* §§13ff.

[103] F. H. Bohlen, *Cases on Torts* (2 ed. 1925) 1-10; F. B. Sayre, *"Mens Rea"* (1931-1932) 45 *H.L.R.* 974.

[104] See Pound, *Philosophy of Law* 79ff.

[105] On the long debated automobile accident compensation plans, *cf.* Stone, *Social Dimensions*, Ch. 6, §§1ff. where the position to 1963 is examined and literature cited; Pound, 4 *Jurisprudence* 505-508.

[106] Printed in (1943) 5 *M.L.R.* 176. *Cf.* this writer's other works cited *supra* Ch. 2, n. 255.

law for his own acts or defaults", as opposed to the common law view of
the workman "as a whole human personality", "a free and lawful man".
And he considered this personality threatened by proposals of the Beveridge
Report on Social Security, which were later nevertheless implemented, and
by other current reform proposals not here immediately relevant.[107] The
underlying theories of justice have indeed become a main point of politico-
economic debate in the last generation, typified in F. S. Hayek's thesis[108]
that proposals for the further extension of social control through law are
destructive of justice and democratic values. They violate "the rule of law",
it is alleged, first because of the resulting growth of discretionary administrative standards,[109] and second because they attempt to realise a substantive
ideal of justice by treating different persons differently, by recognising and
attempting to mitigate the inequalities of economic power in certain cases.[110]
In this thesis it is "the rule of the road", where the content
of the rule is immaterial provided it be uniformly followed, which is
the *true* type of law. The sole function of *true* law is to lay down "the rules
of the game which enable individuals to foresee how the coercive apparatus of
the State will be used, and what he and his fellow-citizens will be allowed
to do and made to do in given circumstances".[111]

§14. REFLECTIONS ON THIS "TRUE" LAW FROM RECENT LEGAL TRENDS.
These ideas are certainly at odds with legislative measures which all
democratic legislatures seem to have found essential. As to the substantive
legal ideal of distributive justice, Professor Pound has summed up certain
modern trends in the phrase "socialisation of law".[112] They include widespread limitations on the *ius utendi,* the *ius abutendi* and the *ius disponendi*
of the owner of property; grave restrictions on the liberty of contract;
numerous provisions imposing liabilities upon individuals regardless of their
exercise of due care; provisions directed to securing to some classes of
persons benefits or opportunities for a full life, not otherwise available to

---

[107] See *ibid.,* noting especially on 182 the attack on the doctrine of vicarious
liability.

[108] Hayek, *Serfdom.*

[109] *Id.* 71ff., 81: "It is more important that there should be a rule applied always
without exceptions, than what this rule is". As seen in Stone, *Social Dimensions,* Ch. 3,
§9, and Ch. 14, §§15ff., however, the answer to bureaucratic power may have to be
found in tightening the limits of discretion and the safeguards of abuse. See Friedmann,
Changing Society 374ff. criticising the Dicey-type position from which Hayek is here
proceeding, and generally the literature cited in Stone, *op. et loc. cit.*

[110] *Id.* 81-82: "To produce the same result for different people, it is necessary
to treat them differently."

[111] In 1960 Hayek somewhat tempers his position, e.g., (1) by admitting differential
treatment that is not "arbitrary" and not favoured only by the beneficiaries (see his
Liberty 133ff., 154ff., 205ff.); (2) by dissociating himself both from liberty of contract
excesses and from social welfare legislation (see *ibid.* and 162ff.); (3) by admitting
(at 193-204, esp. 202-204) that his much-favoured *Rechtsstaat* ideal was less important
in practice than in theory. He seems to concede on 249 and 500 our own point
in Stone, *Province* 261 that his thesis would require reversal of trends in democratic
legislation of the last half-century. But he does not confront the other historical and
philosophical difficulties there raised (*id.* 261-64), nor those discussed below in Ch. 11
§§2ff. And see also E. F. Carritt, "Liberty and Equality" (1940) 56 *L.Q.R.* 61 as to
the philosophical background of the supposed conflict between these last two principles.

[112] See Pound, 1 *Jurisprudence* 429-459; Stone, *Social Dimensions,* Chs. 5, 6,
passim. Obviously, a central political drive of Hayek's argument is against such
trends as seen in the modern "welfare state". For a defence of "the welfare state"
against the "rule of law" notions of Dicey and Hayek's variation, see Friedmann,
cit. supra n. 109, c. xvi; Stone, *Social Dimensions,* Ch. 15, §§17-19.

them in the economic position in which they are placed; provisions spreading losses which happen to fall on individuals in the course of enterprises essential to the community, over the community as a whole—the insurance principle; provisions to prevent or mitigate the evil effects of the operation of economic competition, and of institutions produced by economic competition; the recognition as legal units of associations of individuals for the purpose of equalising bargaining power; provisions substituting the administrative process acting *proprio motu* to regulate social behaviour, for the judicial process acting usually on the motion of the individuals concerned; and the increasing use of broad standards instead of narrow rules as a means both of individualising justice and of providing for situations of unforeseeable complexity. Moreover, as has been seen, in the older legal traditions of both England and America, the ideal of "hands off" is perhaps the exception rather than the rule.[113]

As to the supposed inconsistency between discretionary standards and justice, or "true law", there is similar conflict with what equally appear to be legislative necessities. Legislative discriminations between concrete situations by broad standards requiring the exercise of discretion according to the merits of particular cases have been found, throughout the ages, an indispensable adjunct to the administration of justice. There may be instanced the *bonae fidei* action of the Roman law, the principles of "good faith" and "clean hands", "conscionableness", "fairness" and "due diligence" of equity; the "reasonableness" of care, or of notice of the common law; the "good morals" and "good faith" and "fault" of the German and French Civil Codes;[114] and the standard "arbitrary and unreasonable" under the American Constitution itself, whereby laws embodying the will and affecting the future of tens of millions of its inhabitants, may be struck down. In these and many other cases it has been the experience of men that discretion to discriminate between individual cases "on the merits", far from being unjust, was one vital method of attaining justice; far from being arbitrary may be necessary to avoid the arbitrary operation of general rules of law. And so it may be with legislation which discriminates in advance between different concrete situations and establishes standards for administrative application to this end. These needs should not be concealed by pointing to the dangers of State bureaucratic control of everyone's job, dangers readily recognised by all shades of democratic thought.[115]

§15. Inadequacy of "Impartiality" as a Criterion of Justice.[116] Preliminary to the main difficulty of the position under discussion it is to be observed that "the rule of law" vouched as a criterion of justice is attended

---

113 Curiously, Professor Hayek regards "true" law as more threatened today than "during the last few centuries". How he fitted the law of wage-fixing, price-fixing and regulation of admission to vocations of the sixteenth and seventeenth and eighteenth centuries, into his "true" conception of law is not made clear. Natural law still appears to make its own history, as it did in Blackstone's days. And see as to 18th and 19th century Pennsylvania, *infra* Ch. 4, §11; Stone, *Social Dimensions*, Ch. 7, §17.

114 See Stone, *Legal System*, Ch. 7, §11; *infra* Ch. 6, §1; and Ehrlich, *Sociology* 130ff.

115 See, e.g., on trade union hostility to nationalisation so based, and the related union commitment to collectivist *laissez faire*, B. C. Roberts, "Industrial Relations" in Ginsberg, *20th Century* 364, 385, 389.

116 *Cf.* the critique of "the sporting" theory of social control in Garlan, *Legal Realism* 177-88. And see Cohen, *Ethical Systems* 75ff.

by some confusion.[117] A rule for instance of income tax law applying only to persons with an income of less than £500 would be applicable without exception to all such persons. It might, however, still be a law "treating different people differently" with a view to increasing equality between them. According to the supposed requirement of certainty of application to all who are within its scope, it would be unobjectionable. But according to the requirement that law should not aim at material and substantive equality of different persons, it would be arbitrary and unjust. The supposed single quality of conformity to the "rule of law" is thus really two distinct qualities.

Now the quality of equal application of the rule to all persons within its scope is an attribute of every rule which is duly enforced, and can have reference to formal safeguards only.[118] As a criterion of justice of the rule itself it is unhelpful unless some qualification to it is admitted. It is presumed that no one would wish to sustain the proposition that all rules must apply equally to all human beings (including children) or even to all adults (including, e.g., lunatics). One might, however, require equal application to all persons whose situations, in relation to the reason of the rule, are indistinguishable from each other. The unjust might then be definable as "inequality without intrinsic differences".[119] Arbitrariness on this head would consist in failing to apply equally to all members of society who *as regards the reason* (or *purpose* or *policy* or *end*) of that law are similarly situated; or, in other words, all laws would have to apply equally to all human beings, unless there is good reason to the contrary. All this may seem plausible enough. But when in fact we do try to reduce "the rule of law" to this modified version of "equality", we too often have to invoke fairness, or goodness, or "the merits", or the "rational", if justice is to emerge.[120] The test of "equal application" has to be qualified in order to be applicable to concrete situations. A criterion for comparing those situations must still be found.

But in this, the most feasible sense, Hayek's proposition does not

---

[117] See also on other aspects of "the rule of law" Stone, *Social Dimensions*, Ch. 1, n. 266, Ch. 13, §§9-13; *id.*, *Quest for Survival* (1961) esp. c. i. *Cf.* N. S. Marsh, "The Rule of Law . . ." in A. G. Guest (ed.), *Oxford Essays in Jurisprudence* (1961) 222-264, esp. 245 as to "the equivocal position of equality".

[118] *Cf.* Garlan, *Legal Realism* 89-90; W. I. Jennings, Note (1940) 4 *M.L.R.* 134-35; Macmillan, *Law* 12, 14-15, read together. And see *infra* Ch. 11, §§2ff., where Chaim Perelman's position is also considered.

[119] This formulation is the object of Garlan's attack, *op. cit.* 92. It was necessary, however, for the Supreme Court to reverse earlier cases to hold in 1937 (*W. Coast Hotel Case, supra* n. 67, at 399-400) that legislative differentiation between men and women workers as regards wage-fixing was not "arbitrary and unreasonable"; and even then only by majority. See the dissent at 413.

[120] *Cf.* a main theme of MacDermott, *Protection from Power*. *Cf.* also, since the above was first written, the emergence of the same point in relation to so-called "modified utilitarianism", in which the test of goodness of consequences of an action is redefined to make clear that the critical point lies not in the consequences of the action, but in those of the rule or maxim of the action being made a universal rule, rather *à la* Kant. See J. Harrison, "Utilitarianism . . ." in Olafson, *Social Policy* 55-79, J. Rawls, "Justice as Fairness" *id.* 80-110. Yet almost simultaneously with these writings it was being shown that none of the many versions of the equality principle could be said to constitute a test of justice, even in terms of "fairness". See esp. R. Wollheim, "Equality and Equal Rights" in *id.* 111-127, esp. 125-27, Sir Isaiah Berlin, "Equality as an Ideal" in *id.* 128-150, esp. 129-130, 129ff., 132ff., 140ff. And for an impressive attempt to show how the equalitarian concept of justice may, without inconsistency, admit inequalities as just, and what are these "just inequalities", see G. Vlastos, "Justice and Equality" in R. Brandt, *Social Justice* (1962) 31, esp. 40ff., 70. As with the Trendelenburg line of thought from Kant, the transcending principle thus governing both the areas of just equalities and just inequalities becomes

help his argument. The "equal application" limb of this criterion is no longer absolute. It is qualified by reference to an assessment of the concrete situations of different individuals or classes of individuals. Furthermore, with this necessary qualification this limb flatly contradicts the other limb which, as has been seen, forbids the law to "treat different people differently", "on the merits" of their actual situation. It is not surprising, therefore, that other modern writers, basing themselves also on the concept of equality, have drawn from it a programme of democratic progress which calls for the most vigorous intervention by the state for the elimination of concrete inequalities which, they urge, at present prevent equality of opportunity in the political and economic spheres.[121] For once it is admitted that "equal" application is subject to concrete situations such as infancy or lunacy, no absolute line can be drawn excluding reference to concrete economic situations. The truth is that these modern polemics in terms of what "liberty" requires continue the two divergent interpretations of libertarianism which we have already examined.

§16. BASIC AMBIGUITIES OF THE IDEAL OF THE "FREE-WILLING INDIVIDUAL". Closer analysis indeed reveals an even greater proliferation of ambiguities in concepts of liberty as itself a supreme and sufficient end.[122] First, liberty may mean total absence of legal restraint, but then individuals would still be restrained from their desires by natural limitations of power and environment, and would be abjectly at the mercy of those with greater actual power. Few save the philosophical anarchists[123] would contend for such an ideal. For the rest of us, the question remains: If some activities must be restrained, on what basis shall they be selected? Admittedly, all other things being equal, restraint is an evil; but since all other things are rarely equal, absence of restraint cannot be a sufficient criterion of justice.[124] Second, it may mean a more positive freedom, for instance, to perfect or express oneself, but there has never been any agreement on such positive content, and if there ever were, it would shift the question from lack of restraint to the ultimate good in terms of which one is to be perfectly fulfilled.

Third, if salvation be sought in a Kantian-like formula of equal liberty under law, that is, liberty consistent with an equal liberty of others under a universal principle, the situation is no better. By a circumspect selection of universal principles, it has been well said, one can demonstrate on this theory that most things are good, and also that they are bad. On a principle as

the individual human life as an end in itself, "human worth" as such regardless of "merit". See the fuller discussion *infra* Ch. 11, §§1ff.

[121] See, e.g., Laski, *Politics* 152-165; Macmillan, *Law* 15; R. L. Hale, "Bargain Duress . . ." (1943) 43 *Columbia L.R.* 603. *Cf.* Dr. Lindsay's distinction (*Democratic State* 168) between the puritan ideal of spiritual liberty, and the economic liberty of *laissez faire*, which he thinks ran together in the nineteenth century only to come later into conflict.
    It may be added that the notion of "aiming at equality" as used by Hayek, *Serfdom*, may mean either "aiming to produce absolute equality", or "aiming to produce greater equality", or "aiming to produce absolute equality relative to merit", or "aiming to produce greater equality relative to merit". Mostly he seems to mean all at once, which of course he cannot have.
[122] *Cf.* Cohen, *Ethical Systems* 75-83.
[123] See Stone, *Social Dimensions*, Ch. 9, §6.
[124] *Cf.* as to economic liberty, Lindsay, *Democratic State* 106-107. Bentham himself was in some difficulties precisely on this point. See *infra* Ch. 4, §18.

to badness of "lies", "white lies" will be bad. But if the principle is about the goodness of "white lies", they may be good. On a universal principle that all brunettes may slap once daily the faces of all blondes, the law could be equally applied to all, but it would still be most palpably unfair to blondes.[125] To have value, the idea of "equality" between persons each of whom is uniquely situated in some respects, must be limited to particular comparable aspects of their various situations.[125a] This must ignore inequality as to other aspects. But equality in the chosen respects superimposed on inequality in the ignored respects may produce the most flagrant injustice. In Anatole France's oft-repeated words "the law in its majestic equality forbids the rich as well as the poor to sleep under the bridges, to beg in the streets and to steal bread".

Within narrower compass, of course, the ideal of equality or equal liberty before the law can be given definite and very important meaning, as in the procedural guarantees of Magna Carta, and the original sense of "due process of law".[126] In this sense, which is assuredly also the only precise *lawyer's* sense of Dicey's "rule of law", equality refers to procedural regularity, including the *opportunities* for vindicating those rights which each person considers himself to have under the substantive law, whatever it be. The ill-named "principles of natural justice" such as *"audi alteram partem"* and *"nemo iudex in sua causa",* resorted to by courts to check the proceedings of administrative or domestic *fori,* are of this nature.[127] But even within this narrow compass, it has well been pointed out,[128] no absolute identification of equal liberty with justice is possible. Justice may still be thwarted by *de facto* inequality between the parties in their respective skills and resources in using the procedure for harassment, delay or attrition of the opponent.

---

[125] Ross, *loc. cit. supra* n. 15, quotes as a constitutional guarantee which is thus vacuous the strongly Kantian formula of the Turkish Constitution of Jan. 10, 1945, s. 68: "Every Turk is born free and lives free. He has liberty to do anything that does not harm other persons. The natural right of the individual to liberty is limited by the liberties enjoyed by his fellow citizens. These limits are defined exclusively by the law." And *cf.* Cohen, *Ethical Systems* and the literature on the S. African constitutional crisis, discussed in Stone, *Legal System,* Ch. 3, n. 45, in which of course the present theoretical issues are highly practical ones. All this leaves aside the issues raised, e.g., by F. H. Knight, in *Nomos, Justice* 1, at 6n., of whether "equal liberty" is at all consistent with "universal laws". To act only on putatively "universal laws", he thinks, would strictly speaking "mean first willing away all effective freedom, use of judgment, and spontaneity". The principle that every human being must always be treated as an end, never as a means only, would be similarly violated. The only universal law consistent with "liberty" must be "that everyone shall follow his own judgment".

[125a] R. McKeon, "Justice and Equality" in *Nomos, Justice* 44-61 valiantly seeks to see the pitfalls in interplay of different kinds of equalities (and inequalities) as "an instrumentality of progress, not a defect of analysis". And see *infra* Ch. 11 for fuller discussion.

[126] Garlan, *Legal Realism* 89-97. *Cf.* later statements of this point in Berlin, *op. cit. supra* n. 120; Stone and Tarello, "Justice" 350ff., esp. 352.

[127] "It is chiefly the absence of this protective regularity and ceremonial which distinguishes a lynching party from a court . . ." (E. A. Ross, *Social Control* (1901, repr. 1908) 111). And see the constant stream of cases, commission reports and literature on administrative decision-making, referred to in Stone, *Social Dimensions,* Ch. 14, §§15-26.

[128] Garlan, *Legal Realism* 89-90; R. S. T. Chorley, Note (1940) 4 *M.L.R.* 138, 139.

CHAPTER 4

HEDONIST UTILITARIANISM[1]

I. PERSONAL AND INTELLECTUAL CONTEXT OF BENTHAM'S WORK

§1. LIFE AND CHARACTER OF JEREMY BENTHAM. Bentham's life began in 1748[2] in the early years of the industrial revolution, and ended the very year that the Reform Act of 1832 opened the door to a century of social and legal reform. He himself claims to have perceived the principle of "utility" at the age of eight.[3] He certainly entered Oxford at the early age of twelve, only to leave it, according to his biographer, Montague,[4] even more contemptuous and hostile to its place in English life than when

---

[1] The following is a selected reading list. BACKGROUND OF BENTHAM'S WORK: Dicey, *Law and Opinion* (1 ed. 1905) 69-210; J. Bentham, *Truth against Ashhurst*, in 5 *Works* 234ff.; *id., Indications respecting Lord Eldon, id.* 349-381; *id., A Comment on the Commentaries* (first printed, ed. C. W. Everett, 1928). LIFE AND RELATIONSHIP TO CONTEMPORARY THOUGHT: W. S. Holdsworth, *Some Makers of English Law* (1938) 248-256; *id.* ". . . Reform in the Law, 1793-1832" (1940) 56 *L.Q.R.* 33, 208, 340; N. D. Grundstein, "Bentham's Intro. to the Principles of Morals and Legislation" (1954) 2 *J. Publ. L.* 344-369; A. A. Mitchell, "Bentham . . ." (1923) 36 *Juridical R.* 248-284; F. C. Montagues ed. (1891) of Bentham's *Fragment on Government* (1766) 1-58; B. Horvath, *Théorie Anglaise du Droit* (1943, *Académie Hongroise des Sciences*) 247-489; C. M. Atkinson, *Jeremy Bentham* (1905) 126-155, 212-237; Coleman Phillipson, *Three Criminal Law Reformers* (1923) 26-106; G. Wallas, *Jeremy Bentham* (1922); C. W. Everett, *The Education of Jeremy Bentham* (1931). For the literary history of the *Theory of Legislation* see C. K. Ogden, *Bentham's Theory of Legislation* (1932) xxxi-xli; Bentham, *Theory* 1-87, 88-124, 239-275; *id., Principles of Morals and Legislation* (1780, repr. 1876) (covering much similar ground somewhat more briefly); *id.,* "Table of procedural delays" annexed to *Letters on the Proposed Reform in the Administration of Civil Justice in Scotland,* in 5 *Works* 53ff.; M. Mack, *Jeremy Bentham 1748-1792* (1962). For the literary history of the *Principles of Morals,* etc., in relation to *The Limits of Jurisprudence Defined* (first publ. 1945, and here cited as "Bentham, *Limits*") see C. W. Everett's Intro. to the latter, 4-30, esp. 8-10. ENGLISH LAW REFORM: Dicey, *Law and Opinion;* C. K. Ogden, *op. cit.* ix-x, 511-12; Dowrick, *Justice* 113-131; Keeton *et al., Bentham.* CRITIQUES AND GENERAL: H. Sidgwick, *Methods of Ethics* (5 ed. 1893) esp. bk. iii, c. v, bk. iv, c. iii, conveniently repr. Olafson, *Social Policy* 3-36; F. H. Bradley, *Ethical Studies* (2 ed. 1927) 84-141; M. P. Mack, *Jeremy Bentham* (1962); Baumgardt, *Bentham;* Cohen, *Ethical Systems* 185-220; 131-34; Leslie Stephen, *The English Utilitarians* (1900) vol. i; C. K. Ogden, *Bentham's Theory of Fictions* (1931); Jennings, "Utilitarianism"; G. Wallas, "Jeremy Bentham" (1923) 38 *Pol. Sc. Qu.* 45; *id.,* "Bentham as a Political Inventor" (1926) 129 *Contemporary Review* 308; Dowrick, *Justice* 106-113. BIBLIOGRAPHIES: C. W. Everett, in Halévy. *Radicalism* 522-546; R. Pound, *Outlines of a Course on Legislation* (1934) 55-56, and a shorter one in Pound, *Outlines* 13-14.

The modern standard work of reference on all the aspects enumerated in this note is Halévy, *Radicalism.* Halévy's work as well as that of Dicey is now subject to vital reservations in the light of recent studies in economic history and the history of economic doctrine. See especially Brebner, *"Laissez Faire";* Viner, "Bentham and Mill"; Hartz, *Economic Policy.* B. Russell, *Freedom and Organisation* (1934) cc. ix, x, xii, has good brief accounts of the Mills and Bentham.

[2] Also the year of Hume's *Inquiry Concerning Human Understanding;* the three volumes of the *Treatise of Human Nature* had appeared in 1739-1740.

[3] In F. de Fénelon's *Les Aventures de Télémaque* (1723) quoted C. M. Atkinson, *op. cit. supra* n. 1 at 11.

[4] F. C. Montague, *Bentham's Fragment on Government* (1891) 4-5: "Perhaps the University of Oxford has never sent out into the world another distinguished man who so heartily disliked her." On the state of English legal education and knowledge at the time see W. S. Holdsworth, work first cited *supra* n. 1, lect. xi.

he entered. Of legal forebears and destined for the Bar, he heard Blackstone's lectures in 1763 as a student of Lincoln's Inn, and was inspired with a violent repugnance which he expressed in his *Fragment on Government*.[5]

> If to this endeavour (to improve the laws) we should fancy any author, especially any author of great name, to be . . . a determined and persevering enemy, what should we say of him. We should say that the interests of reformation and through them the welfare of mankind were inseparably connected with the downfall of his work. . . . Such an enemy it has been my misfortune (and not only mine) to see or fancy at least I saw in the author of the celebrated Commentaries on the Law of England.

In this spirit it was, that he was called and went to the English Bar, a Trojan horse of reform within the gates of the chaotic, obsolete, unjust law of his time.[6] He saw his task as one of "clearing away . . . abominations", cleansing "the Augean stables" of the law, worth the devotion of "a thousand lives" if he had them. At twenty-two in his first known publication he was already demanding "new laws" in place of "the cobweb materials of ancient barbarism".[6a]

Bentham, as befitted his genius, had strange methods of work. His energy, vivid and overflowing in the gathering of materials, and the formulation of ideas, would often fail before his work was ready for the printer, so that great periods often elapsed between composition and publication.[7] He was

---

[5] The *Fragment* was a part of a larger MS., *A Comment on the Commentaries*, which Bentham detached and published separately. See the amusing account of the false attribution of the book to Dunning and Lord Camden in Montague, *op. cit.* 4-5. And see H. L. A. Hart, *op. cit. infra* n. 24.

[6] See the unpublished MS. quoted by C. W. Everett, in Bentham, *Limits* 3-4. Everett is correct therefore to stress "that Bentham, the enemy of law *as it is*, was himself a lawyer, and a scholarly one. His dislike came not from prejudice, but from familiarity." It is difficult, however, to believe that Bentham's position on Roman law is equally well grounded. See *op. cit.* 20-21. And *cf.* the late H. F. Jolowicz, in Keeton *et al., Bentham*. 1-19. Bentham is related to have had one brief, which he advised his client to settle and save his money. According to C. K. Ogden (*Bentham's Theory of Fictions* (1931)) he occupied much of his early years with his theory of fictions.

On practising lawyers in English legal reform see Laski, *Politics* 573-74; Macmillan, *Law* 246-47. Names like Brougham, Campbell and Birkenhead warn against over-generalisation. And see a good example of the judicial role in D. Seaborne-Davies, "Child-Killing in English Law" (1937) 1 *M.L.R.* 203, at 213ff.

On the similarly conservative role of the legal profession as a whole in American States see A. T. Vanderbilt, *Famous Firsts in Jersey Jurisprudence* (1956, Inaugural Lecture, Harvard Law School Ass. of N.J.), who points out that while the general vote on the radical judicial reform of 1947 in N.J. was 3½ to 1 in favour, not a single Bar Association supported it. But see *id.* on the earlier roles of "a few—very few—" individual lawyers (5). And see *id., Improving the Administration of Justice* . . . (1957, Marx Lectures, Univ. of Cincinnati) esp. 49ff.

[6a] A letter to *The Gazeteer and New Daily Advertiser*, Dec. 3, 1770, repr. Baumgardt, *Bentham* 551-54, at 552.

[7] Dumont took Bentham's rough notes and hacked, abridged or supplemented, and translated them into publishable shape. See his Preface to Bentham, *Theory*. Professor Ogden, in the Preface to his ed. of the same work, thinks he sometimes hacked ideas as well; and in the end the careful discussion by Baumgardt, *Bentham* 323-26, substantially agrees, while a great deal of his following treatment of the *Theory* (*id.* 326-369) is faintly disapproving. (His treatment of the *Deontology* (492ff.) is more generally critical; and this is no doubt coloured by his assessment at 491-92 of John Bowring's work as editor of that book. For a critique of Bowring's work as editor as compared with Dumont's work, see C. W. Everett, in Bentham, *Limits* (1945) 27-29). The *"Théorie des Peines"* now usually printed with the *Theory of Legislation* was held up from 1777 to 1797. *The Principles of Morals and Legislation*, finished in 1780, remained unpublished until 1789, while *A Comment on*

frequently diverted from his work in the law by inventiveness in other fields, of which his "panopticon"[8] (a most unpleasant labour-saving device for prisons and poor-houses) and his "chrestomatic school" (to impart useful as distinct from literary knowledge) were but two out of many examples. But for his devoted friend and editor, Dumont, even more of his work might never have seen the light.

Much of Bentham's energy was also devoted to foreign countries.[9] He placed great hopes in the despotic power of Catherine II, as an instrument for trying out his ideas; and tendered codes and advice both by correspondence and during his visit to Russia in 1785-7. He was in contact through Dumont with Mirabeau and other French revolutionary leaders, and vainly[10] prepared both a treatise on *Political Tactics* and a code for judicial organisation to aid French reform. He engaged on code-making for Bavaria and constitution-making for Mehemet Ali's Turkey. He was singularly indifferent to the political régime of his clients. Indeed, like the modern analytical jurists, whose pioneer he was, he thought of law as essentially imposed from above. In some senses, therefore, an autocracy was a better instrument for his purposes than a limited democracy, assuming always, of course, that he had the ear of the autocrat. For an autocrat acting on the disinterested principle of the greatest happiness of the greatest number would be at least rational and benevolent. Planning is easier for the planner in an autocracy; and Bentham was in one sense the first full-scale modern planner of the law.[11] It was only after the turn of the century, after the reaction against French revolutionary doctrines waned, and after a change of view on the capacity of the unreformed parliament to pursue the greatest happiness of the greatest number, that Bentham turned to the implications of his thought for political democracy.[12]

Professor Brebner has indeed pointed out, following insights of Halévy, that the identification of Bentham with individualism and *laissez faire* may be a myth springing from his tactical alliance, quite late in his life's work, with James Mill. More than twenty years after he made his basic affirmation of the greatest happiness principle as a guide for the legislator, Bentham

---

the Commentaries remained unpublished until 1928. It is because of Dumont's role that most of Bentham's works first appeared in French, as, for instance, the *Theory*. Bentham's *Limits* was originally written by him as pt. ii of the *Principles*, being intended as a treatise on the basic conceptions of law arising in pt. i. He had with difficulty been persuaded to publish the *Principles* nine years after it was printed. Regarding its reception as poor (it was a failure), he withheld pt. ii altogether, and turned his interest to the Panopticon. (See C. W. Everett, *op. cit.* 3ff., esp. 14.) On the general state of Bentham's publications *cf.* Baumgardt, *Bentham* 13-14 (bibli.).

[8] The English "panopticon" was abortive, but two were built, at St. Petersburg and in Illinois.

[9] See on Benthamite concern and influence in U.S. law, C. W. Everett, in Keeton *et al.*, *Bentham* 185-201; in the Indian codes, S. G. Vesey-Fitzgerald, *id.* 222-232; in international law, G. Schwarzenberger, *id.* 152-184, and in foreign law generally, K. Lipstein, *id.* 202-21. *Cf.* generally on Bentham's overseas influence Baumgardt, *Bentham* 4-7, esp. 4-6 on its slightness in Germany, and 7 n. for Bowring's verse lament of the contrast of Bentham's stature abroad with that in England.

[10] It was perhaps disappointments in these respects which helped to provoke his attack on revolutionary ideology in *Anarchical Fallacies*, 2 *Works* 491.

[11] *Cf.* the remarks of Lindsay, *Democratic State* 140-42. The late Sir Frederick Pollock argued that there was no necessary relation between the imperative theory of law and the utilitarian theory of justice. There is, indeed, no "necessary" one in a logical sense, but there is a very likely one empirically; and they go together in Bentham and Ihering, both of whom were advocates of active reforming legislative activity. On planning by law, see Stone, *Social Dimensions*, Ch. 15.

[12] Halévy, *Radicalism* 490-91. And see *id.* 250, 254ff., fixing the date at 1808.

in 1808 became acutely convinced of the self-preference principle, namely, that those who govern seek their own happiness, not that of those whom they govern.[13] If, therefore, his main affirmation was to be saved, the interests of the governors must be identified with those of the community; and the late alliance of Bentham with the elder Mill to press franchise reform was aimed to produce this result. This alliance, on Bentham's side, was a means to the end of ensuring that Parliament acted for the happiness of the greatest number, if necessary by collectivist legal intervention. For the elder Mill, however, it was to be a step to implementing Adam Smith's ideal of economic *laissez faire* and legislative hands off, now pressed by the rising entrepreneurial class. This ideal assumed that the interests of individuals, when pursued without the distortions arising from legal restraints, would show *natural* mutual "harmony" or "identity", yielding maximum benefits for all. This assumption was not shared by Bentham and his disciples such as Chadwick; they recognised that individual desires often conflict in a manner and degree which require "harmony" to be produced *artificially* by legislative interference and guidance.

This basic difference between Bentham and the elder Mill was covered over (Brebner suggests) by the tactical success of Mill in preaching *laissez faire* under the name of Benthamism.[14] This created a myth that Bentham stood for *laissez faire,* which Dicey's brilliant study of *Law and Opinion in England in the Nineteenth Century* seemed to confirm. But Dicey (it is urged) was deceived by Mill's version, or he failed to read Bentham's own pronouncements sufficiently, or sufficiently open-mindedly. The intervention-ism seen, for example, in Bentham's *Constitutional Code* (1820-1832),[15] and its influence on mid-century legislation, was interpreted (and thus obscured) as a mere manifestation of "humanitarianism". Yet, in historical fact, the Factory Act, 1833, the Mines Acts, 1842 and the Ten Hours Act, 1847, as well as the steady stream of interventionist changes in the Poor Law and the law of public health and police, were not only parts of what Dicey called a "collectivist" programme. They were also parts of such a programme well in line with Benthamite thought. They were not mere humanitarian vagaries in Benthamite *laissez faire,* but natural products of the strain of collectivist interventionism in Bentham, contrasting sharply with the doctrinaire economic *laissez faire* of the age. It was thus misleading to date "collectivism" only from the 1860's, or to regard it as a reaction against "Benthamite *laissez faire*".

§2. CONSPECTUS OF BENTHAM'S WORKS ON ENGLISH REFORM. The wide range of Bentham's critical and constructive work (of which most but not all was collected in Bowring's volumes) included general attacks on what Dicey has called Blackstonian optimism, such as the *Comment on the Com-mentaries,* as well as the *Fragment;* on the criminal law and administration and the theories of punishment, as in his *View of the Hard Labour Bill,* and

---

13 Brebner, "*Laissez Faire*" 62ff. Halévy, *Radicalism* 147, traces this apprehension of Bentham's as far back as 1788. *Cf.* as to Bentham's late interest in franchise reform, Viner, "Bentham and Mill" 363-64.

14 The younger Mill (*Autobiography,* ed. J. S. Coss (1924) 73, 142-43) seems to have recognised this dualism.

15 Which Brebner ("*Laissez Faire*" 63ff.) calls "that forbidding, detailed blue-print for a collectivist state", later executed in part by "that bureaucrat of purest essence, Edwin Chadwick", the disciple and collaborator of Bentham. See *infra* n. 148.

his *Theory of Punishment;* attacks on corruption, procrastination and in-efficiency in the administration of justice, especially in Chancery, as in his *Protest Against Legal Taxes, Rationale of Evidence* and *Elements of the Art of Packing Juries;* attacks on governmental inefficiency, and proposals for political reform, as in his *Radical Reform Bill* (on the suffrage), and his *Pauper Management* (on Pitt's proposals for poor law reform), and the important though later much neglected *Constitutional Code* (1820-32); and finally attacks on restraints on individual liberty, of which the best known are *The Defence of Usury*, written between 1785 and 1787, and *Truth against Ashhurst.* His most famous systematic works, the *Principles of Morals and Legislation,* published in English in 1789, and the *Theory of Legislation,* first published in French in 1802,[16] as *"Traités de Législation Civil et Pénale"*, remain to be mentioned.

More will be said later of the effectiveness of this work. Here it is to be noted that Bentham's penetrating analyses and powerful invective hindered as well as helped his cause. His attack on Blackstone, for instance, made for him both enemies and friends, and so did his later vitriolic attacks on Lord Eldon and the Court of Chancery.[17] The friends included Lord Mansfield during his early life, and in later life Lord Shelburne, Sir Samuel Romilly, and Lords Landsdowne and Brougham, as well as Wilberforce. These and other reformers, for instance the great administrator, Edwin Chadwick, at one time or another, were inspired to act as the political instruments of his reforming schemes. After the publication of the *Principles* in 1789, a small group of disciples and associates had appeared which was to become very wide in the latter part of his life, including the elder Mill, and the son who was later to write *On Liberty,* a classical formulation of individualist utilitarianism.[18] We have already referred to the problematics of *laissez faire* and interventionist trends in the first half of the nineteenth century arising from James Mill's alliance with Bentham. But the mutual support and comfort of these thinkers and the intellectual circles which surrounded them is beyond doubt.

Certainly the full impact of Bentham's ideas was not to be felt in England during Bentham's lifetime. Peel's criminal law reforms were but a meagre beginning. Much was realised in the half-century after his death, but even today much of his grand scheme which was worthy of attention remains unrealised.

§3. INTELLECTUAL CONTEXT: REACTION TO NATURAL LAW. Benthamism stood in a fourfold relation to then existing thought. First, Bentham reacted most vigorously against natural law thinking which had reached its decadent stage during his life, and which he never understood even in its creative phases. Nevertheless, second, he took over uncritically one feature of the decadence of natural law, namely, a supreme faith in the power to lay

---

[16] The *Theory* includes (1) "Principles of Legislation". This covers the ground of the first six Chapters of the *Principles;* (2) "Principles of the Civil Code"; (3) "Principles of the Penal Code". See Dumont's Introduction, Hildreth's transl. (5 ed. 1887) 6. There are other changes. See for literary history Halévy, *Radicalism* 514-521, esp. 518.

[17] See "Indications concerning Lord Eldon" (1825) in 5 *Works* (Bowring's ed.) 349-81. Bentham's relations of conflict or co-operation with contemporary intellectual and political figures and movements are admirably woven into Halévy's exposition.

[18] On their relation to the ruling class, see M. J. P. Plamenatz, ". . . Philosophical Radicalism" in Ginsberg, *20th Century* 27-43.

down by conscious effort, once and for all, a system of law for a given society.[19] Third, the utilitarian criterion was already sufficiently prominent to have influenced (though perhaps only in terminology) the later natural lawyers, and to have received its classical formulation in Hume. Fourthly, even the hedonistic calculus of utility in terms of pains and pleasure had been well canvassed in relation to law reform, for instance by Beccaria.

Natural law was the subject of many biting Benthamite comments.[20] While Bentham well understood and denounced the intuitive quality of natural law thinking, his understanding of its historic role was superficial. He challenged the Grotian view of the "nature of man", pointing out in refutation that law must repress and control natural tendencies of rapacity and the like, and could scarcely therefore be based on them.[21] Further, like Austin, he strongly criticised the natural lawyers' assimilation of positive law to natural law, without recognising that there precisely, in psychological terms, lay much of its creative power.

So too it was entirely proper for Bentham and Austin, both of whom interested themselves in schemes of analysis of legal concepts, as well as in the problem of justice, to view command and enforcement rather than conformity to the moral sense as the essence of law for analytical purposes. But it argued grave misunderstanding for them to refute the natural lawyers' stress on justice as the essence by an argument from their own imperative premises.[22] Indeed no one who understood natural law as a part of the social process could have attacked it as sweepingly as these writers did. Such misunderstandings aside, however, the conflict of substance between Bentham and the natural lawyers was clear. He rebelled, like Kant, above all against their intuitionist position, their assumption that reason applied directly to a given type of situation would provide an answer generally acceptable.

> I propose a treaty of peace with the partisans of natural rights. If "nature" really made such and such a law those who lay it down with so much confidence and have modestly undertaken to interpret it, must believe that nature had some reason for making it. Would it not be safer, shorter and more convincing to give us these reasons at once rather than to offer us the *ipse dixit* of the unknown legislator as being of sufficient authority?

---

[19] In this respect, his view of codification was not dissimilar to that underlying the natural law code of Frederick the Great, the Austrian Civil Code and the Napoleonic Codes themselves. He did not, in this respect, realise the full significance of his own teachings as to the dependence of law on circumstances of time and place. See *infra* §4.

[20] And see *supra* Ch. 2, §25. He thought that what the iusnaturalist would have positive law do for natural and divine law "seems to be much the same as Mr. Andrew in the Puppet-shew does for Mr. Punch: say his good things over again for him, for fear any of them should escape the company . . .". (*A Comment on the Commentaries*, 53-54; *cf. id.* 71, 78ff.)

[21] This is consistent with the modern view, which does not see Bentham's position as that of *laissez faire* and the Manchester School, but rather as regarding utility as *usually* best achieved without State action, but without objection on principle to State intervention when this is necessary. See esp. Viner, "Bentham and Mill" esp. 361ff.; Brebner, *"Laissez Faire"*. On this view the inconsistency attributed by Halévy to Bentham, that on the level of economics Bentham assumed a "natural" harmony of interests, while recognising that on the legal level the harmony must be imposed, is avoided. *Cf.* Halévy, *Radicalism* 11-17, 53-54, 89ff., 499ff., and generally pt. iii, c. iv. Lindsay, *Democratic State* 138ff., suggests that there was a creative ambiguity in Bentham's position. And see *infra* n. 58.

[22] See, e.g., Austin's comments (1 *Lectures* (5 ed.) 217) on Ulpian's definition in *Dig.* 1, 10. See Stone, *Legal System*, Ch. 2.

Such an assumption, it has been said, is only tolerable when circumstances force large masses of men into a common attitude on fundamental matters. Many of these circumstances had disappeared by Bentham's time, and his scorn of natural law was thus as much a mark of changing social and economic conditions as it was of a different temperament.[23] These changed circumstances called for intense and constant ethical criticism of existing law. Yet the apparent monopoly by "natural law" of the function of ethical validation of law, especially when combined with the Blackstonian tendency to identify the common law with natural law, or at least with what was indifferent under natural law (and therefore, by an unwarranted inference, required under natural law), amounted to a cloak immunising the common law from ethical criticism.[24] It was Bentham's determination to tear aside this cloak which made both natural law and Blackstone the targets of his bitterest assaults.

§4. INTELLECTUAL CONTEXT: UTILITARIAN ETHICS. Though utilitarianism in ethics is traceable far into the origins of philosophy, it was only in the eighteenth century, after the wane of both authoritarianism and the rebel natural law, that it came into its own. Hume, the leading English utilitarian philosopher, wrote his *Essays Moral and Political* in 1741-42. Undoubtedly his central thesis that the moral quality of an act was its tendency to produce happiness for the actor (recognising at the same time that man, being a social animal, may be made happy by the happiness of others) was fashionable when Bentham was in his studious 'teens. Bentham, indeed, has told us that he drew the phrase "the greatest happiness of the greatest number" from Priestley's *Essay on Government,* a pamphlet published in 1768, and that when he first read it he "cried out, as it were, in an inward ecstasy like Archimedes on the discovery of the fundamental principle of hydrostatics".[25]

But it is clear that utilitarianism pressed in upon Bentham from other quarters as well. The famous *Lettres Persanes* of the French rationalist Montesquieu, was published as long before as 1731. It consisted of a series of brilliant commentaries by a supposedly Persian visitor, endowed with the eyes of an ideal rational being, on the western civilisation of the time. Among his strictures many were directed to the cruelties, abuses and futilities of the criminal justice of the time, leading up to an assertion of the need

---

[23] On the mutal reinforcement of natural law and *laissez faire* notions in U.S. courts later in the century, see *supra* Ch. 2, and Ch. 3, §§8ff. And *cf.* the materials collected in Simpson-Stone, 1 *Law and Society* 569-584.

[24] *Cf.* H. L. A. Hart, "Blackstone's Use of Natural Law" (1956) *Butterworth's S. Afr. L.R.* 169-174; D. J. Boorstin, *The Mysterious Science of the Law* (1941). And *cf.* on Bentham's attack Baumgardt, *Bentham* 92ff.

[25] 1 *Deontology* (ed. Bowring, 1834) 298ff.; but see as to this account Baumgardt, *Bentham* 36 n. For a detailed pedigree of the "utility" principle see *id.* 35-39; and on the quantification of pleasures and pains see *id.* 224-27. On the influence of Hartley and Hume, and the even closer foreshadowing (with which Bentham himself, however, was apparently unfamiliar) by Francis Hutcheson. *cf.* Halévy, *Radicalism* 7-11, 13, H. A. Bedau, "Justice and Classical Utilitarianism". in *Nomos. Justice* 284, 297ff., and B. Russell, *Freedom and Organisation* (1934) 107. On the link with Benjamin Franklin *via* Priestley, see Viner, "Bentham and Mill" 368; and for an amusing claim to angelic revelation see MS. U.C. written about 1780 and now printed as App. I to Baumgardt, *op. cit.* 549-550: "I dreamt t' other night that I was a founder of a sect: . . . *utilitarians.* . . . As I was musing one night . . . an angel flew in at my window. . . . He put into my hands a book which he said he had just been writing with the quill of a phoenix. it (*sic*) was lettered on the back Principles of legislation. . . ."

for a rational theory of punishment, taking into account the *mœurs* and the accustomed sensibilities of a particular people at a particular time.[26] The relation between law and the manners (*mœurs*) of the particular people at the particular time thus presupposed was, of course, the main theme of Montesquieu's later work, *L'Esprit des Lois*[27] published in 1748, and the relativist view of just law thus implied is obviously closely related to the break from natural law to utilitarianism. Bentham, indeed, dated his first conversion to philosophy from his perusal of the *Lettres Persanes* in 1761,[28] and Montesquieu's influence was clear. For instance, in theory at any rate, Bentham adopted the thesis that law is not to be judged as good or bad in the abstract, but only in relation to the manners, customs and physical environment of the particular people.[29]

§5. INTELLECTUAL CONTEXT: THE HEDONISTIC CALCULUS. The ecstasy with which Bentham read the "greatest happiness" principle in Priestley in 1768 was belated, for this exact phrase had been used as the ultimate test of justice by the Italian penal reformer Beccaria in 1764, in his *Treatise on Crimes and Punishments*.[30] "Good legislation," Beccaria had further said, "is the art of conducting man to the maximum of happiness and to the minimum of misery, if we may apply this mathematical expression to the good and evil of life." Beccaria appears to have influenced Bentham both by acting as a channel for continental thought like that of Montesquieu, and more especially by proposing a measure of happiness in terms of pleasure and pain.

Montesquieu's work, and in particular the *Lettres Persanes*, profoundly influenced Beccaria, whose *Treatise on Crimes and Punishments* was first read to a group of young Milanese intellectuals. Beccaria lacked experience, either in law generally or in criminal law, but his book, published in 1764, had enormous success, being taken up by Voltaire[31] and the Encyclopaedists

---

26 *Lettre* 81: "In a state the greater or less cruelty of punishment does not produce obedience to the laws. In countries where punishment is moderate they are feared as much as where they are tyrannical and horrible. . . . Imagination adapts itself to the *mœurs* of the country one lives in; eight days imprisonment and light fine, are as impressive to the mind of a European brought up in a country of gentle manners as the loss of an arm to an Asiatic."

27 Incidentally to his main thesis Montesquieu expounded ideals of liberty, tolerance and humanity, attacked the degeneracy and secrecy of contemporary criminal procedure and generally linked the problems of criminal justice with those of political liberty. Baumgardt, *Bentham* 41-42, perhaps follows the later Bentham too closely in underestimating the debt to Montesquieu.

28 Letter to Villemain, quoted J. A. Farrer, cited *infra* n. 30 at 6. Amusingly enough, Montesquieu admired almost to excess the English constitutional system which Bentham later attacked so vigorously.

29 J. Bentham, "On the Influence of Time and Place in Matters of Legislation", 1 *Works* (ed. *cit.*) 71.

30 Transl. in J. A. Farrer, *Crimes and Punishments* (1880) Intro. to the *Treatise* c. i (*loc. cit.* 117-18): "We shall see, if we open histories, that laws, which are or ought to be covenants between free men, have generally been nothing but the instrument of the passions of some few men, or the result of some accidental and temporary necessity. They have never been dictated by an unimpassioned student of human nature, able to concentrate the actions of a multitude of men to a single point of view, and to consider them from that point alone—*the greatest happiness divided among the greatest number*". For biography of Beccaria (b. 1738) see C. Phillipson, *Three Criminal Law Reformers* (1923) 3-26, and J. A. Farrer, *op. cit.* cc. i and ii. On the influence of Beccaria, Priestley and Paley, *cf.* Halévy, *Radicalism* 21-23; but see on Paley, C. W. Everett, in Bentham, *Limits* 11-12.

31 See M. T. Maestro, *Beccaria and Voltaire as Reformers of Criminal Law* (1942).

in France.[32] This is not entirely explained as the result of pure virtuosity. "The age of reason" was already agitated by the anomalies and barbarities of criminal justice;[33] Beccaria gave a rallying point in France as Bentham later did in England.

His work in a field close to Bentham's main interests therefore reinforced the influences in the direction of utilitarianism. In addition, however, Bentham was more specifically indebted to him for the idea of calculating pains and pleasures as a measure of utility, for the hedonistic calculus as a measure of happiness.[34] He tells us that "it was from Beccaria's *Treatise on Crimes and Punishments* that I drew, as I well remember, the first idea of this principle (of computation of pains and pleasures) by which the precision and clearness and incontestableness of mathematical calculation are introduced for the first time into the field of morals—the field to which, in its own nature, they are applicable with a propriety no less incontestable". In Mr. Montague's pithy sentence[35] "nothing remained for Bentham but to embody Hume's theory in Beccaria's formula"; and, of course (we must surely add) to translate this eighteenth century thought into a programme of social action.[36]

II. ENGLISH SOCIAL, ECONOMIC AND LEGAL BACKGROUND OF BENTHAM'S WORK

§6. GENERAL OBSOLESCENCE OF THE LAW AND THE INADEQUACY OF THE JUDICIAL SYSTEM FOR THE TASK OF REFORM.[37] When Bentham began to write, the creative influence of natural law in the strict law systems of the continent had virtually ended; and in England, too, the fertilising streams of influence from equity and the law merchant were shortly to run dry.[38] Whereas, on the continent, natural law had begun to inspire

---

[32] It is cited in the first ed. of Blackstone's *Commentaries* in 1765, only one year later (bk. iv, c. i). Its final form was translated into English by J. A. Farrer in his *Crimes and Punishments* (1880). See *id.* 29-68, for Beccaria's influence on legislative reforms and on reform in England. It had been translated into most European languages, and Catherine II had transcribed it into her Code.

[33] See C. Phillipson, *op. cit. supra* n. 30, 27-55.

[34] In a sense, indeed, both Beccaria and Bentham were indebted for this to the French philosopher of hedonism, Helvétius, who flourished 1715-1771. Helvétius' *De L'Esprit,* published in 1758 (first English transl. 1807) was in some degree a rival to the *L'Esprit des Lois.* Its significant thesis from the present viewpoint was that all human faculties may be reduced to physical sensation, and that self-interest founded on the love of pleasure and the fear of pain was the mainspring of judgment, action and affection. It may, indeed, not be far-fetched to trace the famous phrase "the greatest happiness of the greatest number" from Helvétius through Beccaria and Priestley to Bentham. Of Helvétius (on whom see Baumgardt, *Bentham* 37-40, 61, 91, 167-68) Bentham said that "What Bacon was to the physical world, Helvétius was to the moral" (MS. U.C. quoted Halévy, *Radicalism* 19); and that "The idea of considering happiness as resolvable into a number of (individual) pleasures, I took from Helvétius. . . ." He added that Cicero's contrary doctrine in the *Tusculan Disputations* is "nothing but a heap of nonsense" (MS. U.C. now printed Baumgardt, *op. cit.* 554-566 at 557). See *ibid.* on Bentham's debt to Beccaria; and on the influence of Maupertuis see *ibid.,* and the MS. U.C. repr. *id.* 566ff.

[35] *Op. cit. supra* n. 4, 33-34.

[36] *Cf.* Viner, "Bentham and Mill" 360.

[37] The classical account in Dicey, *Law and Opinion,* needs correction by reference to the works of J. B. Brebner, L. Hartz and J. Viner cited *supra* n. 1. And see R. H. Graveson, in Keeton *et al., Bentham* 104ff.

[38] See R. Pound, "The Decadence of Equity" (1905) 5 *Columbia L.R.* 20; H. G. Hanbury, "The Field of Modern Equity" (1929) 45 *L.Q.R.* 196, 207-13.

legislation by autocratic rulers like Frederick the Great of Prussia, Catherine II of Russia, and the Austrian Emperor, in England the great legislative movement for reform of criminal law had not begun.

The whole field of English law was confused and encumbered by obsolete rules created for a feudal land system and a pastoral agricultural and petty industrial economy. It is true that the judges both at common law and in equity had succeeded in making many pressing reforms through the system of precedent, and that belatedly, through Lord Mansfield, the law merchant was being incorporated into the common law. But the productiveness of these sources was limited, and its limits were almost reached when Bentham wrote. With Lord Eldon's Chancellorship, so constant a target of Bentham's shafts, equity ceased to be a main dynamic force: its "decadence" had set in. Though personalities played their part in this, the deeper causes lay perhaps in limitations of judicial techniques, which could build upon existing foundations, but could not, when the whole building proved inadequate, raze the whole and build anew.[39] The success of Mansfield was qualified by similar difficulties of judicial techniques and in addition by the unwillingness of his colleagues and successors to develop or even accept the principles he introduced.[40] Only Parliament could deal adequately with the problem of reform,[41] a state of affairs which perhaps confirmed Bentham's own general prejudices in favour of the legislative power.

The impotence of the courts as instruments of reform was increased by the state of their organisation and procedure. The court system itself was a tangle of fictions and overlappings which concealed and often disturbed the fairly orderly allocation of business beneath.[42] The Chancery and the common law courts still operated in watertight compartments. Appellate instances were even less satisfactory,[43] and virtually absent in criminal cases;[44] fictions and survivals pervaded procedure.[45] Corruption was by no means absent in the courts, and the abuses, procrastinations and extortion

---

[39] See, e.g., Dicey's treatment of the limitations on the development of married women's property in equity, in *Law and Opinion* (2 ed. 1914) 371-398. Bentham in his later years advocated the emancipation of women, though (for him) with unusual caution. See Baumgardt, *Bentham* 466-68.

[40] On Mansfield see Stone, *Legal System*, Ch. 7, §2. Bentham greatly admired and defended Mansfield's work. See Baumgardt, *Bentham* 18-20, and C. K. Ogden, *Jeremy Bentham* (1932) 56-57.

[41] *Law and Opinion* (1 ed. 1905) 166. See generally on the following survey Lord Brougham's famous speech on the state of the law of England in 1828 (2 *Speeches of Lord Brougham* (1838) 319ff.).

[42] The civil jurisdiction of the King's Bench even for debt or contract still rested on the fiction that the defendant had committed a trespass or was in the custody of the marshal. That of the Exchequer in civil cases between subject and subject was largely concurrent, and still rested on the fiction that the cause of action arose in St. Mary-le-Bow or *quominus*—that the plaintiff creditor was unable to pay his debts to the King.

[43] There were unnecessary divergencies according to whether appeal was from the common law, the equity or the admiralty side.

[44] There was no regular instance of appeal, a fact of deadly significance when 160 offences were still punishable capitally.

[45] The staple realty action of ejectment was based on a childish series of fictions, abolished by the Common Law Procedure Act, 1852; the barring of the entail involved refinements and absurdities, abolished by the Fines and Recoveries Act, 1833, which still remain the delight of the legal historian. Trial by battle was still an admissible procedure until 1817, and privilege of clergy was to persist until 1833. A party to a suit or his wife were still incompetent to testify, except by deposition in equity, and a prisoner accused of felony was still denied counsel until the Felony Act, 1836. It is chastening to recall that outlawry was abolished in English law by the Administration of Justice (Miscellaneous Provisions) Act, 1928, s. 12.

of fees and costs familiar to every reader of Dickens, which were to inspire some of Bentham's bitterest polemics, were still tolerated.

§7. CRIMINAL AND PENAL LAW AND ADMINISTRATION.[46] The barbarism of the substantive law of crime conformed in large measure to the contemporary European pattern. On the continent that pattern was dissolving under the influence of men like Beccaria, Montesquieu, and Voltaire, and under the stimulus of French revolutionary liberalism. In 1800 there were 160 capital offences under English law: it was to take fifty years to reduce the number to two. The whipping of women was not abolished until 1820, nor the pillory until 1837. Hanging in chains continued until 1834, and the public execution of murderers even later. Yet neither a prisoner nor his spouse was allowed to give evidence on his behalf until the Criminal Evidence Act, 1898; a prisoner accused of capital felony was not allowed counsel until 1836; and until 1907 there was no regular instance of appeal in criminal cases, and no means whatever of quashing a verdict based on insufficient evidence. The foul conditions of the prisons were notorious. It was only by the most devious and doubtful expedients, like the fictitious extension of the scope of benefit of clergy, and the frequent refusals of juries to convict, that such a state of things was made tolerable at all.

§8. REAL PROPERTY AND COMMERCIAL LAW. The land law presented, perhaps, the most extreme example of changed substance hidden by unchanged form. The idea of a man's land as his absolute property, like his watch, is only the latest of three ideas which have successively moulded the land law. In essence, it had begun in the feudal period as an aspect of government, services being provided to the king in return for tenure of land, which was thus not property in the modern commercial sense. The three centuries prior to the Statute of Tenures, 1660, saw a transition of the land law to suit a new function of land as a basis of family stability and organisation. From about 1660 to 1833, the land law had been moulded to its new function, on the basis of the system of estates, by the Court of Chancery's invention of the trust and the complex of devices known as the family settlement. This transformation of the nature of land had taken place by devious fiction-ridden procedures, only occasionally aided by statutes to clear away the debris. Most of the debris remained, and a major problem crying out for attention in Bentham's time was the expurgation from the law of the fictions and anomalies used by ingenious lawyers to kill the political idea of land, and realise the family idea. This purging process was only to begin with the Report of the Real Property Commissioners in 1828 and the Fines and Recoveries Act, 1833, and was only virtually completed in England by the property legislation of 1922-25. But this was only a part of the urgent need for reform. The family idea of the function of land was itself out of tune with the developing needs of Bentham's age. The industrial revolution brought to the fore the role of land as a commodity, marked by the retreat of family estates before factory sites, and the rise of the industrial middle class, for whom land was worth its market value, no more—no less.

It was perhaps in respect of the rise of commerce in the sixteenth, seventeenth and eighteenth centuries that least credit was due to common

---

[46] See Radzinowicz, 2 *Criminal Law* 33-427.

law judges for successful adaptation of the law. Merchants did not trust the lawyers; while the judges turned up their noses at the new-fangled customs of the merchants. During his Chief Justiceship from 1756 to 1788, Lord Mansfield, it is true, incorporated the law merchant bodily into English law by a brilliant and effective use of juries of merchants. Mansfield's work, however, was done during Bentham's lifetime: and it still left much for the reformist zeal of Bentham to work upon.[47]

In two respects, indeed, commercial law remained particularly unsatisfactory throughout Bentham's life. The first was as to debtors and bankruptcy. The horrors of persecution and imprisonment of debtors are sufficiently familiar to the reader of Dickens. As to the bankruptcy court, a writer of 1837 tells us that it was avoided like the plague, since it endlessly delayed creditors, drained estates, and vexed the unfortunate. The law of joint trading, too, left much to be desired. The regulated companies of the sixteenth and seventeenth centuries had no common stock, nor did they usually share profits. The joint stock company, in which the members contributed to the joint stock and drew profits in return, marked the beginning of modern joint trading. But in Bentham's time it was a mere partnership and could not sue or be sued as such; its human members alone could sue and be sued, and each for the whole debt, with fantastic possibilities of fraudulent manipulation and unjust results where membership ran into hundreds and even thousands.[48] The device of juristic personality with limited liability of members, freely available to all traders at nominal cost, subject to conformity to formal requirements, and to supervision by public officials of the corporate affairs, was still to be invented. Incorporation could only be by special Act or Royal Charter, both limited in practice (because *inter alia* of expense) to public utilities like railways, canals, banks and insurance companies.[49]

§9. LAW OF MASTER AND SERVANT. Perhaps the most abject failure of English law, as the nineteenth century opened, was in the law governing the relation of master and servant in industry. As the factory of the early industrial revolution competed with petty home industries labour conditions degenerated rapidly. The employment of children of five and less for twelve or thirteen hours a day exclusive of meals, and of women to push trucks in coal mines under conditions and for periods which have since been forbidden for pit ponies, are among the notorious crimes of the time. The position was indeed to degenerate further as the price and wage regulating machinery dating from the Elizabethan legislation was swept away before

[47] It needed an "Act for Giving Remedy upon Promissory Notes" 3 & 4 Anne, c. 9, overriding the decision of Holt C.J. in *Buller* v. *Crips* (1703) 6 Mod. 29, to overcome the courts' resistance to such instruments. On matters of insurance Elizabeth in 1601 tempted merchants into a law court created specially for them, but in vain. See F. D. MacKinnon, "Origins of Commercial Law" (1936) 52 *L.Q.R.* 30.

For good brief accounts see C. H. S. Fifoot, *English Law and its Background* (1932); W. S. Holdsworth, *op. et loc. cit. supra* n. 1.

[48] A device of appointing trustees to sue and be sued on behalf of all members provided relief against some of these difficulties.

[49] For important and novel aspects of the transition between the eighteenth century corporation, and that which bases the so-called "corporate system" of modern trade and industry, including the early alignment of "individual" along with "public" enterprise against the "charter corporation" see Hartz, *Economic Policy, passim*. And see Stone, *Social Dimensions*, Ch. 7, §§17ff.

the energy of the new industrial entrepreneur class,[50] while at the same time workers seeking to protect their standards by collective bargaining were struck at through the Combination Act, 1800,[51] and judicial interpretation of the law. The common law as to injuries sustained by a workman in the course of his employment left the loss on the workman unless the master was personally negligent, ignoring the now well-recognised fact that under modern conditions there is a high normal hazard of industry not really attributable to anyone's fault, and that master and man rarely work side by side. The doctrine that the vicarious liability of the master did not extend to the case where one workman was injured by the negligence of a fellow workman of the same master, aggravated the position.[52] This doctrine of common employment was later to be limited somewhat in application by the Employer's Liability Act, 1880, and mitigated by statutory remedies under the Workmen's Compensation Act, 1897; it was but an addition to the incongruity and obsolescence of the law of master and servant as it was in Bentham's time.

In this state of the law of industrial bargaining and injuries, moreover, the regulation of factory and labour conditions was barely begun. The Health and Morals of Apprentices Act, 1802, was only the forerunner of that long series of factory acts designed to set minimum standards of well-being for workers in industry. And until the Factory Act, 1833 (commonly called Hobhouse's Act) set maximum hours (still inhumanly high according to modern standards) for all child workers, apprentice or not, in cotton mills, there was no recognition of the problem of labour conditions as distinct from the pauper question.

§10. GENERAL SOCIAL AND POLITICAL ATMOSPHERE OF THE PERIOD. Bentham's revolt against this state of the law must have been further exacerbated by what Professor Dicey has called its "Old Toryism" and legislative quiescence between 1760 and 1830.[53] This period, Dicey has pointed out, was marked by a placid and priggish "satisfaction with all things English". To Blackstone England appeared to have "a constitution, so wisely contrived, so strongly raised, and so highly finished, it is hard to speak with that praise, which is justly and severely its due". Paley, surveying

---

[50] They were to draw moral support from the Benthamite advocacy of the removal of legal restraints. The whole matter is more fully considered in Stone, *Social Dimensions*, Ch. 7. See for a brief modern account B. Russell, *op. cit. supra* n. 1, cc. vi-vii, xvi. *Cf. id.* 77-78, as to enclosures.

[51] The Combination Act, 1800, according to Professor Dicey (from whom no radical heresies could be expected), "aimed in reality at one object, namely, the suppression of all combinations of workmen whether transitory or permanent of which the object was to obtain an advance in wages, or otherwise fix the terms of employment". Enacted in the panic-stricken reactionary period after the French Revolution, it was replaced, under the influence of Benthamite individualism, first by the Combination Act, 1824, which was in its turn replaced by a slightly less liberal Act of 1825. Section 4 of this latter was to exempt from the penalties of the combination laws any persons combining for the purpose of obtaining improved conditions for their own labour merely. See Stone, *Social Dimensions*, Ch. 7 §§1ff.

[52] Lord Abinger's decision in *Priestley* v. *Fowler* (1837) 3 M. & W.1 is the modern starting-point.

[53] Dicey, *Law and Opinion* (2 ed. 1914) 70ff. And see the late accounts in W. S. Holdsworth, "The Movement for Reform in the Law, 1793-1832" (1940) 56 *L.Q.R.* 33, 208, 340 (including valuable studies of the early reformers Romilly, Brougham, James McIntosh, and the ramifications of Bentham's influence), and (in relation to the criminal law) Radzinowicz, 2 *Criminal Law* 33-167.

the unreformed House of Commons in 1799, was able to ask: "Now, if the country be not safe in such hands, in whose may it confide its interests?" And in 1829, at a time when industrial conditions would not bear description, Macaulay was writing that he found "no record of any great nations past or present in which the working classes have been in a more comfortable situation than England during the last thirty years". And the fire of a Burke was as much a passion for picturesque antiquity as for the principles of government which had emerged from antiquity.[54] This same spirit was driven to reactionary impulses by fear of French revolutionary excesses, and later of Napoleonic domination. The Reform Act of 1832, which marked the first major breach of quiescence, was regarded by influential contemporaries as a final step rather than a beginning.[55]

Yet at a time when such attitudes made rigid the basic features of the flexible English constitution, the industrial revolution was producing drastic social and economic changes at an ever increasing tempo. Large-scale industrialisation brought a whole train of momentous consequences. The rapid growth in population, the shift of the centres both of population and of wealth from south to north and from rural to urban areas, the rise of political power of the new industrial middle class, the disappearance of the personal relation between master and man, the need for efficient trading devices permitting necessary concentration of capital resources for large-scale industry—these and many other consequences exposed the more cruelly the parlous state of English law.

The contrast could not but challenge even less rebellious minds than Bentham's. And when he turned his mind to Parliament in hope of reform, he was confronted by an institution not only marked by corruption, venality and historical anomalies, but in which representation took no account of new concentrations of population. Local government had broken down and its machinery was quite unsuited to the needs of the new industrial areas. The organisation of the Church was not easily adaptable to the new situation. It is but one sample of these inadequacies that great cities came into being long before elementary police and sanitary requirements were even recognised, let alone fulfilled.[56]

§11. INDIVIDUALISM AND COLLECTIVISM IN THE WORK AND INFLUENCE OF BENTHAM. For most of his life, as we have seen, Bentham wrote and worked as if it were only necessary to establish the substantive principles on which legislative reform should proceed, and as if the nature of the legislature itself was irrelevant to the reform programme. These principles, as Professor Brebner has had to remind us, embraced proposals (for example, in the *Manual of Political Economy,* and in the *Constitutional Code*) which were "amazingly prophetic and precise anticipations of the collectivised policies under which so much of the world lives today", as well as demands for the repeal of obsolete legal restraints. From about 1808,

---

[54] Dicey notes a similar mood in Goldsmith among the popular writers.
[55] See, e.g., Lord Macaulay, *Essay on Hallam's Constitutional Law* (1828). For minor changes during the reactionary period see Dicey, *loc. cit.* and for the influence of revolutionary excesses *ibid.,* and W. S. Holdsworth, *op. cit. supra* n. 53 at 33.
[56] See L. Mumford, *The Culture of Cities* (1938) esp. c. iii.

however, he became intensely concerned with the reform of the parliamentary franchise in England, being convinced that only thus could the governors' pursuit of their own happiness be brought to coincide with the greatest happiness of the greatest number.[57] The alliance with James Mill to press for franchise reform led (as has been seen) to confusion of the *laissez faire* drive of James Mill's programme with the more flexible activism of Bentham's, leading to the Dicey-consolidated "myth" that Bentham was a doctrinaire *laissez faire* individualist.

Despite this "myth", Benthamites had "an insistent finger in every interventionist pie from poor law, factory acts, and police, to the century-long battle over public responsibility for public health".[58] They cried "Hands on!" as much as, if not more than, "Hands off!". In particular, as the State in the first half of the nineteenth century took its hands off commerce, it put them onto industry. *Laissez faire* was the battle-cry of industrialists against landowners (and later labourers) rather than a maxim of the State itself. The thesis is, indeed, offered that "in using Bentham as the archetype of British individualism (Dicey) was conveying the exact opposite of the truth. Jeremy Bentham was the archetype of British collectivism".[59]

Yet, of course, it remains true that for much of the nineteenth century and the first half of the twentieth, the Benthamite image pulled towards individualism, whether this rested on truth, or on a myth created by James Mill, or on "the Dicey standard"[60] of later manufacture. If there was not a real Benthamite individualist drive, the pseudo-Benthamite individualist

---

[57] See Halévy, *Radicalism* 147, 257ff.; Brebner, "*Laissez Faire*" 62ff.

[58] Brebner, "*Laissez Faire*" 63-64. E. Halévy, as early as 1901, drew attention to apparent inconsistencies of many aspects of Bentham's work with his supposed *laissez faire* outlook. He sought to reduce them to order by suggesting a dualism of thought. On the legal side, he thought, Bentham was favourable to state intervention, apparently recognising that the necessary harmony of interests must be imposed by law. Whereas on the economic side, he thought, Bentham assumed the *laissez faire* position that once artificial restraints were removed a natural harmony between interests of individuals would assert itself. This dualism, of course, itself raised unacceptable problems, which were not solved by Halévy. Nor were they wholly solved by our own hypothesis in *Province*, Ch. 10 that legal activism was necessary in the actual situation to get rid of obsolete legal restraints. Baumgardt, *Bentham* 10-11, though generally accepting the traditional interpretation of Dicey now brought into question, shows in his discussion of Bentham's attitude to communism (*id.* 468-473, esp. at 471) more sensitivity to the deep dualism in Bentham himself. See generally J. B. Brebner, "Halévy, Diagnostician of Modern Britain" (1948) 23 *Thought* 101-113. Viner, "Bentham and Mill" 360, esp. 368-371, points out that, even as regards economics, the passage in *Manual of Political Economy* (3 *Works* 33) offered to support the *laissez faire* interpretation is in the context too qualified to support it, and that no other evidence of doctrinaire *laissez faire* at all can be found. Dowrick, *Justice* 109-111, still continues in 1961 to see Bentham as uniting *laissez faire* individualism and hedonist utilitarianism, relying on his advocacy of free contracting, and his view that individuals are "the best judges of their own interests".
On the basic influence of the early Factory Act, 1833, see M. W. Thomas, *Early Factory Legislation* (1949).

[59] Brebner, "*Laissez Faire*" 61.

[60] A phrase of Sir C. T. Carr, *Concerning English Administrative Law* (1941) 26, cited *ibid.* On the younger Mill's famous attempt to reconcile his father's position with that of Bentham, see Halévy, *Radicalism* pt. i, c. iii, pt. ii; and on the consistency of the "liberal socialism" and interventionism of John Stuart Mill's later years with the dominance of Bentham's influence or that of Harriet Taylor, over that of his father, see Brebner, "*Laissez Faire*" 63-68. The younger Mill's writings after *On Liberty* (1854-59) are there analysed in this light. And *cf.* as to J. S. Mill's *Principles of Political Economy*, Viner, "Bentham and Mill" 381, and as to J. S. Mill and Bentham generally, *id.* 372-382. On the early history of "the Manchester School" see L. S. Marshall, *The Development of Public Opinion in Manchester* (1946). And see also H. O. Pappe, "The Mills and Harriet Taylor" (1956) 8 *Pol. Sc. Qu.* 19-30.

drive, the myth of Benthamite *laissez faire,* has been real enough in its influence, alongside the very Benthamite interventionism which it concealed. So that we should not now run to the other extreme and allow Benthamite broad interventionism to conceal the genuine strain of practical as distinct from doctrinaire *laissez faire,* of legislative "hands off", which is heard powerfully mingled with his call for legislative activity. At the very time when he was advocating far-reaching legislative activity, he was also proclaiming that all law was an evil, for every law is an infraction of liberty.[61]

What was the reason for this paradoxical position of Bentham and his followers? From one aspect, the dislike of legislation was an echo of American revolutionary anti-authoritarian sentiment. From another it echoed Adam Smith's doctrine of the *natural* "harmony" or "identity" of interests among members of society, which *laissez faire* economics presupposed.[62] But clearly part of the explanation lies in the nature of any hedonistic criterion. Utilitarianism in itself is ambivalent as between collectivism and individualism. There can be a "utilitarian socialism" as well as a "utilitarian individualism";[63] and only if we assume that each individual knows and pursues his own interests best, and that all these several interests and pursuits have a natural harmony which produces the greatest aggregate happiness for the whole group, do utilitarianism and individualism become wholly identified. But in the *hedonist* form which Benthamite utilitarianism took, it did march somewhat with individualism. For pleasure and pain, being felt only by individuals, are in the last resort assessable only by the individual affected,[64] so that each individual is "in the main and as a general rule the best judge of his own happiness". Hence the law should aim rather to decrease pain than increase pleasure, and should limit itself where possible to removing all restrictions on choice not manifestly necessary to protect others.[65] This is still far short of assuming a natural harmony of all individual demands.

Moreover, even apart from his recognition of the need to impose harmony on individual choices when these conflict, Bentham was driven to advocate great legislative activity for the very purpose of making freedom of individual choice possible by repealing existing legal restraints. The mood

----

[61] With due respect for Dicey, this calls for more explanation than a reference to the traditional individualism of the common law (Dicey, *Law and Opinion* (2 ed. 1914) xxviii). *Cf.* W. Friedmann, *Legal Theory* (4 ed. 1960) 270-71.

[62] It was Tom Paine who wrote that "society is produced by our wants and government by our wickedness. . . . Society in every state is a blessing, but government, even in its best state, is but a necessary evil". For the profound influence of Adam Smith's doctrine on Bentham, and its confused conflict with his own early stress on the "artificial" identification of interests, see Halévy, *Radicalism* 11-17, 89ff., 499ff.

[63] *Cf.* Ginsberg, *20th Century* 8ff., 16.

[64] *Cf.* F. H. Bradley, *Ethical Studies* (2 ed. 1927) 101; Lindsay, *Democratic State* 141. On Bentham's own awareness of the essential individuality of pleasures and pains and that "Despotism never takes a worse shape than when it comes in the guise of benevolence", see 2 *Deontology* 288ff.

[65] This is implicit in Mill's classical formulation of the "Benthamite" credo (*On Liberty* (1859)): "The sole end for which mankind are warranted, individually or collectively, in interfering with the liberty of action of any of their number, is self-protection. . . . His own good, either physical or moral, is not a sufficient warranty. He cannot rightfully be compelled to do or forbear, because it will be better for him to do so, because it will make him happier, because in the opinions of others to do so would be wise or even right".

Of course the individualist side is still more complex. Dicey suggested there was an innate English individualism; R. Pound and A. D. Lindsay (*op. cit.* 75, 76, 85-93) have suggested a Protestant or Puritan influence. And see Stone, *Social Dimensions,* Ch. 12.

involved is well expressed in Bentham's polemic against the charge given by Ashhurst J., a puisne judge, to a Middlesex Grand Jury. It is in the form of a dialogue between "Truth" and the learned judge,[66] in which the judge states aphoristically that the law only restrains individual action where safety and good order demand. "Truth" after sundry examples of restraints not so explicable continues:

> The trade I was born in is overstocked: hands are wanting in another. If I offer to work at that other, I may be sent to gaol for it. Why? Because I have not been working at it as an apprentice for seven years. What's the consequence? That, as there is no work for me in my original trade, I must either come upon the parish or starve.
> There is no employment for me in my own parish; there is abundance in the next. Yet if I offer to go there, I am driven away. Why? Because I might become unable to work one of these days, and so I must not work while I am able. I am thrown upon one parish now, for fear I should fall upon another fifty years hence. At this rate, how is work ever to be done? If a man is not poor he won't work; and if he is poor the laws won't let him. How, then, is it that so much is done as is done? As pockets are picked—by stealth and because the law is so wicked that it is only here and there that a man can be found wicked enough to think of executing it. Pray, Mr. Justice, how is the community you speak of the better for any of these restraints, and where is the necessity of them? and how is safety strengthened or good order benefited by them?
> But these are three out of a thousand. . . .

The demand for free movement of manpower required by economic change and frustrated by obsolete laws, stands out clearly, just as the demand for free large-scale capital movement permeates Bentham's attack on the usury laws. In these, as in other respects, Bentham called for legislative activity, not to increase the sphere of legal intervention, but in order to set men free from obsolete legal restraints surviving from an earlier relationally organised society in his own age of social and economic transformation.[67] This was a kind of demand for legislative "hands off" not necessarily tied to doctrinaire *laissez faire,* but capable of making common cause with it over a wide area in the conditions of the particular age.

If this were a correct interpretation we might expect that progressively, as the legislative programme for abolishing unnecessary legal restraints achieved its objectives, the collectivist-interventionist programme would get under way. It follows that the change to legislative collectivism, which Dicey placed about 1860 as a breakaway from "Benthamite" *laissez faire,* may perhaps be more correctly regarded as a point at which the collectivist-interventionist element in the Benthamite legislative drive naturally became more prominent, after achievement of the repeal of the worst obsolete restraints.

---

66 5 *Works,* 234. *Cf.* pt. iii, c. i of "Principles of the Civil Code".
67 *Cf.* the view in D. Lloyd, "The Law of Associations" in Ginsberg, *20th Century* 99, 100ff. The U.S. timetable was different. See Stone, *Social Dimensions,* Ch. 7, §16 on the continued growth there of the older state interventionism past the mid-century. Hartz, *Economic Policy* 13, points out that Benthamite thinking was not popular in Pennsylvania between 1776 and 1860, though many reforms of Benthamite type accompanied open state intervention there.

III. UTILITY AND THE CALCULUS OF PLEASURES AND PAINS

§12. DEFINITION OF UTILITY AS THE CRITERION OF GOOD LAW. "The public good," declared Bentham in opening *The Theory of Legislation,* "ought to be the foundation of the legislator's reasoning." He set out then to define utility precisely and consistently, to show that all other principles of conduct are false, and to find the process of moral arithmetic[68] which would make uniform application of this criterion possible.

He first redefined good and evil in hedonist terms, laying down that "Evil is pain, or the cause of pain, good is pleasure, or the cause of pleasure". On this basis he defined utility as "the property or tendency of a thing to prevent some evil or to procure some good",[69] and more concretely as the tendency of an action "to augment the happiness of the community . . . greater than any which it has to diminish it".[70] All moral judgments of actions, then, must be drawn (as in mathematics from an axiom) from "the principle of utility", which required preference of the action which, out of all possible actions, has most utility in the hedonist sense just defined. Here and throughout his work Bentham tends in this way to weld utilitarianism and hedonism, or better to fix utility and its calculus in hedonist terms, that is in terms of pleasures and pains.[71]

It seems clear (whatever the philosophical difficulties later discussed) that by "happiness of the community" Bentham meant simply the aggregate of individual surpluses of pleasure over pain. His formula "the greatest happiness of the greatest number" suggests this; it would also be an expected result of assessing happiness in terms of "pains" and "pleasures". And his explanation in the same place[72] that "the community" is "a fictitious body" composed of its individual members, and its happiness, the sum of the interest (or happiness) of the several members who compose it, points the same way. It seems clear, too, that Bentham made no difference in value between kinds of pains and pleasures[73] or as between the persons who undergo and enjoy them; each to count for one, and none for more than one, goes equally for persons[73a] and for various kinds of pleasures and pains. For the purpose of his calculus the pleasure of hearing a superb

---

[68] On this matter of calculation see also *infra* §§19ff., and Cohen, *Ethical Systems* 197ff.

[69] Bentham, *Theory* (Hildreth's transl., 5 ed. 1887) 1. References in the succeeding paras. are to this edition.

[70] *Ibid.* These notions of "happiness" and "utility", and the importance of the role which Bentham assigned to them, are well expounded in Baumgardt, *Bentham* 131-34.

[71] *Theory* 1. In ordinary language, of course, "utility" means "usefulness"; and in philosophy, too, its most widely accepted usage is for theories according to which actions are valued by reference to their usefulness, and thus depend on the calculation of consequences. But this calculus need not *necessarily* be conceived of in terms of pleasures or happiness or even wants. *Cf.* on this independence of "the categorical imperative of utilitarianism", Georg Simmel, 1 *Einleitung in die Moralwissenschaft* (1892) 312; and see Ginsberg, *20th Century* 16-19.

[72] *Theory* 3.

[73] But *cf.* J. S. Mill, *Utilitarianism* (1863) 12ff., on which see F. H. Bradley, *Ethical Studies* (2 ed. 1927) 119-122, and Notes thereto. And see J. Viner's important point *infra* nn. 74, 141.

[73a] On the general perplexities of implementing this notion see Sir Isaiah Berlin, "Equality as an Ideal" (1955-56) 56 *Proc. Arist. Soc.* 301-326, repr. Olafson, *Social Policy* 128-150. And *cf.* H. A. Bedau, *cit. supra* n.25, esp. 293ff. And see *infra* Ch. 10 *passim.*

symphony, or reading a divine poem, was to weigh no more and no less than that of watching a boxing match or reading a detective novel;[74] and men and "supermen", the righteous and the wicked, the honest and the criminal, were to be deemed alike. That still left the problems of measuring pains or pleasures in terms first of extensity, that is, of the number of persons affected, and second, of intensity in each person affected.

For Bentham the principle of utility was axiomatic in the fullest sense.[75] His only demonstration was by exposing as fallacious all other principles, as "false methods or reasoning" of the legislator. In this exposure Bentham lays bare some of his antipathies to features of contemporary English law, for instance, to the reliance on ancient authority, intuition and dread of change, the divine will, and the natural law, which he had vehemently attacked in Blackstone—the arch-sanctifier of the legal *status quo*. Even more biting, however, was Bentham's rejection of fictions as a basis (he should rather have said as an instrument) of legislation. A "fiction" Bentham acutely defined as "an assumed fact notoriously false which is reasoned upon as though it were true", and his condemnation was natural in the then state of English law.[76] As to some of the enumerated "false" legislative motives, Bentham admitted that they might properly be weighed as one element in utility since they referred to sentiments of pleasure or pain in men.[77]

---

[74] Assuming, of course, that the *quantity* of pleasure in each case is the same. Much debate has surrounded J. S. Mill's attempt (*Utilitarianism* (1863) 11 ed., 1891, 10-16) to have hedonist utilitarianism take account of qualitative as well as quantitative differences among pleasures, the test of quality being preference of one pleasure over another of greater quantity by those experienced. In his recent discussion ("Bentham and Mill" 277-78) Professor Viner sees the envisaged clash between value-ratings based respectively on quality and quantity as a spurious one for hedonist utilitarianism, and Mill's solution as even more spurious, as well as inconsistent with the utilitarian criterion of maximum pleasure.

Viner, indeed, thinks that Bentham had provided a technique which showed that the quality-versus-quantity problem is not a fundamental moral problem. For actual behaviour, he points out, choices are between "units", not between "classes of objects". Bentham's *dictum* "quantum of pleasure being equal, pushpin is as good as poetry" could therefore be restated: "Desire being equal at the margin of choice, a marginal unit of pushpin is as good as a marginal unit of poetry". A utilitarian using the pleasure calculus could then still consistently say that "since in fact experienced choosers don't plump for even a first unit of pushpin until they are gorged with poetry, in that sense poetry as a class is higher on the scale of values than pushpin as a class". If we understand this correctly it means that to speak of a unit of pushpin which gives the same pleasure as a unit of poetry as having equal value to it, still allows us to recognise that to persons familiar with both, a unit of pushpin *generally* does *not* give as much pleasure as a unit of poetry, so that (in that sense) poetry becomes higher in value than pushpin.

[75] Some writers (e.g., A. J. Ayer in Keeton *et al.*, *Bentham* at 245-46) have treated the principle of utility as inferred from a psychological premise, namely that every man acts with only happiness as his object. Bentham undoubtedly held this to be a valid psychological hypothesis as to how men act, and perhaps as some confirmation of his principle of utility, concerning how men ought to act. We doubt, however, that he inferred the principle *from it*. For the view that the utility principle was itself a (presumably separate) hypothesis, see *infra* n. 186.

[76] "There is no need" he said, "to rest the happiness of mankind on a fiction; to build the social pyramid on a foundation of sand or crumbling clay. Let us leave gewgaws to children: men should speak the language of soberness and truth" (199). For cognate reasons, Bentham denounced the basing of legal rules on metaphors, for instance that of corruption of blood, or the infallibility of the Crown, or the Leviathan or the Social Contract, and above all, as we have seen, he denounced the natural law as but a form of imaginary law. For a *caveat* as to the kind of fictions attacked by Bentham see the thesis of C. K. Ogden, *Bentham's Theory of Fictions* (1931). And see H. Vaihinger, *The Philosophy of "As If"* (transl. C. K. Ogden, 1924); Jones, *Theory of Law* c. vi.

[77] This should have led him to more appreciation of the historical role of

§13. THE KNOWLEDGE OF PAINS AND PLEASURES. Since the systems both of morals and legislation rest on "the knowledge of pains and pleasures" the first task is to identify these. "A reason in morals or politics, which cannot be translated by the simple words pain or pleasure, is an obscure and sophistical reason, from which nothing can be concluded".[78] Bentham's basic tabulation of pleasures and pains manifests, as might have been expected, the state of psychological knowledge of his time. He enumerated a list of "simple pleasures" and another of "simple pains", pointing out that they unite, combine and modify each other in a thousand ways, so that it requires "some little attention and experience" to discover in a complex pleasure or pain all the simple pleasures or pains which are its ultimates.[79]

It should also be observed, however, that what Bentham was attempting in the tabulation outlined in the footnote was not so much an analysis of "pains" and "pleasures" as psychic phenomena, as a description of the typical objective situations from which, in his view, pleasurable or painful sensations resulted. Psychologically, the "pain" resulting from "imagination" might be indistinguishable from that resulting from apprehension of the divine wrath or from unsatisfied desire or (in part at least) of disease. But as a practical matter of legislative calculation the situations (as this writer understands him) were a sufficient criterion of the presence of pains or pleasures.

It should be noted, finally, that Bentham's table of "pleasures" was by no means limited to pleasures of the senses; and if, even then, he did not give enough weight to pleasures of the heart and mind, this may be the fault of insufficient psychological knowledge rather than of any necessary limits of his principle of utility.[80]

---

natural law despite his rational exposure of it. But, after all, he was writing before historical studies had covered the field, and before modern psychology. More surprising is Bentham's failure to appreciate the work of Montesquieu, whose central ideas he occasionally understood so little as to impute much "balderdash" to them. See Baumgardt, *Bentham* 41-42, and generally 44, 125-131, 464-65. The virtue of this defect was of course his fiery impatience with anachronisms. "I would give very little to know the period when Tithes were instituted," he said: "I would give more to see the day when they shall be abolished." (*A Comment on the Commentaries* 136). And he did not see "that we owe any deference to former times that we owe not to our own". (*Id.* 195.)

[78] *Theory of Legislation* 26.

[79] Among the "simple pleasures" Bentham enumerated pleasures of sense, including those of health and novelty; the pleasures of riches, most lively at the moment of acquisition; pleasures of address, that is, of skill or talent; pleasures of friendship and of good reputation, under both of which he frankly included that of "accepting voluntary and gratuitous service" (*id.* 22); pleasures of power over others; pleasures of "piety" including those of what might be called "great expectations"; pleasures of benevolence or sympathy or social affection; pleasures of malevolence, of knowledge, of memory, of imagination; and finally pleasures of relief from pain which might, it is supposed, be as varied as the varied kinds of pain. The simple pains correspond in goodly part to the simple pleasures. They include the pains of privation, whether disappointment, or unsatisfied desire, or regret or ennui; the pains of sense, comprehending diseases of all kinds; the pains of maladdress, that is, lack of skill or talent; the pains of enmity or ill repute or dishonour or social disapproval; the pains of piety, notably the fear of divine punishment; the pains of benevolence, sympathy and the social affections; the pains of malevolence reflecting on the happiness of the hated, and the pains of memory and imagination.

On the uncertainties introduced into hedonism by the inclusion in these lists of items which could refer to *prima facie* non-sensual experiences of virtue and justice see *infra* §§19-21. *Cf.* on this *tabula affectuum* Baumgardt, *Bentham* 236-39.

[80] See Viner, "Bentham and Mill" 366. And see *infra* §§19ff. for difficulties arising from the range of "pleasures". Even Bentham's staunchest admirers acknowledge

§14. THE EXTENSITY OF PLEASURES AND PAINS. Having asserted the principle of utility in terms of the maximisation of pleasures, and detected the mainsprings of pleasures and pains as units of his calculus, the next task was to fix the method of ascertaining the *quantity* of pleasure or pain resulting from a given act.

It is obvious that on Bentham's egalitarian basis, the quantity must increase directly with the number of persons affected. But it is not merely a matter of counting heads. For most acts with which the law is concerned have a range of stimulation of pleasure or pain which goes far beyond what is apparent on the surface. In the case of a robbery, for instance, there are obvious evils of fear and deprivation affecting the victim himself (which Bentham terms "the primitive evil"), as well as those falling on specified individuals directly related to him, as, for instance, his creditors, his family or his insurance company (which Bentham terms "the derivative evil"). Both of these immediate kinds of evil Bentham describes as "evils of the first order".

Less apparent are "the evils of the second order" which, arising from awareness of the former, thereafter spread more or less throughout the community. News of a robbery spreads the alarm among others, lest they too become victims; news of a successful robbery encourages other potential robbers, each new robbery producing new primitive and derivative "evils of the first order", from which spring new "evils of the second order". If waves of such evils become frequent and intense enough a general state of fear and insecurity is produced throughout the society, quite independently of any specific act. It constitutes an "evil of the third order", the pains of desperation and discouragement accompanying the failure of the law to achieve its object of utility.[81]

In the legislator's creation of offences the process is to be one of putting on one side of the ledger the prospective pleasures and pains resulting from the act to the wrongdoer and his victims respectively, and on the other side those resulting from the sanction inflicted and from the prohibition of the act in question; and ensuring that the balance of pleasure is greater on the side of the law. The object is to outweigh the criminal's pleasures with deterrent pains and the victim's pains with pleasures of security and

---

that he was handicapped by his "premature" and "rudimentary" psychology. See, e.g., V. Cohen, *Jeremy Bentham* (1927) 18, and Baumgardt, *op. cit.* 522, 536ff.; but *cf. infra* n. 189.

[81] On the importance of "evils of the first and second order" and the interwoven importance of degrees of intention, see Baumgardt, *Bentham* 283-89.

Bentham composed the amusing doggerel (first published in a note to the *Principles* (2 ed. 1823) c. iv):

"*Intense, long, certain, speedy, fruitful, pure* —
Such marks in pleasures and in pains endure.
Such pleasures seek, if *private* be thy end:
If it be *public*, wide let them *extend*.
Such *pains* avoid, whichever be thy view:
If pains *must* come, let them *extend* to few."

Helen Bevington was perhaps responding in kind when she wrote "A Bomb for Jeremy Bentham" (*Nineteen Million Elephants and Other Poems* (1950) 33-4); with the middle verse:

"He reckoned right and wrong
By felicity — lifelong —
And by such artless measure
As the quantity of pleasure.
For pain he had a plan,
Absurd old gentleman."

retribution. And Bentham warned, in characteristic fashion, that since every law involves an infringement of liberty, the legislator must take care not to administer a medicine worse than the disease.[82]

§15. INTENSITY OF PLEASURES AND PAINS: VARIATIONS IN SENSIBILITY OF PERSONS: The *quality* of pleasure or pain or the "superiority" of the person who feels it are not, as has been seen, regarded by Bentham as proper considerations for the legislator. Nevertheless it was obvious that the same cause of pleasure or pain in Bentham's sense does not create an equal quantity or intensity of pleasure or pain in all individuals. Bentham even admitted that one man's meat may be another man's poison. How could his legislative calculator estimate the quantity of pleasure (or pain) for all the individuals within the ambit of the first, second and third orders, when the sensibility of each varies—and especially when at the moment of legislation, the persons affected are still indeterminate?[83]

Bentham recognised that the primary factors underlying these variations in individual sensibility cannot serve as a basis for the legislator's assessment; for, being in the main psychological features of each individual, they are not easily susceptible of observation and public record. Such primary factors, he enumerated, were temperament, health, strength, corporal imperfections, degree of knowledge, strength of the intellectual faculties, firmness of soul, perseverance, bent of inclination, notions of honour and religion, sentiments of sympathy or antipathy, folly or disorder of the mind and pecuniary circumstances.[84]

The legislator must seek *indicia* which can be more readily observed and recorded, which will permit him to know what number of individuals there are of each class of sensibility. If, then, classes can thus be found with such obvious *indicia,* among whose members certain primary factors affecting sensibility are usually present, the way is open to take account of, at any rate, the more important variations. Such classes Bentham thought he found in sex, age, rank, education, habitual occupation, and religious professions within one nation; and as between nations by reference to climate and type of government.[85] Average variations in sensibility within such broadly defined classes can on this basis be allowed for in the calculus, for instance, in laying down rules of justification, extenuation and aggravation in the criminal law. Of course, particular individuals in a class may not show the variation of sensibility normal to the class. But, in Dicey's later comment, a legislator must calculate in the mass, and Bentham did not propose that

---

[82] *Op. cit.* 48. For a fuller account of Bentham's penal theories, see Halévy, *Radicalism* 54-73.

[83] Persons affected by the second and third order of pleasure and pain *always* remain indeterminate.

[84] The list is obviously somewhat arbitrary but its general nature is clear: it covers the more common attributes (in the main, but not entirely, psychological—pecuniary circumstances being an exception), to which individual idiosyncrasies are referable.

[85] Obviously such classes could be expanded: and at least two of what Bentham termed primary factors affecting sensibility could be used, and might still be used, to define further classes. Thus "folly or disorder of the mind" may clearly so serve; and so, certainly under modern circumstances, may pecuniary circumstances. The graduated income tax itself proceeds in part on the basis of decreasing sensibility to the pain of pecuniary deprivation at successively higher stages of income.

Cf. with these lists his catalogue in the *Principles* c. vi, of 32 "circumstances influencing" moral sensibility, on which see Baumgardt, *Bentham* 239-243.

he should use diamond scales to weigh butcher's meat.[86]

§16. INTENSITY OF PLEASURES AND PAINS: VARIATIONS FROM THE NATURE OF THE ACT. Besides the variations in the number of persons affected, and in intensity of pleasure and pain arising from individual variations in sensibility, there must also be taken into account variations in intensity deriving from the kind of act involved. The quantity of pleasure or pain which it produces will depend on the duration of the act, on the certainty and proximity of its anticipation, as well as on the intensity of the pains and pleasures produced. Thus, when modern income tax liability is shifted to a "pay as you earn" basis, one effect in some countries is to relieve the estates of taxpayers from a prospective liability for income tax in the financial year in which their deaths fall. It might then seem eminently satisfactory to the taxpayer to pay as part of the transition arrangements an additional twenty-five per cent. of a full year's tax now, in lieu of the future 100 per cent. liability of which he is relieved. Yet such an arrangement, it is clear, is not welcomed by taxpayers. For the relief in the year of death is comparatively distant, and owing to possible change in the law also somewhat uncertain, as well as *ex hypothesi* beyond his personal experience. The twenty-five per cent. liability is immediately impending and utterly certain. In Bentham's language, the pain of the immediate certainty of the smaller liability more than outweighs the pleasure of the more distant and less certain, though pecuniarily far greater relief.

Indirectly, the quantity of pleasure or pain produced for an individual by a given act is also affected by the greater or less likelihood of future repetition or productiveness. A pleasure often tends to increase in intensity as it increases in rarity: "look thy last on all things lovely, every hour". A pain, on the other hand, tends to increase in intensity as its repetition and continuance becomes likely. Conversely the quantity of pleasure or pain would also be affected by its "purity", that is, the likelihood that it may be followed by pain if a pleasure, and by pleasure if a pain, the respective quantity being (so Bentham explained) reduced or partly cancelled by an opposite consequent emotion in each case.

§17. LAW AND OTHER SOCIAL CONTROLS. The legislator's power to control conduct, therefore, lies in his use of pleasures and pains as sanctions, for "when we speak of motives, we speak of pleasures and pains". It is, of course, not merely pleasures and pains imposed by the legislator which influence human conduct. Nature, he said, also imposed its sanctions, for instance, of sickness for neglect of health precautions, and in accordance with the maxim "as ye sow so shall ye reap". Second, there are the sanctions of public opinion, the pains of one's fellows' disapproval or enmity or ostracism, and the reverse pleasures. Third, there is the religious sanction

---

[86] Bentham, indeed, was distrustful of judicial discretion, and judicial and administrative discretions are the only means that have been devised in the modern age to overcome the difficulty of legislating for the individual as well as for the mass. See Stone, *Social Dimensions*, Ch. 14, *passim*.

It will be observed that Bentham's sensibility classes correspond somewhat to the law of persons. All of them have at some time, and some still do, carry special incapacities or protections in our law. The correlation is real. For the special sensibilities of the class would result on Bentham's view in a different balance of pains and pleasures and this would direct, on the principle of utility, differences in applicable rules.

arising from the believed disapproval or approval of God and its consequences. The legal or "political" sanctions attached to conduct by human
laws constitute therefore only one of four kinds of controls, and one out
of three social controls. But the legal control, wrote Bentham, thus antici-
pating later sociological opinion,[87] "is the most efficient in its operation and
the most susceptible of being carried to perfection".

Bentham conceived that his principle of utility was the only valid
criterion for all three modes of social control. On the vexed question of
the relation between law and morals his answer was clear and over-simple.
Both had the same central aim, utility, "directing the actions of men in
such a way as to produce the greatest possible sum of good".[88] But though
legislation thus has the same centre as morals, "it has not the same circum-
ference".[89] For first, since in Bentham's view all law is itself an evil, the
evil of the punishment may be greater in certain cases of attempted enforcement of moral precepts than the evil of the offence itself. The provision
of pleasures should be left to individuals, the function of government being
to ward off pains. In the second place, moreover, many moral evils are
of an inward secret nature not amenable to the legislator's sanction even
if he desired to meddle. For instance, it would be difficult either to provide
a definition for legal purposes, or to ascertain the existence in a given
case, of such moral offences as hardheartedness, ingratitude and perfidy.[90]
In substance, this position of Bentham's was also adopted by Austin and
the English analytical school. It is also not far removed from the dominant
position proceeding from Kant.[91] On Bentham's view, the law is concerned
essentially with the reduction of conduct causing pain, and in Kant's view,
with the reduction of conflicts between individual wills in the external
world. It follows naturally, on both views, that law is conceived of as restraint
on action, as having a police function only.[92]

§18. Directives of the Principle of Utility in the Field of the Civil
Law. The principle of utility, Bentham admitted, was more difficult of
application in the civil than in the criminal law because finer assessments
were involved. Nevertheless, utility is still the sole test, and here as elsewhere,
fictions and false reasoning were to be shunned.[93] Every obligation (or
pain) must either be founded on some service (or pleasure) received by
the person obliged, or it must rest on some superior need (i.e., greater
pleasure or avoidance of greater pain) of the person who benefits from
the obligation, or must arise from some mutual agreement which on general
grounds the principle of utility requires to be enforced.[94] While theoretically

---

[87] Cf. E. A. Ross, Social Control (1908) and see Stone, Social Dimensions, Ch. 15,
esp. §§1ff.
[88] Op. cit. 60.
[89] Ibid.
[90] The Romans, however, apparently found no insuperable difficulty in dealing
legally with ingratitude, for instance, in a freedman.
[91] Supra Ch. 3, §6.
[92] See op. cit. 48, 60.
[93] "These same writers acknowledge imprescriptible rights which have always
been prescribed, and inalienable rights which have always been alienated. Take
away their fictions and they know not where they are: for they become so used
to their crutches that they cannot stand without them."
[94] The writer believes there is a latent extra valuation of contract here. But see
the discussion of expectations below.

the law might proceed either by maximising pleasure or by minimising pain, we have seen that on Bentham's hedonistic assumptions the law should where possible limit itself to minimising pain, the provision of pleasure being left to each individual. Rights and obligations distributed by the State involve the individual's sacrifice of part of his liberty; governments are better as the acquisition is greater and the sacrifice less.

The four directives of utility for civil law are, according to Bentham, security, subsistence, abundance and equality. Security he regarded as paramount. He recognised that absolute equality was impossible, though approximation to it was a great aid to happiness; and that abundance presupposed subsistence. Subsistence, abundance and equality, however, all depended, in Bentham's view, on the paramount directive of security. He took great pains to exemplify and warn against attacks on security, for instance, the repudiation of public loans, the imposition of taxes of unfair incidence, the forced raising of the value of money, and forced reduction of interest rates, confiscations of all kinds, and the termination of pensions.[95] Bentham's resort, at this point, to those very abstractions which he had first attacked, is notable. What, for instance, did he mean by "security", and in what sense could it be said that "security" is paramount over "subsistence"? In terms of the individual life man may live without security, but he cannot live without subsistence. If by security he had reference to a collective state then it may indeed be true that security may exist for some or even for many, even if subsistence is lacking for some or even for many.[96] But if that is his meaning he must have permitted the entry of extraneous factors into his egalitarian calculus of individual pains and pleasures.[97] Moreover, of course, the modern tendency is to deny that, in the long run at any rate, security (i.e., social stability) can be achieved except on the basis of subsistence for substantially all individuals.[98] Security of men's expectations, especially as to property, was to Bentham so paramount that he would permit measures for the reduction of inequalities only at the "natural" period of the death of the owner.[99]

Nearer, perhaps, to a long-term truth, was Bentham's assertion that liberty in civil legal relations is merely a branch of security. The argument, of course, is well known, resolving itself ultimately into that of Hobbes' *Leviathan*, that a state of natural liberty not subjected to law is so precarious that the submission of all to a rule, surrendering liberty to the extent necessary for secure social existence, was found preferable. Bentham's reasoning was

---

[95] With one eye perhaps on revolutionary France, he solemnly warned: "You will never win the happiness of nations through the misery of individuals: The altar of the public good no more demands barbarous sacrifices than does the altar of a loving God."

[96] The survival of modern states with nearly a tenth of their population unemployed is perhaps an example.

[97] Viner, "Bentham and Mill", sees Bentham's heavy stress on the security of private property as an exception to his usually flexible attitude towards State intervention, i.e., as not controlled by the plain test of utility. And cf. Ginsberg, *20th Century* 3, 12-13, adopting the view of Halévy, *Radicalism* 366, that finally Bentham's stress on equality was geared to the protection of the middle class.

[98] The twentieth century call for "social security" is a recognition of this impossibility, for it refers in composite fashion to a security which is based upon economic arrangements which ensure subsistence to substantially the whole community. Bentham had asserted that when security and equality come into conflict, there should not be a moment's hesitation. Equality must give way. Modern experience tends to suggest rather that security is unattainable without equality in subsistence, that is, in the basic minimum.

[99] 1 *Works* 312.

barely distinguishable from Hobbes', despite his scornful references to Hobbes' metaphors. This subordination of liberty to security by an approximation to Hobbes' position is the more surprising in view of their different social contexts.[100] Hobbes' tendency was to exalt order after an age of disorder, Bentham's to exalt freedom from obsolete legal restraint at the threshold of an age of great change and expansion.[101] But if the modern view[102] of Bentham's position on *laissez faire* and state intervention is accepted, much of the strangeness disappears. As already seen in his attitude towards natural law,[103] Bentham in the last resort did not adhere to the notion of a natural harmony of interests among members of society, but recognised that harmony may have to be produced by state action.[104]

As to one aspect of security, indeed, namely, tenderness for settled human expectations, Bentham's preference for it is readily understandable on any view of his own criterion. In the conditions of English law in the early nineteenth century, he was able to point out the evil effect upon men's expectations of the then state of English statute and common law.[105] These, he argued, violated the first corollary of respect for expectations—that the laws should be "cognoscible", that is to say, in a form capable of being readily understood by the citizens. Closely linked with this was his demand that the laws be also *accessible,* that is to say, in a form readable without artificial barriers to consulting them, such as those produced at the time by the scarcity of copies of statutes and reports. It was, in part, to meet these needs, as well as to permit necessary reforms, that Bentham was so fervent an advocate of codification.[106] Cognoscibility and accessibility,

---

[100] Cohen, *Ethical Systems* 69-75, esp. 75n, also notes this parallel between Bentham and Hobbes without, however, remarking upon the incongruities of time, place and person.

[101] It was only after the *Principles* that any bias in favour of security, arising from Bentham's known displeasure at the course of the French Revolution, could have operated. And see Halévy, *Radicalism*, App., at 517 on the "anti-equalitarian" bias in Bentham's MS. of 1795 used by Dumont for the *Traités.* And see B. Russell, *op. cit. supra* n. 1, at 120ff. See the *Anarchical Fallacies—An Examination of the Declarations of Rights issued during the French Revolution,* in 2 *Works* 491. *Cf.* Halévy, *op. cit.* 165-175, who does not explicitly connect Bentham's stress on security with these incidents, but attributes it (*id.* 46ff.) to the influence of Hume's doctrine of "expectations" as the basis of justice (citations *ibid.*).

In contemporary terms, of course, the concept of liberty as but a branch of security has implications which cannot fairly be attributed to Bentham, including the trend to limit abstract liberty of contract in order to protect the party in the weakest bargaining position; or more recently, towards economic planning to prevent dislocations which lead to unemployment, and like evils, injuring both general economic security and the concrete individual liberty. For a stimulating discussion of the relation of "liberty" and "equality", see E. F. Carritt, "Liberty and Equality" (1940) 56 *L.Q.R.* 61, 65-66. And see the literature and discussion *infra* Ch. 11, §§1ff.

[102] See *supra* §11.

[103] See *supra* §3.

[104] So *cf.* now Bentham, *Limits* 58ff. In this lately published MS. he reduces liberty virtually to a security granted by law to one person, by the imposition of restraints on others. "Liberty then is of two or even more sorts, according to the number of quarters from whence coercion . . . may come; liberty as against the law, and liberty as against . . . wrongdoers. These two sorts of liberty are directly opposed to one another: and insofar as it is in favour of an individual that the law exercises its authority over another, the generation of the one sort is, as far as it extends, the destruction of the other." The whole important treatment on pp. 58ff. shows no signs either of the natural harmony fallacy or of the *laissez faire* myth.

[105] As well as, incidentally, the disadvantages of the system of unacknowledged judge-made law which he bitterly attacked. See, e.g., the passages collected in Baumgardt, *Bentham* 463-64, 475-78.

[106] Both Bentham and Austin acknowledged at times the need for caution in codification, and the limits on possible simplification of the law for layman or even

indeed, were prerequisites to the formulation of stable expectations for the future. For the rest the legislator's task, in this regard, was to ensure that legislation and administration disturbed these expectations as little as possible. In other words, a pervading element to be weighed in the legislator's scales was the pain caused throughout society by disturbing settled expectations. This pain might veto some changes which otherwise would have a balance of good in their favour.[107] For similar reasons he condemned laws which can be easily evaded as an "immoral lottery" undermining law itself; and also "judge-made" law, and the interpretation of statutes in other than a literal mode.

IV. CRITIQUE OF HEDONIST UTILITARIANISM

§19. BASIC DIFFICULTIES IN EVALUATING BENTHAMITE HEDONIST UTILITARIANISM. As we continue to understand him, Bentham took his stand on the hedonist version of the principle of utility as axiomatic. The only arguments he advanced in support of it were perhaps the following two. First, he did attempt to show all other moral theories to be untenable;[107a] but of course this, even if successful, does not show that hedonist or any other form of utilitarianism is correct. Second, he supported his principle with the psychological hypothesis (which some even regard as a premise from which he inferred that principle) that every man acts with only happiness as his object, taking it for granted, as it were, that the *actual* object of men's actions *is* "the good", *that which ought to be* their object.

As mentioned below, this psychological hypothesis is questionable. But even granting it, there is a further difficulty facing this argument. Even if each man desires *his own* happiness, so that his happiness is a good *to him,* how does it follow that the general happiness is a good to the aggregate of all?[108] For, wrote F. H. Bradley,[109] thus to assume that each

---

lawyer. Both, however, were certain that it could be rendered infinitely more simple than that which confronted them; and both insisted on the accessibility of law as a primary goal. Blackstone, 1 *Commentaries* 45, had found the mode of promulgation of the law to be a "matter of very great indifference", citing the example of the Emperor Caligula, who hung up his laws "in a small character" and on high pillars: for Bentham the point is rather that even Caligula did at least hang up his laws. See *A Comment on the Commentaries* 69. The difference of viewpoint is well stressed by Baumgardt, *Bentham* 111-12.

107 Thus, though Bentham had insisted that "dread of innovation" is not a good reason for the legislator, he recognised that the pain arising from disturbance of expectations centred around the legal *status quo* was always a factor to be weighed.

107a Baumgardt, *Bentham* 180-218, gives an account of Bentham's critique, projected to include contemporary philosophers (see, e.g., 137-150 as to C. D. Broad) among its targets and enriched by reference to unpublished Benthamite MSS. On attempts, particularly by J. S. Mill, to provide positive support for utilitarianism, see E. W. Hall, "The 'Proof' of Utility in Bentham and Mill" (1949) 60 *Ethics* 1-18; H. A. Bedau, "Justice and Classical Utilitarianism" in *Nomos, Justice* 284-305. Bedau charges that utilitarianism fails to indicate what ought to be done in case the directive from utility involves breaking a "moral rule" required by justice to be observed. This question cannot, of course, arise in Bentham's own above terms. But see *infra* n. 143a.

108 J. S. Mill, *Utilitarianism* (1863) 23 argued in effect: (1) General "happiness" is desirable because each desires his own "happiness"; (2) therefore "happiness" is "good"; (3) therefore the "happiness" of each is "a good" to him; and the "happiness" of all a "good" to all. Baumgardt, *Bentham* 499, thinks that the Utopian view involved of "coincidence of all human interests" is most fostered, in Bentham's works, in the *Deontology,* the precise authorship of which is subject to doubts. See *supra* n. 7.

109 *Op. cit. supra* n. 73 at 113.

individual's search for pleasure includes a seeking to give others pleasure, is little different from arguing that if many pigs each have pleasure in feeding at one trough, therefore each pig desires not only his own pleasure but that of all. If pleasure be the end of each, then since pleasure can be felt only by the individual man, the pleasure of others cannot be his end but only a means to his own end, which is his own pleasure.[110] And yet, to satisfy Bentham's theory, not only the legislator but all citizens would have to aim at producing the maximum pleasure for others, which seems contradictory with egoistic hedonism itself. "In the utilitarian doctrine the egoism of the individual is at once explicitly affirmed and implicitly denied."[111]

Underlying the consequential debates concerning hedonist utilitarianism, however, is the preliminary charge that Bentham and his followers shifted back and forth between different meanings of "greatest happiness". It may mean simply what people "most want". On this meaning, it would be necessary (on each application of the principle) to *predict* what the people to be affected (including the actor) would "most want" at the times when the proposed action falls to be taken. Prediction of what others will most want in particular future situations is an extremely difficult undertaking; while the actor's prediction of what he himself will most want at all relevant times is perhaps scarcely less difficult. It seems, indeed, to involve some circularity, because what he will most want will presumably be materially affected by the prescription to be arrived at by the application of the principle of utility. To the extent that it is circular, this formula could provide no guide until after the choices by the person affected and by the actor have been made, nor *ex hypothesi* could it guide before that point.

To escape this, the test may be taken to refer to a particular kind of "wants", the sensations of "pleasures" or the absence of "pains", objectively identifiable as such. In this version, however, the theory loses any confirmation it might have from the psychological hypothesis that men in fact always seek the greatest happiness. For it is clear that in many very important human situations, of which war is only the most dramatic example, men clearly seek something else (for instance, their country's greatness, or the freeing of oppressed peoples) more than they seek to maximise pleasurable sensations.[112] Further, men are generally found to pursue certain interests

---

[110] F. H. Bradley (*id.* 126) applied this with particular ferocity against H. Sidgwick's version of hedonism in his *Methods of Ethics* (1874, 6 ed. 1901).

[111] Halévy, *Radicalism* 503. So, conversely, they are credited with "unselfish and stoical devotion to the doctrine that every man seeks his own pleasure". See B. Russell, *op. cit. supra* n. 1 at 118ff., 137-39. Austin, *Province Determined* 103ff., and esp. 104-118, thought that the difficulties were not in utilitarianism, but in the critics' confusion between the proximate criterion of ethical conduct (utility) (see *infra* n. 167), and the motives of the actor's conduct. "It was never contended or conceited by a sound, orthodox utilitarian, that the lover should kiss his mistress with an eye to the common weal." (*id.* 108.) This, however, scarcely meets the problem in the text. Rather more relevant is Austin's point (*id.* 107) that if each individual set out to pursue the aggregate of happiness of the whole community rather than his own, he would be neglecting those concerns which he knew best, in favour of those he knew least. The net result would be a failure to reach the maximum aggregate of happiness. This, however, seems to be an admission and justification, rather than a denial of the charge of egoism. See, however, the whole of this difficult page span.

[112] In fact, however, Bentham's list of "pleasures" sought to particularise "wants" without reducing them all to pleasures of sense or indicating whether they could be so reduced. It has, indeed, been thought that even the notions of justice, virtue and knowledge, often vouched to bring into doubt Bentham's criterion based on a maxi-

or objects for their own sakes, and not in any search for pleasure. The range of men's interests, or objects, or "wants" in this sense, is so great and variable as between individuals that this meaning may be thought to make the Benthamite calculus illusory. In this version, at least, "we cannot bring all demands to a single 'market' ".[113]

When we try to substitute for pleasures as the objects sought some such range of less determinate "wants", this may leave us with a theory of justice but not with a *hedonist* theory of justice. Thus, because the supporting psychological hypothesis is on the above interpretation discredited, A. J. Ayer[114] and others have suggested that the Benthamite theory may have to be restated as a tautology *faute de mieux*. This restatement solves otherwise insoluble problems by identifying happiness with the objects or ends *in fact pursued*, whatever they be; and by altering the principle of utility correspondingly, so that maximum fulfilment of objects or ends (rather than maximum happiness in any ordinary sense) is what is to be sought. In this version utilitarianism comes to look much like William James' pragmatist ethical theory, adapted into juristic thought by Roscoe Pound. It asserts that all *de facto* wants or demands are valid by the fact that they are made; so that the task of justice is to satisfy as many of them as possible. We shall criticise this version in connection with Pound's pragmatist theory of justice in Chapter 9.

§20. MAIN SPECIFIC CRITICISMS OF THIS THEORY OF JUSTICE. The more important specific arguments brought against Benthamite hedonist utilitarianism must be assessed against the background of these difficulties.

First, hedonism assumes that pleasure is found by being sought, whereas in actual life pleasure comes rather as an incident to the search for other things than as an intended result of the search: "if pleasure is the end, it is an end which must not be made one, and is found there most where it is not sought". And this, it is suggested, is so whether we think of each individual pursuing his own pleasure or the community as a whole seeking the maximum aggregate of pleasure.[115] In answer to this, it has been pointed out that it simply does not conform to experience, which shows that "people who go out for a good time frequently have a good time", and that those who aim to please others do in fact frequently do so.[116] The whole point, however, goes rather to the method of achieving maximum pleasure than to the validity of maximum pleasure as a criterion of goodness.

---

mising of pleasure, will really be found included in Bentham's list of pleasures. See *supra* n. 79, and *cf.* C. W. Everett in Bentham, *Limits* 23-26. At one stage, indeed, Bentham himself essayed a demonstration (MS. U.C., now printed Baumgardt, *Bentham* 566-571) that even "the *practice* of *Justice*" and "the *view* of *Truth*" are in fact "nothing else than pleasures of the body seen at a distance" (*id.* 567). Thus patriotism, he thought, is "partly the sense of the physical benefit" from existence of the polity, or the esteem which redounds from acts so inspired. Or, in the unsophisticate, it is the result of education of the actor by persons so motivated (*id.* 570-71). Bentham later abandoned this extreme view; see Baumgardt, *op. cit.* 221-23, 300.

113 J. Anderson, "Utilitarianism" (1932) 10 *Aust. J. Psych. Phil.* 161, 163; now repr. *id.*, *Studies in Empirical Philosophy* (1962) 227, 229.

114 *Op. cit. supra* n. 75, at 257.

115 F. H. Bradley, *op. cit. supra* n. 73, 87-88. And see the whole of c. iii on "Pleasure for Pleasure's Sake". *Cf.* F. Paulsen, *System of Ethics*, Thilly's transl. (1899), and for a later view opposed to Bradley on most points see Cohen, *Ethical Systems* 185-220. And see on this objection Baumgardt, *Bentham* 537-38.

116 Cohen, *op. cit.* 190.

Second, it is said, if you say "fairly and nakedly" that the goal of society is "feeling pleased as much as possible and as long as possible", then "you cannot . . . bring the hedonistic end before the moral consciousness without a sharp collision".[117] In short, hedonism revolts the general intuition of men. This argument fixes on the pleasure-sensation version of Benthamism. It would be less telling against broader versions of the greatest happiness of the greatest number which Benthamites may adopt. The lamented F. S. Cohen, in some of his best pages,[118] addressed himself to three types of case pressed against hedonism as at odds with the general moral sense. First, that beauty would be better than ugliness though no human being ever preferred it.[119] An introspective judgment on so imaginative an assumption is self-discrediting. Second, that some pleasurable things are clearly not good, as for instance sexually perverted acts. But the hedonist does not say that such an act is good, unless *along with all its consequences* it results in a pleasure-surplus; he would say rather that even for those who derive pleasure from such an act, the act would still be bad if with its consequences it yielded an overall pain-surplus.[120] Third, that there are cases where goodness is clearly not proportionate to pleasure, as in the stock example that the life of the most comfortable pig is not as good as that of the most miserable human being. This begs the question whether satiety in the pig equals maximum pleasure, and absence of it in man maximum pain. However it be with piggish pleasure, it seems clear that men may have a pleasure-surplus in life though full of unsatisfied desires.[121] And as to all these forms of reliance on "the general moral sense", Bentham also gave the general answer[122] of denying the validity of intuitionism—natural law or other.[123]

Third, it is said, pleasure and pain are nothing but names for "a

---

[117] F. H. Bradley, *op. cit.* 89.

[118] *Ethical Systems* 209-220.

[119] *Cf.* G. E. Moore, *Principia Ethica* (1903) 83-84.

[120] See the MS. cited *infra* n. 130 (Baumgardt, *Bentham* 554), on "impure" pleasures. *Cf.* on criminal and related pleasures Baumgardt, *Bentham* 211-15, 259-60, 534-36. Baumgardt's discussion at 212 of the surgeon's pleasure in the patient's pain is, however, unconvincing.

[121] To confront the hedonist with the choice of piggish ecstasy or human misery is like asking: "Do omniscient stones know more than less wise philosophers?" A negative answer must be false since inconsistent with the postulated "omniscience" of stones; an affirmative answer goes against the grain of fact (that stones don't "know"). The hedonist is entitled to pass to the next question.

[122] *Cf.* the account as to both "moral sense" and "common sense" in Baumgardt, *Bentham* 192ff., 527-29. In *Principles* c. ii, §14 Bentham thought that the "common sense" version added only (like the Emperor's new clothes in the fable) an illusion of better coverage, when in fact this is only verbal. *Cf.* Bentham's satirical picture of a hypothetical contest between a "partisan of moral sense" and "a partisan of common sense" or "between two philosophers of the common sense or two partisans of the moral sense", in his *Rationale of Judicial Evidence* (1827) bk. i, c. vii; 6 *Works* 239. *Cf. infra* Ch. 10, §§13-15. And see Austin, *Lectures* (3 ed. 1869) lect. iv, 144-59; *id.*, *Province Determined* 36, 87-100, esp. at 95-96, 98-99; and *infra* n. 167.

[123] Of course, discrediting intuitionism does not establish utilitarianism either. *Cf.* F. H. Bradley, *op. cit.* 90n. In fact, any *positive* argument in favour of utilitarianism would itself probably have to be based on some form of intuitionism. Austin, in his very defence of utilitarianism (*Province Determined* 52), came near to expressing this: "To think that the theory of utility would *substitute* calculation for sentiment, is a gross and flagrant error: the error of a shallow, precipitate understanding. . . . Calculation is the guide, and not the antagonist of sentiment. . . . To crush the moral sentiments, is not the scope or purpose of the true theory of utility. It seeks to impress those sentiments with a just or beneficent direction: to free us of *groundless* likings, and from the tyranny of senseless antipathies; to fix our love upon the useful, our hate upon the pernicious."

series of this, that or other feelings, which are not, except in the moment or moments that they are felt, which have as a series neither limitation of number, beginning or end, nor in themselves any reference at all . . . beyond themselves".[124] They are an "infinite perishing series". Hence to speak of maximum pleasure or minimum pain as an end is to attempt to add up and subtract a series which, until death makes the question academic, is potentially infinite. Hence, hedonist morality is "the striving to realise an idea which can never be realised" and which if realised (i.e., by summation on death) would be *ipso facto* annihilated; it is a striving beyond the present to "an impossible future". Hedonists, even when they admit this difficulty, answer that it does not invalidate that ideal as an indication of the direction in which the good is to be sought. The maximum of pleasure attainable in a concrete situation is said to be measurable, even if the lifetime balance cannot be precisely struck until death. Yet this answer is itself rather inconsistent with the Benthamite stress that the calculus must include all *consequential* pleasures and pains. For consequential pleasures and pains of the actor cannot with certainty be brought into account before death.

Fourth, it is said, the notion of a maximum of pleasure-surplus assumes that pleasures and pains are commensurable *inter se,* whereas in fact they are not. Thus it is not possible to measure a pleasure against a pain, or against another pleasure in the same way as one measures logs or cloth.[125] There were, it must be admitted, strong illusory elements in Bentham's use of terms like "calculus", or "intensity", or "duration". Bentham's zeal to set morality on "scientific" foundations, tempted him to write as if the same methods could be used in moral as in scientific calculations.[126] And critics have seized on this in direct challenge to the feasibility of doing multiplication, addition and subtraction with human feelings. This, however, is not necessarily involved in the hedonist position, which requires us only to assume that pleasures are of quantities "which can be, by direct observation and by inference from such observation, compared and significantly asserted to be equal or unequal".[127] This assumption seems less vulnerable,[128]

---

[124] F. H. Bradley, *op. cit.* 95; *cf.* T. H. Green, *Prolegomena to Ethics* (1883) 359.

[125] Bentham himself contended that this was perfectly possible. "If of two sensations, a pain and a pleasure, a man had as lief enjoy the pleasure and suffer the pain, as not enjoy the first . . . and not suffer the latter, such pleasure and pain must be reputed *equal,* or as we may say in this case, *equivalent*" (MS. cited *infra* n. 130; Baumgardt, *Bentham* 560). On his money equivalations see *id.* 561, and the text following above.

[126] *Cf. id.* 563-64 for his "axioms" of the calculus of pleasures and pains, e.g., that "The magnitude of any given pleasure is as its (number) intensity multiplied by its duration". In the closing pages of this MS. he finally plunges clearly and heavily, and we suspect incorrectly, into mathematics. How, e.g., does a pleasure of intensity 3 and duration 3 attain a magnitude of 27?

[127] F. S. Cohen, *op. cit.* 198ff.

[128] The argument that comparison involves measurement and measurement divisibility, and hence that pleasures being indivisible are not comparable, it is pointed out, is fallacious. For modern thought tends to the view that quantitative comparison, even of distances and duration, does not depend on divisibility (which is always strictly impossible) but on direct observation by means of a conventional and approximate yardstick. (*Id.* 199, relying particularly on B. Russell, *Principles of Mathematics* (1903) 182-83.) The validity of such measurement depends on the assumption that the distance measured remains the same after it has been measured by the yardstick, an assumption only verified by observation of the fact that apparently one distance remains greater or less than or equal to another. There is no reason why, with somewhat less accuracy, pleasures though indivisible may not be compared by reference to "greaterness", "lesserness" or "equalness". Nor does it seem to be a valid objection that observation of quantities of pleasure is subjective, whereas that of space is not. "So far as reality is concerned," Professor Whitehead has written, "all

the more so since (as pointed out in §13) the comparison is not between "pleasures" *in abstracto,* but between amounts of pleasure given by experience as associated with certain objective situations.

Bentham's fullest account of what he calls "Value of a lot of pleasure or pain" is probably[129] in a manuscript of about 1782, first published in full in 1952.[130] That account, for all its marginal fanfares, rests finally and rather anticlimatically[131] on the proposal that pleasures and pains are to be "quantified" by placing monetary equivalents upon them: money is their measure.[132] Lawyers familiar with the morass of the "pain and suffering" damages problem (let alone that in the "vegetable cases") will lift their eyebrows. Bentham himself recognised that a given amount of money may represent more pleasure for one man than for another, and more pleasure *for the same man* at one time than at another; and that the pleasure represented by a million guineas was not a million times more than that represented by one guinea.[133] But the quantities involved were (he thought) comparatively small, and the equivalence to the monetary scale was more likely to be right than that to any other scale, and more likely to be right than wrong.[134] It is perhaps as well that the later Bentham became more cautious on this money version of his moral arithmetic.[135] For whatever else may be said about it, that version could in no way answer the objection that pleasures and pains are not commensurable *inter se.* The fact that amounts of money are commensurable *inter se* does not show that pleasures and pains are so, unless the feeling subject *fixes the quantity of what he feels by reference to* mutually commensurable quantities of *money.* In fact, however, taking Bentham's claims at their utmost, the feeling subject does not do this; he does rather the reverse. He surmises from his own feelings the comparative quantities of the pleasures and pains involved; and only then *converts the proportions he surmises into their equivalents in money.* At most, then, the money equivalation is a precise way of stating the results of a commensuration of pleasures and pains already made; it in no way shows that this commensuration is possible.

Fifth, then, there is the problem of finding and quantifying, whether in general terms of happiness or more specific terms of pleasure surplus, *all* the effects which every one of the alternative actions would have for all

---

our sensations are in the same boat, and must be treated on the same principle." (*The Concept of Nature* (1920) 44, relied on by F. S. Cohen, *id.* 203.) This would not mean that the chances of error are equal as between observations of space, and those of pleasures and pains. But it would answer objections to the *validity* of hedonism on this account.

[129] J. Laird, *The Idea of Value* (1929) 326.

[130] MS. U.C., publ. as App. IV to Baumgardt, *Bentham* 554-566; also partially published in the French original of Halévy, *Radicalism* (*La Formation du Radicalisme Philosophique,* vol. i, 398ff.).

[131] Baumgardt, *Bentham* 557ff.

[132] He thought the money measure necessary for meaningful communication about pleasures and pains, since to say simply that one pleasure was "more" than another might mask such vast differences as to make the statement of little meaning. *Aliter* (he thought) if we say that one pleasure was worth £10, the other £5. *Cf. id.* 560-61.

[133] He also offered an "Apology" for this "mercenary language" on grounds of "necessity", no better measure being available. "Those who are not satisfied with the accuracy of this instrument must find out some other that shall be more accurate, or bid adieu to Politics and Morals. . . . Tis in this way only we can get aliquot parts to measure by." He clearly put all his eggs into this basket; but remained very worried about them.

[134] *Id.* 559.

[135] See Baumgardt, *Bentham* 456 on this aspect of the *Fragment on Government;* and see the quotations illustrative of Bentham's later position at 456ff.

persons affected. Even if the effects under consideration were less ephemeral and more calculable than either happiness or pleasure surplus, and the necessary time and effort were available, the mistakes which must arise with regard to the wider and more distant effects which most concern the legislator would often bar useful decision. This, of course, is a problem facing any criterion which values an action according to its consequences. But it takes on a specially difficult complexion if consequences are thought of in terms of pleasures and pains, and if these are taken to include those arising from feelings associated with virtue and justice.[136] And presumably, since in practice many members of the community affected would still entertain convictions of right and justice on the basis of intuition, a realistic legislator would have to bring into account the pains of guilty conscience even though intuitionism was such anathema to the Benthamite mind. No doubt the Benthamite answer would be that the decision-maker can only do his best, and that he will do better as his knowledge and experience grow, and as the community learns to understand and practise the Benthamite principle of utility.

Sixth, it is said, on the hedonistic basis it is impossible to lay down general rules applicable to more than one individual. "If I am to seek my pleasure, it must be left to me to judge concerning my pleasure,"[137] and despite Mill's "moral Nautical Almanack"[138] one man's meat is another's poison. This criticism has its main substance only if the calculus is deemed to be limited to the actor's own pleasures, whereas the Benthamite calculus aspires to embrace those of all persons concerned. While variations of individual taste and susceptibility still complicate the calculus, both

---

[136] And, of course, insofar as utilitarians often calculated on the basis of the consequences *of actions rather than of rules.* On the "modified utilitarian" position stressing that calculation must be on the "rule" level, see para. 2 of this note, and *infra* Ch. 11, §3. Indeed, Austin's main answer to the charge of unworkability is to say that the calculation must normally be on the level of rules (*Province Determined* 42-58, esp. 47ff.). He says that (for all save the "eccentric or anomalous" cases of crisis, as to which see *id.* 53-54 and *infra* n. 185) we would not calculate on the principle of utility, but on *rules* "fashioned on" that principle. He even tries to explain away the contrary utilitarian language. "In a breath, if we truly try the tendency of a specific or individual act, we try the tendency of the class to which that act belongs" (*id.* 47-48). He also thought that it was not necessary to find out even all the *rules* for oneself: most rules would be taken by most people on trust, though it was still vital to educate people to the principle of utility. See *id.* 60ff., and lect. iii *passim.*

On the "modified utilitarian" principle, adding to the test of good consequence, the rider that the rule of the "good" action shall be practicable as a universal law in a Kantian sense — i.e., that if the action is generally practised its consequences will be good—see J. Harrison, "Utilitarianism, Universalisation and our Duty to be Just" (1952-53) 52 *Proc. Arist. Soc.* 281-300, repr. Olafson, *Social Policy* 55-79. And see the related critique of utilitarianism from the standpoint of the "equal right" to maximum liberty compatible with a like liberty of all, in John Rawls, "Justice as Fairness" (1958) 67 *Phil. R.* 164-194, repr. Olafson, *op. cit.* 80-107.

The distinction here in question between actions and rules as the subject of utilitarian assessment is the basis, e.g., of the "two-level procedure" for judicial decision propounded in R. A. Wasserstrom, *The Judicial Decision . . .* (1961). The distinction cannot, however, be pressed too far; and the attempt of H. A. Bedau, *cit. supra* n. 25, at 289, to correlate it with the distinction between judicial and legislative points of view, encounters rather inevitably the difficulties which he discusses at 289ff. But it is respectfully submitted that the difficulties are Bedau's, not Bentham's.

[137] F. H. Bradley, *op. cit.* 101. A nice illustration, I suppose, is when Mark Twain's Tom Sawyer, being ordered as a punishment to paint the garden fence, instead of doing it himself *qua* pain allowed the other boys to do it *qua* pleasure, on condition that they presented him with a gift in return.

[138] J. S. Mill, *Utilitarianism* (1863) 35.

Bentham and Mill assumed (probably correctly) that there was sufficient uniformity in human reactions, in any particular society, to permit broad statements of probable pleasant or painful reaction.[139] In Dicey's words, for the legislator's purposes butcher's meat can be adequately weighed in butcher's scales, even though diamonds or gases cannot. Replies have, however, also been attempted in terms of individual morality,[140] as well as in economic terms of units of demand at the margin of choice.[141]

§21. SPECIAL DIFFICULTIES IN THE LEGISLATOR'S CALCULUS. Seventh, it is clear that the difficulties of the legislator's calculation of the pleasure-pain consequences of his choices for all members of the community are far greater and more complex (even if not differing in kind) than those of an individual in his own choices for his own conduct. This arises, however, from the more wide-ranging business which concerns the legislator, and not from any difference in the nature of the respective tasks. For the Benthamite criterion requires in both cases the bringing into account of the happiness of all persons affected.[142] There is, nevertheless, one effect of the wider range of the legislator's tasks so great as almost to raise new difficulties.

Bentham's treatment of the principle of utility shows that (in theory at least) he is only concerned with the total quantity of happiness in a community and not with how that happiness is distributed among its members. As Ayer points out,[143] "the greatest happiness of the greatest number" cannot mean any more than the greatest aggregate happiness, for otherwise it would introduce some extraneous criterion, like equality, not turning on preponderance of pleasure.[143a] Yet how, according to this, can we decide between, on the one hand, an alternative which would make three-quarters of the subjects extremely happy and one-quarter rather unhappy, and on the other hand, an alternative which would make all the subjects moderately happy, *the aggregate of happiness being equal in both cases*? And should a fantastically high pleasure balance for half the community be preferred to a more moderate pleasure balance for all, merely because the overall community aggregate will thereby be greater? The problem involved is the most intractable theoretical problem faced by utilitarianism, and for that matter by modern democratic governments, permeated as they are with the echoings and reechoings of the utilitarian theme.

It does, indeed, seem clear that the validity of hedonist utilitarianism

[139] See Bentham's own unpublished critique, quoted Halévy, *Radicalism* 495. They admit in effect the possibility of divergence in application but point out that all criteria of goodness are subject to similar divergencies, and further that these are in large part not the result of conflicting applications of the criterion, but of differing observation or interpretation of the facts to which it is applied.

[140] See, e.g., Cohen, *Ethical Systems* 191. *Cf.* parallel with Dicey's defence, Halévy, *Radicalism* 495.

[141] Viner, "Bentham and Mill" 377-78. And see *supra* n. 74.

[142] It is thus misconceived to argue (as does F. H. Bradley, *op. cit.* 103ff.) that Bentham's *Theory* would lead to a conflict between that maximum of pleasure dictated on the level or norm set by the individual for himself, and that set for him by the legislator. Such conflicts are difficulties of practice in securing loyalty to the Benthamite criterion by the legislator, and not inherent in the criterion itself.

[143] *Op. cit. supra* n. 75, at 250.

[143a] See the main theme of H. A. Bedau, "Justice and Classical Utilitarianism" in *Nomos, Justice* 284-305, esp. 301-305.

as a criterion of just law, is far from unchallengeable.[144] Its modern defenders tend, on the one hand, clearly to repudiate the emphasis on *the actor's own pleasure,* maintaining that the maximum pleasure which is the criterion is that of all concerned, which pleasure may indeed be accompanied only by pain in the actor;[145] and on the other, to claim not *a priori* truth, but only experimental validity for this version of the hedonist hypothesis, that is, that the judgment which it produces accords on the whole with ethical observance, or moral intuition, and is not manifestly false.[146]

When this last way out is sought, further grave problems emerge. For, as Plamenatz has observed as to the philosophical radicals, it never occurred to them that "it might be easier to get men to want what is easily provided, than to provide what they actually want". He asks, "If we can mould men's desires in such a way as to make it easier to satisfy them, why should we not do so?" In this light, the legislator's approach to the greatest happiness of the greatest number has some of the dangers of abuse, as well as the mystery, of the search for the Rousseauesque "General Will". Even if the Benthamite refused to recognise as legitimate the maximisation of happiness by moulding men's desires to fulfillable specifications, the "incalculability" of the "calculus" of the greatest happiness of the greatest number is a strong and constant temptation to those in power to practise such moulding and manipulation.[147] Yet once this point is reached the legislative judgment has come a full circle back into its own arbitrary subjectivity, even if presented without explicit reliance on self-evidence, intuition or natural law.

V. ACHIEVEMENT AND PROSPECTS OF BENTHAMITE UTILITARIANISM

§22. The Benthamite Achievement: Dicey's View with a Caveat. The practical achievements in English law reform traceable directly and indirectly to Bentham's influence received their classical analysis in Dicey's *Relation between Law and Public Opinion in the Nineteenth Century.*[148]

---

[144] F. H. Bradley, *op. cit.* 112ff.; G. E. Moore, *Principia Ethica* (1903) 66ff. *Cf.* also Ehrlich, *Sociology* 208-210; J. Anderson, *cit. supra* n. 113.

[145] Thus seeking to sidestep the subsidiary anti-hedonist argument that right action may be painful to the actor. The difficulty of calculation on the same plane remains.

[146] Cohen, *Ethical Systems* 208; H. Sidgwick, *op. cit. supra* n. 110. See as to David Baumgardt *infra* §23, esp. at n. 186.

[147] M. J. P. Plamenatz, *op. cit. supra* n. 18, at 36. He adds that "even the 'true liberal' wants to guide children". And see also, on the calculus, Viner, "Bentham and Mill" 366ff.; W. C. Mitchell, *The Backward Art of Spending Money* (1937) 177-202; and Bentham himself, cited *supra* n. 64.

[148] *Cf.* Bryce, 2 *Studies* 183. We cannot touch the many important excursions of Benthamites into general governmental reform. Bentham's secretary Chadwick, for instance, was largely responsible for the Royal Commissions on the Poor Law and on sanitary conditions. See generally, for a brief summary, Halévy, *Radicalism* 508-514; and for the classical contemporary account, Lord Brougham, *Speeches* (*cit. supra* n. 41) at 287ff.

For particular aspects see also Keeton *et al., Bentham,* esp. on the Poor Law (M. I. Zaglay, 58-67), civil procedure (*id.* 68-78), law of evidence (G. W. Keeton and O. R. Marshall, 79-100), parliamentary reform (R. C. Fitzgerald, 123-151), penal reform (M. Fry, 20-57), and in general (H. F. Jolowicz, 1-19, and R. H. Graveson, 101-122). For J. B. Brebner's recent reinterpretation, stressing the interventionist drive in the Benthamite programme. see his *"Laissez Faire"* 70ff. On the influence of utilitarianism in the Australian colonies see C. H. Currey, *Influence of the English Law Reformers . . .* (1937) (Science Congress Paper, Auckland).

The English Parliament, unreformed till Bentham's death, was by common recognition incapable of meeting the demand for fundamental legal reform underlying Bentham's work. Of the Reform Act of 1832, which broadly speaking transferred political power from land-owning to the middle classes, Dicey has said that it "was not the handiwork of the Benthamites, but it was in the truest sense the outcome of political utilitarianism".[149] It certainly had the strong support of Bentham and his disciples.

A first group of reforms, in a line descending through Montesquieu and Beccaria to Bentham, was in criminal law and administration, resulting in the elimination of many unnecessary cruelties, or in Bentham's terms, unnecessary pain.[150] They included the beginnings of prison reform, of reform of the lunacy laws, laws for the protection of children and animals, and the emancipation of slaves.

Another even more characteristic group of reforms was directed, in the younger Mill's words, "to secure to every person as much liberty as is consistent with giving the same amount of liberty to every other citizen". Crimes surviving from early regulative laws, such as forestalling and regrating,[151] usury,[152] and crimes under the Navigation Acts[153] and under the Combination Act of 1800[154] were abolished. The doors for large-scale capital investment were thrown open by the abolition of the usury laws and, later, wage-fixing, apprenticeship and other related restraints were abolished.[155] Personal incapacities and inequalities as illustrated by the Married Women's Property Acts from 1872 onwards were removed. The law of real property was gradually recast to conform to the new role of land in the economic process, and in particular to the easy dealings which nineteenth century conditions demanded.[156] Dicey also draws attention in connection with Bentham's influence to the Acts extending religious liberty and freedom of speech.[157]

The reforms perhaps most directly traceable to Bentham were in procedure and evidence. Here, too, perhaps, the practical efficacy of his

---

[149] Dicey, *Law and Opinion* 187. W. S. Holdsworth (*cit. supra* n. 53 at 353) begins the era of law reform at about 1822. It is clear that with the ten reports made between 1829 and 1834 by the two law reform commissions appointed as a result of Lord Brougham's famous speech of 1828 on the state of English law, the era is well begun. For Bentham's constitutional teachings see Halévy, *Radicalism* 404-431.

[150] For instance, the abolition of whipping of women in 1820 (1 Geo. IV c. 57); the pillory in stages in 1816 and 1837 (56 Geo. III c. 138; 7 William IV and 1 Vict. c. 23); hanging in chains in 1834 (4 & 5 William IV c. 263), and by a series of Acts, the death penalty except for murder or treason.

[151] (1844) 7 & 8 Vict. c. 24.

[152] Abolished in stages after 1833. See the Act to Repeal the Laws relating to Usury, 1854, 17 & 18 Vict. c. 9.

[153] Abolished in stages after 1846.

[154] The new Acts of 1824 and 1825, permitted within certain limits, combinations for the purpose of pressing for changes in hours, wages or conditions of labour. For a full account see Dicey, *Law and Opinion* 190-200. On the difficulties erected by combinations for the Benthamite individualists see the final chapter of Bentham, *Theory*, and Dicey, *op. cit.* 153-58. The substance is now dealt with in Stone, *Social Dimensions*, Ch. 7.

[155] See on the resulting inequalities Stone, *op. et loc. cit.*

[156] The Prescription Act, 1832, the Fines and Recoveries Act, 1833, the Real Property Act, 1845, the Acts culminating in the Law of Property Act, 1922, progressively abolishing copyhold, and the Settled Estates and Land Acts, 1856-1925, are all in this aspect but principal stages in increasing and facilitating the alienability of land, and thus, as Dicey properly pointed out, in extending the sphere of contractual freedom.

[157] See, e.g., the Test and Corporation Act, 1828, 8 Geo. IV c. 17; Roman Catholic Relief Act, 1829, 10 Geo. IV c. 7; Non-Conformist Chapels Act, 1844, 7 & 8 Vict. c. 45.

calculus of pain and pleasures was most clearly displayed. He submitted the operations of contemporary courts pitilessly to this test.[158] Reforms of the law of evidence have continued in unabated stream from Denman's Act in 1833 to the Evidence Act, 1938 and later amending provisions. The reform of the court system including the establishment of county courts, the reform of Chancery, and the re-organisation by the Judicature Act of 1873, are familiar, and so is the process of abolition by the Common Law Procedure Acts, 1852, 1854 and 1860 of the forms of action and the main technicalities of pleading.[159]

Argument *post hoc propter hoc* is always a game of hazard. There can be little doubt that in the aggregate, if not in the detail, the role of Bentham's utilitarian theory of justice in the legal reforms of the last century and a half has not been overstated. The distinguished economist Jacob Viner[160] has recently stated the emphatic opinion that Bentham's success as a social reformer is to be reckoned as second only to that of Marx, and that his work inspired both the Fabian socialists and the *laissez faire* liberals. The achievement is the more remarkable because of the crude psychology and the inadequate social data and techniques available to Bentham. But after the full tribute has been paid, a caveat is necessary against too wholesale an indulgence of the *post hoc* argument. The attribution of the extension of liberty of contract to Bentham's influence may serve as an example.

Undoubtedly Bentham remains a champion of liberty of contract, even after modern scholarship has relieved him of the heavy mantle of *laissez faire*. There is a temptation to assume that ideology produced the legal changes involved, notably in the relation of employers and workmen. But in this respect Bentham may often have been merely rationalising changes already proceeding. For example, legislation abolishing wage-fixing and restrictions

---

[158] In his *Official Aptitude Maximised—Expense Minimised* he made an attack on Eldon and equity procedure. In *Legal Taxes* he turned his attention to extortionate legal fees, and his *Rationale of Judicial Evidence* with all its faults has remained a classic ever since (*cf*. Wigmore, 1 *Evidence* (2 ed. 1923) 111ff.). C. P. Harvey's contrary comments ("A Job for Jurisprudence" (1943) 7 *M.L.R.* 42, 51-53) seem unjust to Bentham.

[159] See for a good example of Bentham's work in this field, the tables of procedural delays annexed to his *Letters on the Proposed Reform in the Administration of Civil Justice in Scotland* (1807) in 5 *Works* (ed. cit.) 53ff. On the role of Brougham and Denman in relation to Bentham see H. Wigmore, *op. et loc. cit.* There is a systematic account of Bentham's contributions to the organisation of justice in Halévy, *Radicalism* 376-402.

Lord Bowen was able to write (1 *The Administration of the Law in The Reign of Victoria* (1887) 310, quoted Dicey, *Law and Opinion* 208) that it was "not possible in the year 1887 for an honest litigant to be defeated by any mere technicality, any slip, any mistaken step in litigation. The expenses of the law are still too heavy, and have not diminished *pari passu* with other abuses. But the law has ceased to be a scientific game that may be won or lost by playing some particular move."

On legislative overhaul and simplification of remedies after Bentham see generally Dicey, *Law and Opinion* 205-08 (survey of English procedural reform in the 19th century); F. W. Maitland, "The Forms of Action at Common Law", in *Lectures on Equity* (1913) 374-75 (the decreased importance of the forms of action); the Common Law Procedure Acts of 1852, 15 & 16 Vict. c. 76 (simplification of common law pleading) and 1854, 17 & 18 Vict. c. 125 (dispensation with juries, and equitable defences in common law proceedings); Supreme Court of Judicature Act, 1873, 36 & 37 Vict. c. 66 (re-organisation of the Courts and merger of common law and equity jurisdiction); An Act to Facilitate Remedies on Bills of Exchange . . . 1855, 18 & 19 Vict. c. 67 (summary civil procedure). *Cf.* in the Roman law Jolowicz, *Roman Law* 525-27 (simplification of categories and procedure in the late Roman law), and *id.* 514-15 (practical disappearance of the distinction between *ius civile* and *ius gentium*).

[160] "Bentham and Mill" 361-62. And see 362ff.

on entry to trades, beginning in the second half of the eighteenth century, seems to have resulted from self-interested pressure of new large-scale employers, rather than from any conscious theory of freedom of contract.[161] The work of Adam Smith and Bentham put into circulation ideas which must have seemed to the statesmen to generalise and make explicit the practical measures already in train. Indeed, there is plenty of evidence that later in the century the Manchester School sought to draw support for *laissez faire* policies from the Benthamites, which some of these at least were concerned to repudiate most vigorously.[162] The new policy, of course, by removing the floor beneath wages before collective bargaining had arisen (and indeed when it was still being held illegal by the courts) had ample attraction for employers bent on maximising profits in the early industrial age.

§23. PROPOSALS FOR A TWENTIETH CENTURY REVIVAL OF BENTHAMITE UTILITARIANISM. Although utilitarianism continues to be a potent strain in modern English philosophy,[163] Bentham's hedonist version had long faded from philosophers' esteem[164] when David Baumgardt's *Bentham and the Ethics of Today,* in 1952, called for a return to Bentham as *the* ethical philosopher. This thorough and fascinating reader in Bentham overflows its centrally ethical concern, to illuminate also Bentham's juristic thought.[165] The fluency and formidable scholarship of the book are not, however, equal to the task of philosophical rehabilitation it undertook, even had it been more critical of its subject.[166]

With only mild dissents on some lesser points,[167] Baumgardt is con-

---

[161] See S. Webb, *History of Trade Unionism* (2 ed. 1920) 53ff. referring to the Act 17 Geo. III, c. 35, repealing 8 Eliz. c. 11. This authority points out that almost contemporaneously Parliament was still passing legislation of the old type empowering justices to fix wages by the so-called Spitalfields Acts of 1765 and 1773 (5 Geo. III c. 48, and 13 Geo. III, c. 68).

[162] Thus when the Manchester School quoted J. S. Mill's *Principles of Political Economy* (1848) to oppose state relief of distress, Mill himself, as well as Jevons, Sidgwick and others, rejected such an interpretation.

[163] See *infra* Ch. 11, §3.

[164] See Baumgardt, *Bentham* 9, 10, 11n. for bibli. of views of Bentham as "not a philosopher, but a jurist"; and even as a mere inspirer of the "more philosophically gifted" Mills.

[165] See, e.g., on the hedonistic and utility principles and the table and calculus, 167-181, 211-16, and 223-239.

[166] See the opening encomium at 3, and at 8-9 citations to other admirers comparing Bentham to Napoleon, Galileo, Descartes, Epicurus, Solon and Plato.

[167] E.g., as to his virtual rejection of conscience (110-111); his "exorbitant" praise of logical bifurcations (299); and his intolerance of poetical language in philosophy (90). This last touches one of perhaps the only two major discontents of Baumgardt with Bentham. One is as to Bentham's lack of "any intimate knowledge and understanding of the 'poetical', the finest manifestation of the human soul." And see 480-82. The other is as to his similar lack in relation to religious ideas. See *id.* 104, 317, 480, 482-88, 516-17.

We may here point out that Austin himself developed a religious utilitarianism (which Bentham would scarcely have approved) on a Benthamite kind of base. There had also been earlier religious versions of utilitarianism, e.g., by John Gay, David Hartley, and Thomas Chubb, as well as (contemporary with Bentham himself) William Paley's well-known *Principles of Moral and Political Philosophy* (1785), a kind of "theological" utilitarianism. See Baumgardt, *op. cit.* 313-16 and Austin, *Province Determined* 75-77. Aquinas himself had written, following Justinian, *"Finis autem humanae legis est utilitas hominum."* (*Summa Ia-IIae,* Q. 95 art. 3.)

Austin saw the Divine law, revealed and unrevealed, as "the ultimate test" of human law. (*Op. cit.* 34ff.) The "revealed" laws, as we have seen elsewhere (see Stone, *Legal System,* Ch. 2) are "express commands" and "laws strictly so called", but not human or "positive" law; the "unrevealed" are those discovered by use of some

cerned to re-establish Benthamite doctrine, both generally and in detail. Thus he explains Bentham's attribution of altruistic actions to the actor's ultimate self-interest as "the most consistent philosophy of altruism";[168] supports his view that the free will problem is simply irrelevant to ethics;[169] and adopts his rejection of Grotius,[170] and his sharp but rather uncomprehending and sometimes incomprehensible attack on natural law.[171] As to the *idea* of a hedonistic calculus, while Baumgardt concedes that Bentham underrated some of the grave difficulties[172] and even agrees with C. I. Lewis[173] that experiences which are really "cumulative and consummatory", and in "organic relationship to one another", cannot be handled piecemeal as self-contained arithmetical units,[174] he is still merely spurred by all this to seek a method *à la* Bentham of assessing "our feelings as organic wholes".[175]

Despite all his own riders on it, then, Baumgardt still strongly holds[176] that the case against the Benthamite calculus is not yet proven.[177] He seems to think that the calculus can still be salvaged by recognising that it does not claim to discover "absolute morality" but only *which of two or more alternative* courses of action is *the more* moral;[178] that quantitative thinking in ethics is more common than we think;[179] and that qualitative ethical judgments, however noble, cannot give the precision of quantitative judgments.[180] But in the end, when he has rejected (as needs he must) the

---

human index, such as an "innate moral sense", the principle of utility, or a combination of the two (*id*. 4ff.). The first of these Austin rejected as "halting" (see citations *supra* n. 122), but he still sometimes seemed to admit it in combination with the utility principle (e.g., at 50-51, 52, 102). Clearly he took utility as his main if not only index for the "unrevealed" laws of God, basing this position on "the goodness of God, and . . . the tendencies of human actions". (*id*. 37). Actions are "useful" and therefore enjoined by God, or "pernicious" and therefore forbidden by Him. For God designed "happiness" for men, and created them with faculties by which they can know God's purpose and the tendencies of their own actions, and can thus discover his unrevealed law. Although, as seen in Stone, *Legal System*, Ch. 2, §2, Austin explicitly rejected the natural law conception, his religious utilitarianism sounded many themes of the present-day revival of natural law. See, e.g., *Province Determined* 38ff., and *cf. infra* Ch. 7, §3. Here again, unless we keep separate Austin's analytical jurisprudence ("science of law") from his "science of legislation" and utilitarianism, his position becomes incomprehensible.

This was the setting, so different from Bentham's, which made Austin (in this respect like Bentham) eager to make converts for the "truth and importance" of the principle of utility (*id*. 7; *cf. id*. 74), despite its deficiencies. (See esp. 46, 65, 79-81, 84ff.) Denying as he did that there was any better moral guide, like a "moral sense" or "common sense" or "practical reason", he said that "we must pick our scabrous way with the help of a glimmering light, or wander in profound darkness" (*id*. 46). See also on Austin's utilitarianism *supra* nn. 111, 122, 123, and 136, and *infra* nn. 183, 185. And see as to the neglect of this aspect of Austin's thought Dowrick, *Justice* 177; Bedau, *cit. supra* n. 25, at 286ff.

[168] Baumgardt, *op. cit.* 416-422.

[169] Baumgardt, *op. cit.* 87-88.

[170] *Id*. 85.

[171] *Id*. 106. See, e.g., Bentham, *A Comment on the Commentaries* 54-56.

[172] *Op. cit.* 230; *cf. id*. 459.

[173] C. I. Lewis, *An Analysis of Knowledge and Valuation* (1946) esp. 489ff.

[174] Lewis, *op. cit.* 496, 503; Baumgardt, *op. cit.* 233.

[175] *Ibid*.

[176] *Id*. 531-34.

[177] Yet he is strangely peremptory (see 202-203) in dismissing the tentative appeal in C. D. Broad, *Five Types of Ethical Theory* (1930) 221-22, to a "calculation" of moral rightness by "balancing fittingness on the whole against utility on the whole".

[178] See esp. *id*. 534.

[179] *Id*. 296; *cf. id*. 533.

[180] *Id*. 297. At 459 he adopts as his own Bentham's final summation in 8 *Works* 542, to the effect that however imprecise the calculus it is better than "argumentation in which every idea is afloat, no degree of precision ever attained, because none is ever so much as aimed at".

crudity of Bentham's monetary measuring device,[181] the only account which he can give of the calculus can scarcely be said to be quantitative at all. He thinks that we should proceed by an "inference from performed pleasurable activities to the strength of the preconceived pleasure feelings connected with these activities".[182] The choice of one activity rather than another shows (as it were) the anticipation of greater pleasure from it. We may well agree that to refer thus to kinds of behaviour is more "objective" and "unbiased" than to refer to emotions directly; but unfortunately what can be inferred from such reference is only a fact, not a criterion. And, even more unfortunately, the fact can only be inferred after the occasion for the use of the criterion by the agent, and indeed by the ethical judge of his conduct, has already passed.

Baumgardt's encomium moves to safer ground when it turns to the value of Bentham's method as "perhaps the most instructive signpost, the most objective warning signal against uncritical moralising that we possess in ethical literature".[183] This admiration properly extends to the "censorial" Bentham's radical attack on the conventional presuppositions of popular morality,[184] his striving to clear the foreground of ethical choice from unconscious prejudgments, insisting on moral neutrality while the facts are sought, and his effort to weigh highly emotional matters impartially.[185] And certainly, independently of the validation of Bentham's own hedonistic criterion or even whether it merits the status Baumgardt confers of "a scientific hypothesis",[186] we must regard as salutary the revived concern with the essential Benthamite thought by ethicists, historians and economists[187] as well as political theorists and lawyers.[188]

Ivor W. Jennings (as he then was) had, indeed, already pleaded with lawyers in 1938 for such a revival. The philosophers' challenge to the Benthamite criterion, urged Jennings, does not of necessity mean that it is not a practicable criterion. Though it might not suit a "philosopher-king", those who govern are not in fact philosophers, nor are their peoples

---

[181] Baumgardt, op. cit. 234.

[182] Ibid., and see 533.

[183] Baumgardt, op. cit. 261ff., 374ff., esp. 381, stressing Bentham's labours to produce terminology for human motives that is neutral, i.e., does not beg the ethical questions. See, e.g., Principles, c. x, Table of the Springs of Action (1817), id. 374ff., esp. at 381. Cf. with Bentham's discussion of motives, Austin, Province Determined 109ff.; and Baumgardt's strictures of Dumont, op. cit. 357, 359.

[184] See, e.g., at 24-33, 76ff., 158, 290-91, 299, 492-97, 522.

[185] See esp. id. 280, 353, 534. Though of course there is here little new in Baumgardt's interpretations. Cf., e.g., Stone, Province 295ff. Austin (Province Determined, 54-5) was already very sensitive to this aspect. He thought that even in those rare cases in which we need to "calculate specific consequences" (see supra n. 136), the principle of utility would at least afford "an intelligible test" so that "a peaceable compromise . . . would, at least, be possible"; but that without it, the parties having "bandied their fustian phrases, and 'bawled till their lungs be spent', they must even take to their weapons, and fight their difference out".

[186] Id. 183, where he quotes in support hitherto unpublished MSS., which he thinks would, if known, have forestalled many objections to Benthamite utilitarianism. It is clear at 529-530, however, that by "scientific" he is thinking mainly of the tendency to impartiality and neutralism in analysing acts and movements discussed n. 183 supra.

[187] See the works of J. Viner, J. B. Brebner, and L. Hartz, cited supra n. 1; and the works cited by Baumgardt, op. cit. 233.

[188] The diffidence of English lawyers in the face of ethical disputations had formerly tempted them at least to acquiesce in the philosophers' attack on hedonist utilitarianism outlined above. But see now notably Cohen, Ethical Systems 185-220 and passim, esp. 285; Jennings, "Utilitarianism" (1938) 30-35; Laski, Politics 24-25; and many recent writings of G. L. Williams.

susceptible of government on philosophical principles. Most citizens are willing to be governed in accordance with the principle of the greatest happiness, that is, the maximum of pleasure and minimum of pain of the greatest number; and democratic governors must *ex hypothesi* be ready to conform to it. "A democratic politician has to be in practice a psychological hedonist."

As between the alternatives of indefinitely postponing urgent problems of the law, or approaching them with a criterion of disputed philosophical validity which nevertheless appears to have such great nineteenth century achievements to its credit, Jennings therefore urged acceptance of the latter— especially (he argued) since materials now available in the form of official records and statistics, and the findings of anthropologists and legal historians and the comparative social sciences, would add greatly to the precision of the criterion.[189] It might be added that Bentham's utilitarianism had the great virtue, rivalled perhaps only in modern times by Roscoe Pound's theory of justice, of directing the mind to the full consequences[189a] and implications of the actual or proposed rules of law.[190]

The plea seems strong, but is in the end not as strong as it seems. The argument that this criterion *did prove* workable and valuable in Bentham's century is to some extent deceptive. At least two factors then operating to facilitate reform may be scarcely, if at all, present today. The first factor is that the discrepancy between the eighteenth century legal order and the nineteenth century social, industrial and economic conditions was so great, that even the roughest criterion would have served to expose it and base the needed overhaul, once the emotional reaction had begun.[190a] The second is that the first three-quarters of the nineteenth century were, on the whole, an era of widespread agreement as to the direction in which human affairs were, and ought to be, moving. The convergence for the time being of Kant's metaphysics, Adam Smith's economics, Bentham's utilitarianism, Darwin's evolutionism, and Spencer's positivism, upon the removal of unnecessary legal restraints on individual activity, was clear enough. This convergence, along with the affirmative needs of an industrialised and urbanised era for elementary services such as police, local government, public health and safety facilities, set the direction of a programme dictated as much by facts as by any theory of legislation. In due course, indeed, the organised groups whose activity Dicey thought of as "collectivist", and as diametrically opposed to "Benthamite individualism", also came to adopt the *laissez faire* demand. Kahn-Freund has called it a demand for collectivist *laissez faire,* for hands off by the legislature apart

---

[189] *Cf.* on the irrelevance of Bentham's errors of history and psychology, M. J. P. Plamenatz, in Ginsberg, *20th Century* 39-41; Viner, "Bentham and Mill" 368.

[189a] *Cf.* on the claim that historically utilitarianism offered *an expansion* of the meaning of justice, as compared with the moralist-contractualist criteria whose proponents are often so scornful of utilitarianism, J. W. Chapman, "Justice and Fairness" in *Nomos, Justice* 126, 149ff.

[190] See *supra* n. 185; and see "On the Influence of Time and Place in Matters of Legislation", in 1 *Works* (Bowring's ed.) 171ff.

[190a] See *supra*, §§6-10, §22. *Cf.* I. Jenkins, "Justice as Ideal and Ideology", in *Nomos, Justice* 191 at 199, on "both the short-term fruitfulness and the ultimate incompleteness" of any pragmatic method assuming self-evident goals of social action. "Such a pragmatism can work only . . . when the contrast between the actual and the ideal is both generally compelling and specifically precise. When this is not the case— and it rarely is—reliance on exclusively intuitive and procedural techniques breaks down, for there are then no 'clear and present' ends in view for these to seize and realize."

from the setting of organisational ground rules for collective bargaining, and from fixing standards in cases where bargaining obviously cannot work.[191]

Many legal problems in British countries may be so ripe for consideration that a diligent and consistent application of Bentham's utilitarianism would help in their solution. This is especially so since with Bentham, as (we shall later observe) with Professor Pound,[192] the criterion consisted in part of a comprehensive search for actual facts, and a reduction of them to simple forms, a step in itself conducive to easier solution. There may be many problems on which there would be a reasonable identity of views in the community as to what is desirable, once the factors involved were more fully exposed. But the solutions thus agreed would, as in Bentham's own time,[193] be *endorsed by* the formula, rather than actual consequences of its intellectual content. Over a wide and vital field, moreover, the criterion would probably avail nothing. Here it would produce varied and conflicting results at different hands,[194] thus throwing the protagonists back (in rational discussion at any rate) upon the theoretical problems. The deep immersion of our age in such theoretical fundamentals may, indeed, be the result as much as a cause of its inability to agree on practical measures. In this respect it is reminiscent of fifth century Greece, in which great discoveries commingled with great catastrophes and conflicts of all kinds.[195] The richness and permanence of the speculations which emerged from that ancient world may or may not be equalled in this century. But it seems clear, at least, that the basic twentieth century conflicts are as unlikely to melt away at the touch of hedonist utilitarianism, as those of ancient Greece at the touch of the relativist utilitarianism of a Protagoras.

---

[191] See for an interpretation of U.K. labour relations in these terms, O. Kahn-Freund, "Labour Law" in Ginsberg, *20th Century* 215-263, esp. 227-263, B. C. Roberts, "Industrial Relations" *id.* 364-389, esp. 387-89. And on the resulting perplexities for the 20th century inheritors of 19th century liberalism, see R. B. McCallum, "The Liberal Outlook", in Ginsberg, *20th Century* 63, esp. 66ff.

[192] *Infra* Ch. 9. *Cf.* Bentham, *op. cit. supra* n. 190, at 178; Cohen, *Ethical Systems* 232, who makes this point as to hedonism generally.

[193] See Professor Dicey's notable admission of this, discussed in Stone, *Social Dimensions*, Ch. 12, §7.

[194] As it does, e.g., at the respective hands of Professor Laski (*Politics* 24-25 and *passim*) and a *laissez faire* economist such as Professor F. S. Hayek. Halévy, *Radicalism* (esp. pt. iii, c. iv and pp. 53-54) has made the most penetrating analysis of the contradictory strains within the Benthamite movement, especially of the supposed "natural identity of interests" and the "artificial identification of interests" in society.

[195] *Cf.* Vinogradoff, 2 *Jurisprudence* 20ff. See *supra* Ch. 1, §4.

CHAPTER 5

SOCIAL UTILITY AND SOCIAL SOLIDARITY

I. SOCIAL UTILITARIANISM[1]

§1. SOCIAL AND INTELLECTUAL CONTEXT: THE REVOLT AGAINST INDIVI-
DUALISM. Between the final thought of Kantian and Benthamite individualism
and Rudolf von Ihering's social utilitarianism,[2] lay half a century of rapid
social, economic and intellectual development. During that half-century in
England there came the trend to collectivist legislation and away from exclusive emphasis on freedom from restraint as an ideal.[3] In Germany the issues
involved were raised still earlier.[4] Even as Ihering was writing, a vigorous
doctrinal controversy was proceeding between the socialists and the German
followers of the "Manchester School" of *laissez faire,* with regard to Bismarck's programme of social insurance.

For our present purpose Ihering's scholarly life is sharply divided
around the year 1870. Up to then he was engaged in the orthodox

---

[1] SOCIAL UTILITARIAN THOUGHT: R. von Ihering, *Scherz und Ernst in der Jurisprudenz* (1885) (a collection of papers written from 1860 onwards)—destructive
side; *id., Zweck* (vol. i transl. by I. Husik, 1913, here cited as "Ihering, transl."),
Ihering's Preface and pt. i, cc. i, viii, esp. 325-423; *Der Kampf ums Recht* (1872) (a
small offshoot of Ihering's thinking on the *Zweck*) c. v, section 8 (5 ed. transl. J. J.
Lalor as *The Struggle for Law* (1879, 2 ed. with Intro. by A. Kocourek, 1915))—
constructive side.

BIOGRAPHICAL AND GENERAL: Munroe Smith, "Four German Jurists" in (1895)
10 *Pol. Sc. Qu.* 664-692, (1896) 11 *id.* 278-309, *passim;* J. H. Drake, in Preface to
Ihering, transl. xv-xvii; A. Kocourek, cited *supra;* A. Merkel, 2 *Gesammelte
Abhandlungen* (1899) 744ff., transl. as App. I to Ihering, transl. 427-453; D.
Pasini, *Saggio su Jhering* (1959); E. Paresce, *"Nota su Jhering"* (1960) 37 *Riv. Int. di
Fil. del Dir.* 769-781.

BACKGROUND AS AN HISTORICAL JURIST: Ihering, *Geist* vol. i, Intro. (4 ed. 1878)
1-85 (notice the dedication to Puchta, and *cf.* M. Smith, *cit. supra,* 687ff.); W. M.
Geldart, in his Intro. to Ihering, transl., at xlii-xlv. See citations on the possession
controversy in Stone, *Social Dimensions* Ch. 2, n. 28, and see *infra* nn. 5, 6.

IHERING AND BENTHAM AND THE *INTERESSENJURISPRUDENZ:* J. H. Drake, cited
supra, xvii-xix; W. M. Geldart, cited *supra,* xlvi-ii; P. Heck, *Interessenjurisprudenz*
(1933) (in *Recht und Staat in Geschichte und Gegenwart* No. 97).

[2] Ihering lived 1818-1892, and his writings here mainly in discussion were done
in the 'sixties and the 'seventies. He came of a legal family, trained at Berlin and
was professor successively at Basel, Rostock, Kiel, Vienna, Strassburg and Göttingen.

[3] *Supra* Chs. 3, 4.

[4] See for a good short account, J. H. Boyd, *Treatise on the Law of Compensation
for Injuries to Workmen* . . . (1913) 25-52. As early as 1838, Prussia had enacted a
compensation act for workmen and passengers on railways. In 1854, Prussian statutes
compelled certain classes of employers to contribute to the funds of voluntary sickness
associations formed under statute, and similar provisions were adopted in other
German states. In 1871, Prussia enacted an employers' liability act cutting down
employers' defences. There followed ten years later the famous message to the *Reichstag*
of William I which inaugurated a programme of industrial accident insurance laws,
1883-1887. This legislative programme of Bismarck was, in some degree, an endorse-
ment of the socialist doctrines of Lassalle. And see briefly on the internal German
political situation J. D. Mayer, *Max Weber and German Politics* (1944) c. ii.

German juristic thinking of the age—the mixture of Kantian metaphysics, logical conceptualism and historicism, which characterise, as we have seen elsewhere, the work of Savigny and his followers, the Pandectists.[5] About 1870, as a modern follower has put it, "originally a *Begriffsjurist* . . . from a Saul he turned into a Paul".[6] Gravely dissatisfied with current thought, he published after 1887 *Der Zweck im Recht,* translated into English as *Law as a Means to an End,*[7] which presented at length his social utilitarian position. This thesis was a demand for the reunion of legal conceptions with social realities, and for historians to turn their subject into "a creative force",[8] rather than present it as the working out of inexorable forces before which human effort is helpless.[9] Ihering was also reacting away from the individualist assumptions of the period, which had developed from the Benthamite programme as interpreted by the older Mill, expressed in the younger Mill's *On Liberty,*[10] and elaborated in the programme of the Manchester School. As liberating legislation merged imperceptibly into collectivist regulatory legislation, the vindication of collectivist intervention rather than the vindication of liberty became the question of the day.

In his criticism of individualism Ihering classed together Bentham, Kant and Herbert Spencer.[11] He challenged the negative role attributed to law by the dominant Kantian strain,[12] insisting that positive human purposes, not metaphysical liberty or the "sense of right", are the basis of justice.[13]

---

[5] See Stone, *Legal System,* Ch. 6. Into this class fall all of von Ihering's writings before 1886, which are mainly as follows: *Abhandlungen aus dem römischen Recht* (1844); the 4 vols. of the *Geist* (1852-65, unfinished); *Das Schuldmoment im römischen Privatrecht* (1867). His chief departure from the historical school in the *Geist* is his thesis that the non-national elements in legal systems may be more important in developed systems than the national. See the Preface to vol. i. Even later he joined with gusto in the characteristic dispute as to the ground and conditions for protection of possession in the Roman law: *Über den Grund des Besitzschutzes* (1868, 2 ed. 1869). For a good account see Munroe Smith, *cit. supra* n. 1. He founded in 1857 jointly with the Germanist, von Gerber, the *Jahrbuch für die Dogmatik des heutigen römischen und deutschen Privatrechts,* which is still known as "Ihering's *Jarhbuch*" and was devoted to the orthodox interests of the period. For an account of Ihering's work in the *Dogmatik* see A. Merkel's remarks in Ihering, transl. (*supra* n. 1) at 427-53, esp. 431-35 on the *Jahrbuch.*

[6] P. Heck, cited *supra* n. 1, at 13. Ihering never finished the *Geist* because of this change of approach. See the Preface to the *Zweck.* So his former interest in the refinements of possession gave place to his *Der Besitzwille: Zugleich, eine Kritik der herrschenden juristischen Methode* (1889). His post-1870 destructive works are well represented in the *Scherz und Ernst in der Jurisprudenz* (1895) being a collection of two series of magazine articles written in the 'sixties and entitled *Vertrauliche Briefe über die heutige Jurisprudenz,* and *Plaudereien eines Romanisten.* See the account of these in Stone, *Legal System,* Ch. 6, §11.

[7] A better English title would perhaps have been "The Element of Purpose in Law". Vol. ii of the *Zweck,* which was to work out philosophically the place of purpose in social control generally, was left unfinished. The above translation of vol. i is here cited as "Ihering, transl.".

[8] Saleilles, *"Ecole Historique"* 80. For some account of the specifically English background of the historical school see W. S. Holdsworth, *Some Makers of English Law* (1938) 266-71. And see Stone, *Social Dimensions,* Chs. 2 and 3.

[9] See on these aspects Stone, *Legal System,* Ch. 6, esp. §10, and *infra* Chs. 6, §§11ff., and 10, §§5ff.

[10] (1859). See *supra* Ch. 4, esp. §22.

[11] 2 *Zweck* (2 ed.) 137. On Spencer see Stone, *Social Dimensions,* Ch. 1, §12; *id.* Ch. 9, §§3ff.

[12] Significantly he chose Trendelenburg (on whose criticism of Kant see *supra* Ch. 3, §4) as the philosopher nearest to him.

[13] 1 *Zweck,* Preface, transl. ix. Though he was not familiar with Aquinas in his first edition, he admits in the second (2 *Zweck* 161n.) that his own view of the mutations of law for the attainment of social utility is to be found in Aquinas, and he chides intervening generations for overlooking this. *Cf.* modern Thomist

Ihering addressed himself in greater detail to the prevailing English individualism as expounded by the younger Mill. He challenged Mill's assumed distinction[14] between a man's conduct which concerns only himself, where
his liberty was to be absolute, and that which concerns others, which the
law might regulate. "I know of no example," he wrote, "of a legal rule
which has as its purpose to force an individual against his own will, in
his own interest, for his own good. Where it appears to do so, it is always
in the interest of society."[15] Armed with Mill's formula, he continued:

> I promise so to compress and tight-lace it (individual freedom) that
> it will not have the power to move. If the father squanders his money,
> do not the children suffer? And when the children become a charge
> on the poor box, does not society suffer? Surely it does. Hence I forbid
> prodigality. But not this alone. I forbid also stockjobbing, all daring
> speculations, every extravagant expenditure. In short, I bring the entire
> control of a man's property under police superintendence.

Carrying the attack into the Benthamite camp, he fastened upon Mill's
admission that, even if without family or friends, a man should not be
permitted to sell himself as a slave, since freedom cannot be used for its
own destruction. Ihering commented that in such terms of "the logic of
the concept" every contract contains a partial renunciation of freedom.
He himself, said Ihering, would rather say for such a case that society
has come to recognise that slavery is incompatible with it.

He carried the point further in relation to the social context by asking:
"Has legislation a right to fix the maximum hours of labour?"[16] Mill approved
of this, and of health and safety legislation for factories;[17] yet, says Ihering,
"if the prohibition to work as much or as little as I please does not constitute
an interference with my personal freedom, where does such interference
begin?" He makes the same point concerning Mill's admission of the
propriety of saving the evil-doer from the unintended consequences of his
evil-doing. For Mill had said that though, ordinarily, drunkenness was not
a fit subject for legal interference, still a person once convicted of any act
of drunken violence "should be placed under a special legal restriction
personal to himself". Ihering made this biting comment: "A young man
breaks a window in a state of intoxication. Henceforth, according to Mill,
a special law, issued personally for him, dogs his footsteps, follows him as
long as he lives, and stands as a spectre behind his chair at every joyful
feast."

---

thinking, e.g., T. Meyer, *Institutiones Juris Naturalis . . . secundum Principia S.
Thomas Aquinatis* (1906) 495ff. And see *infra* Ch. 7, §§8ff. *Cf.* F. Gény's position,
discussed in Stone, *Legal System*, Ch. 6, §3.
  14 Transl. 404-06.
  15 *Ibid.* The debatable nature of Mill's principle is seen in its adoption (un-
professed) by the Departmental Committee on Homosexual Offences (Wolfenden
Committee) Report, *Cmnd.* 247 (1957), in the form that "It is not the function of
law to intervene in the private lives of citizens or to seek to enforce any particular
pattern of behaviour". The Committee's recommendation that "homosexual behaviour
between consenting adults in private be no longer a criminal offence" (62) nevertheless was sharply controversial and was not carried out. The point, of course, is
that psychologically, many members of the community are emotionally involved even
by the knowledge of the permissibility of private acts. But see the notable re-
examination by H. L. A. Hart, *Law, Liberty and Morality* (1963), discussed in Stone,
Social Dimensions, Ch. 6, §27. *Cf.* also the analogous indecisiveness of the "peace of
the port" rule in jurisdiction under international law.
  16 *Op. cit.* 407-08.
  17 J. S. Mill, *op. cit. supra* n. 10, at 159, 160, 163, 181.

Yet despite these criticisms of individualism Ihering, as Professor Geldart has written, "stands alone, or almost alone, among German writers in his admiration for Bentham's work".[18] The similarities between them are as great as the differences. Both insisted on penetrating behind the verbal formulae of the law to the social realities which stand behind them and with which they deal—Bentham seeing this reality as individual pleasures and pains, Ihering as interests or purposes of individuals and society. And each of them believed, with naive confidence, that his criterion of justice was novel and epoch-making, the key to both justice and ethics.

By his time context, however, after the first rise of collectivistic legislation,[19] and unembarrassed by the hedonistic calculus, Ihering was led to insist on the primacy of social purposes, and on the valuation of individual purposes, including freedom from restraint, in terms of social purposes.[20] By this context, too, Ihering was given a sense of the role of history and of the idea of evolution as a check upon reason.[21] Whereas Bentham saw in the past mainly the arbitrary and the obsolete, and sought to build on the principle of utility as a new foundation, Ihering, seeing in the past the imperfect realisation of the principle of utility, attempted rather to express this more perfectly.[22] For it must be recalled that the 'seventies and 'eighties were the exciting heyday of the theory of evolution. This theory, which by implication seemed to repudiate claims of absoluteness for philosophical theory, undermined Ihering's old allegiance to metaphysics. It also confirmed him in his view of the purposiveness of legal history.

> One purpose of law is produced out of the other with the same necessity with which, according to the Darwinian theory, one animal species is developed from the other.

> Here is a new inexorability, but not one before which men may remain passive: rather one which requires constant struggle and conscious seeking of ends on the part of men.[23]

§2. THE "LAW OF PURPOSE". Ihering asserts at the outset[24] that the relation between human purposes and human acts plays an analogous role in the moral world to that between cause and effect in the physical world. Within

---

[18] *Cit. supra* n. 1. *Cf.* on this and on its relation to Ihering's imperfect acquaintance with ethical theory, Munroe Smith, cited *supra* n. 1, 11 *Pol. Sc. Qu.* 278, 294.

[19] *Supra* Ch. 3, §§8-10, 12 and works there cited on this. *Cf.* W. M. Geldart in Ihering, transl., *supra* n. 1, xlvi-lii; J. H. Drake, *id.* xvii-xix.

[20] As Ihering himself puts it, Bentham stressed "subjective purposes" while he stressed "objective purposes". It has been said, though with only partial truth, that "the principle of social utility as conceived by Ihering is not inconsistent with, and indeed requires, a due appreciation of the claims of the individual, while Bentham's teaching is capable of conversion to the completest individualism" (W. M. Geldart, *cit. supra* n. 1, xliv). This opinion takes at its face value Ihering's own claim in Volume 2 of the *Zweck* (untranslated) that "*die gesellschaftliche Theorie hat für das Individuum Raum, die individualistische aber nicht für die Gesellschaft—das Ganze schliesst den Teil in sich, der Teil nicht das Ganze*".

[21] The Hegelian philosophy of history went well with this acceptance.

[22] From the same fact springs, perhaps, Bentham's overconfidence in conclusions based on his calculations with a primitive psychology of pains and pleasures. Ihering did not embarrass himself either with the hedonistic calculus, or with the claim to absolutism which proceeded from it.

[23] Preface to the *Zweck*. It is curious that the work of Auguste Comte in the 'thirties and 'forties made little or no impression on Ihering, possibly because it had not yet been taken over into juristic theory. See Stone, *Social Dimensions*, Ch. 1, §11, Ch. 9, §2. And for Comte's greater influence on Duguit see *infra* §8.

[24] Transl. 37-46. The *Zweck* covers four main topics: (1) *Social and egotistic purposes*, including the role and development of human purposes in social life, in

the stronghold of the will the law of causality cannot operate, but the law of purpose operates there instead.[25] While the human will begins, according to Ihering, with an exclusive tendency to further its own individual purposes,[26] men in their mutual relations are led often to perceive that they will further their own purposes by cooperating in the purposes of others. This co-operative mutual furtherance of individual purposes reaches, in the state, its most highly organised form. Law is thus the means whereby the organised purposes of society are achieved, individual purposes serving as levers. Only when the appeal to the individual interest fails, does the state use compulsion. "Unity of purpose and interests on both sides is the formula whereby nature, the State and the individual, gain power over egoism."[27]

To show the relations one to another, "the higher to the lower", of the purposes of which human life consists, and how one purpose is inexorably produced out of another,[28] is therefore a main task. Conscious somewhat of the danger of too sharp a contrast of individual and society, he explained that by his social-individual distinction, he meant merely that a concrete individual living in society has some purposes which have regard solely to his separate life, and others ("higher") which pertain to his social life.[29]

§3. INDIVIDUAL AND SOCIAL PURPOSES. Individual purposes, or "egotistic self-assertion", include above all that of self-preservation. This animal reaction is sublimated and elaborated in man, showing itself for instance in efforts to ward off future as well as present dangers. It is thus an important base of the law of property, economic self-assertion being, in Ihering's view, merely a wider extension of self-preservation to the future, the necessary basis for all the higher needs of human life. But since nature in general only

---

particular the modification of the individual's self-regarding purposes by reference to the purposes of others (cc. i-v).

(2) *Social mechanics,* being the means of securing social purposes, including (a) the largely extra-legal use of reward to mould individual to social purposes, and (b) coercion as a means to the same end, this being the characteristic though not exclusive field of law and the state, which are the coercive instruments of human purposes, the "politics of force". Here Ihering sought to show how, for its own efficacy, law though a means of coercion became a control over force, and a check on the violence of the state itself (cc. v, vii and viii).

(3) *A survey of the conditions of social life,* or rather of the human purposes which mature systems of law as he knew them had attempted to fulfil (c. viii in part).

(4) In his ninth Chapter, which consists of the whole of the second volume of the *Zweck,* he considered at large the role of morals in social control, that is of non-legal coercion. In morals, he points out, society uses the individual's sense of his ethical destiny, his ethical self-assertion, as a means of inducing his co-operation in the realisation of social purposes. See on this second volume, which is mainly of sociological interest, Stone, *Social Dimensions,* Ch. 12.

[25] Even a lunatic, he says, acts with a purpose though it may be a peculiar and abnormal purpose.

[26] Ihering thus seemed to open with the unnecessary assumption that society has developed only by modifying the natural egoism which human beings share with the animal world. The real primitive man, in Ihering's view, lived outside all social bonds, recognised no social injunction. This, it will be seen, is Hobbes' "nature" as contrasted with that of Grotius or Rousseau, propounded with a charming innocence of how debatable and debated it was.

[27] Cc.i and ii.

[28] Ihering, transl. 43.

[29] *Id.* 44. *Cf.* his long discussion of the personification of society, in vol. ii (2 ed.) 192ff. The student will do well to make a mental reservation on this head, and reconsider it along with Roscoe Pound's attempt to avoid the trap by referring to claims asserted "in title of" individual life, "in title of" social life, and "in title of" life in politically organised society respectively. See Stone, *Social Dimensions,* Ch. 4, §§3ff.

yields fruits to labour, consistent labour develops with the claim to property. Property produces inevitably *law,* for without *law* there is no security of life or property, and law presupposes organised society. So exchange, with the contract as its form, is a by-product of economic self-assertion; for exchange is the means whereby what is produced is directed to him whose purposes it best serves. The social function of contracts is, from this view-point, to secure the original purposes of the parties against later prejudicial shifts of purpose or evaluation of purposes on the part of one of the parties.[30] These two urges of physical self-assertion and economic self-assertion lead up to the urge for what Ihering called juristic self-assertion, which, however, transcends them. For the growth of the conception of law brings with it a struggle by men to vindicate and protect their position under the law, which goes beyond the mere protection of economic or other interests which may be involved.[31]

Individual purposes or interests, by the very effort to realise them, create more complex group or social purposes.[32] Whether men are conscious of it or not, every one exists, not for himself alone, but at the same time for others and through others. His contribution to social purposes is secured either in the free processes of social life, or by force, the state and its law occupying the sphere of force. Ihering thus made the vital distinction between "society" and "the state", between social control in general, and social control through law.[33] Society is the indispensable form of individual life. It is only for those social purposes which cannot be achieved by free interplay of individuals and groups, and where external force is thus needed, that the organisation of the state and its law is created.[34]

§4. SOCIAL MECHANICS: COMPETITIVE POWER AND ASSOCIATION. "Social mechanics" is Ihering's term for the means used by society for controlling individual purposes and moulding them nearer to social purposes. These means, he thought, included on the one hand law (with its organised coercion), and on the other the free processes of social life (with their non-coercive levers of reward, and the potentialities of association for the more efficient realisation of individual purposes).

First, then, as to reward, which Ihering saw as the dominant modern means for securing the satisfaction of economic wants.[35] "There were times when one got services for nothing which now one can get only for

---

[30] Ihering sums up this "inexorable" emergence of purposes one from another thus: "The person, i.e., the purpose of his physical self-preservation, produced property, i.e., the purpose of the regulated and assured realisation of that purpose. The two together lead again to law, i.e., to the purpose of securing their mutual purposes, otherwise solely dependent upon the physical strength of the subject, by the power of the state".

[31] Ihering elaborated this idea of the struggle for the vindication of legal rights as factors in legal progress in his *Kampf ums Recht* (1872) transl. J. J. Lalor as *The Struggle for Law* (2 ed. 1915).

[32] See generally c. vi.

[33] Society, on the one hand, he said (transl. 68) "must be defined as the actual organisation of life for and through others and (since the individual is what he is only through others) as the indispensable form of life for oneself. Society is therefore really the form of life in general. Human life and social life are synonymous".

[34] "But it needs it only in small part. Commerce and trade, agriculture, manufacture and industry, art and science, the usage of the home and the customs of life organise themsleves. Only occasionally does the State interfere with its 'law' so far as it is absolutely necessary to secure against violation the order which these interests have evolved independently" (68).

[35] See generally c. vii.

money", as with the public officials and jurisconsults in ancient Rome where the equivalent rendered was in honour and respect.[36] The change to money rewards was a change to a system of organised compensation, and tended towards more reliable and complete satisfaction of wants, substituting, for instance, the reliable service of the modern hotel for the less reliable private hospitality.[37] Commerce, then, he concluded, is the organisation of social rewards by competition,[38] which "is the social self-adjustment of egoism", that is, the social means of ascertaining equivalence between the parties.[39]

It will have become apparent that Ihering attributed to competition for commercial reward an indispensable role in social development.[40] He saw in it an emancipator of the poor man, making services from the world over available to him; the vindication of human equality, since commerce knows no respect for persons, and money entitles the holder to the support of others for his purposes; and a pioneer of justice generally.[41]

Such a note, reminiscent of Bentham's greatest single blow for *laissez faire, The Defence of Usury*,[42] is perhaps explained by the expansion of production and markets at the end of the nineteenth century. The eloquence is indeed rather misleading, for it is clear that Ihering is not withdrawing his strictures on *laissez faire*. His praise is directed rather to the *past* achievement of commerce. For he insisted on the "right" of society "to check the excesses of the selfish motive when these become dangerous to the success of society", and that no error was more serious than to assume that a contract as such, merely because it was not illegal or immoral, *must* be legally enforced. In terms of their respective social and economic contexts, therefore, Ihering's qualifications in the 1870's upon Bentham's positions of the 1780's are entirely natural. His kinship with twentieth-century thinkers (for example, Duguit, shortly to be discussed) is clear from his further insistence that "duty is that side of a man's vocation which addresses itself to society", and that this must increase as economic specialisation increased the dependence of society as a whole on the proper function-

---

[36] *Cf.* the custom of hospitality in undeveloped societies, and the now largely fictitious theory of legally gratuitous services of members of the bar in some British countries; and the considerable modern use of this "ideal reward" in certain spheres, such as "social work", public office, the arts and the sciences, to supplement inadequate economic reward. Ihering considers this at length (transl. 136-57).

[37] At 90.

[38] At 89. Just as, he adds, "retribution of the socially evil becomes criminal justice".

[39] On occasions, indeed, his praise of it is sharply reminiscent of the far-sighted propaganda campaigns of large-scale business enterprises, which were to become frequent in the present century. "If I ask myself where the idea of justice is most perfectly realised in our social institutions, the answer is, in business" (174).

[40] In the contract of exchange both parties getting what immediately serves his purposes better; in sale or contract of service, the other getting money which potentially does so. It is not necessary to consider here Ihering's elaborate analysis (transl. 118-36) of the social purposes filled by credit in modern economics. His thesis that the smooth operation of the system of exchange could not be assured without modern credit devices was not new.

[41] "While the states were fighting one another, trade found out and levelled the roads that lead from one nation to another, and established between them a relation of exchange of goods and ideas; a pathfinder in the wilderness, a herald of peace, a torchbearer of culture" (transl. 174).

[42] (1785-87). See *supra* Ch. 4, §1; and *cf.* Stone, *Social Dimensions*, Ch. 7, §3. Note however (*supra* Ch. 4, *passim*) that traditional portrayals under Dicey's influence of Bentham as a champion of *laissez faire* must now be greatly qualified, Bentham himself being at least ambivalent on this matter. In Ihering the ambivalence seems more striking still, since he seems simultaneously to eulogise the past role of *laissez faire* and to refute its claims to a major future role.

ing of each part.[43]

The other non-coercive means of furthering social purposes Ihering saw in the phenomenon of association. Competition fosters socially useful purposes by making each individual's purposes fit sufficiently with those of others to command reward. In association the egoistic interests are harnessed differently. First, association for a given purpose increases proportionately the strength available for its fulfilment. Second, the advantages of this strength provide a powerful incentive to individuals to pursue purposes which others can share. Association in all its forms thus "throws a bridge between egoism and self-denial", and between individual and social purposes.[44]

§5. SOCIAL MECHANICS: FORCE AND ITS SELF-LIMITATION. "The second lever of social order is coercion. . . . Coercion organised makes the State and law".[45] By coercion Ihering meant the realisation of the purposes of one person by mastering the will of another. Such mastery might be mechanical, where the will is broken and the act is therefore virtually done by the coercing party; or psychological as where by various pressures "the resistance of the will is overcome from within", so that the subject himself wills the act, albeit under pressure.[46]

In Ihering's view, not only is the measure of justice the fullest possible effectuation of individual and social purposes, but the State and its law, the most organised form of coercion, are themselves a product of the operation of individual and social purposes.[47] Men, said Ihering, precisely because their behaviour is purposive, cannot rest content like animals with a crude interplay of force. The history of force on the earth is the history of human egoism, but this history is summed up in the fact that egoism becomes wiser by instruction, and accepts self-denying ordinances. "Force produces law immediately out of itself, and as a measure of itself, law evolving as the politics of force."[48] Failure to appreciate this was, in Ihering's view, the root error of dominant theories of justice which under-estimated the element of personal energy, of force, of the struggle of interests behind concrete legal growth, treating it as a mechanical unfolding of truth.[49]

At this point Ihering proceeded to ask how it came about that "the preponderance of force is on the side of right"? His answer was as uncon-

---

[43] Ihering, transl. 109, 113, 115ff. Cf., on E. Durkheim and L. Duguit, infra §§8ff., and Stone, Social Dimensions, Ch. 3, §§8-9.

[44] Ihering, transl. 161. He stressed the modern advance on the Roman law by the use of large associations in trade (164), thus combining the social mechanics of reward and association. Even here, however, it is characteristic of Ihering that he found it necessary to stress the need of safeguards against abuse of this modern device (167-170).

[45] Id. 176.

[46] Ihering's psychology seems hazardously based on the distinction made in the Roman law of metus where the maxim was "coactus volui".

[47] At this point, as later with Roscoe Pound and Léon Duguit, it becomes impossible to separate distinctly Ihering's theory of justice from his contribution to early sociological thought. The present brief account is supplemented on the sociological side in Stone, Social Dimensions, Ch. 9, §1, Ch. 13, §7.

[48] Transl. 182.

[49] "The process of legal evolution is not a matter of mere knowledge, as in the case of truth, but the result too of a struggle of interests, and the weapons by which the fight is won are not reasons and deduction, but the actions and force of the national will." See transl. 195-218 for the full development of this theme. See also the Geist, vol. i, para. 10 and Kampf ums Recht (1 ed. 1872).

vincing[50] as the question was, *in terms of his own positions,* unnecessary. Ihering was entitled to rest on his explanation of the State and law as instruments of the common purposes of members of society.[51] For him, as we have seen, individual purposes develop into associational purposes and social purposes. Social purposes generate coercive norms regulating their pursuit, which operate upon members of society, creating rights and duties independent of the wills of the parties, and enforcing them. The theory of justice implicit in this analysis is that the *justness* of law is measured by *the extent to which it fulfils the common purposes* of the society it governs. And since *he has already taken the position* that State and law are an expression of the force behind these common purposes, and that this force is preponderant in the society, then the very existence of the law, supported as it is by such force, proves that the law is just *in terms of his own criterion.* Since he has (in effect) defined both "right" and law in terms of what the "preponderant force" which lies behind "common purposes" supports, his purported demonstration is really circular.[52]

In the long run, Ihering also thought (though in what relation to his unexplained notion of "right" is not very clear) that those who wield the state's monopoly of force themselves become bound by the legal norms created. For they cannot ensure stability and respect for law so long as it is merely a unilateral direction to the subjects. The need for stability leads them to make it a bilateral standard binding also those who exercise organised social coercion. And he formulated strikingly the conception of the *Rechtsstaat* prominent in the German public law writings of the time:

> The outer guarantee of respect for law by the state lies in the administration of justice—justice changes its abode, and the mere removal has the consequence that if the state authorities desire to lay violent hands upon it, they must first cross the street; whereas as long as it lived under the same roof with them they could have done the thing within the four walls without being noticed.[53]

§6. LAW AS ONE MEANS OF SECURING THE CONDITIONS OF SOCIAL LIFE. The task of each legal system, then, is to secure "the conditions of social life" as conceived and lived by the men of the particular society at the particular time—a compendious way of referring to the conditions required

---

[50] Transl. 218.

[51] Unless he started from his own question-begging criterion, Ihering would have had to ask a preliminary question, namely, "*Is* the preponderance of force always on the side of right?" If he answered this question in the negative, his whole thesis would fall. If in the affirmative, it could only be on the basis that law always effectuates the common purposes of the society as a whole, and *by definition,* therefore, would both be "right" and marshal preponderant power. But that would be merely saying (circularly) that "right" being what the preponderance of force supports, the preponderant force always supports what is "right". For another interpretation which, however, rather depends on ignoring Ihering's actual purported demonstrations, and substituting a different speculative one to meet the above difficulty, see I. Jenkins, "Rudolf von Ihering" (1960) 14 *Vanderb. L.R.* 169-190, esp. 169ff., 182-190. And see on Jenkins' thesis *infra* §7.

[52] And in a terminological universe in which "force" and "right" are thus linked *by definition,* questions about this linkage cannot significantly be asked or answered. This is apart from our suggestion in *Province* 308 that the essentially pragmatic nature of Ihering's approach at this point would excuse him from asking such questions at all.

[53] Transl. 293. For Ihering's influence on German analytical thought see W. Friedmann, *Legal Theory* (4 ed. 1960) 213-14. For this side of Ihering's theory in relation to the nature of power, see Stone, *Social Dimensions,* Ch. 13, §7.

to meet common purposes. Hence, the same content of law can be now just, or unjust, and contrary laws both just, in different systems.[54] Ihering, indeed, admitted that the conditions which the legislator at a particular time seeks to ensure may in fact be contrary to the "true" interests of that society, as with medieval laws against witches and sorcerers. He was clearly not aware of the gap opened up in his theory by this admission.[55]

While law is a means of securing the conditions of social life, it is not the only means. These conditions may exist independently of law, either in part or (more rarely) altogether, but the degree of independence and therefore of legal support is itself variable, as with the law against suicide in relation to the security of human life, or laws encouraging marriage and propagation. Laws are here ancillary to natural drives of self-preservation, sex-expression and the like.[56] Again, performance of work is in large part assured by the "instinct of acquisition", linked no doubt with those of self-preservation and sex, the law playing a minor role.[57] Finally, some of the conditions of social life are secured entirely or almost entirely by the law, as for instance, respect for property, the raising of the public revenue, and military service. This, Ihering thought, was the sphere in which individual egoism seeks to have the benefits of society without the burden[58] and only by organised coercion can social interests be secured.

Ihering identified five main classes of purposes, or interests (as he interchangeably terms them)—those of the individual, the State, the Church and associations generally, and the indeterminate mass he termed society. He reduced these to three—those of the Individual, the State and Society; a division later adopted by Roscoe Pound.[59] He illustrated their operation from the modern Roman law, and at this point traced the variety of human purposes which may be served in a single branch of technical law. Property law, for example, protected not only individual economic interests but also many social and public interests, like general access to certain resources, the public control of others and the interests of the fiscus. So also with contract and delict and quasi-contract and quasi-delict; and these in addition protected also individual physical integrity and honour and personality generally.

The criminal law is on the same footing.[60] It resorts to the use of punishment rather than compensation only as a matter of "social politics".[61]

---

[54] Thus, he says, pointedly, Rome first repressed Christianity by force and then imposed Christianity by force, while modern law regards both of these courses as violative of modern conditions of social life.

[55] This gap will be later considered in relation to the theories of justice of Kohler and Pound, *infra* Chs. 6, 9.

[56] Connect in this regard the field opened up by E. Durkheim's *Le Suicide* (1897). *Cf.* also non-legal measures to meet the same problem, for instance, the "Save a Life League" formed in the United States during the depression to help prospective suicides. The degree of legal aid required today, in a sense, was a deep underlying issue in *Beresford's Case* (1938) A.C. 586. See Stone, *Social Dimensions*, Ch. 4, §7. This is now a regular field of social work and church activity.

[57] From the abstract standpoint of individual liberty, Ihering commented (transl. 342) that legal interference in any of the above three respects would not be justified. "That it does take place as a matter of fact shows . . . that the appeal of the individual to his freedom is met by the command of social self-preservation".

[58] Transl. 344.

[59] See Stone, *Social Dimensions*, Ch. 4, §§3ff. for reservations, and criticisms of the division.

[60] See Stone, *Legal System*, Ch. 3, §13, and for Austin's anticipation of this *id.* Ch. 2, n. 94.

[61] Ihering, transl. 363.

Whereas in civil liability the law need only supplement egoistic impulses, "the criminal law begins where punishment is necessary in the interest of society. . . . Crime is that which endangers the conditions of social life, and of which the legislator is convinced that it can be removed only by punishment". The gist is not merely, or even mainly, the concrete danger of the particular act, but the abstract danger from the whole category of acts. The criminal law protects individual bodily integrity, property interests, honour and family relations. But it also protects the physical security of society generally in meeting threats of arson, flood or riot; it establishes the prerequisites of economic activity by suppressing false currency, false documents and fraud generally; and seeks to protect society generally by striking at immorality, perjury and blasphemy. And finally, the criminal law is aimed to protect the state, that is, the system of organised coercion of which it is a part, its territory and power by the law of treason; its revenue by the law of tax offences and embezzlement, and its honour and prestige by punishment of contempt, bribery and corruption of its courts and officials. Law, concluded Ihering, was "the sum of the conditions of social life, in the widest sense of the term, as secured by the power of the state through the means of external compulsion".[62]

§7. CRITIQUE OF IHERING'S THEORY. For the age in which he wrote Ihering's penetration behind legal conceptions to the complex of interests secured by law was spectacular.[63] His theory of justice, with which we are here concerned, has been labelled almost universally as social utilitarian.[64] He pressed the "fundamental idea that the highest principle of classification from the philosophical point of view is the subject for whose sake the law is made; and that in addition to the individual and the State . . . society also, in the narrower sense, must be recognised as a subject".[65] Looked at from the viewpoint of the subject this was an assertion of the primacy of interests or claims; from that of the legislator of the primacy of the purposes to be fulfilled by law. One part at least of justice must be stated in the relativist terms of the relation between human purposes for the time being and the means, legal or other, existing for their fulfilment.[66]

Of the main criticisms urged against Ihering two notably merit some discussion. The first is that Ihering built his system upon an assumed egocentric individual who gradually develops into the socially-minded member of the group, and that in the modern view such sharp opposition of individual and society is false. Ihering's explanation of how individual purposes are transmuted into social purposes is perhaps a reaching out for Pound's point that in final resort all demands are demands of human beings, and can be looked at as either "individual" or "social". Ihering was almost on the very point when he said against Mill (§1 above) that any society has an interest

---

[62] Transl. 380.

[63] This extended not only to generalities but to particular doctrines. For instance his leap behind the contemporary juristic debates as to the nature of public charitable and other foundations, to the social interests which legal recognition of the foundations secures, is a model of anti-conceptualism.

[64] He himself in the volume of the *Zweck* devoted to law did not adopt such a label, though he does refer in the second volume, devoted to morals, to his "*gesellschaftlichen oder objektiven Utilitarismus*" (2 *Zweck*, §ii (1) (2 ed.) 192ff., 215-23).

[65] Transl. 375.

[66] Munroe Smith, cited *supra* n. 1, 11 *Pol. Sc. Qu.* at 294.

in almost every individual purpose, and every individual a deep interest in the fulfilment of those purposes which Ihering termed "social" and "public". He did not carry the matter through; but as we shall see even Pound found it difficult to carry through consistently this correct insight.[67]

Another related and far more central criticism is that Ihering did not provide a criterion of justice at all. While he drew attention to the conflicting purposes[68] which lie behind law and to the fact that law is but the resultant of the adjustment for the time being of these conflicts, he gave no satisfactory guide for deciding whether this compromise embodied in the law is a just one, or how a more just one could be attained. To say, as he frequently does, that individual purposes must give way to social purposes is no answer. For, first, how much way shall they give? He clearly cannot mean that whenever the smallest tittle of social interest conflicts with the gravest individual interest, the latter is to be completely overridden. Furthermore, how is a social interest to be distinguished from an individual interest? Nor does it assist to say that social utility decides. For what is social utility? It is not something given and known: it is precisely what is sought to be discovered.[69]

Like Duguit's notion of "social solidarity" next to be discussed, Ihering's "social utility" remained an inaccessible mystery to the end. Once Ihering takes it for granted that its dictates are self-evident there is no way to follow him, unless we assume (as recent writers sometimes do) that he intended to set forth not merely the "conditions of life" and "social purposes" in the sense of what is empirically found in a given society, but the "universal necessities of man's actual lot and the objective goals of his ideal fulfilment".[70] To regard this as the main drive of Ihering's contribution, however, would reduce his role to that of a very inarticulate and socially-minded neo-Scholastic—a kind of Gény who never got to the point. And whether this is or is not warranted, such speculation should not conceal that his actual contribution and influence were in quite other directions.

Fundamentally the importance of Ihering's *Zweck im Recht* lay in powerfully drawing attention to the stuff to be weighed in the scales of justice—the earthy materials of human conflicting purposes in a particular time and place. He did for German, and perhaps for continental thought, what Bentham and his disciples had already done for English thought. But

---

[67] See *infra* Ch. 9, §§6ff. and Stone, *Social Dimensions*, Ch. 4, §§3ff. Ihering was led by his position to think that the pressure of society on the individual is continually increasing. In fact, as E. Durkheim pointed out, though the activities of the state are constantly increasing, *the intensity* of the social pressure upon the individual may rather have decreased with the growing complexity of state functions. *Cf.* Munroe Smith, *op. cit. supra* n. 1, at 296ff.

[68] For a criticism of Ihering's use of the term "purposes" as unduly stressing men's intentions, as distinct from the concrete effects of what they seek to do or do, see Cohen, *Ethical Systems* 68n.

[69] If "society" were something clearly and precisely known, apart from its members, and if that something and what is useful for it were known, social utility might provide a test. But Ihering does not adequately explain whether it is, and if so, how to recognise what would be useful for it.

The *Interessenjuristen* like Professor Heck, though following the method of Ihering's sociological analysis, acknowledged that Ihering's claim to have established a criterion of justice by his doctrine of "social interest" or "social utility" was unwarranted. See Stone, *Legal System*, Ch. 6, §12. *Cf.* I. Jenkins' stricture on them (*op. cit. supra* n. 51, at 172ff., 184ff.) for doing so, instead of attempting to clarify "the ends" which law "should ideally serve" (p. 172). But as to Jenkins' interpretation of Ihering see *supra* at n. 51, and *infra* n. 70.

[70] See the thesis of I. Jenkins, *op. cit.*, esp. 187ff.

he did more. He insisted on the relativism of justice, which Bentham's calculus of pains and pleasures tended in practice to obscure. And he insisted that there were some important interests to which the law must have regard which cannot easily be fitted into a calculus of pains and pleasures. Thought in terms of society, he insisted, naturally finds room for the individual; but thought in terms of the individual tends to overlook many interests which are not *easily* identifiable in terms of the individual. In particular social conditions the appeal to "social utility" may seem to produce, we must admit, a consensus as to what justice requires on particular problems, as appeal to Bentham's utility notion formerly did. The great Holmes himself thought that "social utility" was a real guide to judgment. But this consensus is a function of the circumstances of the time, and of men's reactions to them, not of any decisive guidance afforded by the notion of "social utility" itself. Once the conflicts have been identified, the general agreement of men as to the desirable result settles the matter. The reason given for that agreement may be termed "utility" or "social utility"; the actuality may still be merely that on the conflicts revealed there is consensus as to the "merits".

Ihering's social utilitarianism remains finally one of the important bridges between the nineteenth and twentieth centuries. Ihering had drunk deeply from the orthodox nineteenth century juristic springs. When he attacked his former teachers he did so in terms which they could not but understand, and his criticisms thus entered the main stream of juristic thought. Though men like Stammler and Kohler later scoffed at his poor philosophical equipment (which he himself admitted), their own very different criteria of justice still reflected both the collectivist preference and the relativist mood of Ihering's overall position. Gény and Pound in their diverse ways carried both this preference and this mood fully into our present century.[71] All of these, with their diverse ways of thought, eased the nineteenth century into the twentieth; and a main bridgehead for their passage was that won by Ihering's *Zweck im Recht*.

This is not to suggest that Ihering's teaching dominated these later writers. Indeed, few important jurists have had so few disciples: Ihering left no "school" behind him.[72] But if there was no disciple, there was equally none who was able to write as if the *Scherz und Ernst* and *Zweck im Recht* had not been written. With Ihering, as with Bentham, the destructive work was almost as important as the constructive. And the constructive work itself, though philosophically vulnerable, was a reflection of social and economic trends which none dared ignore once they had been pointed out.[73]

II. SOCIAL SOLIDARISM

§8. LIFE AND BACKGROUND OF DUGUIT.[74] Léon Duguit was Professor of

---

[71] See the succeeding Chapters on these other writers.

[72] On the *Interessenjurisprudenz* see Stone, *Legal System*, Ch. 6, §12.

[73] The following may be added as selected background material for twentieth century theories: Saleilles, *"Ecole Historique"*; *id.*, Preface to Gény, *Méthode*; R. Stammler, "Fundamental Tendencies in Modern Jurisprudence" (1923) 21 *Mich. L.R.* 623, 765, 862; *id.*, *Über die Methode der geschichtlichen Rechtstheorie* (1888) (a critique of "the historical method"); Haines, *Revival* 310-349; R. Pound, "Law and the Science of Law . . ." (1934) 43 *Yale L.J.* 525.

[74] LIFE AND BACKGROUND: H. J. Laski's Intro. to his translation (with Laski) of

Constitutional Law at Bordeaux in the first quarter of the twentieth century. Each of these facts is of some significance. He wrote after the full effect of Comte's sociology was felt,[75] immediately after and under the direct influence of the work of Emile Durkheim[76] and of Ihering.[77] His age was characterised in France as well as in England by the rise of what Dicey termed "collectivist legislation", the age (in Roscoe Pound's term) of "the socialisation of law". All this must have been particularly borne in upon one who worked in the industrial metropolis of Bordeaux. As primarily a constitutional lawyer, moreover, he tended to think of the whole legal system in terms of the broad concepts of public law and to treat somewhat lightly the refined conceptions of private law.

Like Ihering, Duguit rejected metaphysical and intuitive theories of justice. Indeed, he also denounced all the major juristic conceptions such as "sovereignty", "right", "public" and "private" law, as excrescences of metaphysics. He was both voracious and undiscriminating in the sources of his thought, leaning, however, towards the mechanical almost fatalist view of the social process put forward by the pre-Darwinian Comte. His ideal of law as *"la règle de droit"* based on social solidarity through division of labour, and as *"le produit spontané des faits"*, dominated his whole scholarly life. Yet he was also deeply impressed by Ihering's view of law as the effectuation of dynamic human purposes. He did not clearly perceive

---

Duguit, *Droit Public* as *Law in the Modern State* (1921) ix-xxxiv; *id.,* "Note on M. Duguit" (1918) 31 *H.L.R.* 186-192; A. W. Spencer, Editorial Preface to *Modern French Legal Philosophy* xliv-xlvii (*Modern Legal Philosophy Series,* vol. vii); L. Duguit, "Law and the State" (1918) 31 *H.L.R.* 1-185, esp. 1-26, 145-185 (Duguit's basic antipathies); Duguit, *Droit Objectif,* transl. in part in *Modern French Legal Philosophy, supra,* see esp. 251-53 (relative influences of Comte and Ihering); J. Stone, Book Review of E. Durkheim, *Division of Labour in Society* (1893) transl. G. Simpson (1934) 47 *H.L.R.* 1448 (influence of Durkheim).

SOCIAL SOLIDARITY: THE POSITIVIST BASIS OF HIGHER LAW: Duguit, *Droit Objectif* c. i, transl. in *Modern French Legal Philosophy, supra* 258-284 as "Objective Law Anterior to the State" (confessedly inspired by Durkheim, *supra,* see 258n.). And see R. Bonnard *"Les Idées de Léon Duguit sur les Valeurs Sociales"* (1932) 2 *Arch. de Phil. et Soc. Jur.* 7.

THE HIGHER LAW: DUGUIT'S *"Règle De Droit":* Duguit, *Droit Objectif* c. ii, transl. in *Modern French Legal Philosophy, supra* 285-339, esp. 290ff.

DEMONSTRATION OF THIS THESIS BY REFERENCE TO THE NINETEENTH CENTURY DEVELOPMENT OF FRENCH LAW: Duguit, *Droit Privé,* transl. in *Progress of Continental Law in the Nineteenth Century* 65-146 (*Continental Legal History Series,* vol. xi); Duguit, *Droit Public.*

CRITIQUES OF DUGUIT: H. J. Laski, "M. Duguit's Conception of the State" in Jennings (ed.), *Theories of Law* 53-67; Gény. 2 *Science et Technique* (1915) 190-272; Cohen, *Ethical Systems* 21-24; J. Stone, "Theories of Law and Justice of Fascist Italy" (1933) 1 *M.L.R.* 177 (as to Duguit's ideas in Fascist form); R. Pound, "Fifty Years of Jurisprudence" (1938) 51 *H.L.R.* 444, 466-471; R. Bonnard, "Léon Duguit" (1926-27) 1 *Rev. Int. T. du Droit* 18ff. (both these last contain full bibliographies); J. Bonnecase, *La Pensée Juridique Française* (1933) 348-588.

There are a series of appreciations of Duguit's work in (1932) 2 *Arch. de Phil. et Soc. Jur.* by M. Réglade, O. Ionescu and L. Le Fur (21, 269, 175—general), N. Politis (69—influence on international law), G. Jèse (135—on administrative law), G. Morin (143—on private law), and R. Bonnard (7—theory of social values).

Some critical comparisons of Duguit's and Kelsen's thought will be found in articles by G. Davy in the same journal for 1933 at 7, by J. L. Kunz in (1926-27) 1 *Rev. Int. T. du Droit* 140, 204, and by U. Scheuner in (1929) 3 *id.* 220.

Reference should also be made to Stone, *Social Dimensions,* Ch. 3, §§8-9 (for Durkheim's and Duguit's correlations of legal and social types), and to *id.* Ch. 9, §5 (as to Duguit's doctrine of the identity of "law" with "social facts"). On Duguit's influence abroad see G. Langrod, *"L'Influsso delle Idee di Léon Duguit . . ."* (1959) 36 *Riv. Int. di Fil. del Dir.* 640-672.

[75] See Stone, *Social Dimensions,* Ch. 1, §§10ff.
[76] See *id.,* Ch. 3, §§8-9.
[77] *Supra* §§1-7.

the partial contradiction, nor did he ever resolve it.[78] The confused merger of sociological analysis and the theory of justice runs throughout his work.[79]

§9. BACKGROUND: DUGUIT'S VIEW OF THE TRANSFORMATION OF LAW IN MODERN SOCIETY. Duguit's criterion of justice is not really severable from his view of the contemporary relation of law to society; and for this in turn (as we have seen more fully elsewhere)[79a] he depended on Emile Durkheim.

The progress of human society, wrote Durkheim in his *De la Division du Travail Social*,[80] presents a shift from mechanical to organic solidarity, from a solidarity based on homogeneity of needs and functions to a solidarity based on a highly specialised heterogeneity of functions. A modern industrial society had as its very foundation a complex economic organisation. The *sine qua non* of the efficient conduct of that organisation was the unbroken carrying on of all the functions involved, by the human beings to whom they are respectively assigned. What the individual had was a function to perform in this economic enterprise; that was his primary attribute as a member of society, and all others followed from it. Law thus becomes an instrument for securing and regulating the operation of a complicated but close-fitting system of specialised functions.

Duguit developed these basic ideas, throughout his life, with all the earnestness of his temperament, and all the equipment of his training and study as a professor of constitutional law.[81] On their basis he demolished to his own satisfaction the entire system of private law, substituting for individual rights the protection of social functions, and denounced such notions as "a right", "sovereign" and "subject", "public law" and "private law" as "metaphysical" or "natural law" survivals unrelated to the facts of social life. The role of law was part of the observed fact of social solidarity in the above organic sense. Insisting that his method was positivist only, he declared that the validity of law depended neither on sovereign command, nor on natural law, but on the fact that acts done in violation of social solidarity cause social disorder and a spontaneous, almost a reflex, movement towards readjustment. Under this law the individual had, not rights, but only functions dictated by social solidarity to which he is held, and in which he is protected. The distinction between public and private law vanished,[82] public officials being merely individuals, like all others, who were held

---

[78] Duguit did attempt to overcome the difficulties of the mechanical view but only by uniting with it elements essentially inconsistent with it. See, e.g., *Droit Objectif* 16ff., where, after praising the achievements of "social biology", and "social statics and dynamics" in showing that society is not at all a willed and artificial fact but a spontaneous and natural one, he declared them in error in "wishing to identify social facts with physical and biological phenomena". Yet he proceeded forthwith to say that man's conscious will towards certain goals is "the essential factor in social matters", accepting Ihering's position explicitly. No doubt, such incongruities also explain at least in part why, though his language often resembles that of the Thomists (see, e.g., Gény, 2 *Science et Technique* 251), he was the *bête noire* of some of them. See Stone, *Social Dimensions*, Ch. 11, §2; and for an indication (with bibli.) of these early sociological trends mentioned by Duguit, see *id.*, Ch. 1.

[79] For this reason his ideas also fall to be considered in our separate work on *Social Dimensions of Law and Justice*. Recognition that Duguit's philosophical and juristic background was deficient, and his dogmatism excessive, should not exclude the importance of his contributions, certainly in terms of actual influence. See esp. among the citations *supra* n. 74, H. J. Laski, in Jennings (ed.), *Theories of Law* 52.

[79a] See Stone, *Province*, Ch. 19; and see now Stone, *Social Dimensions*, Ch. 3.

[80] (1893).

[81] *Cf.* his *Droit Objectif* c. i, with his *Leçons de Droit Public* (1926) 73-94.

[82] Duguit, *Droit Public* 279-280.

to and protected in the performance of the functions allotted by social solidarity.[83] All have duties, or rather functions, and rights so far only as correlative to those functions.[84] Duguit regarded the idea that individuals have "subjective rights" as itself an obsolete relic of natural law and metaphysical thought. He pushed these ideas to the point of saying that even the supreme legislator is in no different position, so that (independently of any written constitution) his acts do not bind unless they conform to social solidarity—*la règle de droit*. In this sense he even denied the existence of sovereignty, and he devoted two able books to drawing out what he thought were the "transformations" of public and private law arising from the compulsions of "social solidarity".[85]

§10. THE OBJECTIVE LAW. Duguit, then, posed for himself the problem of finding "the principle and the formula" of "the objective law", *"la règle de droit"*,[86] a supreme law of society. This, he conceived, must be neither a physical law nor a moral law, but one appropriate to the complex of social life, which imposed itself as an observed fact on all members of society, requiring each to do nothing to infringe social interdependence, and to do what was necessary to ensure it.[86a]

It is an observed and inescapable fact, he argued, that men must live in society. Their daily needs, where not similar, are reciprocal, and the increasing modern specialisation of functions in filling these needs is constantly making men more and more dependent on social organisation. This "social solidarity" is, in substance, Durkheim's organic solidarity through community of needs and division of labour[87] as the basis of cohesion in modern society. The supposed needs of this social solidarity determine the content of *la règle de droit*. Law exists to ensure fulfilment of these needs, and the "State" is mere machinery to this end, *la règle de droit* being binding *proprio vigore* on all its officials and organs.[88]

Whence did this supreme law derive a quality so obligatory that any positive law inconsistent with it is by that fact invalid? Duguit's answer was direct, but remains difficult still to grasp. He insisted that the principle was part of the observed "fact" of social solidarity, obligatory independently of, and even adversely to, any sovereign command. Violative conduct, he said, caused social disturbance, and a resulting spontaneous social movement to restore equilibrium. Yet even if the re-equilibration were so effective and inevitable as automatically to rectify the breach, it is difficult to see *why this should create an obligation*. It might rather, indeed, make this seem unnecessary.

---

[83] See his *Droit Objectif* cc. iv, v; *Le Droit Social* . . . (*cit. infra* n. 93) lecture ii; *Droit Privé* and *Droit Public, passim.*

[84] *Cf.* Laski, *Politics* 94, and cc. iii, iv and *passim,* who also pointed out (in Jennings (ed.), *Theories of Law* 59) that Duguit's denial that individuals have "subjective rights" was verbal merely, since Duguit laid down conditions which must be ensured to individuals performing their functions which are in nature if not in content indistinguishable from "rights".

[85] *Supra* n.74. For a fuller statement on this see Stone, *Social Dimensions,* Ch. 3, §9. And see Duguit, *Droit Public* and *Droit Privé, passim.*

[86] Of course this phrase is not to be confused with Dicey's notion of "the rule of law", which has reference to equal treatment under positive law. Stone, *Social Dimensions,* Ch. 14, §§17-19.

[86a] See, e.g., L. Duguit, "Law and the State" (1917) 31 *H.L.R.* 178.

[87] See Stone, *Social Dimensions,* Ch. 3, §§8ff.

[88] The present author is deliberately using "law" ambiguously as Duguit frequently did. The resulting errors will be examined below.

§11. THE OBJECTIVE LAW AND POSITIVE LAW. Can the assertion that the supreme law of solidarity is paramount over the positive law itself stand as a proposition of positive law? It may, as we shall see, stand as a criterion of justice or even as a generalisation (more or less exact) of the sociology of law. But Duguit himself urged it as a proposition of law, and it is necessary first to see what sense this can make.

He insisted that this supreme law limited the legislator even where there was no rigid constitution embodying it. "The legislator," he wrote in his *Traité de Droit Constitutionnel*,[89] "is still, even in countries without rigid constitutions, limited by a law superior to himself. Even in England . . . there are certain superior rules which the very conscience of the English people will not permit to be violated by Parliament."[90] The crucial test would be on a conflict between a statute of an unlimited legislature like the English, and the "objective" law of solidarity. On such a test Duguit stalwartly insisted that the statute must give way. He denied in advance the charge that anarchy would result if the "objective" law prevailed, insisting with delightful inconsequence that anarchy is individualist while his theory is social.[91] He admitted the unsatisfactory history of attempts in France to create tribunals to pass even on conformity of statutes to the written constitution.[92] But he said:

> Whether or not there is in these countries an organ charged with passing upon the conformity of statutes to the "objective" law, and declaring that statutes contrary thereto are invalid, we ought not to hesitate to draw all the consequences from our proposition, and to say that it is perfectly legitimate to refuse to obey a statute which is contrary to this "objective" law.

He even, in a later work, suggested rather vaguely that the courts should have the power of striking down such statutes inconsistent with the "objective" law whether written or not; and he proposed for this purpose the establishment of "a high tribunal composed equally of representatives of all the social classes, which would judge, so to speak, of the legality of the law".[93] He does not appear to have got beyond this somewhat amorphous proposal.

Insofar, then, as Duguit presented *la règle de droit* of social solidarity as positive law of overriding force, his thesis was not sustained and it is properly to be rejected.[94]

§12. THE OBJECTIVE LAW AND NATURAL LAW. The truth appears to be[95]

---

[89] (2 vols., 1911) vol. i, 154.

[90] This bitter critic of natural law thus innocently took a position indistinguishable from that of proponents of a natural law in nineteenth century constitutional decisions. See *supra* Ch. 3, §§5ff. It seems clear, however, that he favoured written constitutions as the natural mode of subjecting legislative power to *la règle de droit*. *Cf*. H. J. Laski in Jennings (ed.), *Theories of Law* 57ff. On the corollary of the subject's "right of insurrection" and the contradictions in Duguit's position on this point, *cf. id.* 55, 59-61.

[91] *Op. cit. supra* n. 89 at 153.

[92] *Id.* 156-57.

[93] *Le Droit Social, Le Droit Individuel et la Transformation de l'Etat* (1910, 2 ed. 1911) 58. On the overwhelming difficulties of providing some mode of scrutiny of governmental acts, whether by standards embodied in written constitutions, or of "natural" or moral rights see Laski, *Politics* 134-41; and *cf.* the same writer in Jennings (ed.), *Theories of Law* 59-63.

[94] See, e.g., Cardozo, *Growth* 49ff.; R. Saleilles's view adopted in Vinogradoff, 1 *Jurisprudence* 150-51, and F. Gény and H. J. Laski, cited *infra* §14.

[95] Gény, 2 *Science et Technique* 242ff.

that Duguit, who so denounced the natural lawyers, built his own system upon a central feature of the classical natural law, namely, an assertion of the self-evidence of values immanent in experience. When he asserted that there is a supreme *règle de droit, un droit objectif,* to be found in the very facts of social life, this *droit* was neither positive law, the legislator's law, nor any other positive law; for this could not test its own validity. Furthermore, as we have seen, Duguit strenuously denied that this objective law was to be identified with merely moral law. Whence did it derive? What kind of obligation did it impose? How, indeed, did he draw from *the facts* of social solidarity any norm or imperative at all?[96]

It has to be concluded that a measure of values asserted as self-evident because immanent in the facts, and given the force of overriding "law", which is nevertheless not positive law, must be understood as a cryptic natural law criterion of justice.[97] In Duguit, as well as in the older natural lawyers, the legally obligatory force of the supposed "law", and the contents attributed to it,[98] stand or fall with the original assumption that the "objective" law or "the law of nature" are respectively binding independently and adversely to the positive law. On rare occasions, indeed, Duguit made explicit this intuitive nature of his system, as when he declared, in his Introduction to the French translation of Woodrow Wilson's *The State*,[99] that since "all social manifestations" are finally traceable to acts of individual conscience, the political thinker defaults if he does not determine "the eternal and stable principle of conduct, binding upon governments.[100]

§13. THE OBJECTIVE LAW AND SOCIAL FACTS. Was it possible, finally, for Duguit to draw the obligatory force of his objective law from the certainty of social reaction to breach of it, the compulsion of the facts of social re-equilibration?

Such a suggestion will not bear examination. First, no such exact social equilibrium exists as would provoke any spontaneous movement for

---

[96] *Cf.* W. Friedmann, *Legal Theory* (4 ed. 1960) 183-84.

[97] *Cf.* also H. J. Laski in Jennings (ed.), *Theories of Law* 64. Indeed, in the attempts of his successors at Bordeaux, Roger Bonnard and Marc Réglade, to reinterpret Duguit acceptably, a position is taken which is overtly (if not quite explicitly) a natural law position. See esp. Réglade's *Valeur Sociale et Concepts Juridiques* (1950) recognising Duguit's failure to show how his "social facts" gained normative force (p. 3); and seeking to remedy this deficiency by postulating that "objective" values "exist behind . . . the social fact" (*id.* 20-21, quoting Bonnard, *"L'Origine de l'Ordonnement Juridique"*, in *Mélanges Hauriou* (1929) 31-77). The supporting argument cannot be distinguished from well-known natural law positions, except that Duguit's stress on the "social" is carried through into a distinction between moral and legal norms, in which the ideal of the former are concerned with "the individual as he ought to be", and the latter with "the social being as it ought to be". And see also on Réglade's efforts to show how the facts are *valorisés, op. cit.* 31, and on the claimed "scientific" nature of his value concept, *id.* 36. He inevitably finds himself invoking "the common good", recognised by "our moral conscience in all time and in all human society", which he calls *"morale juridicale"* but admits to be ordinarily called "natural law". See *id.* 46-47, 53. R. Théry observes that Réglade is thus attempting the feat of restoring " 'metaphysical duty' at the heart of a positivist doctrine" ("Ten Years of the Philosophy of Law in France" (1956) 1 *Nat. L. Forum* 104, 105). *Cf.* H. Motulsky in (1952) *Arch. de Phil. du Droit* (N.S.) 223, 228. It is unnecessary to debate the aptness of the term "metaphysical" in this context.

[98] See, e.g., *Droit Objectif* 18-19.

[99] (1902).

[100] *Cf.* his occasional introduction of the "sentiment of pity" as a subsidiary test of justice, e.g., in n. 68 of *op. cit. supra* n. 93, criticised by H. J. Laski in Jennings (ed.), *Theories of Law* at 61-62.

re-equilibration of a degree of a refinement significant for legal purposes. At the most the "solidarity" or "equilibrium" in most societies is a rough, momentary compromise of conflicts in constant dynamic change. Second, in any case, Duguit himself is at much pains to deny that his objective law is a mechanical one analogous to the physical or biological laws so popular with Comte and his followers. Third, and even more fundamental, Duguit nowhere explains how the fact of social solidarity or any other fact, for that matter, can create an obligation.[101] The fact that the "mass of men" may regard the supposed rule as imperative, which Duguit sometimes seemed to vouch as a source of its legal obligatory force, is, if it exists, a social-psychological fact. It may be relevant to a criterion of justice, but it cannot in itself constitute an obligation either of law or of justice. If what *is* is to be the test of goodness, then everything that exists is good, and nothing can be bad: *ergo* no evaluation of what *is* is either necessary or possible.

§14. THE OBJECTIVE LAW AS A CRITERION OF JUSTICE. Duguit's thought, when stripped of its extravagant garb of positive law, still leaves a twofold contribution, first to the sociology of law, and second to the theory of justice. Our fuller consideration of the former is in the separate work entitled *Social Dimensions of Law and Justice* (Chapter 3, §9 and Chapter 12, §1). The latter may here be assessed. Even as to this, the obstacles of Duguit's dogmatism have to be overcome. For he himself denied that his theory was concerned with justice, as distinct from the compulsions arising from the "law" of social solidarity, and in particular the reaction to "social disorder" arising from its breach.[102] But, of course, neither dictates of social solidarity,[103] nor the social disorder arising from breach, are observable facts, objectively recognisable without reference to any standards of values.[104] The truth is that Duguit's exclusion of values, ideals, and the like was illusory: ideals entered, but as "crypto-idealism".[105]

Viewed as relevant to a theory of justice, Duguit's thesis as to "social solidarity" drew attention at a crucial time in Western industrial development, to an ideal of justice implicit in much modern legislation. It directed attention to reasons for then current adjustments in the valuing of "social" as against "individual" interests, and the heavy economic component in those social interests. In the last resort, indeed, he was largely repeating Ihering's message in richer form, insofar as "solidarity" and "social services" may seem more nearly related to the complex interdependence of modern industrial society than was "social utility".[106] Yet the test of "social solidarity" itself remains subject to vices similar to those we have seen to affect "social utility". The phrases "social solidarity" and "social utility" may and do direct attention to important facts to be considered in the process of evaluation; but neither provides a measure of values necessary to complete the judgment. Duguit stopped short of enumerating the concrete

---

101 *Cf.* Laski's comments in *id.* 58ff.; and see Krabbe, *The State* 206ff., and G. H. Sabine and W. J. Shepard, Transl.'s Intro. thereto, lii-liv.

102 *Droit Privé* 187.

103 *Cf.* 1 Pareto §§418, 449-450 (Livingston's ed. (1935), 251, 269-270).

104 The fallacy is cognate to that indulged by Huntington Cairns and discussed in Stone, *Social Dimensions*, Ch. 1, §8.

105 *Cf.* Cohen, *Ethical Systems* 21ff.; H. J. Laski, in Jennings (ed.), *Theories of Law* 62-63.

106 *Cf.* Sabine and Shepard, *cit. supra* n. 101, at livff.

dictates of his principle of social solidarity[107] just as Ihering stopped short of enumerating the dictates of social utility. The latter is question-begging: the former, though in some cases it might serve, would help very little over large branches of the law, such as family law, where alternative solutions might be quite different so far as social solidarity is concerned. And even in the economic sphere, for which such a test seems apt, it may give little guidance, even on such central matters as compulsory recognition of collective bargaining, night work for women, or "employers' liability".[108]

Despite its service, therefore, as a theory of justice adapted to modern complex industrialised societies, and as a bridge between politico-economic thought and juristic thought of the present century,[109] Duguit's thought stands tainted at the heart with intuitive thinking. Yet, for all that, he was able (as natural lawyers have often been) to wield a powerful iconoclastic influence upon settled conceptions and attitudes, opening the way for major change. "What was lacking in the work of Duguit is not a metaphysic, but rather the consciousness and acknowledgment of his metaphysic".[110] And Harold Laski rather praised Duguit's work just for its iconoclasm and its affinity to medieval natural law, and has pronounced as its main lack the failure to make this explicit and draw the consequences.[111] Yet it also has to be added that when we strip the extravagances from Duguit's "social solidarity" notion to reveal his insights for the modern problems of justice, we still do not cancel the evil misuses to which these extravagances lent themselves in the fascist totalitarianisms of the second generation of the twentieth century.[112]

---

[107] There are signs, however, of a formative economic content. See J. Stone, "Theories of Law and Justice of Fascist Italy" (1933) 1 *M.L.R.* 177, and Duguit, *op. cit. supra* n. 93, 105-147.

[108] *Cf.* H. J. Laski, despite his admiration of Duguit, in Jennings (ed.), *Theories of Law* 62-63.

[109] See J. Stone, *cit. supra* n. 107.

[110] F. Gény, *op. et loc. cit. Cf.* Cohen, *Ethical Systems* 23: "Duguit has not gotten rid of his ethics at all . . . but he has agreed not to use the word ethics lest his extremely shaky ethical system be challenged".

As sober a historian of English law as Professor Vinogradoff wrote in 1920 (1 *Jurisprudence* 97-98) that neither the courts nor the theory of law could stand indifferent before "the social struggles of the time"; that it was "more and more evident that the time-honoured opposition between private law and constitutional law is not appropriate to the present state of legal thought", that a comprehensive overhaul of traditional concepts to take account of the newer ideals of "public utility" and "social solidarity" was urgently necessary. And this was despite his general rejection of Duguit's positions. See *id.* 151.

[111] In Jennings (ed.), *Theories of Law* 64-67. So W. Friedmann has wittily observed that Duguit's "social solidarity" is "what Kelsen would call an 'initial hypothesis' . . . [It] is not, however, hypothetical but categorical".

[112] *Cf.* Stone, *op. cit. supra* n. 107; Friedmann, *op. cit. supra* n. 96, 186.

CHAPTER 6

SOCIAL IDEAL OR CIVILISATION AS CRITERIA OF JUSTICE

I. NEO-KANTIAN SOCIAL IDEALISM

§1. JURISTIC BACKGROUND: PROBLEMS OF CODIFICATION. During the formative period of Rudolf Stammler's life[1] the German juristic scene was agitated by controversies surrounding the long preparations for the enactment of the German Civil Code of 1900. Such a code, first proposed early in the last century, had been postponed as a result in part of the influence of Savigny and the historical school. When the first draft was published in 1887 the subject was still hotly disputed, but on somewhat changed issues—first, the nationalist issue, and second, the economic issue.[2] On the former issue, Stammler ranged himself in 1888 in support of the draft Code, against the nationalist position led by Otto von Gierke, thus rejecting the fatalistic assumption that the self-unfolding of a people's law should not, and indeed could not, be consciously diverted. On the economic side, the draft Code came under attack from opinion surrounding Lassalle and the socialists, and Bismarck's programme of social legislation, for allegedly pro-capitalist bias. Stammler set himself against the thesis of economic determinism.[3]

---

[1] Rudolf Stammler was born in 1856 and died in 1938. From 1919 to his death in 1938 he was a professor at the University of Berlin, where he had succeeded Josef Kohler. He had studied at Giessen and Leipzig, and had taught successively at Leipzig (1880), at Giessen (1884) and at Halle (1885-1919). The main work here involved is Stammler, *Lehre*, transl. by I. Husik (1925) as Stammler, *Theory of Justice*. See esp. pt. ii, cc. i, ii (133-166), cc. iv, v (188-234), and for application of his criterion, pt. iii, c. ii. The basic lines of Stammler's thought were therefore published before Kohler formulated his main theories in 1904 and 1907. Stammler's other important works are: *Wirtschaft und Recht* (1896), *Theorie der Rechtswissenchaft* (2 ed. 1923); *Lehrbuch der Rechtsphilosophie* (3 ed. 1928). And see R. Stammler, "Fundamental Tendencies in Modern Jurisprudence" (1923) 21 *Mich. L.R.* 623 at 623-24.

CRITIQUES OF STAMMLER: F. Gény, "The Critical System of Rudolph Stammler", transl. from his *Science et Technique*, vol. ii, in *Theory of Justice* 41-52; H. Kantorowicz, *Zur Lehre vom richtigen Recht* (1909) (a short, keen analysis of the *Lehre*); M. Ginsberg, "Stammler's Philosophy of Law", in Jennings (ed.), *Theories of Law* 38-61; and later work cited *infra* n. 10; Hocking, *Law and Rights* c. ii. For an important line of thought influenced by Stammler's theory of just law—the "free law school" (*Freirechtsschule*) see Stone, *Legal System*, Ch. 6, §12. For comparisons of Stammler and Pound see *infra* Ch. 9; J. C. H. Wu, in *Theory of Justice* 573-86, and later work cited *infra* n. 57. For fuller bibliographies on Stammler see (1923) 21 *Mich. L.R.* 623-24, and Pound, *Outlines* 16-17, 200-201.

[2] See on the earlier codification controversies Stone, *Social Dimensions*, Ch. 2, §§3ff.

[3] His first major work, the *Wirtschaft und Recht* (1896), was devoted to combating the Marxist assumption that economic forces determine law. Though admitting that economic factors were powerful, he denied that they were decisive, and unless they were decisive, he argued, the problem of justice still remains independent and urgent. See M. Weber's critique, "*R. Stammler's 'Überwindung' der materialistischen Geschichtsauffassung*" (1907) 24 *Arch. Sozialw. und Sozialpol.* 94-151. *Cf.* on Weber's reaction to neo-Kantian formalism, Parsons, *Social Action* 502, and Strauss, *Natural Right* c. ii.

Other aspects of the draft Code, quite apart from notions like *contra bonos mores* (Art. 138), and the inevitable problem of the *casus omissus*,[4] made a theory of just law a practical necessity.[5] In his *Lehre* Stammler returned again and again to the point that the application of such phrases as "good faith" or "bad faith", for instance in the performance of obligations (Arts. 242, 320),[6] "abuse of rights", as in family law and property law; "reasonableness", for instance in fixing time-limits or measuring the fulfilment of obligation; "practicableness", as in the giving of notices; "fairness" or "equity", as in the adjustment of partnership or boundary partitions, all involved a creative application of some measure of justice, and were in this sense "lenient". The tasks of justice in short were as endemic in the new Code as they were in the old Roman law instruction to the *iudex* to decide according to the *bonum et aequum, bona fides, aequitas, ius naturale, boni mores, benevolentia, humanitas, pudor, pietas* or *iustitia;* or the Anglo-American lawyer's need to grapple with "good faith" and "conscionableness" at a dozen points in equity, with "clean hands" in the law of equitable remedies, "reasonableness" in the law of negligence, or restraint of trade, and "public policy" in its creative aspects.

§2. PHILOSOPHICAL BASIS OF STAMMLER'S THEORY OF JUSTICE. Though no school of thought named itself after Stammler, his influence in the first third of the present century cannot be doubted, especially among European and Latin-American thinkers, and also (as we shall see) in Pound's work in common law countries as well. Nor can we explain the absence of a clear juristic succession by the oft-noted ponderosities of his style, and the difficulty of grasping his highly abstract substance,[7] nor even by the unsolved mysteries (which we stressed in *The Province and Function of Law*, and shall further develop below) of the relation between his "pure" principles and the earthy problems to which they are presumably finally addressed. More persuasive explanations must be sought, then, of the fact that while the *Lehre* is among the modern juristic classics, its influence scarcely goes beyond that of a mood beckoning to the future in the language of the past.

The main answer lies probably in Stammler's strategic position at the turn of the century, when the first excitement of bringing the problems of law within the order of positivist social knowledge had subsided, without being matched by any revolutionary break-through in either the older or the newer problems of law and justice. Marxism apart, neither the Hegelian and pseudo-Hegelian philosophical interpretations of history, nor the Benthamite, Comteian, nor Darwinist nor any similar positivist programmes of moulding law and justice to the facts of social life, maintained their full early vigour into the twentieth century. It is no accident, in this

---

[4] See on the parallel problems under other European systems, Stone, *Legal System*, Ch. 6, §§6ff., and literature there cited.

[5] H. Kantorowicz, *Vorgeschichte der Freirechtslehre* (1925) 5-6; *id., op. cit. supra* n. 1. *Cf.* besides the indeterminate standards of the common law, the problems of justice involved in applying this law "so far as applicable" to former dependent territories. See the symposium in A. L. Goodhart (ed.), *Migration of the Common Law* (1960), repr. from (1960) 76 *L.Q.R.* 39-77.

[6] See also Art. 826. And *cf.* the Code of Civil Procedure, Arts. 14, 328, 723. Under Art. 242 the *Reichsgericht* took power to make most radical adjustments in contractual obligations during the inflation of 1922. Stammler also termed such rules "abstract" as distinct from "casuistic". See pt. i, c. iii of the *Lehre*.

[7] As Sir C. K. Allen, *Aspects of Justice* (1958) 87ff. seeks to do.

connection, that in the earlier of his two best known works Stammler set himself against the Marxist thesis that men's ideas of law, justice and ethical duty are but reflexes of the economic, and in particular the class structure, of society. For economic determinism had already shown itself as a dynamic challenge to nineteenth century individualist theories of justice, and an aspirant for dominance in the twentieth. The challenge issued by Marxism was by way of denying the independent reality of ideals of justice. This denial Stammler rejected in the *Wirtschaft und Recht;* then, in the *Lehre*, he issued his own challenge to the dominant nineteenth century theories.

His challenge was directed both against justice conceived in terms merely of individual rights; and against the prevailing philosophical bases of speculation. As to the former, the restatement of the problem of justice in terms of the *social* order, Stammler reinforced and also shared in the stream of influence from Ihering's social utilitarianism. As to the latter, the prevailing philosophical bases consisted, for the most part, of various shades of positivism and Hegelianism. Against these, Stammler sought to re-marshal certain doctrines of Kantian philosophy which, after a long eclipse, were again becoming a focus of philosophical interest in the Marburg[8] and Heidelberg[9] schools of neo-Kantianism. Here again, therefore, Stammler's theory gathered around it some of the influence of a movement of thought already in train.

Neo-Kantian philosophy, which Stammler re-directed onto the problems of law and justice, rejected both natural law and positivist standpoints. At the end of the nineteenth century it was particularly concerned to reject the positivist view that knowledge is exclusively based on sensory experience. The central position of neo-Kantians was that knowledge proceeds on its own principles, which are independent of sensory experience. The neo-Kantians in general sought therefore to discover *a priori* categories of thought, in the sense of concepts pre-ordinated to and independent of experience, which make experience possible,[10] these being the keys to the universal validity of knowledge. Stammler's legal philosophy must be understood as concerned with law as an object of knowledge in this sense, aiming to discover the pre-experiential categories or "pure forms" of thinking about law, to be applied thereafter to law as found in experience. While these categories are for use in the field of experience of positive law, *they do not arise from* this experience, but are rather *a priori* to it in the above sense.

Despite the fact that Stammler thought that Ihering was a poor legal philosopher, the "pure forms" of thinking from which Stammler starts,

---

[8] For example, H. Cohen (1842-1918) and P. Natrop (1854-1924). See, e.g., H. Cohen, *Ethik des reinen Willens* (1904).

[9] For example, W. Windelband (1848-1915) and H. Rickert (1863-1936). See, e.g., W. Windelband, *Über Willensfreiheit* (1904, 2 ed. 1923), H. Rickert, *Kulturwissenschaft und Naturwissenschaft* (1899, 2 ed. 1926).

[10] *Cf.* the Kantian origins *supra* Ch. 3. See K. Larenz, *Rechts- und Staatsphilosophie der Gegenwart* (2 ed. 1935) 25-26. See also M. Ginsberg, *Reason and Unreason in Society* (2 imp. 1956) 214, who nicely summarises "the critical method" as concerned with the question what must be presupposed if there is to be any knowledge at all, rather than with the historical or genetic inquiry into growth in time, or the psychological inquiry into the elements constituting belief in ideas and conditioning their occurrence in individual minds. It seeks these presuppositions by inquiring into the "formal" elements of knowledge, that is, those which "do not vary with its matter or content".

F

namely, "cause and effect", and "end and means" were also those from which (we may recall) Ihering also started. For Ihering, however, the relation between cause and effect was an empirical physical fact, and the relation of ends and means was an empirical fact of psychology; while for Stammler, these are the categories through which the appropriate contents of consciousness are ordered in their mutual relations.[11] Causality is pre-ordinated for knowledge of objects of natural science, finality (end and means) for that of norms of conduct, embraced within teleological science (*Zweckwissenschaft*).[12] Because Ihering conceived of ends and means as empirically-given phenomena, the "social utility" which he offered as the supreme norm or criterion of justice remained in the end rather undis-coverable. For Stammler on the other hand, the "volition" ("*Wollen*") which emerges from the end-means relation is not a psychological fact but rather a basic category of thinking about law and justice, "a pure method of ordering . . . to determine changes according to purpose and means as conditioning fundamental thoughts".[13] It remains to be seen whether Stammler, starting from this pure normative method, succeeded in reversing the journey of Ihering and travelling from normativeness to empirical facts.

A further preliminary point concerns the semantic maze in which Stammler involved himself and his readers, by his way of using the terms *Recht, gerecht* and *richtig* in relation to a legal precept. The word *Recht* itself of course, as opposed for example to "*Gesetz*" or "*Satzung*", connotes an element of rightness or morality or justness in the rule referred to. What are we then to say of such a sentence as the following? "*Ein gerechtes Recht ist eine rechtliche Satzung dann, wenn sie in festem Wollen bestrebt ist, das in kommenden Streitfällen richtige im voraus allgemein zu sagen.*"[14] Clearly, the third word "*Recht*" must in the context be stripped of its usual connotation and mean simply "a rule" (*Satzung*); otherwise the adjective "*gerechtes*", whatever it means, is redundant. On the other hand, this adjective itself must clearly have some import of rightness, morality, or justness, and it is therefore to be distinguished from the sixth word "*rechtliche*" (*Satzung*), which must be read like the third word "*Recht*" to mean "legal" without the connotation of rightness which the word "*Recht*" usually has.

At this point the sense appears to be: "A just (or moral? or right?) law is a legal rule which strives, in firm volition, to express generally in advance what is '*richtig*' for future cases". One question which then arises is whether "*richtig*" is used by Stammler as a synonym of "*gerecht*". If it is, we would still have to ask whether its reference is to what is "moral", or what is "right", or what is "just" (however these be delimited) or whether more than one are embraced, and if so, which. But the more serious question would be, if Stammler *were* intending some distinction between "*gerecht*" and "*richtig*", to ascertain quite what this distinction is. For it is to be noted that the *Lehre* here under examination, is a *Lehre von dem richtigen Recht* (not (be it noted) "*gerechten Recht*").

The answer to this last question is exasperatingly obscure. From the fact that he generally uses *richtig* but also occasionally uses *gerecht* and its derivatives, one would guess that he must intend some distinction in

[11] See R. Stammler, *Lehrbuch der Rechtsphilosophie* (3 ed. 1928) 57.
[12] *Id.* 55-57.
[13] *Id.* 66, n. 11.
[14] *Lehre* (2 ed. 1926) 174.

meaning. But his only explicit attention, besides the passage above quoted, seems to be in his *Theorie der Rechtswissenschaft*,[15] in which he speaks of justice (*Gerechtigkeit*) as being the "rightness in principle of a law", and as its "correspondence with the guidance (*Richtung*) of the *Gemeinschaftsgedanke*". If this last word were understood to mean "thought of the community" in the psychological sense, namely, the thoughts or opinions *held by* the community, this would give a clear meaning. But it would be one so drastically at odds with Stammler's whole approach that it must surely be rejected. *Gemeinschaftsgedanke* must therefore rather be understood as meaning "the idea of the community", or the "social ideal" in that sense. The whole passage would then mean that *Richtigkeit* is a kind of abstract guide-line pointing from the still more abstract "idea of the community" to the more concrete *Gerechtigkeit* of a concrete rule in relation to a concrete situation. This, in turn, is not identical (though it may be quite consistent) with the flat assertion in the *Lehre*[16] that "right law" (*richtiges Recht*) can also be called "moral law" (*"sittliches Recht"*).

In general, however, the meaning of *Richtigkeit* as "guidance towards just law" marches well enough with Stammler's exposition, and with his statement that *Richtigkeit* is the Kantian notion of the "regulative idea" of law. Stammler's distinction, then, between "justice" and "rightness" in relation to law, seems to be that "just law" is concrete law which has been enacted in pursuance of the guidance received from "right law" as a "regulative idea". This guidance falls short of being a criterion, for it points *in the direction of* just solutions, rather than fixes their locus and description. And the word "law" in the phrase "right law" has correspondingly no reference to positive or even concrete law. Yet while these distinctions may be important for some purposes, we believe that in the contexts of the present Chapter "right law" may be rendered, without serious distortion, in terms of "justice" or the "criteria" or "principles" of "justice".

The legal "standards", indeed, which Stammler (as seen in §1) designated as "lenient", create an unavoidable need for seeking a test of what is just in the particular situation. It is not only the legislator, he urged, who needs such a test for formulating new rules or revising existing rules. The judge also needs it—(1) in applying "lenient" legal standards to concrete situations,[17] and (2) in dealing with situations not covered by any existing legal provision.[18] In addition, Stammler urged the need, where legal rules as distinct from standards existed, for the recognition of a residual discretion in the court, which he termed "grace". For even the ideally just law, he said, may yield unjust results in the particular case, since every change of circumstances changes the content of justice, and its embodiment in rules becomes, therefore, necessarily imperfect immediately afterwards.[19]

---

[15] (2 ed. 1923) 288.

[16] (2 ed. 1926) 77.

[17] He perhaps went too far in that some of these standards (e.g., "good morals") may merely incorporate by reference prevalent ethical custom, which just as often as not will diverge from Stammler's criterion of justice. See Cohen, *Social Order* 286.

[18] On this analysis Stammler in effect said with Saleilles (*"Ecole Historique"* 102): "I believe that the adequate interpretation of the wide powers which we claim for the judge are only admissible, socially and scientifically, if at the side of the text, and in addition to the text, and in default of the text, we can furnish certain objective bases of interpretation". And *cf.* Ehrlich, *Sociology* 186ff. and c. viii, on the relation of these provisions to judicial law-making.

[19] He defined "grace" as "the realisation of just law without legal compulsion

And, furthermore, human law can never be perfectly ideal, and "grace" is needed for this reason as well.

§3. MAIN VARIATIONS ON THE KANTIAN APPROACH TO JUSTICE. Stammler accepted the major distinctions made by Kant in the fields of law and justice. Like Kant he rejected the natural lawyers' subjection of positive law to just law, recognising explicitly that positive law is binding[20] independently of its goodness or badness, and that the study of it is a part of legal science.[21] So with Kant he set off the justice of law from the ethical good, the former as concerned only with external conduct, the latter with conduct from the aspect of the purity of the actor's will.[22] And the Kantian basis is clear also in Stammler's initial proposition that no "conduct must be approved as right, which, if it became universal, would destroy the fundamental idea of a legally organised society".

Kant, however, had stated his categorical imperative in terms of the principle of action of each free-willing individual harmonious with that of all others. For Stammler the harmony was to be within "the idea of society", it being incorrect to think of society as an aggregate of individuals "with whose natural freedom the state interferes".[23] Moreover, as early as his *Wirtschaft und Recht* in 1896, he had insisted that while the ideal of justice was absolute, its application must vary constantly with time and place. It was in this work that Stammler proclaimed the search for a "natural law with a changing content". In the *Lehre* his design was to seek, not universal *rules* of just law (which he thought quite unattainable), but merely a universal *method* of ascertaining just law in empirically conditioned situations. In theory this *method* should be absolute and universal, though even as to this, Stammler was sufficiently a twentieth century child to admit that "a systematic and universal view of law may also undergo change and progress".[24]

Even with these riders the point of departure of Stammler's idea of justice still remains close to the Kantian position. What is preordinated to justice is not the psychological will (which Stammler would regard rather as *Willkür* (arbitrariness)) but the harmonised- and harmonising-will. We must be careful to understand his *Wollen* in this sense when the context

---

on the basis of ethical duty", and regarded it as the one respect in which the theory of justice depends on ethics. The point is by no means clear. If his "rules of just law" are formulated as he claims they should be in the light of the circumstances of the time and place, is not the problem merely to make it "just" for the later time? Yet he insists that "grace" as distinct from "justice" is here involved.

20 *Theory of Justice* 12, and see generally 1-19.

21 "Law in general is the necessary condition for organising harmoniously the social life of man" (*Theory of Justice* 23). Justness in particular legal rules is inconceivable except in society organised under law. Law therefore being a prerequisite of just law, legality must be a quality independent of justness. Stammler goes so far at one point as to deny that there can be a moral or "natural" duty to disobey the law, since law is a necessary condition of justice, and just law requires it to be obeyed so long as it is not legally changed (*id.* 80-85).

22 Ethical good stands, then, he points out, in relation to actual or positive morality, as justice stands to the actual or positive law, the two being parallel, not coincident. Ethics, he added, does play an important role in inspiring men to seek justice. "It is not sufficient to know the just; one must have the enthusiasm to carry it out, and this enthusiasm is furnished by ethics." Conversely, ethics requires just law for its realisation, since without it the ethical injunction to will freely can be given no content for men's external relations.

23 *Theory of Justice* 190.

24 *Id.* 92.

requires it; for in this sense it imports not so much psychological acts of willing, but norms of right-willing for judging such acts. For clearly "rightness" (or *Richtigkeit*) here involved is a "regulative idea" in relation to law in the Kantian sense,[25] an idea, in turn, related to the "concept of law", which for Stammler serves in the "procedure of intellectual ordering",[26] summing up the different ways in which means are related to ends in social volition.[27] The idea of justice or right-willing in this sense, as Ginsberg has well said, is the ideal "of a complete harmony of all striving or endeavour", towards which the will must continually aspire afresh, and in which particular ends must be subordinated to the universal harmony of all ends whatever. And here again we must be careful to avoid hasty conclusions; for this explanation, too, is entirely formal, offering a way of approaching choices we have to make, rather than indicating precisely which choice we *should* make.[28]

§4. THE "IDEA OF SOCIETY" AND THE "PRINCIPLES FOR JUST LAW".[29] The universal element of purpose in all legal rules consists, Stammler wrote, in the adjustment therein made between the purposes of the community and those of its individual members, so that each member is serving himself best in joining the community to carry on the common struggle for existence. The community itself represents the formal unity or harmony of all individual purposes: and justice is achieved when the individual purposes in a particular controversy are brought into harmony with the fundamental purpose of society, viewed as this formal unity.

Obviously, to be capable of realisation in this way individual purposes must not be merely subjective and arbitrary—in Kant's terms "free will" involves not merely volition but reason. In Stammler's words: "The aim of a legally organised community can only be the union of the individual members so far as their volitions are ends in themselves (*Selbstzwecke*)". It is in this sense that we are to understand, at the first stage in Stammler's method, his conception of a "community of free-willing men" (*Gemeinschaft freiwollender Menschen*).[30] Stammler claims for this "idea of society" the purity, freedom from specific content and therefore universal validity, which Kant had claimed for "the free will" as a universal conception. It is a conceptual prerequisite for reaching just results; yet in order to use it we have "to span the bridge between the idea of just law and its significance for specific legal questions".[31] The first part of this span consists of the

---

[25] That is, according to Kant, a principle which orients us to what we should think or otherwise do about a subject-matter, as in this case, law. A "regulative idea" is thus not empirically given. Nor is it "constitutive" of the subject-matter in the sense of being necessary for knowledge of it, as, for example, are cause and effect and time and space for knowledge of the subject-matter of natural science; or (in Austin's theory) sovereign person, rule and sanction for knowledge of law. See H. Schmidt, *Philosophisches Wörterbuch* (11 ed. by J. Streller, 1951) 485, *sub voce "regulativ"*. And see *infra* n. 35, as to the possible linkage of the notion "regulative" with the notion of a "community of neighbours".

[26] *Theory of Justice* 55.

[27] Stammler's definition of law is: "*Das Recht: das unverletzbar selbstherrlich verbindende Wollen.*" (*Theorie der Rechtswissenschaft* (2 ed. 1923) 66). Translated (so far as possible) this might read: "Law: the inviolable self-authoritative binding volition". *Cf.* Ginsberg, *op. cit. supra* n. 10 at 216.

[28] *Id.* 217.

[29] As to this rendering of "*Grundsätze des richtigen Rechts*" see *supra* §2.

[30] *Theory of Justice* 153. On this see also Hocking, *Law and Rights* c. ii.

[31] *Theory of Justice* 158.

"principles for just law", the second of the notional "special community", thus making, with "the idea of society", three stages in all.

"The principles for just law" as Stammler conceived them are drawn directly from the idea of a community of free-willing men. They are therefore equally empty of empirical content and equally absolute in their validity. That idea, involving the harmony of individual and common purposes, consists of two elements; in the first place, mutual respect of individuals for each other's purposes, and in the second place the participation of each in the achievement of the common purpose. Stammler thus deduced from his idea of society two sets of principles of just law, the "Principles of Respect" and the "Principles of Participation".

The principles of respect are two:

"(1) The content of a person's volition must not depend upon the arbitrary will of another."

"(2) Every legal demand can only be maintained in such a way that the person obligated may remain a fellow-creature (*der Nächste sein kann*)."

The first of these principles sets the limits within which one man may assert control over another through legal obligation. It seems clear enough, apart from the qualification "arbitrary" later to be examined.[32] The second principle is explained by Stammler[33] to mean that the person obliged must remain "an end in himself, so as to make possible just willing". The effect would then be that a legal demand, even if not based on the demander's "arbitrary" will, must not be pressed to the point that the person obliged ceases to have the character of a member of a community of free-willing men.[34]

Stammler stated the principles of participation as follows:

"(1) A person legally obligated must not be arbitrarily excluded from the community."[35]

"(2) Every lawful power of decision may exclude the person affected by it from the community[36] only to the extent that that person may remain a fellow-creature (*der Nächtse sein kann*)."

[32] Stammler's explanation of "arbitrary" as referring to a will which says: "You shall will what I will because I will it" does not resolve the difficulty. See *infra* §7.

[33] *Lehre* 285; *Theory of Justice* 218.

[34] The text might literally also mean that no demand is to be made on A by virtue of A's special situation which would not be made generally on other persons. Though the Kantian flavour is here apparent, Stammler has abandoned the effort to limit one individual's rights by reference to the equal rights of other individuals. His limits are derived from the notion of community of purpose in social life which he uses as the touchstone of individual purposes. He avoids, it may be noted, talking of "rights" at this stage, using instead terms such as "claims" or "demands" or "purposes". He thus avoids the danger of confusing "natural" or "moral" or "ideal legal rights" with those actually conferred by positive law.

[35] Husik says "a legal community". Strikingly recalling this, and surrounded by similar difficulties, is Kitto J.'s suggestion (in part dissenting) in the *Second Hughes & Vale Case* (1955) 93 C.L.R. 127. "Regulatory" laws now held to be permissible under s. 92 of the Australian Constitution (he thought) are those "by which an individual's latitude of conduct is circumscribed in the interests of fitting him into a neighbourhood—a society, membership of which entails, because of its nature, acts and forbearances on the part of each by which room is allowed for the reasonable enjoyment by each other of his own position in the same society" (218). To impose liability for activity which respects this principle (Kitto J. went on) is "to meet" the person liable "outside the field of regulated conduct in an ordered society and, in effect, to deny flatly that he may enter it as of right", and therefore to violate s. 92 (219). And *cf*. 220.

[36] Our paraphrase of very difficult words which seem to mean literally, "may be exclusive only, etc.".

Both these principles, Stammler explained, forbid exclusion of any person from the benefits of social life, thus making explicit the co-operative aspect of "the idea of society". "Just as we may bind him and make claims on his conduct, so everyone should act towards him in a similar way, allowing him to share in the common life."

§5. THE SPECIAL COMMUNITY (MODEL FOR JUST LAW) AS A MEANS OF ORGANISING THE CONFLICTING INTERESTS IN A PARTICULAR CASE. Stammler found corresponding difficulties in his neo-Kantian theory of *justice* to those which have faced Hans Kelsen in his neo-Kantian theory of *the internal structure of the law*,[36a] namely, difficulties of application to the existential world. Even after he had deduced his principles for just law, Stammler confessed that they could not be applied to concrete problems unless the empirical material involved could be organised to make this possible. For this task he offered "the Model (*Vorbild*) for Just Law" in these terms.

> The principles for just law are universal propositions which start from the heights of the absolute idea of law and bring its commands down to earth and divide and distribute them; whereas it is the function of the model for just law (the special community) to come up to meet them from below. Its business is to gather in unitary fashion the conditioned material of legal experience and lay it before the plenipotentiaries of the appellate monarch—the idea of just law.[37]

The "model for just law", we are told, is the idea (*Gedanke*) of a special community among those whose conflicting claims are to be passed upon and resolved conformably to the criterion of justice. Conversely, it is supposed, the "special community" is the "model for just law" *in the particular case*. This conception is sufficiently difficult to warrant further examination.

Neither the "special community" nor the "model for just law" is a part of any actual legal order. They are merely notional means of "subordinating concrete subject-matter to the abstract principles for just law",[38] the *a posteriori* to the *a priori*. The "special community", for example, derives from the "idea of society", of a community of free-willing men. Yet it is to include the actual claims of actual men in their role as "neighbours" to each other in the particular situation,[39] conflict among whom calls for a just solution. The range of persons thus involved will vary according to the nature of the conflict, and may or may not be superimposed upon an existing social unit, such as the family.

Thus far Stammler's mind has been directed essentially to the administration of justice in particular cases; but he also adapted his criteria into the form of three "postulates for legislation" dealing respectively with "personality", "provision" (of the conditions for just-willing), and "measure" (of permissible legal exaction); and covering much the same ground as the "principles for just law". For the legislator, as for the judge, the mediating device of the "special community" is necessary. But since

---

[36a] See Stone, *Legal System*, Ch. 3.
[37] *Theory of Justice* 212. The lapse at such a crucial point into almost theological metaphor is most significant.
[38] *Id.* 215.
[39] *Id.* 217-223.

legislation tends to affect more persons at one stroke (and more radically) than do judicial decisions, the "special community" would be more complex and the pressure and conflicts of claims are there more intense. The legislator's task is thus correspondingly difficult.[40]

§6. LORD ATKIN'S "MY NEIGHBOUR" AND STAMMLER'S "SPECIAL COMMUNITY". The conception of "my neighbour", which is perhaps the most crucial part of Stammler's system, though familiar to religious thought, has a certain alien ring in lawyers' ears.[40a] For this reason it is well to recall that in a famous formulation of Lord Atkin it has now been, for more than thirty years, a focal centre of the problematics of the law of negligence.

In *Donoghue* v. *Stevenson*[41] the House of Lords addressed itself to the essentially practical question whether Mrs. Donoghue was to be compensated by the manufacturer of a bottle of ginger beer for injury resulting from the impurity of the contents, when, though that impurity was due to his negligence, the purchase was made, not from him, but from a third party, the retailer. Lord Atkin, in the course of his speech, said:

> At the present I content myself with pointing out that in English law there must be, and is, some general conception of relations giving rise to a duty of care, of which the particular cases found in the books are but instances. The liability for negligence . . . is no doubt based upon the general public sentiment of wrongdoing (*sic*) for which the offender must pay. But acts and omissions which any moral code would censor cannot in a practical world be treated so as to give a right to every person injured by them to demand relief. . . . The rule that you are to love your neighbour becomes in law, you must not injure your neighbour, and the lawyer's question "Who is my neighbour?" receives a restricted reply. You must take reasonable care to avoid acts or omissions which you can reasonably foresee would be likely to injure your neighbour. Who, then, in law, is my neighbour?[42] The answer seems to be—persons who are so closely and directly affected by my act that I ought reasonably to have them in contemplation as being so affected when I am directing my mind to the acts and omissions which are called into question.

---

[40] It is for this reason that Stammler limits himself to the administration of justice in illustrating the application of his method in pt. iii of the *Lehre*. He does not illustrate it for the legislative process. For similar reasons he excludes the administration of criminal justice.

[40a] On its use in Hebrew law see *supra* Ch. 1, §5. While many of the rules of liability for damage in *Exodus* cc. 21ff. are stated in terms of liability to a man's neighbour *(re'ehu)*, that word there seems to embrace not any delimited group (e.g., those foreseeably affected) but any fellow members in the community to whom the damage is in fact done. But the Talmudic exegesis imported a distinction between *garmai* (where liable without more shown) and *grama* (where not liable unless damage was generally to be expected even if not inevitable in the context of action) (*Sanhedrin* 76b, *Babba Kama* 60a, *Babba Bathra* 22b, *Gloss of Tosefoth*). This latter category in effect cut down the range of persons to whom there will be liability, and thus approximated to each other the two notions of "neighbour". *Cf.* a similar narrowing as between Hooker's *Laws of Ecclesiastical Polity*, I, 8, sec. 7, and Locke's *Treatises of Government*, II, secs. 5-6; and see Strauss, *Natural Right* 221n.

[41] (1932) A.C. 562, at 580, and see Stone, *Legal System*, Ch. 7, §§11-12; *id.*, *Social Dimensions*, Ch. 6, §1.

[42] It is submitted that the noble Lord's meaning would have been better rendered by "for purposes of law"; "in law" suggested that the criterion consists of a rule of positive law; whereas it is clearly extra-legal in its nature. This distinction seems to be the basis of the difficult opinion of the P.C. in *Commr. for Rlys.* v. *Quinlan* (1964) 2 W.L.R. 817. See esp. 825, 832, 837.

Lord Atkin postulated that "there must be and is some general conception of relations giving rise to a duty of care". But why? The answer would be clear in terms of some *a priori* assumption such as that lying behind Stammler's postulate of a community of free-willing men. And the principle that "you must take reasonable care to avoid acts or omissions which you can reasonably foresee would be likely to injure your neighbour" will, without excessive strain, bear comparison with Stammler's principles of just law. The parallel is the more remarkable in that Lord Atkin is led, as Stammler was, to a conception of "my neighbour" as the crucial meeting-point of the *a priori* principles and the empirical facts to which they are to be applied. It is, moreover, clear that Lord Atkin's "neighbour" is a concept of justice rather than of law. For he continued:

> I do not think so ill of our jurisprudence as to suppose that its principles are so remote from the ordinary needs of civilised society and the ordinary claims it makes upon its members, as to deny a legal remedy where there is so obviously a social wrong.[43]

Both Lord Atkin's and Stammler's positions, when stripped as far as may be of mystical garb, appear to amount to this. One step in just solution is always to penetrate beneath the confusion of the claims of human beings that are involved. These claims must be stated in terms which comprehend them all, as well as render them mutually comparable, and adjustable.[44] In short, the "special community" is a notional arrangement of the disputants and their purposes, as a model on a smaller scale of society as a whole, thus permitting them to be tested against the idea of a society of free-willing men and the principles for just law.[45]

§7. CRITIQUE OF STAMMLER'S SOCIAL IDEALISM: CIRCULARITY OR SHORTFALL IN THE PRINCIPLES. Stammler himself admitted that he had not produced a criterion of certain or easy application, that there is no "mathematical basis" for the judgment of justice, that more than logical deduction is involved, that remarkable variations in judgment are to be expected, and that there are no ready-made pigeon holes for doubtful cases.[46] Even all this, however, cannot disarm those of his critics[47] who find his criterion equivocal and, in the last resort, impossible of application. Our own criticisms fall into two principal groups. First, in his principles for just law Stammler uses words such as "arbitrary" as if their meaning were given. It is necessary, according to Stammler, to know what is "arbitrary" in order to know what is "just". And as to this it must be asked whether we *can* know what is "arbitrary" without some notion of what is "just". And also if, *so far as we can,* it is helpful to know what is "arbitrary", in order to know what is "just". We will try to answer these questions according to the possible meanings of "arbitrary" in Stammler's contexts, with alertness for the circularities which some meanings may involve. Second, Stammler does not satisfactorily bridge the gap between his *a priori* "idea of society", "the

---

[43] At 583. Adopted as a test in *Bourhill's Case* (1943) A.C. 92, *per* Lord Porter at 117.

[44] *Theory of Justice* 230.

[45] It will be observed in Ch. 9 that there exists a striking resemblance between this device and some portions of Professor Pound's sociological criterion of justice.

[46] *Theory of Justice* 233, 242.

[47] *Cf.* notably Gény, *Science et Technique* 190; H. Kantorowicz, *op. cit. supra* n. 1, at 33-35, 36-37; G. Fraenkel, *Die kritische Rechtsphilosophie bei Fries und bei Stammler* (1912) §§17-19.

principles for just law" derived therefrom, and the empirical conflict of claims to which they are supposed to offer a just solution.

The charge of circularity in some respects cannot, it is feared, be rebutted. Thus the very "idea of society", the pre-ordinated source of his entire criterion of justice, is defined as the idea of a community in which each member joins in furthering the "objectively justified" (*objektivberechtigte*) purposes of the others. Thus at this first stage of defining what is "just" Stammler presupposes some notion of what it is. This, however, need not be fatal, provided that similar difficulties do not afflict his subsequent elaborations in "the principles for just law". His first "principle of respect" forbids the subordination of one man's will to the "arbitrary" will of another. His first "principle of participation" limits the "arbitrary" exclusion of a person from the community. A will, Stammler said, is "arbitrary" if it says: "You shall will what I will because I will it".[48] But men are rarely so foolish as to will without any reason whatever, and taken thus literally, his principle would be reduced to a negligible scope. After we had determined that what was willed was "arbitrary" in this sense, we would still be very far from determining whether it was just. For while it is true that what I will merely because I will it can only be just by accident (as it were), the mere fact that I *can* honestly vouch *some other reason than my own will,* in no way assures that what I will *for that reason* is just. If this were all that "arbitrary" imported we would have to conclude that these principles could contribute nothing to the understanding of justice save the truism that when we pursue our own will, regardless of the justness of what we will, then what we will can only be just by accident.

"Arbitrary" may, however, have other meanings than the one indicated by Stammler. It may mean, in the second place, "at random", as when the choice is determined by drawing lots or pricking pins into alternative formulations. The analysis here would be little different from the preceding. But there are still two more possible meanings other than either personal whim or randomness. There is, in the third place, the meaning of "arbitrary" which imports the absence of any "good" or "justifiable" or "fair" or "proper" or (some other synonym of) "just", reason. Stammler nowhere explicitly indicates that this is what he meant by "arbitrary". If nevertheless this *were* what he meant, we would have to observe that as a guide to what is "just" *this* notion of "arbitrariness" would be circular. It is true that under the due process clause of the United States Constitution as interpreted by the courts the validity of a statute depends on the deprivation of life, liberty or property involved being "not arbitrary and unreasonable".[49] But even if the courts had given to the phrase "not arbitrary and unreasonable" the meaning "just", they would not have been open to the charge of circularity to which Stammler is vulnerable. For they would be using this formula

---

48 He uses *Willkür* for arbitrariness, and "*subjektive Laune*" for personal whim, etc. See the *Lehre* (2 ed. 1926) 22, 149. Little seems to turn (and we therefore take no position) on the point whether a despot governs "arbitrarily" in this sense, or obeys a precarious legal régime consisting of one norm sanctifying the despotic will. See L. Legaz y Lacambra, *Filosofia del Derecho* (1953) 493, 495. This author seems, further, to identify arbitrariness with non-application of a rule to a case falling within it. "Law can be unjust but it cannot be arbitrary", since "arbitrariness is non-law, the contrary to law, the negation of law in its form." (494-95.) On this view, equitable derogations from *legal* rules would be both arbitrary and *just*. This may be a relevant view for the study of internal structures *of law;* but Stammler is here surely concerned rather with the structure of justice.

49 See *supra* Ch. 3, §§6ff.

not to test for what is "just", but to test for what is valid law.

In fact, the American judicial view which actually prevails is not this; it is rather that a deprivation is "not arbitrary and unreasonable" if *any reason based on facts* can be offered to support it.[50] This presents still a fourth possible meaning of "arbitrary". In this meaning, to say that something *is* "arbitrary" is certainly to say that it cannot be just. Yet to say that it is *not* "arbitrary" gives no assurance *that it is just.* So that even if there were reason to suppose (and there is not) that this is what Stammler meant by "arbitrary", his principles for "just law" which centre on this notion would again fall vastly short of a guide towards just law.

Difficulties, moreover, also affect Stammler's second "principle of respect" which forbids legal demands to be pressed to the point when the person obliged ceases to be "a neighbour" or "a fellow creature". Stammler explains this difficult phrase as meaning that the person obliged must remain "an end in himself so as to make possible *just* willing". But the precise purpose of the principle being to define what is "just" it is scarcely helpful to define it in terms of what makes possible "just" willing. A similar difficulty affects the second "principle of participation."[51]

§8. CRITIQUE OF STAMMLER'S SOCIAL IDEALISM: THE GAP BETWEEN *A PRIORI* PRINCIPLES AND CONCRETE SITUATIONS. The second group of criticisms, it will be recalled, concern Stammler's purported *rapprochement* of the *a priori* "idea of society" and its derivative "principles for just law", to the concrete conflicts for the solution of which they are to provide guidance. François Gény pointed out long ago that Stammler had not succeeded in bridging the gap involved. The formulae, he said, which Stammler had elaborated—

> are merely abstract, aiming simply at unity, generality and universal validity. Hence if you try to adapt them to the tangible circumstances of life they refuse their service; at the very least they show themselves unequal to the task, because they demand of the facts a deconcretisation that is impossible to attain.

From this, concluded Gény, proceeds the necessity in which Stammler found himself, of resorting in his illustrations[52] consciously or unconsciously to a more concrete method. His attempt to close the hiatus by the concept of "the special community" achieved little more[53] than to add a new formula

---

[50] *Ibid.*

[51] There is a surprising but real similarity between this conception of Stammler and the superficially very different outlook of H. J. Laski. The latter's recurring reference to the ultimate moral rights of each citizen to "fulfil his best self" (see *Politics* 92, 187, 195, 488 and *passim*) and to a "common civic minimum" (*id.* cc. iii, v, 197 and *passim*) are only not subject to a similar objection of *petitio principii* because Professor Laski follows the principle with more concrete applications. In these applications they represent in substance various aspects of what we have elsewhere termed, following Pound, "the social interest in the individual life" of all members of society. See Stone, *Social Dimensions*, Ch. 6, §§23ff.

[52] In pt. iii, for an account of which space is not here available.

[53] Though I have suggested an analogy between Stammler's "special community" and one aspect of Pound's theory of justice, the analogy may not extend so far as to subject the latter to the same objection. See *infra* Ch. 9, §3.

Disciples of Stammler have for this reason sought substitutes or supplements for the principles of just law and the notional special community. (See, e.g., L. Brütt, *Die Kunst der Rechtsanwendung* (1907) which seeks to interpose ends presupposed by a people's civilisation. See esp. 125-140, and *infra* n. 97). *Cf.* Cohen, *Social Order* 173, 194, 256, who observed that "you cannot construct a building merely out of the rules of architecture".

to all the others. And Luis Recaséns Siches has referred to Stammler's "formalist illusion", by which he purported to derive from the idea of human personality as an end in itself a universal guide independent of the concrete contents of human experience, and yet somehow admitted into his thought "as a kind of *deus ex machina,* a body of ideas of value with concrete content".[54]

Recaséns seems to link this imperfection with certain deeper alleged errors. He believes that Stammler wrongly transferred Kant's theory of *knowledge,* as expounded in the *Kritik der reinen Vernunft,* to the legal and moral fields, overlooking the specific characteristics of these areas of the practical reason.[55] And he suggests that Stammler was also in error (this time following Kant) in equating the formal-material distinction to the *a priori—a posteriori* distinction. In other words, Stammler did not recognise that there might be formal ideas which were not *a priori,* and therefore not absolute, necessary and universal; nor, conversely, that material content need not necessarily be *a posteriori* and therefore contingent and empirical. This suggestion, if correct, may be relevant to the unsolved mystery in Stammler of the relation of "pure" ideas to empirically given problems.[56] And it may be that Stammler himself came near to acknowledging such an error. John C. H. Wu relates[57] that while studying with Stammler he wrote an article maintaining that "the concept of law presupposed the law as a thing in itself" (*sic,* meaning presumably an empirically found entity), so that not only conceptual knowledge, but also perception and indeed "intellectual intuition" as well (in short, the use of "the *whole* mind") were necessary for knowing about law. Stammler commented (Dr. Wu recalls) that "this is so far the most formidable criticism that my philosophy has met with!"

§9. Stammler's Contributions to Twentieth Century Theories of Justice.

Stammler's achievements remain nevertheless considerable.[58] First, his work heralded revival of efforts to analyse justice in philosophical terms. Ihering had revived the hue and cry after justice, but Stammler it was who, for good or ill, reset the respectable badge of Kantian philosophy on the enterprise. He brought over into the twentieth century the age-old craving for a better foundation for justice than any man's arbitrary will.[59] Second, Stammler posed clearly for the first time the problem of finding a "universally valid method for the attainment of just law on a given question at a given time".[60] His call for "natural law with a changing content" has become a slogan of twentieth century jurists,[61] ministering as it does

---

54 See Recaséns, *Filosofía del Derecho* 458.

55 But see *supra* Ch. 3, §1 on Kant's position as to use of the "transcendental method", which was *par excellence* the method for the theory of knowledge.

56 See Recaséns, *op. cit.* 459. This criticism is advanced from the philosophical positions of M. Scheler and N. Hartmann on the theory of values.

57 See J. C. H. Wu, *Fountain of Justice* (1955) 51, n. 79.

58 *Cf.* Pound, *Outlines* 23.

59 *Cf.* Gény, *Science et Technique. Cf.* R. Pound, "Fifty Years of Jurisprudence" (1937) 38 *H.L.R.* 444, 448, id., 1 *Jurisprudence* 154. It seems extravagant, however, as does Brütt, *op. cit supra* n. 53, at 118, to match his stature in legal philosophy with that of Kant in the theory of knowledge.

60 H. Kantorowicz, *op. cit. supra* n. 1, at 37ff.; Gény, *loc. cit.*

61 *Cf.* the general tenor of L. Fuller, *The Law in Quest of Itself* (1940); and see *infra* Ch. 7. J. C. H. Wu, *op. et loc. cit. supra* n. 57, stresses precisely Stammler's encouragement to natural law thought when it was at a low ebb in the struggle with positivism. We doubt, however, Dr. Wu's suggestion that this came about by his

both to the yearning for a universal ideal, and the caution of scientific relativism. He offered, it has been said, "an harmonious articulation of the rational exigencies, which are universally valid, with the concrete necessities proper to every social situation".[62] Third, Stammler sought to adapt the Kantian philosophical tradition to juristic problems of a century later. As Ihering's social utilitarianism stands to Bentham's individualist utilitarianism, so Stammler's social metaphysics stands to Kant's individualistic metaphysics. Ihering and Stammler together, in addressing themselves to the question of their age—What restrictions on liberty does social living require?—helped to set the tone for twentieth century thought.

There is also to be credited to Stammler his arresting statement of the need for conscious evaluation of the just in creative judicial activity even under a code. In this his prospective work on the German Code matched Gény's retrospective work on the French Code, and the work of Holmes, Pound, and Cardozo on the common law. Moreover, as Pound once put it, Stammler "added a theory of the just decision of causes to the theory of making just rules", and contributed materially to the twentieth century understanding of the process of application and "individualisation of justice" within the framework of a system of law.

§10. JUSTICE ACCORDING TO NELSON'S NEO-KANTIAN "SCIENCE OF ETHICS".[63] Leonard Nelson's claim to have worked out a "science" of ethics must be understood in his own sense, namely that ethics can be presented as "a system . . . rigorously logical in structure".[64] As his admirer Julius Kraft observes, he demonstrates *"more geometrico"* what a system "logically derived from ethical rules would look like".[65] This claim to be able to *deduce* a system of ethical rules constitutes here a special interest of Nelson's neo-Kantian version of justice. Nelson did not claim that he

---

persuasiveness for positivists, rather than by providing a respectable philosophical position on which *anti-positivists* could stand.

[62] Recaséns, *Filosofía del Derecho* 457, 474, comparing Stammler in this respect with Suarez.

[63] Leonard Nelson was born in Berlin in 1882. In 1919 he became Professor of Philosophy at the University of Göttingen. He had by then already published the first volume of his *lectures on the foundations of ethics*, under the title of *Kritik der praktischen Vernunft* (1917). Part of a later volume, the *System der philosophischen Ethik und Pedägogik* (1932), is now transl. by N. Guterman as *System of Ethics* (1956) here cited as "Nelson, transl.". The earlier *Kritik* is concerned with Nelson's basic ethical postulates. His ideas on justice are in the translated *System*. He died in 1927 after a distinguished academic career.

[64] He rejected the contrary view of Henri Poincaré, *"La Morale et la Science"*, in *id., Dernières Pensées* (1913) 221-247. His other issues with Poincaré, quoted Nelson, transl. 3-4, seem beside the present point. One was that the word "science" should not be appropriated to natural science, merely because that was the usage in the French language (*sic*—we doubt this either then or now). Another was that the fact that the "rigorous logic" of the science of ethics must start from "some unproved imperative" was no objection, since natural science also starts from "unproved premises" this time in the indicative mood (4-5). While one chain of argument was through imperative and the other through indicative propositions, to allow the grammatical difference between imperatives and indicatives to decide the argument was (he thought) a *petitio principii*. We ourselves would have thought that the availability of experimental proof of indicative propositions was relevant to the debate. The fact that Nelson does not think so seems to mean that he is using "scientific" in the narrow sense of "derived by logical deduction from given premises". In this sense, of course, the word asserts nothing about the truth or justness either of premises or conclusion. See Stone, *Legal System,* Ch. 6. As to whether there can be a logic of imperatives, and if so how, see *id.* Ch. 2, §19. And on the relevance of grammar to the argument see Nelson, *loc. cit.*, and *infra* Ch. 10, §9.

[65] Intro. to Nelson, transl. at xiv.

had proved the premises from which his logic proceeded.[66] Stammler, as we have seen, admitted that mere logical deduction was insufficient.[67]

Nelson offers, then, a reconstructed ethics (including justice) derived by "rigorous logic" from "a few clearly formulated assumptions".[68] His ethics is a "practical science of nature".[69] It is broader than morality, which for him deals only with norms prescribing duties, whereas ethical norms embrace not only these but also those of "wisdom" with its less rigorous injunctions which he called "optatives". This elaboration expresses, then, the assumption that we should do not only our duty, but also what is worth doing[70] as measured by an additional norm, which Nelson calls the "ideal". Duty observance is morality; cleaving to the ideal is "culture"; both together are "wisdom". This, no doubt, puts it all in a nutshell. Our problems then, however, are whether we can keep it there, and whether (even if we can) any guidance can come from it.

What is in the nutshell is quite complicated. First, while the two branches of ethics ("duties" and "ideal"-"optatives") are co-ordinated, nevertheless, in pursuing the ideals, it is assumed that the duties have been fulfilled. This is a condition precedent for *any* value of the action concerned. Secondly, in neo-Kantian fashion he insists that each of the norms both of duty or ideal has two aspects, distinguishable only by a vitally important process of abstraction.[71] These are the "form" and the "content". The formal aspect of such a norm comprises what is implied in the concept of it, *regardless* of the specific task it sets us; the content is this specific task. In his development of this distinction Nelson acknowledged, in a chapter entitled "Transition to Material Theory of Duties",[72] an apparent paradox. From the formal aspect of duty only the agent's *sense of duty* is in question, regardless of whether his ideas about duty are "true" or "false". Yet in the material (content-pertaining) theory of duties the search is for a criterion of what *is "true"* duty. What is *here* crucial is precisely what is irrelevant to our evaluation of the ethical performance of the agent. And it is this latter obviously which is of greater interest to lawyers' justice, the lawyer being concerned with the content of duties rather than with evaluating the actor's ethical performance. Nelson's resolution of the paradox is that we must

---

[66] See *supra* n. 64. There is involved here, of course, the old problem of "bridging the gap" between the "Is" and the "Ought". *Cf.* on modern attempts to bridge this gap, *infra* Ch. 7 *passim*.
Despite these limits (which seem quite clear on pp. 4ff.) Nelson also slips into language which seems to claim more. He makes much, for example, of the facts that Socrates was proved wrong in his conviction that the gods did not grant man the ability to penetrate the mysteries of *natural* science, and that only because certain bold thinkers dared to disregard his view did *natural* science emerge. This scarcely proves more than that Socrates was wrong, and that some positions firmly held *may* be wrong. It cannot prove that any particular position as to the nature of ethics *is* wrong.
[67] See *supra* §7.
[68] J. Kraft, Intro. to Nelson, transl. at xiv. *Cf.* his Intro. to L. Nelson, *Socratic Method and Critical Philosophy* (transl. 1949), repr. Nelson, transl. 263-275.
[69] Nelson used the term "theoretical" in the sense in which a cognition is called "theoretical" when it refers to the *existence* of things, and "practical" when it refers to the *purposes* or *values* of things. Thus his "practical science" of ethics is also described as a "subjective teleology". But then in transl. 21 he speaks of his "science" being "practical in the original, narrowest, and most rigorous sense of the term".
[70] A. R. Blackshield, "Empiricist and Rationalist Theories of Justice" (1962) 48 *Arch. R.- und Sozialph.* 25, at 38-39, has tried to make sense of this kind of position. *Cf.* L. L. Fuller's construction of a dual level of morality, the "morality of duty" and the "morality of aspiration" in his *The Morality of Law* (1964, Storrs Lectures on Jurisprudence, Yale University, 1963) *passim*, esp. 3-32.
[71] Nelson, transl. 36.   [72] *Id.* 86-87.

here recognise a direct link between the material and formal aspects. Duty in its formal aspect imposes on us a kind of liaison-duty to strive for knowledge of the content of duty. This duty, though quite different in philosophical texture, has directives for judges and legislature harmonious with the assumptions of most modern theories, for instance that of Pound concerning the importance of bringing to awareness all the *de facto* interests affected.[73]

Within this general framework of ethics justice itself is for Nelson part of the "material theory of duties". It is approached in three steps. First, the principle of personal dignity subjects our freedom of action to the condition that we *respect* (without our being told how much) the "true" interests of persons affected by our action. Second, the principle of equality of persons gives us the measure of how far one person's interests may be restricted by another's. Third, there are the "law of adjustment" (or "principle of equity") and the "law of just retribution" whenever (as is always implied) there is a conflict between the interests of the agent and those of the person affected by his action.

The "law of adjustment" (or "principle of equity")[74] obliges us to refrain from actions injuring another's interest unless our own interest in such actions is "preponderant". "Never act in such a way that you could not assent to your conduct if the interests of those affected by it were also your own." If this duty is violated, a different situation arises, bringing into operation the "law of just retribution". In order to restore equality, the unfair advantage must be offset by requiring the malefactor to suffer injury equal to the one inflicted. To the malefactor the law of just retribution says that he must assent to a disregard of his own interests equal to what he has shown for the interests of others.

Since the "law of retribution" presupposes (as it were) the "practicality" of the "law of adjustment", the latter is what we shall here examine. At first sight it is far from "practical". For A, in a situation affecting B, to act as if B's interests were A's would (if taken literally) still leave A with no guidance at all; only instead of acting in his own interests he would now act in B's interests. This might be just or more than just to B; but there would be no reason to think it just to A. Moreover B, if he were actor, would have to follow the reciprocal procedure. And wherever this kind of reciprocal surrender of interests may lead, it does not seem to lead to justice. What Nelson should rather be understood to mean is that the actor must put the other's interests *alongside* his own, to ensure that his preference does not automatically favour his own interests *because they are his own*. Thus interpreted the position not only recalls Stammler's "special community", but also accords with the central point of Pound's theory just mentioned which we shall fully examine in Chapter 9.

We shall see that Pound's theory is plagued by many difficulties because it requires the conflicting interests to be stated in quantitative terms before the criterion of maximum satisfaction of all the interests affected can be applied. The difficulties with Nelson's position are even graver. First, it is by no means clear what he means *in this context* by "interests". In his substantive treatment of the notion he seems to say that a person's "interests" determine the "value" of an action to him. But he is also at pains to make clear that in his sense "it is entirely incidental" whether

[73] See, e.g., *id.* 108-109.
[74] *"Das Gesetz der gerechten Abwägung".* See *id.* 120ff.

the party affected is "directly conscious of the interest", and that the actor need not take into account that other's *actual* interests if they are not his "true" interests; for they are then only "putative" interests. Nelson also says that the actor must take into account the other's "true" interests even if they are not the other's actual interests.[75] If reduction to quantities of interests is a hard problem with Pound's theory, where at least the interests are said to be *de facto* psychological phenomena and presumably observable, it must be quite chimerical with Nelson's "interests". For these appear themselves each to involve a value-judgment before we can even say whether and how far they exist at all in a sense in which the actor ought to consider them.[76] Yet the whole crux of his "law of adjustment" (or "principle of equity"), and indirectly also of his "law of retribution", is to enjoin us to determine our decision according to which "interests" are "preponderant".[77]

These difficulties are for the lawyer so conclusive that we should perhaps not linger over the further point that Nelson's entire discussion of the duty of justice is in terms of a conflict between the interests of *two* parties. Problems of justice as they confront lawyers and legislators involve a competition far more complex; and the adaptation of his model to real legal problems would compound all the difficulties of quantification. In these circumstances, and since we have already raised the matter in Chapter 3, and will consider its modern position in Ch. 11, §§2 and 3, we also need not do more than mention that his adoption of the test of equality (or of what can become "a general rule") is inadvertent to many of the difficulties with which modern thought has confronted these Kantian positions.

II. NEO-HEGELIAN CIVILISATION THEORY[78]

§11. FACTS AND JUSTICE: KOHLER'S APPROACH THROUGH THE PHILOSOPHY OF HISTORY. Ihering had thought that social utility as the test of

---

[75] *Id.* 97. And see generally 103ff., esp. for his discussion of "obscure" interests. These difficulties are far greater than that of conceiving of one man regarding as his own the interests of the other person affected, which worries A. Ross, *On Law and Justice* (1958) 278-280.

[76] The point is rather confused in Ross, *op. et loc. cit.* and his *Kritik der . . . praktischen Erkenntnis* (1933) cxi. He charges in effect that Nelson's test of justice is tautologous because it requires us to satisfy those interests which are justified. A better interpretation, though still open to the difficulties for lawyers mentioned in the text, is that an "interest" for Nelson must be tested for its ethical value before it can be brought into consideration for adjustment of its conflict with other interests. The testing of each interest for ethical value is not necessarily tautologous with the later testing of the conflicting interests for adjustment in accordance with justice.

[77] Nelson, transl. 120.

[78] The following reading list is suggested.

LIFE AND BACKGROUND: A. Kocourek, editorial preface in Kohler, transl. xv-xxiv; Kohler, transl. 12-19 (his ideological antipathies and sympathies); W. Sauer, "*Hegel und die Gegenwart*" (1931) 25 *Arch. R.- und Wirtschaftsph.* 1-8.

CONCEPTION OF "CIVILISATION" (*KULTUR*): Kohler, transl. 28-64; Kohler, *Moderne Rechtsprobleme* (1913) 1-15; Hocking, *Law and Rights* 24-36 (a very important interpretation); R. Pound, "Scope and Purpose of Sociological Jurisprudence" (1912) 23 *H.L.R.* 140, 154-58. THE "JURAL" OR RATHER "CIVILISATIONAL" POSTULATES (*Rechtspostulate*): Kohler, transl. 4 (badly translated as "postulates of law". They are either "postulates of civilisation" or "postulates for law"). RELATIONS OF STAMMLER, KOHLER AND POUND: *Infra* Ch. 9 on Pound's theory of interests and jural postulates; Hocking, *Law and Rights* 1-11, 36-46, 84-97; Pound, "Social Interests" 1; *id.*, *Outlines* 168-186 (on jural postulates I-V) and *cf.* his *Social Control* 118ff.; Stone, "Pound's Theory of Justice" 531, 540-550; J. C. H. Wu in Stammler, *Theory of Justice* 572.

justice was discernible from observation of the play of human purposes; and on a different level of empirical inquiry Duguit confidently assumed that the directives of his criterion of social solidarity were self-evident and even self-applying in a complex industrial society. Examination revealed no basis for their confidence that social facts carry any built-in directions for placing them within the order of justice. To Stammler the error leading to such failures was obvious. The norms of justice must be sought, not in observing social facts, or indeed any facts; but rather in an understanding of what is presupposed when men think about justice, namely the "social ideal" or "community of free-willing individuals", and in what is then to be implied from this ideal. The "principles for just law" thus revealed, may then guide us to just solutions of the problems raised by particular social facts. Here, however, as we have seen, Stammler encountered difficulties converse to those of Ihering and Duguit. Their vision of the facts, with all its power, did not yield a normative "take-off". Stammler's normative vision of the pure "idea of society" and its derivative principles soar down, as it were, from above, but find no clear landing-place amid the social facts.

Josef Kohler strove valiantly to infuse social facts with the power of normative take-off, by integrating them (as it were) into a non-empirical conception of "civilisation". His discussion of justice merits attention for at least three reasons. First, this notion of "civilisation" as normative for law, and its derivative notion of "jural postulates", have become part of the currency of subsequent juristic thought. His *Lehrbuch der Rechtsphilosophie,* first published in 1908, is therefore among the modern classics of the theory of justice.[79] Second, as we have just seen, this work presents itself as still another secular effort to solve the problem of the relation between social facts and the norms of justice. Third (and subsidiarily for the present work, which is a work on juristic theory rather than on philosophy itself), Kohler's efforts are in the line of Hegelian philosophy. Indeed, Communist theory apart, they are the most ambitious contribution to the theory of justice framed in Hegelian mood during the first third of the century.

In a life-span stretching from 1849 to 1919, Kohler held until his death the Chair at the University of Berlin in which Stammler then succeeded him. Kohler's main work until the end of the century was in comparative legal history; not until after the turn of the century did he take up directly the problems of the *Lehrbuch,* and indeed that work appeared only some years after Stammler's *Lehre.* The basis of the *Lehrbuch,* so far as Kohler's own awareness went,[80] is the Hegelian philosophy of history, asserting that history has absolute meaning. "The idea", the highest form of reason, was postulated to be unfolding beneath the tangled mass of events and processes of which world history, at first sight, seems to consist. As

---

[79] For a recent tribute see O. Brusiin's Address on the 50th Anniversary of the *Internationale Vereinigung für Rechts- and Sozialphilosophie* (1960), publ. *Beiheft Nr. 38 Arch. R.- und Sozialph.* 1, at 1-5. And see Pound, 1 *Jurisprudence* 158-170.

[80] The influence of Darwin and Savigny can, of course, scarcely be excluded. See Stone, *Social Dimensions,* Chs. 1, 2. O. Brusiin, *op. cit. supra* n. 79, at 2, doubts whether "the philosophy" of Hegel, as distinct from his "artistic-metaphysical genius", really influenced Kohler. The present author leaves open whether Professor Brusiin's test is not too severe. For the revived influence of Hegel in the 1930's see J. Binder, M. Busse, and K. Larenz, *Einführung in Hegels Rechtsphilosophie* (1931), and Binder's *Grundlegung zur Rechtsphilosophie* (1935). Binder's earlier work (*Philosophie des Rechts* (1925)) was neo-Kantian. This *Hegelrenaissance* was apparently accommodating enough to flourish in Nazi Germany.

Kohler understood Hegel—

> the world process was progressive logical thought with a constant
> thesis and antithesis and their reconciliation, so that in this way a
> continual progression takes place from one to the other: a progression
> in the development of the great cosmos as well as in humanity. . . .
> And this is done not so that past and future stand in a neutral relation
> to each other, but so that the future is formed by the progress that
> has its rise in the past.[81]

It is, indeed, clear enough that human thought and institutions which
appear firm and final are constantly found to disintegrate from the impact
of changes in men's relation to their environment and to each other.[82] A
tension arises with the answers formulated in existing thought and institutions
to the problems of the previous age, producing what is often called a
"reaction" to them. This insight is present in Hegel's teaching that the
world of existence is ever in dynamic transformation, that the world of
thought shares this quality, both spheres being aspects of the same reality.
The philosophical apparatus of Hegel, however, imposed upon this theme
the incumbrance of the dialectic linked with his name. Each institution, or
conception (the *thesis*) contained as it were within itself an opposite institution or conception (the *anti-thesis*). Change was conceived to be the
process whereby this inner contradiction is resolved by the emergence of
a new conception (the *synthesis*), which in turn, forms the thesis for further
development progressively revealing the unfolding Idea.

The Hegelian philosophy of history[83] provided a technique whereby
an apparent sanction of inexorable development could be put behind many
historical facts and many human aspirations. The charge is notorious that
history, according to Hegel and many of his followers, had reached its
culmination in the German state of his day, in which the idea of ordered
liberty in its full development was thought to be made manifest. The
Scots jurist, Miller, saw English history as the unfolding of the idea of
individual liberty, and the gradual abdication by the state of its control
over individual action, culminating in the unshackling legislation of his
own day.[84] Maine saw in the past history of human relations a movement
from status to contract.[85] Left-wing Hegelians saw in history a long and
inevitable struggle to resolve the successive inner contradictions of "capitalism", to culminate in the emancipation of the "working class".[86] Natural
rights of men were seen to grow inexorably from acorns into oaks.[87]
After the middle of the century the theory of evolution seemed to some
to add nature's support to this way of thought. And the joint influence
of Savigny's *Volksgeist* and the biological analogy was also to suggest the
predestined dominance of particular nations, preshadowing the travesty of

---

[81] Kohler, transl. 19. The Hegelian "dialectic" represents, of course, only one of
a series of varied and changing phases in the growth of this notion since its early
Greek use. See P. Foulquié, *La Dialectique* (1956); and for a brief account M. D.
Kirby, "Dialectics and Law" in *Australian Studies in Legal Philosophy* 91-116. And
see Stone, *Legal System*, Ch. 8, n. 126.
[82] *Cf.* generally Stone, *Social Dimensions*, esp. Chs. 12, 13, 14, 15 *passim*.
[83] See Hegel, *The Philosophy of History* (delivered 1830-1831; transl. by J. Sibree,
rev. ed. 1944) Intro. *passim*, esp. iii, "Philosophical History", 9-27, 63-65.
[84] Miller, *Lectures* 63, 68-69, 71-72.
[85] H. Maine, *Ancient Law* (1861, 5 ed. 1916) 174.
[86] See Stone, *Social Dimensions*, Ch. 10.
[87] E. L. Campbell, *The Science of Law according to the American Theory of
Government* (1887) 16-20, esp. 17. *Cf.* W. S. Holdsworth's criticism in Book Review
(1941) 57 *L.Q.R.* 475, of a similar assumption which he sees in A. J. Carlyle, *Political
Liberty . . . in the Middle Ages and in Modern Times* (1941).

national sentiment of twentieth-century Fascism.[88]

Clearly Croce was right to remind Hegelians that while history can be treated philosophically, that does not make philosophy and history identical.[89] The Hegelian trend, when it sought to force particular events or ideas into an inexorable dialectical frame, over-reached the truth that ideas and moralities are themselves part of the historical process. As a result, the Hegelian school gave rise not only to great historians, but also to "petulant and comic contemners of history".[90] And C. J. Friedrich has correctly added that there has emerged from the dialectic a central exaltation of the power of negation, supporting drives of "the destructive character" to raze to the ground whatever stands in the way, but affording no wisdom for the journey beyond.[90a]

§12. RIDERS ON THE HEGELIAN VIEW OF HISTORY. Kohler, for his part, insisted that "it is not true that the development of the history of the world is so logical and that everything goes forward in three-part time".[91] What is magnificent often perishes, ages decline, trends appear not "in line with" but "opposed to the course of our development", and the multitude of ramifications of each event in history forbids the simple view. While accepting the Hegelian view that true insight would show a persistent trend in the unfolding of the Idea, he insisted that this trend was not necessarily manifest at any particular moment. For, "side by side with reason, stands its opposite, and the greatness of the world's history is attested simply by this, that in the final development, it is reason that triumphs".[92] Moreover, second, even when the ultimate goal is clear, the path is not logically predestined, but may vary infinitely. There can be no escape from the need to examine the details of men's life in each age.[93]

Kohler's third rider upon the Hegelian doctrine lies in his concretisation of "The Idea" which is unfolding in history. For his legal purposes Kohler translates this universal idea into the idea of "Civilisation" (*Kultur*),

---

[88] See, e.g., V. Gioberti, *Del Primato Morale e Civile degli Italiani* (1843); id., *Sul Progresso*, c. iii, and other literature cited H. W. Schneider, *Making the Fascist State* (1928) 21ff.; J. Stone, "Theories of Law and Justice of Fascist Italy" (1937) 1 *M.L.R.* 177, 189ff.

[89] B. Croce, *What is Living and What is Dead in the Philosophy of Hegel* (1912). It has often been suggested (see, e.g., Cohen, *Ethical Systems* 6), that "Hegelian pictures of inevitable trends are offered as substitutes for the delineation of the desirable" in many quarters not usually associated with Hegelian philosophy, for example, in a court's tendency to extend a line of decision further in the direction in which it has been extended in the past, or in the general idea of the march of progress.

[90] French transl. by Burot c. vii, at 121. *Cf.* W. Friedmann, *Legal Theory* (4 ed. 1960) 114-15, and the discussion *ibid.* of Hegel's spurious opposites in the juristic field. No account of Hegel's doctrines of legal philosophy as such is here attempted. The attempt has been made *inter alia* by Friedmann (*op. cit.* 114-127), Cairns (*Plato to Hegel* 503-547) and Barna Horvath, *Hegel und das Recht* (1932). And see Hegel's *Grundlinien der Philosophie des Rechts* (1821) transl. as *Hegel's Philosophy of Right* by S. W. Dyde (1896), and under the same title by T. M. Knox (1942, 2 ed. 1953). As to the state and liberty Hegel thought that any "mature" state, though "this or that defect may be found in it", yet "has in it the moments essential to the existence of the state". Just as we recognise the affirmation of life even in the "ugliest of men, or a criminal, or an invalid, or a cripple", so we must always remember the "inward organic life" of the state. (Knox's transl. 279). Such conciliatory qualifications still raise more problems than they solve, either for Hegel or Kohler.

[90a] C. J. Friedrich, "The Power of Negation", in D. C. Travers, *A Hegel Symposium* (1963) 13-35, esp. 33-35.

[91] Kohler, transl. 21, 39.

[92] *Id.* 20.

[93] And see *infra* §§16-17.

which he defines to mean the raising of man's powers over external nature and over his own nature to the highest possible level. His neo-Hegelian thesis then becomes that civilisation develops inexorably, and man's powers over himself and over external nature are constantly extending even though hampered from time to time by elements of chance, illogicality and back-sliding. The purpose of law is to assist in this development and in the reduction or neutralisation of the obstructive elements. Although, for instance, law cannot eliminate chance elements obstructing development, it can alter and distribute the incidence of risk over society as a whole so as to neutralise it. The device of insurance is a concrete example of this neutralisation, but it is manifested in many other ways.[94]

§13. BACKGROUND: RELATION TO JURISTIC PREDECESSORS. Kohler characterised Ihering's *Zweck im Recht* as an amateurish platitude; and scarcely noticed Stammler's elaborate theory of justice. From our present distance, however, these three writers have deep affinities despite their philosophical variety. All of them, for example, and Roscoe Pound who built on them, were convinced that nineteenth-century historical and logical-analytical work was at a dead-end.[95] All of them, too, including even Stammler, were careful to discount any claim of natural law to fix, once and for all, the content of just law. Again while Ihering's "social utility" was regarded by the other three as deficient, all four were at one in asserting that law is a means to *social* ends, moulded thereto by the conscious efforts of men. They were also agreed in rejecting economic determinism: Stammler on the ground that without co-operative effort any social economy was impossible, and hence that the problems of law and justice must precede and cannot be determined by the social economy;[96] Pound on the ground[97] that law often runs counter to the interests of the dominant economic class, the latter being only a segment of the operative influences; and Kohler for similar reasons. And we shall see that Pound was able to give to the other theories a fair degree of summation within his final position.

Kohler's own position was neo-Hegelian in the sense above indicated. He denied that *all* events could be shown dialectically to be a part of the unfolding of a universal "Idea". Kohler insisted that, off the main line of development and often hostile to it, the presence of these illogical elements must be recognised, arising above all from the elements of time and space.[98] This it is which gives its creative force to Kohler's Hegelianism. For him man is not merely observing an unfolding destiny but is struggling to overcome illogical elements which threaten and obstruct that destiny. At this point Kohler seems to be invoking, despite himself, the original historical doctrine of Savigny. For beside the ultimate ideal of civilisation developing in human experience, there stands for him the civilisation actually achieved

---

[94] Kohler, transl. 28. For instance in private law, he points out, quasi-contractual liability may be regarded as eliminating the effects of mere chance.

[95] See e.g., *id.* 10-11: "After the historical school of law under Savigny had demolished natural law, and Hegel had taught the idea of evolution, we might have hoped that a new period of growth of Philosophy of Law would set in. . . . Great ideas were replaced by hairsplitting discussions of petty details. . . . The philosophic jurist was gagged and bound: it was inelegant to speak of the Philosophy of Law at all."

[96] This seems a *non sequitur* since the social economy and the problems of law and justice might appear simultaneously.

[97] As to which, however, see Stone, *Province* 333; and see now *id., Social Dimensions,* Ch. 3, §6, Ch. 10, and Ch. 12, §8.

[98] Kohler, transl. 28.

in the particular time and place. That is the immediate concern of the jurist, and to it, with all its "illogical" elements, his proposals must have regard. His proposals, therefore, being relative to that civilisation, cannot have universal validity.[99]

§14. RELATION OF LAW AND OTHER SOCIAL CONTROLS TO "CIVILISATION". For Kohler, then, the general function of law was, like that of custom, morals, religion and other social controls,[100] to preserve further and transmit "civilisation" in a sense somehow embracing[101] both the ultimate ideal, and the social facts of the embodiment of it in a given time and place. The particular functions of law were mainly three. First, the law is a framework for all progress, assigning each his post and task, and protecting existing values and creating new ones. Second, the law attends to material and intellectual needs of civilisation, in which it is a particular problem to ensure that material civilisation, or control over the external world, does not stray into paths where the mind cannot follow it.[102] Third, within the ambit of the above objectives the law must delimit for the time being the sphere of individual rights as against the sphere of "civilisational" values. It is for the law to decide how far the advantages of life are to be distributed among men, and how far held in the immediate control of society as a whole.[103]

§15. "JURAL POSTULATES" OF A CIVILISATION AS THE CRITERION OF ITS JUST LAW. Since the law must ever be tested by these functions, it must constantly change as it is adapted to promote changing needs of civilisation.

> Thus every civilisation has its definite postulates for law, and it is the duty of society, from time to time, to shape the law according to these requirements. . . . The law that is suitable for one period is not so for another; we can only strive to provide every civilisation with its corresponding system of law; what is good for one would mean ruin to another.

We are thus introduced to Kohler's central notion of "jural postulates" or "postulates for law"[104] of the civilisation. What is meant by this notion may be stated briefly thus. A particular civilisation is, sociologically speaking, a complex of physical, psychological and socio-economic conditions and inter-actions, along with the tendencies, forces or movements which arise there-from. In part these are produced or modified by conscious human controls over men's behaviour, such as those of ethics and law. The civilisation as a whole is constantly changing, both because of the appearance of new elements, of which time is a constant one, and because of changing relations within the complex. But not every element in the complex is changing at

---

[99] The evolutionist flavour of this position, close though it is to "social Darwinism" must, it is believed, be traced rather to Hegelian anticipations of that doctrine.

[100] His account of the lack of differentiation in early society, and of compulsion as the specific mark of law, is not very different from Ihering's and Bentham's positions on the relation of law and morals. For Kohler's view of the relation of egoism to the advance of civilisation see, e.g., transl. 60ff. Despite his expressed contempt for Ihering, it is difficult to see what advance he makes upon him in this regard either. See *supra* Ch. 5, §3.

[101] *Cf.* Hocking, *Law and Rights* 24.

[102] Kohler, transl. 59.

[103] *Id.* 59-60.

[104] *Rechtspostulate*: Either of the above renderings are preferable to "postulates of law" in Albrecht's translation. The postulates originate from *outside* the law and *not* from within it.

an even rate, and the conscious controls over human behaviour in particular are never adapted and cannot in the nature of things be adapted *pari passu* with the rest. For the law this means that there is always a lag between the ends actually pursued by law in a particular time and place and the actual tendencies of its civilisation as a whole.

This is not merely an elaboration of the truism that lawyers tend to be conservative. It also states one cause of this conservatism, and points to the constant need for effort to adjust law to "civilisational needs", in the double sense of achieving suitable interpretation of existing law if possible, and of altering it suitably, if this is not possible.[105] The jural postulates are devices to assist this relative and progressive[106] effort. They are generalised statements of actual tendencies, presuppositions of the particular civilisation and the tendencies of change within it. They are a kind of ideals presupposed by the whole social complex, which may serve to bring the law into harmony with it, so that the law "promotes rather than hampers and oppresses it". They may therefore serve to guide those who wield lawmaking power.

§16. AMBIGUITY OF THE CONCEPT OF CIVILISATION: RELATIVIST OR ABSOLUTIST? The assertion that the maintenance and advancement of civilisation is the function of law has been thought capable of any or all of the following distinct meanings.[107] First, that law should serve existing civilisation by moulding all behaviour to the dominant pattern. Second, that the law should serve the civilisation emerging from the present, moulding behaviour to the tendencies toward change as they appear. Third, that law should serve those tendencies in present civilisation which tend to make it more harmonious with some ultimate ideal of civilisation, an ideal which being timeless is presumably absolute. It is clear that Kohler's conception included both of the first two possibilities. Law must not only minister to present civilisation, but also foster in the civilisational complex *those tendencies* whose fulfilment will bring it *"nearer to its own ideal"*.[108] Equally clearly he believed that this double meaning in his criterion of law did not affect its relativist nature. For he wrote, with emphasis and without qualification, that "Law must be different in every different civilisation, in order to realise its own object". All we are able to do, he thought, is to see "the general outlines of the world process" and prepare for "the progress of law in the immediate succeeding time".[109]

While this emphatic relativism would seem to negate any absolute value elements in the tasks of furthering civilisation in these first two senses, the present writer has doubted whether such elements can really be excluded when the task requires a choice from among the tendencies of the present, of those which will assist present civilisation to realise "its own ideal".[110] But be that as it may, it is certain that at any point where Kohler must invoke the *third* meaning of civilisation, as an ultimate ideal,

---

[105] Kohler, transl. 5.

[106] Even though law at a given time will, of course, still continue to lag behind the civilisation of that time.

[107] *Cf.* Hocking, *Law and Rights* 30-35.

[108] *Ibid.*, relying on J. Kohler, *Moderne Rechtsprobleme* (2 ed. 1913) 10.

[109] J. Kohler, *id.* 11 (transl. and quoted Hocking, *op. et loc. cit.*).

[110] *Pace* Hocking's contrary view *ibid.* See Stone, *Province* 338ff. Our dissent, if it have merit, equally applies to Professor Pound's theory of justice, and discussion of it will for that reason be postponed to Ch. 9, §§ 9ff. For the present the assumption of Kohler and Professor Hocking is accepted.

an absolute criterion enters. The question is—Does Kohler include this third meaning within his criterion of good law? He recognises that the actual trends of a given civilisation may be hostile to the raising of human powers over internal and external nature which is his ultimate conception of civilisation. A consistent relativist would have to say that nevertheless the law must be adapted to civilisation as it is, retrogressive though this might be. Clearly that is not Kohler's position, nor from his stress on the ultimate ideal was this to be expected. And he asks explicitly whether the lawgiver should, in uncivilised or retrogressive periods, adapt law to the backward tendencies, or try to reverse these tendencies and restore "the normal condition of progress". These, he declares in answer, are "the times when the lawgiver's mind that stands above the people is especially called upon to wrestle with the popular mind, and to diminish its illogical efforts".[111] Here, in his uneasy settlement with the Hegelian philosophy of history, Kohler's relativism broke down. By admitting the disturbing role of the "illogical" elements, Kohler was cut off from reliance on the Hegelian dialectics of history to keep civilisation and the law as its mentor on the path of evolutionary progress. Yet to adapt the law to a civilisation which has run off the dialectical path is treasonous to that ultimate ideal of civilisation, to which, even as a *neo*-Hegelian, Kohler owed fealty.

§17. The Absolutist Element in the Civilisation Criterion. Insofar, then, as Kohler has a relativist criterion, he was not willing to use it for social conditions in which the trends were antagonistic to the ultimate ideal of civilisation. But this may be only another way of saying that Kohler is not in the last analysis a relativist. He is a relativist only within the manœuvring space left to him by his ultimate ideal of civilisation; and only within this space is his criterion for just law relative to the conditions and tendencies of time and place. The fuller meaning of all this is that conformity with the conditions and tendencies of a given civilisation is only a valid criterion of good law insofar as these are consistent with the absolute ideal of civilisation. Above and controlling the relativist jural postulates of the civilisation of the time and place, are the absolute jural postulates of all civilisation whatsoever, of the ultimate idea of civilisation itself.

If we ask what are these absolute postulates we are thrown back upon the definintion of civilisation as the raising to the highest possible level of man's control over himself and over external nature. From this definition Professor Hocking has suggested two directions or postulates of an absolute nature which may accurately represent Kohler's thought. The present author adds a third.

I. Among contradictory possibilities that one is always to be chosen which promises to further human knowledge to the greatest degree.

II. No step shall be taken, however profitable at the moment, which threatens to lower the level of human creative power.

III. In applying Postulates I and II regard shall be had to the fact that the furtherance of human knowledge, and the raising of human creative power, depend upon the maintenance both of social cohesion and of intense individual development. No measures tending to secure social cohesion should be taken without careful

---

111 Kohler, transl. 58-59.

estimation of their effect on individual development; nor *vice versa.*[112]

We shall see in Chapter 9 that even the humbler task of assessing the tendencies of an actual civilisation requires talents among the leaders of men such as are rarely to be found. Yet Kohler's criterion not only requires the constant presence of such leaders, it also requires that they should, at any moment, be ready and able to detect major trends antagonistic to the ultimate ideal of civilisation (always assuming this ideal is known and agreed). If a sociological seer with a strong strain of the mystical is required for the first and more modest of these functions, a combination of sociologist, saint and near-divinity would be required for the other.

Kohler, indeed, seems to assume that each civilisation will throw up its own wise legislative mentors. That in itself is an assertion of mystical faith. When he goes further and suggests that in retrogressive periods the lawgiver may be relied on to detect the tendencies prejudicial to the ultimate ideal of civilisation, it is also clear that the relation of Kohler's proposed lawgiver to his standard is a mystical relation, depending on the lawmaker's subjective vision, and not on objective demonstration. So that "Kohler, then, as well as Stammler, falls back upon intuitive judgment and upon the intuitive judgment of specially qualified minds".[113]

---

[112] This third postulate is based on *id.* 49. See Hocking, *Law and Rights* 25.

It is perhaps of interest that a disciple of Stammler, Lorenz Brütt (*op. cit. supra* n. 53), starting with Stammler's pure "idea of society" has reached, from the other direction, a similar ambiguous position between relativism and absolutism by incorporating the idea of civilisation (125-38) and its "intermediate ends" (139-40) into this system in the place of Stammler's "principles of just law" and "notional special community" (*supra* §§4ff.).

[113] Hocking, *Law and Rights* 30.

CHAPTER 7

REVIVED NATURAL LAW

I. CONTEMPORARY VERSIONS OF NATURAL LAW

§1. "Revival" or Reappraisal of Natural Law. The so-called "revival" of natural law has now been a topic of juristic discussion for nearly half a century,[1] and after some waning between the two wars it is again being prominently discussed. The "revival", of course, is not strictly of natural law thought itself (which as the juristic branch of the Roman Catholic *philosophia perennis* can scarcely be said to have died at all), but of general juristic concern with it. If, indeed, it were to be assumed that the revival of natural law itself were in question (that is, that natural law was dead and sought to be revived) it might be difficult to avoid Norberto Bobbio's cruel conclusion that the limited success of current efforts has come rather to resemble the examination of a corpse.[2] Clearly what confronts us is a notable recanvassing of the history, philosophical foundations and practical applications of natural law, the value of which must not be pre-judged by assuming that it is an autopsy rather than a biopsy.[3]

---

[1] For the earliest monograph see J. Charmont, *La Renaissance du Droit Naturel* (1910), and (in the U.S.) Haines, *Revival*; and for the best recent surveys, with bibli. of the by now considerable literature, see Pound, 1 *Jurisprudence* 178-191, and C. du Pasquier, *Introduction à la Théorie Générale et à la Philosophie du Droit* (3 ed. 1948) 267. The purpose here is rather to examine in depth some of the principal issues, when not merely derivative or repetitious, which the revival since World War II has thrown up, and to assess any resulting additions to the body of knowledge.

Both Charmont and du Pasquier date the so-called revival from Charles Beudant, *Le Droit Individuel et l'Etat* (1891), but Pound (1 *op. cit.* 179) thinks that that work was merely a late echo of the "political theory of natural law", of the revolutionary Declaration of the Rights of Man. He prefers to date the movement in Germany from Rudolf Stammler's *Wirtschaft und Recht* (1895), and its introduction to French lawyers as a *rapprochement* between historical and metaphysical thought under neo-Kantian and sociological influence, by Saleilles, "*Ecole Historique*". On Stammler and Duguit in relation to the revival of natural law see *supra* Chs. 5, 6.

[2] See N. Bobbio, "*Alcuni Argomenti contro il Diritto Naturale*" (1958) 4 *Riv. di Dir. Civ.* 253-271, at 262.

[3] See, e.g., Freiherr von der Heydte, "Natural Law Tendencies in Contemporary German Jurisprudence" (1956) 1 *Nat. L. Forum* 115, at 116-120; H. Rommen, *The Natural Law* (transl. T. R. Hanley, 1947); Welzel, *Naturrecht*; J. Messner, *Das Naturrecht* (4 ed. 1960); E. Wolf, *Das Problem der Naturrechtslehre* (2 ed. 1959). And see A. Nussbaum, ". . . German Legal Philosophy since 1946" (1954) 3 *Am. J. Comp. L.* 379-396; G. Del Vecchio, *Philosophy of Law* (transl. T. O. Martin, 1953); A. Verdross, *Abendländische Rechtsphilosophie* ... (1958) 232, 257ff. (reducing natural law, however, to *morality* based on "the common good"); G. Lumia, "*Su Alcune Recenti Concezioni del Diritto Naturale*" (1959) 36 *Riv. Int. di Fil. del Dir* 428-443.

On German law since 1945 see also H. A. Rommen, "Natural Law in Decisions of the . . . Courts in Germany" (1959) 4 *Nat. L. Forum* 1, 25 including references to constitutional provisions; E. von Hippel, "The Role of Natural Law in . . . the German Federal Republic" *id.* 106-118. Caveats on some of these interpretations may arise from the account in H. O. Pappe, "On the Validity of Judicial Decisions in the Nazi Era" (1960) 23 *M.L.R.* 260-274.

And see in the Anglo-American setting, A. P. D'Entrèves, *Natural Law* (1951); Hart, "Law and Morals" 593-629; Fuller, "Positivism" 630-672; Wild, *Plato's Enemies*; and the new periodical *Natural Law Forum* (Notre Dame Law School, 1955-) (here

Even if this work has lost some of the momentum it had gained after the Nazi-perpetrated horrors of the Second World War,[4] and may indeed have been rather a flash in the pan,[5] the contemporary phenomenon holds jurisprudential interest for reasons independent of its success as a revivalist movement. For iusnaturalism (if we may adopt this convenient term for a natural law type of approach to justice) must be admitted, at the least, to have had a notable degree of social operative power in the history of law and of thinking about law. Some of the notable aspects recently agitated certainly involve attempts to revive this operative force, sometimes by adjustments of theory to meet the persistent challenges of positivism, sometimes by recognising more clearly the dead-ends of previous lines of thought. History does not warrant any advance assumption that this re-agitation of issues must be necessarily barren.

§2. GERMAN NATURAL LAW THINKING AFTER WORLD WAR II: TRADITION-ALIST AND THEOLOGICAL APPROACHES. The most dramatic and problematic outcropping of recent German natural law thought, that of Gustav Radbruch, will be considered in the next Chapter. Its drama will be seen to be compounded not only of his supposed "conversion" in the aftermath of the horrors of the Nazi period, but of the deep tensions in his final positions and thought, and the unsolved mysteries in his positions as a whole.[6] His doctrine of the nature of things will be referred to in a later section, along with the somewhat related doctrines of Gény and the existentialist Maihofer. But Radbruch's approach to natural law was but one case of the prevailing mood of the German legal culture after 1945,[7] which saw philosophers as well as theologians, Catholics as well as Protestants, neo-Kantians and neo-Hegelians as well as existentialists, making a new and urgent approach to natural law.

Heinrich Mitteis, in a post-war survey,[8] approached natural law as a historian, but with an ardour perhaps rather unhistorical. It is, he thought, all around us "like the air we breathe".

> We speak today often of a rebirth of *natural law.* . . . This can mean, however, only that we have become again fully conscious of it, that we declare our faith in it; there can be reborn only what once has died. But natural law never died. . . . It has been very unrightfully (*zu Unrecht*) declared to be dead. . . . We have become tired of hearing that lawyers are called arid (*öde*) formalists, whose brittle (*spröde*) and sterile thinking burdens the world like a curse. We again place natural law against all formalism and cult of concepts; we place justice and

cited as *"Nat. L. Forum"*). And *cf.* for a reconstruction of international law in the creative mood of natural law H. Lauterpacht, *International Law and Human Rights* (1950).

[4] J. Messner, "The Postwar Natural Law Revival and its Outcome" (1959) 4 *Nat. L. Forum* 101, at 101, 105.

[5] See N. Bobbio's review of A. Verdross, *Abendländische Rechtsphilosophie* (1958) in (1959) 50 *Riv. Fil.* 484, at 485.

[6] For discussion of Radbruch's relevant positions see *infra* Ch. 8, §§11ff.

[7] H. A. Rommen (article cited *supra* n. 3 at 5, 13) asserts that "conversions" to "natural law" came much earlier in reaction against the Nazi "system of injustice", but could not express themselves. He instances the first edition of his own book (cited *supra* n. 3) which, though published in 1936, was forbidden to be advertised or displayed, and was only sold from under the counter. Dr. Rommen himself, of course, as a Catholic thinker, was not a case of "conversion".

[8] H. Mitteis, *Über das Naturrecht* (1948). Lecture at the *Deutsche Akademie der Wissenschaften zu Berlin*.

humanity against legalised barbarianism which we have overcome (*überwunden*) for ever.[9]

Professor Mitteis thought that the weaker followers of Savigny were guilty of a radical turn from historicism to extreme positivism, the worst abuse (he wrote) in German legal history and thought.[10] In words recalling Radbruch's famous pronouncement he declared that when a positivist law fails even to *seek* after what is right (*das Richtige*) but with "cynical openness" adopts "the principle of egoism", of mere "usefulness" (*Nützlichkeit*) for any purpose whatsoever, then it is not law at all. It is "not even a defective and revocable law, but a *sham-law* (*ein Scheinrecht*), a non-law (*Nichtrecht*)", usurping the claim to validity to cover "the reign of arbitrariness".[11] While Mitteis makes a brief but useful addition to the historical surveys of natural law which characterise the current literature,[12] his replies to the positivist critiques of natural law do not go further than mere eloquence can take them.

The modern Catholic exposition of natural law builds, as is to be expected, on the traditional Thomist position which, due to the small number of its principles, its inner tensions, and its concessions to the role of positive law, is highly adaptable to modern conditions. The Austrian neo-Thomist Johannes Messner of Vienna, indeed, shows a patient willingness to examine modern secular philosophical thought, even of legal positivists.[13] But the theme remains "both the faith in and the search after absolute and timeless law", and the antinomic relation of this with "the historical character of positive law".[14]

In contrast to the Catholic doctrine, that the norms of natural law are immanent in and can be known from the essential order of created nature, Protestant natural law, of which Erik Wolf of Freiburg in Breisgau is the most distinguished exponent,[15] emphasises the disability of man, by dint of his sinful, fallen nature, to perceive true natural law without the aid of the divine word. The effect, it has been properly said, is that such Protestant theories depend on a kind of theological anthropology and theological ethics, transmitted by revelation. Acceptance of revelation establishes the reality of natural law; but there is by the same token nothing for discussion with anyone who rejects it.[16] As von der Heydte acutely comments, on examining the Protestant position, "the Word as a revelation of law stands in the midst of the world and of a history conceived as a process of salvation".[17]

---

[9] *Id.* 5.

[10] *Id.* 29.

[11] *Id.* 37.

[12] Surveys by Erik Wolf, A. von Verdross and Felix Flückiger will be referred to below.

[13] See his works cited *supra* nn. 3 and 4, esp. *Das Naturrecht* (4 ed. 1960) 23-30, 93ff., and his article "*Naturrecht im positiven Recht*" (1958) 9 *Oest. Z.ö.R.* 129-150.

[14] Messner's open-minded contributions are rather a rethinking of Thomist doctrine on particular substantive questions, than on the general problems of the status of natural law and its relations to positive law with which we are here concerned. See esp. the chapters treating various aspects of social ethics 467-622. *Cf.* Von der Heydte, article cited *supra* n. 3, at 116.

[15] For Protestant conceptions of natural law see E. Wolf, *Rechtsgedanke und biblische Weisung* (1948); U. Scheun, *Kirche und Recht* (1950); W. Schönfeld, *Über die Gerechtigkeit* (1952). As to theological ethics, *cf.* R. Niebuhr, *Children of Light and Children of Darkness* (1945).

[16] *Cf.* J. Messner, *op. cit. supra* n. 4 at 104. *Cf.* also Ambrosetti, *Riforma* 36, suggesting that the Lutheran concept of man as fundamentally corrupt had as its immediate consequence a sort of "irrationalism" in which the authority of the state is "not freely instituted by men in recognising an objective social order" but is "directly established by God".

[17] Article cited *supra* n. 3, at 117.

The Protestant version thus still leaves its exponents with the unresolved antinomy between Christian and worldly existence, between the two Cities of St. Augustine.

Despite the willingness of some modern theologically based expositions to incorporate elements of secularist theory, they have not achieved any such theoretical basis transcending that of the classical doctrines of natural law.

§3. SECULARIST "DYNAMIC" NATURAL LAW THEORY: JOHN WILD. The urgent search of contemporary natural lawyers for a negotiated peace with the positivists and empiricists is reflected in the American scholar John Wild's notable exposition of a "dynamic" theory of natural law.[18] It is notable, indeed, not only for its attempt to accommodate some empiricist demands, but also for its attempt to bring into the open (as we shall shortly see Arthur Kaufmann to have done in Germany) the metaphysical basis of the respective positions, and generally to maintain a reasoned theoretical position throughout, avoiding excessive resort to rhetorical and emotional arguments concerning the role of natural law in the control of modern forms of arbitrary power.[19] It has in these circumstances received appropriate attention (appreciative as well as destructive) from outstanding legal positivists such as Hans Kelsen and Norberto Bobbio.[20]

Wild himself sees his theory as departing radically in the following ways "from others now familiar to us".[21] First, it opposes the tendency to see value as "a peculiar quality or property", which he thinks leads either to reductionist ethics such as hedonism and utilitarianism, or to chaotic moral pluralism, or to a flight to ineffability and intuitionism.[22] Second, as to positive objectives, it is "a primary duty" to have "perspectives" accommodating "all the immediate data of experience without incoherence". Third, as to method, resort must be had to "phenomenological description" and careful analysis of the ontological data inaccessible to methods of natural science, and to the framing of hypotheses testable by these data.[23]

He thinks, then, that value and disvalue are "empirical", "ontological" facts, that is, facts directly observable in the data of experience. He thinks that these are facts, in the same sense that they are asserted in "protocol statements", describing what is directly observed.[24] He further thinks that though value and disvalue are not the kind of facts which are the subject of "restricted sciences", they are nevertheless facts capable of being recorded, albeit in "metaphysical protocols".[25] For metaphysics, he says, is the philo-

---

[18] Wild, *Plato's Enemies*.

[19] Cf. N. Bobbio, *"Ancora sul Diritto Naturale"* (1956) 47 *Riv. Fil.* 72-82.

[20] See H. Kelsen, "A 'Dynamic' Theory of Natural Law" (1956) 16 *Louisiana L.R.* 597-626 repr. in his *What is Justice?* (1957) 174-197. Linguistic analysts have also, of course, paid much attention to the revival. See, e.g., the discussions in A. G. Chloros, "What is Natural Law?" (1958) 21 *M.L.R.* 609, at 614-616; Hart, "Law and Morals"; M. Charlesworth, "Linguistic Analysis and Language about God" (1961) *Int. Phil. Q.* 139.

[21] Wild, *Plato's Enemies* 234.

[22] Instancing G. E. Moore. Cf. the critique in Jacob-Flink, *Value Decision* 17-18.

[23] *Id.* 232-233.

[24] For a brief characterisation of "protocol statements", see B. Russell, *An Inquiry into Meaning and Truth* (3 imp. 1948) 20-21. Cf. the *intentio recta* notion of N. Hartmann, *Zur Grundlegung der Ontologie* (3 ed. 1948) 49ff.

[25] We find Professor Wild's blending of phenomenology and logical positivism especially difficult at this point. Surely facts recorded in protocol statements are the foundation of all sciences dealing with Being, whether "restricted" (whatever he means by this) or otherwise. In that case, protocol statements concerning value and disvalue would not be "metaphysical" in any sense in which statements about other observable facts were not equally so.

sophical discipline "most eminently empirical and closest to the brute facts actually given",[26] without guidance from which "the basic concepts and theorems of all other disciplines lapse into vagueness, unintelligibility and meaninglessness",[27] and we ourselves into "either reductionism or disintegration".[28] As to method he is concerned to show that moral law can be "founded on nature" (or "value" on "fact"), even though it cannot be deduced from "nature" in the sense of the tautological process of modern logic.[29] Founding norms on "nature" involves a process of "moral justification" which, though it involves logical processes, is distinguishable from deductive argument,[30] in that its drive is persuasive or rhetorical rather than towards stringent proof.[31]. Deductive argument proceeds from premises to conclusion or, in checking our steps, from conclusion back to premises. "Justification" however, begins with the feeling of "obligation"; and "insofar as this feeling is justified, we are able to pass back to certain values which require the acts, to certain needs which the values satisfy, and to factual evidence showing these needs to be essential rights of man".[32]

Wild believes that his theory continues five basic doctrines characteristic of the "authentic" doctrines of classical natural law,[33] all of which proceed on the assumption that "norms are not invented by man", but are "grounded on nature".[34]

1. The world is an order of divergent tendencies which on the whole[35] support one another.

2. Each individual entity is marked by an essential structure which it shares in common with other members of the species.

3. This structure determines basic existential tendencies that are also common to the species.

But if this is to be the case, then value and disvalue must be observable. If they are observable, in what sense are they so, other than a sense in which what are observed are certain psychological phenomena? Insofar as they are psychological phenomena they should be approachable by the methods of the appropriate restricted sciences. But Wild seems to deny that they are so approachable.

Wild may, of course, be using the terms "value" and "disvalue" to carry also elements which are not reducible to facts recordable in "protocol statements"; and it may be these unrecorded elements, rather than the recordable facts, which produce the appearance of coalescence of the "is" and the "ought". Cf. as to a probably related ambiguity in Professor Fuller's position infra nn. 109, 149, 148.

[26] Wild, Plato's Enemies 181. Cf. id. 185ff., 211, 233.

[27] Id. 181.

[28] Id. 183-184.

[29] Id. 134, 231.

[30] Id. 224.

[31] Unless this is what Wild means we find it difficult to follow him. For what otherwise is the distinction from deductive logic? Is not "passing back" to "values which require the acts" merely a re-checking of deductive steps? And how, without deductive logic, can "facts" be made to "evidence" that "needs" are "essential rights of man"? Yet if the supposed difference lies in the phenomenological attention to "facts" and "needs" referred to in the premises, what is the difference from the use of deductive logic in natural science? Finally, then, the difference comes to be in the kind of "facts" which Wild thinks can be taken as the starting-point of logical reasoning for moral law, as distinct from natural science. And see, on the difference between deductive (stringent) and rhetorical (persuasive) argument which may perhaps be involved, Stone, Legal System, Ch. 8.

Cf. N. Bobbio, cit. supra n. 19, at 73.

[32] Wild, Plato's Enemies 228.

[33] Which he associates with Plato, Aristotle, the Stoics, St. Thomas Aquinas, Grotius, Hooker, and Thomas Paine, but not inter alios with Hobbes and Locke. See generally his chapters on the theory of natural law and its history in the West, at 103-177, and cf. on Hobbes and Locke the attitude of Strauss, Natural Right c. v.

[34] Plato's Enemies 150, 169.

[35] Does not this qualification seriously impede the writer's thesis?

4. If these tendencies are to be realized without distortion and frustration, they must follow a general dynamic pattern. This pattern is what is meant by natural law. It is grounded on real structure, and is enforced by inexorable natural sanctions.

5. Good and evil are existential categories. It is good for an entity to exist in a condition of active realization. If its basic tendencies are hampered and frustrated, it exists in an evil condition.[36]

Wild, therefore, is undertaking squarely to establish that natural law is a pattern of action binding on all men everywhere, grounded on basic common existential tendencies issuing from their common "structure", i.e., human "nature" in this sense. And he acknowledges that this requires him above all to throw a bridge between value and existence. His effort proceeds by asserting that "*goodness is some kind or mode of existence*", and "*evil some mode of non-existence, or privation*". By the "non-existence" of evil he does not apparently mean what he says, for he proceeds immediately to add that "empirical evidence shows us that evil in some sense exists, as well as what is good", and therefore that the mere fact of *existence* cannot itself distinguish good from evil. If it is said, moreover, that "non-existence" refers really to the classical natural law notion of privation of a good which the subject is naturally apt to have, the difficulty remains that he is then rather begging the question, What is "good"?[36a] At any rate, Wild seems to say that it must be another fact, additional to that of existence, which distinguishes good from evil, namely the tendency of an existent entity to complete its being. That which furthers this tendency is "good" and has "value". The tendency is *the fact* on which *the value* is grounded.[37] Moreover, since (in his view) all existence is tendential, and, indeed, "active tendency is a third metaphysical principle co-ordinated with essence and existence",[38] a value-judgment may be grounded on fact as to every existing entity. The fact of tending to fulfil the entity grounds a judgment of goodness; the fact of tending to warp and impede it, a judgment of badness. "Such existence is said to be unsound and incorrect".[39]

It being a fact, then, that all men share a "determinate structure or nature", which in turn produces certain "tendencies towards fulfilment", these are "the root of the human feeling of obligation". This obligation is felt because man has "the capacity of human reason to apprehend this essential common structure and the perfective tendencies characteristic of the human species". These perfective tendencies, "expressed in universal propositions . . . are norms or moral laws",[40] and presumably they mean the same as tendencies towards "fulfilment" or "completeness". Presumably, too, their presence or the presence of their negation are the facts which ground the value, though it is difficult to see why Wild should press the point vaguely further[41] to say that "values" and "disvalues" are themselves facts *of some kind*.[42] Is not his point sufficiently made if he shows that the value can be

---

[36] *Id.* 132-33.
[36a] *Pace* P. M. Farrell, O.P., "Evil and Omnipotence" (1958) 67 *Mind* 399. *Cf.* Blackshield, "*Pensiero Umano*" 480, concluding that even if we adopt as our standard of value that one should "be what one *is*", we in fact tend to value "not everything that exists, but only what exists in a way that is pleasing, comfortable, or otherwise satisfying to a human being in the light of his (other) human values". See also *infra* Ch. 11, §§4-5.
[37] Wild, *op. cit.* 64-65.
[38] *Id.* 197.
[39] *Id.* 231; *cf. id.* 65.
[40] *Id.* 66.   [41] *Ibid.*
[42] Nor is it responsive to any current view (other than perhaps that of some

grounded on the fact of an "actual urge" common to human nature towards realisation, together with a common human cognition of this "urge",[43] man's "reason" being thus "cognitive" as well as "desiderative"?

Wild concludes that according to rational insight:

> We are physically moved or bound by the urge of obligation or ought-ness. This is neither a pure theoretical judgment, having no basis in natural desire, nor a mere appetitive bias, having no connection with cognizable fact. It is rather a union of the two—a natural urge, together with the rational justification of this urge or, as Aristotle put it, "a desiderative reason, a reasoning desire".[44]

Here again it is difficult to say why he would not have been on safer (but not necessarily safe) ground to say rather that the sense of obligation as felt by all men is an empirically found fact—a psychological datum; that the presence or negation of "perfective tendency" for this nature is also an empirically found fact; and that on these two kinds of facts values for all men, that is, natural law, may be grounded. The difficulty for him, of course, is that this would only give him (assuming these facts were indeed empirically based), a set of propositions by which all men are "physi-cally moved . . . by the urge of obligation", by a "desiderative reason". It would still not demonstrate that these norms have whatever is meant by saying that men are *morally bound* or—in other words—*why they ought* to obey "the urge".

It is therefore somewhat premature, from the present standpoint, for Wild to feel that he can sustain his thesis on an entirely secular basis by rejecting what he calls any "metaphysical" or "theological" theory of the "natural order as having been imposed by the command of God".[45] This, he rightly says, is not the basic issue between the defenders and opponents of natural law; the basic issue is rather "the nature of moral norms". Yet on this basic issue his own theory, even if (as we shall see is not the case) it had been sustained by him in his own terms, would have established only that norms of a certain content can be found which all men tend to observe insofar as they tend to wish to fulfil their nature. It would have met the objection that the content provided for natural law is subjectively arrived at by natural lawyers; but it would not have shown *why natural law is a binding system*—that is, why there is an obligation on men to self-fulfilment.

Yet the mere demonstration of an objective factual ground for an assumed content of "natural law" would itself be a considerable achievement, and the main estimate of Wild's work must be precisely on this point. Has he sustained even this part of his thesis within his own terms?

First, then, despite commendable care in formulation, Wild's reasoning is impeded at critical points by his language. It is critical, for example, in assessing this theory to know what he means by fulfilment or completion of an entity. If he is to sustain the thesis that value-judgment is grounded in *the fact* of tendency towards these conditions, then the meaning of their fulfilment must be given precision. Yet at some points he seems to identify fulfilment (and therefore goodness) with continued existence, as opposed

---

Scandinavian realists) for him to add, even more vaguely, that "if values do not exist in some way, ethical reflection is much ado about nothing", that it is "by no means obvious that value is totally divorced from fact", and that all that can be said is that "they are distinct, but inseparable". See *id.* 99.

[43] *Id.* 97.

[44] *Id.* 68 and *cf.* 83.

[45] See *id.* 104.

to decay and destruction;[46] at others he seems to say that a tendency is evil if it "warps and impedes" the entity even if the entity "still goes on existing". What can "warped" mean *as mere fact*, if tendency to continued existence is not the test for "fulfilment"? What is *the fact-other-than-existence-tendency* which bases the judgment that "warping" (or for that matter "impeding") is evil? Or for that matter which tells us what "warping" and "impeding" consist of, and how we recognise them?

Second, as Kelsen has pointed out, even if norms or values "exist", it does not follow that they exist in the sense of "facts" embodied in "reality". They may exist only in the sense that they are valid, that is, have been created by a human act, representing its specific meaning. The act of creation can be described by an "is"-statement; but its meaning, that something ought to be or to be done, is not a "fact", and can be described only by an "ought"-statement. So that to say that norms are embedded as facts in reality is to confuse an act with its meaning. This point is converse to that already made above, that Wild wrongly assumes that if he can show ground in facts *for the contents* of the supposed rules of natural law, this proves that this "natural law" is a binding order. He overlooks that the one fact which he takes as grounding natural law is a process of human creation; namely, the fact (in his own words) "that we are physically moved or bound by the urge of obligation". He not only overlooks this human creation, but denies the relevance of any divine act. This leaves it still open for Kelsen to reply that only a being endowed with reason and will can issue norms, and if the being is not human it must be divine.[47] We would add that Wild's argument that natural law as a system of binding obligations is neither man-made nor God-made but is embedded in existential reality, may perhaps be explicable as proceeding on a concealed assumption that this law was laid down indirectly by God, insofar as God created reality and fixed its "nature" and "structure".

Third, as already hinted, grave ambiguities, opening the door to full-scale subjectivism, surround the notions of "completion", "fulfilment", "perfection", "sound" and "correct" tendencies, and what are "fitting" ways of pursuing these. We do not go with Kelsen in complaining that while the "sound or healthy state" of an entity is a fact, when Wild says that such a fact is good this assumes a value-judgment, and a norm by reference to which it is rendered. For insofar as we accept (as we must, in arguing with him) Wild's meaning of "sound, etc." namely "tending to self-fulfilment of the entity", he *has* provided the norm by reference to which the state of affairs may be said to be good. The difficulty is that the objective grounding in facts which Wild claims for this norm is rather illusory. For the only *fixed core* of the meaning of self-fulfilment of an existing or living entity is that its life should continue, and this would yield at least the natural law of the preservation of existence. But, as already seen, Wild

---

[46] Space permits only one detailed example. In one sentence on p. 231, he says; "Existence is tendential. This tendency may proceed towards its natural fulfilment. The entity is then said to be sound and correct." Does "its" here refer to the existent entity, or to the tendency? In the next sentence he says: "On the other hand, it may be warped and impeded and still go on existing". What is "it" here? Presumably the existent entity? And he increases the difficulty by interposing after "proceed" the weazel phrase "in a fitting manner". Can an entity proceed "towards its natural fulfilment" in an "unfitting" manner? If so, would this be *bad*? And if it would, what is *the fact* which corresponds to the adjective "unfitting"? If it would be good though "unfitting", why insert the condition at all?

[47] H. Kelsen, cited *supra* n. 20, at 602-603.

sometimes indicates that continuing existence "may be unsound and incorrect".[48] This, therefore, does not carry us very far, even if we overlook Kelsen's sharp point that as between the existent life of men, and the existent life of a poisonous snake, we have no hesitation in concluding that the acceptance of natural law (in Wild's sense) for men, is equivalent to absolute denial of it for poisonous snakes. The point is equally sharp even when Wild states his position in terms of the healthy or unsound condition of an existent entity.[49]

But the main point is still graver. When we ask what, apart from bare preservation of the life of man, constitutes its "self-fulfilment", it becomes obvious that all the divergent views as to the correct ideals by which men shall live, and as to the goals that they should pursue, including the problems of immediate and more remote goals, and means and ends, are available as competing desiderata of "self-fulfilment". Past this point, then, what is indicated as natural law must be grounded not as an objective fact of reason-cum-desire shared in common by all men, but on the millennially chronic conflict between the different subjective reasons-cum-desires of men's varied conclusions, among themselves and down the generations. This is perhaps a better reason than Kelsen has given for his conclusion that Wild's "identification of the fact of soundness with the moral value of goodness is . . . the projection of a subjective value in objective reality".[50] For Wild does not identify "soundness" *simpliciter* with goodness, but rather soundness in the course of the tendency of "self-fulfilment". It is that notion of "self-fulfilment" which ensnares Wild's main thesis that there are facts which *objectively* ground natural law; and it is this weazel phrase against which warning is necessary.

The difficulty is not overcome when Wild changes his ground to the distinction between what is "essential" and what is merely "incidental" to the existence of man, or between "natural" existence and "mere" existence, between "nature" and "existence".[51] For these distinctions in substance merely restate that between mere continuance of life and "self-fulfilment". Insofar as the difference is not the difference between what "is" and what "ought to be" (as Wild is striving to prove it is not),[52] it is subject to the multiplicity of competing reasons-cum-desires of men—the pluralism and subjectivity which it is his main object to exorcise.

The difficulty which Wild fails to overcome by his notion of "tendencies" reflects those that have also been well-recognised in the Thomist notion of "inclinations". Among these Aquinas included "inclinations" towards self-preservation, procreation of offspring, and also those common to mankind only, such as living rationally and socially, doing justice and the like. As to self-preservation and procreation "inclination" appears to have an existential reference, and to mean something like "instinct". The last mentioned group of "inclinations", however, seem to have a different kind of reference, incorporating in what are ostensibly facts of behaviour, a reference to the

---

[48] *Supra* n. 46.

[49] *Id.* 606.

[50] *Id.* 607. *Cf.* N. Bobbio, article cited *supra* n. 19, at 73, 76-79. And see Bobbio's comment on Wild's claim that he has established "ethical realism", that it could be equally described as "ethical rationalism" in the sense that it assumes that there are "a few very general self-evident principles of ethics from which by deductive procedures it is possible to recover all concrete norms of conduct". (*Id.* 73.)

[51] See Wild, *Plato's Enemies* 77, 76.

[52] And as Professor Kelsen thinks it is. See article cited *supra* n. 20, at 612.

G

norms of "reason", "sociality", etc., as if these were already given.[52a]
When natural lawyers explain on this point that the natural law "has as
its end an *ordered* system of human relations and cannot be identified with
spontaneous activity alone",[52b] this seems to involve an acknowledgment
that values are not immanent in the mere existential facts of human nature.
For they then have to explain further that what gives rise to the normative
precepts implied is what Aquinas calls "*synderesis*", a kind of sympathetic
understanding found in men, a habit of the practical intellect inciting them
to the good and murmuring against evil (*Summa* Q. 94 art. 1), or what
Suarez calls "*recta ratio*" (*De Legibus* 2, 5, 14), or something like "conscience". The question then becomes whether in any sense comparable to
that in which the instinct of self-preservation is *an objective fact*, men have
an instinct to find concrete moral precepts binding on *all of them in common*.
Even, however, if the psychological fact of "conscience" (in the sense of
synderesis) be admitted for each individual, this could not be an existential
basis *for a single body of natural law*.

For this we would also have to establish *as being existent in fact* a kind of
"universal conscience" of all individuals. But *as a fact* natural lawyers have
to add that men's "consciences" do not always come together in this
way, and it is to meet this problem that they have to resort to the
explanation that men's "consciences" may "err" and their reason be
"corrupt". So that if the "*universal* conscience", the *synderesis*, be offered as
a fact from which values emerge, it is a fact whose existence
is apparently not testable by either external observation or introspection.[52c]

§4. SECULARIST APPROACHES TO NATURAL LAW: EXISTENTIALIST ELEMENTS.
While some influence of existentialism on legal philosophy can be traced
back to shortly after publication of Martin Heidegger's *Sein und Zeit* in
1927, and of Karl Jaspers' *Philosophie* in 1932,[53] leading existentialists have
mostly eschewed the problems of law. Heidegger himself treats law only incidentally to his doctrines of man's inauthentic being and of the fall of
man.[54] Yet the fact that some existentialist themes bear on legal thought
is increasingly manifest in jurisprudential literature.[55]

Existentialism is, of course, not a unitary movement of thought. There
is intellectual tension between its main exponents, and one of its leaders
(Heidegger) rejects the label,[56] while another (Jaspers) would now prefer

---

[52a] *Cf. Summa Ia-IIae*, Q. 94 art. 2.

[52b] R. D. Lumb, "The Scholastic Doctrine . . ." (1959) 2 *Melb. U.L.R.* 205,
209 and see generally 207ff.

[52c] Lumb's offered solution, *id.* 217-221, does not meet the difficulty. Nor is
the difficulty avoided by placing precepts of natural law in terms of Aquinas' other
category, of knowledge or recognition of situations as congenial or inimical. For here
too he has to admit grades of self-evidence, or evidence to particular persons or
communities, or at various levels of reflection, education, etc.

[53] See, for example, E. Husserl, *Recht und Welt* (1929); E. Wolf, *Das Wesen
des Täters* (1932).

[54] See I. Tammelo, "On the Space and Limits of Legal Experience" (1958) 11
J. Leg. Ed. 171, at 176. *Cf.* W. Maihofer, *Recht und Sein* (1954) 15ff.

[55] See, e.g., G. Cohn, *Existentialismus und Rechtswissenschaft* (1955) on which
H. Kelsen ("*Existentialismus in der Rechtswissenschaft?*" (1957) 43 *Arch. R.- und
Sozialph.* 161) somewhat cruelly (and debatably) observes that the approach of
existentialists to jurisprudence was like a fashion coming to the provinces after it
has waned in the metropolis. And *cf.* the slightly different point in A. Kaufmann,
"*Recht als Mass der Macht*" (1958) 163 *Stimmen der Zeit* 22, 23.

[56] See W. Bock's Prefatory Note to M. Heidegger, *Existence and Being* (ed. W.
Bock, 1949) 18.

to call his philosophy "periechontology".[57] The difficulties of approach to it are increased by the abstruse expression of much of its literature, especially arising from the necessity which existentialists feel to create new words in order to convey what they regard as a new outlook on man and his world. The import of the word "existentialist" is in any case problematical,[58] and the name is perhaps best understood as referring to the effort of this body of thought to answer Kant's call for a philosophical anthropology to explore the question, "Who am I?".[59] Existentialists have attempted to reconstruct ontology—much shaken by intervening neo-positivist philosophies —by reflecting upon the cares of men, seeking thus for a new "humanism"[60] or "transcendental humanism".[61] The name then refers to man's turning to his authentic being and potentiality abstracted from all preconditioned purposefulness.[62] "What I am authentically", says Jaspers, "is the encompassing of the self-being. Self-being is *Existenz*." This is "the axis" around which turns everything that a man is, and that can gain authentic and fundamental meaning for him.[63] This meaningful self-being (*Selbstsein*) comes through communication, including communication with oneself,[64] and through suffering and frustration, rather than consummation.[65]

There is implied in this, as Thyssen well observes, that *Existenz* is a value-connoting entity, an excellence to be attained to whereby a man's present situation is seized in all its uncertainty of origin and goal, and its anxiety for the future.[66] Its attainment implies the individual's repeated ascent out of "everydayness" (*Alltäglichkeit*) (from which, however, he cannot escape once and for all, but each time anew) to his own self-being.[67] This last point, as Fechner observes, means that man's authentic being is actualised not in a vacuum, but in concrete historical situations of strife (*Auseinandersetzung*) with tradition.[68] The strife is accompanied by *Sorge*, a term embracing not only our word "care" standing alone, but its other main contextual uses, what we "care for", and "care about", as well as whether we "care" at all.[69]

"Natural law", understood as embracing absolute and eternal norms superior and preordinated to all law, would seem very alien to these and other basic positions of existentialism.[70] These basic positions imply negation

---

[57] K. Jaspers, *Von der Wahrheit* (1947) 160.

[58] *Cf.* P. Foulquié, *L'Existentialisme* (1955) 56; J. Thyssen, *"Staat und Recht in der Existenzphilosophie"* (1954-55) 41 *Arch. R.- und Sozialph.* 1, at 2. J.-P. Sartre, *L'Existentialisme est un Humanisme* (1946) 17, says that the name refers simply to the belief "that existence is prior to essence". But he seems to be here speaking only as a populariser; and it seems difficult (perhaps partly because of the confusions mentioned *infra* n. 61) to make his formula meaningful in existentialist terms.

[59] See M. Buber, *Between Man and Man* (1947) 119-121.

[60] J.-P. Sartre, *op. cit. supra* n. 58.

[61] Used by Spanish existentialists of their own position. See L. Recaséns Siches, *Human Life, Society, and Law* in vol. iii, *20th Century Legal Philosophy Series* (1948) 1, at 23. In the German, the term *"Existenz"* creates additional difficulties. The common usage word "existence" in English would be rendered by existentialists as *"Dasein"*, not as *"Existenz"*.

[62] *Cf.* E. Fechner, *"Naturrecht und Existenzphilosophie"* (1954-55) 41 *Arch. R.- und Sozialph.* 305, at 307ff.

[63] K. Jaspers, *supra* n. 57, at 76.

[64] *Id.* 374.

[65] K. Jaspers, *Philosophie* (2 ed. 1948) 879.

[66] J. Thyssen, *supra* n. 58, 3.

[67] *Cf.* E. Fechner, *op. et loc. cit. supra* n. 62.

[68] *Id.* 309. *Cf.* on the divergencies among existentialists from this point onwards, A. Kaufmann, *cit. supra* n. 55, at 22ff.

[69] The existentialist term *"Sorge"* would be rendered in Latin by *"sollicitudo"*.

[70] For the view that the main themes of existentialism are not consistent with

of any eternal verities, such as absolute norms of natural law, however many philosophers may believe that there are such, and testify to that effect.[71] Indeed, existentialism seems rather to march with positivism in stressing the duty of ethical criticism, rather than recognising any natural law annulment of positive law. Correspondingly, as Fechner also observes, where natural law sees orderly coexistence as pre-existing and demanding only recognition, the existentialist sees man as confronting in anxiety the chaos and void into which he is thrown, struggling always "to build . . . new islands of Being into Nothingness". Yet this is not the positivist position either. For the existentialist man is not the measure of law. Man has not the power to enact the law he deems good: he enacts whatever he can manage to pull together for his extreme need and distress.[72]

When, therefore, existentialists purport to develop natural law conceptions (as does Werner Maihofer in the doctrine examined in the later section on "The Nature of Things") the explanation is likely to lie either in a certain abandonment of existentialist positions,[73] or in a loose understanding of the term "natural law", or both.

On the other hand, however, nothing in the existentialist position obstructs an approach from this standpoint to the problem of "good law", that is, of the relations of law and justice. The "authentic being" or "self-being" of man is no less promising a basis for a theory of justice than the unfolding of the human personality long popular with nineteenth century natural lawyers. Yet in the countless pages dedicated by Jaspers, Sartre, and Heidegger to these notions, and the related fall into "everydayness", little explicit can be found about good law. No doubt much wisdom relevant to the search for good law could be distilled from such earnest thinkers, so keenly observant of their world and sensitive to the great ethical systems. But it has defied the present efforts to provide the flavour even in paraphrase.[73a] The distillation would be a labour of Sisyphus, requiring endless time to become naturalised into existentialist language, endless tolerance of Jaspers' verbosity, of Heidegger's linguistic plays, and Sartre's dramatic paradoxes and effects. By a paradox of our own, therefore, we have to confess that the nearest approach we have found to an openly existentialist theory of justice, is in the "inauthentic" form of Maihofer's theory of "the nature of things". And by a converse paradox, the best essay in vindicating natural law in "authentically" existentialist terms is that of the German judge, now Professor Arthur Kaufmann, who avoids explicit invocation of general existentialist philosophy.

§5. EXISTENTIALIST REASSESSMENT OF NATURAL LAW AND HISTORICISM. The post-war German juristic enthusiasm for natural law had sufficiently

---

iusnaturalism, see G. Quadri, *"Giusnaturalismo o Paradossia come Problema per la Filosofia dell'Esistenza . . ."* (1955) 32 *Riv. Int. di Fil. del Dir.* 327, at 329-330. *Cf.* the related point in A. Brecht, "The Ultimate Standard of Justice" in *Nomos, Justice* 62, at 68: "Only after fully recognizing that our humanitarian ideals . . . cannot be extracted from nature . . . are we mature enough to comprehend our personal responsibility, individually or in groups, in choosing our ultimate . . . norms."

[71] See E. Fechner, *supra* n. 62, at 314.

[72] See *id.* 315.

[73] *Cf.* E. di Robilant, *"Richiami all' Esistenzialismo nella Recente Filosofia del Diritto"* (1957) 34 *Riv. Int. di Fil. del Dir.* 18 at 39.

[73a] Jaspers, it may be recalled, came to philosophy from psychiatry, where his experience no doubt yielded rich insight into the "inauthenticity of man", and thence into horizons of man's potentiality as an authentic being (*eigentliches Seinkönnen*). Sartre has given literary and dramatic form to the unseizable elements of man's

waned by 1955 for Peter Schneider to observe, in his inaugural lecture at Bonn,[74] that Heinrich Rommen's book of 1936, *The Eternal Return of Natural Law* (*Die ewige Wiederkehr des Naturrechts*) might well be replaced by one entitled *The Eternal Return to Positivism*. The natural law phase had, he thought, yielded no univocal ethical principles for law, but a confusing plurality of opposed *Weltanschauungen*; and he repeated Georg Jellinek's warning that jurists should not become involved in the struggle of gods.[75] Arthur Kaufmann's important lecture of 1956[76] is to be read not only as an academic deliverance, but also as the reflection of a man of judicial experience upon the indecisive, motley, and often contradictory variety of ethical evaluations which had been produced in German courts themselves during the post-war hey-day of natural law.[77] And it is written significantly enough by a successor of Radbruch in the teaching of legal philosophy at Heidelberg.

In opening his thesis on natural law and historicity, Professor Kaufmann took note that post-war awareness of the dangers of legal positivism had not prevented increasing scepticism and even rejection of natural law. The decisive reason, he thought, was the concurrent awareness of *"the historical conditioning of the law"*, that a legal order arises from and is part of a given historical situation, and that this was true also as to the concrete content of norms claimed to be natural law.[78] Historicism is an arch-opponent of iusnaturalism, a version of value-relativism, as to which it has been said "the relativity of every kind of human conception is the last word of the historical conception of the world".[79]

Kaufmann is concerned, therefore, to remind us that Aquinas did not see natural law as a rigid body of ethically based legal principles (*starre Prinzipienrecht*) as he thought modern neo-scholastics tended to insist. For St. Thomas, Kaufmann thought, natural law acquires its role (*kommt zustande*) only where the general and immutable principles are connected with concrete, historical situations. While the nature of men and the nature of things have a central role, "nature" is to be understood as including not only the immutable essence of men and things, but also their historically mutable situations. Did not St. Thomas state at the very outset, *"natura autem hominis est mutabilis"*?[80] A true Thomist was therefore still entitled to see that the real problematics of law starts where most of the modern natural lawyers have stopped, namely after the *eternal* principles are formulated and the question is asked, What content of positive law is required by these principles? They start, in other words, with the concrete content of law.[81]

The decisive mistake of historicism lay, Kaufmann thought, in inferring

---

agonies in situations from which there is "no exit". And the classical philologist in Heidegger has given precious, if untranslatable, expression to civilised man's endless efforts to rise above everydayness.

[74] Published as *"Naturrechtliche Strömungen in deutscher Rechtssprechung"* (1956) 42 *Arch. R.- und Sozialph.* 98.

[75] *Ibid.*, referring to G. Jellinek, *Ausgewählte Schriften und Reden* (2 vols., 1911), vol. i, at 208ff. Rommen's book above referred to has, in the English transl. of 1947, the title *The Natural Law*.

[76] Published as *Naturrecht und Geschichtlichkeit* (1957).

[77] See *id.* 6-7.   [78] *Id.* 8-9.

[79] *Id.* 15, quoting Wilhelm Dilthey.

[80] *Id.* 12 (quoting *Summa IIa-IIae*, Q. 57 art. 2). For additional qualifications on the "rigidified" picture of St. Thomas now traditional, see *supra* Ch. 2, n. 100. But on the misleading nature of modern attempts to present him as an "existentialist", see F. Copleston, 2 *History of Philosophy* (1950) 308.

[81] *Op. cit.* 12-13.

from the empirically found changefulness of factual circumstances, that the "*ontological* history of Being" must be correspondingly changeful. Historicism assumed that since our perceptions or experience of law (*Rechtserkenntnisse*) are mutable and subjective, law itself (that is, the *subject* of such knowledge) cannot be fixed (*feststehendes*) and objective. It thus assumed that its purely empirical finding of the variability of knowledge about law grounded an absolute holding that law itself cannot be immutable. This conclusion, he urges, contradicts its own fundamental thesis. It must in its own terms be a purely speculative assumption, leaving open the issue whether there are immutable principles of natural law, even though men's findings as to what these are have changed, and may still change further, in different historical situations. "For the history of knowing never means simply the same as a history of the object of knowledge".[82] *Error multiplex veritas una.*

Kaufmann recognised that demonstration of this error merely disposes of one attack on iusnaturalism; it does not establish the truth of iusnaturalism and absolutism as against the positivist and relativist standpoints. Moreover, he admits that its truth cannot be shown by producing a minimum number of immutable and eternal ("abstract") principles of natural law. Yet he is concerned to show that there must be *some* such principles that are not completely indeterminate in their influence on the content of law. Let us assume, he suggested, that a legal order takes its departure from principles completely opposed to current notions of abstract natural law, for instance, "Injustice ought to be done" and "[Wanton] killing is permitted". No legal order could be built on such principles; and yet, if the postulates of justice were completely devoid of content, this should be possible. This consideration showed, he thought, that the function of immutable and eternal principles of law is not so much the positive one of giving contents to law, as the negative one of excluding immoral and unjust laws. Awareness of such limits was not to be underrated, for to know what a thing is *not*, may be a great deal. Indeed, he thought that perhaps the view of '*philosophia negativa*' that metaphysical cognition must be limited to the not-so-being (*auf das Nicht-so-sein*), might be a general truth.[83]

As between the supposed absoluteness or relativity of the contents of law, he thought that there was a law of human life barring the driving of any idea to extremes, and forcing extremes to "meet each other again as complementary theories". There must, therefore, be a foothold for law between *relativity* and *absoluteness*; perhaps, in the *ontological structure* of law itself, absoluteness *and* relativity, permanence (*Beständigkeit*) *and* change, eternity (*Ewigkeit*) *and* historicity are all active as *polar* forces. This would mean that positive law and natural law are neither mutually exclusive, raising questions of which prevails, nor identical, in the sense that one merely expresses the other. They are rather in a polar relation of mutual reference and tension. The historicity of law would then not be merely a function of empirically observed contingencies fixing mutable contents, but rather "a mode of being of law founded on the ontological form of every concrete legal order".[84] The "essence" (natural law, pre-

---

[82] *Id.* 17. *Cf.* on this point A. Kaufmann, "*Der Mensch im Recht*" (1958) *Ruperto-Carola* 2-8, praising Radbruch's position for respecting this distinction; G. Radbruch, *Rechtsphilosophie* (5 ed. 1956) 106ff.; A. Verdross-Drossberg, "*Die systematische Verknüpfung von Recht und Moral*" in *Forum der Rechtsphilosophie* (1950) 9-19, esp. 16.

[83] *Op. cit. supra* n. 76.

[84] *Id.* 24-25. And see *id.* "The Ontological Structure of Law" (1963) 8 *Nat. L. Forum* 79-96.

sumably) and the existence (positive law, presumably) of law do not necessarily coincide; there is tension and *ontological difference* between them. And while this tension and difference cannot be resolved by man, because of imperfect human cognition of "the perfectly true and just law", it is when man ceases to *aspire* to such resolution, that the law sinks into "the deficiency called legal positivism".[85]

According to Kaufmann, "the temporality and historicity of man as well as of law are a form of structure of their being". Man is aware of his temporal and historical situation, that his Being is in time and through time. He must see his tasks in time, distinguishing yesterday from today and both from tomorrow. Yet since his tasks are never complete, he is always "on the way". This perpetual wayfaring can only have a meaning if directed to an end (*Ziel*), "on the background of the supra-temporal (*Ueberzeitlichen*) and the absolute"; but "the wayfaring itself means that man's existence is historical". Similarly "law" itself constantly has its Being determined by time, being "actualised always anew to come to itself", and is thus "historical", in the sense that it is moving towards an end (*Ziel*) which must not be arbitrary. It is always "on the way to. . . natural law". The historical nature of law does not make it an enemy of natural law, but rather opens it to the influence of natural law, this unachievable goal still serving the essential purpose of measuring what law is for the moment achievable, "*das zeitgerechte Recht*".[86]

On this balanced and movingly written view of historicity and natural law, natural law becomes but a guiding star for *homo viator* in mutable historical situations; and *das zeitgerechte Recht* is not so much natural law, as actual positive law oriented to natural law principles. And while this view of natural law may be unacceptable to many natural lawyers, it may also be less vulnerable to the attacks of positivists. The fact is that it presents a version of natural law in which are incorporated not only a certain Radbruchian strain, but also (less explicitly) a number of important existentialist ideas. Jasper's notion of *Existenz* as an ever recurring struggle to rise from the world of "everydayness" to authentic self-being, Gabriel Marcel's notion of man the wayfarer with goal but no set course, and Heidegger's ideas on the historicity of Being supply the essential guides to the nature of Kaufmann's revision.[87] Clearly the result is not natural law in the traditional sense, for it reduces natural law finally to a critique of positive law in terms of justice, rather than insists that positive law derives from it through natural justice its standing as law. After all, despite his important principle of "*prudentia*", Aquinas did say categorically that "every human law has just so much of the nature of law as it is derived from the law of nature. But if in any point it departs from the law of nature, it is no longer law, but a perversion of law".[88]

§6. "THE NATURE OF THINGS" AND THE "CONCRETE NATURAL LAW". After the Second World War, the ancient idea of "the nature of things" (*physei*

---

[85] *Id.* 28-29.

[86] *Id.* 30-31.

[87] My friend Father P. M. Farrell, O.P. draws my attention to the possibility that if its full role were given to Aquinas' principle of *prudentia*, this interpretation may not have been too unacceptable to Aquinas himself. And see T. Gilby, *Principality and Polity* (1958) cc. vi-viii, esp. 324-28. But see next note.

[88] *Summa Ia-IIae*, Q. 95, art. 2, *corpus*.

dikaion)[89] as a source of good law, much discredited in the last century,[90] provided a further channel, mostly in Europe, of natural law revival.[91] Besides Radbruch's treatment, the doctrine has been favoured with a flood of monographs and articles, and with a full-fledged Conference at Saarbrücken in 1957 of the International Association for Philosophy of Law and Social Philosophy.[92]

The notion of "things" in this body of doctrine is used widely to embrace not only things in the ordinary sense, but also men and their life situations. The doctrine might thus perhaps be better referred to as "*les données reélles*"[93] or "the nature of facts".[94] Karl Engisch sees its thesis to be that the natural properties and circumstances of the objects of legal regulation "indicate . . . immediately the guiding lines of its content".[95] Herbert Schambeck thinks that it is concerned with "the determining ground" ("nature") of a given entity ("thing"), which is "anchored in the facts to which a positive legal norm refers".[96] Ilmar Tammelo, as interpreter rather than advocate, sees this doctrine as centred on the thesis that appropriate legal norms can be derived directly from the essentials of the fact-situation which they are to regulate;[97] that mere factual existence implies a normatively ordered existence.[98] It can be read out of (or into) ancient philosophical aphorisms, or out of (or into) Judaeo-Christian religious beliefs that creation presupposes the Creator, and that the creature manifests His will.[99] It is certainly present in the Thomist ideas of *conaturalitas*,[100] and of concrete legal norms as flowing from the "*natura rei*", immanent in legal states of

---

[89] See E. Wolf, *Griechisches Rechtsdenken* (3 vols. 1950, 1952, 1954) vol. ii, 78-94.
[90] E.g., by B. J. H. Windscheid, 1 *Pandekten* (9 ed. 1906) §2, n. 1; K. Bergbohm, 1 *Jurisprudenz und Rechtsphilosophie* (1892) 353.
[91] For early signs of revival see Gény, 2 *Méthode* 92.
[92] See with titles all referring to "the nature of things", A. Asquini, in (1921) 76 *Archivio Giuridico* 129-167; M. Gutzwiller, in *Festgabe der juristischen Fakultät . . . Freiburg (Schweiz)* (1924) 282-302; G. Radbruch, in (1941) 21 *Riv. Int. di Fil. del Dir.* 145-156; *id.*, in *Laun Festschrift* 157-176; G. Stratenwerth, *Das rechtstheoretische Problem der Natur der Sache* (1957); W. Maihofer, in *id.* 145-174; A. Baratta, in (1959) 36 *Riv. Int. di Fil. del Dir.* 177-228; H. Schambeck, in (1959-1960) 10 *Oest. Z.ö.R.* 452-474; and I. Tammelo in *Australian Studies in Legal Philosophy* 236-261. For Radbruch's treatment see *infra* Ch. 8, §13.
[93] Gény, *Science et Technique* 371.
[94] See articles of Baratta and Tammelo, *supra* n. 92. And see Schambeck's caveat, *op. cit.* n. 92, at 457ff.
[95] See K. Engisch, *Die Idee der Konkretisierung in Recht und Rechtswissenschaft* (1953) 116.
[96] *Supra* n. 92, at 452.
[97] See Tammelo, *supra* n. 92, at 236.
[98] *Cf.* E. Wolf, *Das Problem der Naturrechtslehre* (2 ed. 1959) 25: "*Alles, was ist, ist auch als Seiendes in Ordnung*". Perhaps something like this could be read out of Anaximander's pristine precept (6th century B.C.) to the effect that justice is a balancing principle governing the course of events in the world at large. See Freeman, *Ancilla* 19: *cf.* on Heraclitus *id.* 28, fragm. 5, and 32, fragm. 112, on which see *supra* Ch. 1, §§3-4. A. Verdross reads out of some of them that man's task is "to behave in accordance with Nature, hearkening to her". A. Verdross, "*Die Rechtslehre Heraklits*" (1942) 22 *Z.ö.R.* 498ff.
[99] As by Schambeck, *cit. supra* n. 92, at 453.
[100] The idea seems not to have emerged explicitly in St. Thomas' own writings, but to have been developed by later followers working out his concept of *synderesis*. It is much emphasised by contemporary Thomists, e.g., J. Maritain, *Man and the State* (1951, 4 imp. 1956) 91-93; and see *id.* 91, n. 11, for the view that the ideas thus expounded are "the real meaning implied by St. Thomas" in his references (e.g., *Summa Ia-IIae*, Q. 94 arts. 2 and 3) to knowledge through inclination. See also *id.*, *The Range of Reason* (1953) 22; and B. Miller, "Being and the Natural Law", in *Australian Studies in Legal Philosophy* 219, esp. at 223 n. 6. And see *infra* n. 122b and Ch. 11, n. 105.

affairs,[101] which continue in the contemporary natural law teaching that "morality . . . is that which is 'naturally right' for man according to 'existential purposes' predesignated for him in his nature".[102]

The most detailed attempt to show how this notion of "the nature of things" might be put to work is the rather dispiritingly sanguine thesis of Werner Maihofer. His attempt at a purely secular account of it is not rendered any easier to understand, however, by his choice of Martin Heidegger's philosophy as a vehicle of exposition. The reader's task of distinguishing difficult ideas from unacceptable ones is also made almost impossible by a Heidegger-like resort to unusual word-formations and the deliberate choice of words for their often untranslatable overtones, or for their punning qualities, earnestly indulged.[103] For Maihofer, at any rate, "the nature of things" is a main and not merely subsidiary source of law, affording a standard for appraising abstract rules according to a "concrete standard of material justice". He urges lawyers to work out a body of doctrine incorporating the findings of "philosophical anthropology", and "the doctrine of the legal *a priori*", and mirroring "the nature of things" in "concrete natural law".[104] The worthwhileness of such a mission depends of course on the sensibleness of the goal, and the means offered of reaching it.

Space forbids a detailed critique of Maihofer's particular doctrine here. Most readers unfamiliar with the existentialist language he uses will find it difficult to render his words into grammatical English free of clumsy paraphrases. Even then, much of the meaning which Maihofer's German original would convey to an existentialist reader would be lost. Our fuller examination elsewhere convinces us that Maihofer has simply not made good his claim to have "bridged the gulf between the Is and the Ought" by the notion of *"die Natur der Sache"*.[105] The mystery of how facts become value-endowed is still unsolved at the end. In secularising the notion he does avoid the theological mystery of a transcendent Will and Purpose manifest in world order by which facts are value-endowed; but he only does so by substituting a series of lesser mysteries, concealed under the delphic cloak of his esoteric word- and thought-formations.[106]

---

101 *Summa IIa-IIae*, Q. 57 arts. 2-4.

102 See J. Messner, *Das Naturrecht* (3 ed. 1958) 75.

103 The difficulties being, of course, always aggravated in translation. In *Identität und Differenz* (1957) (*Vorwort* 10), to give but one simple example, Heidegger says about metaphysics that *"Beweisen lässt sich in diesem Bereich nichts, aber weisen manches."* In K. F. Leidecker's transl. (1960) this is rendered: "Nothing in this sphere is it possible to prove, but much can be hinted" (*sic*). *Inter alia* this completely misses the shade of meaning probably intended by Heidegger arising from the homonomy of *"weisen"* as meaning "to indicate", and *"Weisen"* as meaning "sages". It also of course loses the "poetry" value of the rhyming of *"beweisen"* and *"weisen"*. At any rate, the difficulties involved may similarly surround Maihofer's use of *"Verweisungen"* (e.g., in *"Die Natur der Sache"* (1958) 44 Arch. R.- und Sozialph. 145, at 165) which we render below in n. 106 as "referrings".

104 *Id.* at 145.

105 See J. Stone, "An Existentialist *Natur der Sache*" (1964) 50 *Arch. R.- und Sozialph.*

106 Thus the single, well-known, and vast mystery of the Transcendent Will, underlying most natural law thought (including its "nature of things" version) is distributed in Maihofer's secular version into a number of minor verbally hidden mysteries in his process of giving meaning to "concrete natural law" by exegesis on the phrase "nature of things". We draw attention to the following *loci esoterici*: (1) The use of the word "things" in senses going beyond even the widest range of physical and psychological facts, and the word "facts" similarly. (2) In particular, the paraphrase from "thing(s)", to "fact-relations of life" (*Lebenssachverhalte*), to "cultural fact-relations" (*Kultursachverhalte*). (3) The movement from these in turn to "qualities" of men as such (*Alssein*) which are "not apprehensible" but "touch the core of their meaning" (*Sinnmitte*). (4) The movement from such "qualities" to

We remain, all in all, sceptical of the claims made by the various exponents of "the nature of things". But as long as some of the wise and learned continue to express themselves in these terms the rest of us must continue to listen to what they say. This notion remains, at any rate, a kind of *tópos* or seat of argument.[107] And the fact that a conclusion purporting to be based on it is not really so, does not exclude the possibility that the conclusion may have better bases for which that phrase is an elliptic formula. Yet if there are better bases, we are entitled to ask for them, and to withhold assent in the interim.

II. ISSUES RAISED BY THE NATURAL LAW REVIVAL

§7. IDENTIFICATION OF THE ISSUES RAISED BY THE REVIVAL. No one busy with other matters, or otherwise lacking time or patience, should wed jurisprudence; and natural law is perhaps the best test of a well and truly wedded jurisprudent—whether he be its friend, its foe, or (as is the present writer) a rather sceptical admirer at some distance. Certainly distance will continue to temper admiration as long as natural law proponents persist in denying that those who reject natural law can be concerned, and even coherently concerned, with justice. Can it not become common ground that belief in natural law is *one way* of trying to make positive law conform to justice; but that there are other ways of trying to do this, and that positive law may be challenged in the name of justice even if natural law is not invoked?[107a]

Wild purports to prove the importance of natural law by virtually claiming that unless natural law is acknowledged, the "very existence of ethics as a rational discipline" would be questionable and the dream of a world community based upon rational foundations would become pure fantasy.[108] Such a claim might conceivably be the final conclusion of a long contemporary debate between positivists and natural lawyers. Yet it is scarcely self-evident enough to form a presupposition of the debate.[108a]

"referrings of entities to each other", which yield their reciprocal meanings for each other from which follow reciprocal "expectations". (5) The movement from such "referrings" (*Verweisungen*) to the "'natural' and 'reasonable' interests" in the "value or disvalue" of the reciprocal behaviour of each "as such" (*Alssein*). (6) And, finally, the movement from these to "justified demands" and "justified obligations".

[107] See Tammelo, *cit. supra* n. 92, at 256-59. Its bases may also merit attention in relation to other *conclusions*. See, e.g., as to some parallelisms in terms of descriptive social analysis with Parsonian positions, Stone, *Social Dimensions*, Ch. 1, n. 53a.

[107a] As to the conclusion that what he terms "legal positivism" and "natural law philosophy" are "complementary" in major respects, *cf.* J. Hall, ". . . Integrative Jurisprudence (1964) 33 *Univ. of Cin. L.R.* 20-53, esp. 38-39. We, however, would not base this (as Hall does) on identification of legal positivism with a theory of justice as "order".

[108] See Wild, *Plato's Enemies* 72. The emphatic and explicit claim that neither ethics nor justice nor "true law" can be seriously sought after unless the natural law standpoint is accepted, is the main theme of Micklem, *Law*. See esp. 1-29, 98-105. That writer seeks as a theologian to reintegrate "Theology, Moral Philosophy and Jurisprudence". See *infra* Ch. 10, §3.

[108a] A. P. D'Entrèves, *Natural Law* (1951) 108, indulges a common form of this error when he asserts—as itself almost self-evident—that "recognition that the ultimate test of validity of law lies beyond law is itself nothing but a natural law proposition". This would only be plausible if we were speaking of the "validity" of the basic norm (that is of a legal system as a whole) in the same sense as we speak of the "validity" of subordinate legislation or of a contract. In fact it means

If we reinterpret natural law, as R. M. Hutchins has recently done,[108b] as involving in essence merely commitments to "purpose", to the use of reason in adjusting ends and means, and to "the ends that are discovered", and to distinguishing good and evil, accepting a duty to do one and avoid the other, and accompany all this with a declaration of independence from all earlier specific natural law teachings, we commit really an act of imperialist appropriation by "natural law" of the whole ethical and justice field. We do so, moreover, by shedding some of the specific features of natural law theory as historically given.

The same is to be said of theses such as that of J. C. Murray, S.J.,[108c] that "natural law" has the same meaning as A. A. Berle's "public consensus", referring to assent of the "public" (but not necessarily the majority) "mind" to what is found "by the careful enquiry of the wise to be in accord with reason". Can only professing natural lawyers be "wise", or exercise "reason"? And, even more obviously, the mere use of the phrase "nature of man" as a focus of thought is quite inconclusive as a mark of natural law thinking.[108d] The divisions between natural law and other thinking about justice still lurk within ambiguities of the word "nature". The present writer is concerned rather to ask for recognition of the common concern with human justice of all men (whether "positivists" or "natural lawyers")[109]

---

an entirely different thing (see Stone, *Legal System*, Ch. 3, §§5ff., 14ff.), namely that the basic norm stands in a certain relation with the facts of social life, and with the ethical convictions current within society, so as to be "effective" in this sense. The inquiries necessary to test effectiveness in this sense do not necessarily involve reliance on natural law. *Cf.* the recurrent overtones in Cogley (ed.), *Natural Law* suggesting that only a return to "natural law" can save mankind from the ethical wilderness. See, e.g., J. Cogley, Intro. 11-15, 28; R. M. Hutchins, 29-47 (identifying "normative jurisprudence" with "principles of natural law which are intended to be universal", and all recognition and pursuit of the good with the natural law position); J. C. Murray, 48-81, esp. 75-81; S. Buchanan, 82-153, esp. 82. Professor (Rabbi) R. Gordis, *id.* 240-276, identifies ethical principles so exclusively with "natural law", that he is constrained to reinterpret the whole humane ethico-religious tradition of Judaism as one of "natural law". See esp. 260-276, and contrast *supra* Ch. 1, §7.

When the tangled histories of the words "nature", "natural right", "natural rights", "natural society", "natural law", "state of nature", and the like are set aside, the thesis of Strauss, *Natural Right* is that history and theory have neither disproved man's uninterrupted concern with "the good life" including "justice", nor provided any sensible translation of this concern into the mere empirical data of past human behaviour. We regret that earnest philosophers should continue to provoke the dissent of their fellows by seeming to insist that this truth can not be expressed nor grasped without the intrusion of the adjective "natural" in some more or less unnatural sense. Strauss's book is itself a notable attempt to liberate the human aspiration towards the good and the just from the morass of verbal cross-purposes in which earlier attempts at articulation by certain lines of thinkers have buried it. But to present the liberated truth in terms which immediately threaten it with a historicist reburial, and this under the very banner of anti-historicism, borders on perverseness. And in one who appears to recognise that the Hebraic stream of influence concerning justice neither needed nor found place for the notion of "natural right", the perverseness wraps itself in even deeper mystery. See *id.* 81ff.; and *supra* Ch. 1 §7.

[108b] In Cogley (ed.), *Natural Law* 28-47, esp. 34ff.

[108c] In *id.* 48-81, esp. 79-81.

[108d] *Pace* R. M. Hutchins, *op. cit.* 31, J. C. Murray, *loc. cit.* 63, R. Gordis, *op. cit.* 240, 244, 253.

[109] We agree with Nagel, "Fact and Value" esp. at 77-78 that it produces little but confusion to label as "natural law" every view proposing objective standards of moral evaluation of law. And see *id.* "Human Purpose" 33ff., 43, suggesting that Professor Fuller's "animus" against "positivists" springs from the "curious" and unwarranted belief that anyone who accepts the distinction between the "is" and the "ought" is "barred in principle from evaluating the law in terms of objective moral standards". (One trouble here, of course, is that "objective" can mean either empirically found and verifiable, or merely justifiable by communicable reasons.)

Cf. the emphatic assertion of this concern for a clearly thought out "legal positivism" in S. I. Shuman, *Legal Positivism* (1963) 41-65, 192-193, 200-202. See esp. *id.*

who strive to identify, describe, test for and actualise those qualities of human law which render it worthy of men's acceptance and support.[110]

The decisive issues between positivists and natural lawyers are mainly three.[110a] Have the natural lawyers shown that they can derive ethical norms from facts? Have they explained how positive law ceases to be law simply by virtue of its violation of natural law? Are they entitled to claim that

202-204 on the contribution of Kelsen's confused terminology to contemporary cross-purposes. And see the argument that "legal positivism" and "natural law philosophy" are "complementary" in major respects, in J. Hall, ". . . Integrative Jurisprudence (1964) 33 *Univ. of Cin. L.R.* 20-53, esp. 38-39, more dubiously based on Hall's identification of legal positivism with a theory of justice as "order".

    Cf. H. Kelsen's moving statement in his *What is Justice?* (1957) 24, and N. Bobbio, article cited *supra* n. 2, at p. 13. Even A. Lundstedt deeply concerned himself with man's destiny, while simultaneously making a bitter denunciation of natural law: A. V. Lundstedt, "Law and Justice", in Sayre (ed.), *Modern Legal Philosophies* 450-483; *id. Legal Thinking Revised* (1956), esp. 131-216; *id., Superstition or Rationality in Action for Peace?* (1925) 129-158.

    [110] *Cf.* P. A. Freund's point ("Storm Over The American Supreme Court" (1958) 21 *M.L.R.* 345, at 357-58), that whether we see the moral criterion outside or immanent within the law, the important thing is to see it, so that we do not "rest the case for obedience on positive law alone". And conversely those who reject a natural law argument ought still to attend to the claim of justice which it symbolises. See also generally Ch. 8, §§10-11; N. Bobbio, article cited *supra* n. 19, at 82. On the historical record of the role of positivism as a critique of social institutions *cf.* generally E. Nagel, articles cited *supra* n. 109. Correspondingly, N. Bobbio has pointed out, men fought, killed, tortured each other even *nei beati tempi* when natural law was proclaimed in unison by jurists, philosophers and theologians (article cited *supra* n. 19, at 80), so that any special responsibility of positivism for recent human barbarism is still to be proved. It seems certainly true (as Hellmut Pappe showed in the article cited *supra* n. 3) that many outrageous judicial decisions of the Nazi period are to be attributed not to positivist amorality but to corrupt applications of the then positive German law. That very element of deeply felt faith which has often made natural law ideas so effective in action may easily distort them in certain social phases into rationalisations of the violence which men bring (under whatever banner of theory) to impassioned causes. And see *infra* Ch. 8, §11, and literature there cited, on certain other aspects of this matter.

    [110a] We are here concerned only with positivism as it confronts natural law thinking. But of course the label "positivism" is often applied in other confrontations to characterise other positions. Hart ("Law and Morals" 601-02) distinguishes (1) the view of laws as human commands; (2) the denial of necessary connection between law and morals; (3) stress on analysis of legal concepts as distinct from concern with the social relations of law, or its evaluation; (4) exclusive concern with logical interrelations of legal precepts in seeking applicable rules; (5) denial that moral judgments can be based on rational proof ("noncognitivism" in ethics). S. I. Shuman's monograph, *Legal Positivism* (1963) 15, 44, seems to take only numbers (2) and (5) as essential. And see *id.* 184-185, 187-88 discussing the distinction between "formal" and "substantial" positivism stressed by M. Rheinstein," . . . Relations of Morals to Law" (1952) 1 *J. Pub. L.* 287, 291, discussed S. I. Shuman, *op. cit.*, 184-185, and also the offered distinction between "legal" and "philosophical" positivism, work last cited at 187-88.

    N. Bobbio, after a Seminar in 1961 (attended among others by H. L. A. Hart, A. Ross, and A. P. D'Entrèves) deplored the continuing vagueness of the notion used to embrace such diverse ideas as those of sociology, Hegelianism, Marxism, Italian historicism, or American neo-realism. See his *"Sul Positivismo Giuridico"* (1961) 52 *Riv. Fil.* 14-34. He would distinguish positivism as (1) *in method* stressing the "scientific" approach to law, apt for a descriptive and explicative science, unhindered by value-judgments; (2) as a *conception of law* associated with state power, and focused on command, coercion and self-sufficiency of state law; (3) as an *ideology of justice* asserting that "obedience to legal norms is a moral duty". He says (correctly as we have seen) that this last has not in fact been an important positivist doctrine, and that its true paternity is disputed. See *id.* 14-22.

    Like A. Ross (". . . Legal Positivism and Natural Law" (1961) 4 *Rev. Jur. de B.A.* 46, 48) Bobbio denies that a legal positivist can be held to every so-called "positivist" position, or that all such positions necessarily go together. So with M. A. Cattaneo, *Il Positivismo Giuridico Inglese* (1962) 282-83, and in (1960) 94 *Rendiconti* 701-742 (Istituto Lombardo). In this last lucid account the three recurrent positivist themes are seen as (1) ethical neutrality in describing legal phenomena; (2) stress on the duty to obey law as such; (3) and on the relative nature of judgments of justice and morality, Cattaneo thinks that (1) and (2) contradict each other.

what they assert as self-evident must be recognised as self-evident by all? These issues remain central with revived natural law, as with the classical natural law, and there is perhaps more to be gained by confronting them directly than by entering the lists for or against the great philosophers, ancient or modern. Insofar as this tendency to direct confrontation grows, the contemporary debate on natural law may well be more fruitful than formerly, and may even prepare the way for some degree of *rapprochement*, or at least a basis for coexistence, between natural lawyers and positivists. We must, however, before discussing these issues in §§9-11, recall certain distinctions within iusnaturalist positions, and especially (in §8) within Thomist doctrine itself.

1. *Multiple References of "Nature", "Law", and "Natural Law"*. It first needs saying that in a body of doctrine surrounding what the term "natural law" symbolises, in which nine different meanings can be found attributed to "nature" and no less a number of meanings to "law",[111] we have (without adding the meanings of the two words "natural law" as a single symbol) about eighty-one possible meanings. This, no doubt, represents for the natural lawyer a rich currency; but it is a currency from which neither daily life nor theory generally can derive much benefit, until it is vastly simplified and adapted to contemporary mental commerce. As it is, anyone who tries to speak of the doctrine must specify what he is attributing to it; and if he is talking about it generally he must try to deal only, but truly, with the central core and the most characteristic common features (if these can be found) of at least the majority of the doctrines. And these are the aspects we have already tried to raise.

2. *Immanence of Values in Reality: Discovery not Creation by Man*. Second, then, it seems recognised on all hands, that one of these common features (if not the central one) is the claim that immutable values (or norms) are immanent in existential facts, which yield (in this sense) norms from "nature", independently of any acts of human will creating them.[112] And it is perhaps almost equally a part of this core of common doctrine (though analytically it may be quite distinguishable) that these immanent norms confronting positive law have a particular virtue to override positive law, over and above any enjoyed by the principles of "justice" or of "good law" as such.[113]

3. *Direct Divine Revelation*. Even on such core matters, some natural law theories can be found to dissent, and the most important of these may perhaps be recalled at this point. Contemporary Protestant conceptions, as has been seen, may even deny man's capacity to perceive any natural law order immanent in reality. The ground of this incapacity lies (it is said) "in the original sin, which enables us to have only a disturbed knowledge of the true, the beautiful and the good, and no less of the just".[114] It

---

[111] E. Wolf, *op. cit. supra* n. 98, at 22-153. Norberto Bobbio, (*supra* n. 2, at 12), if he is right in comparing this concern with natural law with concern with a corpse, would have to think of a vast army of corpses, with widely different histories.

[112] *Cf.* H. Kelsen, *"Justice et Droit Naturel"*, in *Institut International de Philosophie de Politique*, 3 *Annales de Philosophie Politique* (1959) 1, at 68-69. *Cf.* his article cited *supra* n. 20, at 597.

[113] Readers of Leo Strauss' vindication of "natural right" against "history", even when they accept the substance of its thesis, will often wonder if both its difficulty, and the resistance to it, are not vastly increased by the complexities buried within the adjective "natural" itself. See Strauss, *Natural Right, passim*: and see *supra* n. 108a. *Cf.*, as we understand him, K. Engisch, *Die Idee der Konkretisierung im Recht* . . . (1953) 228. N. Bobbio, article cited *supra* n. 2 at 13, perhaps insufficiently stresses the natural lawyer's claim to special superiority of the power of such immanent principles *over* positive law, as compared with the power of the mere ideals of "justice" or "good law".

[114] E. Wolf, *Rechtsgedanke und biblische Weisung* (1948) 28-29, esp. at 29.

follows in this view (as contrasted with the Catholic or Thomist view) that for the "natural" man there is no access to the absolute justice other than in "transcending" ("*Uebergang*") into the Kingdom of God. This transcending comes, it is said, not from man himself, but rather "the other way round: God seizes man and makes him just through justifying mercy (*rechtfertigende Gnade*)".[115]

4. *Independence of Divine Revelation: Secular Version.* The above position is manifestly at the opposite pole to the dominant secular versions of natural law. It is as concerned to assert the entire dependence of natural law on the divine revelation as John Wild is to deny it. It is also quite different from the natural law stemming from the positions of Aquinas. The seminal discussions on natural law and human law (Questions 94-97 of the *Prima Secundae* of the *Summa*) are set in the framework of deo-centric cosmology.[115a] Yet Aquinas' positions in these Questions can probably be argued for, as Aquinas did indeed to a remarkable extent succeed in doing, independently of theology, by appeal to the philosophical traditions originating in Greece, and to the kind of evidence associated with those traditions.[116] Thomist doctrines thus form grist to the intellectual mill both of the adherents and of the opponents of "theologification" of natural law. Even secularists such as Arthur Kaufmann, Werner Maihofer, and John Wild are clearly indebted to inspirations derived from the *Summa* of St. Thomas. On the other hand, and by contrast, the Protestant theories, insofar as they can move only within the limiting directives of written revelation, are scarcely capable of discussion with those who do not accept these directives.[117] And no real discussion seems possible between such Protestant theorists and positivists for another very different, but still very good reason: that natural law of this type is really a kind of extreme positivism, in which God plays God, instead of man playing God.

5. *Dual Import of Claims of Immanence of Value in Reality.* Coming then to the natural law claim that binding principles of morality and justice can be found by the human reason, since these principles are immanent in reality, we have first to recall that two different sub-claims are here implied. One is that any principles so found are binding by that fact. The other is that the content of such principles is objectively found, and therefore universally recognised by men generally. The former sub-claim we have sufficiently shown, in connection with Wild's recent effort, not to be yet demonstrated on any *secular basis*. As to the latter, the

---

[115] *Id.* 27-28.

[115a] See P. M. Farrell, O.P., "The Location of Law in the Moral System of Aquinas", in *Australian Studies in Legal Philosophy* 165-194; and *cf.* on the relation between philosophy and theology in Aquinas, F. Copleston, 2 *op. cit. supra* n. 80, 306-307, 310-323, 399-405.

[116] In the answer to Objection 2 in I *pars*, Q. 1 art. 1, Aquinas takes the position that certain sciences according to the diverse nature of their knowable objects can be known by the light of "natural reason", unaided by direct revelation. (And he dealt of course with the Decalogue not under "natural law" but under "The Old Law" (*Ia-IIae*, Q. 100).) If the term "theology" be used to embrace also knowledge gained by sciences of the above kind, we must then distinguish this part of it as "theology which is part of philosophy" as distinct from "sacred doctrine". Of course, Aquinas recognised that precepts of the natural law may also have been directly revealed.

[117] Despite E. Wolf's somewhat ambiguous assertion (*id.* 28) that since "free" research can proceed within the limits set by the directives, Protestant legal thought is independent of "ecclesiastical systematics". Rabbi Gordis is probably correct to argue (Cogley (ed.), *Natural Law* 240-276, esp. 252, 255ff.) that there is an inescapable link between the presuppositions of most iusnaturalist positions and "a religious world view".

concealed subjectivity of the standards (e.g., of self-fulfilment or "completion") which Wild makes crucial, impels us to add a few words as to the concealed *locus* of subjectivity. Natural lawyers' usage of the word "nature" itself, Bobbio has (perhaps too caustically) remarked, is "an elegy of folly";[118] a remark which becomes even apter if "nature" is taken to embrace pessimistic conceptions of the world such as that of Schopenhauer. On the level of degree of convergence or diversity of views, no clear line can be drawn between versions of natural law and (as Kelsen's and Perelman's studies have recently shown)[119] versions of justice itself. But of course the element of subjectivity is less concealed when we talk in terms of justice.

Is it an adequate answer in support of the second sub-claim above-mentioned that the many diverse versions of nature and therefore of justice are simply the result of ignorance, or aberrations from the "true" or "authentic" natural law, from (as it were) *the* natural law"?[120] Unless some special authority can be shown for one version as "true" (which would involve the necessity of reliance on some version of revelation which secularists are concerned to deny)[121] this is surely not adequate to establish any existing version. Even if we grant that this is a case of *error multiplex veritas una*, what men live *with* is the error, even when they live *by* the distant vision of *veritas*. For each sincere exponent of a version of natural law, that version is *the* true one. This leads to the paradox well-noted by Radbruch, that it is in the nature of conflicting versions of absolute justice that they tend to neutralise or at least to relativise each other. Each then becomes subject to examination as a theory of justice offered for acceptance, rather than imposing itself as value immanent in the facts. Aquinas himself recognised that the uncertainty and "admixture of many errors" gave great *convenientia* to divinely revealed truth, even where truth was directly accessible to the natural reason itself. The critical point becomes whether there cannot be a *tertium quid* as between divine revelation and natural law on the one hand, and utter moral scepticism on the other.

§8. UNIVERSALITY, INDETERMINACY, FLEXIBILITY AND *PRUDENTIA* IN THOMIST TEACHING. To offer a set of principles as proceeding simply from the divine will or reason, and made known to men simply through revelation, affords a weighty, or at least a comprehensible, ground for claims that the principles so offered are the "true" natural law. But such claims are attended by special elements inviting obfuscation when they are made from positions which attach central importance to human reason as participating in the divine reason. If Thomist natural law, like the Protestant version, were unambiguously asserted as an expression of God's revealed will, the claim of a particular version to be the sole "true" version might perhaps be sustained; at least for all those who accepted that particular version of revelation. Certainly on such assumptions the *possibility* of a sole "true" version would be undeniable. Yet to restrict natural law thought to such grounds would involve jettisoning much of the fruitful body of thought

---

118 N. Bobbio, article cited *supra* n. 2, at 7.
119 H. Kelsen, article cited *supra* n. 112, at 12-63; Ch. Perelman, *De la Justice* (1945) 15-19, 28-40.
120 *Cf.* Arthur Kaufmann's view, discussed *supra* §5.
121 See for attempts to deal with this aspect, G. W. Goble, "Nature, Man, and Law: The True Natural Law" (1955) 41 *A.B.A.J.* 403-476, esp. 404n.; W. J. Kenealy, S.J., "Whose Natural Law?" (1955) 1 *The Catholic Lawyer* 259-266.

concerning natural law and "human" law which the world owes to St. Thomas Aquinas.[122] And it should also be remembered that in any event exclusive and definitive possession of a "true" natural law, sufficient to meet all problems, is not necessarily claimed by the natural law theorist; and that in Aquinas himself a constant and important role is assigned to a flexible *prudentia,* both in the framing of general principles of natural law, and in application of these principles to changing situations.

Yet, it may be asked, is it not true that Aquinas has given us an unexcelled version of the content of many of the principles of natural law, as these have won wide recognition by men throughout the ages? And does this not show that the values thus expressed are indeed immanent in the facts of "nature"? The latter question only arises if the former is answered in the affirmative, and even then the possibility could not be excluded that while such recognition has been wide it has been far from universal. The degree of consensus might then be explicable without concluding that values must be immanent in the facts of nature.[122a]

It is more important, however, to observe that the answer even to the former question is far from unambiguous in its import. Many of the principles that may be said to have general acceptance, for instance, are in such general and abstract terms that men would have little occasion really to challenge them. Who is interested in denying what Aquinas asserts in *Ia-IIae* Q. 94 art. 2, namely that "good is what all things seek after" and that good ought to be pursued and evil avoided, at any rate as long as he is not thereby committed as to precisely what is good? The precepts about "good" and "evil" as they figure in the primary principle of natural law turn on indeterminacy, if not circularity: for these are but *names for* "the first thing that falls under the apprehension of the practical reason", and for "that which all things seek after". The principle is really only a kind of "preamble".[122b] So too with the alternative formulation, "Act according to reason". Who would not agree that men should act according to "reason", as long as he is not committed to any particular concept of "reason" or version of its requirements? Of course the secondary and tertiary precepts to which Aquinas then proceeds, such as those concerning man's self-preservation, the fulfilment of his physical nature, and the exercise of his reason in pursuing knowledge of God, shunning ignorance, and living socially among his fellows, may still be free of these difficulties even then. Obviously, however, not all of them are. So that even if it be said that the main principle as to the pursuit of good is an ultimate *moral* principle which need not justify itself in the *jurisprudential* universe of dis-

---

[122] And see for a somewhat different consideration, H. Kelsen, article cited *supra* n. 112, at 84-87.

[122a] The mere fact that instances are found "confirming" a theory means little if we have not tried and failed to discover contrary evidence, or if we do not take it seriously. *Cf.* Popper "Historicism" (12 *Economica* (N.S.) 79).

[122b] J. Maritain, work first cited *supra* n. 100, at 90, adopted R. D. Lumb, cited *supra* n. 52b, at 213-16. Lumb stresses that natural law must refer to "concrete precepts" which are not deducible from the primary principle, but are rather drawn by "an intuition . . . prompted by *synderesis,* or sympathetic understanding . . . supported on rational grounds". See esp. 216. *Cf.* Maritain, *op. cit.* 91-92: "Knowledge *through inclination* . . . is not clear knowledge through concepts and conceptual judgments; it is obscure, unsystematic, vital knowledge by connaturality or affinity, in which the intellect, in order to form its judgment, consults and listens to the inner melody that the vibrating strings of abiding tendencies awaken in us". Contrast Dr. Micklem's more conventional interpretation in *Law* 30.

Cf. on the indeterminacy of the 1948 Universal Declaration of Human Rights, Benn and Peters, *Principles* 101.

course, the same difficulties often remain as to the consequential natural law precepts.

Who, for example, would contest that knowledge should be striven for and ignorance should be abolished? Could not even a confirmed positivist agree that men should act socially and yet feel uncommitted to many natural lawyers' precepts drawn from this? The point, obviously, at which general acceptance of a particular precept becomes significant for conduct is at a certain level of concreteness; and it must surely be acknowledged on all hands that as we approach the concrete level, general acceptance of natural law precepts often tends to fall away. We are here concerned, the reader may recall, not with the merits of any particular precepts, but with the question whether there is any such general acceptance of them as demonstrates the immanence of the values they express in the facts of human nature. Once we have to acknowledge that disagreements increasingly arise at the more concrete levels, and are often left by Aquinas to *prudentia*, this leaves the general acceptance at the level of the more abstract principles of rather ambiguous import.

This ambiguity of *agreed* abstract principles, from which *controverted* subordinate precepts then often emerge, is of course well illustrated in the millennial puzzle set for natural lawyers by the institution of slavery. St. Thomas did not go so far, as did the classical natural law, as to seek to justify slavery. His discussion of it is not by way of laying down formal precepts, but by way of testing his own positions against objections based on the existence of slavery. Yet though men throughout the ages have struggled and convulsed social life to banish slavery, Aquinas felt compelled to hold it always to have been embraced within natural law, since though not *brought in by nature*, it was (like private ownership) "devised by human reason for the benefit of human life".[123] Men, of course, even the greatest, must be understood in the context of their age; and St. Thomas is entitled, like The Philosopher himself, to this full understanding. Such an understanding requires it to be assumed that masters in their turn would be bound to observe the principles of natural law in the treatment of their slaves.[124] Yet we are left with the main difficulty, that on the concrete level even of precepts with which mankind has the vastest experience, and on which we might expect what is "good" as proceeding from the facts of human nature to have the clearest meaning, natural law has left the door open for opposed conclusions.

The principles concerning private possessions and against stealing may be thought to represent a clearer focus of general acceptance, and therefore a better testing point. Yet here, too, it is well to remember that until precepts setting the limits of the *suum* are laid down the master precept, *suum cuique*, may be accepted as right by men mortally opposed to each other concerning what is the just distribution of material goods. *Suum cuique* may be a battle-cry common to both sides, though each utters it with radically different concrete implications. It is agreed in short that there should be a *suum*, and that the range of what is attributable to each must

---

[123] *Summa Ia-IIae*, Q. 94 art. 5, Reply 3. And see *IIa-IIae*, Q. 57 art. 3, Reply 2, and commentary on Aristotle's *Politics* (c. 1255) lib. I, lect. iv. Duns Scotus, on the other hand, took a comparatively firm stand against slavery: see *Reportata Parisiensia*, IV, dist. 36, q. 2, nn. 5ff. And see C. R. S. Harris, 2 *Duns Scotus* (1927) 349-350.

[124] He may also have used *servitus* in some different sense than that which we now associate with "slavery", in a sense, for example, cognate to that in which we speak of penal *servitude*. *Cf.* also Arthur Kaufmann, *op. cit. supra* n. 76, 12ff., raising the question of the relevance of the historical context in which Aquinas was thinking.

somehow be delimited. Yet the questions "How?" and "What limits?" should, after all, be where the study of justice begins rather than where it ends. Indeterminacy (and sometimes circularity) in the Thomist principles and precepts, may, then, even on the secondary and tertiary levels, explain much apparent general acceptance of them. This, we repeat, is not a complaint as to their substantive merits. All rule-making involves a degree of abstraction, and therefore of indeterminacy, in concrete cases. But it does mean that general acceptance, when it exists, may still be of ambiguous import for the argument whether values are immanent in facts.

We have to add that allowance must also be made for the use by St. Thomas, as by exponents of law of all kinds, of precepts in antinomic relations to accommodate conflict of principles in an offered universal ordering which must maintain some consistency in the varied and changing circumstances of concrete applications. Thus, the principle requiring the stability of marriage has been hitherto clear as a directive, even if we attribute the prohibition of divorce to divine positive law. So far as concerns the stability principle alone, however, it is not too hard to argue that the primary principle that we should do good and avoid evil *could* require divorce in certain circumstances, since we should not perpetuate evils (broken-down marriages) which can be remedied.

Finally, the great flexibility of precepts, and therefore the room for disagreement beneath apparently stable and agreed content, is increased further by St. Thomas's wise stress on the contextual application of principles, and by the important role he gives to *prudentia* of the interpreters and of the positive law-givers who apply the precepts derived from natural law.[125]

All this can be regarded, indeed, not as evasion of hard questions by Aquinas, nor even as systematic faults, but as a recognition dictated by *prudentia* itself of the degree of precision which the various orders of precepts can tolerate, having regard to the tasks of law and legislation.[125a] The greatest juristic and legislative work is subject to similar observations. So that even recognising its flexibilities, Thomist natural law sets an agendum of problems requiring further thought, and of essential themes requiring elaboration and qualification. Accepted on this basis, it is an invaluable stimulus to moral deliberation. Scholarship would benefit if it were received for discussion in this sense, both by its proponents and opponents.[126]

---

[125] In *Summa Ia-IIae*, Q. 95 art. 2, St. Thomas himself recognised that, apart from "derivation" as a conclusion from "premises", there was involved "determination of certain common notions". And he seems to refer the latter, in Reply 4, to "the judgment of expert and prudent men", who "see at once what is the best thing to decide". *Cf.* D. Granfield in *Nomos Justice* 229, at 232; and on the Thomist *prudentia* generally see J. Pieper, *Prudence* (1959). The otherwise varied contemporary natural law viewpoints collected in Cogley (ed.), *Natural Law* concur the more strikingly in stressing "the changing and changeable factors of human existence" (J. Cogley, Intro. 17); in seeing natural law as "sustained, as it was born, of argument and persuasion" and to be validated by "experience and reflective thought" (J. C. Murray, 48-81, at 59 and *passim*); in eschewing "doctrinal answers", and following "the dialectical method" of "endless mutual persuasions" (S. Buchanan, 82-153, at 90-91 and *passim*). And *cf.* also *id.* 136, R. M. Hutchins at 38, 44-46; P. Selznick at 174-75, 181, 183-86; and R. Gordis, at 251, 274-75. And see *supra* n. 122b.

[125a] In this it remains thoroughly in the modern juristic mood. See Stone, *Legal System*, Chs. 5-8, *passim*. And see the earnest plea for more overt acknowledgment of the doubt and indeterminacies involved, admitting candidly the indeterminacy of the "equality" concept even while retaining emphasis on equality, in J. F. Coons, "Approaches to Court-Imposed Compromise" (1964) 58 Northw. *U.L.R.* 750-794, esp. 793-94, and the overall theme of the symposium, *ibid*.

[126] *Cf.* on a more abstract level, Tammelo, "Justice and Doubt" 379.

§9. PHILOSOPHICAL STANDING OF THE DOCTRINE OF IMMANENCE OF VALUES IN REALITY. If moral values cannot be shown to be immanent in factual reality by reference to men's general recognition, proof might still conceivably be available in terms of philosophical, or rather metaphysical, theory. Neo-Kantians, of course, as we saw with Kelsen, reject such a possibility as repugnant to their basic doctrine of the distinctness of the realms of the Is and the Ought. Yet even apart from so rigid a position, the difficulties are serious. If it be granted, as John Wild insists, that values themselves are a kind of facts, they would still have to be distinguished from actual human tendencies, inclinations, propensities, as such, just as they would from the facts dealt with in chemistry or geology. And if facts as such are not values, and yet some have values embedded in them, the question must be faced how this embedding comes about.

The positivist standpoint, no doubt oversimply, answers that it comes about when sentient beings perform value-endowing acts; it insists that the creation of these values *for men* still requires acts of human evaluation. For men committed by religious faith, the positivist would say, this remains true though the commitment arises (as it were) from a single act of faith, endowing with value whatever is valued by the teachings of the religion concerned. This, of course, is no more acceptable to a religious man than the positivist's flat denial that values can be immanent in reality, independently of men's own evaluations, could be acceptable to the sincere natural lawyer. In the terms in which the positivists press this point against the iusnaturalists, it is unanswerable, for it proceeds on the positivist conception of value.

Natural lawyers, however, have after all no duty to proceed on positivist assumptions. They are entitled to reject these assumptions, and assert some way of creation or at any rate discovery of values, not dependent on human value-endowing acts. They do appeal to the nature of man as setting ends for his pursuit and to his exercise of reason in the clarification and pursuit of these ends. In Aquinas' terms they see this "final" causality as metaphysically necessary and rationally vindicated by both the "speculative" and the "practical intellect".[126a] They urge that what reason shows to be thus involved in the nature of man is not man-made but only man-discovered; that what is thus discovered is what they mean by "value", that "value" in this sense proceeds from human reason and not from human will, and that it is discovered in the world of factual reality which comprehends the nature of man himself. Nor is the fact that all this rests upon a conclusion of the speculative intellect, necessarily fatal to it; all positions on such ultimate matters must probably rest on a metaphysic, whether disclosed or not.

Yet this, after all, would amount only to an agreement to differ, and would simply leave unjoined the issue whether value is discovered by human reason, or made by human will. Each side would then mean a different thing by "value" and in the result there could be between them no useful discussion of that issue. What they could then disagree about is only which of them is entitled exclusively to possess and interpret the symbol "value".

§10. CAN THERE BE A POSITIVIST-NATURAL LAW *RAPPROCHEMENT?* HOW

[126a] *Summa I pars*, Q. 79 art. 11. These matters fall, of course, within moral

far, if at all, can the alienation between positivism and iusnaturalism be reduced by mutual concessions?[127] Norberto Bobbio has argued that moderate positivists could accept the view that there are rules of human conduct outside those of positive law, and ethically more commendable, by which the latter can be evaluated.[128] The present writer, while agreeing, cannot see that this would be any concession save as regards those positivists, probably a small minority, who deliberately deny that law can be evaluated by reference to an objective standard of any kind.[129] At any rate, natural lawyers might certainly bring to such an accommodation the renunciation of the doctrine that natural law prevails *as law* over positive law, that "*lex injusta non est lex*". If they substituted for this the tenet of Aquinas that "unjust law does not bind in conscience", this would bring them into the common ground with moderate positivists that there is a constant duty to measure positive law by standards of justice.[129a] The two sides could then, it might be thought, debate the merits of their respective standards of justice as other competing groups have done from time immemorial.[129b]

The natural lawyer's doctrine of the immanence of value in reality would, however, still present difficulties, insofar as debate about the characteristics of an entity is difficult between one man who says he sees it, and another who says that there is nothing there to see. Yet this is a point which natural lawyers cannot give up and remain natural lawyers, nor can positivists accept it and remain positivists. It is not enough here for the onlooker to say that the point is trivial anyhow, since no particular concrete decision depends on it. Even if this were so, and if most of mankind did not know what either the immanence of value in reality or its negation meant, the integrity of this doctrine would still remain, for the earnest natural lawyer, the integrity of his own moral outlook. Nor is it enough to say that it should be given up because it only leads to cross-purposes; for this is one point on which the issue is truly joined.[130] The difficulty is that there is no way of deciding it *which will bind the conscience of the natural lawyer*. One main series of cross-purposes between natural lawyers and positivists follows when failure to decide an issue is followed by discussion of sub-issues which depend on how that one is to be decided.

What of the relativism of the usual positivist, and the claim of natural lawyers on the other hand that they can discover eternal immutable or,

---

philosophy and theology, and they involve in application the virtue of prudence. See *supra* §8.

[127] N. Bobbio has recently discussed this question in his review cited *supra* n. 5, at 485.

[128] *Id.* 489.

[129] *Cf.* Nagel, "Human Purpose" at 32, 43.

[129a] This seems the position taken by A. Verdross (see *op. cit.* n. 3, 232, 257ff., noting his recognition of the uncertainties arising in the absence of acceptance of revelation). On the other hand, passionate demands like that of Micklem (*Law* 79ff., 112ff.), speaking as a theologian, that all lawyers and juristic thinkers accept the doctrine of a transcendent natural law will not help the learned to find common ground. *Cf.* on Aquinas' own careful qualifications of his position *supra* Ch. 2, n. 107.

[129b] This in substance seems to be a major point of A. Kaufmann in his 1963 article cited *supra* n. 84, esp. 92-93. Yet if, as he there says, "justice and natural law are, indeed, the same", and the difference between mere *Gesetz* (*lex*) and *Recht* (*ius*) can be stated in terms of either, it would be an even greater aid to communication if the side-issues and cross-issues raised by the term "natural law" itself were avoided altogether. And see *id.* "*Gesetz und Recht*" in *Existenz und Ordnung* (*Festschrift für Erik Wolf*) (1962) 327-397, esp. 381-393.

[130] In the tangled exchanges between Professors Fuller and Nagel further discussed and cited *supra* n. 109, and *infra* nn. 143ff., this issue at least is clearly joined, and, indeed, well illuminated for most readers. See Fuller, "Human Purpose"; Nagel, "Fact and Value"; Fuller, "Rejoinder"; Nagel, "Human Purpose".

as it is often said, absolute values? Is this a point on which one or the other or both might yield somewhat? Kaufmann's point is here, perhaps, worth pondering, that even the positivist's relativism itself cannot be absolute. Even if values do arise only from human value-endowing acts, it may still be that men invariably do perform acts creating certain values. There need only be a small range of such constantly occurring acts to come some way to meet the natural lawyer. Conversely, moderate natural lawyers admit, in any case, a wide variability of the concrete contents of subordinate precepts of natural law, arising from interpretation of principles in various contexts of time and place. Natural law as well as "human law" are treated by Aquinas as spheres of the "practical intellect" in which, as principles have to be brought down to precepts for concrete situations, "prudence" plays an increasing role. Positivists might not deny immutability to abstractions of sufficiently high order, nor find it difficult to accept Arthur Kaufmann's conception of "natural law", by which he concludes that there must be absolutes in the changing law.[131] As Fuller has wisely observed, if "absolute" refers to something not related to anything else, it is difficult to conceive such an "unrelated" thing. While if it refers to a moral principle that yields a clear rule of decision under all circumstances, this too is difficult to conceive. So that the notions "absolute" and "relative" as employed about natural law may be "unanalysed terms of censure and praise" which do not clarify "essential problems of law and justice".[132]

§11. HUMAN PURPOSES, "FORMS OF SOCIAL ORDER" AND NATURAL LAW. Yet when we discuss *rapprochements*, we must bear in mind that natural lawyers (rather more even than the rest of mankind) escape their inheritance only with difficulty. Sometimes, indeed, the very aspects of natural law achievement which moderate positivists might wish to emulate, are by-products of other aspects which they shun or even repudiate. There must be few moderate positivists who have not been drawn from time to time to the energies and dedication manifest in the best natural law searchings. While Lon Fuller would not defend "all the things which have been said in the name of that excellent philosopher, St. Thomas Aquinas",[133] he thinks that if we must have illusions, that of "natural law . . . at least . . . liberates the energies of men's minds", and sustains "our spiritual needs".[134] But the refusal of further intellectual commitment is no less striking. It is not only that "for many the term 'natural law' has about it a rich deep

---

131 At the same time they may find rather unconvincing his statement that "we cannot have a consciousness of relativity if things are relative in their Being", that "relativity can exist only in relation to something non-relative", and that "a point of reference which itself is relative, which evades me is no more a point of reference; to such a point I can have no relation, with it I can have no cognitive relation". See A. Kaufmann, *op. cit. supra* n. 76, at 18. And *cf.* I. Tammelo, *Drei rechtsphilosophische Aufsätze* (1948) 8. For this seems to overlook the possibility of a point of reference which is only relatively constant, this relative constant being relative in its turn to other relative constants. Justice may be relative to *Weltanschauungen*, *Weltanschauungen* relative to social and economic conditions, social and economic conditions relative to technology, techniques of organisation, etc. This would involve, of course, a *regressus ad infinitum*, but why should not there be such a regress? We may follow it as long as it is needful, or fruitful of results, always admitting that the final point of reference is not the ultimate point.

132 Fuller, "Mid-Century" 467. See *supra* Ch. 1, §10; *infra* Ch. 8, §1, and *infra* Chs. 10 and 11, *passim*.

133 *The Law in Quest of Itself* (1940) 101; and *cf.* 100-101, 116-17.

134 *Id.* 110; and *cf.* 116-17.

odor of the witches' cauldron . . .".[135] He also wishes it to be clear that the common ground he shares with natural lawyers, of concern with "good order and workable arrangements" (to which he gives the name "eunomics") involves no commitment to "ultimate ends".[136]

The emulation extends, however, not only to the older natural law's direction of concern, but to its ways of thinking, its "broader and freer method", where "reason" uninhibited by positivism pushes on "naturally" as far ahead as it can, and "tends inevitably to find anchorage in the natural laws which are assumed to underlie the relations of men".[137] Unless this is merely a play on the expressions "natural law", "naturally" and "natural laws",[138] its praise must be directed to the range of facts and arguments brought into consideration by the natural law jurist.[139] At a later stage[140] Fuller felt that he shared the classical natural law acceptance "of the possibility of discovery in the moral realm", and the aim "of discovering those principles of social order which will enable men to attain a satisfactory life in common". This process of discovery he thinks to be close to the "collaborative articulation of shared purposes" for clarifying men's ends, and the means of achieving them,[141] central to his own science of "eunomics".

Since, however, Fuller criticises the natural law concentration on human "ends" and their implications for law, as not "holding means and ends open for a reciprocal adjustment with respect to each problem",[142] his expressed preference for this way of thinking cannot refer to any exemplification of the interplay of ends and means. What precisely, then, are the elements of thought in respect of which he regards "the older natural law" as a model? Two possibilities remain. One is its attention to "the principles of social order", by which men can live "satisfactorily" together. This, however, would credit natural law with a kind of monopoly of concern with matters in which, as we have already suggested, no such monopoly can be recognised. The other possible reason for Fuller's preference for the natural law way of thinking might be the process of "casuistic" and "dialectical" discussion found in the best natural law treatises.[143] But if

---

[135] L. Fuller, "Reason and Fiat in Case Law" (1946) 59 *H.L.R.* 376, 379.

[136] "Mid-Century" 473-481, 477.

[137] *Op. cit. supra* n. 133, at 100ff., 103-104.

[138] No doubt this has contributed to unclarity as to whether Fuller's position is finally a natural law position, despite his denial that it is. See *infra* this section *passim*.

[139] Fuller had earlier observed (*op. cit. supra* n. 133, at 101-102) upon the paradox that a body of doctrine with this range of reference should have come into such disrepute in an age which insisted that fruitful work in the law "presupposes a familiarity with the other social sciences, such as psychology, economics, and sociology".

[140] "Rejoinder" 84.

[141] *Ibid.*

[142] *Cf.* his "Mid-Century" at 479.

[143] Certainly in his "Rejoinder", at 97-98, Fuller seems to regard this kind of casuistic discussion as the best way of explaining, by ostentation as it were, what it is that joins him to natural lawyers in insisting on the "confusion" of the "is" and the "ought" in legal discussions proceeding from "the collaborative articulation of shared purposes". To show how principles emerge from such discussion he offers a sequence of hypothetical cases. In *Case No. 1*, the *bona fide* purchaser is not protected lest this create a "market for stolen goods". In *Case No. 2* the purchaser is denied title because of his own fraud. In *Case No. 3*, the *bona fide* purchaser from such fraudulent party is protected lest purchasers of property be compelled to scrutinize details of their vendors' chain of title. In *Case No. 4*, even a *mala fide* purchaser from the *bona fide* purchaser is protected in order not to permit the property to be rendered valueless in the latter's hand. In *Case No. 5* (which Fuller leaves for speculation) the *mala fide* purchaser from the *bona fide* purchaser is not only aware of initial fraud,

this were all that is meant, the conclusions which natural lawyers reached by this process, working from immutable principles based on man's "nature", would not necessarily coincide with those which Fuller thinks emerge from the play of ends and means in men's pursuit of their actual purposes.

This leads us to the third respect in which Fuller praises natural law thought, namely, to its "coalescence of the *is and the ought* . . .",[144] its tolerance of "a confusion of them in legal discussion". Indeed, in 1954[145] he thought that his own position on this was substantially similar to that of Wild.[146] Since "coalescence" or "confusion" is not *as such* a virtue, it may be asked what precisely Fuller thinks *to be the common virtue* here.

Wild's grounding of the "ought" and the "is" springs from the doctrine that entities as they actually are tend towards self-fulfilment and completion, and that whatever aids that tendency is good, and what distorts or obstructs it is evil. The "is" and the "ought" are here embedded together in the "nature" of man, since "nature" embraces *ex hypothesi* both its actual condition and what it requires for self-fulfilment. This union, moreover, and therefore the norms which arise from it, are independent of human will, purpose or expediency, and it is this independence after all which bases the claimed universality and immutability of the main principles of natural law. But Fuller's doctrine of the "is" and the "ought", which he thinks "similar" to Wild's, is very different indeed. He starts with the human purpose or "congeries of purposes" which (he says) is the essential meaning of a legal rule. Since he says, a purpose is a direction-giving *fact*, it "is at once a fact and a standard for judging facts", and "in any interpretation which treats what is observed as purposive, fact and value merge", and no sharp dichotomy can be maintained.

This is surely vastly different from Wild's position. There the level of merger would yield principles universal and immutable because the "nature" of man is not dependent on man's purposes, but on the condition in which man finds himself with its potentialities for his fulfilment. Fuller's resolution can on the face of it yield only various functions and transmutations of actual human purposes, as ends and means clarify themselves in the unfolding process of reciprocal testing.[147] These are part of the facts of social life which bear upon the law, and the study of them and their interactions is strictly not a normative or evaluating activity but rather part of the sociological enquiries concerning the relations of law and society.[148] For however hard reason may work to clarify these ends and

---

but was a party to it.

But the didactic value of this process as a means of clarifying all kinds of principles (moral *and other*) is a commonplace, especially in common law courts, not to speak of other legal systems. Is it not, therefore, rather carrying coals to Newcastle, to press common lawyers so hard with the natural law casuistic model? And is this process peculiar to defining "*moral and* legal ends", as distinct from any other ends implicit in whatever purposes, moral or otherwise, human decision-makers set before themselves? We agree therefore with Nagel, "Human Purpose" 38-40, in seeing no particular connection between the "collaborative articulation" subthesis, and Fuller's main thesis of the merging of fact and value which it is offered to support. And see further, on this point, H. L. A. Hart *infra* n. 149.

[144] *The Law in Quest of Itself* (1940) 5-6. *Cf.* his "Positivism" *passim*.

[145] "Mid-Century" 471, n. 26.

[146] Citing Wild, *Plato's Enemies*.

[147] *Cf.* Fuller, "Human Purpose" 68ff.

[148] See Stone, *Social Dimensions*, Ch. 1, on the basic distinction between sociological study of what moves men to action (including their "operative ideals"), on the one hand, and a normative or evaluating study of such ideals on the other.

means, the materials it works on are humanly set purposes or goals, the product of human will, not of rational discovery. They do not *necessarily* have either universality or immutability, nor, indeed, any necessary relation to morals or justice. They might indeed, conceivably, be part of "some hideously immoral code of oppression whose immorality is appreciated by those called in to interpret it".[149]

This contrast, despite his own belief that his position is similar to Wild's, is confirmed by Fuller's insistence that "eunomics", his science of "good order and workable arrangements", has "no commitment to 'ultimate ends' ".[150] By this he means not that eunomics is "indifferent to ends", but only that after study of the relations of means and ends on a particular problem, "men may still differ as to what ought to be done and that eunomics cannot promise to resolve all such differences."[151] Thus far, then, Fuller's "eunomics" cannot transcend men's actual purposes at the given time, and the interplay of ends and means in their pursuit. It smacks indeed somewhat of positivism, as he understands and frowns on it, rather than of the natural law, to which he feels drawn. As Ernest Nagel very correctly observes, "the mere existence of purposes and goals does not settle the question what ought to be done when a moral problem arises."[152]

So far, however, is Fuller from recognising such positivist implications of his positions that he rejects "the cultural relativist" view that "man's 'nature' is shaped entirely by the cultural matrix".[153] If that view were correct, he thinks, breach or disturbance of the matrix would cause man to disintegrate and fall apart drastically; and if regularities nevertheless persist despite change in social forms, these must reflect some constancy in the "nature" of man. This latter inference, however, is only warranted if such regularities survive a sudden traumatic breach of the matrix. Mere social change, even if substantial, will not quite do, since the cultural matrix might itself be moulded by the change, as the matrix in turn moulds men.[154] The survival, moreover, would have to be so persistent as not to be explicable as due to the continuing effects of the preceding conditioning. On neither head does his argument support the conclusion as to constancy in the nature of man, on which he wishes to think that

---

[149] *Cf.* H. L. A. Hart, "Law and Morals" 629, who also acutely observes at 613 that the "intelligent" decision which emerges from the mutual testing of ends and means, is equally to be found "inside a system dedicated to the pursuit of the most evil aims". We add that insofar as Fuller seeks to distinguish his "eunomics" from natural law by starting from men's actual purposes, he would, to be consistent, have to take account of the learning (controversial, yet surely too important to be ignored) concerning men's persistent drives to death and masochism such as that which Theodor Reik built on that of his teacher Freud. See Reik's *Masochism in Modern Man* (transl. M. H. Beigel and G. M. Kurth, 2 impr. 1949) developing the thesis that "two instincts dominate organic life and determine life and death of every living being—the sexual urge, the Eros, and the death instinct, the aggression", and that masochism emerges as an accommodation of the death instinct with the Eros, "diverting its destructive effects from the ego into the outer world". (*Id.* 31ff.) If this aspect is brought into account, it would become very clear that Fuller's position on the relation of the "is" and the "ought", if he really carried it through, would leave him very far from the theory of Wild with which he purports to agree.

[150] "Mid-Century" 478.

[151] *Id.* 480.

[152] Nagel, "Fact and Value" 81.

[153] "Mid-Century" 481. We discount, as trivialising the whole point, any suggestion that its gist rests on the word "entirely".

[154] Even sudden change might not suffice as a test case, if the disturbance were not grave enough. We must surely, on any view, and in any case, recognise that conditioning by the matrix will continue to have effects even after breach of the matrix.

"eunomics reaches common ground with the natural law theory of the source of ethical judgments".

This leap over from his own "is-ought merger" grounded on *humanly set* purposes to the assertion that such a merger arises from constancies and regularities in *"the nature of man"* seems to indicate an implicit commitment to the core doctrines of natural law which, explicitly, Fuller rejects. Either his "eunomics" is a kind of speculative social-psychological description of the transformation of men's purposes, in which case it is wrong to confuse the psychological operations described with the doctrine of the immanence of moral values in reality. Or, if his "eunomics" is to have a bearing on this doctrine, it must take him squarely into the assertion that *there are ultimate ends*, which we can discover, towards which the results of this process *ought to move*, and by which these results are to be evaluated. It is surely a *non sequitur*, if not a contradiction, to deny that "eunomics" can say anything decisive about ultimate ends, and then also to assert that men's efforts "to explain and justify their decisions" will generally "pull those decisions towards goodness, by whatever standards of ultimate goodness there are",[155] and that the common law *must* "work itself pure from case to case" towards "a more perfect realisation" of "equity" rather than "iniquity".[156] All sides in these controversies would surely agree that *men ought to strive* towards more perfect equity, rather than iniquity, but the questions here are how this "ought" can be drawn from the facts of men's striving, and how, anyhow, we should recognise "equity"? Once Fuller excludes, as he does, the question of "ultimate ends", and rests on men's actual purposes, he cannot resolve the dichotomy of "is" and "ought" in a similar manner to Wild's.

Where, then, are we to place Fuller's position in the present context of possible *rapprochements* between positivism and iusnaturalism? In his own later version, obviously carefully considered in view of the "misunderstanding" of his position of which he complains,[157] he *rejects* the following notions:

1. the notion that the demands of natural law can be the subject of an authoritative pronouncement;
2. the notion that there is something called "the natural law" capable of concrete application like a written code;
3. the notion that there is a "higher law" transcending the concerns of this life by which human enactments must be measured and declared invalid in case of conflict.

Furthermore, from earlier statements[158] we might also cull: 4. that he is not "advocating the doctrine of natural rights"; 5. the omnibus but rather un-

---

[155] "Positivism" at 636.

[156] *Cf.* Nagel, "Fact and Value" 81.

[157] "Rejoinder" 82, replying to Nagel, "Fact and Value". The deep obscurities and inconsistencies we here examine may perhaps explain some of the "misunderstanding" and failure of "communication" of which he has complained. And see "Rejoinder" 83, 84, 86, 87, 95. Intellectual contact is difficult enough between self-conscious natural lawyers and their colleagues: the difficulty is vastly increased with the unselfconscious natural lawyer, and multiplied again when he explicitly denies his implicit position. The full value of Fuller's contributions is unlikely to emerge unless these difficulties are faced.

Cf. as to Fuller's assumptions concerning the term "positivist", E. Nagel, articles cited, esp. "Fact and Value" at 77, 78, and "Human Purpose" at 32ff., 43. Fuller's view has led him (Nagel thinks) to do battle "with straw men" (32), when he charges positivists, merely because they are such, with rejecting the objective nature of values, or the relevance of facts to values.

[158] *Op. cit. supra* n. 133, at 100-101.

helpful declaration that he is not undertaking to defend "all the things that have been said" in the name of Aquinas.

It is unfortunate, in view of the potential fruitfulness of the questions raised by Fuller's work, that these rejections do not explain the internal contradictions above examined. They are also in themselves indecisive on several critical points. Thus, No. 1 tells us that he rejects any authoritative pronouncement, but does it also deny the possibility of discovery and demonstration? No. 2 denies that natural law can be "capable of concrete application like a written code"; but does it also deny that natural law exists as a binding order? No. 3 denies that there is a "higher law" transcending "the concerns of this life" declaring human laws conflicting therewith invalid: but does this mean that he believes that there is such a "higher law" but that it does not declare such laws invalid? Or that there is a "higher law" *not* transcending these concerns, declaring such human law invalid? Or that there is no such "higher law" at all?

We have to conclude, therefore, that an approach through actual human purposes and "the forms of social order", does not seem to lead to any well-based *rapprochement* between the revived natural law and its critics. It may, indeed, in its present form, introduce additional polemical cross-purposes, so long as it continues explicitly to deny basic positions on which it nevertheless implicitly proceeds.

§12. CREATIVE COEXISTENCE? We have been speaking hitherto about points of possible *rapprochement* between bodies of ideas to which most positivists and natural lawyers are respectively committed. Obviously, quite apart from the bodies of ideas on which the standpoints divide, individual thinkers of each side may find points of orientation in the store of ideas of the other. Not even the most fanatical positivist can really deny that the *Summa* is a vast reservoir of ideas relevant to reasoned argumentation on ethical matters. And while the constant prodding of positivists to "stand up and be counted" ethically cannot vindicate natural law against positivist attack, it forces their common attention to their common concern with justice, and the criticism of positive law. This in itself should reduce distance, and suggest possibilities of continued dialogue. For, as already observed, most positivists have not denied the problems of justice. Some today hold to modern shades of utilitarianism, others adhere to "good grounds" ethics, others frankly affirm a personal faith and commitment, others have existentialist tinges. All may have reached merely staging-posts, and even mistaken ones at that; and some may be entirely sceptical about the journey which they nevertheless feel bound to make. Yet it is important that all thoughtful men should continue along this road; for wherever its end may be, there lies, in important part, the destiny of man in an ominously changeful world.

CHAPTER 8

UNCOMMITTED RELATIVISM IN MODERN THEORIES OF JUSTICE

§1. MODERN TRENDS TO RELATIVISM. Relativism, in general, means rejection of absolute standards, principles, or values; and this rejection may be explicit, or it may be only implied in the assertion of standards, principles or values which vary with time and place. In ethical relativism, and in related theories of justice, the moral values are not absolute, but are determined by certain variables, usually some aspects of particular historical situations. Insofar as scepticism tends to reject assertions of truth or value made in absolute terms, relativism and scepticism usually go together. Insofar as the variables stressed are usually in the stream of time, relativism often accompanies historicism (using that term in a non-pejorative sense). Insofar as these variables are usually of social phenomena, relativism often accompanies sociologism (in a similar sense). Insofar as the rejection of absoluteness tends to press judgment on to the level of practical experience, relativism is also closely related to pragmatism.[1]

Relativist ideas bearing on justice may spring (in an intellectual sense) from any of the great variety of ideas current in the wide field of thought in which ethical relativism is found. When, in 1917, Max Weber denied that values could be scientifically demonstrated in the fields of sociology and economics, and asserted that social phenomena could be explained only up to the point of ultimate valuation, he was denying the availability for ethical judgment of such absolute criteria as he thought to be available in the natural sciences.[2] A year later, Oliver Wendell Holmes Jr. bathed the classical natural law in relativist acid, proclaiming truth for him to be the system of his own intellectual limitations. The appearance of objectivity (he thought) associated with natural law arose from "the fact that I find my fellow man to a greater or lesser extent (never wholly) subject to the same *Can't Helps*". The "Can't Helps" of each man have a common root in time, what we most love and revere being generally determined by our early associations. It followed for him that "deep-seated preferences cannot be argued about", and that "beliefs and wishes have a transcendental basis in the sense that their foundation is arbitrary".[3]

In this, as on so many other matters, Holmes showed an oft-noted sensitivity to contemporary movements of juristic thought. Already, indeed, as the *fin de siècle* moved fully into our own century, intellectual, political, social and religious life in Europe moved into a phase of wide-ranging

---

[1] There is, of course, no significant connection between ethical relativism and the relativity theory of modern physics.

[2] See M. Weber, "*Der Sinn der Wertfreiheit der soziologischen und ökonomischen Wissenschaften*" in his *Gesammelte Aufsätze zur Wissenschaftslehre* (1922); and see the edited transl. by E. A. Shils and H. A. Finch, in *Max Weber on The Methodology of the Social Sciences* (1949).

[3] See O. W. Holmes, Jr., "Natural Law" (1918) 32 *H.L.R.* 40, at 40-41.

and deep divisions. Whether this was due to the spread of literacy, the implications of liberal democracy, the unsettlement of impending war and technological innovation, or to a dialectic of reaction against the comparative stability of Europe since the Congress of Vienna, or to the disillusionment which accompanied and followed the First World War, need not detain us. What is here important is that amid the growing conflict of ideologies, some intellectuals, being unable to identify themselves (or for that matter the intellectual function itself) with the circulating ideologies, began to devote themselves, not to the elaboration of more conflicting ideologies, but to what might now be called an uncommitted or non-aligned examination of the existing ones.[4]

Movements such as culturalism, historicism and relativism were each of them types of uncommitted approach, studying the relations between asserted values and the environments in which values are asserted and in which they operate. Such uncommitted activity, no doubt, also had its attractions as betokening an appreciation of the richness and variety of intellectual and spiritual life in modern society,[5] so that the open-minded path of uncommitted analysis did not appear to the intellectual as alienating him from his society. On the contrary, the uncommitted examination often presented itself as an effort to mitigate or find an escape from the struggle of intransigent dogmatisms, by seeking common grounds, or at least sufficient common terms to permit dialogue to be resumed, and sufficient tolerance to encourage its resumption.[6] It is as a part of the movement for analysis and comparison of ideologies or of concepts or terms whose use is normally ideologically conditioned, that we can best understand the work of Gustav Radbruch.[7]

One further preliminary point is to be made. The relativism with which we are here concerned is one which reaches to the climax of judgment, and does not merely affect the interlocutory processes preceding judgment. We agree with Arnold Brecht that "if one were to call a relativist everyone who holds that *something* in justice is relative, is dependent on customs, laws, history, climate, environment or the like, there would be no writer on justice from ancient to recent times who would not deserve that description".[8] At any rate, in the specific sense of relativism in the theory of justice, its essence is the explicit or tacit denial that there are any absolute standards of justice. So that even theories, such as that of Rudolf Stammler, which stress the variable content of natural law from age to age, are not within the present topic.[9] For even if Stammler had given more attention to this variable content, he would still insist that this content is held within certain absolute values of natural law, which he formulates as the principles of respect and participation.

§2. RELATIVISM IMPLICIT IN OFFERED CRITERIA OF JUSTICE. Weber and

---

[4] The traditions of aristocracy and enlightenment still associated with European intellectual movements also encouraged postures of non-commitment to ideologies which came to have wide plebeian currency.

[5] See P. Valéry, 4 *Variétes* (1937) 35, 36.

[6] See H. Bergson, *Les Deux Sources de la Morale et de la Religion* (1932). And see on this positive contribution of relativism as fostering "objectivity, tolerance, and sympathy for the varieties of human experience", R. Gordis, "Natural Law and Religion" in Cogley (ed.), *Natural Law* 240, at 241-42.

[7] See *infra* §§6ff.

[8] See Brecht, "Relativism" 49ff.

[9] See R. Stammler, *Wirtschaft und Recht nach der materialistischen Geschichts-*

Holmes illustrate the display of relativism in ethics by explicit rejection of absolute values. In a multitude of other modern writers from William James[10] to our own day, the relativist position is seen as an affirmative assertion of certain criteria of judgment in their nature non-absolute, whether or not they are *asserted* to be relativist. Thus, the hedonistic criterion of Jeremy Bentham, although Bentham offered it as universally valid and therefore in a sense absolute, was by its very dependence on individually felt pains and pleasures a relativist criterion. Certainly Roscoe Pound's view of justice as expressible in terms of a scheme of interests pressing in a society at a particular time and place, was as devoid of absolute elements as its distinguished and lamented author could make it.[11] And because of the great influence of this writer through virtually the whole of the first half of the twentieth century, his position (to be examined fully in the next Chapter) may serve here to characterise briefly a kind of relativism in practice which nevertheless acknowledges no allegiance to it in theory.

In his comparatively late work, *Justice According to Law*, in 1951,[12] Pound came as near as he ever did to the taking of an explicit position as between relativism and absolutism. While he generally agreed that justice is best thought of in terms of an "ideal relation between men", he was concerned to stress that it is better to think of "*an* ideal relation", rather than "*the* ideal relation". The contrast thus pointed to is presumably between a relation asserted as the *only* one deserving to be acknowledged, and a relation asserted as so deserving even though other relations may *also* correctly be said to be "ideal relations". In that case each such "ideal relation" would presumably be valid for particular social situations. And this "relativist" reference seems also indicated by Pound's observation that it is no longer possible, as nineteenth century thinkers assumed to do, to offer theories of "*the* ideal relation", since any such theory is now "not the settled and no longer debated question" we thought it was.[13]

Yet his same discussion went on to characterise as "give-it-up philosophy" or "post-war theories of futility", the view "that an ultimate theory of values cannot be found", that "values are purely subjective" and that "objective values cannot be reached".[14] The illustrations of such "post-war" phenomena, from ancient Greece onwards, put beyond doubt the reference to "relativism" at this point; and this is again confirmed by Pound's contrast of these with "the Kantian idea of justice, the liberty of each individual adjusted to the like liberty of others" which (he asserted) under various verbal guises became "*the*[15] ideal relation" for most nineteenth-century jurists. From the explicit dislike and the implicit disagreement in such terms as "futility" and "give-it-up philosophy", it would appear that Pound was here rejecting what he appeared a few pages before

---

auffassung (1896) 185. And see the *Lehre* discussed Brecht, "Relativism" 52; and *supra* Ch. 6, §§1-9.

  10 See *infra* Ch. 9, §2.

  11 See R. Pound, *Justice According To Law* (1951) 1-31. And see for other contemporary examples, H. Kelsen, *What is Justice?* (1957) 1-24; W. Friedmann, *Legal Theory* (4 ed. 1960) 303-324.

  12 Pound, *op. cit.* 19-31. The positions here discussed had been taken by Pound for more than a generation before then. They are best assembled in the cited work.

  13 *Id.* 19-21.

  14 *Id.* 22-23: On the merits of this kind of criticism, as aimed e.g. at Kelsen, see Stone, *Legal System* 135-36; *supra* Ch. 7, §7. esp. n. 109; S. I. Shuman, *Legal Positivism* (1963) 182-190, esp. 182-83. And see also on the strain of absolutism in Pound's own theory *infra* Ch. 9, §8, esp. n. 51.

  15 Itals. supplied.

to accept when he insisted that justice is "*an* ideal relation" rather than "*the* ideal relation".

Finally, however, Pound's theory of justice must be characterised by its own orientation and elements rather than by Pound's description of it. Our analysis in Chapter 9 will show that its apparatus is offered above all *both* to minimise subjectivity, *and* to avoid the need for resort to absolutes. And in his 1951 discussion he repeats this basis of his theory, justifying it as a method based on "experience developed by reason, and reason tested by experience". These, he says, "have taught us how to go far toward achieving a practical task of enabling men to live together . . . with the guidance of a working idea, even if that working idea is not metaphysically or logically or ethically convincingly ideal".[16] For in the ordering of human relations through politically organised society, the search is for "the more inclusive order", and this "down to the present" means "to reconcile and adjust (men's) desires or wants or expectations so far as we can, so as to secure as much of the totality of them as we can". Insofar as the exposition of his essentially practical method discloses a theoretical basis, this must finally be regarded as a relativist basis, as fuller analysis will show; and Pound's position is thus an interesting example of explicit non-acceptance of relativism, by a jurist whose theory is basically relativist.[17]

§3. THE ANCIENT BEGINNINGS OF RELATIVISM. Pound's view that the denial of ultimate values is a recurring phenomenon of post-war disillusionment, from Pyrro's doctrines after the Peloponnesian War down to our own times, is probably very oversimplified. In any case, it must be clear that the roots of ethical relativism are to be found far back in the ancient world, notably with Protagoras of Abdera (485-411 B.C.) in the golden age of Pericles.

With Protagoras, it was perhaps the interplay of Greek and foreign customs in a city on the northwestern periphery of the Hellenic world which inspired relativism. "Of all things," said Protagoras, "the measure is Man, of the things that are, that they are, and of the things that are not, that they are not."[18] Read with other texts of Protagoras,[19] this is thought to mean (as regards law and justice) that the question what is law in a political society depends on approval by the citizens duly assembled, for as long as a later assembly does not express a different opinion. Flückiger

---

[16] *Id.* 29.

[17] No doubt the explicit non-acceptance of relativism is intended to reserve his position in case some absolute ideal ("*the*" ideal relation among men) acceptable to him might eventually arise by agreement among the philosophers. See *ibid.* Yet it is clear that he regards this contingency as too remote to have much bearing on juristic problems.

Radbruch commented in this connection that Pound's "observations about the purpose of law stop where a real legal philosophy ought to begin". ("Anglo-American Jurisprudence through Continental Eyes" (1936) 52 *L.Q.R.* 530, 542). He attributed this to "Anglo-Saxon mistrust" of "general theories of legal philosophy", the tendency to believe that the individual case "bears its law in itself", and the fear that "preconceived ideas" may block "the teaching of infinitely varying experience" (*id.* 543).

[18] See Freeman, *Ancilla* 125, fragm. 1; Plato, *Theaetetus* 152. Alfred von Verdross (*Abendländische Rechtsphilosophie* (1958) 17), accepting Wilhelm Nestle's view that the word "*chrema*" in this fragment means, not "thing" but "quality" or "value", would translate it as: "Man is the measure of all qualities and evaluations". He supports this by another *dictum* attributed to Protagoras by Plato, *Theaetetus* 167: "Whatever appears to a state to be just and fair, so long as it is regarded as such, is just and fair to it". See A. von Verdross, *op. cit.* 17.

[19] See *ibid.*

points out that the relativism of Protagoras refers primarily not to the fact that judgment is subjective to each individual, but to the perpetual change-fulness of the world. "Nothing is in itself *one* but everything is always in becoming in relation to something else"[20] (*"dass nichts an sich eines sei, sondern alles ist immer werdend im Verhältnis zu anderem"*). In the context of his age, Protagoras' doctrine was a revolutionary break from the conception of *Themis*—a law divine in origin, and therefore immutable. And as a radical he was fortunate in enjoying the tolerance, protection and patronage of Pericles, himself a statesman of high intellectual capacity and integrity.[21]

Erik Wolf makes the point, which it is well to keep open for most relativists, that Protagoras was neither a nihilist sceptic nor a frivolous juggler with ideas, but was inspired rather by a real love of truth driving him to inquire critically into hitherto unexamined claims to universal validity.[22] The moral doubting which he brought to rigid traditional beliefs rested on the intellectual conviction that truth in the field of ethics and politics was relative. But though relative, these truths were not for him arbitrary, much less non-existent. In his reported dialogue with Socrates,[23] there is a myth about the birth of the state which makes clear that in Protagoras' view lawmaking does not rest on the arbitrariness of men, but on their sense of law. It is as a means of deriving unequivocal norms from this sense that assemblies of the people are necessary to settle the law for that people. And Protagoras saw his own role, along with that of educators and rhetors, as that of ensuring that the people in their assemblies were well advised in matters of state, and the art of public affairs.[24] This is very different from the radicalism of a Gorgias, who, according to Isocrates, "had the hardihood to say that nothing whatever exists",[25] and who set in the place of justice (*dike*) the equity (*epikeia*) of each case based on the opinions (*doxai*) to which the rhetors are able to lead the assembly or tribunal.[26]

§4. GENERAL CHARACTER OF TWENTIETH CENTURY JURISTIC RELATIVISM.
We shall see that the most elaborate modern relativist theory of justice is that of Gustav Radbruch. Of course, relativist theories have been no more homogeneous in the twentieth century than they were in ancient Greece. Yet it is clear that there are certain features which seem to recur whenever relativists take the stage, even when their entry is from quite opposite directions.
A. *The Mood.*

One of these features is to be characterised in terms of mood, rather than intellectual doctrine—a mood of humility and self-abasement in face of the achievements of natural science, and of the apparent limitations of social (including juristic) science. This humility is often accompanied by a deep sense of responsibility before tasks unfulfilled, of which impatience

---

[20] Flückiger, 1 *Geschichte* 99, referring to Plato, *Theaetetus* 157.
[21] Pericles entrusted to him the making of laws for the daughter-city of Athens, Thurioi in Lower Italy. See E. Wolf, 2 *Griechisches Rechtsdenken* (1952) 20.
[22] *Id.* 24.
[23] See Plato, *Protagoras* 320 C ff. We assume for our purposes that the Platonic Protagoras is at least as accurate an intellectual portrait as the Platonic Socrates. For fuller analyses of the meaning of this myth, see W. Jaeger, "Praise of Law", in Sayre (ed.), *Modern Legal Philosophies* 352 at 362; and Wolf, *op. cit. supra* n. 21, at 35-44.
[24] See A. von Verdross, *op. cit.* 17ff.
[25] See Freeman, *Ancilla* 127, fragm. 1.
[26] A. von Verdross, *op. cit.* 18; E. Wolf, 2 *op. cit.* 62.

with the continued philosophical debates about ultimate values is only the reverse side. Some of this mood lies, as we have seen, behind Roscoe Pound's wavering stance between relative and absolute values. But the best expression of this, at a crucial point in the growth of twentieth-century relativism, is Hermann Kantorowicz's characteristically passionate manifesto of 1908. Science, he said, cannot remove the need to choose between various viewpoints; it can only enlighten choice by demonstrating the consequences of each alternative offering.

> As practical lawyers we have long been accustomed to being conscientious trustees of other people's interests. As theorists we must, in severe self-discipline, assume the corresponding procedure, that is, relativism. Only through relativism, confining itself strictly to theory, will our science become a science. Only through relativism, sufficiently limiting the field from the outset, can results of general validity be attained. Only through relativism will the insoluble controversy on ultimate value judgments be eliminated to make room for the only worthy controversy—that on facts and relations. Only through relativism will the pernicious impulses of our discussions become their harmless subjects. Only through relativism will 'normative science', that fruitless hobby of zealots, become the 'science of the normative'.[27]

B. *Intellectual Recoil from Assertion of Absolute Values, especially of Natural Law.*

While the relativist impatience of mood confronts all theories of justice offered as absolutes, it tends to recoil most vigorously from natural law formulations. And the influence of Hans Kelsen's intellectual campaign against natural law has fallen little short of that of his theory of law as a pyramid of norms with a "hypothetical" basic norm at its apex. As Kelsen saw it, indeed, positivism and epistemological relativism stand together against the doctrines of natural law and metaphysical absolutism. As a matter of epistemology, positive law can have only relative-hypothetical foundations; to seek absolutely valid foundations is to confuse positive law and natural law.[28] Epistemology requires us to recognise (he urges) "the ultimate enigma" and the unsurpassable limitations of human knowledge before it. For him even validity of a norm as law is validity only within the system, and since each legal system rests only on a hypothetical basic norm, is only relative to that basic norm.[29] This is even more the case for questions of justice (and similar values) which "cannot be answered by means of rational cognition", but are "determined by emotional factors . . . valid only for the judging subject and therefore relative only". Answers will vary with men's religious, philosophical, and political outlooks, and will thus often be "different from one another and mutually irreconcilable". And they will still be only relative even if, in a particular society, there may be a wide consensus on the answers at a particular time.[30]

---

[27] H. Kantorowicz, *"Probleme der Strafrechtsvergleichung"* (1907-08) 4 *Monatsch. für Krim. und Strafr.* 65, 102-103, quoted and transl. Brecht, "Relativism" 54, 67. The influence of Kantorowicz on Radbruch will sufficiently appear hereafter; Radbruch dedicated the *Rechtsphilosophie* to him in 1932, as well as two editions of the preliminary *Grundzüge der Rechtsphilosophie.*

[28] Kelsen, *Theory* 396 (Appendix on "Natural Law Doctrine and Legal Positivism"). See also his *What is Justice?* (1957). Of course, these doctrines had been repeatedly declared in the preceding decades.

[29] *Theory* 433-34; and for the last sentence, *id.* 394-95.

[30] *Id.* 6ff.; *What is Justice?* (1957) 4, 7.

C. *Tolerance of Pluralism of Values as a Relativist "Absolute".*

We shall see that Radbruch, in a lifetime of thought centred on relativism, believed at certain points that he had wrought the "miracle" of drawing certain absolutes out of the *"Nichts"* of relativism.[31] However this be, the principle of tolerance of divergent value-standpoints is certainly a specific feature of most relativist positions. And this is only superficially a paradox. For obviously the relativist rejection of absolutes implies that no one can be dogmatic about his answers; moreover, from another stand-point, the survival of relativism itself as a social force depends on the vindication of this principle.

Few passages in Kelsen's voluminous writings have approached in noble emotion his recent statement of this point:

The particular moral principle involved in a relativistic philosophy of justice is the principle of tolerance, and that means the sympathetic understanding of the religious or political beliefs of others—without accepting them, but not preventing them from being freely expressed. . . . I cannot say what justice is, the absolute justice for which mankind is longing. I must acquiesce in a relative justice and I can only say what justice is to me. Since science is my profession, and hence the most important thing in my life, justice, to me, is that social order under whose protection the search for truth can prosper. 'My' justice, then, is the justice of freedom, the justice of peace, the justice of democracy—the justice of tolerance.[32]

D. *The Uncommitted Examination of Competing Values, as Expressions of Competing Ideologies or Weltanschauungen.*

If it is denied that any of the various competing systems of ultimate values are capable of rational demonstration, scientific examination is relegated to lesser (though still important) tasks. These include (1) identification of the postulates upon which each of the main competing systems proceeds; (2) the placing of each such postulate in the social setting in which it has arisen, including the ideologies and *Weltanschauungen* with which it is associated; (3) exposure of the consequences which respectively flow from such postulates if these are consistently maintained; (4) clarification of the means appropriate for carrying out the directives from such postulates.

Among the earliest of the modern juristic relativists, Georg Jellinek in 1900 offered the generalisation that the principal conceptions of the state, and of the values which the state is a means of realising, were two great *Weltanschauungen*—the individualistic-atomistic, on the one hand, and the collectivistic-universalistic, on the other.[33] And in 1904, Emil Lask applied this specifically to the conception of "justice", which was, he said, a repository of the judgments rendered on law by the various *Weltanschauungen* prevailing in the course of history.[34] We shall observe these themes reechoing in the systems of Radbruch, and others.

§5. RELATIVISM IN ANGLO-AMERICAN JURISPRUDENCE. Writing between the world wars, Gustav Radbruch somewhat sweepingly declared that even the most advanced Anglo-American juristic thought of that time stopped where a real philosophy of law ought to begin. He attributed this to distrust lest general theories of legal philosophy should impede the rather intuitive

---

31 See *infra* §10.   32 *What is Justice?* (1957) 10, 22-24.
33 G. Jellinek, *Allgemeine Staatslehre* (1900) 174.
34 E. Lask, *Rechtsphilosophie* (1904) 24, quoted and transl. Brecht, "Relativism" 53.

process of developing law through the experience arising from the decision of concrete individual cases. But he thought that "when shattered social conditions press for quick regulation through the legislature, general theories about the aims and instruments of law, a legal philosophy and a legal policy, must be at hand".[35] In this respect, he thought that the more "volcanic" conditions of the United States explained the rebirth of legal philosophy earlier in that country. And he commended to that country a shift from the "all too rigid natural law principles", and the adoption of a type of thought which he described in terms which obviously summarised his own thinking at the time.

> Its legal philosophy must do justice to the paradoxes, antinomies and relativities of life. It must be *antinomic*, that is to say, it must not cloud the irremovable contradictions between the highest legal values, such as justice, expediency, legal security. . . . It must be *relativistic*, that is to say, it must present the various conflicting concepts of law and life, such as the authoritarian, the liberal, the democratic and the socialist concept side by side, without one-sidedly identifying itself with the one or the other. And it must be *decisionistic*, that is to say, it must vigorously appeal to responsible decision of the individual legislation between such antinomies and relativities. Such a philosophy of law can become a driving force of its own in the striking struggle of conflicting social energies.[36]

If Radbruch hoped for any results from this blueprint for an American philosophy of law, he must have been disappointed *as a relativist* (though perhaps later in his life, as an advocate of natural law, he may have been glad of this disappointment). As between "higher law" and relativist philosophies in the United States, the movement since 1936 has tended, as Arnold Brecht still observed in 1954, not to favour relativism in political and juristic thought.[37] Whatever may be "the anti-dogmatic attitude of Americans in other precincts of life", Brecht said, "their acceptance of inalienable individual rights and of general democratic principles and ideals is highly dogmatic in character. . . ." And he added that this "unconscious dogmatism is a very valuable antidote against the political dangers of relativism . . .", even when it results in superficiality in scholarly work.

Indeed, the relativist strands in American juristic thought have, if anything, weakened since 1936. Though pragmatism and relativism are not the same thing, the pragmatisms of William James and John Dewey, insofar as they refuse to accept absolute values as controlling experience, represent a similar mood. These, along with the related juristic pragmatism of Pound, were perhaps at their strongest in the decade before Radbruch's plea; if anything, they have waned in influence since. In Pound himself a certain drawing back from the relativist implication of his theory of interests was to be apparent in the 'forties and 'fifties. The more notable American declarations of the relativist position virtually all antedate 1936. It was in 1913 that George Santayana declared that

> to speak of the truth of an ultimate good would be a false collocation of terms; an ultimate good is chosen, found, or aimed at; it is not opined. The ultimate intuitions on which ethics rests are not debatable, for they are not opinions we hazard, but preferences we feel; and it

---

[35] G. Radbruch, "Anglo-American Jurisprudence through Continental Eyes" (1936) 52 *L.Q.R.* 530, 543-44.
[36] *Id.* 544.   [37] Brecht, "Relativism" 60, 62.

can be neither correct nor incorrect to feel them.[38]
It was in 1917 that Holmes described values as our "Can't Helps", and the
underlying thought had been present in his writings long before. It was
before 1935 that Morris Cohen, whose every word was studied by lawyers
as closely as by philosophers, said that "reason . . . cannot determine the
ultimate ends that are a matter of ultimate choice".[39] John Dickinson had
already in 1929 given to the relativist position something of an antinomical
form, declaring that "competing interests have an unexpected habit of
expressing their conflict precisely in the form of an apparent conflict between
these accepted fundamental principles of the law", that "axioms clash",
that general principles have a "significant habit of travelling in pairs of
opposites", and that "all questions of law are ultimately questions of
policy, or rather of opinion about policy".[40] And Karl Llewellyn's call in
1931 for the separation of the study of the "Is" from that of the "Ought"
of law, and the deferment of the latter at least until more knowledge of
the former was accumulated, was based essentially on relativist grounds.
For him "value-judgments" were "in the airy sphere of individual ideals
and subjectivity", of "the flux of changing opinion as to social objectives",
none of which (he thought) science can confirm.[41]

§6. LIMITS OF KNOWLEDGE IN THE REALM OF JUSTICE. The most comprehensive and systematic modern attempt to validate relativist theories of
justice is still that of the German legal philosopher Gustav Radbruch. With
a background of the neo-Kantian philosophy of values of the Heidelberg
school, Radbruch was still sensitive to a wide range of contemporary trends
of thought ranging from Marxism to neo-Thomism, and embracing most
of the major problems of modern law and society which underlie these.
In a sense he accepted the mission of staking out a place in the sun
for the uncommitted but conscientious man in an age of internecine partisanship of closed and conflicting ideologies. This is an important reason for his
prominent place among modern legal philosophers, for the stimulation he
has given to others, and for the fruitfulness of his influence even in its
vicissitudes.[42] This place of his thought as a point both of convergence

---

[38] *Winds of Doctrine, Studies of Contemporary Opinion* (1913) 144.
[39] *Law and the Social Order* (1933) 173, 194.
[40] J. Dickinson, "The Law behind the Law: II" (1929) 29 *Columbia L.R.* 285,
at 296, 298, 313, n. 62.
[41] K. Llewellyn, "Legal Tradition and Social Science Method: A Realist's
Critique", in *Essays on Research in the Social Sciences* (Brookings Institution, 1931)
89, 100, 101, 102, quoted by Brecht, "Relativism" 70, n. 49.
[42] The principal legal-philosophical writings of Radbruch are: *Rechtsphilosophie*
(3rd and "conclusive" edition 1932; posthumous editions expanded with notes added
by the editor, Erik Wolf, and with additional essays, 4 ed. 1950, and 5 ed. 1956);
Einführung in die Rechtswissenschaft (9 ed. 1952); *Der Mensch im Recht* (1957—a
posthumous collection of his essays); *Vorschule der Rechtsphilosophie* (1947—
students' notes of a seminar of Radbruch, authorised by him and publishe₫ under
his name, here cited as *Vorschule*), "La Sécurité en Droit d'après la Théorie
Anglaise" (1936) 6 (Nos. 3-4) *Arch. de Phil. du Droit* 86-99 (here cited as
"*Sécurité*"). For a list of writings about Radbruch's *Rechtsphilosophie* see *Rechtsphilosophie* (5 ed. 1956) 312-313.
    The writer has been fortunate to have at his side while preparing the present
Chapter, his colleague Dr. Ilmar Tammelo, of the Faculty of Law at Sydney. During
the rather critical years in Radbruch's thought, 1944-1948, Dr. Tammelo was in
close scholarly contact with him, as a graduate student and then *Privatdozent* in Legal
Philosophy at Heidelberg. The information and ideas which have thus been made
available to me, both orally and in the form of his lecture notes, have greatly
enriched my treatment, though of course I must accept sole responsibility for the
final analysis.

and irradiation[43] of contemporary juristic ideas is also deeply relevant to an understanding of his relativism.

Radbruch's adult life[44] spanned a period which saw the transformation of European civilisation by the rise of Marxist socialism, Soviet communism, German and Italian fascism, and two disastrous World Wars. Educated at Leipzig and Berlin, he counted the German criminal law reformer Franz von Liszt among his professors, and from 1914 to 1933 himself taught criminal law and legal philosophy in the Universities of Königsberg, Kiel and Heidelberg.[45] During his forced retirement, after being purged in 1933 by the Nazis from his Heidelberg post, he declined several calls to chairs in foreign universities, though he spent an important year of study at Oxford, a fruit of which was his book on the spirit of English law.[46] The book reflected the important influence of this law on his legal philosophical conceptions.[47] Yet in the overall texture of his thought the inspiration which he drew from general philosophy, poetry, mythology and art was no less important than that which came from the law and legal literature of Europe. And this explains much, not only of the wide appeal of his work, but also of the difficulty of finally assessing its intellectual contribution.

Radbruch saw his ethical and political relativism as opposed to "the irrationalist fashions of the times";[48] but by taking his stand on rationalism he did not mean to assert that the world analysed by reason leaves nothing unexplained. He meant that he saw his task as that of "rationally revealing ultimate conflicts and not irrationally befogging them".[49] From this standpoint he thought that legal history and comparative law had discovered a vast manifoldness (*Mannigfaltigkeit*) in the reality of law, and not that

---

[43] Erik Wolf ("Revolution or Evolution in Gustav Radbruch's Legal Philosophy" (1958) 3 *Nat. L. Forum* 1, at 19) and Cattaneo, "*L'Ultima Fase*" at 69 think that "for Radbruch relativism was . . . a corridor, . . . a way of transcendence, necessary to reach beyond interpretations of life and law which had prematurely and uncritically crystallised into so-called philosophical systems".

[44] 1878-1949. *Cf.* on the importance of relating Radbruch's philosophy even more than that of most thinkers to his life and personality, W. Friedmann, "Gustav Radbruch" (1960) 14 *Vanderb. L.R.* 191-209, esp. at 192.

[45] He was Minister of Justice of the German Weimar Republic, 1921-1922 and again in 1923, and was the author of the project of the *Allgemeines Strafgesetzbuch* of 1922.

[46] See G. Radbruch, *Der Geist des englischen Rechts* (3 ed. 1956). Radbruch was mainly influenced, on the philosophical side, by the Heidelberg neo-Kantian philosophers Wilhelm Windelband, Heinrich Rickert, and Emil Lask, and by the Heidelberg sociologist Max Weber. (See *Mensch im Recht* 21.) From the three former he adopted views on the relations between reality and value and on the classification of man's intellectual concerns. From Weber he took perhaps his main relativist posture, as well as the device of using type-concepts ("ideal types") for analysing social reality. See Stone, *Legal System*, Ch. 1, §11; *id.*, *Social Dimensions*, Ch. 3, §§6-7. Later Radbruch found points of contact with existentialist and personalist philosophies, with phenomenology, and with theology influenced by these philosophies. See E. Wolf, article cited *supra* n. 43. He also shows the influence of Karl Jaspers, who had a similar fate at Heidelberg under the Nazis, and of the theologian Paul Tillich, with whom he cooperated at one stage. See *id.* 22, n. 124. Thus, Jaspers' philosophy of "open horizons" or "periechontology" (see his *Von der Wahrheit* (1947) 158-161) and Tillich's meditations on love in relation to justice (P. Tillich, *Love, Power and Justice* (3 imp. 1954)) were congenial for Radbruch. And see for his interests in poetry the collection in G. Radbruch, *Lyrisches Lebensgeleite* (2 ed. 1958).

[47] In 1945 he resumed his academic position at the University of Heidelberg, and as Dean of the Faculty participated in its rehabilitation.

[48] Preface to third and later editions of the *Rechtsphilosophie*.

[49] See the English translation of the third edition of Radbruch's *Rechtsphilosophie* by K. Wilk, in vol. vi, *20th Century Legal Philosophy Series* (1950) 45-224, hereafter cited as "*Legal Philosophy*", at p. 48. Where not otherwise indicated, quotations in English are from this translation.

unitary unequivocal (*eindeutige*) ideal of justice assumed by the doctrines of natural law. The judgment that the content of a particular law is just can be made only for a society at a given time and place, acknowledging a given set of values.[50]

This relativism he thought to be presupposed by democracy. For "democracy refuses to identify itself with a definite political view", since it has no final test of correctness, but accepts the view which for the time being commands majority support. And, conversely, relativism as a practical political programme "demands a democratic State".[51] Certain implications followed. First, relativism imports "a renunciation on the part of theoretical reason", and the recognition of limits on what can be expected from "scientific" thinking. Second, it imports liberalism in the sense that while the state is authorised by majority support to implement a particular policy, the state must also respect the freedoms of opinion, of the press, of science and of religion, through which majority opinion may be brought to change.[52] Third, it imports general tolerance of the viewpoints of others; though Radbruch was eager to stress that this did not mean "cowardice or indolence of moral will", or that tolerance should be granted to intolerance.[53] As a relativist he sought to teach "both determination in one's own attitude and justice toward that of another"[54] though (the present writer would add) it is by no means clear how a relativist can teach this save by exemplarship.[55]

On its negative side, as an unmasking of what Erik Wolf has termed the "conventional lies of civilized humanity", and of the claim that moral values are already finally determined, Radbruch's thesis was scarcely revolutionary, though it was of special importance in disposing of the artificialities of much nineteenth century German idealistic thinking about justice. In its time and place, and as a juristic doctrine, however, its negations were necessary to clear the ground for a new approach to justice from the aspect of the substantial content of law, seeking to avail itself of empirical, social, and practical data for clarifying just solutions.[56] When we seek, however, more positive indications from Radbruch's relativism for the tasks of justice, great difficulties will be found to confront us, due in part to his own intellectual vicissitudes.[57]

---

[50] See *Mensch im Recht* 80-81.

[51] See *Mensch im Recht* 85, *Legal Philosophy* 48, *Rechtsphilosophie* 84 (4 ed. 1950 or 5 ed. 1956: these two editions have identical pagination over their common ground, the fifth, however, including some additional matter at the end. Both will here be referred to simply as "*Rechtsphilosophie*").

[52] See *Mensch im Recht* 83-84.

[53] See *id*. 84-86.

[54] See *id*. 81 and *Legal Philosophy* 48, *Rechtsphilosophie* 84.

[55] It illustrates this difficulty that Radbruch was also convinced that relativism merges into (*mündet in*) socialism, socialism meaning, according to him, "the destruction of all irrational and unreasonable (*irrationellen und unrationalen*) forces", as well as "the liberation of the innate ideological force of the idea, and the leap (*Sprung*) from necessity to freedom". See *Mensch im Recht* 87.

[56] See E. Wolf, article cited *supra* n. 43, at 18-19. Wolf is thus correct in linking Radbruch's work with what Hermann Kantorowicz characterised as "the free law movement", on which see Stone, *Legal System*, Ch. 6, §12.

[57] He took pains in the 1932 edition of his *Rechtsphilosophie* to designate that version as his final word, providing, in case of his death, for a new edition to be issued without changes but supplemented by a postscript which he intended to write. See the Editor's Preface in *Rechtsphilosophie* (4 ed. 1950) at 7. This posthumous edition contained in fact no substantial change, but his editor, Erik Wolf, placed in brackets within the footnotes materials by Radbruch relating to the 1932 edition. He also included four essays by Radbruch apparently written after 1945, and presumably reflecting Radbruch's latest thought. In 1947, however, Radbruch had also authorised the publication of students' notes of his seminar under the title *Vorschule*

Along Heidelberg neo-Kantian lines[58] Radbruch asserted that reality and value are drastically commingled in the "unformed raw material of our experience". "The first achievement of the mind consists in the ego withdrawing from and confronting what is given, and thus distinguishing reality from value." With respect to reality, the mind has four attitudes: the value-blind, the evaluating, the value-relating, and the value-conquering. "By a value-blind attitude of ours, the realm of nature is created out of the chaos of what is given; for nature is nothing but that which is given, as it presents itself when cleared of falsifying evaluations". Deliberate "value-blindness" is thus essential to the thought of natural science.[59] The "evaluating attitude", conscious of the norms which make up the realm of values that confront nature, characterises, when systematically adopted, the philosophy of values in its three branches of logic, ethics and aesthetics.[60] The "value-relating" and "value-conquering" attitudes lie, at very different points, in between the value-blind and the evaluating attitudes.

The "evaluating" attitude within the "value-relating" attitude is "the methodical attitude of the cultural sciences", these "sciences" being dedicated to understanding the relation of all other phenomena to the promotion, maintenance or destruction of values.[61] This attitude is relativist also in the deeper sense, in that values are seen to vary not merely in time and place, but according to discoverable relationships with other social phenomena. The value-conquering attitude, on the other hand, denies both this variability and these relations, and is typified by the major religions, which, he thought, amounted to "ultimate affirmation of whatever exists, smiling positivism that pronounces its 'yea' and 'amen' over all things, love without regard to the worth or worthlessness of whatever is loved".[62] This kind of indifference to the distinction between worth and worthlessness was (he thought) the result of conquest by value over worthlessness, not of blindness to value.

Insofar as "law is a cultural phenomenon, that is, a fact related to value", it can only be understood "like any human creation" as meant to realise its "idea". The question of the justice of law only arises because (as will be discussed in §7 below) "the idea" of law in its final meaning is to be just.[63] This "idea" of law is the standard of evaluation for legal reality, and pertains to the "evaluating attitude".[64]

Methodical dualism led Radbruch, as it led Kelsen and others, to deny the logical derivability of value from reality, of the "ought" from the "is", though he was careful to warn that this did not exclude the "causal" influence of existing facts upon values actually held (in the sense that

der Rechtsphilosophie. While, from a formal point of view, Erik Wolf may be correct in insisting that Radbruch did not regard this last as "a substitute for his main work or even an advance to a new level of his thought transcending the Rechtsphilosophie" (article cited supra n. 43, at 3), this does not establish that on any particular point the Vorschule can be ignored.

[58] See supra n. 46. And see on the present point Legal Philosophy 49, n. 1, Rechtsphilosophie 91, n. 1.

[59] See Legal Philosophy 49-50, Rechtsphilosophie 91-92.   [60] Loc. cit.

[61] Legal Philosophy 50, Rechtsphilosophie 92.

[62] Legal Philosophy 50, Rechtsphilosophie 93. This is one point at which his own love of poetry and mythology led Radbruch into paths difficult to follow. He builds the above on the text of Genesis 1.31: "And God saw every thing that he had made, and, behold, it was very good".

[63] Legal Philosophy 51-52, Rechtsphilosophie 94-96.

[64] Radbruch wished to appropriate the term "philosophy of law" to this evaluating view of the law. It seems desirable to avoid such side-issues. See Stone, Legal System, Intro. §8.

"ideologies are determined by their social settings"). Conversely, he recognised that ideas, once they emerge, are "like Homeric gods" which "descend to the battlefield and fight, powerful forces themselves, side by side with other forces".[65] All this, however, could not alter the *logical* truth that since "statements concerning the Ought may be established or proved only by other statements concerning the Ought . . . the ultimate statements concerning the Ought are incapable of proof". They are "axiomatic",[66] and any argument between opposite views must be scientifically inconclusive.

In such a field the functions of knowledge are limited. First, it may establish the means necessary to realise posited ends, and consider the means proposed with a view to clarifying the end sought. Second, there is the task of clarifying a legal value-judgment by exposing its ultimate presuppositions in terms of *Weltanschauungen*. Third, in systematic development, this would expose all the "conceivable ultimate presuppositions and, consequently, all starting-points of legal evaluation". It would present exhaustively, in their similarities and contrasts, all possible systems of legal evaluation, along with the various types of conceptions of law; all within the framework of the various types of possible *Weltanschauungen*. It would seek not "*the* system of legal philosophy, but the complete systematisation of its possible systems".[67] These functions are consistent with "relativism". They are not concerned with determining the rightness in themselves of a value-judgment or an outlook on values or on the world, but only with rightness in relation to a particular postulated supreme value-judgment, in the context of a particular postulated outlook on values and the world.

Relativism, in short, according to Radbruch, while it aims to produce a body of cogent theoretical knowledge, insists on the limits within which such knowledge is possible. In particular, it requires the renunciation of attempts to establish "scientifically certain" ultimate decisions. Radbruch is careful always to add that this does not exempt the inquirer *as a man* from the duty of reaching such decisions as best he can, by choosing between the possible legal views which emerge from alternative ultimate presuppositions as they are systematically exposed. He even insists that this choice is not at the individual's pleasure but rather according to his conscience. But he thinks that short of the genius who alone could choose with scientific exactitude, the choice cannot be based on demonstrable knowledge.[68]

§7. "JUSTICE" AS THE REALITY OF THE IDEA OF LAW. For Radbruch law is a reality whose meaning is to serve the values (*Rechtswerte*), that is "the idea of law (*Rechtsidee*)". "The idea of law", he thinks, can be none other than "justice".[68a] He further thinks that "the just, like the good, the true, and the beautiful, is . . . a value that cannot be derived from any other value".[69] In relation to justice, Radbruch distinguishes, as have many

---

[65] "All great political changes were prepared or accompanied by legal philosophy". (*Legal Philosophy* 55, *Rechtsphilosophie* 100.)
[66] "They may not be discerned but only professed" (*nicht der Erkenntnis, sondern nur des Bekenntnisses fähig*"). Loc. cit.
[67] *Legal Philosophy* 56, *Rechtsphilosophie* 101.
[68] *Legal Philosophy* 57-58, *Rechtsphilosophie* 102-103. *Cf.* H. Kantorowicz's manifesto, *supra* n. 27, W. Friedmann, *Legal Theory* (4 ed. 1960) 290.
[68a] But see the end of this Section.
[69] *Legal Philosophy* 73. But it is surely confusing to add as Radbruch there does that *in this sense* justice is an "absolute" value.

others since Aristotle, justice as a virtue, or personal quality (as of a "just" judge), which he calls "subjective justice", and justice as a quality of a relation between parties (as of a "just" price) which he calls "objective justice". He regards "subjective justice" as the mentality (*Gesinnung*) which is orientated to the actualisation of "objective justice", as truthfulness is towards the actualisation of truth.[70] It is thus justice as a relation between men (objective justice) with which Radbruch is mainly concerned.[71]

At the core (*Kern*) of justice Radbruch places equality, and he interprets Aristotle's classical distinction between commutative (synallagmatic) justice and distributive justice as an elaboration of the principle of equality. Commutative justice is the absolute equality of performance (*Leistung*) and counter-performance (*Gegenleistung*) between two co-ordinated parties: for example between seller and buyer as to goods sold and price, between damage and compensation, or between guilt and punishment. It is synallagmatic, a reciprocated equality between men viewed as being already *in pari passu*. Distributive justice, on the other hand, refers to the equality which is sought to be achieved through super-ordinated authority as between men in their concrete differences of situation. Here the achievement of equality may have to be sought on the basis of differential treatment grounded upon preexisting inequalities, for instance, of capacity to pay in taxation, or of seniority of service and experience in promotions.[72] Hence "equality" as the core of justice means in this case equality of standard (*Massstab*), having in mind differences of situation preceding the application of the standard. It thus implies difference (*Verschiedenheit*) of treatment according to the differences between situations, not absolute but proportional equality.[73]

Radbruch sees an insurmountable (*unüberwindliche*) paradox in the fact, on the one hand, that the essence of justice is some kind of equality, and therefore implies more or less general standards (*Massstab*);[74] and the "aspiration", on the other hand, that justice must also have regard to

---

[70] What meaning he (as a relativist) would give to "orientation" towards "objective justice" is not elaborated by Radbruch.

[71] Radbruch further distinguishes: justice according to positive law, which he calls "legality" (*Rechtlichkeit*), and justice as the pre- and supra-legal "idea" of law (*vor- und übergesetzliche Rechtsidee*). This is, of course, only Kant's distinction between legality and justice in different words. See *supra* Ch. 3, §§1-2.

[72] See *Vorschule* 23.

[73] See *Mensch im Recht* 90. Some of his elaborations as well as these points themselves seem dubious or unsound. Thus he thought that commutative justice assumes two persons legally co-ordinated (*gleichgesetzt*), whereas distributive justice also assumes at least a third super-ordinated person to determine the differentiation of treatment required. But his further hypothesis that private law is law between co-ordinated persons, based on commutative justice, whereas public law proceeds on distributive justice, seems only approximate if not quite hazardous. And even more serious doubts must be expressed as to the value of the assertion that distributive justice—the *suum cuique*—is the primary form (*Urform*), whereas commutative justice is the secondary form of justice (*Vorschule* 23-24), since before there can be the transactions between co-ordinate parties which commutative justice presupposes, equal legal capacity must have been allotted to them. For if this means merely that legal transactions presuppose capacity of the parties, this is a commonplace; while if it means that there must *necessarily* be differentiation among the legal capacities conferred by the law, it is simply insupportable.

As to Aristotle's formulations, see generally *supra* Ch. 1, §3.

[74] *Id.* 24. He refers to the aspiration to full individualisation as *Billigkeit*. But see for a rather different view, *Rechtsphilosophie* 27, where he sees "justice" as involving deduction from principles, and *Billigkeit* as the intuitive perception from the "*Natur der Sache*" of the "*richtiges Recht*". But these ambiguous concepts leave us still at large. On "the nature of things" doctrines. see *supra* Ch. 7, §6.

individual cases and the nature and situation of individual persons.[75] Though justice can admit different treatment as between different sub-classes of people, this still presupposes at least the comparability (*Vergleichbarkeit*) of the individual persons within the same sub-classes, and therefore some generalisation from their ultimate individuality.[76] He thinks like Stammler (to whom, however, he does not refer at this point), that "justice" as an idea of law is "absolutely and universally valid",[77] but recognises, also like Stammler, that it is only a formal idea, and that therefore it is impossible to derive ready-made legal norms (*fertige Rechtssätze ableiten*) from it. This idea itself cannot tell us, for example, who are to be regarded as equal or unequal in particular respects. Neither does it determine (beyond the requirement of equality) the treatment to be accorded to each sub-class as compared to the others. To fix the content of specific rules implementing equality, other ideas than that of justice must therefore enter. For while justice is "the specific idea of law" the idea of law embraces also two other ideas, namely purpose-conformity (*Zweckmässigkeit*) and legal certainty (*Rechtssicherheit*).[78]

§8. MAIN FACTORS CONTROLLING THE CONTENT OF LAW. As between these last, the fixing of a content for law conforming to its "idea" can be expected, according to Radbruch, only from the element of purpose-conformity; for legal certainty, like justice, is, he says, a universally valid, and hence a formal idea.[79] And since, as will later be elaborated, he thinks that there is no single unequivocal answer to the question what is *the* purpose of law, but only certain alternative answers, corresponding to various *Weltanschauungen*, with no objective means of choosing between them, this content would be reduced to a chaos of divergent individual choices unless this process were checked. It was to keep choices within check that Radbruch saw the idea of legal certainty as the third component of the idea of law. First, this postulate (he thought) is the ultimate justification or validation of positive law, that is of law laid down by established political authority.[80] Second, it directs that rules be so framed that their meaning is objectively determinable and not dependent on subjective value-judgments. Third, it directs that the facts on which the rules are to operate be such that proof of them is practicable. Finally, it directs that the positive law be not lightly or easily changed. The slowness (*Schwerfälligkeit*) of the parliamentary apparatus was, from his point of view, a guarantee of legal certainty.[81]

---

[75] "*Und dennoch wohnt ihr das Bestreben inne, dem Einzelfall und dem Einzelmenschen in ihrer Einzigartigkeit gerecht zu werden.*"

[76] *Mensch im Recht* 91. The present writer does not find this argument cogent insofar as it is directed to justice, as distinct from justice according to law. The basis for individualisation of justice alone could be a norm wholly imagined or divinely laid down, for example, and which *in theory* could differentiate between every case submitted to it, e.g., "love thy neighbour according to his deserts". The association of generality with justice is an imperative not of *justice* as such but of justice according to law. But see *supra* Ch. 1, §6.

[77] *Legal Philosophy* 108-109, *Rechtsphilosophie* 169-170. *Cf.* on the relationship between Radbruch and Stammler, Friedmann, article cited *supra* n. 44, esp. at 196-7.

[78] *Legal Philosophy*, 90-91, *Rechtsphilosophie* 146-147 and *Vorschule* 25.

[79] *Legal Philosophy* 109, *Rechtsphilosophie* 170.

[80] *Legal Philosophy* 108, *Rechtsphilosophie* 169.

[81] See *Vorschule* 28-29. *Cf.* "*Sécurité*" 89, where he stresses that the coverage is not merely security *under* law, but security *of* the law and its institutions. He there specifically included the "vested rights" principle under it.

There is an apparent contradiction between Radbruch's flat assertion, on the one hand, that since legal certainty is only a formal idea it cannot determine the content of law, which must thus be left to the postulate of purpose-conformity, and his insistence, on the other hand, that without the postulate of legal certainty the content of law would be surrendered to the chaos of divergent views of what purpose-conformity demands. What he presumably means is that any legal system, whatever the ethical-purposive basis of its content, must respect the need for legal certainty. But this must surely mean that to that extent the idea of legal certainty (whether or not it is only "a formal idea") not only can but *must* determine part of the content of law. Nor is it any answer to this to try to draw a further distinction between material content, which *Zweckmässigkeit* must control, and *formal* content which the needs of legal certainty must control. For in the present view, the truth rather is that the desiderata of legal certainty are a part of what is involved in the purpose-conformity of particular contents of law, whatever version of the purpose of law be chosen.

It becomes very clear, when Radbruch's notions of "the purpose of law" (*der Zweck des Rechts*) and "purpose-conformity" (*Zweckmässigkeit*) are examined, that they are very different from the superficially related notions of Rudolf von Ihering. Ihering's "purposes", like Pound's "interests", purport to describe the empirical phenomena; and more concretely the psychological phenomena of men's purposes and demands. And insofar as their respective criteria of justice are determined by what these actual purposes and demands are at a particular time and place, these criteria of justice are relativist in the sense that they will yield different contents for "just" rules at each particular time and place.

Radbruch's notion of *Zweckmässigkeit*, on the other hand, has a much less clear empirical reference, even though he himself regarded it (as it has also been regarded by others) as the focal point of relativist modesty and restraint within his entire theory.[82] Indeed, he purports to exclude from it any empirical reference at all. He insists that by *"Zwecke des Rechts"* he does not mean empirically found purposes (*empirische Zwecksetzung*), but rather the idea of the-purposes-that-ought-to-be (*die gesollte Zweckidee*). And this impression is confirmed by his view that the idea of the *Zweck des Rechts* must be sought in ethics,[83] and that it embraces the notion of the common weal (*Gemeinwohl*).[84] In view of this, careful readers of Radbruch are left perplexed as to why he so persisted in treating *Zweckmässigkeit* as if it were an independent notion coordinate (as it were) with *Gerechtigkeit*, rather than a part of that notion,[85] especially in view of the virtual impotence of his notion of formal justice even to check the most outrageous discrimination until content is given to it from

---

[82] *Legal Philosophy* 108, *Rechtsphilosophie* 169.

[83] *Vorschule* 26.

[84] Thus the English translations of *"Zweckmässigkeit"* as "expediency" by K. Wilk, *op. cit.* and as "utility" by W. Friedmann (*op. cit. supra* n. 11, at 145ff., and *supra* n. 44, at 199ff.) cannot be considered as quite adequate.

In Radbruch's own article, *"Sécurité"*, at 87, in 1934, he equivalated his own "Justice" to values expressed in English legal literature as equality and generality, his *Zweckmässigkeit* to those of utility, happiness, subsistence, abundance and well-being; his "legal certainty" to those of authority, peace and order. He translates *Zweckmässigkeit* in his French articles as *"le bien commun"*. But even if the French tongue offered no better alternative, the misunderstandings which this translation has produced with French scholars indicate that this, too, may not be a fortunate translation.

[85] And see *infra* as to Radbruch's later revision of his view.

elsewhere.[86] This, however, appears to have been his position.

The "ethics" in which the *Zwecke* and *Gemeinwohl* were to be sought, Radbruch divided into the theory of moral duties and a related theory of moral goods.[87] There are (he thinks) three types of ethical goods: those of the individual, those of the collectivity, and those of created values. Underlying the first is the individual personality, underlying the second the collective personality of the whole group, and underlying the third the creations of culture (*Kulturwerk*).[88] From the individualistic standpoint, individual values are given highest rank, and those of the *Kulturwerke* and of the collectivity are subservient to personality values. Culture is there but a means of cultivating personality or freedom; the state and the law are but means to secure and promote personality. From the collectivist (or national or supra-individualistic) standpoint, the values of personality and of *Kulturwerke* merely subserve collective values, that is, those of the state and its law. From the standpoint of the creations of culture (which Radbruch also calls the "transpersonal" standpoint) personality values and collective values, including law and the state, subserve cultural values.[89]

This typification of ethical goods, though professedly not empirically derived, bears ample signs of Radbruch's preoccupations during and between two world wars. This is even clearer from his further descriptions. Individualism, he thinks, has three sub-types—the liberal, the democratic, and the socialist. In the liberal sub-type the personality values are, as it were, of infinite worth, so that conflicts involving them cannot be settled merely by counting votes. The democratic sub-type, by contrast, reduces personality value to a level of finite worth so that the combined personality values of a majority prevail over those of a minority. The socialist sub-type tends to enlarge the economic content involved in the promotion of personality values or freedom. He sees the collectivist or *supra*-individualistic view of the group as the foundation of modern authoritarianism, under which the tasks of the state prevail even as against the wishes or interests of the citizens. The transpersonal standpoint of the *Kulturwerk* Radbruch admits to stand apart from the other two in its relation to actual political life. It is not, he thinks, "a programme but a feeling for a way of life".[90] For empirical reasons it seems adequate only for partial communities such as universities, churches or orders.[91]

---

[86] Suppose processed adult brunette female human skin, taken *durante vita*, were found to be a perfect canvas for artists, and a law provided that all female brunettes should on their sixteenth birthday be flayed alive and their skins handed over to appropriate agencies for processing and sale to artists on the register of the Ministry of Culture. Assuming this law were applicable equally to the whole subclasses involved (adult female brunettes and registered artists) the terms of Radbruch's description of formal justice would, we believe, present no obstacle. Perhaps some inkling of these difficulties lies behind Radbruch's invocation, after 1945, of love and mercy. See *infra* §§10, 12. *Cf.* our discussion of Perelman's "formal justice" in Ch. 11, §2.

[87] *Legal Philosophy* 91, *Rechtsphilosophie* 147.

[88] We prefer the above to K. Wilk's rendering as "work value", *Legal Philosophy* 91ff., *Rechtsphilosophie* 147ff.

[89] *Legal Philosophy* 94, *Rechtsphilosophie* 150-151. A group in which individualistic values are dominant Radbruch (following Tönnies) called a "society" (*Gesellschaft*); one dominated by collective values, a "collectivity" (*Gesamtheit*); and one dominated by the culture-bearing group, a "community" (*Gemeinschaft*). *Cf.* on these various *Weltanschauungen* Tammelo, "Justice and Doubt" 392-93.

[90] And therefore (see *Vorschule* 26-27) easier to think of in relation to past societies of which only the cultural patrimony has survived; and even then, we may add, only as reduced to a traditional and easily manipulable form from which many richnesses and antinomies of the original have been sifted off.

[91] *Legal Philosophy* 96-97, *Rechtsphilosophie* 154-155. He denies that, except

As competing sets of ultimate values, these three types of ethical goods press upon each decision-maker. Nor does any hierarchy between them decide the choice in any given social situation. The choice must vary not only with time, place and situation, but also with the sentiment of law (*Rechtsgefühl*), political and party platform, religion or *Weltanschauung*, of the decision-maker. Relativism as a theory exposes the alternative ultimate values and their implications, but the choice between them comes finally from the depth of the chooser's personality, a decision of conscience. Relativism teaches man not what he ought to do, but what is properly involved in what he wants (*was er eigentlich will*); that is, what he wants if he is really consistent with himself once he has decided to adopt one basic purpose rather than another (*wenn er sich dem Gesetz der Folgerichtigkeit unterwirft, konsequenterweise wollen muss*).[92]

Yet at the same time as he presents these as competing values for choice by the individual conscience, Radbruch asserts that

> each of them can be attained only by striving for another. The ultimate end of society is the personality, but personality is among those values which can be attained only if they are not striven for. Personality is but the unexpected reward of selfless devotion to the cause; it is a matter of gift and grace alone . . . acquired by self-forgetting objectivity.

So with national character which is a product of "self-forgetful devotion to universally valid tasks", that is, the tasks not of the supra-individual collectivity but of the culture-bearing transpersonal community. And so with the creations of culture, which finally are the result of an overflow of richness of personality. These three apparently separate purposes of law (says Radbruch) are therefore in reality one single unbreakable ring of purpose, and the choice between them is really only a matter of emphasis on one of the three links or elements of an indivisible whole.[93]

Here again it seems to this writer that Radbruch is sacrificing good sense to dramatic effect. If, indeed, it is the case that the three *Zwecke des Rechts* are but different elements of an indivisible whole, so that at no one time can one be chosen to the exclusion of the other, then this must surely be reflected in the manner in which they should be presented to the choosing mind. There would not then be competing choices in any real sense at all—the alternatives would rather constitute aspects of a single *Zweck*, aspects which must all be considered together, the emphasis as between them being always inspired by what seems necessary to furthering that single *Zweck* in the particular time, place, and circumstances. Yet Radbruch insists that the choice to be made from "the depth" of the chooser's "personality" is not between emphases within one *Zweck*, but between distinct competing *Zwecke*. These contradictions can only be reconciled if we assume that in presenting them as competing *Zwecke* he is talking in terms of *Zwecke* as actually but erroneously pursued by members of a given society, and that he is knowingly repeating their error. But this way of removing the apparent contradiction seems barred to Radbruch by his great insistence (already noticed) that the *Zwecke* which *he* has in mind are not those which men are empirically found to hold, but rather *die gesollte Zweckidee*, the idea of the purposes-that-ought-to-be. And whoever else may be free to neglect the normative import of the competing

---

as a spurious façade for collectivism, it has ever formed a basis of state organisation.

[92] See *Vorschule* 26-27.

[93] *Legal Philosophy* 95-96 *Rechtsphilosophie* 153-154.

"purposes" in this sense, Radbruch certainly is not. He is left therefore asserting that men *must choose among* these competing purposes (which imports that they *can* choose), and simultaneously asserting that these purposes are only an indivisible whole, equal "links in a closed chain" (which surely imports that they *cannot choose one without the others*).

§9. ANTINOMIES BETWEEN THE ELEMENTS OR "IDEAS" OF LAW. Justice, legal certainty and purpose-conformity as elements or ideas which make up "the idea of law", stand, according to Radbruch, in inevitable tension with each other. Despite this common relation to "the idea of law" their directives often come (he says) into conflict, with no principle for determining which shall prevail. This leads to his much-admired (and perhaps over-admired) doctrine of the antinomies within the idea of law.[94]

First, he says, there is an irremovable antinomy between "justice and purpose-conformity". Since, he argues, justice is some kind of equality, it requires some degree of generality of legal rules. Yet the equality achieved even by general rules remains "but an abstraction from actual inequality". And this inequality must be taken into account in seeking purpose-conformity as a basis for the necessary individualisation.[95] The best example of such conflict which he offered was between, on the one hand, the needs of individualisation in administrative action for achieving purpose-conformity; and those of judicial review of such administrative action, for protecting the equality required by "formal justice". Yet the point is not as impressive as it seems. For, as he has himself argued (with more than respectable predecessors), his "formal justice" embraces also distributive (proportional) justice, admitting differentiation of applicable rules, for different concrete situations.[96] If this is so, the argument from justice to "equality" and from "equality" to "generality" of rules, and thence to the antinomy of justice with purpose-conformity by dint of the latter's directives for "individualisation", loses much of its dramatic, as well as its practical, importance. This remains only within the limited area in which purpose-conformity requires the administrator to treat each individual case as unique, that is, where he is given no rule or standard whatever for his guidance. Moreover, there is no self-evident reason at all why, for the most part, purpose-conformity should not require some degree of generality of rule, just as does "equality" itself. And this refers us to the more basic difficulty with Radbruch's position, already adverted to, that his treatment of "justice" and "purpose-conformity" (in the *non*-empirical sense of "purpose") is rather incomprehensible.[97]

Second, Radbruch pointed, with somewhat more cogency, to the antinomy between justice and legal certainty, the latter demanding that

---

[94] Many modern writers, of course, tend to expound juristic problems in terms of sets of antinomies or polarities. See, e.g., W Friedmann, *Legal Theory* (4 ed. 1960) 28ff., and A. Kaufmann, "The Ontological Structure of Law" (1963) 8 *Nat. L. Forum* 79-96. And see Stone, *Legal System*, Ch. 1, §3, esp. nn. 15ff. Work on antinomies in legal thinking is proceeding at the Free University of Brussels under C. Perelman's direction.

[95] See *Legal Philosophy* 109, *Rechtsphilosophie* 170. Radbruch offered as a further illustration the contrasting maxims *"salus populi suprema lex esto"* interpreted to mean that only purpose-conformity counts, and *"iustitia fundamentum regnorum"*. (See *Vorschule* 30.) This assumes, of course, that *"iustitia"* in the second maxim carries the directive for general rules which is really in issue.

[96] His inclusion of *Billigkeit* as a part of justice reinforces the present point. See *supra* n. 74.

[97] See *supra* §8.

the law be applied even if it is unjust (*unrichtig*). On the one side, he says, is the call, "*fiat iustitia pereat mundus*"; on the other, "*summum ius summa iniuria*", in the sense that the strict application of positive law may lead to the worst injustice.[98] Even here, however, Radbruch rather over-played the drama. After all, most of the cases (all of which are in any case marginal) in which the directives of legal certainty would lead to *summa iniuria*, are cases of some defect in the formulation of the rule which was designed to promote legal certainty. If the formulator had shown sufficient skill and foresight, the injustice would not have been perpetrated,[99] and the antinomy would not have arisen at all. On the concrete level of an actual legal system, of course, some contingencies are bound to be so remote that they escape even the wisest human foresight, and to this extent an antinomy is bound to arise. But this is a far less dramatic range than Radbruch suggests; and further, insofar as he is talking on the level not of actualities, but of what is theoretically inescapable, his thesis is questionable even for this modest range.

Third, Radbruch thought that directives of legal certainty must inevitably raise conflicts with individualising purpose-conformity, drawing sharp lines "where life knows only flowing transitions", or defining a situation by *externalia* when what purpose-conformity is really concerned with are inner psychological facts.[100] Though this comes nearest perhaps to a real antinomy of principles, two observations must be made. A part of the field of conflict which Radbruch indicates could be removed by better design of the definitions of positive law. Another part, that touching inner facts, could be removed by due recognition by the legislator of the limits of effective legal action. That "the devil himself knoweth not the mind of man" may sometimes be ground for relying on *externalia* to evidence states of mind; but it is even more often a good reason for not trying to meddle at all with states of mind.

These conflicts which he thought to exist between the directives of justice, legal certainty, and purpose-conformity, could not, in Radbruch's view, be settled by regarding each as having its own self-contained field of operation.[101] Although there are legal rules and situations for which each of them respectively may be the only relevant value, there are also numerous others where more than one of them may operate together and where these irremovable conflicts may therefore arise.[102] And his conclusion in the *Rechtsphilosophie* with respect to the antinomies between the elements of the idea of law, is that in principle (as it were) they "jointly govern

[98] See *Vorschule* 30.

[99] Supposing, for example, the legal definition of accessory to the crime of kidnapping is such as to catch, without qualification, any person assisting the kidnappers to receive without detection the demanded ransom, and a minimum penalty of imprisonment is prescribed for this offence. When the assistant is a minister of religion who knowingly carries the money to them, under pledge not to inform the police, in order to reduce the chance that the kidnappers will, to escape detection, otherwise kill the victim, he might conceivably be prosecuted and convicted. And this would be *summa iniuria*. But this would indicate no inevitable antinomy of legal certainty with justice; it would rather indicate that the rule of positive law was drafted with inadequate care and providence about possibilities that were surely foreseeable.

[100] See *Legal Philosophy* 109-110, *Rechtsphilosophie* 171.

[101] For instance, by saying that justice only tests whether a precept may at all be brought within the concept of law; that purpose-conformity only determines whether its contents are right (*richtig*); and finally, that the directives of legal certainty only determine whether to ascribe validity to it. And see *infra* §§9ff. as to the relation of the first proposition above to his post-1945 positions.

[102] *Legal Philosophy* 110-111, *Rechtsphilosophie* 175.

law in all its aspects" despite these conflicts.[103] They exercise, he said in another place, "a condominium over the law—not in tensionless harmony, but on the contrary in a living relation of tension".[104] And wherever such antinomies arose, the decision-maker must choose between them. This was no defect of a philosophical system. "Philosophy is not to relieve one of decisions, but to confront him with decisions. It is to make life not easy, but on the contrary, problematical".[105] *"Je n'ai pas peur"*, he said in 1937, *"des antinomies irreconciliables; se décider c'est vivre"*.[106]

§10. ABSOLUTES FOR RELATIVISTS. There are many earlier foreshadowings of the now famous search for absolute standards of justice which marked the later years of Radbruch's life, after he had witnessed the horrors perpetrated in Nazi Germany under cover of enacted law.[107] While insisting generally that his relativism was quite formal, he frequently showed drive to give its notions some material content. Erik Wolf has pointed out that Radbruch contemplated, as early as 1906,[108] the possibility that he must recognise some *"supra*-positive" norms. In his Lyon lecture on relativism in legal philosophy, published in 1934, Radbruch drew from his relativism "absolute consequences, namely the traditional demands of the classical natural law",[109] including the principles of liberalism, the rule of law, the division of state powers, the sovereignty of the people, tolerance, and socialism.[110]

Even hints of his more celebrated assertion that enacted "law" which is too outrageously unjust is not law at all, may seem to be found embedded *alio intuitu* in the *Rechtsphilosophie*.[111] But the determination of the relation of this to Radbruch's later position would still be attended by many pitfalls. The earlier proposition has reference to the requirements of the formal idea of justice: while he there insisted that the "idea of justice" cannot determine the contents of legal rules except in connection with the further directives of the chosen *Zweckmässigkeit*, he suggested that the idea of justice might nevertheless provide a test of whether a given norm is law. But he might here be saying no more than that certain formal requirements

---

103 *Legal Philosophy* 111, *Rechtsphilosophie* 175.

104 *Mensch im Recht* 104. ("*üben das Kondominat über das Recht aus—nicht in spannungsloser Harmonie, sondern umgekehrt in einem lebendigen Spannungsverhältnis*".) Perhaps he was not familiar with the international lawyer's jingle that "condominium is pandemonium".

105 See *Legal Philosophy* 112, *Rechtsphilosophie* 175. Radbruch goes on to say: "A philosophical system is to resemble a Gothic cathedral in which the masses support each other by pressing against each other. How suspect would be a philosophy that did not consider the world a purposeful creation of reason and yet resolved it into a rational system with no contradiction! And how superfluous any existence if ultimately the world involved no contradiction and life involved no decision!"

106 See G. Radbruch in *Le But du Droit: Bien Commun, Justice, Sécurité* (1938) 162. In "*Sécurité*" 87, Radbruch speculated rather vaguely on the relation of choices made at various past epochs to "the juridical conscience" of each epoch.

107 *Cf.* K. Engisch and E. Wolf, in the latter's article cited *supra* n. 43, at 5, and at 3, n. 11.

108 E. Wolf, article cited *supra* n. 43, at 5, quoting Radbruch's "*Rechtswissenschaft und Rechtsschöpfung*" (1906) 4 *Arch. Sozialw. und Sozialpol.* 355-370. And *cf.* K. Engisch, "*Gustav Radbruch als Rechtsphilosoph*" (1949-1950) 38 *Arch. R.- und Sozialph.* 305.

109 "*Absolute Folgerungen . . . nämlich die überlieferten Forderungen des klassischen Naturrechts.*"

110 *Mensch im Recht* 87. With characteristic over-dramatisation he declared that "*ars nesciendi . . . has performed a logical miracle: out of Nothing the All was born*" (*Die ars nesciendi hat sich wieder einmal fruchtbar erwiesen. Ein logisches Wunder hat sich vollzogen: das Nichts hat aus sich heraus das All geboren*).

111 See *supra* n. 101.

(including whatever he means by those of the-idea-of-justice-as-distinct-from-the-quality-of-the-contents-of-legal-rules) are part of his definition of law, as Austin said that generality of the command was part of his. And in that case, this early assertion that conformity to "the idea of justice" serves as a test of "lawness" would have only an illusory connection with his supposed later revolt against positivism.

But in fact even this would be an over-simplification. As suggested above, Radbruch's inclusion of distributive justice within "the idea of justice", stands rather ill with his virtual relegation of the whole content of legal rules for determination by reference to *Zweckmässigkeit* (as distinct from justice). So far, however, as Radbruch *did not in 1932 refer the content of law to justice for determination*, his readers would be in error to identify the "justice" by which he thought in 1932 that the quality of a rule as law might be tested, with the "justice" whose outrageous violation by the content of a rule he thought, after 1945, would denude the rule of the quality of "law". Yet if, as we believe, Radbruch were not self-consistent in 1932, when he adopted the neo-Kantian commonplace that his "idea of justice" *did not* determine the content of legal rules, even though he included distributive justice within it, another fascinating possibility emerges. Perhaps the reader's erroneous reading of his *words* may still yield a *correct insight* about *the substance* of Radbruch's earlier and later positions, the later being an elucidation of his earlier inconsistencies, deepened by his intervening experience of the world.

The traumatic nature of this experience of Radbruch as a man in his own generation would need little recalling here, but for the happy oblivious-ness of the *postnati*. The German nation had apparently come to its full political unity and maturity, its jurists and jurisconsults had dominated legal scholarship ever since the nineteenth century opened, it was the beneficiary of a Civil Code praised as the most careful statement of a nation's law that the world had ever seen, and the teachings of its publicists concerning the *Rechtsstaat* had merged with Dicey's "rule of law" doctrine as seem-ingly a broad highway to the civilised human future. Its legal academies and research institutes were as renowned as its individual scholars, and their renown and vitality survived the disasters and aftermath of the First World War. Despite all this, and much more, this people, for the most part docilely, under a "legal" régime itself arguably lawful under the Weimar Constitution, accepted (to use Radbruch's own phrase) a supra-individualist or totalitarian order. This order denied in practice every precept which he had claimed to issue from democracy, and from the relativist philosophy which he had constructed to match it. From this relativism, it is recalled, he had claimed to draw as late as 1934 the "absolute consequences" of "liberalism, the rule of law, the division of State powers, sovereignty of the people, tolerance and socialism".[112] Yet between 1933 and 1945 he was to see hundreds of thousands of his fellow-Germans excluded by "law" from the ordinary rights of citizenship, and tens of thousands thrown into concen-tration camps. He saw or later learned of several millions of Jews, and hundreds of thousands of other Europeans, marshalled, herded like cattle, looted and stripped by other human beings as by scavengers in a junk yard, driven to mass murder chambers, and destroyed with more brutality than accompanies the slaughter of animals, or the execution of lawfully condemned criminals. In the halls of justice he witnessed tribunals and

---

[112] See *supra* n. 110.

procedures which, still under the formulae of law and justice, reversed and perverted principles which had formerly seemed so much part of the necessary order of society as to have been tacitly presupposed by his relativism.

Such reversals and perversions might well have forced the articulation of what had already been taken tacitly for granted. And the activities of German lawyers and judges in the areas where choices were left by his relativism, must inevitably have led him to reexamine his confidence that the exposure to view through relativism of the full range of choices tolerated by a legal system, must exalt and ennoble men or must confer on them the dignity and responsibility of decision according to conscience. These, at any rate, were some of the events which intervened between the last edition of the *Rechtsphilosophie* in his lifetime, and the now famous pronouncements of 1945 and 1946, notably his lecture *"Fünf Minuten Rechtsphilosophie"*,[113] and his article *"Gesetzliches Unrecht und übergesetzliches Recht"*,[113a] respectively.

Radbruch had hitherto stressed the irremovable antinomies which could arise between the directives of legal certainty, and the directives of "justice". In this earlier phase Radbruch apparently made no qualification on the court's duty to enforce the positive law. "Justice", he then wrote, "is the second great task of law; the closest one (*die nächste*), however, is legal certainty". And he added, quoting Goethe: "I would rather commit injustice than stand disorder (*Unordnung*)".[114] In his later pronouncements, however, he sought to resolve the gravest of such conflicts by declaring that the supremacy of positive law ceases where the contradiction of positive law and justice assumes intolerable proportions. In that situation the positive law must give way to justice, not merely in the sense that the positive law is to be regarded as unjust, and not *morally* compelling, but also in the sense that it is not to be regarded as positive law at all; it is not even *legally* compelling. "Where justice is not even striven for, where equality which is the core of justice is constantly denied in the enactment of positive law, there the law is not only 'unjust law' but lacks the nature of law altogether."[115] Turning his attention explicitly to positivism, he declared in 1945 that the positivist conviction that "the law is the law" (*Gesetz ist Gesetz*)[116] had rendered German lawyers defenceless against laws which were

---

[113] Now published in *Rechtsphilosophie* (4 ed. 1950) 335-37.

[113a] First published in *Süd-Deutsche Juristen-Zeitung*, No. 5. August 1946 reprinted in *Rechtsphilosophie* (4 ed. 1950) 347-357, and in *Mensch im Recht* 111-124.

[114] *Rechtsphilosophie* 181-82. *Cf*. Cattaneo, "*L'Ultima Fase*" 64.

[115] See repr. in *Mensch im Recht* 119: "... *wo Gerechtigkeit nicht einmal erstrebt wird, wo die Gleichheit, die den Kern der Gerechtigkeit ausmacht, bei der Setzung positiven Rechts bewusst verleugnet wurde, da ist das Gesetz nicht etwa nur 'unrichtiges Recht', vielmehr entbehrt es überhaupt der Rechtsnatur".*

[116] Spelled out in the sense in which Radbruch attributed it to German lawyers, the slogan "*Gesetz ist Gesetz*" means: "*Was als Gesetz niedergelegt ist, gilt als Recht*". Insofar as it asserts the validity of *Gesetz* as such, that is independent of any further ethical test, it imports the separation of law and morals. Hart, "Law and Morals" 593, is concerned to assert that it does not import a demand to follow the norms of law rather than the norms of morals. Except insofar as "law" or "*Recht*" in the second clause carries in common usage a sense of ordering, which, in Fuller's view of common usage, must be *good* ordering, this may be accepted. It must be added, however, that the syntactical form "*Gesetz ist Gesetz*" has in other sentences a connotation in common usage which is quite different, and which may be called "resignative". When a German says "*Kind ist Kind*" ("A child is a child"), "*Narr ist Narr*" ("A fool is a fool") he imports acceptance while recognising deficiencies or dangers of what is spoken of. In this sense of the phrase, Hart would certainly be correct in thinking that the citizen's acceptance of the rule as law

arbitrary and even criminal in their contents.[117] And in his contribution to the Carnelutti *Festschrift*, published in 1949,[118] he sought to develop the more positive implications of this position by trying to relate the idea of Justice to the ideas of God and love.[119]

Radbruch's post-final doctrine that certain absolute minima of justice must be deemed to be built into the very concept of law, thus stands as an apparently unintegrated and perplexing rider to his system as a relativist. Formerly Radbruch saw a clean-cut antinomy between his "legal certainty" and "justice" (the latter, be it remembered, being in his view merely formal), and he had disposed of it by saying that he "would rather commit injustice than stand disorder". But at the later phase he saw the demand for certainty and constancy of interpretation as a demand *of justice*.[119a] So that behind what appears to be "a conflict . . . between legal certainty and justice, between a materially (*inhaltlich*) revocable (*anfechtbar*) but positive law and a just but as yet only potential law, the real conflict is of justice with itself, a conflict between a seeming (*scheinbar*) and an actual (*wirklich*) justice". He thought now that the conflict was similar to that between the evangelist's command that we simultaneously acknowledge "the authority which has power" over us, and yet also "obey God more than man". And he thought that the solution to be followed was "that the law secured by enactment prevails even when it is in content (*inhaltlich*) unjust and *unzweckmässig*, except when the contradiction of positive law with justice reaches such an intolerable measure that law as 'unjust law' (*unrichtiges Recht*) has to give way (*weichen*) to justice".[120]

It is now clear that this position imports at least two variations on the earlier position. First, it purports to resolve the antinomy which he earlier treated as insoluble, by making justice prevail over legal certainty in the indicated situation. Second, it adds to the earlier directives of justice for positive law, namely the principles of synallagmatic and distributive justice, certain other controls of its content, which, so far as Radbruch stated them, come close to the current declarations of certain human rights.[121]

While this is not the place to canvass the analytical issues here involved

---

leaves intact the moral duty to judge the law in terms of justice, and finally, to resist outrageously unjust law.

[117] Repr. in *Mensch im Recht* 118: "*Der Positivismus hat in der Tat mit seiner Überzeugung 'Gesetz ist Gesetz' den deutschen Juristenstand wehrlos gemacht gegen Gesetze willkürlichen und verbrecherischen Inhalts*".

[118] Entitled "*Gerechtigkeit und Gnade*" repr. in *Rechtsphilosophie* (4 ed. 1950) 337-343.

[119] *Id*. 310. The literary evidence seems to support a degree of correlation between Radbruch's views and his observation of the rise of Nazism implied in the text. His "final" version in *Rechtsphilosophie* in 1932 left the antinomies irremovable. In 1936 when Nazi innovations were but threatening, we find him delivering an unqualified encomium on legal certainty as the supreme value, especially as against *Zweckmässigkeit*. See "*Sécurité*" 99. But in 1945, when he had witnessed the full arbitrariness of Nazi law, his "legal certainty" became subjected to the over-all check of justice. On the Hebraic ideas of God and love in relation to justice, see *supra* Ch. 1, §§5-9, esp. §9.

[119a] Friedmann, article cited *supra* n. 44, at 205, however, points out that Radbruch's attitude to Nazi "law" might be influenced by the fact that his notion of "legal certainty" had always included a requirement of orderly relations between organs of government, and a hierarchy of norms. So that, merely in formal terms, he might view the overruling of law by a Hitler's enraged pronouncements as anarchy and not law.

[120] "*Gesetzliches Unrecht und übergesetzliches Recht*" in *Rechtsphilosophie* (5 ed.) 353.

[121] See Cattaneo, "*L'Ultima Fase*". *Cf*., equivalating "natural law" as the minimal satisfaction of the subjects' values with the "natural" fact (in another sense) of the tendency of the community to rebel if pressed hard enough to overcome

concerning the "correct" definition of law,[122] certain comments may be offered. The first is that Radbruch is at this stage stating the relation of law and justice essentially in the terms of the classical natural law, that law is not law unless it conforms to certain minimum norms of natural justice.[123] Second, whether or not he had been correct in saying in 1934 that he had derived certain ethical "absolutes" from his "relativism", he was probably correct in describing such an operation as "miraculous". Third, even if the position that outrageously unjust law is not "law" cannot be reconciled with his earlier position that this antinomy was irremovable, this does not in itself discredit or accredit either position. Each position has still to be judged on its merits. Iusnaturalist arguments that the position *posterior in tempore* (as it were) is *potior in jure*, and positivist arguments that the period in a man's life when he prepares to meet his Maker is not the most conducive to clear intellection on worldly matters, are equally mere exercises in public relations.[124] Fourth, provided we could find some clear measure of when injustice becomes intolerable in Radbruch's sense, his repudiation of positivism could be regarded as operative only beyond that point. His earlier and later positions could then stand together—one on one side of the line, the other on the other.

Finally, if the view that outrageously unjust positive law is not law at all has any importance, it raises a number of consequential problems always associated with a "higher law" theory. One is the problem of drawing the line between the level of injustice which is tolerable within positive "law", and the level which disqualifies a rule as law. For clearly neither Radbruch nor, indeed, any other theorist of natural law, has ever insisted that a rule must render *perfect* justice in order to qualify as "law". No doubt situations arise, of which barbarous excesses such as those of the Nazi régime are happily not too frequent an instance, in which the line is clearly crossed. But there are also many positive laws of many countries, and many positive laws even of the most barbarous régimes, where the line is more difficult to see. Radbruch, perhaps due to the lateness of his approach to this problem, contributed little if anything to its solution.

§11. HIGHER LAW ABSOLUTES AND RESISTANCE TO POWER. The situations in which clear lines can be drawn are those, such as characterised the Nazi era, where at least from an ethical if not from a legal standpoint, society is

---

"inertia and fear", Hughes, "Legal System" 1022ff. That author correctly points out that the level of justice so assumed may still be outrageously unjust law (1023).

[122] See Stone, *Legal System*, Ch. 5; *infra* §11; and literature cited *infra* n. 124.

[123] It is not important to the present point whether Radbruch thought that his *supra*-legal law was the classical natural law or (as Cattaneo, *"L'Ultima Fase"* 73, thinks) some new *"Naturrecht mit wechselndem Inhalt"*. Cattaneo is relying on G. Radbruch, *"Neue Probleme in der Rechtswissenschaft"* in *Eine Feuerbach-Gedanken-rede sowie drei Aufsätze aus dem wissenschaftlichen Nachlass* (ed. E. Schmidt, 1952) 33. It may be added that as late as 1947 in the *Vorschule*, Radbruch still let himself be quoted (at p. 70) as saying that "natural law" had the "life-giving power of an illusion", even when on p. 109 his peroration is a passionate invocation of natural law. *Cf.* Cattaneo, *op. cit.* 68.

[124] Cattaneo, *"L'Ultima Fase"* 72, makes the shorter point, which may be more debatable, that Radbruch's thought cannot in either of its phases be regarded "as completely iusnaturalistic or anti-iusnaturalistic". The focus of discussion in English has been H. L. A. Hart's Holmes Lecture of 1957. See Hart, "Law and Morals" 593-629; Fuller, "Positivism" *id.* 630-673. And see Cattaneo, *op. cit.* But see on the German cases involved H. O. Pappe, "On the Validity of Judicial Decisions in the Nazi Era" (1960) 23 *M.L.R.* 260-274. There is a thoughful analysis of the Hart-Fuller debate in S. I. Shuman, *Legal Positivism* (1963) 61-93, and *passim*. And see *infra* §11, and *supra* Ch. 7, §7, and literature there cited.

in revolution or dissolution or both. At such moments the analytically correct view of the status of "outrageously unjust law" is scarcely likely to be a matter of social or political or even legal importance. In the assumed situation those who have the vision, the courage and the means should equally resist the putative "law", whether it be regarded as *law* which is outrageously unjust, or be regarded as not law at all.[125] For, on the one hand, law or not, the minions of political authority *will* try to enforce it by power; and, on the other, this power *should be resisted,* whether it is enforcing law which is outrageously unjust, or whether it is enforcing outrageous injustice which is only spuriously "law".

In the present view, then, the more important question concerning Radbruch's post-1945 position, which piety presents to the many whose minds his thought has enlivened and enriched, is not a question of theoretical superiority as between the positivist-relativist, and natural law-absolutist, positions. The important question concerns rather the comparative social efficacy of adherence to one standpoint or the other in preventing human backsliding, especially in periods of revolution and social transition and disintegration. This surely is the question which the ordeal of the Nazi period thrust into the delicately equilibrating structure of this mature scholar's relativism. And this surely was why the climactic point of the 1946 article is the assertion that it had been the positivist conviction that *Gesetz ist Gesetz* which rendered German lawyers "defenceless" against arbitrary and even criminal "laws".[126] Can it indeed be said that at such times the defences of men against outrageously unjust laws will be stronger if these laws can be denounced as not law at all, rather than merely as "outrageously unjust law"? This is not merely a verbal or even epistemological question of the correct definition of the word "law". Nor is it an ethical or ethico-political question turning on which of the duties bearing down upon men from different normative systems of law, ethics or religion ought to prevail. It is rather a question of social-psychological fact, or prognosis of such, and this means that even if answers to it may be no more accessible than answers to those other questions, they certainly may be very different answers.

It should be said at once that it might be better if the issues raised by Radbruch, and later taken up by Professor Hart, were not described in terms of "fusion of law and morals". What the older Radbruch asked for, and what natural lawyers also ask for, is that "law-ness" be tested for *by certain standards of justice.* Fusion of law and morals (or justice) only arises insofar as their demand is fulfilled; but the making of the demand is not its fulfilment. The demand is addressed in particular to all concerned with fixing the content of the law, including legislator and judge; and insofar as these tend to be lawyers, or to use lawyers' language, it is a demand for a change in their usage of the word "law"—that it shall only be used to qualify rules which conform to certain minimum standards of justice.

It is assumed by those who press this demand that by withholding the title "law" from them, outrageous rules will be denied the potency of

---

[125] Cattaneo, *"L'Ultima Fase"*.
[126] Cattaneo (*id.* 73) suggests that this "neo-iusnaturalism of Radbruch is founded on the accentuation of the importance of the function of the judges as depositories and interpreters of the principles of the suprapositive law". While in the historical context this may be so, Radbruch would scarcely have so limited it; nor does it add much to say that Radbruch's "natural law" is a special natural law of judicial creation.

the symbol "law" for evoking obedience, and that this will tend to make
more effective resistance to the rules, or attempts to amend them, in
title of justice. And this assumption seems indubitably correct for all people
who understand the demand and conform to its terms—that is, as long
as they refuse to treat rules as "law" which fail to meet the standard of
justice by which they themselves independently test it.

How then is it possible for this view, held by many men of piety,
including scholars of undoubted sincerity and integrity, to be denounced
by other scholars as naive, wrongheaded, and in certain circumstances dangerous to both freedom and morality? Professor Hart has presented perhaps
the most cogent argument. It is that to say that "law" is not law unless
it conforms to minimal standards of justice, is to invite all persons to whom
"a law" is presented, not only to accept it as law, but to *believe* that it is
a *just law*. It merges, as it were, the decision as to the justice of the rule
with the acceptance of it as "law", and in the resulting confusion it reduces
the *spatium moralis* deliberandi which would otherwise be available *between*
recognition of the rule as "law" *and* the decision whether the law should
be obeyed.

This line of argument cannot, however, be accepted in quite its own
terms. If the demand is met that outrageously unjust rules shall not be
recognised as law, then there is no inescapable reason why this should
have the effect of reducing the interval for moral deliberation. On the
contrary, fully to meet Radbruch's demand would require there to be
such an interval, and (what is more) would impose on every addressee
of a putative law *the duty to avail himself of this interval before ever he
accepts the offered rules as veritably law*. And where this is so, it is simply
not true that there is "a fusion" of law and justice which endows the
offered rules with the combined power of evoking obedience of both the
symbol "law" and the symbol "justice". *If social-psychological processes
conformed to Radbruch's demand,* the evocative power of the symbol
"justice" would do its work in checking obedience before the power of the
symbol "law" to stimulate obedience could even come into operation. Indeed,
the symbol "law" could only make its power felt if the censorial power of
the "justice" symbol allowed the rule in question to be qualified as "law".

Yet the issue cannot be allowed to rest here either; for this replication
is itself dependent on certain assumptions about social-psychological processes
which are hazardous in the extreme. Can it be expected that the addressee
will pause, as each rule purporting to be law is presented to him for his
obedience, and ask himself—Is this particular rule sufficiently in conformity
with justice to qualify as law? If we assume that Radbruch's demand has
already come to be accepted in the particular community, it is feared that
the matter will present itself rather differently to the addressee. The addressee
will then take it for granted that the law as a whole (that is, the legal order)
conforms to "justice"; and he will be told that the rule presented to him
for obedience is "law". Even if he is not told that it is also "just law",
he will then tend himself to make this translation because he will share
the general belief that the legal order of which this rule is a part is just.
Whenever this happens, the danger envisaged by Professor Hart *is* likely
in fact to occur—the fact that the symbol "justice" has become associated
with the symbol "law" will lead most people further to translate the
general belief that the legal order as a whole is just, into an assumption
that the particular rules which purport to be rules within that legal order

are also just. Where this double step occurs (and it may have to be expected as a matter of social psychology, however unwarranted logically) the *spatium moralis deliberandi* would in fact be frustrated. The censorial power of justice as a symbol checking the obedience-producing capacity of the symbol "law" would then be neutralised *a limine,* and converted into a reinforcement by rationalisation of the obedience-response.[126a]

The likelihood that this will occur is of course vastly increased by the fact that those who promulgate what purports to be law are also in a position to promulgate a version of justice to match their enactment, and to give it currency among people along with the enactment. To adapt Bertrand Russell's striking phrase in a related context, "the Satan will speak in their hearts" with the voice of God. For there to be a more hopeful outcome of the demand that law must qualify as just, therefore, we would have to suppose a society in which the leadership of voluntary organisations, for instance of churches and universities, is sufficiently enlightened, courageous, resolute and powerful to prevent or reverse the operation of these social-psychological tendencies. And this leadership would have to be a continuing leadership, for these tendencies are always likely to recur. Yet it may well be said that if such leadership is available, it could make itself felt with at least equal effectiveness even though Radbruch's view is rejected, and the "law" is recognised as law, but subjected to scrutiny and criticism for its conformity to minimal justice, as Hart thinks it ought to be.

For Hart is clearly correct to insist that the doctrine of the separateness of law and morals does *not* import for him that it is morally indifferent what is the content of positive law. It is, indeed, possible to graft onto the "separation" doctrine the further view that law and morals are of equal axiotic dignity, or even the Pyrrhonic view that there is no reason for believing that one course of action is better than another; but these are not necessary nor even the usual versions. More usually the separation doctrine is held by thinkers who have a keen sense of responsibility and great moral earnestness. As Hart himself observed, a goodly part of Austin's famous lectures were devoted to what we would now call the theory of justice. All that this separation doctrine necessarily asserts is that legal evaluation and moral evaluation involve different processes and criteria, and that it is better, if we are to avoid confusion, to attend to them separately, even though we must still attend to both. For such thinkers, even though what is morally invalid may be legally in force, it may still be the prevailing duty of the addressee to disobey the law which is morally objectionable.

Obviously, Radbruch interpreted the separation doctrine in a sense which excluded the possibility that moral duty might have to prevail over legal duty. And this would have been natural for Radbruch if he was reacting against his own earlier relativist view that when justice, legal certainty and *Zweckmässigkeit* conflict, there can be for the intellect no rational ground for preferring one over the other—that there was an irremovable antinomy. Yet we may come to think that, if this were so, his message might have been more productive of real exploration if he

---

[126a] It is thus only by dint of and within the limits of these complex psychological probabilities that we would agree with S. I. Shuman, *op. cit. supra* n. 124, at 204-209, esp. 207, that natural law results in the diminution of individual, moral and political responsibility. And see *id.,* 191-99 for a valuable analysis of the "obedience to law" aspect of L. L. Fuller's position.

had put it in precisely those terms.

Of course, neither Radbruch's view (even if implemented), nor Hart's view, could assure us that outrageously unjust law will always be resisted, much less successfully resisted; the most that is in issue is the degree of probability of resistance under each. Nor is it in issue between them that the moral duty to resist must be any weightier under one than under the other. It seems unlikely, moreover, that we can find conditions that will permit us to measure any added social-psychological power which unjust law might receive from the erroneous assumption that it is "just" because it is "law", as against the weakening of unjust law which could be brought about by seeking to deny to it the standing of "law". For (and this is the added dimension which must be given to the Radbruch-Hart controversy), we fail to see how any situation could arise in which either theory could marshal empirical evidence in its own support. In Nazi Germany, even if all its lawyers and most of its people had taken Radbruch's later view, the result would probably still have been the same. The ruthless use of physical power and propaganda techniques by the Nazis for the *Umwertung der Werte* would probably have overborne in any case the moral resistance of most German lawyers. And what the Nazi régime displayed in horrifying caricature remains true in lesser degree for any society in which the law-making power is vested in a stable central authority. For, almost *ex hypothesi*, and under both democratic and dictatorial governments, those who make the law do so by virtue of the fact that they wield, for the time being, the predominant political and (at a pinch) physical power in the community. The capacity of "law" to command obedience, therefore, is always in some degree a function not of the emotive power of the symbol "law", but of the *de facto* predominance in the community of those who are in a position to manipulate the symbol. How much of the tendency to obey what is "law" is to be attributed to its power as a symbol, and how much to the tendency of most people to submit to actual power, and even to the "normative tendency of the factual",[127] is probably at best rather problematical.

The liberation of men from tyrannically unjust law is a function, in short, not so much of *a theory* of rebellion, nor even of *a theory* of law, or of law and justice. Liberation is a rebellion against facts, including the facts of vested political and physical power. No doubt these facts take theories unto themselves by way of reinforcement; and so do those who rebel against such facts. But to suggest that, in a particular time and place, it can be decisive for the success of a rebellion against unjust law whether people regard this "law" as not law at all, or whether they regard it as a law which is intolerably unjust, is to overlook what is too frequently the stark reality. This is that what rebellion must finally overcome is not only the emotive power of the symbol "law", but the political and physical power of those who have enacted it and seek to enforce it. Compared to this, and to the energy and sacrifice necessary to overcome it, any differential advantage as between Hart's view or Radbruch's and Fuller's views on the relation of law and justice (if we could be confident that there was one) might well be regarded as too small to merit further protraction of

---

[127] See Stone, *Social Dimensions*, Chs. 12-13, and on the "normative force of the factual" see G. Jellinek, *Allgemeine Staatslehre* (1922) 337-44. *Cf.* generally Austin, *Province Determined* 186, discussed Hughes, "Legal System" 1026-27. There may of course be other good reasons for preferring one of the views here discussed rather than the other. See now Hart, *Law* 201ff., esp. 203-207.

this debate. Historical instances must be rare indeed in which the elements in struggle are so delicately balanced that the refinements under discussion have been decisive.[127a]

§12. THE ANTINOMIES OF LAW AND THE SOLILOQUY OF JUSTICE WITH ITSELF. A second related shift in Radbruch's position that may be detected in his later writings, concerns his understanding of the antinomical notion itself, at any rate as applied to the conflict of legal certainty with justice. His earlier analysis placed the ideas of justice, legal certainty and purpose-conformity on a somewhat[128] level basis as the constituent ideas of law.[129] On these assumptions he seemed to declare the contradiction between justice and legal certainty in the outrageously unjust positive law to represent an antinomy which was irremovable. In his 1946 article, however, he pronounces that such a conflict is "in truth a conflict of justice with itself, a conflict between apparent and actual justice" (*liegt in Wahrheit ein Konflikt der Gerechtigkeit mit sich selbst, ein Konflikt zwischen scheinbarer und wirklicher Gerechtigkeit vor*).[130]

Erik Wolf is thus correct in observing, in his posthumous edition of *Rechtsphilosophie*, that for Radbruch the conflict between justice, legal certainty, and purpose-conformity, appeared finally as a soliloquy of justice with itself (*als Gespräch der Gerechtigkeit mit sich selbst*). And it both conforms to the editor's learned piety towards his author,[131] and to the tenor of Radbruch's essay of 1949 on "*Gerechtigkeit und Gnade*" for him to add that finally Radbruch regarded the conflict as surmountable by love.[132] But in the present view a still more important point is to be made. For the fact that Radbruch finally resolved such conflicts into a soliloquy of *justice with itself* means that in the end he *elevated the rank* of the idea of justice as against legal certainty, in a manner which left justice as the final and decisive idea of law. This, after all, is only a reflection in his methodology of his final revolt against positivism. But insofar as it is correct, Radbruch ought to have rewritten, a great deal less dramatically, his whole theory of "irremovable antinomies".[133]

§13. "THE NATURE OF THINGS." Even more problematical among the notions which become prominent in Radbruch's later thought was his invocation of "the nature of things as a juristic thought-form". (*Natur der Sache als juristische Denkform*.)[134] "Nature", Radbruch says, in the phrase "the

---

127a *Cf.* on some aspects of this indecisiveness for the question of resistance, S. I. Shuman, *cit. supra* n. 124, at 61-93, 188-190, 205ff., 211-222. In the light of the present analysis the concession on 188-190 to the Fuller standpoint, that it may be decisive as to "lazy and morally weak people", may even seem too generous.

128 Hints that justice is somehow primary can be found, but unclarified.

129 Or as constituents of the idea of law. His language is quite ambivalent on this matter.

130 See repr. in *Mensch im Recht* 118-19. *Cf. Vorschule* 31.

131 See *Rechtsphilosophie*, ed. Preface, p. 72.

132 Cited *supra* n. 118, esp. at 340, 343. At 338 he asserts that in essence mercy and love are identical.

133 And see *supra* §9 for other reasons why this was called for.

134 Radbruch addressed this problem twice after the war: "*Die Natur der Sache als juristische Denkform*" in *Laun Festschrift* 157, at 164ff. and in *Vorschule* 20-22. It has been noted that Radbruch's idea of English law was that it is "on the basis of the whole legal reality and the 'nature' of the thing" that the English law is created and legal issues decided. See E. Wolf, article cited *supra* n. 43 at 20, esp. n. 114. See also Radbruch, *Der Geist des englischen Rechts* (3 ed. 1956) 35. On other contemporary doctrines of "the nature of things", related to the so-called "revival of natural law", see *supra* Ch. 7, §6.

nature of things" means "the essence, the meaning of the thing, the objective meaning which is to be taken from the conditions of the situations of life".[135] He thought the notion of the nature of things answered the question, "How can . . . a situation of life meaningfully be thought of as an actualisation of a certain notion of value?"[136] By "thing" in the same phrase, Radbruch meant the objective content, the raw material (Stoff, for which he sometimes also uses "substratum" as a synonym), which the law tries to handle; and this certainly embraced the physical and social context and the human relations within the context, and the legal situations with which the law-maker is confronted and which he seeks to subject to his regulation.[137] Taking up a thought of Emil Lask that every idea of value is ordinated to certain objective circumstances,[138] Radbruch finds that the ideas of law are conditions limited or held in by the raw materials which law must handle (Rechtsstoff) as these emerge in the particular time and place (including the Volksgeist), by what Erik Wolf has called "the material determination of the idea" (Stoffbestimmtheit der Idee).[139] But the word "determination" must obviously not be taken literally, since he is at pains to say that while the process reduces somewhat the sharp (schroff) dualism between the ought and the is, it does not remove it. The nature of things, which refers to the objective meaning of the given facts as they are, still leaves the last word to the idea of law. The nature of things sets the limits of possibility of actualising certain ideas of law; just as, from a different angle, it consists of the resistance of the obtuse world,[140] to which ideas of law must adjust themselves if they are to be realised. Moreover, by the same token, every legal idea that is realised carries on itself the marks of the "historical climate" in which it arose, and remains enclosed within the limits of the historically possible, which is another way of saying that it is bound by "the nature of things".[141]

It is surprising that a spirit of Radbruch's sensitivity and literary range should have chosen to express an important insight by an overworked and ambiguous phrase, such as "the nature of things", particularly as he was at pains to deny that he used it in a natural law sense. And even accepting every writer's liberty to use well-hallowed phrases to express his own ideas, it is still a matter of surprise that he should not have made any mention of related and more aptly named doctrines, such as Roscoe Pound's quite old and well worked out doctrine of the "limits of effective legal action". Perhaps some part of the explanation lies in the original texture of Radbruch's relativism. Eager as he was to teach that the validity of evaluative ideas was relative to the validity of other ideas, he was ever fascinated by apparent stalemate situations, to the point of over-dramatisa-tion. It is no accident that, apart from his late alleged "conversion", it is his doctrine of the irremovable antinomies between legal ideas which is best known. His final system, as he regarded the 1932 edition of the Rechtsphilosophie, scarcely carried through beyond the relativity of the

---

135 "Der Sinn der Sache . . . der aus der Beschaffenheit des Lebensverhältnisses selbst zu entnehmende, objektive Sinn."
136 "Er ist die Antwort auf die Frage, wie dies so beschaffene Lebensverhältnis sinnvoll als Verwirklichung eines bestimmten Wertgedankens gedacht werden kann." See Vorschule 20.
137 Loc. cit.
138 "So ist jede Wertidee auf einen Stoff hingeordnet."
139 Article cited supra n. 43 at 21; Rechtsphilosophie (Ed. Preface) 54.
140 "Widerstand der stumpfen Welt."
141 See Vorschule 47.

evaluative ideas to each other, into the confrontation of such ideas by the concrete factual contexts, physical, social and technological, of diverse societies at diverse times.[142]

Yet clearly some of the most constructive, influential and practical juristic contributions of modern times have been directed precisely to showing that ideas of justice are relative to factual contexts. If we go no further back than Montesquieu's *L'Esprit des Lois* and enumerate only the *juristic* milestones, we would still have to name Beccaria, Bentham, Savigny, Maine, Holmes, Pareto and Pound. Perhaps, therefore, we should not just read Radbruch's doctrine of *Natur der Sache* as a curious unintegrated rider on his doctrine of the mutual relativism of ideas of law. Perhaps it is better understood as an acknowledgment that, besides the problem of the relative validity of evaluative ideas in relation to each other, there is that of the "value" of evaluative ideas relative to concrete physical, social, and technological contexts (or, as he himself put it, relative to "the resistance of the obtuse world").

That acknowledgment would, of course, still do much less than justice to its subject. Mainly Radbruch saw "the nature of things" as a brake on legal ideas; and when he espoused the claim of justice to subjugate positive law, he still did not specify the valid *casus subjugandi.* "The nature of things" was a warning against impossible law, but it left the question of justice still indeterminate. Certainly he provided no clear indications about "the nature of things" as a positive guide to the requirements of justice in the actual facts of social life. Yet, at any rate, it is well to be thus reminded that the achievements of relativist theories of justice transcend Radbruch's own version of them.

§14. THEORIST'S ANTINOMIES AND MAN'S DUTIES. Radbruch's contribution to the theory of justice rests primarily on the challenge by his dramatic doctrine of "irremovable antinomies" to the terms in which classical ideas were framed, and the resultant opening of new perspectives of inquiry. But the most irremovable antinomy of all, perhaps, is the one which Radbruch left for his successors to explore; we mean his own apparent espousal of some of the central natural law doctrines, while purporting to maintain all the rest of his relativist system. In these circumstances, as history gives its due place to piety and personal admiration, his place in thought may well remain problematical. For Roscoe Pound (who was, in the present view, not entitled so to down-grade his own stature), Radbruch was "the foremost philosopher of law . . . in the present generation".[143] Even before Radbruch's *rapprochement* of law and morals, neo-scholastic writers had given similar place and praise to "the truly classical beauty and aesthetical restraint" of Radbruch's style, to his "profound and mature wisdom", to his "erudition . . . tolerance . . . comprehension of . . . logical and epistemological difficulties, and . . . absence of . . . intellectual arrogance".[144] But to

---

[142] It is true that his classification of *Zwecke des Rechts* as either "individualist", "supra-individualist" or "transpersonal" reflected the ideological and political travail of Europe between the wars; but that this was, as it were, *malgré soi*, is apparent from his insistence that his statement of these *Zwecke* was not to be regarded as empirically based. See *supra* §8. *Cf.* on Radbruch's assertion that relativism leads to socialism, as an expression of his faith rather than rational thinking, Friedmann, article cited *supra* n. 44 at 204.

[143] See Pound, *op. cit. supra* n. 11, at 19.

[144] See A. H. Chroust, "The Philosophy of Law of Gustav Radbruch" (1944) 53 *Phil. R.* 23, at 23.

other scholars his doctrine, especially as before 1945, has seemed but "relative cynicism", "sophistical skepticism", "spirit turned profoundly uncreative", "one-dimensional thinking devoid of any understanding of social reality", "intellectually exhausted subjectivism", and "weak and wretched philosophy".[145] This violent contrast of judgments is no doubt in part the natural reaction of orthodoxies to a body of deliberately provocative thought; but, in part too, it must be attributed to the somewhat paradoxical state in which Radbruch finally left his own intellectual positions.

Radbruch's earlier relativism not only reiterated the well-known but constantly forgotten precept that life is not easy but problematical, and that above all else it is the rational and honest understanding of the problems which is the beginning of wisdom. Applying this to ideas of law, he displayed dramatically the indecisive nature of many ostensibly absolute ideas of law and justice, not only in the "contradictions" between them when each is followed through, but in the related but unsuspected evils that may spring from attempting to follow them through. And the deep lesson for which moderns correctly hail him, in an age properly described as one of "total" ideological struggle, is that to remain open-minded and open-hearted in the contemporary world of law and morals, and to be conscious of where even the best of intentions may actually take us, is a strenuous intellectual undertaking. His stress, perhaps over-stress, on the role of the antinomies, as Erik Wolf well observes, creates a constant stimulus to test and re-value judgments, for (in Radbruch's own words), a jurist who finds and keeps a system must have a "bad conscience"; only by constantly re-challenging his own system of ideas can he keep his conscience "clear".[146]

It was not necessarily inconsistent with this last precept that Radbruch thought that his own relativism, from which it sprang, was in its final form as early as 1932. For the precept was directed, as it were, to the practitioner's challenge to the practitioner's own conceptions of justice, whereas his own relativism was but an onlooker's body of theory about these problems of practice. The onlooker's body of theory was relativist for it showed that since a number of the purportedly absolute ideas resorted to in practice were in irreconcilable conflict with each other, their directives may not be compelling. When this was so, the practitioner must make his decision, finally, according to the dictates of his conscience, informed but not coerced by theory. So far, therefore, as decision-making goes, Radbruch's doctrine of antinomies merely alerted the practitioner to the areas where ideas of law and justice might lead only to uncertainty. From that point onwards, insofar as decisions must still be made cutting through the conflicting values, Radbruch left the decision-maker to the dictates, or as Holmes might have said, to the "Can't Helps" of his own conscience.

Had Radbruch been concerned with the sociology as well as the philosophy of justice, he could not have stopped at this point. He would have had then to make "the depths of personality" and "conscience" a matter of serious scholarly concern, together with the questions what these are, and how they are to be fathomed. His interests would no doubt have led him to such contemporary inquiries as those whose concern is with "the Authentic Self".[146a] On these matters Radbruch himself developed no

---

[145] For a compilation of these characterisations see E. Wolf, *supra* n. 43, at 15-16.
[146] *Id*. 11. And see G. Radbruch, "*Juristen—böse Christen*" (1916) No. 9 *Die Argonauten*.
[146a] He did in fact feel close affinities with the work of Karl Jaspers: see

organised body of ideas, though he left some precious occasional *dicta* to other contemporary movements of thought, including existentialism, personalism, and neo-scholasticism. Whatever the objective value of his relativism so far as it went, its searching humanist drive well deserved the *ave pia anima* which even his classicist critics spoke after him.[147]

It has a certain gentle irony to observe that the relativist who conceived his theory as final in 1932, and who made the contradictions of absolute ideas in practice a main theme of this theory, should in the end have drawn attention to such startling contradictions within his own positions, as to throw again into obscurity the very problems of practice which his theory was designed to illuminate. Certainly, the "logical miracle" which Radbruch claimed in his Lyon lecture to have worked, of deriving from the *"Nichts"* of his relativism *"das All"* of the classical principles of natural law, is not to be explained by the rational processes to which his theory of justice claimed to limit itself. And perhaps, as the experiences of totalitarian law and justice merged with those of advancing years, the line between the rational processes of theorising about justice, and the duty of the theorist as a man to take his stand, ceased to be as clear as it had formerly seemed. Certainly, these latterly discovered absolutes seem to have proceeded from the depths of his humanist conscience rather than from the rational teachings of his relativism.

§15. THE FINAL SOLILOQUY. It is significant in this connection that, even apart from any later change of position, his assertion of an irremovable antinomy between justice, legal certainty, and purpose-conformity was very much over-dramatised. If, as our analysis seems to show, his equality-as-the-core-of-justice was rather indeterminate, and could not settle the concrete content of positive law, many of the alleged conflicts between justice and the other two ideas of law could have been solved by giving to the idea of equality such content as would not conflict with the other two ideas of law. If the idea of justice is really (as he claims) a purely formal idea of justice, then, apart from the directive of generality of rules of law which he draws from it, it can always be harmonised with purpose-conformity. Moreover, insofar as he admitted to "formal justice" distributive justice proportional to merit or needs, most conflicts could certainly be avoided by reshaping the criteria of differentiation whereby different treatment is assigned for different concrete situations. A conflict between the "idea" of "formal justice" and the other two "ideas of law" can really only be asserted to exist to the extent that "formal justice" has *some* effect, other than what equality under the rule imports, on material content.

Some vague perception of these difficulties may have lain behind the early beginnings of Radbruch's concern with supra-positive norms, and the principles of classical natural law, even when they seemed at odds with all his main positions. Certainly, as we have pointed out, the full admission of "higher law" norms into the thinking of his later years was also accompanied by his re-interpretation of the relations between these three ideas which control "the idea of law". The younger Radbruch had seen these relations as co-ordinate, even though justice was (as it were) *primus inter pares*. The older Radbruch came to see these relations as finally but a soliloquy within the heart of justice itself. Legal certainty and purpose-

---

supra n. 46 and *cf.* Friedmann, article cited *supra* n. 44, at 198, 199.
[147] See W. Fuchs, *Neo-klassik in der Rechtsphilosophie* (1954) 60.

conformity must finally, as it were, make their case within the forum of justice itself, and it is the final judgment of justice which controls the law. This re-interpretation too, of course, on Radbruch's assumptions, still leaves open the question what content this judgment of justice is to have on a particular matter. And, as to this, his very latest theme, that the conflict of legal values is not ultimate, but penultimate, and that it is to be transcended by love, is a statement rather of the limitations of reason in this problem of justice than a rational contribution to its solution. Appeal to love as the ultimate arbiter still leaves the conflict at large; as Paul Tillich has well said,[148] there are many forms of love, and love itself may not be free of antinomic character.

These may be among the reasons why Radbruch has been said to have struggled for a legal philosophical system without finding one,[149] and to have remained to the end a "questing soul".[150] His writings as a whole disclose antinomies within his own personality and intellectual positions quite as *unüberwindliche* as any which he exposed in his theory of relativism. The themes of the subjugation of positive law to justice, of the "higher law" or "*supra*-positive norms", certainly stand in apparent, and probably in real, contradiction to the essential positions of his relativism. They were present in muted notes even as he elaborated his relativism, rising in the end to the heights of a dominant but unharmonised theme.

The reconciliation has, indeed, been suggested that Radbruch's relativism, being merely epistemological and not ontological, refers only to the relativity of our knowledge, and does not exclude the possibility that the existences of which we have this relative knowledge may themselves have absolute truth. It knows no dogma (it is said) except the one that there are no dogmas. Arthur Kaufmann thinks, for this reason, that Radbruch's approach should be termed "perspectivism" rather than relativism; it is "relativism" limited to the field of knowing that (he thinks) breeds genuine tolerance.[151] For it admits that there may be absolute truth about a subject-matter, and recognises that variable knowledge about it may arise from errors which are inevitable (as it were) on the road to this absolute truth.[152] Whether Kaufmann's interpretation be acceptable to us or not, it is one to which Radbruch himself would probably have been much attracted.

All this leaves him still a great thinker of his age, the inspirer of

---

[148] See P. Tillich, *supra* n. 46, pp. 118ff. See also I. Tammelo, "*La Relatività della Giustizia ed il Principio della 'Sollecitudine'*" (1958) 35 *Riv. Int. di Fil. del Dir.* 350, at 364ff.

[149] See F. von Hippel, *Gustav Radbruch als rechtsphilosophischer Denker* (1951) 51ff.

[150] W. Fuchs, *op. et loc. cit. supra* n. 147.

[151] In this connection Friedmann, *cit. supra* n. 44, at 203, quotes the *Mensch im Recht* 86 where Radbruch excluded from the duty of tolerance opinion which "claims absolute dominion" and the right to seize or retain power without regard to the majority. "Relativism is general tolerance—but not tolerance towards intolerance." *Cf.* Kelsen, *What is Justice?* (1957) 22-23. And see for the present writer's related positions on some of the matters in the text Stone, *Legal System*, Intro., §3; *infra* Ch. 11, §§7-8; Stone, *Social Dimensions*, Ch. 15, §24.

[152] A. Kaufmann, "*Der Mensch im Recht*" (1958) *Ruperto-Carola* 2-8. He thinks, therefore, that it is only "a relativity of value in respect of the subject", not "value-relativity as such". See A. Kaufmann, "*Gedanken zur Überwindung rechtsphilosophischen Relativismus*" (1960) 46 *Arch. R.- und Sozialph.* 553-569, esp. 558-59, 566-67, where he develops the thesis that tolerance arising from relativism which does not recognise "ontological truth" of values is "the false tolerance of the coexistence" of mutually exclusive "absolutisms". Relativism should summon us not to renounce cognition but to redouble cognitional efforts (567).

many important contemporary juristic inquiries. We owe his ideas at least that patience which he thought his relativism showed to be necessary in man's approach to the essential problems of social life.

Patience gains the value of permanence for the transitory. It holds firm the fleeting instant; it means victory over Time, because it has no fear of losing time. At every point of its road it is at its destination and enjoys the product of work already when the work is being done. It means balance, faith, and trust. It has created the Persian carpet and the Gothic cathedral. It is the gentle mother of culture.[153]

---

[153] Quoted in A. Kaufmann, *Naturrecht und Geschichtlichkeit* (1957) 31.

CHAPTER 9

PRAGMATISM

§1. BACKGROUND: RELATION OF POUND'S THEORY OF JUSTICE TO HIS SOCIOLOGICAL THOUGHT. Roscoe Pound's theory of justice, by reason of its pragmatic nature, is interlocked with his theory of the social phenomena behind law—his sociological theory of interests.[1] There was long an insufficient awareness of his theory of justice itself,[2] aggravated by the absence of clear demarcation of it in Pound's earlier scattered writings,[3] and even now in his great treatise *Jurisprudence*.[4] We believe it the more important to maintain the separate examination of his position on justice which we initiated in 1935, leaving the sociological aspect for our work on *Social Dimensions of Law and Justice*. For we believe that in his thought relating to justice, few branches of Anglo-American law lack the effects of half a century of persistent pressing by Pound and his disciples of the

[1] This is more fully discussed in Stone, *Social Dimensions*, Chs. 1 and 4ff. For a biography of Pound see P. Sayre, *The Life of Roscoe Pound* (1948), with bibli.

[2] See, e.g., P. Lepaulle, "The Function of Comparative Law . . ." (1922) 35 *H.L.R.* 383, 845-851, and F. K. Beutel, "Some Implications of Experimental Jurisprudence" (1934) 48 *H.L.R.* 169, 177, 186-89; Cohen, *Social Order* 327; Sir Maurice Amos, "Roscoe Pound" in Jennings (ed.), *Theories of Law* 86; W. L. Grossman, "The Legal Philosophy of Roscoe Pound" (1935) 44 *Yale L.J.* 605; J. C. H. Wu, "The Juristic Philosophy of Roscoe Pound" (1923) 18 *Ill. L.R.* 285. But see, in later writings, Stone, *Province*, Ch. 15; G. W. Paton, *Jurisprudence* (2 ed. 1951) 197ff.; Patterson, *Jurisprudence* 516ff. For a systematic stricturing of Pound's general pragmatic position from the Thomistic natural law standpoint, see L. J. McManaman, "Social Engineering: The Legal Philosophy of Roscoe Pound" (1958) 33 *St. John's L.R.* 1-47.

The present writer was first led to attempt a coherent account (Stone, "Pound's Theory of Justice") by the give and take of oral discussion with Dean Pound when teaching the Jurisprudence Seminar at Harvard from 1931 to 1936. That article benefited from Pound's comments before publication. The present revision takes account of Pound's further comments on the writer's position, and restatements of his own position, in various articles (see, e.g., "Juristic Theory in the Atomic Age" (1955) 9 *Rutg. L.R.* 464, 466ff.), and in his 5 volume *magnum opus, Jurisprudence* (1959). It seeks also to confront this theory with social changes which have proceeded in Western and other countries since the *Province* was published. As we wrote it, Pound continued to make his contributions to the law (see, e.g., his "Critique" in (1961) 46 *Minn. L.R.* 117 of Friedmann, *Changing Society*; "The Fourteenth Amendment and the Right of Privacy" (1961) 13 *W. Res. L.R.* 34-55; and "Runaway Courts in the Runaway World" (1963) 10 *U.C.L.A.L.R.* 729-738). The hope that he might be moved to clarify some of the newer issues here raised is unhappily defeated by his lamented death in July, 1964, as we are on the press.

[3] Notably relevant are his *Legal History* esp. lect. vii; *Law and Morals* (1924); "Scope and Purpose of Sociological Jurisprudence" (1911) 24 *H.L.R.* 591, (1912) 25 *id.* 140, 489; "Social Justice and Legal Justice" (1912) 75 *Cent. L.J.* 455; "The End of Law as Developed in Juristic Thought" (1914) 27 *H.L.R.* 605, (1917) 30 *id.* 201; "The End of Law as Developed in Legal Rules and Doctrines" (1914) 27 *id.* 195; "Ideal Element in American Legal Decision" (1931) 45 *id.* 136; "A Theory of Social Interests" (1921) 15 *Proc. Am. Soc. Society* 16; "Twentieth Century Ideas as to the End of Law" in *Harvard Legal Essays* (1934) 357; "A Comparison of Ideals of Law" (1933) 47 *H.L.R.* 1; *Social Control*; "Social Interests"; *New Paths of the Law* (1950); *Justice According to Law* (1952); and *Philosophy of Law*. See for biographical material and fuller bibliographies, the celebration volume for Pound's 75th birthday, Sayre (ed.), *Modern Legal Philosophies* Intro. 1-13. *Cf.* in many respects with Pound's positions Krabbe, *The State* esp. iv, v, and transl's Intro. lvii-lxxxi.

[4] See 3 *Jurisprudence* 3-373, esp. 3-30.

question, "What are you good for?" This is a question which challenges theories of justice, if indeed it is not the question of justice itself. And we are also indebted to three score and ten years of Pound's cultivation and exposition of contemporary theories responding to the challenge, across the insular boundaries which formerly separated not only Western legal cultures from each other, but also juristic from ethical and sociological thought.[5]

The core of Pound's theory of justice, justifying its description as "pragmatist", may be stated at the outset in his own words. Justice as applied to law is not, he writes, "an individual virtue". Nor is it "the ideal relation among men". It is merely "such an adjustment of relations and ordering of conduct as will make the goods of existence . . . go round as far as possible with the least friction and waste".[6]

§2. LINKS WITH KOHLER, IHERING AND JAMES: CIVILISATION OF THE TIME AND PLACE AS MANIFEST IN HUMAN CLAIMS. Pound repeatedly incorporated in his system as a focal point Kohler's conception of civilisation.[7] Like Kohler, Roscoe Pound sees in law an attempt to maintain, further and transmit civilisation (meaning by civilisation the raising of human powers over internal and external nature to constantly greater completeness, yielding the maximum control of which "men are for the time being, capable");[8] and, like him, sees in the law of a particular society an instrument for maintaining, furthering and transmitting civilisation as embodied in that society.[9] He would observe, therefore, the phenomena of a given society which constitute its efforts towards civilisation, and draw from them by dint of objective synthesis the principles concerning human conduct which those efforts presuppose. These principles he, like Kohler, terms the jural postulates of the civilisation of the time and place. Their general nature, with examples of Professor Pound's suggestions, are discussed in §§4 and 11 below.

While Kohler is never very definite as to the nature of the phenomena from which the jural postulates are drawn, Pound sees them to be *de facto* claims made by human beings. This difference is carried through to the scheme of interests to be secured by law which is fundamental in Pound's criterion. In this latter respect he goes entirely beyond Kohler. In fact, it may properly be said that his debt to Kohler ceases with the adoption, as *one way* of presenting the phenomena of the civilisation which press upon the law, of the idea of the jural postulates of the civilisation of the time and place. He seems to feel the need for some alternative way of bringing the notion of civilisation to bear upon the detailed problems of administration of justice; and it is here that he has recourse to the scheme of interests to be secured by law. At times he presents this scheme of interests as part (along with the jural postulates) of the apparatus for one method, the two elements then functioning together, in a sense to be examined below, to provide his method of adjusting the conflicting *de facto*

---

[5] See the fuller appreciation in J. Stone, "The Golden Age of Pound" (1962) 4 *Syd. L.R.* 1-27.

[6] *Social Control* 65. *Cf.* now Pound, 3 *Jurisprudence* 5ff. (§80), on this and the other intellectual linkages mentioned above.

[7] Kohler, *Lehrbuch* 1-3, Albrecht's transl. as *Philosophy of Law* (1914) 3-6; and see *supra* Ch. 6.

[8] *Social Control* 16.

[9] As to the hidden plurality of meanings here see *supra* Ch. 6, §16. Besides the predecessors here mentioned the direct influence of others like Jeremy Bentham, Lester F. Ward, and Oliver Wendell Holmes Jr. might be urged as equally important.

claims. At other times, however, the scheme of interests is regarded as providing in itself a sufficient means to this adjustment, and the jural postulates are then relegated to the role of an alternative method of analysis and criterion, of equal, but separate, validity, on which the efficacy of the scheme of interests is in no way dependent.

For the "scheme of interests" in either of these roles, as well as for the drawing of the jural postulates themselves from the *de facto* human claims, it is to Rudolf von Ihering[10] and William James that we must trace his thought. That law is a means of securing interests was a theme so effectively revived by Ihering that in less than half a century it had ceased to be a discovery. What is basic in any particular problem is the conflict of interests, i.e., that the claims of individuals for themselves, for society as a whole and for the state, are in mutual and reciprocal conflict. James put it thus for ethics:

> Any desire is imperative to the extent of its amount, it makes itself valid by the fact that it exists at all.[11] Since everything which is demanded is by that fact a good, must not the guiding principle for ethical philosophy (since all demands conjointly cannot be satisfied in this poor world) be simply to satisfy at all times as many demands as we can?[12]

So, Professor Pound, putting it for law, says that in any given society its legal system represents an attempt to adjust the interests of individuals with each other, including those interests asserted on behalf of society and the state, with the least possible sacrifice of the whole.[13]

It is therefore both possible and (he thinks) necessary to set out in an ordered scheme for any given society, the interests to which its law ought to give effect. This scheme will include not merely those interests which the law actually enforces, but those also which this particular society recognises as interests to which effect ought to be given. In Pound's classification of interests for the purpose of convenience into social, public and individual, there is a definite similarity to Ihering's analysis of "the conditions of social life" into those pertaining to the individual, the state and society.[14] He does not, however, fall into the trap of maintaining such a classification at the moment of comparison, for he asserts (as we shall more fully see) that for this purpose it is first necessary to reduce all the interests conflicting in the particular case to the same terms, individual or social. Such interchangeability is possible, he thinks, from the very definition of the term "interest" as a *de facto* claim of a human being.[15] The resemblance to Ihering on this point therefore is quite superficial.

§3. ADJUSTMENT OF CONFLICTING CLAIMS BY REFERENCE TO ALL THE INTERESTS PRESSING IN THE PARTICULAR CIVILISATION: LINKS WITH STAMMLER. The next step brings us to the final stage of the solution of particular problems. The question, what is a just solution, whether legislative or judicial, of a particular controversy or type of controversy, involves

---

10 See, e.g., *Social Control* 65.

11 W. James, *The Will to Believe* (1897) 195, and see the pages following.

12 *Id.* at 205.

13 *Cf.* Garlan, *Legal Realism* 41; Laski, *Politics* 288: "Our rules of conduct are justified only as what they are in working induces our allegiance to them".

14 See Ihering, 1 *Zweck* 427-500, c. viii, §12, Husik's transl. 325-81.

15 But see Stone, *Social Dimensions*, Ch. 4, §§3, 6, for further discussion of this matter.

an evaluation of the interests, that is, the concrete human demands, which are in conflict. Such conflict there will certainly be, for *ex hypothesi* that is precisely how the problem of justice arises. How are we to evaluate the conflicting interests as against each other? Here, in a most interesting way, Pound's thought has echoings of Stammler's device of the "special community".[16]

By this device, as we have seen,[17] Stammler attempted to match the concrete human interests involved in a particular controversy against his abstract *a priori* conception of law as the harmonisation of individual purposes with each other and with those of society. He notionally placed the assertors of the conflicting interests in a "special community". This notional group he offered as a concretisation in the world of matter of "the Idea" of society, or the "Social Ideal", and the adjustment of the conflicting purposes within it will be a just one if and only if it realises "the Idea" of society, or the "Social Ideal".[18] And this he purported to ensure by saying that the conflicts of purposes within the group are to be resolved by applying the "Principles of Just Law", which he purported to have drawn by pure reason from the "Social Ideal". We have seen, however, the insoluble difficulties in this procedure arising from the gap between the *a priori* nature of these "Principles of Just Law" and the empirical nature of the subject-matter to which they are to be applied.

Roscoe Pound seeks to avoid this kind of objection by interposing a mediating device in order to put into concrete terms what Stammler put abstractly. This mediating reference, it appears, may be *either* to the scheme of interests *or* to the jural postulates. In either case, the first and vital step in resolving a given controversy is to see what interests are in conflict. But in terms of the former device, the scheme of interests, these conflicting interests are already, in their generalised form, part of the scheme of interests in which the level of the particular civilisation is manifest. The conflict must, therefore, be resolved by choosing that solution which will do least injury to the scheme as a whole. Or, as James would put it: "That act must be best . . . which makes for the best whole, in the sense of awakening the least sum of dissatisfaction."[19] In terms of the latter alternative, the jural postulates (or presuppositions for the law) of that civilisation, the conflict must be resolved so as to conform as nearly as possible to those postulates.

§4. JURAL POSTULATES DRAWN FROM THE HUMAN CLAIMS OR INTERESTS ACTUALLY PRESSING. The pattern of Pound's method and its relation to previous thought may now therefore be stated as follows: (a) The observation of *de facto* claims, demands or interests in the given society which are to be regarded as valid in themselves: from Rudolf von Ihering and William James. (b) The discernment of the jural postulates presupposed by the *de facto* claims, demands or interests in that society at a given time: from Josef Kohler. (c) The construction of a scheme of *de facto* claims, demands or interests asserted in a given civilisation arranging in a different and more orderly way the pressing human claims from which the jural postulates were also drawn: no direct source. (d) The analysis of interests conflicting

---

[16] Stammler, *Lehre* 281-84, 292-98. I. Husik's translation as *The Theory of Justice* (1925) 215-17, 223-28, seems not entirely adequate in these sections.
[17] See more fully on the following points *supra* Ch. 6, §§1-9.
[18] See Ch. 6, §§7ff.
[19] W. James, *op. cit. supra* n.11 at 205.

in a given case, and reference of the conflict for adjustment to the jural postulates or to the whole scheme of interests for a solution: vaguely foreshadowed by William James and Rudolf Stammler, but only indirectly based on their work. Pound's writings suggest[20] that the testing by reference to the jural postulates, or by reference to the whole scheme of interests, are alternative ways of proceeding. But of the two he finally seemed to prefer the scheme of interests,[21] and the study of interests is in any case essential to either approach. So that, despite the traces of other philosophical approaches in his work, its deepest formative strain, as well as its over-all mood, seem best described as pragmatist.

We may now explain more fully these steps in Pound's criterion of justice, reserving major criticism, for clarity's sake, for §§9-12. First, then, as to the observation of claims pressing and the formulation therefrom of the jural postulates.

In a given society at a given time individuals are asserting interests as worthy of protection by the law of that society. Men have certain wants, desires, claims, interests (Pound uses the words as synonymous), and they require the law under which they live to secure those wants to them. In order to understand what law in that society should do, the first step, therefore, must be to observe and record the social phenomena with which the law is concerned, namely, the interests which human beings are actually pressing for recognition by law. From this comprehensive picture the jurist can also draw out, by as impersonal a synthesis as possible, the fundamental principles concerning human conduct (or "the jural postulates") which substantially all of the phenomena presuppose. The phenomena are claims actually made by men, regardless of the claimants' or the observers' own moral evaluations of them. But it must be apparent that even in a relatively stable and homogeneous society "minority" claims always exist which are quite at odds with those generally prevalent, and inexplicable by the same set of postulates. The jural postulates then are distinct from the actual claims in two respects. First, they are *rationalisations* of these claims, not necessarily coinciding with the actual psychological origins of the claimants' behaviour. Second, they are rationalisations not of all the actual claims but only of *substantially* all.[22] These presuppositions, then, of the mass of claims,

---

[20] *Cf.* now quite explicitly 3 *Jurisprudence* 7-8 (§80), and earlier his *Legal History* 141ff. and *Social Control* 112ff. The point is still subject to some ambiguities and cross-purposes: see the valiant attempt to cope with these by Braybrooke, "Roscoe Pound" 310-12, marred unfortunately by his attempt to make room also for Edwin Patterson's view that "social interests" are themselves Pound's criterion. We shall show (*infra* §6) that this must be ruled out as a third criterion. We add that Braybrooke, in our view, misreads (at 311) Pound's late reformulation of the "scheme of interests" version in non-Jamesian terms (see Pound, "The Role of the Will in Law" (1954) 68 H.L.R. 1 at 19) as a rejection of it; and also that it is oversimple to take our own *Province,* Ch. 15, as asserting Pound's adoption of the "jural postulates" version *simpliciter* (see Braybrooke at 312). Though the "scheme of interests" and "jural postulates" devices are strictly alternative, they are also to be stated as cumulative because Pound also seems to imply that their use may be mutually confirmatory.

[21] See, e.g., 3 *Jurisprudence* 15. We agree with Braybrooke, *op. cit.* 312, n. 68, that at 3 *id.* 32 Pound appears implicitly to pass over recourse to jural postulates altogether; yet it is difficult simply to ignore so much of Pound's exposition.

[22] In addition to the difficulties just mentioned as to the *functional* relation between the jural postulates and the scheme of interests, difficulties arise as to the *contentual* relation between them. On the assumption that the postulates represent the *same materials* as the interests, raised to a higher level of abstraction, the failure of the former to cover quite the same ground as the latter gives rise to problems which are admirably illustrated by Braybrooke, "Roscoe Pound" 312. We would say rather that while Pound presents the former as arrived at *more* by a process of abstraction, he presents the scheme of interests as produced rather by means of classification. Yet it is

are what Professor Pound, following Kohler, terms the "jural postulates" of the civilisation of the time and place. What is their utility when found?

On the one hand, they are working hypotheses which have been found by observation to rationalise, within the limits above stressed, the claims, demands or interests pressing in a given society. They are, therefore, not *mere* speculation. On the other hand, the process of drawing the jural postulates from the mass of claims can scarcely be a very exact one; if it can be described as "induction" it would be so only in a rather impressionistic sense. It must be noticed, further, that they are working hypotheses, not of what law *is*, but of what the *men* in the given society *want law to do*. They are postulates *for* law, not postulates *of* law. Being drawn not only from that small corner of the field of social phenomena which we call the legal order, but from the entire field, they are not merely rationalisations of the *legal status quo*. They can serve also as a gauge of the actual achievement of the law by reference to *all* the claims, in the given society at the given time, which the law ought to try to secure.[23] The jural postulates, as working hypotheses, are maintainable only until new facts show that they are no

---

still important to realise that the latter process also involves abstraction; and the discrepancies between the scheme of interests and the jural postulates must finally be explained by laying the stress on *those elements* in the abstraction of the postulates which are referred to in the text. *Cf. infra* §5.

[23] Braybrooke, "Roscoe Pound", esp. at 292-93, offers two criticisms of the postulates which are saved from square self-contradiction only by tentativeness of statement. One, that the postulates offered by Pound are not in fact restricted to any specific time and place, will be discussed *infra* §11. The other is that Pound's formulations merely "reflect developmental tendencies already present in the law. But to say that law in a civilized society *is* developing in a particular way, and to equate the lines of that development *ex post facto* with necessary conditions for the attainment of 'civilization', appears hardly to be the heroic task which Kohler envisaged as that of the jurist." (*Id*. 293; *cf. id*. 297). So Beutel, *supra* n. 2, at 177, dismisses both the postulates and the interests as "little more than rational speculation based on the legal *status quo*". This kind of criticism gains apparent support from Pound's early formulations of "jural postulates"; see, e.g., Postulates III, IV, and V (*infra* §11) as to contracts, negligence and the "general principle" of *Rylands* v. *Fletcher*. And see *infra* n. 68a.

Insofar, however, as such comments are offered as expressing Pound's criterion rather than occasional lapses in statement, they are wide of the mark. Admittedly the point is often slurred, even by Pound himself. Thus at 3 *Jurisprudence* 7-8 he describes the alternative approaches *via* the jural postulates and the scheme of interests. The former, he says, refers to the grant or denial of legal recognition to "jural presuppositions of life in civilised society"; it "shows us what we may expect to find asserted . . . as well as the basis of recognition and securing". The latter (the scheme of interests) displays "the claims . . . asserted and calling for recognition and securing"; it shows "what (claims) are pressing . . . *so far as the course of legislation and adjudication can indicate*". (Italics supplied.) Clearly, apart from this last phrase, the sense is that attributed in the text; the postulates and the scheme may embrace claims even not yet legally recognised, or even still legally denied. That, too, surely, is required by the very stress on the *de facto* nature of the claims as *not* creatures of the law but valid by the fact that they are made. The phrase italicised above, however, referring to the course of legislation and adjudication, may mislead us (if carelessly read) into thinking that Pound would only admit to the scheme such claims as are already recognised by the legal order. In fact all that it appears to mean is that the legislative proceedings and judicial reports are for lawyers the most convenient evidence of claims pressed for recognition, whether this recognition has been granted or denied. He would certainly not say that they could be *the only* evidence.

The slurring, unless correctly understood, may produce vast misinterpretations. Thus F. K. Beutel, *supra* n. 2, at 186-89, speaks of Pound's analysis of "law" into the elements of "precepts", "techniques" and "received ideals", as if the "received ideals" were Pound's criterion of justice. In fact that analysis merely stresses that the *authoritative materials* include not only rules as Austin assumed, but also the other elements mentioned. Far from being a criterion of justice, the received ideals themselves may be or may become unjust. In short, Pound's criterion is directed to the criticism of received ideals as much as to that of precepts and techniques. This slurring may also have contributed to many neo-realist disagreements with Pound,

longer apt. Meanwhile they are to be put to the practical work of bringing
the legal institutions of a particular society into a condition of harmony
with themselves or with the scheme of interests, and therefore into a condition
of harmony with the actual demands made by men in that society.

§5. THE SCHEME OF INTERESTS PRESSING IN THE PARTICULAR CIVILISATION.
As an alternative and supplementary device for this same purpose Pound
offers his "scheme of interests". This again is an attempt to mediate between
the detailed problems of administration of justice and the civilisation of the
time and place. He would draw up a classified inventory of the interests
which claim recognition and enforcement by law in the given society. It is
clear that the drawing up of such a scheme involves a degree of abstraction
from the actual *de facto* demands. For the very purpose of schematisation
is to simplify and stabilise, to a form usable in the judgment of justice, the
dynamic and rather formless mass of men's *de facto* claims as they actually
confront us in society. At best, therefore, in the device of the scheme of
interests, as in that of the jural postulates, not all *de facto* claims but only
substantially all will be embraced. There will be a margin of excluded claims
in each case, not necessarily quite identical. Those claims which fall between
the "all" and the "substantially all" will be the victims of this guillotine
procedure. For instance, in a society for which an apt jural postulate is
that "in civilised society men must be able to assume that they may control
for beneficial purposes what they have created by their own labour, and
what they have acquired in the existing social and economic order,"[24] claims
for an equal share of each individual in the world's riches, or for all things
to be enjoyed in common, are likely to figure as little in the scheme of
interests as they could in the jural postulates.

Subject to this, however, the jural postulates should take into account,
and the scheme of interests should include, all the *de facto* claims actually
made. This, of course, is not to say that every *de facto* claim or interest
which finds a place in the scheme of interests will be given effect in all
circumstances. Claims within a reasonably homogeneous legal order which
are not *necessarily* mutually incompatible may nevertheless come into conflict
in particular situations. Indeed, most of the problems in which the judgment
of justice is called for arise from a conflict of two or more of such *de facto*
claims, none of which can be given effect to completely without prejudice to
the others. The scheme of interests, like the jural postulates, is a device for
presenting to the mind of the judge and legislator a rough picture of the
actual claims made by men in a given society at a given time, to which
justice requires them to give effect so far as possible. Pound adopts as a
convenient mode of classification of these claims the division into individual,
public and social interests. This does not mean that he opposes individual to
social or public interests, for he insists that all are claims made by individual human beings. The difference is that some are more readily thought
of as made on behalf of individual, some on behalf of social life, and some
on behalf of the life of politically organised society. Each, he says, is
convertible into the other, and must be so converted for purposes of com-

despite the fact that their stress on "squeals" as a guide to justice seems to follow
Pound, when he is correctly understood as here presented. See Garlan, *Legal Realism*
122ff.
[24] Pound, *Outlines* (4 ed. 1928) 108.

parison and evaluation,[25] though finally it seems to be into either "individual" or "social" terms that he seems to translate them.

In a given controversy (as we have seen) the first step is to ascertain what interests are in conflict and to state them in common terms, and as a practical matter it is usually simplest to put them all in terms of social interests. These conflicting interests, in a generalised form, are already included in the scheme of interests. Since they are in conflict, it is obvious that any solution of this particular case is going to give legal effect to part of the scheme at the expense of some other part. That solution must, therefore, be chosen which will cause the "least" disturbance to the scheme of interests as a whole, or will "secure all interests as far as possible with the least sacrifice of the totality of interests or the scheme of interests as a whole".[26] The process, in a word, is one of evaluating the conflicting interests as against each other *in terms of the quantitative impairment,* resulting from one solution or the other, *of the scheme of interests as a whole.*

§6. QUANTIFICATION PROBLEMS IN POUND'S CRITERION. Whether we use "jural postulates" or "the scheme of interests", construction of such devices which are apt for a particular society will involve a number of seemingly quantitative judgments. The formulation of the jural postulates involves a judgment as to what the *preponderant* mass of claims presupposes, and conversely as to what claims may be ignored because of this preponderance. The scheme of interests insofar as it involves a static abstraction from the dynamic complex of concrete claims, must also involve a corresponding discrimination. The conflict of interests in a particular case is to be referred either to the jural postulates, for maximum conformity therewith of the solution; or to the scheme of interests to test which solution will least injure (or most fully effectuate) the "totality" of the scheme of interests. All these words, "preponderant", "maximum", "least", "most", and the various synonyms and correlatives which we find in Pound's expositions are hornets' nests. Do they point to a counting of heads, an arithmetical computation on each side of the ledger of the number of human beings affected, and the number and intensity of interests of each? Or are we to assume some higher value (in a qualitative rather than quantitative sense) of some parts of the scheme of interests as compared to others? Even apart from the point that such quantifications would be difficult to make and to calculate with, are we to understand Pound as intending to make them? And this is but another way of asking how far the criterion of justice here offered is a relativist one, relative to the quantities of human claims here and now pressing, and how far it contains elements of absolute valuation. For insofar as we cannot give reality to the appearance of quantification, and no other relativist basis is offered, elements of absolute valuation must be present, even if unacknowledged.

Pound himself has now replied to this last point, by saying (in effect) that while his theory is a relativist one some absolute elements must be expected to enter, just as we find conversely that "absolute" standards have often in fact been an idealisation of the "relative".[27] This answer does not, however, dispose of our real concerns, which are that the theory of interests can only fulfil its apparent promise if somewhat greater precision can be

---

25 But see as to the difficulties involved Stone, *Social Dimensions,* Ch. 4.
26 3 *Jurisprudence* 334 (§100).
27 3 *Jurisprudence* 13 (§80), which really only reaffirms his *Social Control* 79-80.

given to the implied notions of quantity. Without this we cannot tell *what degree* of objectivity (and therefore of verifiability) can be attributed to the apparently quantitative determinations on which, in Pound's theory, every judgment of justice seems to depend.

These doubts surrounding the possibility of quantifying interests are not unrelated to the major difficulty which must now be raised concerning what Pound means by "social interests". If quantification is to be taken seriously, arithmetic (even if not "simple" arithmetic) supplies the method of justice. And the present writer, after years of treasured association with Pound at Harvard, had no doubt that this was indeed Pound's position, until 1947, when Professor Edwin W. Patterson, himself a student of Pound, published his article in the first Pound *Festschrift*,[28] itself following on Pound's article "A Survey of Social Interests" in 1943.[29]

Patterson's central assertion is that "Pound's theory of social interests . . . represents a teleological axiology like that of Bentham and Ihering". He means by this (he says) that for Pound, "social interests" are the final yardstick for adjusting conflicting interests in the judgment of justice. Each of Pound's "social interests", he tells us, is a measuring or testing device for "individual interests"; and (again) a "social interest is a means to the maintenance of a civilised society". As Patterson sees it, then, each of Pound's "social interests" is itself a measuring instrument, rather than a part of the phenomena (that is, the *de facto* human interests) to be measured. We shall see shortly that when this leads him into an *impasse*, Patterson offers a supplementary version which, however, seems even more at odds with the meaning which Pound has generally conveyed.

Patterson's main version (of which we now speak) would necessarily imply that "social interests" (as he thinks Pound uses that term) consist of different stuff from his "individual interests". If Pound's "individual interests", as is certainly clear, are always *de facto* human claims made at a given time and place, valid by the very fact that they are made, then "social interests" must (if Patterson is right) be something more (or, at any rate, something *other*) than this. Yet the present writer has always understood Pound to say that all *de facto* human claims can be stated as either "social interests" or "individual interests". Pound recognised that our ways of thought and speech often make it easier to think of some human claims (for instance, the claim to security of the physical person, or to free individual self-assertion) in terms of *individual* interests; but he has insisted that even these can be stated also in *social* terms, for instance, in terms of the social interest in the general security, and in a minimum individual life, respectively. And he has urged almost *ad nauseam*, that before the judging of a concrete conflict of interests, we must always bring *all* the conflicting claims to one same level, "social" or "individual". The purpose presumably is to neutralise any emotional prejudice stirred in the judge by either symbol.[30]

Professor Patterson, however, asserts that "a social interest" is not

---

[28] "Pound's Theory of Social Interests" in Sayre (ed.), *Modern Legal Philosophies* 558-571. And see his *Jurisprudence*. Patterson has not revised his interpretation in his recent review article, "Roscoe Pound on Jurisprudence" (1960) 60 *Columbia L.R.* 1124-1132, esp. 1128-29; nor has he adverted to the present writer's dissent from it in J. Stone, Book Review (1955) 50 *Northw. U.L.R.* 130ff., esp. 134-37.

[29] (1943) 57 *H.L.R.* 886.

[30] See Pound's earlier statements cited in J. Stone, Book Review, *supra* n. 28. Braybrooke, "Roscoe Pound", by including the Patterson version as one of Pound's own versions (see *supra* n. 20), sometimes rather distorts Pound's analysis; see, e.g., at 317.

merely a way of referring to a *de facto* human claim. He says that Pound would not recognise as a "social interest" any "interest" which was not a means of maintaining "a civilised society" on "a mature level of culture".[31] This means that "social interests" are not *de facto* claims or interests, but rather claims *deserving of approval*; it turns them, in other words, into criteria for judging *de facto* human demands.[31a] He has not explained how this can be true if, as Pound constantly insists, the interests that *he* is talking about are what *people de facto claim,* not what *the legislator thinks they ought to claim.* Not unexpectedly, in the circumstances, this main version of Patterson, even as he utters it, lands him in a confessed *impasse.* For he has to pose in the end, without offering any answer, the question how it can be possible for Pound to weigh "social interests" against each other. This conundrum could only arise because of the deviant version of "social interests" which Patterson adopts. On Pound's own version, as we have always understood him (and as he continued to write in 1959) it simply does not arise. He has never suggested that we should weigh either "social interests" *or* "individual interests" against each other as categories, but rather that we should ascertain how far the whole scheme of *de facto* human interests pressing for recognition in the particular society will be secured or frustrated by the alternative solutions offered. The words "social" or "individual" are to be discounted or (which is the same thing) neutralised before the moment of judgment. Pound's theory, as we have just shown, raises questions of quantification and commensurability of interests; but they are not the questions in Patterson's conundrum. And they make (we submit) a good deal more sense.

The fact that Patterson's main version, namely, that of evaluation by reference to a plurality of "social interests", ends in an *impasse,* is somewhat concealed by his introduction (almost inadvertently) of a rather different test of value. According to this, judgment is according to "the social conse-quences which *the social interest* designates as good or bad". In the present context this distinction between "good" and "bad" cannot turn on maximum satisfaction of demands. If "the social interest" is to determine whether "the social consequences" of one solution or another are "good" or "bad", the term "*the* social interest" must be but a symbol for whatever *final* evaluation is reached in the concrete case. Like Ihering's "social utility", and like the vulgar use of the terms "the public interest",[31b] and "the common good", "the social interest" is a name for the conclusion reached, and not a method of reaching it. It is difficult to see how such a meaning of "social interest" can stand along with his simultaneous main version, whereby Pound recognises many "social interests", each of which is "*a* measuring or testing device for individual interests". But, however that be, just as we have seen the main version to end in an *impasse,* so this supple-mentary version ends in a circularity.

§7. POUND'S POSITION IN 1959. What light does Pound's *Jurisprudence* (1959) throw on these central notions of his sociological doctrines? We

---

31 Patterson, *Jurisprudence* 525.

31a It is as to this sense of interests that, in the context of administrative decision making Jacob-Flink, *Value Decision* 31, concludes that to treat "interests" as "norma-tive standards of the desirable" is finally confusing, and that "values should . . . be viewed as *one component* of interest, rather than as synonymous with it".

31b As to the use of which in administrative policy-formulation see Stone, *Social Dimensions,* Ch. 14, §23.

hope we may show here, once and for all, that the only view which makes sense of Pound's main exposition is the one we have always understood him to hold. This is that his "social interests" are not (*pace* Patterson) a measuring device at all, but rather a way of referring to *de facto* human claims, just as the term "individual interests" is another way of referring to the same claims.

The main exposition of the theory of interests is in the third volume of the work (§§80-102). We look first to §81, where Pound restates his theory of interests as a criterion of justice. He there insists without quali- fication that the "interests", or "claims" or "demands" with which he is concerned are *de facto* psychological phenomena which pre-exist and are not merely the creations of the legal order. "A legal system," he says, "attains the ends of the legal order (1) by recognising certain *interests, individual, public and social*; (2) by defining the limits within which *those interests shall be recognised.* . . ."[32] Clearly, the measure for defining the limits of recog- nition cannot consist of "social interests", for these are expressly listed among the phenomena[33] for which a measure is required. And, later in the same section, Pound is even more emphatic that these "interests" are the subject-matter to which "the principles of valuation" are applied, adding that apart from these principles of valuation, the securing of interests is limited also by "the limits of effective legal action".[34] He gives an account of individual interests, public interests and social interests unchanged from that presented in previous pages, including the intertranslatability of "social" and "individual" interests.[35]

Furthermore, this intertranslatability is given major reaffirmation in §100:

> In weighing or valuing claims or demands with respect to other claims or demands, we must be careful to compare them on the same plane. If we put one as an individual interest and the other as a social interest we may decide the question in advance in our very way of putting it. For example, in the "truck act" cases the claim of the employer to make contracts freely may be thought of as an individual interest of substance. In that event we must weigh it with the claim of the employee not to be coerced by economic pressure into contracts to take his pay in orders on a company store, thought of as an individual interest of personality.[36]

"In general, but not always," adds Pound, "it is expedient to put claims or demands in their most generalised form, i.e. as social interests, in order to compare them." But it may also, he thinks, be possible to look at them all as individual interests.[37] Nothing, we suggest, could be more at odds with

---

[32] Pound, 3 *Jurisprudence* 5-24, esp. 16-21.

[33] See this made even more explicit in §93, esp. 289-91.

[34] At 3 *Jurisprudence* 288-89, he analogises his "interests" (both social and individual without discrimination) to the "instincts" of W. McDougall, *Social Psycho- logy* (12 ed. 1917) 55ff. On "The Limits of Effective Legal Action", see Pound, 3 *op. cit.* 353-373.

[35] *Id.* 23-24 (§81). On the slight obscurity at one point, see Stone, article cited *supra* n. 5 at 18.

[36] *Id.* 328 (§100).

[37] See 3 *op. cit.* 31, 328-29. *Cf.* his "Theory of Social Interests" (1921) 15 *Proc. Am. Soc. Society* 16, 32, and his Book Review (1948) 61 *H.L.R.* 721, 735. Even as to "public interests" he now also writes in §92 (p. 236) that "ultimately they come down to a social interest in the security of social institutions". This, perhaps, is a response to the present writer's view in *Province*, Ch. 20, §4, as to which see now Stone, *Social Dimensions*, Ch. 4, §3.

either of the two versions which Patterson gives to "social interests". Far from Pound's "social interests" being the measure for valuing, they are presented along with "individual interests" as ways of referring to the same subject-matter, the *de facto* human claims, which are to be measured. It is to ensure that the measure will be impartially applied that the conflicting interests must be looked at as all of them "social", or all of them "individual".[38]

Finally, any doubt left by two or three curiously ambiguous turns of phrase,[39] must surely be wholly and finally removed by the last three paragraphs of §100, where Pound sets out his own departures from "social utilitarian" thinking.[40]

He first deals with Holmes' well-known formulation that "the true grounds of decision are questions of policy and of social advantage",[41] a formulation obviously cognate if not identical with Patterson's version of Pound which says that the test for valuing claims is whether "*the* social interest" designates the "social consequences" of the claims as "good or bad". Yet Pound is here concerned to reject this kind of test altogether. It is, he says, not a test at all. Since we do not know, and the test does not tell us, what "social advantage" is, to invoke it is merely to convert the inquiry about "justice" into an inquiry about "social advantage".

If, therefore, that Patterson version were to represent Pound's position, it would only do so against Pound's better judgment. Moreover, the final paragraph of §100[42] gives a similar flat rejection to the other main version of "social interests" attributed by Patterson to Pound, whereby "*a* social interest" must be a means of maintaining "a civilised society" on "a mature level of culture", so that "social interests" serve as a plurality of measures for evaluating conflicting individual interests.

Pound attributes this kind of notion also to the "social utilitarians", and says it is "very generally assumed in recent practice". He describes it

---

[38] This means, conversely, that *once we are in control of any prejudices associated with the symbols* "individual" and "social" it does not matter *in what verbal terms* we make the comparison. Thus at 3 *Jurisprudence* 38, Pound directly confronts the individual claim to nervous integrity with the social interest in the general security. And *cf. id.* 58 as to privacy.

[39] In §100 itself (at 329) Pound says that "often" the terms "individual" and "social" refer to "the same type of claims as they are asserted in different titles". This word "often" (if we were astute to hold him to every word) may be said to deny implicitly his preceding assertion that the "social-individual" intertranslatability is absolutely essential. It is, however, a flimsy inference to reverse so emphatic an explicit assertion. So is his reference at the same point to the "subsumption" of "individual interests" under "social interests", as a basis for reversing his explicit statement that there is no reason why conflicting interests (where this is convenient) should not all be translated into terms of individual interests for purposes of comparison. Later in the section, too (at 331), he speaks of the legislator's problem as "a practical one of securing the whole scheme of *social* (italics supplied) interests so far as he may". And in §8 (at 24) there is a sentence: "Every claim does not *necessarily* go, once and for all, in one of these categories" (i.e., "individual", "social", etc.). But to say that *every claim* does not *necessarily* so go, seems impliedly to deny, what in the immediately preceding paragraph he has squarely asserted, namely, that these categories are merely different ways of referring to the same *de facto* human claims. There is also a curious passage, 3 *id.* 27, to be contrasted with 3 *id.* 31.

We do not trouble to canvass side-references such as those in the corollary to his Jural Postulate I, as to liability for intentional damage. He there describes the privilege situation as one where the act is shown to be done in accordance with "some recognised public or social interest". This traditionally sanctified usage is obviously off the present point.

[40] At 331-34.

[41] See *id.* 331.

[42] *Id.* 332-333.

carefully, preparatory to rejecting it. According to this view, he says: "Individual interests are to be secured by law because and to the extent that they coincide with social interests, or better, because and to the extent that social interests are secured by securing them."[43] According to it, he goes on, "we secure individual interests so far as conduces to the general security, . . . to the security of social institutions, to the general morals", and the rest. On this view "while individual interests are one thing and social interests another, the law, which is a social institution, really secures individual interests because of a social advantage in doing so. . . . No individual may expect to be secured in an interest which conflicts with any social advantage unless he can show some countervailing social advantage in so securing him".[44] If Pound had deliberately focussed on the main Patterson version he could not have described it more clearly; nor could his rejection of it which follows be much clearer.

> My objection to this way of putting it is that it assumes demands may be referred absolutely and once and for all to a category of individual or one of social interests. Instead, I should say, we look at the individual demand in its larger aspect, as subsumed under some social interest in order to compare it with other individual demands treated in the same way.[45]

And his last word on the matter is an unambiguous reaffirmation of the *quantitative* basis of his own method of evaluation. "I should ask" he says—

> How far, if at all, may a *de facto* interest be recognised without substantial impairment of the scheme of interests as a whole? Accordingly, as I see it, the principle should be: Secure all interests so far as possible with the least sacrifice of the totality of interests as a whole.[46]

§8. INSTRUMENTAL VALUE OF THESE DEVICES. Roscoe Pound's proposals seem, in the last analysis, to be an attempt to implement the familiar thought that there should be a correspondence between the demands made by men in a given society at a given time and its law at that time. He generalises this thought, draws out its implications, and suggests devices by the use of which an approximation to the desired state of affairs may be attained. There is no magic in the discovery of "the civilisation of the time and place", nor in its "jural postulates", nor yet in the "scheme of interests" to be secured. Most serious proposals for law reform, most opinions as to the "soundness" of rules, and as to their "policy", are based on a similar mental process more or less coherent, more or less well-understood. The very commonplaceness of the thought, perhaps, adds importance to any endeavour to fashion it into a mental instrument from which vagueness and caprice are, so far as possible, eliminated. Commonplace thoughts do much of the work of the world. They will do it even if they are not, but they will do it better if they are, thoroughly understood. And the instrumental value in giving background and context remains, despite the fact that quantifying procedures stop short of guiding the final evaluative judgment.[47] Whatever these final difficulties, Pound is saying, the law-maker should be as conscious as possible

---

[43] *Id.* 332.
[44] *Id.* 333.
[45] *Ibid.*
[46] *Id.* 334.
[47] *Cf.* Garlan, *Legal Realism* 114, which perhaps underrates, however, the "elasticity, indeterminateness and ubiquitous relevance" (*id.* 106) of Pound's approach; and less clearly, Braybrooke, "Roscoe Pound" 301.

of the objective factors involved, and should make an honest attempt to take them into account. The position marches with Llewellyn's demand that "action should be bottomed on all the knowledge that can be got in time to act".[48] It marches also with Laski's demand[49] that decisions shall be "the largest empirical induction it is open to them to obtain", so that their power shall be built "from the experience of all persons affected by its exercise", and provide "the maximum guarantee available that the wants of each individual receive their due recognition in the totality of wants supplied".[50]

Yet at the same time it must be frankly acknowledged that the cry for bringing law into harmony with the conditions of the times tacitly assumes that the law will be better law when this has been done, that "good law" means law which is in harmony with the conditions of the time. But if there have been, and are, as few will deny, retrogressive civilisations, that is, civilisations which have moved in time from a higher to a lower level of powers over internal and external nature, it must be obvious that the process of bringing their law into harmony with their later state, is a process of degradation of the law from the level of harmony with a higher to that of harmony with a lower civilisation. Though a betterment in the sense of this pragmatist definition, it is not a betterment in the sense of more effectively maintaining, furthering and transmitting human powers over internal and external nature.

This, it will readily be seen, is the difficulty in which Kohler was involved by the ambiguity of the term "civilisation" which may mean (1) the civilisation that is, here and now, and (2) the civilisation which is about to be, perceptibly emerging from the trends of the present, or (3) some ultimate ideal of civilisation. Kohler made but a half-hearted attempt to meet this difficulty by urging in Hegelian fashion that ages which are retrogressive in relation to the ultimate ideal were but accidents in the course of human history, and that we would have to rely on the vision of the far-sighted ruler to use the law as an aid in reversing the downward movement. In the last resort he subordinated (1) and (2) to the absolute test of an ultimate ideal—the raising of human powers. But Pound seems to have abandoned any conscious attempt to qualify the *de facto* civilisation by reference to an ultimate civilisation.[51] And what is perhaps even more decisive is the implied attitude (for the most part)[52] that an attempt by

---

[48] Using K. N. Llewellyn's terms, "Some Realism about Realism" (1931) 44 *H.L.R.* 1222, 1223. F. S. Cohen's courageous if somewhat overconfident exposition in his *Ethical Systems* is, in the present writer's view, not basically different from Pound's, even though Cohen classifies his position as either "absolutistic-non-natural hedonism" or as "relativist-natural hedonism". His criticisms of Pound's position (see, e.g., 20 n.) seem with respect to be based on a partial understanding of it, as to the reasons for which see *supra* §1; and *cf.* a similar dissent from Cohen's view in Garlan, *Legal Realism* 114.

[49] Laski, *Politics* 241, 266-69, 272ff., and c. vii.

[50] Despite the many words of disagreement between Pound and Laski no close student can avoid being struck by the similarity of their apparent assumptions. See *id.* (3 ed. 1938) ix-x.

[51] Agreeing thus with the efforts in sociological thought generally to eliminate the evaluative element from the concept itself. See, e.g., the definition of "culture" in Cairns, *Legal Science* 29-30 as "the composite of products which result from human association". Later sociologists tend to recognise that this neutralisation of value-concepts is unworkable: see Stone, *Social Dimensions*, Ch. 1, §2, Ch. 4, §5. But in terms of Pound's consciously offered criteria, the desire to avoid such concealed evaluations as that here discussed is clear, even when he does not succeed in doing so. And see *supra* Ch. 8, §2.

[52] Pound obviously maintains certain personal absolutes. See his discussion (*Contemporary Juristic Theory* (1940) 29-56) of what he terms "skeptical realist" or "give-it-up Philosophies". *Cf.* his *Social Control* 28ff., 37, where he makes the

the law to pull in the opposite direction to that in which the society is moving is anyhow doomed to failure, that the wise legislator will "not act in vain", that the law is forever a handmaid to society.

§9. Difficulties of a Time-and-Space-Conditioned Criterion. We pointed in 1935 and 1946 to the requirements, for satisfactory application in practice, that the "civilisation-area" and "civilisation-period", which constitute the unit of application of this kind of theory, shall be adequately defined, and that the degree of transitional movement shall not be too great. For the theory assumes that in the area within which and the time at which legislative power must be exercised, there is in the society concerned a certain minimal homogeneity in men's demands, that is, in their experience, environment and aspirations. That is not to say that there may not be considerable variations of cultural, economic, religious, political and moral characteristics within one civilisation. Clearly, however, those variations, if they pass a certain limit, will make it necessary to recognise not one but two (or more) civilisations, or "civilisation-areas" as we may term them.

Now it is obvious that within one law-making area there may be many such civilisation-areas, and the finding of jural postulates and construction of schemes of interests would have to be a separate process in each.[53] Bantus and whites form no single civilisation in South Africa, nor negroes and whites in the Southern States.[54] And generally it might be difficult to

point that we "must not take relativism absolutely" if we are to avoid the faults of the "give-it-up Philosophies". In 1959 (3 *Jurisprudence* 9 (§80)), acknowledging a certain obsolescence in his Jural Postulate II as to the title of the discoverer and the creator, he adds that nevertheless "each proposition responds to what are still deep-seated ideas of justice". *Cf.* Stone, *Social Dimensions*, Ch. 5, §12. Value judgments seem already implicit in the words "in civilised society" and "reasonable" as they appear in Pound's formulation of jural postulates. They also seem quite explicit in the item of his 1931 sociological programme for jurisprudence (as to which see Stone, *Social Dimensions*, Ch. 4) calling for "a theory of values for the valuing of interests, consistent with modern psychology and philosophy, without being tied fast to any particular . . . psychological or philosophical dogma . . .". Pound may, of course regard his theory at present under discussion as such "a theory of values"; but in view of the continued "urgent" demand in "Philosophy of Law and Comparative Law" (1951) 100 *Univ. of Pa. L.R.* 1, at 16, it seems more properly regarded as his view of a necessary interim (or even stop-gap) method of proceeding. See the valuable discussion of some of these points in Braybrooke, "Roscoe Pound" 308ff.

We may add that even the conception of goodness as a resultant of adjustment of conflicting impulses within one individual, encounters serious difficulties. See, e.g., R. B. Perry, *General Theory of Value* (1926) c. vii.

[53] This is the central but often overlooked problem of the role of the Privy Council in a variegated range of British countries, and of the weight to be given to U.K. decisions in dominion and colonial courts. See Stone, *Legal System*, Ch. 7, §8.

For a controversy on the H.L. as a court of appeal in Scots matters from this standpoint, see D. M. Walker, "Some Characteristics of Scots Law" (1955) 18 *M.L.R.* 321, esp. at 334ff.; R. E. Megarry, and T. B. Smith, Notes, (1956) 19 *M.L.R.* 95, 425-26, and 427-432. Yet, conversely, we may well wonder what differences in the respective civilisations justify the fact that habitual drunkenness is a ground for divorce in Scotland, but not in England; or for that matter the differences in the respective laws as to Crown rights discussed in *Glasgow Corp.* v. *Central Land Board* (1955) S.L.T. 155, (1956) S.L.T. 41. And for a discussion perhaps tending to minimise the difficulties here in question see Latham, "Commonwealth" 540ff.

On a miniature symbolic scale civilisational conflicts within the same jurisdictional area are also involved as to polygamous marriage in Western states. See, e.g., the problems in *Bamgbose* v. *Daniel* (1954) 3 W.L.R. 561; G. W. Bartholomew, "Polygamous Marriages and English Criminal Law" (1954) 17 *M.L.R.* 344-359.

[54] The pre-Civil War North-South struggle over the federal law imposing penalties on abolitionists manifested the conflict of plural civilisations within a single lawmaking unit, just as does the continuing southern resistance to the various desegre-

treat the United States as a whole as one civilisation-area, while any attempt to sub-divide it into distinct legislative areas might face formidable political and constitutional difficulties.[55] So, too, with the time-factor. Pound's approach assumes that change is sufficiently slow to allow effective use of the jural postulates, and the scheme of interests, derived from a survey made at a somewhat earlier time. In any case, of course, these begin to grow obsolete as soon as they are formulated. Their period of useful service may be a year, a decade, a generation, or conceivably a century; only time can tell. This necessitates an unceasing re-examination of the postulates and scheme of interests in the light of changes in society, in order to ascertain the degree of incompatibility, and the exercise of judgment as to what degree of incompatibility will dictate a scrapping of the old and the formulation of new ones.

A third aspect of this problem we identified in 1946 as that of the transitional "civilisation-area-period". This is where, because of the rapidity of change, there is such an undermining of old demands and such an incoherence of new ones, that it is impossible to formulate the presuppositions of the "civilisation-area-period", except in the form of mutually incompatible sets of jural postulates and schemes of interests, the ones obsolescent, the others speculative. In such a situation between the obsolescent and the speculative all solutions must be tentative, and must await the end of the transformation period for determination upon any other than a hand-to-mouth basis. Neither Professor Pound's theory nor any alternative theory of adjusting law to time and place can oust Judge Time from his exclusive competence over such *interregna*.

Today, a generation later, these questions loom even greater. We live in a world of legal orders that are turbulently restive even among the stabler and maturer peoples. For the younger peoples, who now make up a substantial part of the world, the legal orders under which they will come to live lie still gestating in the womb of time. In any case the inheritance which these legal orders will bear is still often as speculative as the degree of guidance which they will tolerate as they move into independent life. This changefulness raises a number of awkward questions for any theory of justice centred on the degree of satisfaction of articulated claims. Can legislative policy rely for guidance simply on the *de facto* human claims actually pressing in the newer democratic countries such as India, when the objectives of national planning must apparently, according to all informed opinions, be geared rather to stimulating people *to make demands not yet made*, or to *changing the demands made* to accord better with national objectives? Can the subject-matter of law be adequately stated even for the older democracies in terms of articulated claims, when articulation becomes as controlled, distorted, amplified, stultified, stimulated, or even created and simulated, as it is becoming under the operations of modern instruments of mass communication, high pressure advertising, per-

---

gation rulings. Somewhat different problems arise from civilisational differences between the society and alien law-enforcing and law-ascertaining authorities. See, e.g., A. N. Allott, "The Judicial Ascertainment of Customary Law in British Africa" (1957) 20 *M.L.R.* 244-263.

[55] *Cf.* s. 99 of the Australian Constitution forbidding preference to "one State or any part thereof over another State or any part thereof". Dixon C.J. in *Commr.* v. *Clyne* (1958) 100 C.L.R. 246, at 265-266, had difficulty in appreciating "the distinction between the selection . . . of an area in fact forming part of a State for the bestowal of a preference upon the area, and the selection of the same area for the same purpose 'as part of the State' ".

suasion and indoctrination?[55a] In both kinds of society, can the notion of justice centred on the maximum satisfaction of *de facto* human demands be moulded, without losing its sense, to a shape tolerant of the *deliberate* manipulation, stimulation and diversion of demands through the means of social control (including law)?

§10. INAPTNESS OF THE THEORY FOR CONTEMPORY PLURAL AND TRANSITIONAL CIVILISATIONS. Many developing countries of Asia and Africa now illustrate these problems almost to the point of caricature. Here again, India provides an eloquent example. Within the stream of time, to which the present point relates, the comparatively educated and Westernised minority which provides executive and legislative government makes demands in terms of industrialisation, democratisation, and modernisation. These demands simply cannot stand in a single scheme or postulate system, with the worldly inertia and other-worldly expectations which characterise in the same stream of time the attitudes of the vast majority of India's people. As we shall later see, the actual path that is here being trodden turns the theory of interests upside down, a main objective of legislative policy being to create a structure of demands among the hundreds of millions such as will further the development plans. The creation of demands and the creation of the means of satisfaction of demands proceed in an uneasily staggered synchrony.

The uneasiness is made more acute by the courageous and (in a literal sense) successful experiment in political democracy based on adult franchise. For while the Indian parliament has assumed the role of Kohler's "far-seeing legislator" in seeking to raise the level of human powers over external nature well ahead of the *de facto* aspirations of most of its people, it cannot move too far ahead. Adult franchise still forces the governing party into constant compromises with attitudes and *mores* and institutional patterns which resist the implications of development, and the modification of traditional inertias. Those who set themselves the task of guiding India in the modern world are thus likely, for a long time, to carry this role amid a world of co-existence, not always peaceful, between old traditional civilisations struggling to preserve themselves, and a new one painfully seeking to prove itself viable. There are also involved in this complex, as already seen, besides the problems of retrogressive, those of transitional civilisations, as well as of a plural civilisation-area, embracing not only diverse older cultures, but that of the more Westernised minority in whose hands political governance largely rests.

What has Pound to say about these difficulties in 1959? He has, indeed, in Volume III of his *Jurisprudence*, discussed these and some other matters raised by the writer. He there declares that of course new claims emerge and press upon the legal order, and that what these new claims are can be identified from current law reports, legislative committee reports, legislative debates, and proceedings of the various trade, labour, and voluntary associations. While he admits that it may be difficult to decide how far they should be given effect by reference to the prevailing jural postulates or scheme of interests, he thinks that evaluation would be no easier by any absolute measure of values. As to whether evaluation by any absolute measure would be easier, we make no argument. The point surely is that an absolute measure (supposing we accepted it) would *ex hypothesi* not be

---

[55a] See *infra* §12; Stone, *Social Dimensions*, Ch. 3, §13.

relative to the phenomena of the time and place; it is the difficulties which spring from such *relativity* with which we are here concerned. As to the main point, we respectfully think that his response is helpful only for societies moving at a moderate rate of change. It does not really confront the problems raised for the theory of interests by either "transitional" or "retrogressive" phases of a society's life, in the present writer's sense. Pound himself, indeed, concludes that "jural postulates of an era of transition are not readily discovered", and that "until the change to a distinct civilisation era is complete, formulation could hardly be profitable". We can see the jural postulates, he says, of a civilisation "complete for the time being", and also "how those postulates are ceasing to be those of the times and places in which we are living". We must "seek to understand these times as well as we may in an era of transition without expecting to lay down final formulations". Perhaps the word "final" still slurs the difficulties.

§11. PROBLEMS OF TRANSITION IN WESTERN SOCIETIES. It is, of course, somewhat unfair to expect theories to prove viable in contexts so vastly different from that in which they were conceived. Pound's theory of interests as a measure of justice was designed to meet the failures and abuses of the American legal order of the last quarter of the nineteenth century, and of the first quarter of the twentieth century. Although, as compared with India, the pace of change has been more moderate, it has still been great in an absolute sense. Pound formulated in 1919[56] five jural postulates for American law, which he still maintained in substance in 1942[57] and indeed in 1954 and 1959.[58]

I. In civilised society men must be able to assume that others will commit no intentional aggressions upon them.

II. In civilised society men must be able to assume that they may control for beneficial purposes what they have discovered and appropriated to their own use, what they have created by their own labour, and what they have acquired under the existing social and economic order.

III. In civilised society men must be able to assume that those with whom they deal in the general intercourse of society will act in good faith and hence

    (a) will make good reasonable expectations which their promises or other conduct reasonably create;

    (b) will carry out their undertakings according to the expectations which the moral sentiment of the community attaches thereto;

    (c) will restore specifically or by equivalent what comes to them by mistake, or (failure of the presuppositions of a transaction, or other) unanticipated[59] situation, whereby they receive at another's expense what they could not reasonably have expected to receive under the actual circumstances.

IV. In civilised society men must be able to assume that[60] those who

---

[56] *Introduction to American Law* (1919).

[57] See *Outlines* (5 ed. 1943) 168ff.; *Social Control* 118ff. Textual changes will be indicated in the footnotes.

[58] Pound, *Philosophy of Law* 85ff., 107-08; 3 *Jurisprudence* 8-10 (§80).

[59] The words "or not fully intended" were inserted at this point in 1942, but were omitted again in 1959, while the words in brackets above were added.

[60] The 1919 formulation read from here onwards: "others when they act affirmatively, will do so with due care, with respect to consequences that may reasonably be anticipated".

engage in some course of conduct will act with due care not to cast an unreasonable risk of injury upon others.

V. In civilised society men must be able to assume that others who maintain things (or employ agencies, harmless in the sphere of their use but harmful in their normal action elsewhere, and having a natural tendency to cross the boundaries of their proper use)[61] will restrain them or keep them within their proper bounds.

These postulates have been regarded by a distinguished philosopher[62] as not only stating the characteristic ideals of American civilisation at the time but as having done so *sub specie aeternitatis*, combining the relative values of the time and place with the absolute values embodied in his own philosophy, as the "liaison between philosophy and the science of law". The writer is not concerned to assess this tribute.[63] What is more important is to observe how between 1919 and 1959 Professor Pound himself has found it necessary to modify some postulates, and to contemplate additional postulates, more or less inchoate; and that these further postulates necessitate radical revision of the 1919 ones, in some respects to the point of discard. Thus in 1942[64] Professor Pound thought he saw in formation a postulate entitling men to security in their jobs, removing the employer-employee relation from the domain of contract. If so, what grave modifications must Postulate II, as to control of property "acquired under the existing social and economic order", and possibly also Postulate III (a), undergo![65] He thought he saw also formative, in 1942, a postulate imposing on enterprise the burden of human wear and tear. But if so Postulates IV and V as they stand become misleading half-truths.[65a] A further formative postulate in 1942 he thought might be that the risk of misfortune to individuals is to be borne by society as a whole, a postulate which if it were established would require radical revision of all the five 1919 Postulates, except perhaps Postulate I.

As Professor Pound pointed out, the conflicts of interests involved in these inchoate postulates are not sufficiently worked out to permit them to be formulated. It must be clear, however, that the 1919 postulates had by 1942 more or less ceased to represent the presuppositions of mid-twentieth century society. In 1959 he further observed that "there may well be some question" about the whole of Postulate II (as to property) except

---

[61] The words "likely to get out of hand or to escape and do damage", included at this point in 1919, are replaced in 1959 by the words in brackets above.

[62] Hocking, *Law and Rights* 93. *Cf.* T. E. Davitt, "St. Thomas Aquinas and the Natural Law", in A. L. Harding (ed.), *Origins of the Natural Law Tradition* (1954) 26 at 42-43, suggesting that Pound's "jural postulates" "are, for the most part, nothing but Natural Law Judgments". And *cf.* the first limb of Braybrooke's twofold criticism cited *supra* n. 23, that the postulates are neither "peculiarly American" nor "peculiarly twentieth-century" (293). This criticism is rather flimsily grounded if it rests on the prefatory words—"In civilized society . . .". It is also incongruous with his further charges (p. 295) that Postulate II is "outdated", that the main set of five postulates consists simply of "rationalizations of positions already reached" by the law; and that the three further postulates which Pound suggested as emergent in 1943 have only partly transcended these limits.

[63] And see the comments in Stone, *Social Dimensions*, Chs. 5 and 6 *passim*, esp. Ch. 5, §§11ff.

[64] *Social Control* 115. *Cf.* in the U.K., B. C. Roberts, "Industrial Relations", in Ginsberg, *20th Century* 364, esp. 382-84, 388.

[65] 3 *Jurisprudence* 9 (§80). And see *supra* n. 24.

[65a] *Cf.* Braybrooke, "Roscoe Pound" 304, who draws out the implication of the above comment that the formulation of the new postulates is necessary precisely because the law "has not been able to assure men of the security contemplated by the fourth and fifth of the original jural postulates".

for its third limb as to what has been "acquired under the existing social and economic order". The propositions as to the titles of the appropriator and the creator, he thought, were significant in "pioneer America", but have lost significance in "urban, industrial society".[66] By the same token that new postulates are still incapable of formulation, the old ones are still incapable of adequate revision. For Western contexts also, therefore, Judge Time may have exclusive jurisdiction, and with an adjournment *sine die*.

§12. PROBLEMS OF GENUINENESS, AND ADEQUACY OF ARTICULATION, OF INTERESTS. The changes in technology, industrial organisation and ideology, whose effect Pound thus so courageously acknowledges, are however only a part of the difficulties now faced by his theory. Others also arise as effects of the growth of modern instruments and techniques of communication and persuasion, which bring fully into the open certain latent ambiguities in the position of both Pound and James.

For some very hard questions are concealed by the multiplicity of terms which Pound used interchangeably for the subject-matter of law. To speak of a "claim" or "demand" that is unarticulated seems self-contradictory; to speak of a "desire" or "expectation" or even "interest" that is unarticulated, is not. Clearly when Pound speaks of "claim" or "demand", it is still the "desire", and not the articulation of it, which is significant for the theory of interests, and the search for justice through that theory. Insofar as his position rests on that of James, it is absurd to suppose that articulation should either increase or decrease the ethical merits which attach to the human desire as such. Yet for Pound, even more than for James, nothing can be done about demands that are not articulated. And it is also difficult to see how, under modern conditions, legislators can learn to distinguish when an articulation corresponds to a genuine human desire, and when it does not.

There is more, therefore, in the prefix "*de facto*" in the term "*de facto* interests*" than appears on the surface. We ordinarily take this prefix as stressing that the interests relevant to the legislative judgment are those as actually felt by the subjects, not as the legislator might think they should feel, or might think was good for them, that it is the wearer who knows where the shoe pinches, and that the squeal is evidence of the pinch. In 1911 it was still possible to think that in the ordinary workings of democracy under universal franchise the squeals would correspond closely with the pinches, and the legislator be responsive to all of them. So that, in a sense, Pound's theory of interests and the practical working of democracy would run together.

Yet already in America, and increasingly in other Western countries, grave problems arise. The prefix "*de facto*" should now not only warn us against confusing the legislator's own desires and his views of what *should be* those of the subjects, with their *actual desires*. It should also alert us to the difficulty of distinguishing *articulations by the subjects* which express their own desires, from those which are the result of manipulation[66a] by operators of various sorts, especially those who are able to use the expensive

---

[66] So *cf*. the implications of this as bearing upon the legal liberty of the great corporation to abandon a particular locality, leaving it as only "a ghost town". See Berle, *Capitalist Revolution* 22. *Cf*. also *id*. 64-85, esp. 83-84, as to the power of the corporation to dismiss as compared with traditional employer-employee relations.

[66a] Such manipulation takes place through selection and activation of certain predispositions at the expense of others which might otherwise countervail. See Stone, *Social Dimensions*, Ch. 3, §13, esp. nn. 163, 167b.

instruments of mass communication and mass persuasion. If there can be no effective screening of articulations to ensure that they do indeed express the *de facto* desires of the subject, would not the theory of interests surrender justice to the competing groups of organised professional persuaders, open and hidden? And the more the powers of government intervene to check or counteract such manipulations, the more are we likely to face an even greater perplexity. For the legislative power itself is then likely to increase its own resort to the stimulation, suppression, diversion and manipulation of human demands. No doubt some forms of state persuasion are less unacceptable than others, and at a certain point this difference divides totalitarianism from democracy. But in principle *any* degree and kind of conscious legislative stimulation, suppression, diversion or manipulation, strikes at the vitals of Pound's whole theory of justice. The legislator's task cannot be said to lie in giving maximum effect to the *de facto* interests pressing in his society, if he himself is getting people to press the "*de facto* interests" *which he thinks good.*

De facto interests which are *ersatz* or phoney, in other words, must abuse or abort the theory of interests as Pound conceives it. The converse difficulty of genuine interests which lack articulation is also very grave, though not perhaps insuperable. If it is men's desires which are valid by the fact that men hold them, the legislator must ensure that he is advertent to these desires. This presupposes that they will be evidenced by some form of articulation. But channels of articulation that will ensure that genuine demands are not unheeded become daily less accessible to individual initiative. No doubt these tendencies are not irreversible. Pound himself has been urging for half a century the establishment of true Ministries of Justice to serve precisely to open such channels of articulation for the individual citizen.[67] The late Harold Laski was confident that parliamentary constitutionalism could be recast to ensure interest representation of all members of the community.[68] Neither of these answers, however, has been put into effect; and Pound is left for the most part to rely on the claims that are pressing "so far as the course of legislation and adjudication can indicate".[68a] Beyond this, we must make do with a medley of channels of articulation through voluntary associations, supplemented by public opinion surveys, and public relations operations.[69] And, as long as we do, more and

[67] 1 *Jurisprudence* 356-357 and earlier writings there cited, esp. "Juristic Problems of National Progress" (1917) 22 *Am. J. Soc.* 721. This is the deeper ground for the criticism of Pound's theory, that it is unduly tender to those elements in society that are vocal (see, e.g., Cohen, *Ethical Systems* 20, 89-90), which otherwise seems based on an over-literal reading. Pound has repeatedly attacked the evils of lobbying in the legislative process, and his whole gist is that the search for men's *de facto* claims must be on the widest and most open basis. There is perhaps no more (if no less) difficulty in ascertaining these "interests", or in saying what the preponderance of them presupposes, than there is in ascertaining (as Cohen proposed) what view "most" people take as to the "pleasurableness" or otherwise of an entity (*id.* 204-05, 218ff.), or in measuring quantities of pleasure (195ff.). For later thought on the ministry of justice see Stone, *Social Dimensions*, Ch. 1, §§22-25.

[68] Laski, *Politics* (3 ed. 1938), c. vii.

[68a] 3 *Jurisprudence* 8; *cf.* Braybrooke, "Roscoe Pound" 298-99. This predominant reliance on the *actual legal* materials leaves the practical working of the theory (rather than the theory itself as such) open to a host of criticisms. See Beutel and Braybrooke discussed *supra* n. 23, as well as the latter's point (*op. cit.* 314) that its conjuncture with rigid versions of *stare decisis* may cause interests asserted in wrong fact-situations, or prematurely, to be " 'driven underground', repressed and overlooked". *Cf.* also W. Kennedy, "Pragmatism as a Philosophy of Law" (1925) 9 *Marqu. L.R.* 63 at 75.

[69] Demands, especially from voluntary associations, are of course frequently not self-serving. Pound makes no distinction between them on this basis. Non-self-serving

more demands are likely to find it more and more difficult to make themselves heard. Is the legislator justified in ignoring demands that cannot
make themselves heard?

§13. "DEMOCRATIC PLANNING" AND *DE FACTO* DEMANDS IN DEVELOPING
COUNTRIES. "Planning" by totalitarian states has obviously presented some
problems for Pound's theory of interests. Yet insofar as totalitarian planners
could be regarded as imposing their own values by naked power, the problems
could be dismissed as irrelevant to the validity of Pound's theory, and as
illustrating merely the obvious fact that legislators may be unwise, or
may legislate for other ends than social justice.

Much more difficult to handle is "democratic planning" of the kind
to be found in the Indian Five Year Plans, on the third of which that
country has entered. It is equally indubitable that India has a democratic
form of government, and that many of the principal demands to the satisfaction of which the Plans are directed are not the *de facto* demands of
any but a small segment of India's 430 million people. What, if anything,
can Pound's theory of interests say about such a situation?

This kind of society adds further complexities to those of the articulation
of interests in the maturer democracies which we have just discussed. It
can be said in defence of Pound's position *vis-à-vis* totalitarian societies
that the difficulties arise from excesses and abuses which we must struggle to
check. But the situation in a democracy such as India simply does not lend
itself to this kind of answer. Suppose those who guide the destiny of India
tried to make their decisions by reference to the maximum satisfaction of
the *de facto* demands of India's 430 million people. What facts would they
face?

First, they would have to face that about three-quarters of India's
430 million people have no particular demands which they are concerned
to press on politically organised society. Claims within the family and caste
are, of course, a part of the pattern of life, but beyond this the inertia of
tradition and of acceptance of the inherited worldly lot dominates the
lives and attitudes of individuals. This inertia is reinforced by centuries
of remoteness from the main centres of urban civilisation and culture; there
was a deliberate shunning of such contacts when they were likely to entail
official contact with alien rulers, Muslim or British. For the oral tradition
of the elders associated rulers rather with looting, punishment, exile and
forced labour, than with welfare and the satisfaction of human demands.
These inhibitions also have deep roots in the teachings of Hinduism, which
enjoined acceptance of one's inherited lot, and even of the misfortunes of
life, as a punishment for some earlier unworthy existence or preparation for
a happier and more worthy one. Such an ethic left little room for the
pressing of *de facto* interests of individual human beings for recognition
by organised society. Where there was room for it, the business was not

---

groups, such as the National Campaign for Abolition of Capital Punishment, the
Abortion Law Reform Association, Voluntary Euthanasia Association, Magistrates
Association, Howard League for Penal Reform, are among the more articulate. And
see, conversely, for a view of U.K. labour relations as an area in which the group
concerned regulate their interests outside the ambit of law, O. Kahn-Freund, "Labour
Law" in Ginsberg, *20th Century*, 215-262. See generally W. J. M. Mackenzie, "Pressure
Groups in British Government" (1955) 6 *Br. Jo. Soc.* 133-148.

On the specific use of public opinion polls in detecting unarticulated demands
see E. Noelle *et al.* in *I.S.S.J., Communication* 283-302, S. N. Eisenstadt in *id.* 337-348,
and in balancing demands through pressure groups and the mass media, see *id.* 290.

hat of individuals but of the head of the joint family, and the received radition was that the interests were to be mediated and negotiated, rather han pressed or litigated. To add to all this, the rather static rural economy at subsistence level was not likely to stimulate new demands, which are a function of a mobile and dynamic rather than of a static, relationally-organised, society. Finally, the dominance of the national struggle for independence joined with indigenous traditions to prevent any effective contention for national leadership which might have led, through competing bids for popular votes, to the stimulation of popular demands.

Those elected to govern such a country could scarcely be expected to wait for guidance in their policies from the pressure of demands by these hundreds of millions, most of whom are still, in any case, illiterate and innocent of civic ambitions. They took their directives from simple indubitable statistics — of births and deaths, of an average rural workday of only two hours, of 25-30 million people constantly unemployed, of food supply and deficiency diseases, of buildings and sanitation arrangements, of famine and flood, ignorance and sickness. One irony is that even as the minority of Indians who guide the nation's destiny pursue their plans for Village Community Development, and for Small and Heavy Industry Projects, and the like, governmental paternalism, and the interposition of the system of cooperatives, are likely to leave individual demands and initiative as recessive as ever. Even down to the level of attention to the stagnant puddle in the village lane, the Indian picture remains, fifteen years after independence, one of legislative striving to stimulate and even create a structure of *de facto* human demands. As late as 1959, indeed, the entire rural Village Community Plan was overhauled precisely with this aim in view on the principle of "democratic decentralisation". It was sought to shift responsibility for the initiation of projects from the Block Development Officers of the State Government to the villagers themselves organised in tiers upwards from the village *panchayat*. Initiated in Rajasthan in 1959, this attempt from above to make way for or even stimulate a pattern of demands corresponding to the legislative recognition of "objective" needs, may or may not succeed.[69a] Either way it represents a stage or condition of democratic society in which Pound's theory of interests, without some drastic adaptation not yet in sight, can give little guidance.[70]

§14. THEORY OF INTERESTS AND INTERNATIONAL LAW. The tendency to interdependence of nations on a world scale, not only in a military, but in a social, economic and psychological sense, is, of course, noted by Pound. He has long written and continued to write in 1959 as if the claims of state entities were assimilable in his theory to the *de facto* claims of human beings, or at least could be dealt with in a rather analogous way as "public" interests. We have criticised this both from the aspect of the "interests" of "the state" within its own society,[71] and at more length

---

[69a] See S. K. Dey, *Panchayati Raj* (1961); and the Indian Law Ministry's *Report of the Study Team on Nyaya Panchayats* (1962). In fact the continued economic dominance of high caste villagers may often make the "decentralisation" gravely undemocratic for the lower (untouchable or scheduled) castes.

[70] *Cf.* generally on the civilisational base in countries of rapid development, M. Ginsberg, "The Growth of Social Responsibility" in Ginsberg, *20th Century* 3-26, esp. 23-26; Myrdal, *Welfare State* 88-99; and in terms of transformation of a people's social inheritance, Stone, *Social Dimensions*, Ch. 2, §18.

[71] Stone, *Province*, Ch. 20, §4; *id.*, *Social Dimensions*, Ch. 4, §3.

from that of the interests of the state *vis-à-vis* other states.[72] We are left
still, by his 1959 exposition, with the questions whether such easy assimila-
tions and analogies are not an evasion of the real questions; and whether
on the axiom (which is Pound's as well as James') that human demands
are valid by the fact that they are made, the theory of interests must not
always reckon with *de facto* demands of human beings, rather than with
supposed demands of *juristic* persons; and whether in these circumstances
the theory of interests can be of much use internationally unless we are
able to translate what is claimed in title of state entities into terms of
de facto claims of human beings.

§15. *CHERCHEZ L'HOMME.* Finally, even if all other difficulties were overcome, we would still need the human intellect capable of surveying and
interpreting the complexities of each modern civilisation-area-period. For this
theory demands more than mere observation and recording of all major
trends in society, more than the mere application of the methods of science,
whether physical or social, to the phenomena clustering about the legal
system. It calls for the mental stature to view the entire phenomena in an
adequate sweep for objective interpretation, so far as this is humanly
attainable, of what the social phenomena as a whole presuppose concerning
human conduct. Moreover, it demands the permanent services of such
minds, for the task is always unfinished.[73] The difficulties reviewed show,
indeed, that the vicissitudes of phenomena in time and space defy any very
accurate measurement or control by human understanding and foresight,
even if human understanding and foresight were constantly at their greatest.
In fact they are rarely at their greatest, and times and places with lesser
intellectual equipments must be content with lesser accuracy.[74] But none
of these drawbacks justifies a refusal to search for what accuracy is attainable, with the best instruments that can be devised, and with the fullest
appreciation of the difficulties revealed by the earnest search of those who
have devoted themselves to the theory of justice.[75] Roscoe Pound's death,
even as we closed this Chapter, concluded a life which will stand as a model
of human aspiration to master the tasks of justice.

---

[72] J. Stone, "International Law and International Society" (1952) 30 *Can. B.R.*
170; *id.*, "Morality and Foreign Policy" (1954) 13 *Meanjin* (Australia) 485; *id.*, ". . .
Sociological Inquiries Concerning International Law" (1956) 89 *Hague Recueil* 65-175
passim. And see the fuller examination in Stone, *Social Dimensions*, Ch. 2, §19, with
biblio. in n. 124.

[73] *Cf.* Ehrlich, *Sociology* 207-08; Laski, *Politics* 277ff. As to cognate formulations
of Bosanquet and Lindsay facing similar difficulties see Stone, *Social Dimensions*,
Ch. 15, §§16-17.

[74] It may be added that Huntington Cairns' ambitious project for the construction, on the basis of verified hypotheses as to the interplay between changes
in systems of legal relations and in human activity, of ideal types of orders of legal
regulations, involves fundamentally similar difficulties. See Cairns, *Legal Science*
c. viii, esp. 106-11.

[75] Commons (*Capitalism* 360-388, esp. 360, 382-84) properly recognised the
kinship of his "economic" theory of the state, as "a going concern based on the
authoritative proportioning of inducements in a world of limited resources", to
Pound's theory of justice. Its difficulties are similar. And see for other linkages
Stone, *Social Dimensions*, Ch. 15, §§10ff.

CHAPTER 10

THEORIES OF JUSTICE AND MEANING OF JUSTICE

I. CARDINAL DIVISIONS AMONG THEORIES OF JUSTICE

§1. MAIN PATTERNS AND CONTRASTS FOUND IN THEORISINGS ABOUT JUSTICE. We have sought in this study of theories of justice, as we did in *Legal System and Lawyers' Reasonings* with theories of the logical structure of the legal order, to see both the content of each theory examined, and the limits within which this was to be understood. It is unnecessary to recanvass, therefore, in the present Chapter the meanings, strengths and the weaknesses of any particular theory. Nor will an attentive reader of what has gone before expect the present writer to adopt as his own any of the particular positions examined. There are few of these theories which do not, in the present view, draw attention to important aspects of justice; there is equally no one of them which we can hail as adequate for the second half of our century. There may nevertheless be some gain from our survey of such theories, quite apart from the merits of any particular one of them; and to this we must now turn.

The questions of the uses of theory, and of the limits of theory, press also for theories of justice in general. The preceding Chapters, in short, challenge the role of theory in the enterprise of securing whatever is meant by justice. Or perhaps we should rather say that they challenge the role of *theories of justice* in this enterprise; for of the role of *psychological* and *sociological* theory in understanding justice there can be little doubt at all.[1] Yet to the challenge, "What are you good for?", the theories of justice seem also to have an answer. For to explain how and how far men come to profess and even act on a particular theory of justice is only an ancillary part of the tasks of doing justice; the main onus must still lie with some theory of what these tasks ought to be. The necessity therefore for what we have called "theories of justice" is inescapable. But this necessity in its turn does not prove that an adequate theory can be developed, let alone that it has been. In short, we have to ask whether there are any general reasons which limit the performance by theories of justice of the tasks of guiding the practical doing of justice in any legal order.

The source of one of these general limits must be clear enough. However much we struggle to place the components of theories of justice in the order of knowledge, some of these components escape, for they are the products of emotion not of intellect. Even emotive components of theories of justice can of course be examined—but scarcely for the purpose of assessing their *normative validity*. So far as these components are concerned, the examinable questions are those concerning the causes stimulating the particular emotions, and the consequences thereof. Both these

---

[1] See *infra* n. 90; Stone, *Social Dimensions*, Ch. 12.

questions are in a strict sense questions concerning the operation of law in society, and fall to be considered in various aspects in our work on *Social Dimensions of Law and Justice*. Yet they are also involved somewhat at the present juncture, when we seek to come to some balance of view as to the uses, and the limits on the uses, of theories of justice in general. For this requires us to look at these theories from the standpoint, not merely of their validity *as theories*, but also of their relation to human behaviour, including that of the theorists themselves.

In approaching these broader questions we may venture the generalisation that any theory of justice as offered or held at a particular time and place represents a certain point of equilibrium achieved in the mind of him who professes it. The theorist takes a stance somewhere along the lines of tension and strain between the actual conditions of society as he has experienced it, and what he might conceive *in abstracto* as the ideal conditions of an ideal society. Four of the more cardinal contrasts of position found in the various theories of justice already examined illustrate this generalisation.

(1) *Natural law* as contrasted with *other* (usually what is called "positivist") *theories of justice*, raises questions as to whether justice must be thought of in terms of norms transcending the human addressees, and if so, the range and power of this transcendence. And even here the role usually assigned to "reason" in such theories leaves ground on which, despite the theoretical transcendence, the human theorist still has to take his own stance.

(2) *Metaphysical* (or "*a priori*" or "*pure*") theories such as Kant's, on the one hand, stand in contrast to empiricist theories such as Duguit's on the other. The former claim to impose obligation by virtue of their supposed *non*-derivation from the social facts to which they are to be applied, and their deduction from a pure idea. The latter claim to impose obligation by virtue of the precise contrary, their derivation from social facts. This contrast is as to the role of observed facts in framing the criterion.[2]

(3) Theories which seek *absolute* standards valid for all times and places, such as most natural lawyers' or Kant's or Stammler's or Kohler's, stand in contrast with *relativist* theories, such as those of Ihering, Radbruch, or Pound, which insist on the variability of the criterion with variations in time and place and the accompanying variations in social context. This contrast has reference to the range of facts deemed relevant in framing and applying the criterion.

(4) Finally, theories which seek to achieve justice by some general or universal formula (such as Kant's or Stammler's) stand in contrast with those such as Bentham's (on its hedonistic side), or Pound's, which are directed to the uniqueness of the judgment of justice in each particular situation. The contrast here is in the degree of abstraction from the facts in the criterion of justice.

These four lines of contrast cut across some of the distinctive features of the various theories which were stressed in the preceding Chapters. They do not, indeed, cut across from four entirely different angles; the four lines of division lie rather in the same latitude and fairly close together. A "typical" natural lawyer will be embraced by the former arm of all

---

[2] See generally J. Hospers, *An Introduction to Philosophical Analysis* (1956), esp. 86-90, 114-15, 134-144; and *cf.* A. R. Blackshield, "Empiricist and Rationalist Theories of Justice" (1962) 48 *Arch. R.- und Sozialph.* 25 at 43-46.

four distinctions; a "typical" sociological jurist by the latter arm in each case. But flesh-and-blood jurists are not always such typical figures; and to reduce the four distinctions to one would be dangerously over-simple. The third and fourth distinctions may, perhaps, in the last resort be the same; but even if that were so, the distinction in its latter form is so much more familiar to common lawyers that it would merit brief discussion as such.

§2. NATURAL LAW AND OTHER CRITERIA: SPECIFIC FEATURES OF NATURAL LAW CRITERIA. Both "natural law" and other criteria of justice emerge historically side by side. Their common origins, and their common or at least overlapping concern with the criticism of law, necessarily entail many confusions and cross-purposes. Each term, for example, is sometimes taken to refer to the whole ambit of discussion of "good" or (in that sense) "desirable" law. In the competitive situation thus arising, "justice" is sometimes even offered to provide the contents of "natural law", and (even more frequently) "natural law" to provide the contents of justice.[3] Conversely, insofar as the criteria reached under each *may* fundamentally coincide, the statement of these in terms of "justice" *simpliciter*, or of "natural law" *simpliciter*, may depend entirely on the accidents of the exponent's personal background and of the age in which he lives. What is the fashion of thought may also determine the choice; it may even lead to the designation as "natural law" of theories, such as that of Duns Scotus, and perhaps even St. Augustine, in which what is involved is neither "natural law" nor "justice" in general, but rather some other standard or symbol altogether (in their case "love").

For these and other reasons it would be a task of despair to try to sustain historically any consistent and meaningful distinction between the terms "justice" and "natural law".[3a] Nor would it be appropriate here to think that we can sufficiently identify an entity "natural law" of which we can give an ontological account, independently of historical usage of that term. Nevertheless, with a concept so deeply woven into all the literature, it seems essential to offer some indications of the salient marks which have been or can be offered for identifying a criterion of justice as having a "natural law" character. Even here we must be careful not to assume that we are doing more than suggesting general characterisations of "natural law" helpful towards understanding it. And it may further be thought (as we indeed do think) that the doubts and variations at the core of the doctrine as taught require alternative though overlapping typifications. For while some uses of the term "natural law" can be dismissed as adventitious to its doctrinal core, no one can really be dogmatic as to what contributes the whole of this core. The range of uses that we cannot thus dismiss may still be so wide as not to allow of one single typification.

It goes, of course, without saying that we are not concerned anywhere in the present Chapter with the substantive criteria of justice offered respectively by natural law and other theories. The purpose is only to give some indications, and these only approximate, of the boundaries which (within the tolerances of a variable historical usage) seem to distinguish

[3] *Cf.* E. N. Cahn, *The Sense of Injustice* (1949) 4.

[3a] For major descriptive literary histories see Del Vecchio, *Justice*, and works of E. Wolf, esp. his *Griechisches Rechtsdenken* (3 vols., 1950-1954) and his *Grosse Rechtsdenker der deutschen Geistesgeschichte* (3 ed. 1951). And see for a briefer sketch, Recaséns, *Filosofía del Derecho* 422-477.

criteria of justice presented through a natural law framework from those presented directly. Such clarification as we achieve in these regards must stop short of doing violence to existing bodies of thought and the accustomed usage of language within them. With some prudence this may be avoided while yet assisting a free flow of communication concerning criteria offered in the different ways.

One mark, certainly, of a natural law frame of justice is that it presents the criteria in the form of *norms* of justice, rather than in terms of justice itself. This can in itself be regarded as a reliable mark, though obviously not a sufficiently distinguishing one; for exponents of other theories may also express them by way of norms, although, as we have seen, they often do not. Second, natural law theories of justice are transcendent from the point of view of the judging subject. They present the individual as "held in a framework which transcends him, where what is important and valuable is the framework, and the individual only has importance, or even reality, insofar as he belongs to the framework".[4] Where, on the other hand, a theory does not proceed through such a transcendent framework, the judging subject is somehow himself involved in the content of the criteria of justice. The content of the criteria, the method of operation with them, and the hierarchical order of priority among them, are all then matters to which, in some degree at least, the individual valuing agent contributes.

Third, and perhaps consequentially, insofar as natural law criteria of justice are expressed in a transcendent normative order, the contents of these criteria are deemed to be objective and universal; they never admit to being in any degree a creature of each judging subject. No doubt, natural law criteria may differ among themselves as to the range and detail of the norms through which they are expressed. Much may be caught by one natural law order which is not caught by another. But within the range of what is caught, objectivity and universality are a mark of the criteria expressed. Even "natural law with a changing content" presents an important part of its content as unchangeable.

The position on this third point is much more complex with direct criteria of justice. Here, the judging subject operates directly with conceptualisations of various manifestations of his inner sense of reasoned (or even unreasoned) approval or disapproval. This does not necessarily mean that each judging subject will have a different criterion or that his criterion will be whimsical or arbitrary; but it does mean that values are not likely to be objective and universal in the above sense. It may nevertheless be that the criteria held by all men are sufficiently similar to be called "objective" in the different and much more modest sense that the content of the criteria concerned is in fact the same for all men (or for all the men for whom it is said to be an objective criterion) regardless of how this sameness is derived, and regardless of whether it is possible that this sameness may disintegrate.[4a]

For outside the matrix of some transcendental normative system, such as natural law, the factors operating on the valuing individual to determine the contents of his criteria are of three different clusters. Partly they are

---

[4] *Cf.* I. Murdoch, "Metaphysics and Ethics" in D. F. Pears (ed.), *The Nature of Metaphysics* (1957) 99-123, esp. 114-17.

[4a] See Lamont, *Moral Judgment* 17-18, for yet another meaning of "objectivity" as "not dependent upon the testimony of any single person", and capable of being "correlated with other facts".

peculiar to the valuing individual; partly they are common to all men in a given time and place, but still peculiar to the time and place; and partly they are common to all mankind. A given theory which offers directly a criterion of justice may emphasise one or another of these clusters of factors. Insofar as the first or second are emphasised at the expense of the third, the result is obviously to detract from "objectivity" in the sense just specified. But conversely, so far as the third cluster comes to be stressed, the criteria might become more "objective" in the present limited sense.

No degree of such objectivity, however, would alter the conceptual point that such a theory is not a natural law theory. For the content of the criteria, the method of operation with them and their hierarchical order among themselves, would still in some degree be matters for the individual judging subject. Yet we repeat the caution that the present effort to distinguish natural law from other criteria of justice does not mean that their respective contents *must* be different; nor is it specifying any distinction by way of these contents, much less by way of their respective merits.

§3. NATURAL LAW AS AN OVERRIDING LEGAL ORDER. At this point the effort to isolate the specific marks of a natural law theory requires some flexibility of approach. What has gone before is, we believe, an acceptable differentiation in itself. Yet it does not include what in the view of many, and in its actual social operations, is the most dramatic, and even a sufficient, characterisation of natural law. This is that when criteria of justice are put into the framework of a system of natural law, and used to test the justice of positive law, the duplication of the word "law" in both phrases has an additional effect rather independently of the criteria of justice themselves. This effect is that a theory of natural law tends not only to criticise positive law by reference to whether it realises justice; but also *to deny that its norms are valid law at all* unless they are in keeping with certain norms of natural law.

This characterisation of natural law thought certainly has historical as well as operational bases. The juxtaposition involved of "law" in the one sense (*natural law*) over against "law" in the other sense (*positive law*), may be traceable to that stage, seen most clearly in ancient Greece, when a customary law hitherto accepted as the expression of a divine or cosmo-centric order, controlling man but not controlled by him, first comes under rational control. Prior to the fifth century B.C., as we have seen, "law" was the analogical expression of man's blind submission to decrees of fate. These were not only inescapable, but also inaccessible to rational under-standing, so that even "guilt" was regarded as an infliction imposed by the gods on the man they wished to destroy.[5] The formative stage in the later polarity of natural law thought may well have come with the positing by the fifth century philosophers of an analogical relation between the nature of man and the order of the cosmos,[6] and hence of an active participation of man in the process of the unfolding of that order.[7] For, once order as such had become accessible to the rational understanding of man, the nature of man's participation in the formation of an order, and therefore

---

[5] *Cf.* the fragment from Aeschylus quoted by Flückiger, 1 *Geschichte* 42.

[6] See *supra* Ch. 1. *Cf.* A. Verdross, *Abendländische Rechtsphilosophie...* (1958) 11: "The hidden harmony of the world creates the eternal *Logos*.... But man has the ability to know the *Logos*, because it dwells in the depths of his soul."

[7] Solon accepts the existence of a law of causality in the social order. See *id.* 5. An order based on causality is not a sacral but a rational order.

the nature of law also, became the central problem of political and social thought.

After the decisive step of rationalisation of sacral law had been taken, law could be regarded as the expression of a universal system of which man was an integral part by virtue of his active and voluntary participation in it. It is true that this development also opened the way to the down-grading of law to become an order valid merely for a particular situation, or, at worst, a mere instrument of coercive power; and that this positivist view was to have its long flowering from at least the Sophists onwards into our own times. But its more dominant effect was to consolidate the belief in a "law" which was not only set over against the positive law of the *polis*, but superior to it *as law*. The historical truth was recognised by Aquinas himself that the core problem of natural law is the conflict of two "laws".[8] Natural law as one of these "laws" also embodies, as we have seen, the criteria of justice; but its special feature *as natural law* is that the "law" which embodies these criteria is thought to prevail over the positive law. The special gist, therefore, of this kind of characterisation of natural law is not merely to juxtapose a norm of *law* with a norm of *justice* but rather to juxtapose these as belonging to *two legal orders*.

Moreover, as we have seen, it is implied in the traditional natural lawyer's juxtaposition of "legal" orders that, where these conflict, only one of them can prevail. And it follows somewhat paradoxically that *in application* these two legal orders then merge at any point of conflict into one governing order. In the common language positive law is "struck down" when it violates natural law. Or, in Aquinas' words, "it is no longer law, but only a perversion of law".[9] However it is put, the result is *one legal solution*, and one only, whenever natural law and the natural justice in which it issues permits only one solution.

When we approach the relation of law and justice otherwise than through natural law, however, the outcome is very different. Even when justice is then seen as an absolute and eternal value, its criticism of a law is not an act of legal annulment or cassation, but a demand on the lawmaker, and an appeal to all members of society to do whatever is necessary to bring about the repeal or other withdrawal of the impugned law. Until that appeal is answered, justice and law stand together in mutual conflict—not strictly in duplication but in the struggle of two norms to govern a situation, neither norm having any virtue by which it can prevail over the other, except in the forum of society, and by the decision and action of the men whose attitudes and action operate or control or constitute the social process.[10]

Conversely, if we accept a natural law approach, the standing of both positive law and its positive justice is to be referred back (on the more critical matters) to natural law and its natural justice. These latter are then seen as basic concepts of all jurisprudence, for whose definition and analysis we are then referred back to philosophy, including metaphysics, and possibly

---

[8] Positive law for Aquinas derives its validity as "law" from "natural law" by dint of its conformity to "natural justice" which is a kind of corollary of natural law. See *Summa I pars*, Q. 21, art. 2; *Ia-IIae*, Q. 95, art. 2: "the force of law depends on the extent of its justice" or conformity to "the rule of reason". And see the discussion in L. Lachance, *Le Concept de Droit selon Aristote et St. Thomas* (1948) c. 6.

[9] *Summa Ia-IIae*, Q. 95, art. 2 *corp.*

[10] As to Aquinas' exceptional duty to obey even "positive law" which is not "law", see *supra* Ch. 7, §8.

to theology also.[11] This is why natural law adherents tend to accuse those who reject natural law doctrine of indifference and even callousness towards justice. But the inference they thus draw would only be warranted where (if we may be rather Irish) the recusant was himself rejecting natural law *on the basis of a natural law credo*. For if (as is generally the case) the rejection is on the basis that justice consists of certain criteria or ideals to which men are personally committed, which they press for realisation through the positive law, and for the sake of which they may have to change or even defy and overturn the positive law, no such inference is warranted. And it has indeed been plausibly charged in reply that the natural law approach, by thrusting the problems of justice back into the abstract sphere of a supposedly objective "natural law" and "natural right", submerges and confuses the inescapably individual responsibility of men to resist and correct injustice.[11a]

We believe that not merely for natural lawyers, but for all who agonise to understand justice, residual elements not intellectually reducible to specific criteria or norms always remain. Natural lawyers, it is true, hope to occupy this residual area by insisting (for example) that "Justice and Reason, Nature and Law are terms that must be held together", and that (theologically speaking) all these terms "rest upon an intuition . . . of the Transcendent God", as "Lord of Nature", and "as the divine Reason and Source of Justice".[12] But it is simply not clear how this can justify their demand that anyone who aspires to find a more perfect idea of justice than any theories (including natural law) have hitherto produced, shall be condemned (as it were) as a renegade from justice if he refuses to declare himself a natural lawyer.

The argument that without "natural law" we cannot see justice as bound to men's most cherished values and therefore finally to God, through whom most men envisage these, must have the reverent answer that the Hebrew prophets have inspired men's dedication to the highest ideals of justice without resort to a mediating "natural law".[13] If the argument is that "Justice is not that which man ordains; it is that which he seeks to discover",[14] the answer is also clear. Many theories of justice, besides natural law, are efforts at such discovery. Common dedication and exchange of intelligence among all who search are more important than recrimination against those who refuse to join one's own particular expedition. Nor can the argument be that natural law as historically given *has already produced* the answers to all the problems of the practical tasks of doing justice. Indeed, we can find natural lawyers simultaneously lamenting the "obscurities", and the "static, abstract, *a priori* and unhistorical form" of natural law writings, from the classics to the present day, in the same breath as they insist that unless men accept natural law they are not concerned with justice.[15]

---

[11] See generally *Summa Ia-IIae*, Q. 95, esp. arts. 1-2.
[11a] See, e.g., S. I. Shuman, *Legal Positivism* (1936) 185-186, 194-222, esp. 207-209.
[12] Micklem, *Law* 118-19, and see generally 113-119.
[13] We leave aside as perhaps a flourish Dr. Micklem's appropriation of credit for Western concern with the rights of individuals to "the Christian religion" as teaching that men are made in the image of God and are his children (*Law* 82). We add only the rider that the pre-Christian Pentateuch and the Prophets conveyed these ideas adequately enough to transmit them, without the aid of natural law. See *supra* Ch. 1, §5.
[14] Micklem, *Law* 15.
[15] See, e.g., Micklem's criticisms of Suarez in *id.* 30ff., esp. 38.

The present work is not concerned to question the value of seeking justice through natural law ideas.[16] What is needed is that all of us should recognise that justice *can* be sensibly and sincerely inquired about without using the notion of "natural law", and that mere aspiration for certain and workable criteria is not the same thing as achievement of them, even when the aspiration is associated with the time-hallowed name "natural law". The difference, often enough, between the natural lawyers' attitude towards the *summum bonum*, and that of jurists who are not natural lawyers, is mainly that the former *claim* that its full contents can be found while the others admit great areas of doubt. At this point, theologian natural lawyers may rest; but jurists must, while still continuing the ultimate search, also provide solutions as just as they can make them for the problems raised here and now under the legal order. And, indeed, we find in the most earnest of present English theologian natural lawyers, when he brings his theories near the concrete level, that same relative and tentative mood in applying justice, which he severely castigates in other kinds of thinkers.[17]

Sometimes, no doubt, in the centuries and millennia of discussions of justice, natural law was the preferred way of talking of justice as a criterion of good law; or, where justice was still invoked, its content was preferably or even exclusively sought to be derived from natural law. In effect, at these times, the function of natural law as providing criteria of justice for criticising positive law seemed to occupy the whole field of justice. This was due to a variety of reasons, including the inspirational force of a "law" assumed to govern the order of the universe and to bind men to the divine reason, and the power of overriding positive law attributed to natural

[16] A surprising aspect of Dr. Micklem's thesis (see *id*. 38) is that he comes near to thinking that the obscurities of much natural law doctrine and the mis-understanding and rejections surrounding it might indicate that the term should be abandoned altogether. On balance, however, he would retain it.

[17] See Micklem, *Law*, *passim*. Thus at 66ff. he attacks as "perilous" Pound's use of maximal satisfaction of claims as a practical criterion of justice. But with no apparent awareness of the incongruity, he falls quite enamoured of Dr. E. F. Carritt's point (*Ethical and Political Thinking* (1947) 155ff.) that the notion of "natural rights" as "absolute" and "inalienable" should be replaced by that of "natural claims", since what can be granted depends on "the situation", on "the claims of other men, all of which must receive equal consideration" and on "the good of the whole", and since such "claims" can only be met as far as possible. This way of doing justice is not really distinguishable from Pound's which he has seemed to censure. Dr. Micklem goes on, very properly for a theologian, to declare that this pursuit of justice is based on a "spiritual" conception of human nature, the fatherhood of God and the brotherhood of man. But would it not help all concerned, and justice too, to recognise that for the doing of justice here and now his approach is really very close to Pound's, though rather less precise?

The confusions in Dr. Micklem's treatment of the present writer's position are also increased by certain incorrect statements. On p. 62 he asserts that we make "social interests" the criterion of the justness of individual interests, in the face of our direct contrary expression in *Province* 493, now elaborated *supra* Ch. 9, §§6ff. On p. 64 he asserts that our criterion is "social utility", which is not understandable in the light of our whole Ch. 11 of the *Province* (see now *supra* Ch. 5, §§1-7) criticis-ing this kind of theory. On pp. 64-65 he lifts our analysis of the psychological nature of ethical conviction quite out of its actual context of sociological analysis (p. 68) and presents it as if we had offered it as a theory of justice, a topic dealt with hundreds of pages before. Then, in a way which illustrates the very point *we* make as to the psychological nature of ethical conviction, he states (114-15) as *his own* final overall position, that the fact that "it is the end of law to do justice . . . is a matter of faith, not proof. . . . The lawyer like the saint must live by faith". (*Cf*. his own reference of the search for a standard of justice to an "instinct" on 80-81.) Finally, on p. 63, to prove his assertion that we fail to distinguish the theory of justice from "empirical science" he erroneously transposes what we said (*Province* 490) was the gist of *theory of justice*, and quotes it as being our statement of the gist of *sociological jurisprudence*. He then suggests how nonsensical the result is. We agree with him; but the nonsense is not ours.

law. But we believe that the assumption that concern with justice is some-how the exclusive preserve of natural lawyers is unwarranted at this stage of history, and needs to be abandoned if dialogue of any value is to continue.[17a]

§4. Norms as the Form of Criteria of Justice. We have presented the supposed operation of natural law criteria as a juxtaposed and overriding legal order, as an alternative specific mark of natural law. It is not, however, our intention to deny the obvious linkages or overlappings between this and our first alternative characterisation in terms of a transcendent system of norms objectively and universally valid. Obviously, the norm-system is common to both characterisations, and so are objectivity and universality. If the meaning of transcendence were defined so as to hold within the inviolable matrix of natural law not merely the conscience and reason of all men, but the authority of the positive law legislator, the two alternative specifications would become virtually identical. Insofar as this meaning may be disputable, and it is not to our present point to argue it, no harm is done by leaving the two sets of characterisations as alternatives. We would, however, add our belief that unless such a meaning is given to transcendence, the first alternative characterisation would fail to refer to what we tend to regard as *the* most specific single mark of natural law. Certainly, the mere fact that criteria of justice issue from natural law in the form of norms is no sufficient contrast with other criteria of justice. For, on the one hand, there may be very few such norms in a natural law system; and, on the other hand, what are clearly non-natural law systems may issue their criteria in the form of a multitude of norms.

Perhaps it is unfair to offer Duns Scotus' "Love God" as an example of a natural law system consisting of one single precept, though this is how he presented it and it is often understood. For it may be said that this very paucity of norms is a circumstance which raises the question whether, apart from its historical placing, it is really proper to regard Scotus' theory as one of "natural law" at all. Yet it is clear that Aquinas' natural law, which is certainly as near the core of whatever natural law is as the more elaborate systems of the 18th century, contained comparatively few fundamental principles.[17b] And it also appears that nothing clear can be said about the number (between one and a few) at which a body of norms ceases on ground of paucity to qualify as a legal order. Nor can we escape this difficulty by saying that "natural law" doctrine in essence postulates that there is immanent in reality, in one way or another, a legal system analogous to the system of positive law, and that the former is the criterion of the latter in the sense that positive law is "just" (and thereby is "valid law") only to the extent that its norms are consonant with those of natural law. For this assumes rather than explains how *the mere fact that natural law consists of norms*, whether "immanent" or not, comes to entail the *overriding* of positive law by natural law when they conflict. The assertion of this overriding power is therefore, we believe, better expressed as a separate specific mark of natural law.

On the one hand, then, natural law, though it is characteristically (or even necessarily) expressed in norms, may consist of very few norms. On the other hand, non-natural-law criteria of justice, though they are often

---

17a And see *supra* Ch. 7, §§7, 12.
17b See *supra* Ch. 2, esp. §6, and Ch. 7, esp. §8.

expressed in the direct form of "the idea of justice" and ancillary value ideas (such as equality or fairness), may also be expressed in the form of a series of norms. Indeed, it is probably the correct analysis, as we saw in Chapter 1, that even such ideas must imply norms corresponding to them. Equality stated as an ideal is equivalent to at least a norm that we should strive to preserve equality or bring it about. It is only because many of these ideals, and what they entail by way of criticism of the *status quo*, are so well-known, that it is often unnecessary to give them normative expression. The norm is taken for granted. Moreover, varying with the particular idea of justice, many ancillary ideas may cluster about it, which may be stated either as clusters of value-ideas or as clusters of norms. In either form the clustering may be heterogeneous, or structured in some way as a jointed or rationally-connected unity. In the latter case, the rational pattern which is imposed on the materials will usually be one of logical deduction and implication, much resembling in this superficial respect a body of natural law norms. It may also, however, be structured on antinomy.[18]

The structure of Giorgio Del Vecchio's theory of justice well illustrates that value-ideas can be stated either directly or also by drawing out the norms which are implicit in them. At the apex of his hierarchical arrangement of value-ideas is the idea of inter-subjectivity;[19] this, says Del Vecchio, necessarily implies (if indeed it is not the same thing as) the idea of bilaterality.[20] From bilaterality there logically follow for him the ideas of parity (or equality) and reciprocity;[21] the latter in turn leads to the ideas of requital[22] and of reward.[23] The articulation of what is meant by inter-subjectivity is presented primarily as a statement of fact about man's rational nature; the articulation of the subordinate value-ideas of justice is presented in normative form. Either factual or normative *propositions* must be used if the relation between various value-ideas is to be one of logical implication;[24] and Del Vecchio is able to confer the mantle of logical derivation from the value-ideas stated as norms upon a striking number— perhaps too striking —[25] of the norms actually found in positive law.[26] And he is able flexibly to reconvert the derived norms back into further value-ideas within justice, giving us contributory justice, social justice, penal justice, international justice and the like.[27] Yet this notable example from

---

[18] *Cf.* for Gustav Radbruch's antinomic theory of justice *supra* Ch. 8.

[19] In other words the idea that "there is a specific form of consciousness which we may term *trans-subjective* consciousness, through which the subject posits himself as an element in a net of interrelations between selves; that there is, in short, an *objective consciousness of self whereby the subjective self becomes co-ordinated with other selves*". See his *Justice* 80.

[20] Meaning that for just decision, the two or more subjects involved are placed notionally at the same time on the same plane, and each seen as a function of the other. See *Justice* 83.

[21] Meaning that what is just for you to do must be just for you to be done by in similar circumstances. See *id.* 84.

[22] That is, the act authorises a similar act with roles reversed. This, of course, is a possible basis of a *lex talionis*. See *ibid.*

[23] Pursuant to the formula "To each his due", and consequential on the postulated bilaterality. See *id.* 84-85.

[24] The postulated fact of man's rational nature is linked to the subordinate normative ideas by presupposing a norm requiring man to act in accordance with his rational nature. See G. Del Vecchio, *Philosophy of Law* (transl. T. O. Martin, 1952) 431-440, esp. 436-37.

[25] Inasmuch as it is not free of the tendency to ascribe to ideal principles the particular rules familiar to us, as to which see Stone, *Social Dimensions*, Ch. 12.

[26] See Del Vecchio, *Justice* 117-121.

[27] For the meanings of these see *id.* 119-121. And see generally on Del Vecchio's theory, A. R. Blackshield, article cited *supra* n. 2, at 54ff.

Del Vecchio's work should not, it is believed, be taken as a satisfactory way of picturing the *actual structure* of men's value-ideas in the justice area. For though such an ordering is valuable for analytical, pedagogic and even mnemonic purposes, much of the actuality is simply not tractable to it.[28]

§5. METAPHYSICAL AND EMPIRICIST CRITERIA. To assign a theory of justice to either side of our second kind of contrast seems to subject it to insuperable philosophic objections.[29] The "apriorists" accept as absolute the division between the existential "is" and the normative "ought"; they conclude that therefore their criteria must not include any existential elements. They then assert a supposedly "pure idea" as unchallengeable, such as Kant's categorical imperative or universal maxim of equal freedom, and they deduce the principles of justice from that "idea". We have here seen the apparently inevitable inconclusiveness of such systems divorced from the existential universe; and we have also seen the failure of attempts, like that of Stammler, to remedy the fault by bringing the facts of existence half-way to meet the *a priori* principle.[30]

No lesser difficulties were seen to affect theories which identify the criterion of justice with the observed facts of social life. This in effect was what Duguit did when he insisted that his criterion, "the objective law", or *la règle de droit*, emerged spontaneously from the social solidarity[31] manifested in the facts of social life. More covertly a similar enthroning of the facts is to be seen in the social utilitarianism of von Ihering, and perhaps even in Bentham's utilitarianism. For both of them assumed that once the facts are analysed and catalogued, the just solution will emerge as the dictate of "utility".[32] Ihering certainly did not succeed in giving any further precision or in showing how it could issue from the facts.[33] In lesser degree even Pound's pragmatism faces similar difficulties,[34] though he was certainly not unaware of them.

Philosophically the *a priori* criterion which is "pure" of all reference

---

[28] *Cf.* Cahn, *op. cit. supra* n. 3, at 22, stating the matter in terms of "the sense of injustice". There are, of course, dangers in systematisation, as when the ideal of honour was "capitalized into Honour", as in the *code duello*. See Curtis Bok, *Star Wormwood* (1959) 57-58.

[29] *Cf.* A. R. Blackshield, *op. cit. supra* n. 2, at 61-64.

[30] So also with the *a priori* limb of the natural law position claiming to find principles of justice by applying "reason" to the (ideal) nature of man as a social being. So far as state justice is concerned, the common view that Kant "undermined" the "rationalist" position of the natural lawyers is not helpful. In the juristic context what Kant mainly did was rather to pin down the roving natural law commission to the idea of the free will. On the ready alliance of the two positions see *supra* Ch. 3 *passim*. In short, on the precise question of the relation of either the natural law or the Kantian positions to empirical reality, their similarity may be more significant than their differences. On Stammler see *supra* Ch. 6, §§1-9.

[31] *Cf.* as to "solidarity" in the political field, 1 Pareto §§449-453 (transl. Livingston *et al.* (1935) 269-273). And *cf.* for the general identification of "good law" and "fact", A. V. Lundstedt, *Superstition or Rationality in Action for Peace?* (1925); and K. Olivecrona, *Law as Fact* (1939), which proceeds on the basis that legal rules "are completely vindicated by the simple fact" that they "are necessary to the existence of the community" (27). And see esp. 128-158. On Duguit see *supra* Ch. 5. §§8-14.

[32] Any appeal to utility raises the question, utility to what end? If as in some modern English approaches the answer is sought in a teleological view of nature, then at this stage too the answer will be purportedly rooted in the facts, e.g., in Bentham, of the incidence of pleasure and pain. See *supra* Ch. 4, §§12ff. And *cf.* Hart, *Law* 184ff. On Ihering see *supra* Ch. 5, §§1-7, and on Bentham *supra* Ch. 4.

[33] *Cf. supra* Ch. 5, §7.

[34] *Supra* Ch. 9, §§6ff.

J

to the existential world, but yet is claimed for that very reason to be binding on all human conduct in the existential world, remains a mystery. It may perhaps be too harsh to say that demonstration of this kind of theory is a proceeding by which one "first invents a false theory as to the nature of things, and then deduces that wicked actions are those which show that his theory is false".[35] It is true, however, that the only way in which the *a priori* can bind the world of existence, is either in the same way as a law of natural science, or as some kind of ethical obligation. The former is, of course, out of the question; for if conduct were subject to *a priori law* in that sense, it would have to obey willy-nilly; no *ethical* consequences of such an *a priori* law could ever arise. As to the latter sense, such *a priori* principles could indeed have ethical consequences, but the manner in which they could be given a *content* relevant to conduct in a particular time and place remains difficult to see. And even greater philosophical difficulties affect those positivist theories which purport to derive their criterion exclusively from the scientifically observed facts. Validity is claimed for such a criterion by reason of its correspondence with the observed facts. But *ex hypothesi* if the facts do not correspond to it, it is invalid; while if they do, the criterion would have no ethical effectiveness, there being no possible disobedience that could call it into play.

All this does not entail that the holding of such theories may not give rise to consequences of the utmost importance for law and society in particular times and places,[36] or that these effects are bad rather than good. Indeed, the reason why there can be such consequences, despite the unpromising philosophical basis, is precisely one of the present concerns. Part of this reason certainly lies in the fact that the strategic plans and logistical equipment on which each position purports exclusively to proceed, are often only a part of what they actually use.[37] The knowledge on which the positivist proceeds, whether or not he is conscious of it, often has foundations which are only *a priori*. Equally, what the metaphysician purports to construct *a priori* often has foundations which are only empirical, revealed by his own experience. The fact is that the world operates through the mind and experience of the philosopher himself to give content to what *he* believes and earnestly insists are pure *a priori* propositions. Even when they struggle hardest to exclude the world of existence, the authors of *a priori* systems still operate within the framework of conceptions and preconceptions which a social context irresistibly impresses upon the thought of those within it.[38] The influence of the observed facts is nonetheless present, even if concealed in a "crypto-positivism".[39] And conversely, as has been seen, the sole reliance upon existential facts claimed by positivists like

---

[35] Cf. Bertrand Russell, *Sceptical Essays* (1928) 91, noting that Russell's scepticism does not extend to empiricism. In *Wisdom of the West* (1959) 219, he likens an "*a priori* system" to a pyramid "built upside down", an empirical one to a pyramid standing "on its base". The *a priori* one (he says) "topples over if you so much as squint at it". The empirical one will survive crumbling or even removal of whole slabs. See also the very different but no less challenging examination by H. Prosch, "The Problem of Ultimate Justification" (1961) 71 *Int. Jo. Ethics* 155, 164-170, of Kant's efforts at exclusively *a priori* demonstration in the *Grundlegung zur Metaphysik der Sitten*, and the *Kritiken*.

[36] Cf. on the influence of Duguit and Kohler, Laski, *Politics* 577.

[37] See Stone, *Legal System*, Intro., §3.

[38] Cf. Stone, *Social Dimensions*, Ch. 12, and Cairns, *Legal Science* 91. Cf. as to cryptic empirical bases of *a priori* systems, A. C. Pigou (ed.), *Memorials of Alfred Marshall* (1925) 108, discussed *id.* 71-72. And see generally the thesis of L. Bagolini, "Value Judgments in Ethics and Law" (1951) *Phil. Q.* 423-432, esp. 423-426.

[39] M. R. Cohen, *Reason and Nature* (1931) 416ff.

Duguit conceals an unavowed use of ideal presuppositions—a "crypto-idealism".

It is usually because directives from the theorist's unavowed experience operate through his ostensibly *a priori* intellectual apparatus, that he is able (if at all) to make his work seem relevant to other men of his age. For similar experience promotes a sympathetic hearing, and the bolstering of the directives by *a priori* principles is naturally welcome to those who sympathise with the directives. And similarly, the emotional preferences offered by theorists for the ostensibly simple directives of the empirical facts, are also likely to have contemporary appeal quite independent of any philosophical value. For these emotional preferences insofar as they spring from experience of the time and place are likely to be shared by others also; and all of us are inclined to embrace rather readily positions which seem to give an objective base to what *we feel* to be right.

It will already have become apparent in the details of the preceding Chapters that the significance of a particular theory of justice as a socially operative force is often a function of the problems of the social context, rather than of the intellectual tenability of the particular theory. We now place this fact in the context of the broader hypothesis that we can best understand most theories of justice as their authors' struggle to establish a *modus vivendi* between the inner vision of Utopia and the world of actual experience, the inner vision itself being also partly moulded by experience. *A priori* theories and the kind of positivism here under discussion seek, by standing at extreme poles, to avoid the tension here involved. The *modus vivendi* emerges nevertheless. Few *a priori* thinkers can approach their problems with a mind quite innocent of the world, nor even as innocent as was that of Kant. And no positivists who have insight enough to explore the facts of their own society can be so sterile of emotions and ideals that they draw nothing from the facts observed but what is warranted by the facts, as a mere matter of empirical inquiry.

§6. ABSOLUTIST AND RELATIVIST CRITERIA. The difficulties facing criteria of an absolute nature on the one hand, and relativist on the other, have already been discussed at length. Absolute criteria face great and perhaps insuperable philosophical difficulties and, for the most part, great practical ones as well. With relativist criteria, the philosophical difficulties are equally great,[40] but they do seem to have a measure of practicality *in certain kinds of social situations*. For relativist theories, including here not merely various forms of utilitarianism, pragmatism and scepticism, but also some versions of "natural law with a changing content", are often designed precisely to accommodate both a changing environment and changing human reactions to the environment.

Yet it by no means follows that such theories must have the greatest influence. Indeed, their very sophistication tends to reduce the efficiency of their bid for social influence. Apart from hedonism, which could use the independently attractive symbols of "happiness", "pleasure" and "utility", the ideals which relativism usually offers have not the glamour which surrounds principles which present themselves as absolute. Their complexities also place them at a disadvantage with the comparative simplicity

---

[40] We cannot enter fully into the philosophical doubts affecting both demonstration and refutation of both the absolutist and the relativist positions. The fullest juristic analysis in relation to justice is in Cohen. *Ethical Systems*, c. iii, 113-229.

of most absolutes. Moreover, most generations of most societies resent the suggestion that the values they cherish are transient, and when they cease to resent it they still do not really believe it. A relativist theory of justice, then, is likely to be more influential as an instrument in the hands of a governing class, than as a programme which comes to express a people's idea of justice.

Moreover, relativist theories tend to lose their helpfulness in periods of rapid change, or of acute and evenly balanced social division. The present generation, it must be admitted, finds itself unusually perplexed in providing clear directions for the powerful engine of the law. We are perhaps less able to agree than in previous centuries upon an absolute criterion of justice. Yet, even on a relativist basis, and even admitting the full role of time and place in basing a criterion for the time being, our case seems little better. Roscoe Pound's theory of justice still, perhaps, comes nearer than any other to a relativism which is not merely at large. But Pound himself in 1942 recognised the waning of its usefulness "because of transition from a social order . . . the jural postulates of which were clearly understood, to one which has not sufficiently found itself to admit of formulating an ideal which all accept".[41] We have given reasons, in the Chapter on Pound's theory of justice, for believing that the difficulties are even greater than these, especially if we try to use it to meet the grave legislative problems of newly established states in Asia and Africa.

§7. GENERAL FORMULAE AND CONCRETE APPLICATIONS OF JUSTICE. When justice is sought in some formula such as reason, or due process, or equal liberty, or natural law, or utility, which shall embrace the particular applications of it and yet allow for varied social contexts, it becomes increasingly indeterminate, that is, increasingly inapt for directing judgment towards a *single* assured result in a given case.[42] On the other hand, when we seek justice in the particularity of decisions on the special situation in a given time and place, "on the merits" of the particular case (as the common lawyer shy of abstract ideas would phrase it), it would appear not to be capable of application to the decision of other cases. For the contexts of no two cases are identical, and the decision whether differences are "material" seems to prerequire a kind of criterion related to justice in general which those who distrust abstractions strive above all to avoid.[43] Indeed,

---

41 *Social Control* 133; see now 3 *Jurisprudence* 14-15.

42 *Cf.* the very able thesis of Garlan, *Legal Realism* c. iii. This seems, however, both too sweeping in the indeterminacy it regards as inevitable, and too narrow in suggesting that "due process", "reason", "the common good" and "public policy", there dealt with, are any less determinate than the formulae of "Legal Justice" (c. iv) and of "Philosophic Justice" (c. v). The implied distinctions seem rather vain. *Cf.* as to the varied content of abstract principles of law giving a superficial appearance of stability in change, Stone, *Legal System*, Ch. 6, §§13ff., and Ch. 7; and Ehrlich, *Sociology* c. xv, n. 38, 132-34.

43 "Justice" in this particularist view, it has been well said, assumes "the appearance of a collective concept open at both ends with a membership list of rights and pressures that is constantly changing", old members often being expelled, and new admitted, and yet not always as soon as they would be if the aggregate membership at a particular moment were different. Title to membership appears to reside in a relation between the member rule and a given social context but what that relation is, is not definable on an empirical basis. Nor is the expulsion of old or the admission of new members a reliable guide: for "new members fail of admittance frequently because of cliques of old members who oppose them". Garlan, *Legal Realism* 53, developing the thought of F. V. Harper, "Some Implications of Juristic Pragmatism" (1929) *Int. Jo. Ethics* 269, 281. We have dealt fully with this matter in the legal context in Stone, *Legal System* Ch. 7, esp. §§12-14, and Ch. 8, esp. §§7-10.

at some point in both processes, the results of generalisation of the formula of justice become essentially similar to the results of particularisation. Formulae such as "the merits" of the case, of "doing justice between the parties", may be regarded simultaneously as the extreme of generalisation and the extreme of particularisation. "Reasonableness", "public policy", "the good", "the public interest" or "convenience", "social utility", seem also to have this quality in operation. They go little beyond restating the problem of justice.[44]

Not that these notions leave matters quite at large. First, neither "justice" nor, say, "reason", is *wholly* indeterminate; each conveys to the hearer at least the mood and flavour of what is meant. "Reasonableness" juxtaposed with "justice", indeed, does far more than add our (partial) understanding of justice to our (partial) understanding of reason. It rather multiplies than adds, so that understanding is noticeably *less* indeterminate, though it may still be *very* indeterminate. Second, such standards encourage us to view the particular case in a larger context embracing others, and require issues to be generalised before decision. Thirdly, by their very indeterminacy they promote stability during change by appealing to a "constant" ideal.[45] And fourthly, they serve as instruments whereby situations, not fully understood or assessable, can be resolved without undermining faith in justice by open confession of our inadequacy.[46] And conversely, of course, the criteria which centre on doing justice in the particular case fill the important function of focusing attention on the concrete situation in which justice is to be done, on the "changing content" of justice, requiring different rules of law for different situations.[47]

§8. INTERNAL AND EXTERNAL SOURCES OF THE CONTENT OF "JUSTICE". The theories which we have thus far here recalled, whatever their tendency in terms of the above divisions, seek to derive a content for our judgments of justice from some source external to the concept or practice of justice itself: either from higher "ideas" by which the concept of justice is to be controlled and shaped, or from the social facts on or with which it must operate. The idea of justice must indeed be controlled and shaped by other ideas, and also by the techniques of its application to social facts and of manipulation and

---

[44] So *cf.* the demand for abandonment of concepts altogether, though what sense this makes in practice is dubious. See for an extreme thesis claiming that concepts should be abandoned because they interfere both with the realities of knowledge and our capacity to know G. Cohn, *Existenzialismus und Rechtswissenschaft* (1955). *Cf.* in relation to morality *id., Ethik und Soziologie* (1911, 2 ed. 1919).

There is a linkage, of course, between this kind of modern position and Hume's famous statement of the approval basis of ethical value, that while ethical value is "a matter of fact", it is "the object of feeling not of reason" (*A Treatise of Human Nature* (Everyman's ed. 1911) vol. ii). *Cf. infra* n. 91.

[45] *Cf.* on fictions in early law, Stone, *Social Dimensions*, Ch. 3, §3. We do not, of course, by this comparison, intend to suggest that justice is itself a fiction.

[46] *Cf.* the general thesis of Stone, *Legal System*, Ch. 7, and Garlan, *Legal Realism* 69-74. These functions are equally subserved, however, by what that learned writer terms "the sense of justice", "decency", "benevolent justice", "natural eternal justice", which he considered under the separate rubric "Philosophic Justice" (*id.* c. v).

[47] *Cf.* in particular the individualising standards of equity. See, e.g., *Jenyns v. Public Curator (Q.)* (1953) 90 C.L.R. 113, at 118-19, recalling that the equitable principles as to setting aside gifts because of undue influence, etc., call for a precise scrutiny of the particular facts, relations between the parties, and "the mental capacities, processes and idiosyncrasies of the donor", and that determination is not by clearly defined "legal categories" raising "definite issues of fact". And see for an attempt to build an "indeterminacy-equality" concept of justice-decision-making, J. F. Coons, "Approaches to Court-Imposed Compromise" (1964) 58 *Northw.* U.L.R. 750-794. esp. 793-94.

organisation of those facts for the purpose of such application. But such studies can only lay down the *conceptual boundaries within which* the idea of justice can play. If such studies, supposing that they could be carried out with full thoroughness and conviction, were sufficient to tell us all that need be known about justice, the result would be that the doing of "justice" would continue to raise problems only in the gaps or "free spaces" left by the theories concerned. Yet experience, including experience with such theories, suggests that the full meaning of "justice" and of the doing of justice is more than this, and that indeed, however able the theories, the problems involved continue to be secreted around and within their very boundaries. It is perhaps for this reason that recent years have seen increasing efforts to analyse "justice", not in the light of such concepts as Natural Law, or Free Will, or Utility, or Interest, but in the light of something that is postulated as the core of the notion of "justice" itself, and our human ways of operating with it.

It is more important to make this point as to the *postulation* of a core notion of justice, because the studies concerned sometimes purport by their terms to be based merely on empirical observations, for instance, of operations with the idea or impulse it denotes. Yet when such studies do actually reach the problem of what "justice" is, they *assume* that it is some idea or impulse, rather than induce this idea or impulse from the empirical data. The linguistic and psychological behaviour marshalled is asserted, not so much to base a scientific hypothesis, but rather as illustrative aids to understanding this postulated idea or impulse. Thus, when Chaim Perelman adopts a "linguistic" approach to justice, he really makes no serious effort to study all the different semantic shadings that the word has historically assumed in usage. He searches rather for a kind of nucleus of justice, which shall be independent of varying usage-associations, and of the ideological implications of such usage. His assumption manifestly is that "justice" has a core of meaning independent of associated usages or ideologies, that in fact there is some *determinate and correct* communication that takes place when men speak of "justice", whoever speaks and whoever listens. For those who make this kind of assumption, the problem of "communication" does not involve the problems of knowing what is the set of experiences or associations for which in a given speaker's mouth in a given context the symbol "justice" stands, or of knowing the ideological or psychological implications of particular predications of justice. It is reduced to the problem of what is the nucleus analytically implied in using "justice" as a symbol; on this basis, this attitude insists, we can always count on getting agreement upon such a nucleus. So, equally, when the late E. N. Cahn embarked on an "anthropocentric" study of psychological and biological reactions to injustice, his assumption is still that there is a "justice" which is "an ideal value of highest rank". "Anthropocentricism" is seen merely as a safer and surer way to capturing its content.[48]

Neither of these linguistic and psychological approaches to "justice", therefore, offers an analysis of "justice" on strictly empirical foundations, though each does make use of empirical materials. Still less is either approach necessarily "positivistic". For despite the play of empirical data and empirical techniques, the only "empirical" matter which they take as a basis consists of men's appeals and reactions to the symbol "justice" (or "injustice") itself. Now, certainly, such use is empirical evidence of a

---

[48] See E. N. Cahn, *op. cit. supra* n. 3 at 11-13.

possibly discoverable psychological law concerning men's behaviour when confronted by these symbols, or by situations characterised in terms of these symbols. It could not, however, unless the range of empirical data consulted were on a vastly different scale, and the techniques of handling them infinitely more stringent, base a claim that we can discover empirically the meaning of these symbols for *all* men, or even a claim to have proved that there is one such meaning.[49] In fact, the approaches involved fall so much short, on both heads, that whatever either may discover still has to be *interpreted* by non-empirical methods; and the interpretation supplied by the thinker may still be of metaphysical empirical or other tendency. This alone confirms that our four distinctions between theories of justice, though they may be closely related, cannot be unified; for although the "linguistic" or "psychological" theorist of justice is most likely to be a relativist,[50] he need not advocate individualisation or treating each case on its merits; and indeed in terms of our fourth distinction the tendency may often be towards claims of universality.

II. LINGUISTIC INQUIRIES AS TO THE MEANING OF "JUSTICE"

§9. THE LIMITATIONS OF SEMANTIC AIDS TO STUDY OF JUSTICE. Both philologists and philosophers in the past fifty years have paid an increasing amount of attention to the study of semantics; some of the implications which this concern has for the law have been considered in our work *Legal System and Lawyers' Reasonings*.[51] Both philologists and philosophers have tended to concentrate upon the meaning of given words at a given time ("descriptive semantics"),[52] and to neglect the continuity of meaning and change of meaning which accompany the etymological history of words ("historical semantics").[53] But insofar as both aspects of semantics are sources of acceptable scholarly knowledge, both may have relevance to a philosophic or jurisprudential inquiry; and in what follows both will receive some attention.

At the same time, for such an inquiry, we cannot accept the methods and results offered by either kind of language study without a certain degree of adaptation and modification. Language *alone* is not a safe guide for philosophical inquiry; if we do consider it alone, indeed, it is a fruitful source of error.[54] It can be a fruitful source of knowledge; but only within certain limitations which must be briefly stated at the outset.

As to the descriptive branch, the English thinkers whom Wittgenstein first inspired to linguistic philosophy did actually proceed, by a simple inquiry as to what words *mean*. But it was found that when imported into the philosophic universe of discourse, this emphasis on meaning led to a series of insoluble problems. For this reason, the philosophers abandoned

---

[49] Indeed, "positivists" in the sense used by Lloyd, *Jurisprudence* xvi, as essentially denying the possibility of establishing "a scale of absolute values . . . without distinction of time and place", would probably find the assumptions of Cahn's thesis concerning "the sense of injustice" quite repugnant.

[50] Since his theory will *ex hypothesi* be relative to the particular concepts of justice empirically occurring in particular times and places which he takes as his starting-point.

[51] See Stone, *Legal System*, Ch. 1, §§5-10.

[52] S. Ullmann's "synchronistic approach". See *The Principles of Semantics* (2 ed. 1957) 36. Though we here characterise the concerns involved in terms derived from the philological side, the point seems valid for linguistic philosophy as well.

[53] Ullmann's "diachronistic approach" (*loc. cit.*).

[54] See Del Vecchio, *Justice* 3, n. 6.

their emphasis on the *meaning* of words and concentrated instead on the *use* of words. Semantics *as a science* continues to be concerned with meaning, but the question for semantic *philosophy* has become rather "What is the function of this word in the typical utterances in which we employ it?"[55] Wittgenstein himself arrived at this conclusion only at a comparatively late stage.

So long as this limitation is kept in mind, linguistic philosophy can provide many useful insights. Also, however, once the limitation is brought to mind, it becomes apparent that though such inquiries can tell us how the word "justice" is used, they cannot tell us what thing it is that is denoted by the word. In some areas, indeed, concern with the function of linguistic utterances can lead us back to information about their meaning. For one function which such utterances can serve is as a means for dealing with knowledge; and the question that arises when an utterance is considered in this aspect is still under what conditions the utterance can be said to be true.[56] But this first kind of approach yielded little of importance in relation to words like "justice". For in fact it has mainly been directed to the language of natural sciences, and of logic and mathematics; and those employing it have tended to regard other kinds of utterance, especially those about values or in terms of values, as meaningless,[57] unless they were translatable into propositions of the cognitive type.[58] This was, indeed, one of the very difficulties already referred to which led to an increased emphasis on the function of words.[59]

A second main approach has been to concentrate on the function of utterances as conveying information, even though the information may not strictly qualify as "knowledge".[60] Here too the main question which arises is

---

[55] See Hart, "Definition" for this approach to the concept "law" and such concepts as "right", "possession", "state" and "corporation".

[56] We refer, generally, to the philosophical trends which analyse propositions as truth-functions; such as atomism and neo-positivism. On atomism see B. Russell, "Logical Atomism", in *Contemporary British Philosophy* (First Series, ed. J. H. Muirhead, 1924). On neo-positivism see J. Weinberg, *An Examination of Logical Positivism* (1936). On the relation between atomism and neo-positivism, the problem of reductive analysis, the problems of propositions about generals, and of logical constructions, see J. O. Urmson, *Philosophical Analysis* (1958) pts. 1, 2.

[57] See, e.g., A. J. Ayer, *Language, Truth and Logic* (1946) 107: "If I say to someone 'You acted wrongly in stealing that money', I am not stating anything more than if I had simply said 'You stole that money'. . . . If I . . . say 'Stealing money is wrong', I produce a sentence which has no factual meaning—that is, expresses no proposition which can be either true or false. It is as if I had written 'Stealing money!'."

[58] Of course, this is not so if the value is in effect defined as a name for verifiable facts. So imperatives also raise no difficulty if they may be understood as an elliptical form of asserting that undesirable consequences will follow disobedience. But neo-positivists — especially English — did not regard imperatives as disguised indicatives—perhaps due to the general influence of Moore's attack on the "naturalistic fallacy", though not necessarily involving acceptance of Moore's consequential ethical intuitionism. Pragmatism, and especially Dewey's instrumentalism, have shown that the distinction between cognitive propositions and imperatives and norms is not so sharp, insofar as a proposition is seen as a function of a whole process of inquiry. If the whole process is cognitive, then propositions which occur in it receive cognitive character, even when norms. *Cf.* H. Fingarette, "How Normativeness can be Cognitive but not Descriptive . . ." (1951) 48 *J. Phil.* 625-635, at 634; A. Sesonske, "Cognitive and Normative" (1956) 17 *Phil. and Phen. R.* 1, at 5. But it also follows that on the other hand, norms are thus a product of the process. *Cf.* G. Tarello, "*Norma e Giuridificazione nella Logica di Dewey*" (1960) *Atti del IV Congresso Nazionale di Filosofia del Diritto* 280.

[59] For fuller treatment of this and the other difficulties see G. Ryle, "The Theory of Meaning" in C. H. Mace (ed.), *British Philosophy in Mid-Century* (1957) 239, esp. at 250ff.; and Urmson, *cit. supra* n. 56.

[60] For the beginnings of this way of analysing see J. O. Urmson, *op. cit.* pt. 3, with

of the conditions under which the employment of an utterance is correct. But this kind of analysis still tended to direct its study to those sorts of utterances which most obviously had the function of conveying information, that is, to cognitive utterances. When confronted with evaluative or normative or imperative utterances, exponents sought to transfer to study of them, the methods used for handling cognitive utterances. Naturally, for this purpose, they chose as subject-matter those imperatives which are more easily amenable to handling by either the logic of indicatives or the patterns of usage of indicatives, that is, those which are part of a set or system of utterances. They thus tended to discard from study those instances not so amenable, including mere expletives and ejaculations.[61]

A third approach which has recently been prominent both in England and on the Continent is that which concentrates on the function of utterances as a means for conveying emotions, and in particular that of "approval". Here, clearly, the main concern is squarely with the evaluative type of utterance; but as it has so far turned out the result has been mainly to reformulate demonstrations in terms of "persuasion" rather than to cover new ground.[62]

In short, though linguistic analysis has collected and systematised considerable information, and though some of it has worked well and hard on the logic of value-judgments (or imperatives or norms), yet its main concern still remains remote from the problem of the meaning or meanings of emotionally charged words.[62a]

As for the application to philosophic problems of the *historical* branch of semantics, and in particular of the old-established science of etymology, rather graver caveats are required.[63] The comparative neglect by recent generations of this area of linguistic study has some good cause. No doubt the traditional techniques of etymology can give us valuable insights into the "contents" of a word, but it is extremely doubtful how much philosophic or even linguistic significance can be attached to such insights. The derivation of most words is very ancient, often extending back to roots in the early Indian and Persian forms of Sanskrit words; and (particularly with regard to words of juristic significance) it may well be that the implications which

bibli. On "dealing with knowledge" as distinct from "conveying information" see A. Sesonske, cited *supra* n. 58, at 2-3.

[61] There are, of course, some authors who do *not* believe that the study of the logical structure of imperative sentences is part of the study of the imperative function.

[62] In recent years this trend has become very strong both in England and on the Continent. In England the title of Stephen Toulmin's book, *The Place of Reason in Ethics* (1950), might be more clearly expressed as—"In what sense a moral statement can be said to be supported by a reasoned argument". The resulting reconsideration of argument in the sciences led to his essays now collected in *The Uses of Argument* (1958), considered in Stone, *Legal System*, Ch. 8. On the Continent, too, the relevant theses have been closely related to the revived interest in rhetorics which we have also there considered.

[62a] Even if a *significatum* like "the idea of justice" be assumed to have a prescribed and fixed content, there is no way of warranting the relation of men's usage of the *signa* "justice" and "just" to this content. See Stone, *Legal System*, Ch. 1, §§6ff. Any meaning of "justice" yielded by mere study of linguistic usage cannot, in short, escape the limits of its relation to men's linguistic, emotional, and evaluative habits of the time and place. And see the next § on these limits.

For the above reason we do not here enter the controversy surrounding the functions of paradigms in the ascertainment of meaning. See A. G. Flew, . . . *Conceptual Analysis* (1956), esp. 19; A. J. Ayer, *The Concept of a Person* . . . (1964); A. R. Blackshield, "The Game They Dare Not Bite" (1963) 3 *Jaipur L.J.* 44, 78-83; J. W. Watkins, "Farewell to the Paradigm Case Argument" (1957) 18 *Analysis* 25.

[63] *Cf.* on this matter A. R. Blackshield, article cited *supra* n. 2 at 34, n. 29.

we seek to draw from primitive word-formations import primitive, magical ideas. Are we then to suggest that the preservation in our language of the primitive word-forms imports the survival also of the primitive ideas? Clearly so mechanical a procedure would be unwarranted, and could only be adopted by fad, fashion or idiosyncrasy.

Must we, then, go to the other extreme and conclude that the primitive concepts embodied in certain word-formations do not even have significance? Certainly this is what many of the most distinguished philologists would themselves have us do.[64] Yet, again, this seems to be going too far. The lawyer (influenced perhaps by the comparative smoothness of English legal history) cannot conclude when he turns to verbal history that the primitive concepts embodied in our words are totally devoid of significance. However greatly such concepts may have been overlaid or expanded by later intellectual and cultural developments, we cannot wholly exclude the possibility or even probability that they retain some residual significance in our modern verbal concepts. Nor can we agree with any easy assumption that that residue always and necessarily merely "fetters" rather than is an essential part of the present concept.[65] What we would rather say is that, whichever be the case, to make such residues explicit can only help to make knowledge of the phenomena more accessible and adequate. We cannot, therefore, exclude etymology, *for what it may be worth*, as evidence of the meaning of justice.

§10. THE USAGE OF THE WORD "JUSTICE". In the present Sections we are addressing ourselves as separate sources of information to our *linguistic* operations with the *word* "justice", and to our substantive emotional or evaluative operations with the idea or impulse which the word denotes. Linguistic analysis is primarily concerned with the former inquiry into the function which is served by utterances containing the word "justice". Insofar as use of language can *also* be a kind of emotive or evaluative operation, linguistic analysis may also carry information of the latter kind; but it is then rather subsidiary to direct psychological and sociological observation. Even if this is one of the areas in which linguistic analysis can make some contribution to "descriptive sociology",[66] it is not a particularly distinctive contribution.

Yet when we therefore limit ourselves in the present Section to the distinctively *linguistic* contribution to our understanding of "justice", one which a mere study of the usage of that word can provide, this contribution becomes rather dispiritingly small,[66a] and in any case dangerously unreliable.

---

[64] Including O. Jespersen in *Mankind, Nation and Individual* (1946) 217, who characterises resort to etymology as based on "a learned form of superstitious belief in the power of the name, related to the primitive superstition that the name has a magical potency". See also Sir Ernest Gowers, *The Complete Plain Words* (1954) 39; H. W. Fowler, *A Dictionary of Modern English Usage* (1926) article "True and False Etymology"; S. Stephenson Smith, *The Command of Words* (1936) 112 (but *cf.* 44).

[65] *Pace* A. Ross, *Towards a Realistic Jurisprudence* (1946) 256 (in the context of a discussion of the "magical" ideas at the basis of the Roman law concept of "rights"). And see *id.* 233 discussing the relevance of the etymological consideration of German *Schuld* (old Norse *skuld*) to the meaning of the concept of obligation.

[66] *Cf.* Hart, *Law*, Preface, vii.

[66a] Though valuable no doubt as a way of showing the inadequacy of "fairness" as the criterion of justice, J. Chapman's conclusions (after a rather laboured comparative study of the usage of this word with that of "justice") that "justice" is a vaguer, more comprehensive and more complex notion than "fairness", seem slight. See his "Justice and Fairness" in *Nomos, Justice* 147, at 157; see generally 154-163.

It is unreliable because linguistic data, without the checking and substantiation of reference to other data, seem peculiarly susceptible to unconscious manipulation to fit whatever thesis the analyst may wish to expound. One writer has recently concluded on the basis of usage that "we readily apply 'fair' in the context of a process and we tend to reserve 'justice' for use with reference to outcomes alone", and that as between the two elements of equality and reciprocity, "justice" tends to be appropriated especially to the former, and "fairness" to the latter.[66b] For our part, if we attached any importance to quibbling about the words "justice" and "fairness", we would doubt this version of lay (or even of lawyer) usage. We even doubt that usage provides any *specific* differentiation between them at all. It is precisely because of the variety of usage of the word "justice" that the usage argument is so easily adaptable to so many philosophical positions. Its uses are so varied and ubiquitous in contexts that we can only begin to think significantly about them if we severely limit the ambit of our inquiry. For there is "scarcely a single relationship of life into which the question of justice does not enter".[67] But while we must set some limit by *fiat*, this must not be arbitrary, lest we thereby increase the danger of selecting that usage which aids the particular analyst's thesis.

One possible course is to say that we should look only to those uses of "just" or "justice" in which these words cannot be replaced, without some shift in meaning of the whole utterance, by any other word: since it is in these uses that what is characteristic of the meaning of "justice" is most likely to be embodied. This would provide us with a warrant (if warrant were needed)[68] for excluding such uses of the phoneme "just" as in "just a moment!", "just here", "just right" and "as we have just said"; for in all these cases the word "just" may be replaced by some paraphrase or circumlocution without any change in meaning. Similarly, though less obviously, it would enable us to exclude such usages as "he complained with justice", "a just observation", and "just indignation". Yet we would still be left with a host of usages (such as "to do justice", "there is no justice in this law", "a just man", "just conduct", "a just punishment", "a just law", "a just price", "a just reward") so diverse that the only possible conclusions would be both exceedingly general and already known: for example, that "justice" refers to a social situation[69] or a quality of an enactment and the like; and that "just" means a quality of a person, of a segment of behaviour, of a norm, or of a value.[70]

Another possible limiting fiat would be to confine ourselves to those usages of "justice" which have some connection with law. Again, this fiat

---

[66b] *Id.* 155, 156, 158. At 162 he is led into a further distinction (still based on usage) between "fairness as equality of treatment" and "fairness as reciprocity". As to the support which he seeks at 160-62 from the linguistic analysts' recurrent game analogy, see A. R. Blackshield, *cit. supra* n. 62a, at 71-73.

[67] C. K. Allen, *Aspects of Justice* (1958) 4.

[68] On the remote connection existing even here see Blackshield, article cited *supra* n. 2, at 32-33. And see the attempt to reach the meaning of justice linguistically, taking account (*inter alia*) even of such usages, in L. Lachance, *cit. supra* n. 8, 25ff., esp. at 26.

[69] Even this (at least on the basis of usage) probably cannot be pressed beyond the point that a "justice situation" always involves at least two people. See Aristotle's discussions cited *supra* Ch. 1, §3; and *cf.* Lamont, *Moral Judgment* 174: "Justice could, at least theoretically, exist when the relations between individuals are so purely external and accidental that no question of co-operation for common ends ever arises."

[70] See Tammelo, "Justice and Doubt" 315-17.

seems warranted—both by the purposes of our inquiry and by the usage itself. But the relevant usage here perhaps raises more problems than it solves. There is no doubt that in ordinary usage "justice" is in fact connected to "law" in a double way. In some contexts "justice" is a synonym of "law" or of the legal process: "penal justice", for example, may mean "penal law". In such cases the word "justice" is homonymic,[70a] covering both law and justice. The differentiation of these two concepts stimulated by legal positivism is leading today to a disuse of this double meaning of "justice"; but this very differentiation merely reinforces the homonymic clash in contexts where the word was formerly of clear and single but undifferentiated meaning.

Yet it should by now be obvious that, in the present view, a usage which merges "justice" with "law" as two names for the same thing cannot be regarded as helpful. This is not to suggest that such a thing as "justice" and such a thing as "law" are in themselves obviously distinct, as Professor Hart sometimes seems to suggest in the Hart-Fuller discussion;[71] it is simply to suggest that the very fact that a position like Hart's is taken implies that the two concepts have to be distinguished. And this is so even for those who insist on the old truth now argued again by Fuller, that in the concrete processes of law-application considerations of "justice" and "law" cannot always be distinguished.

A further question, if the present fiat were imposed, would be whether we should limit ourselves merely to usages of "justice" connected with law or to usages of "justice" in law. There is no doubt that "justice" and "just" do occur in legal contexts, and even in privileged propositions of the law field. Statutes[72] and even constitutions[73] contain the expression "just" in some sense or senses which concern us; and such usages, and judicial exegeses upon them, may indeed be highly illuminating. Yet on the whole[74] the pronouncements of judges will tend to be rather in general terms, and will be relevant to the present inquiry as little more than hints which we must follow up elsewhere, or reflections of what we and they have found

---

[70a] Or at least polysemic, tending towards homonymity. See S. Ullmann, *The Principles of Semantics* (2 ed. 1957) 117-138; and on the critical situation when such semantic phenomena occur *in the same universe of discourse*, see literature cited *id.* 132, esp. J. Gilliéron and M. Roques, *Etudes de Géographie Linguistique* (1912) 149ff.

[71] See Hart, "Law and Morals" *passim*.

[72] E.g., ss. 1-3 of the Law Reform (Frustrated Contracts)Act, 1943, as to the circumstances in which money can be recovered by or from a party incurring expenses, or receiving a valuable benefit (respectively), before time of discharge of the contract.

[73] E.g., the Fifth Amendment to the U.S. Constitution, and s. 51 (xxxi) of the Australian Constitution, as to (respectively) "just compensation" or "just terms" for the acquisition of private property for public purposes.

[74] So, apart from the various shades of assimilation of "justice" to law or legal process discussed *infra* n. 79 (and sometimes even there), F. E. Dowrick's pioneering *Justice According to the English Common Lawyers* (1961, here cited as "Dowrick, *Justice*") is constrained to use mainly non-judicial, especially juristic articulations. And sometimes these have to be as remote as Bracton and St. Germain. See, e.g., 17-19, 46ff. As to the other kinds of justice-theorising by common lawyers which he can detect he cites mainly: (1) for natural justice, R. O'Sullivan, Q.C., and Sir Henry Slesser (see *op. cit.* 46-72, esp. 49ff., 69; and see also as to O'Sullivan *supra* Ch. 2, n. 267; Ch. 3, §§4, 13). (2) For "moral justice" (*op. cit.* 73ff., esp. 79, 87-93), the judicial use of various legal standards such as "reasonable", "just and reasonable", "good sense", "decency", etc., implying (in his meaning of it, which is that of Pollock, discussed *infra* nn. 93, 111) an incorporation by reference of "the common sense of justice" (on which latter see *infra* §§13-15). (3) For Benthamite utilitarianism (despite its undoubted influence on law and lawyers—see *supra* Ch. 4, §22) he offers mainly Bentham's own articulations (*Justice* 106-134). These, of course, with Bentham himself, were usually not made in terms of "justice". See the *Principles of Morals* . . ., c. x, §40n.; and H. A. Bedau in *Nomos, Justice* 284, at

elsewhere. When for instance in the *Grace Brothers Case*[75] Latham C.J.
said[76] that the Court should not invalidate acquisition legislation as not
being on "just terms" unless it is "such that a reasonable man could not
regard the terms of acquisition as being just", he was pointing to the
importance of the common human "sense of injustice" as an index of
justice, an index we shall briefly consider in §14 of this Chapter. And
when in the next paragraph he said that "justice involves consideration
of the interests of the community as well as of the person whose property
is acquired",[77] he was pointing to the weighing of individual and social
interests as a criterion of justice, which we have examined more closely in
the preceding Chapter.[78] It may be added that even if all the interests referred
to occasionally coincide, this is certainly not the same thing as the common
human sense of justice and injustice; or perhaps one should say that
whether it is, remains an open question.

In any event, the *legal* uses of "justice" are likely either to refer to
"justice-according-to-law",[79] which at least ought not to be assumed to

---

288. (4) As to "social justice", or related notions of "social utility", "public interest"
and the like (135-175), he finds these notions not so much *articulated* by English
judges, as *used* to rationalise and refine judicial methods. (See *Justice* 143, and also
150-59.)

No doubt Dowrick is right to see a blend of these various approaches underlying
English judicial thought. Our present point, confirming the position in the text, is
that the primary evidence he can find of the articulation of them is usually non-
judicial. For a fuller demonstration see A. R. Blackshield, Book Review (1963) 4
Syd. L.R. 332-37.

[75] *Grace Brothers Pty. Ltd.* v. *Cwlth.* (1946) 72 C.L.R. 269 at 280.

[76] Thereby restating the well-known test laid down by Starke J. in *Minister for
the Army* v. *Dalziel* (1944) 68 C.L.R. 261 at 291.

[77] *Loc. cit. supra* n. 75. See also Dixon J. at 290.

[78] Other cases on the meaning of these constitutional provisions for "just terms"
or "just compensation" give some information about the meaning of "justice", but
little of major significance. On the whole the Australian cases are more helpful,
because in the American cases there is an admixture of the problem of "due
process" with that of "justness" of "compensation". On the other hand, "just compensation" is a narrower requirement than "just terms". See in the *Huon Transport
Case* (1945) 70 C.L.R. 293, Rich J. at 307-308, McTiernan J. at 327, and Williams J.
at 337; and in the *Grace Bros. Case* Dixon J. at 289-290.

Cf. on the phrase "just and reasonable", in England: the cases from *Simons* v.
G.W. Rly. (1856) 18 C.B. 805 to *G.W. Rly.* v. *McCarthy* (1887) 12 App. Cas. 218,
and *Sutcliffe* v. *G.W. Rly.* (1910) 1 K.B. 478 (Kennedy L.J.). In the U.S., see *Reagan*
v. *Farmers' Loan and Trust Co.* (1894) 154 U.S. 362; *San Diego Land & Town Co.* v.
National City (1899) 174 U.S. 739.

[79] *Cf.* Callaway C.J. in *McManus* v. *Fulton* (1929) 85 mt. 170, 278 Pac. 126
at 134 (justice "is in a legal sense 'that end which ought to be reached in a case
by the regular administration of the principles of the law involved as applied to the
facts' "); and many of the cases collected by Campbell J. in *City of Sioux Falls* v.
Marshall (1925) 48 S.D. 378, 204 N.W. 999 at 1002. *Cf.* in conclusion Dowrick, *Justice*
215, that "the stock notions in the working philosophy of the typical English judge
in the modern era" are those of "justice as judicature" (17-29), "justice as fair
trial" (30-45), and "legal justice" (176-204); and *cf.* the position of H. R. S. Ryan
in (1960-61) 3 *Crim. L.Q.* 194-97. See the comments of G. Wilson, (1962) 78
L.Q.R. at 434, on the nature of Dowrick's collection, and contrast a philosopher's
defence of lawyers against their self-depreciation in this respect in Lamont, *Moral
Judgment* 129-131.

It is clear that common lawyers usually shy away from abstract thought about
justice. See Tammelo, "Justice and Doubt" 318; Dowrick, *Justice* 5-8; Wright, *Essays*
392; and Lord Denning, Intro. to W. Friedmann, *Law and Social Change in Contemporary Britain* (1951). G. Wilson justly says of Dowrick's survey of English judicial
utterances that "it is not his fault that the gleanings are thin". See (1962) 78 *L.Q.R.*
434, 437. And see generally the views discussed in Stone, *Legal System*, Ch. 8, n. 62.
Greene M. R., *The Judicial Office* (1938) observes on the judicial "sense of justice"
that judicial denials of concern with "justice" are true insofar as they excuse inability
to reach "a just result in an individual case because the state of the law prevents
it". See also *infra* n. 96.

be identical with "justice";[80] or to have no *specific* reference at all, but only an indeterminate reference.[81] For in all these contexts it is clear that the introduction of "justice" is conditioned by the limits of its application; and within these limits the reference to justice usually amounts to the inclusion within the logical structure of law of an indeterminate standard.[82] In other words, the reference to justice—as to the "*équité*", "*equità*", "equitable", or "*equo*",[83] of systems where equity has not been crystallized into law—marks the boundary where the judge stops speaking the language of law and begins speaking the common language (and begins thinking therefore in terms, not of legal sense, but of common sense).[84]

We would therefore say that even if we limit our study to usages of "justice" which are somehow related to law, this limitation cannot be taken in the sense of referring only to those usages which occur within the fabric of the law itself. For this could be done only if the language of law were identified with the language of justice, or were at least accorded some special right to speak with final authority of justice. As to this latter alternative, it is sufficient to say that the concept of justice is not a prerogative of the lawyers, but is in fact used by all men; as to the former, the point we have just made is that (except in relation to "justice-according-to-law") there is no special lawyers' usage of justice as distinct from the common usage. There is, of course, such a special lawyers' usage of "law",[85] and this finds a place in a special "language of law"; but since there is no such special usage of "justice", it would be wrong to identify the language of justice with this "language of law" and thereby to limit ourselves to lawyers' usage.

§11. "JUSTICE" A WORD MAINLY OF COMMON LANGUAGE: "LAW" MAINLY OF TECHNICAL LANGUAGE. The consequences of the growth of this special "language of law" are illuminating, even if not always encouraging. First, the "language of law" has tended to become more and more a technical language; and a clear result of this is that propositions employing reference to "law", or to "legal rights" and the like, tend to become fixed, rigidly defined, and differentiated from each other. Further, and in part consequentially, the relations between them tend to become (though of course without ever finally becoming) *logical* relations. In the result, the word "law" tends to become not the substantive corresponding to an adjective— an apprehensible concept corresponding to an apprehensible quality—but

---

[80] It may of course be so identified, even in popular usage. See Lamont, *Moral Judgment* 163, regarding this as "quite inappropriate".

[81] See Tammelo, "Justice and Doubt" at 318. *Cf.* Lamont, *Moral Judgment* 27-28.

[82] Which has long been discussed in common law countries. See Pound, 2 *Jurisprudence* 127ff., 4 *id.* 28, and his "Theory of Judicial Decision" (1923) 36 H.L.R. 641. And see Stone, *Legal System*, Ch. 7 *passim*.

[83] In civil law countries there has recently been much interest in these tendencies. See, e.g., C. M. de Marini, *Il Giudizio di Equità . . .: Premesse Teoriche* (1959). *Cf.* on the similar vague use in English of "equitable", "*ex aequo et bono*" and the like, Dowrick, *Justice* 74.

[84] *Cf.* as to the phrase "suffer an injustice" in s. 171 (1) (c) of the U.K. Law of Property Act, 1925, *In re Freeman* (1927) 1 Ch. 479 where the C.A. distinguished between an injustice in the strict sense of involving the violation or withholding of a legal right, and the extended and popular sense as meaning "be unfair to". Sargent L.J. (490-91) held that it must include a violated "moral claim", or "disappointment of a well-founded expectation", despite the vagueness involved until cases are decided. *Cf.* Lawrence L.J. at 493-94, and Lord Hanworth M.R. at 487, quoting Shakespeare, *King John*, Act V, Sc. ii.

[85] See Stone, *Legal System*, Ch. 5 and *cf.* Stone and Tarello, "Justice", esp. at 372-76.

the label for a field, with a set of logically interrelated substantives taking the place of the original law-adjectivations. On the one hand, this makes it increasingly difficult to find any single concept which may be identified as "law"; on the other hand, it means that each of the interrelated substantives within the law field, and to a lesser extent the relationship between them, can be defined with some precision.

Neither of these propositions is true of "justice". It is true that we indubitably see correspondences between the proposition of law-language, "I have a legal right to . . .", and the proposition of common language, "It is just that I be allowed to . . ."; and between other similar pairs. But in the types of sentence referring to "legal *rights*", etc., the meaning receives a certainty and predictability from the conventional legal definitions of "rights", etc., and from the logical relations between this and other legal conceptions, which are simply not present in the sentences uttered in terms of what is just. On the other hand, if the usages of "justice" are less well articulated, they remain by the same token more homogeneous, and thus in principle more amenable to a *single* articulation if only it can be found.

Second, in the law field, whether or not we commit ourselves totally to an analytical view of law, it is at least true that *some* propositions of law are treated as privileged, so that other propositions can be said to be law only if they are analytically derived from, or from an interpretation of, the privileged ones.[86] To identify a proposition of law, therefore, it may suffice to state the privileged norm or norms, and the rules of derivation and interpretation. The privileged norms themselves, insofar as they are not derived from or otherwise dependent for their identification on any other norms, will in the terms of linguistic analysis be "primitives". But when we try to identify a proposition of justice, this method is not available. *Any* statement about justice may in fact be unrelated in any systematic way to any other statement; that is, *any* such statement may in fact be a primitive statement. Nor is there any way of determining whether a particular statement about justice is a "primitive" one or not, for even if it were not a "primitive", common usage gives us no principles for discovering what it might derive from. One statement of justice may in usage be "derived" from another in the same or in a different sphere in any of numerous senses, from logical deduction to the merest association of ideas. To say that the ground of one statement of justice must be another *more general* statement of justice amounts to saying that the language of evaluations in common usage *ought to be reduced* to a particular system of formal logic. But it is not in fact so reduced; nor is the tacit assertion that it *ought to be* so reduced even a plausible reason for accepting the reduction as in any way useful.

Further, insofar as linguistic analysis of utterances will tend to concentrate on analysis of their syntactic structures and of only the *kinds of purposes* for which they are employed, linguistic analysis of common-language usages of "justice" cannot distinguish "justice" from the broad class of values in general. For the *kinds* of purpose of value-utterances are common to all such utterances; while at least in common language the syntactic structures by reference to which we can talk analytically about

---

[86] See N. Bobbio's paper in the section on theory of proof of the *Colloque International de Logique* at Brussels, 1953, in "*Considérations introductives sur le raisonnement des juristes*" (1954) 8 *Revue Int. de Phil.* 67.

"justice" are only those syntactic structures by reference to which we can also describe the usage of other valuational terms and perhaps abstract terms in general. The statements about "justice" which could be made by reference to such syntactic structures would be the same statements as could be made about other abstract terms, and would thus say *nothing specific about justice*. Here again the "justice" usage differs from the "law" usage, for a description of "law" in terms of syntactic structures does amount to a specific description of an important part of the special language-field for which, in lawyers' usage, "law" has become a comprehensive name. "Justice" is neither the name for a special language-field nor itself a term whose meaning is only clear in such a field.

§12. FUNCTIONS OF LINGUISTIC STUDY OF "JUSTICE". In short, a study of the usage of "justice" seems able to tell us only what we already know: that "justice" is assigned or appealed to in evaluative operations; that the application of these operations is fairly ubiquitous, but that it tends to focus round certain poles of application such as social situations and the legal regulation of them; and that in particular (perhaps with the help of a fiat limiting the range of our relevant inquiry) it tends to focus on situations which are relevant to law. But if this last piece of information is to be given anything approaching universal tenability, it must be very loosely expressed, as for instance by saying that the situations in which it is appropriate to employ "justice" are those situations in which it might reasonably be thought appropriate to employ "law", whether or not the particular situation is actually within the purview of law for the time being.

It may, indeed, be possible to draw from the usage one further suggestion: to infer from the usage, as Edmond Cahn has inferred from his meditations on the "sense of injustice", that "justice" always applies to *individual* situations—"that it arises only to meet the challenge of the here-and-now, the real or imagined haecceity of the occasion. It responds to each human predicament as ultimately important".[87] It is no doubt possible to collect hosts of instances in which "justice" is applied to individual situations. But there are also the more general usages of "justice". We may admit that in "a just punishment", "a just law", "a just price", "a just reward", "a just act", the reference is still clearly to an individual instance. And even when we speak of "a just man", so that our utterance is of individual application in respect to that man, but of general application in respect to his conduct, we may admit that the general element is merely a generalisation from, or simply a convenient shorthand expression of, the fact that on two or three individual occasions we have known him to act in a manner which might appropriately be described as "just". We do not really mean to suggest that invariably his actions always have been and always will be "just". All this may be admitted. Yet there still seem to be also many instances in which "justice" is used with more truly general intention; and at least on the basis of usage Cahn's suggestion that justice *only* arises to meet individual situations seems dubious.

Similarly, when we turn to the etymological history of the word "justice", we find not only that (for reasons already mentioned) the information available must be employed with circumspection, but that in any case this information is negligible. Such scanty and speculative information as

[87] E. N. Cahn, *op. cit. supra* n. 3, at 176. For discussion of Cahn's thesis see *infra* §14.

is available[88] suggests that the central idea of justice is its binding, obligatory character, and perhaps also that it is associated with the idea of well-being or welfare. No further inferences, and certainly no specific inferences, seem possible.

Indeed, on the purely linguistic level it seems impossible to go further. To try to extract some general *meaning* from the usage of "justice" and its derivatives in all the various contexts in which they actually occur would seem to be a hopeless and even preposterous enterprise. There is no sufficient uniformity in their usage to provide a universal characterisation which would be more than vacuous. To catalogue all the *different* meanings also seems unfeasible. Nor do definitional fiats seem appropriate; for once it is agreed that our attention must be directed to *common* usage, we really have no legislative power to issue fiats to command the usage in question. It may still be possible to list some characteristic kinds of feeling which the word is usually used to express; but such a list cannot be exhaustive, and cannot pretend to cover the whole field of "justice" except in terms of pervasive flavour. And even this cannot be done on the basis of linguistic usage alone. Some of the more articulate usage may help us to characterise the feelings and impulses that are expressed; but for the most part the function of linguistic usage will be merely to identify for us the kinds of situation that we ought to be examining.[89]

III. THE "SENSE OF JUSTICE"

§13. LIMITS ON THE USEFULNESS OF THE HUMAN "SENSE OF JUSTICE" AS A GUIDE. The fact that value-ideas conceptualise at the least human feelings of approval and disapproval and resulting human impulses, and that value-terms at the least symbolise such feelings and impulses, grounds the hope that examination of these feelings and impulses may reveal the content of values.[89a] Such an examination might disclose what kind of situations stimulate the kind of approval or disapproval expressed by the value in question, and to what kinds of action we are then impelled, without begging the question whether all the feelings and impulses related to a certain value have something essential in common, or whether they are merely a heterogeneous cluster associated with the common term only by cultural and historical accident. Despite the psychological flavour[90] of this kind of

---

[88] By which "just" is traced back through the Latin "*ius*" either to the Sanskrit "*yu*", meaning "to join" or "to bind", or alternatively to the Sanskrit "*vós*" or "*yós*", an old sacral word somehow connected with the human "weal" or the divine "will". See the note by Professor J. Puhvel of the University of California, published in I. Tammelo. "Justice and Doubt" 324; and *cf.* G. Del Vecchio, *Justice* 3, n. 8; and Blackshield, article cited *supra* n. 2, at 34.

[89] Lamont, *Moral Judgment* 134, believes that though many people's expressions about justice cannot withstand theoretical analysis. the concurrence of appeals to certain principles at various levels of experience may still show that "these principles are fundamental". The role of linguistic usage here is a little vague.

[89a] The growth, structure and operation of ethical convictions in human groups represent, of course, a different study, on which see Stone, *Social Dimensions*, Ch. 12, and *id.* Ch. 1, §§3-4.

[90] See, e.g., F. R. Bienenfeld, *Rediscovery of Justice* (1949), esp. pt. i, "Justice in the Nursery". On the special value of children's reactions in such an inquiry see Lamont, *Moral Judgment* 35-36. Both Lamont and Bienenfeld of course acknowledge debt to Jean Piaget's pioneering studies in child psychology, esp. *The Moral Judgment of the Child* (1932). For criticisms of Bienenfeld's approach, esp. the assumption of parallelism between individual and societal stages of development, see

inquiry, its approach to justice really continues a long-standing attitude which sees the roots of all conceptions of justice not in anything yet formulated, but in a peculiar human sentiment or instinct.[91] This, said Gény half a century ago, "is a kind of instinct which, without appealing to the reasoning mind, goes of its own accord straight to the best solution, the one most conformable to the aim of all juridical organization".[92] Such a notion of justice is obviously attractive to "the common man" (with whom we should perhaps couple many common lawyers), for it erects into a theory his very inarticulateness about justice.[93] It encourages in him, too, the prideful if not condescending belief that the vast web of theories of justice advanced during millennia by philosophers and jurists are but attempts to articulate that common sense of justice which comes naturally to him. And it allows him to dismiss such theories if he thinks they do not reflect this "common sense", and even to condemn them as obscuring the intimate and personal sense of justice by misleading artificial ideals.

The very intimacy of this intuition and the mystery of its inaccessibility to rational checking is, however, anathema for the earnest rationalist or scientific thinker. From this standpoint, even when some related sentiment in the human soul is admitted, its competence to reach correct valuation is doubted. In the first place, the doing of justice presupposes a knowledge of what are the true facts relevant to judgment; and inner feelings do not either gather or interpret statistics. In the second place, even assuming all relevant facts are known, the "sense of justice" which operates upon

---

W. Friedmann, Book Review (1949) 65 *L.Q.R.* 91. And on the "psychodynamics" of justice see Tammelo, "Justice and Doubt" at 399-403.

Lamont's work is an inquiry into ethics rather parallel to the present section's inquiry into "justice", being concerned not with what ought to be, but with *what actually are*, men's moral standards. See *id.* 9ff., esp. 10; and on the psychological nature of his interest *id.* 20, 24ff., 35ff., 137ff. *Cf.* also D. Snygg, "The Psychological Basis of Human Values", in A. P. Ward (ed.), *Goals of Economic Life* (1953) 335-367.

[91] See Cohen, *Ethical Systems* 100. David Hume himself, after the most famous proclamation in English philosophy of the unbridgeable gap between the "is" and the "ought" (*A Treatise of Human Nature*, bk. iii, pt. i, §i), went on immediately to imply that such a bridge might be found in the "agreeable" "feeling or sentiment" of "satisfaction" evoked by virtue, and the "uneasy" one of "blame" evoked by vice. See *id.*, §ii; and *cf.* Benn and Peters, *Principles* 40-41. And *cf.* J. Feinberg's suggestion (*Nomos, Justice* 69 at 92) that judgments of moral appropriateness finally resemble "aesthetic judgments—for example that crimson and orange are clashing colors—more than they resemble judicial pronouncements". See also I. Jenkins in *id.* 191 at 194, 196, linking the work of Cahn and Gény here cited with similar emphases there detected in Krabbe, Stammler, Rommen and Del Vecchio.

Jacob-Flink, *Value Decision* 16, offer as "operational indices" for the identification of values "(1) 'Ought' or 'should' statements in rationalizations of actions. (2) Statements indicating guilt, shame, or diffuse anxiety association with specific actions. (3) Statements indicating moral indignation or approbation of actions on the one hand, and of esteem or praise on the other."

[92] See Gény, 3 *Science et Technique* 215. *Cf.* H. Sidgwick, *Methods of Ethics* (1874) 236: "Scientific ethics can be only the organization and systematic elaboration of principles and methods implied in the moral reasoning of common men".

[93] See F. Pollock's apotheosis (*Essays* 288ff.) of "the moral sense", as "the invisible and informal judgment-seat of righteous men" (*id.* 297), a "habit of instinctive moral judgment, acquired by living in society" (*id.* 275). He also maintained that competence for ethical judgment was independent of knowledge of "moral philosophy" (*id.* 266), the latter being merely an attempt to explain the former (*id.* 294). He thought that "the proper task of the philosopher" was to "assign principles on which to give a rational account of the morality already familiar to him"; and (simultaneously) "that ethical judgments are not organized, and that we do not expect them to become so" (*id.* 272-73). For an attempted rationalisation of these positions, and on some other aspects of Pollock's notion of justice, see Dowrick, *Justice* 103, 74. Pollock saw all this in the context of "the *English* moral sense", hostile to "scholastic and quasi-legal method" and the final authority which this latter presupposed (*id.* 272). And see *infra* n. 111.

these data is "largely a composite of accepted moral doctrines". As such (it is correctly pointed out) "it is no more impregnable to intellectual criticism than the beliefs upon which it is based". The "sense of justice" in this light requires critical examination by philosophy and science. It cannot be the final test of justice; and to make it such would be "simply to assign ultimate authority to our moral ignorance".[94]

Even this stern view, of course, has to recognise that theories of justice are in some degree attempts to articulate and refine this sentiment, and lack something when they wander too far from it. Yet it is also undeniable that our modern feelings and impulses of justice are themselves influenced (if not determined) by the philosophical theories of justice which have entered, in more or less corrupted versions, into the cultural heritage of our societies.[95] To this extent, the "sense of justice" has rational, cognitive, and reasoning elements; and even its emotional, irrational and intuitive elements may be capable of being reasoned about, expressed in rational form, and even perhaps brought within the order of reason.[96] By the same token, we have to recognise that while the feelings and impulses which are comprehended by "the sense of justice" are likely to vary with time and place, and to a degree from man to man, the fact that these feelings and impulses are in part a function of an ongoing cultural tradition means that they also tend to have a certain homogeneity. And insofar as there is contact, confluence, convergence, diffusion, and separation from common sources, as between the various streams of human culture, there may be some elements in the "sense of justice" common to men of every time and place, even if one excludes any biological basis for universality. In short, it is possible to generalise about *some aspects of* the "sense of justice", but not about the "sense of justice" seen as a sufficient guide of what is just. For, conceived in this last way, the concept not only encounters grave difficulties as to "universality". It simply ends discussion, for it blocks all further inquiry.[96a]

If further inquiry and discussion are to grow in fruitfulness they must be both tolerant and alert to the different elements operative within the plaited influence-mesh which bears on the choices commonly regarded as "moral" or "value-determined". Social science has come to distinguish three main classes of "vectors" of such influence. These of course include "values",

---

[94] Cohen, *Ethical Systems* 100-101. *Cf.* the criticisms of Austin and Bentham, *supra* Ch. 4, nn. 122, 123, 167. And see generally the criticisms discussed by Dowrick, *Justice* 101-105; I. Jenkins, in *Nomos, Justice* 191, 195-203. So Sven Ranulf gave to his work, *The Jealousy of the Gods and Criminal Law at Athens* (1933), the subtitle "A Contribution to the Sociology of Moral Indignation", aiming to analyse the emotions and passions beneath ostensibly rational arguments, so as to reduce their force and clear the ground for utilitarian calculation in practical decisions. See *id.* at 2. *Cf.* the different and supplementary point in J. Feinberg, article cited *supra* n. 91, at 93, who sees the utilitarian superstructure as contributing also the desideratum that our attitudes and appraisals, once expressed and acknowledged, be cast in public and conventional forms. Simply to "feel sympathy toward the unemployed . . . would not prevent food riots".

[95] On the interaction between "speculative" and "practical" standards, see Pollock, *Essays* c. x, esp. at 284-85.

[96] So Greene M.R. (*op. cit. supra* n. 79, at 7) sees the operation of "the sense of justice" as dependent on what are finally rational qualities: "openmindedness, patience", ability to withhold judgment, and to recognise that a position taken has been proved wrong. Indeed, just as Coke envisaged "reason" as not "natural reason", but that acquired by long study and experience, so Lord Greene (*id.* 8-9) denies the efficacy of the merely "natural" sense of justice.

[96a] C. J. Friedrich's point as to the central role of prevalent values in political justice (*Nomos, Justice* 24-61, esp. 30ff., 43) is not open to this objection since not *necessarily* tied to the assumption of a universal common sense of human justice.

that is, normative propositions supported by internalised sanctions and operating as imperatives in judging, and as standards for evaluating and rationalising choices made. They also include, however, motivations or impulses of action not arising from values, whether innate (as in the impulse to self-preservation) or learned (as in the conventional expediencies or proprieties of going cultures). They include, third, a class of vectors corresponding to the rational and cognitive elements in justice-decision already stressed, consisting of "existential propositions held by individual human beings regarding the structure and operation of the social and physical universe and one's place in it." These consist of cognitive standards (used as criteria of the tenability and applicability of information), appreciative standards (used as criteria of the potential results of an act), and knowledge (accepted existential propositions even when these are regarded as subject to further verification).[96b]

§14. THE "SENSE OF INJUSTICE". It is a fact, no doubt regrettable, that the common man's feelings and impulses of justice seem to come to vigour mainly in reaction against injustice personally confronted, whether in the individual's own life[97] or in some *cause célèbre* inflaming the imagination of a nation or of the world.[98] An inquirer into the "sense of justice" therefore tends to see it manifested in passionate emotion rather alien to his own mood as an impartial observer. Are we to say that the inquirer's sense of justice fails to reflect the common sense of justice? Or that somehow the passionate emotion is really alien to the feelings and impulses which express the common sense of justice, even though it empirically accompanies them? Apart from these problems, how far is the inquiry affected simply by the fact that what is usually aroused is the sense of *in*justice rather than that of justice?[99] How far are conclusions about injustice translatable into terms of justice? Justice and injustice are not logical contradictories. An injustice is not a negation of justice in general; it is only one particular in which justice has not been realised. Even the clearest elucidation of particular "injustices" will give us only, at best, a limited number of individual particulars of what justice is not.

Despite all these discomforts and difficulties, the sense of injustice has been recognised as an index to the idea of justice ever since Aristotle. "The many forms of injustice," he thought, "make the many forms of justice quite clear."[100] A contemporary American writer, E. N. Cahn, set out in 1949

96b See the notable statement in Jacob-Flink, *Value Decision* 22-23, building on Parsons-Shils, *Theory of Action*, in which see esp. C. Kluckhohn *et al.*, "Values and Value-Orientations in the Theory of Action" at 390ff., and on K. Lewin, *Field Theory in Social Science* (1951). More dubiously Jacob-Flink also places under "beliefs" a category as to "power", treating this as embodied in existential propositions "regarding man's perception of his relative capacity to influence and/or control" his social and physical world. And see Stone, *Social Dimensions*, Chs. 9, 12.

97 See, e.g., most of the examples employed by E. N. Cahn, *op. cit. supra* n. 3 at 13-28.

98 See, e.g., the examples used by Timasheff, *Sociology of Law* 96-97. And *cf.* on this point A. R. Blackshield, article cited *supra* n. 2 at 29-30.

99 *Cf.* Friedrich, *Philosophy of Law* 199, who like Cahn accepts this as a fact, and thinks that the ontological ground for this fact is "the value system" held by each man, whether personally or as part of a wider group. The value is most consciously held when most clearly threatened. Friedrich concludes "that justice and injustice cannot be related to any *one* value, be it equality or any other, but only to the complex value system of a man, a community, or mankind". *Cf.* now his important essay cited *supra* n. 96a, at 30 and esp. at 39-40. And *cf.* Dowrick, *Justice* 74.

100 *Nicomachean Ethics* v. I; *cf.* Aquinas, *Commentary on the Nicomachean*

to revindicate this thesis, which he expressed in the title *The Sense of In-justice*. He envisaged an empirical study of the sense of injustice as a "familiar and observable phenomenon", disclosing "how justice arises" and "its biologic purpose". He thought that its "active, vital, and experiential" nature was regrettably overlaid by the beclouding natural law notions of "ideal relation, static condition or preceptual standards". The response to such notions is "merely contemplative, and contemplation bakes no loaves"; while the response to injustice (Cahn thought) "is alive with movement and warmth in the human organism".[101] It is, no doubt, both stirring and reassuring, in an era marked by the most massive cruelties by men to men for two millennia, and the no less massive indifference of vast sections of onlooking mankind, to think (as Cahn does) that "the human organism" emphatically identifies injustice suffered or witnessed as a kind of attack on itself.[102] It is also natural that this thesis was well received by "the common man". But the resulting empirical inquiries into this pheno-menon contribute little more to our knowledge than these vague generalities themselves. Such thoughts and theories about law and society as do emerge seem mostly derived from sources other than "the sense of injustice".

The unhappy truth is that this kind of inquiry, even if otherwise promis-ing, faces rather insuperable difficulties. First, the question, "What do people consider to be unjust?" directs us to the whole range of human behaviour, within and beyond the ambit of a particular law. Such principles as lie ready here for discovery, lie somewhere inside a "bottomless pit", filled with an endless chaos of individual acts and motives, set in endless multitudes of sets of particular circumstances. Moreover, second, even if we try to delimit a more precise observation chamber within the "bottomless pit", we find that what particular people feel as just or unjust varies accord-ing to how much chance they have to think about it, and how far they are made aware of the implications of what they say, they feel or think.[103] This difficulty has been found to remain, even when inquiry was focused on those particular situations in which each of a limited number of persons was aware of or concerned about injustice.[104]

Clearly, any light which can be shed on the content of the idea of justice by empirical evidence of the operation of the sense of injustice of men generally is to be welcomed; but the prospects are certainly not such that we can assign to the "sense of injustice" the role of *primum mobile* of our whole understanding of justice. "Its disclosures are neither generalized nor systematic, so they cannot offer the coherent direction that purposive action requires." It is "largely retrospective and corrective; the deficiencies it identifies can be finally repaired only by a body of doctrine that is prospective and creative".[104a] Even those who most stress "the sense of injustice" have perforce to admit that this is not an answer to the problem

---

Ethics . . ., 5, 1, No. 893. Earlier still, Heraclitus said that "were there no injustice, men would never have known the name of justice". *Cf.* Plato, *Republic* 440c-d.

[101] Cahn, *op. cit. supra* n. 3, at 13.

[102] *Id.* 136.

[103] A. Barton and S. Mendlovitz, "The Experience of Injustice as a Research Problem" (1960) 13 *J. Leg. Ed.* 24, 25. *Cf.* for other difficulties with this approach Lamont, *Moral Judgment* 25.

[104] Barton and Mendlovitz, *loc. cit.* In these circumstances, we find it unnecessary to do more than register warm agreement with A. E. Sutherland's able demonstration (*The Law and One Man among Many* (1956) 72-74) that "an unmerited sense of outrage . . . counts for nothing. The sense of injustice must not only be felt; it must also be righteous".

[104a] I. Jenkins, *cit. supra* n. 91, at 197.

of justice, but is "only one of the several causes that are *constitutive* of particular answers".[105] The present writer believes that even in an inquiry centred on "the sense of injustice" (or of "justice"), fuller understanding still has to be sought by more varied, less precise and less oversimplified paths. And we suggest these not as independent ways by which explorers of "the sense of injustice" should *supplement* their main concern, but as pointing to matters of which they should be more explicitly aware as being *in fact* important elements in their main concern itself.

Among these paths, a central one certainly is introspection, not only of the inquirers' personal experience,[106] but of experience drawn indirectly by them from other persons[107] and from the streams of culture of which they are a part. And as part of these last there cannot be ignored the socially inherited theories of justice, both as manifesting the content from time to time of the supposed "common sense of justice", and as influences which continually mould and remould that content.[108]

Perhaps, indeed, these varied sources of mutual confirmation and mutual checking are the only bases on which we can commit ourselves to the assertion that any substantial directive is a directive of justice, as well as the only standards to which we can finally resort for testing of such assertions. Whether it is possible at all to assert substantial directives of material justice with reasoned commitment, and some of the specific directives that might be so asserted, will be considered in the next Chapter. We shall suggest that in any case even those directives which we can agree upon might better be thought of as but parts of the "enclaves of justice" controlled for the time being by the particular society, articulated in but also moulded by the theories of justice by which the members of that society explain and justify what they hold to be right. What is certainly clear is that such directives cannot be thought of with assurance as *innate* human attitudes, but rather as the end-products of interactions of individuals and cultural inheritances in particular segments of mankind.[109]

No doubt each man has a "sense" of justice which might conceivably be articulated in a set of (for him) "absolute" directives of justice; and no doubt in any given society (if only because of the common social matrix and cultural heritage) there would be considerable overlapping and common ground amongst all such sets of such directives elaborated for all the

---

105 Cahn, *op. cit. supra* n. 3, at 175.

106 See Lamont, *Moral Judgment* 22ff.

107 See *id.* 24ff.

108 This is, we take it, the heart of Sutherland's point (*supra* n. 104, 73-74) that while the "sense of injustice" of judges and others cannot be ignored, this is not merely a matter of what shocks a judge, but of a sophisticated awareness of "participation in the errors and passions of the rest of mankind", and that "only when justly aroused is their own indignation a guide to justice". See the discussion *id.* 69ff. of the opinion in *Rochin* v. *California* (1952) 342 U.S. 165, and other cases. See also the late F. S. Cohen's questions on Cahn's thesis, in (1950) 63 *H.L.R.* 1481, esp. 1484: "Do we have here, in truth, a 'sense of injustice'? Or do we have simply the 'fact of resentment'?" And see F. H. Knight in *Nomos, Justice* 1 at 16-17, recalling the relevance of the fact that as civilization has progressed, culture has progressively overlaid and obscured men's primal sensibilities. His point that men may romanticise and sentimentalise these is an additional one.

109 Though there is much of interest rather unevenly spread in R. B. Brandt, *Social Justice* (1962), the implications on which the title and some of the contributions proceed remain dubious. As we have seen in Ch. 9, §§9ff., and above, and as P. A. Freund again brings out (in *id.* 93, esp. 102-106) to talk about "justice" at all implies a community context and a community frame of criteria, or what we ourselves have termed a "justice-constituency"; see Stone, *Social Dimensions*, Ch. 2, §§18-19, Ch. 15, §§10ff.

society's members. Insofar as the supposed "*common* sense of justice" is not merely chimerical, there must be at least some such directives which can be said to be common to the "senses" of justice of "every man", that is, of members of the group generally. And if, as with some recent writers, this community is assumed to be humanity-wide, it must be possible to say this about "every man" in the world.

But the fact that reliance on the "common" sense of justice, taking account of "modern" (including psychological) knowledge, leads us thus to a position not far from those of classical natural law,[110] should not encourage iusnaturalist complacency. For it is also a fact that no one can really be in a position to show the content of a "common sense of justice" even in his own society, much less in the whole world, nor even (as we have seen) to offer a method whereby its existence can be tested. We have, therefore, to regard assertions about it for what they are worth, as impressionistic insights (of value varying with the experience, introspective power and imagination and wisdom of the particular author) of what we can expect from our fellow men by way of spontaneous feelings and impulses. Their unscientific nature does not warrant our dismissing them as useless; but by the same token we should not allow them to be posed as universal or quasi-universal absolutes based on empirical evidence.[110a]

We should be aware, finally, of the temptations to deceive ourselves into the pretence of empirically based discovery, by pushing the uncertainties of the empirical data behind the obscurities and circularities of our formulations of any particular directives. As to the "quasi-absolute" directives offered in Chapter 11, §6, for instance, it might seem plausible for us to present these as absolute truths empirically grounded in every man's sense of justice. We could then counter any empirically based doubts as to any of them by saying that, of course, these directives are necessarily only approximate and not exhaustive; and that even small differences in different men's senses of justice may lead to differences in their judgments of justice. This would plausibly dispose of the cases to which our opponents could readily point, in which a course of action genuinely just according to the actor's sense of justice is equally clearly unjust to the sense of others, observers, who meditate upon his action. Any remaining objections of this type could be disposed of by saying that the source of such differences is not the contents of the directives given by the respective "senses of justice",

---

[110] For a good example see Lamont, *Moral Judgment* c. vii. And see Brecht, "Relative Justice". *Cf.* Friedrich, *Philosophy of Law* 197, who observes that "the concept and the image of the common man are rooted in natural-law notions".

[110a] This basic point is insufficiently regarded in A. A. Ehrenzweig's plan ("Psychoanalysis of Justice", esp. 163-65) for discovering what is " 'just' in itself" in a community, by "refining" through psychoanalytical techniques the "justices" (that is, the justice-attitudes) manifest within each individual. These "justices" he sees as childhood "primitive communism", moving through "progressive communism", "conservative" justice, "liberal" justice, to adult "nationalist" justice, and as "necessarily irreconcilable with each other" (163). They seem in themselves, to the present writer, rather vague for *juristic use*. But in any case, presumably, they would be cumulative rather than cleanly successive in each individual's attitudes, for otherwise there would not be the "irreconcilable conflict" within the individual which Ehrenzweig seems to assert. Yet, on that presumption, what could be "refined" from conflicting "justices" within one individual would show no *necessary* relation to what is refined from conflicts within others. Finally, therefore, Professor Ehrenzweig's assertion that this "refinement" would somehow reveal a community judgment of justice, of what is " 'just' in itself", seems based on some unexamined postulate, analogous perhaps to the now discredited assumption that there is a "natural harmony of interests". See *supra* pp. 107-08, and 118ff., and bibli. there cited. And see also as to Ehrenzweig's thesis *infra* Ch. 11, n.2.

but the fact that the critics' judgments of justice will be based upon *their* cognition and *their* evaluations of the situation in which the action was taken, and the actor's on his. Differences of this kind, it could be added, will almost always be present among human beings, whether through differences in cognitive and evaluative acumen and experience, or through differences in the amount of information available as to the facts of the particular situation. Hence, it could be concluded that, in practice at any rate, almost all of the differences in men's judgments of justice are traceable to such sources. In effect, the result of these plausible caveats would be to save the pretension that the contents of a universal "common sense of justice" had been empirically found; yet to shield the pretension from any feasible procedures for testing it.[111] Further, insofar as the directives we offered were stated from the viewpoint of the *actor* in a justice-situation (and it is difficult to see from what other viewpoint such directives could usefully be stated), we would be faced with the consequence that even while we thus claimed to have wrought out of men's subjective "senses" an "objective" meaning for justice, we would be committed to recognising as "just" an act which accorded with the actor's own sense of justice, however objectively unjust it might be.[112]

We must be aware, too, of the grave social dangers which we may create by these self-deceptions. Most Indian leaders, following the great Mahatma Gandhi, were quite convinced that "non-violence" (meaning acceptance of the really much richer Hindu precept of *ahimsa*) was a kind of datum of the common sense of justice of the Indian people, even up to the hideous mutual slaughter of the partition period in which hundreds of thousands perished. And most educated Indians have maintained this conviction into our present day, being repeatedly taken by surprise as bitter communalist violence repeatedly broke out into the very year in which we write. To claim an unwarranted empirical basis for supposed directives of "the common sense of justice", is to conceal the actuality of their normative and inspirational function, and to invite default both in forestalling and confronting the actualities of man's behaviour to man. It may also be to substitute the illusions of *spontaneous* human self-control, for *the duty to educate ourselves* in self-control. And for these reasons the present writer, while acknowledging the sincerity of the belief that "the common sense of justice" can somehow be empirically found, cannot share this belief.

He would regretfully conclude that the central human task is rather to create the understanding and self-control which that belief assumes to exist, and to maintain and extend it outwards from those limited enclaves of men's life together, and those communities, where some ground for justice has been painfully won and held. In this continuing struggle for justice men's "senses" of justice, and their habits of appealing to and operating with particular standards of justice, may have important parts to play. Yet to clarify, perpetuate, spread and sometimes even to create these

---

[111] We can avoid this fault, of course, as did Pollock, *Essays* 270, by openly identifying "the moral sense of mankind" with only that part of it "whose character and circumstances are like enough to our own to make their opinions worth considering"(!). But we then fall into another, of sanctifying for mankind our own "national versions". See *id*. 270, 272.

[112] Yet the present writer would agree with C. J. Friedrich (in *Nomos, Justice* 24 at 26) that justice must be "objective" at least in the sense that it depends on "a certain objective relation" of the decision "to the setting in which it occurs", and not on any mere motivation of the judge.

inarticulate "senses" and standards remain still and ever tasks for the *theories* of justice. So that theories of justice, in all their rich diversity of content and mode of presentation, cannot safely be discarded even from the most practical concern.

CHAPTER 11

JUSTICE IN IDEA AND JUSTICE IN HISTORY

§1. Theory and Practice of Justice Presupposes the Identification of Justice as a Normative Component of Social Action. A main concern of the theory of justice is to give a degree of rational structuring to men's ideas of justice, and in particular to relate these to some accrediting source, be this "nature", "utility", or "the categorical imperative", "human interests" or other of the rich offerings of man's intellectual history. Involved in this is the effort to explain why the idea offered imports an obligation to conform; and what this obligation directs as regards the actual and desirable relations between the ideas and the law in force. The sociological jurist has among his tasks the study of the formation of ideas of justice, and their impact on law and society.[1] Even theories of analytical jurisprudence (as seen in *Legal System and Lawyers' Reasonings*) often proceed on assumptions (usually inarticulate) about justice; and they may also be designed even by their authors as a means of refining the tools, or processing the materials, requisite for doing justice.

The idea of justice, then, seems to give sense to legal and juristic work at many points and levels, just as the idea of beauty does to artistic work.[1a] Paradoxically, this very multifariousness of activity around the idea puts it in danger of becoming lost from sight. So that the theorist of justice himself may need, as we do, to make a conscious effort to return finally to the cardinal question, What is justice? Not only as a legal philosopher, but also as a human being, the lawyer and the jurisprudent must each try to penetrate beyond intellectual and sociological issues to face frontally the question, "What, if anything, can be said about the substantive requirements or contents of the idea of justice for me and for my fellow human beings?"[2]

The dilemmas confronting attempted answers have been familiar since the time of Plato;[3] they remain disturbing today, as we have seen in Chapter 10, §§5-7.[4] Insofar as we move towards precepts which shall direct with

---

[1] The purpose of the present Chapter is to set the body of ideas concerning justice in the context of the actual history of that part of social action which has expressed men's strivings towards justice, and to summarise as best we can the products of these strivings as they appear to stand in our generation. In our later work *Social Dimensions* we shall seek to provide a more detailed and contemporary setting for these ideas, not merely in that part of men's activities which is explicitly directed towards justice, but in their whole social situation. *Cf.* esp. in conjunction with the present Chapter *id.*, Ch. 12, Ch. 13, Ch. 14 and Ch. 15, §23.

[1a] See Stone, *Legal Controls* 54. And *cf.* W. Sauer, *Juristische Elementarlehre* (1944) 28, who thinks that justice is the highest aim of every juristic activity, forever unattainable and veiled in mysterious obscurity, though it seems clearer as it is approached.

[2] *Cf.* A. Brecht, "The Ultimate Standard of Justice", in *Nomos, Justice* 62, at 62-63. On the call in Ehrenzweig, "Psychoanalysis of Justice", esp. at 163-65, to transcend the positivist-iusnaturalist tension by using psychoanalysis to refine out of the "justices" (i.e. justice-attitudes) of men what is "'just' in itself", see *supra* Ch. 10, n. 110a.

[3] See *supra* Ch. 1, §§3-4.

[4] *Cf.* I. Jenkins, "Justice as Ideal and Ideology" in *Nomos, Justice* 191, at 191-92.

clarity for all problem-situations, we are driven to levels of abstraction and vagueness which leave decision at large. We seem to escape this only at the cost of stipulating conditions and solutions which by their very details lose the quality of general applicability. To a degree, no doubt, the above-mentioned inquiries of sociology, analysis and ratiocination *about* justice may help to ease, or at any rate reconcile us to, this dilemma. As to the conceptual "placing" of justice, for example, we have already suggested in Chapter 1 (§11) that justice is best seen as a positive, ethical, social (inter-personal) value; and this at least circumscribes the area for which we seek directives. But it still leaves us with the mystery of "the norma-tive"; if "justice" has some definite distinctive meaning, this must lie in precepts or values[4a] addressing themselves to men generally and prescribing what kinds of behaviour and procedures are worthy of acceptance as governing their inter-personal relations.[5] If such precepts cannot be formu-lated, "justice" may be but a convenient way of referring to the maximum of acceptability or even of acceptance, neither of which tells us what is "worthy" of being ("ought to be") accepted. Yet it must be to this last that the normative finally refers.

At this point temptation has always been well-nigh irresistible to trans-late the question into other forms, in which the mystery is preserved, but the mind diverted by different formulae. A recent writer, for example, finally offers the solution that justice is basically "the perfect accomplish-ment of the tasks of law". This, of course, tells us of the involvement of justice with "perfection" and "law"; but for the rest, it merely transfers the problem to the correct meanings of "*perfection*" and of "*the tasks of law*".[6] And when this earnest account finally reaches its "exact statement" of "the essential tasks committed to law", this amounts merely to posing pairs of antinomies, qualities and aims, stated as setting the arena and criteria of justice. Regrettably, it is an arena within which each of us could in most of the really perplexing situations find justice to be where we wished it.[7]

[4a] *Cf.* C. Kluckhohn *et al.*, "Values and Value-Orientations in the Theory of Action", in Parsons-Shils, *Theory of Action* 390: "The only general agreement is that values somehow have to do with normative as opposed to existential propositions". But *cf.* W. Goldschmidt and R. B. Edgerton, "A Picture Technique for the Study of Values" (1961) 63 *Am. Anthrop.* 26. And see generally Jacob-Flink, *Value Decision*, taking the above proposition as the basis for a notable attempt "to delineate the value concept . . . for use as an analytic tool in the policy sciences" (*id.* 7).

So, even the "legal positivist" and "ethically non-cognitivist" may properly insist on the importance and the "reality", for purposes of scholarly discussion, of the "non-cognitive" elements. See, e.g., S. I. Shuman, *Legal Positivism* (1963) 95-118, 121-153, 193.

[5] *Cf.* the demand of I. Jenkins (*id.* 219-220) that the answers should "illuminate and guide our dealings . . . with the actual things and situations that we encounter in life"; and should "animate and direct our efforts as they reach into the future." They cannot reduce our problems to "logical deductions", or "depict beforehand the final and finished result"; but they can offer "a general destination and program", "a full and clear view on which to base our decisions". Of course, such prescriptions (as it were) for the prescriptions of justice do not make it much easier to specify the latter. Too often, indeed, they but restate the "generality" horn of the dilemma from which she starts.

[6] See *id.* 203-228. Interesting as this may be, it scarcely warrants the author's claim (*id.* 203) to establish a conception of justice based on "scientific knowledge" and not on "mere personal preference". Her use at critical points of notions of "com-pleteness" (e.g., at 209), of "order" and "disorder" (*passim* and esp. 207-208) are open to difficulties similar to those criticised *supra* Ch. 7, §3 and in Stone, *Social Dimensions*, Ch. 1, §8. And see *supra* Ch. 1, n. 89a.

[7] Jenkins, *op. cit.* 214ff., e.g., at 214: "Law must effect a reconciliation (*sic*) of similarity and differentiation, of subordination and participation, of action-reaction and

In the search for normative precepts of justice which can guide us more than this, the theories of justice offered by jurists and philosophers are of course deeply relevant. And it is helpful (and unavoidable in any case) to consult the experience and intuitions both of individual observers of the situation to be judged and of members of their community generally.[8] Indeed, as we saw in the last Chapter, our knowledge of the whole of whatever we mean by the "culture" must be brought into play. We have at once a dearth of direct information about "justice", and an *embarras de richesses* of clues. We shall offer in §6 below certain directives of justice which the present writer would regard as "quasi-absolutes", and as commanding general acceptance as such in Western societies at the present stage of their development. Yet, even then, the attempt to assert these as "absolutes" independent of time and place faces formidable difficulties.[9]

The extent to which "absoluteness" is really essential in directives offered as useful for spelling out the content of justice is, of course, itself open to question. For most purposes in most societies it may well be a sufficient answer to the question "What is justice?" to specify what kinds of conduct and procedure, in what situations, will be held "just" for that society. Certainly, it may not be necessary to show that these would *always* and *everywhere* be evaluated as "just", nor even that such evaluations are more than a matter of *shared* subjective feelings for the time being. Yet there may also be purposes for which it does seem important to show that the offered precepts are "absolute", in the sense that they are a "universal" minimum.[10] And even where universality is not strictly a requirement, the needs to make the offered precepts persuasive, and to infuse cognition of them with a sense of ethical obligation, are a constant source of demands for "absoluteness" in a double sense. One is that the offered precepts be rooted in or derived from unquestionable and unchanging higher principles or values; another, that the precepts offered be themselves unquestionable and unchanging, even apart from any such derived authority.[10a]

Such demands are answered, but rarely quieted, by the hard truth that as soon as we supplement theory (as the search for justice inevitably requires us to do) with references to social facts and social experience, and human interests and feelings and desires, we are admitting to our reasoning elements which by their very nature cannot be absolute. For it is in the time and place dimensions that it is true to say, with Friedrich,

---

self-determination, and of rigidity and flexibility." We do not see, either, that the addition of the related concepts of "Cultivation", "Authority", "Responsibility" and "Continuity" does much to resolve these antinomies in a way supporting the claim to "scientific knowledge". When we are told that purposiveness creates "authority" to prevent men turning participation to their own ends thus reducing "waste" of efforts in friction, the pejorative term "waste" begs all the questions of where the individual's "own ends" ought to be submerged in the "participation". See *id.* 215-216; and *cf.* I. Jenkins, "The Matrix of Positive Law" (1961) 6 *Nat. L. Forum* 1-50.

[8] *Cf.* the four tests for "absolute postulates of justice" offered by A. Brecht, "The Myth of Is and Ought", in M. D. Forkosch (ed.), *The Political Philosophy of Arnold Brecht* (1954) 102-123, *id.*, "The Search for Absolutes in Political and Legal Philosophy" (1940) 7 *Social Research* 201, namely: (1) our own experience as immediate evidence; (2) general confession to the same evidence by everyone who is in earnest; (3) our own inability even to imagine a view not containing these elements; (4) the inability of anyone else to imagine a view not containing them.

[9] *Cf.* Jenkins, *op. cit.* 193, which is unduly sombre, however, in thinking that "most" of the ideas by which we direct our lives are "to a high degree friable and volatile".

[10] *Cf.* A. Brecht, *cit. supra* n. 2, at 64; and see as to the varied uses of "justice" in the U.N. Charter our discussion in *Legal Controls* 50ff., esp. 52, 53n.

[10a] *Cf.* on the meaning of "absolutist" *supra* Ch. 10, §§1, 6, and R. Firth, "Ethical Absolutism and the Ideal Observer" (1952) 12 *Phil. and Phen. R.* 317-19.

that "justice is never given; it is always a task to be achieved. Its incomplete realisation does not result from the complexity of the criteria, but from their fluidity. In fact, fluidity is not the right word either, for it is the steady evolution and devolution of values which cause the difficulty".[11] The resulting difficulties ever multiply as men's cultural traditions become more complex, and commentation more massive, men's values becoming, as at present, often quite obfuscated. When we add to this the endless ramifications of problems which the law seeks to govern in our complex economically organised democratic societies, "justice" seems sometimes to embrace the whole ambit of social idealism, in all aspects and all versions.[12] As it thus spreads the concept becomes necessarily thinner and vaguer, falling back into the centuries-old obfuscation which merges the more limited and specific problem of "justice" into that of the good society in general.[13] Yet the widened ambit of men's demands on the law makes all this increasingly difficult to avoid.

This part of our conclusion from the sociological history of ideas is reinforced by Kant's still unanswered thesis that in the ethical sphere (as probably in epistemology generally)[14] the only propositions that can be made "absolutely and without qualifications"[15] must be merely formal, and that to strip them of all variable content is to strip them of all content. So that the prescriptions for justice which can be offered as absolute will be found on examination to be either merely formal, or not really absolute. And we have already seen and will now further show that when, as with "equality", an offered prescription *seems* to carry both formal and material implications, only the former will prove to be really "absolute".[16]

§2. EQUALITY AS AN ABSOLUTE FORMAL SPECIFICATION AND ITS LIMITS. The theme that "equality", as somehow properly understood, is the key to justice continues re-echoing from its Greek and Hebraic origins into

---

[11] C. J. Friedrich, "Justice: The Just Political Act", in *Nomos, Justice* 24 at 34. Cf. on the "dynamizing function of justice" *id.* 40.

[12] See F. H. Knight, "On the Meaning of Justice" in *Nomos, Justice* 1, at 3. At 3-23 Knight offers various considerations to support this position, not all of which seem relevant or significant. But at least three are of crucial importance. These are (1) the fact that democratic organisation offers no "ideal society" for attainment but only a "direction of change" in the course of which injustices may be remedied; so that the question of attainment of "the" ideal of justice does not arise, this being by the nature of democracy an open ideal (though Knight seems to go too far when he puts this (at 3) in terms that there is now no such thing as "justice in general"); (2) cultural relativism—the surprising tolerance of human society for cultural growth (*id.* 10-12); and (3) our lack of the knowledge required for agreement on means and ends.

[13] See *supra* Ch. 1, §3.

[14] See J. Hospers, *An Introduction to Philosophical Analysis* (1956) 106ff.

[15] Kant, *Grundlegung zur Metaphysik der Sitten* (Reclam ed.) 31-32. Cf. O. Bondy, "The Moral Law Theory . . ." in *Australian Studies in Legal Philosophy* 139, esp. 147. And see *supra* Ch. 3. §2.

[16] To say that "absolute" directives of justice can only be "formal" or at least "non-material" is not, of course, to say that they are unimportant. Thus C. J. Friedrich, *cit. supra* n. 11, concludes that even if justice be seen merely in terms of accord with prevalent values, three absolute criteria are inherent in it. These are (1) truth of the basing facts; (2) non-arbitrariness in the relation of the basing facts to values; and (3) non-impossibility of performance of the norms derived. We may think that "non-arbitrary" is here question-begging (but see *infra* §2), and that "non-impossibility" (as regards law) is in practice rather unimportant (but see I. Tammelo, Book Review (1959) 13 *J. Leg. Ed.* 550 at 553, and citations *infra* n. 90). But the "truth" criterion is clearly both informative and important (see *infra* §6, directive I). So, too, the requirement that men should be free to express their interests is probably only "formal", or at least "procedural"; yet it is an indispensable presupposition of justice. See *infra* §3; §6, directive I. And *cf.* generally J. Cogley, Intro. to *id.* (ed.), *Natural Law* at 25.

modern thought and practice. In the present review of possible precepts of
"justice", its central position in contemporary concern[17] warrants some
final attention.

As with the "common sense of justice" discussed in the last Chapter,
the "equality" principle meets *ab initio* the problem of variable interpretations of it. It may *seem* to carry, at a given time and place, an unambiguous
directive because of the operation of some other ideal strictly extraneous to
equality itself, as when that of the dignity of every human being confronts
a social *status quo* in which some human beings are excluded from membership or otherwise grossly subject to the will of others.[17a] But this apart,
the variabilities are endemic. Is there some way of redefining equality which
will remove these variabilities and disclose some core of consensus? This,
in effect, seems to have been Chaim Perelman's starting-point, though
stated rather in the form of reducing the complex and controverted notion
of "justice" into "formal justice", on the one hand, and men's conflicting
notions of "concrete justice", on the other. Insofar as all conflicting concrete
notions are thus put aside, Perelman's "formal justice" (which he also
terms "*la règle de justice*") resolves itself into the equality principle, requiring that "beings considered to be essentially similar ought to be treated
in the same manner".[18]

Insofar as we might seek to use this principle as a self-sufficient substantive criterion of justice, Perelman himself recognises that it will not
do. For, taken alone, it would justify most outrageous laws, for instance a
law penalising all persons who are deemed (by any single criterion) to be
inferior, provided the penalty for all of them was the same. Obviously this
is not what he means.[19] Yet, on the other hand, if we do not use it as
a self-sufficient criterion, the formula seems to amount only to this, that
however we delimit a class of persons for differential legal treatment from
other classes, justice requires that *all members of that class should fall*
within the rule applicable to that class. And while this is unquestionable,
it is so by dint of a principle of logic rather than of a precept of justice.[20]
Certainly, if we linger unduly on this as a precept of justice we risk neglecting
the really hard problems, which arise precisely in determining *which* beings
are "essentially similar" for the purpose of allocation to that class.[21]

---

[17] The last major pre-war study was R. H. Tawney, *Equality* (1931); the contemporary explicit concern with equality as such is a post-war development, perhaps
paralleling the revived interest in natural law (as to which see *supra* Ch. 7), and
beginning in the U.S. with H. A. Myers, *Are Men Equal?* (1945), and in England
with D. Thomson, *Equality* (1949). And *cf.*, for an attempt to specify the role of equal
franchise in the selection of leaders in limiting hierarchy *within* the collective decision-
system, Parsons, *Political Power I*, esp. 807-813.

[17a] See *supra* Ch. 3, §§14-16. This, it seems to us, is the substantial point of
J. Rawls' demonstration (*Nomos, Justice* 98, 107ff.) that "rational individuals" would
not contract into a caste society in which the place of each were to be assigned
by chance.

[18] Ch. Perelman, "*Rationalité*", at 10. See also his earlier statements as to
"formal justice", beginning with his *De la Justice* (1945), and including the Unesco
study, "*La Justice . . .*" (1957) 41 *Revue Int. de Phil.* 344, discussed at length in
Stone and Tarello, "Justice" *passim*, esp. 347ff., 355ff. The Unesco study has been
reprinted as "*L'Idée de Justice . . .*" (1959) 3 *Annales de l'Institut International de
Philosophie Politique* 128. This reprint will hereafter be cited as "*L'Idée de Justice*".

[19] Though occasionally he writes as if he is rather inadvertent to the possibility
See, e.g., "*L'Idée de Justice*" 135. *Cf.* Dowrick, *Justice* 14, who observes of the
related classical axioms that they "presuppose an extremely detailed system of ethical
or legal rules defining what is due to individuals, and which individuals are equals".

[20] See Stone and Tarello, "Justice" at 359; Benn and Peters, *Principles* 124-25, 126.

[21] *Cf.* Friedrich, *Philosophy of Law* 195, observing that since interests and passions
make up a large part of what is vital for man, it is as well that a community

Perelman's later restatements of these ideas[22] have sought to meet the difficulties which we have elsewhere raised. In a much valued exchange of letters of 23rd January, 1962, he has pointed out that "*de plus en plus, je centre le fondement de la philosophie sur le problème de la justification*". This does suggest promisingly that his notion of "formal justice" (or equal treatment under a rule), may be given body by reference to his other notable work on non-stringent reasoning (or "argumentation"),[23] in particular by referring to this kind of reasoning the critical question of justice, which must be answered before equality or "formal justice" can come to life. This question is: When are beings or situations "essentially similar" in a sense which warrants their subjection to one same rule, which is different from the rule applied to other beings or situations?[24] How far the notion of "formal justice" can be made adequate by this resort to non-stringent reasoning depends, of course, on the potentialities of this kind of reasoning. So far as Perelman has yet taken these potentialities, success is still perhaps in doubt.[25] For, as we saw in our work on *Legal System and Lawyers' Reasonings* (Chapter 8), his theory of argumentation leaves the essential point of when the conclusion of non-stringent reasoning is to be regarded as acceptable (or in his word "rational") in rather an impasse.[26]

His criterion of "rationality" is "worthiness of a universal audience of the totality of reasonable beings". Now we must not expect, of course, that the reasoning of the new rhetorics can be as precise as that of stringent argument; it is apt by definition especially for those subject-matters not susceptible of the more severe methods. At best it can produce, not proof, but a greater "intensity of adherence".[27] Yet, however imprecise be its indications, they are scarcely helpful if they are not at least indications in one direction or another. How much help, then, can we expect from taking as our forum of appeal on the "rationality" of an argument concerning justice, "a universal audience of the totality of reasonable beings"? If this "universal" audience includes every one in the world, all men being (in the classical sense) distinguished from other creatures by their reason,

---

in which every member really acts according to the categorical imperative is not realisable.

[22] See Perelman, "*Rationalité*"; *id.*, article cited *infra* n. 28a.

[23] He has himself recognised in general terms that his "theory of argumentation" is largely focused on clarifying the manner in which we apply reason to values. See *id.*, "How Do We Apply Reason to Values?" (1955) 52 *J. Phil.* 797-802, esp. 798; *id.*, *Justice et Raison* (1963) 235-243, esp. 243. In his article of 1960, repr. *id.* 224, at 230-31, he is explicit that his "*règle de justice*" cannot guide in concrete cases without resort to value-laden "*argumentation*". And see the discussion and citations in Stone, *Legal System*, Ch. 8. Perelman uses "reason" as a general term, identifies stringent (logical) reasoning with "the analytical", and refers to the other areas as "the field of those reasons which, according to Pascal and according to contemporary logicians, reason does not know". See *id.* 802.

[24] See *infra* n. 58 for further citations as to the kind of argument involved. And *cf.* from the natural law viewpoint J. C. Murray in Cogley (ed.), *Natural Law* 48, esp. 74-79; S. Buchanan in *id.* 82, esp. 117-120; and other references *supra* Ch. 7, §8.

[25] See his *Justice et Raison* (1963) 244-255. So *cf.* in terms of reasoned elaboration of preferences based on practical consequences, Friedrich, *cit. supra* n. 11, esp. 37ff., 43.

[26] We do not linger on the danger of merely verbalising our problems away by play on the word "reason". See, e.g., R. McKeon in *Nomos, Justice* 44, at 61: "Justice is the adjustment by rational means of the use of reason to secure material goods to the use of reason to establish a common treatment of men in the community. Justice is the adjustment by rational means of the use of one's own reason in making decisions to the use of common reason and consensus to analyse truths and to achieve goods." All of which proves at least the importance of keeping the use of reason within reason unless there is the clearest reason to the contrary.

[27] See article first cited *supra* n. 23, at 799.

the difficulties of getting any verdict from it are obvious. And the very proposal to address such a forum would also seem at odds with the now accepted reality that as often as not the dynamics of consensus in mass societies may reinforce irrationalities, rather than discover a common reason. If, on the other hand, this "universal audience" of which reasoning (if it is to be "rational") must be worthy, consists only of some limited class of human beings who are somehow "reasonable" in a different sense from all their fellows, what does "reasonable" in this special sense mean? We are seeking (be it recalled) to delimit an "audience" to serve (notionally) as a forum to judge the question of "rationality"; yet the mark offered to delimit this forum is "reasonableness". Both the words "rational" and "reasonable" are slippery and even treacherous in any Western language, as well in common as in philosophical usage. To avoid falling into circularity, the "reasonable" would have to be distinguished from the "rational" far more clearly than Perelman has done in this context.[28]

Stephen Toulmin, as we also saw in Chapter 8 of *Legal System and Lawyers' Reasonings*, avoided this kind of difficulty by giving a kind of ostensive definition of "rational" argument about values, offering as his model for this purpose the way in which common law judges reason from and to their decisions. In his more recent restatements Perelman, too, seems to move towards a similar escape from the problem of delimiting the "universal" audience of "reasonable" men. "The rules of justice", he urged in 1960, "arise from a tendency natural to the human mind, to consider as normal and *rational*, and thus *as requiring no other justification*, behaviour in conformity with precedents."[28a] Unfortunately, as lawyers have come to see, the question whether an earlier case *is* a "precedent" for the present situation depends on an assessment of "essential similarities" and "differences" between the two, which is really not very different from the assessment which is a central concern of Perelman's new rhetorics. And, in any case, as we also observed in the above cited work, so far as this kind of idea is offered *to lawyers* as an aid to finding justice, it seems to amount to telling them that what they need to do in order to decide problems of justice is *to act as if they were lawyers*. So that, so far as Perelman has yet brought his theory of argumentation to bear upon his theory of justice, it seems only

---

28 This matter of "reasonable men" is certainly not clarified in *id.* 800, where, indeed, Perelman suggests that what is addressed to a "universal" audience, e.g., Kant's categorical imperative, is necessarily "rational". Yet he simultaneously says that he means a more or less perfect human audience and that this must mean that it consists of "reasonable beings". *Cf.* the common lawyers' appeals to "the best sort of citizens" (Sir F. Pollock, *First Book of Jurisprudence* (6 ed. 1929) 48), or "the right-minded members of the community" (Lord Denning, *The Road to Justice* (1955) 4). See generally Stone, *Legal System*, Ch. 7, §11; and as to Pollock *cf.* his "Judicial Caution and Valour" (1929) 45 *L.Q.R.* 293, at 294-95, defining "reasonable" in terms of "right-minded and rightly informed men" and "the enlightened common-sense of the nation". For some of the deep perplexities involved in the notion of "rational" decision or action see the basic analysis in Hempel, "Rational Action", where the modern theorising is assessed. See esp. 7-18. Hempel's conclusion that "the explanatory power of the concept of rational action is in fact rather limited", and that more specific explanatory hypotheses must be found to complement it, marches generally with juristic experience.

How indeterminate a guide to justice it is to say that the "justification" must be worthy of an audience of reasonable men, is well illustrated in *Poulton* v. *Cwlth*. (1953) 89 C.L.R. 540. There, following earlier authority, it was held that "just terms" are any terms "not so unreasonable" that "they cannot find justification in the eyes of reasonable men". Otherwise no one could see what terms represented "ideal justice". See esp. 574-78. Whatever be said of this as a matter of interpretation of a statutory term, it reads strangely as a comment on the notion of justice.

28a See *"La Règle de Justice"* (1960) 14 *Dialectica* 230, 237.

to have led him back to a main thesis of his initial work on justice of 1945. This, it will be recalled, is that all that can be "rationally" said about justice is that it consists of adhering to a rule, that is, treating similarly all situations which are essentially similar.[29]

So that these lines of thought, as they bear on the role of equality as a criterion of justice, amount to this. Beginning with the equality notion, Perelman has warned that this is merely formal and cannot guide us in concrete cases, the crucial question there being the delimitation of the class of equals. To guide us the equality-governed class must be somehow "justified", and whether it is or is not is to be tested by the adequacy or worthiness of argumentation by which it can be supported. The test of this adequacy or worthiness (he then insists) is whether the arguments are worthy of a "universal audience" of "reasonable" men. Finally, in response to the problem of identifying this audience, we are told that the best guide in a given time and place to such adequacy or worth is that of conformity with precedents. To this, however, *we* have had to add, from the standpoint *of the lawyer's concern with justice,* that for the lawyer the most general problem of justice-valuation arises precisely in determining whether or not, in view of the similarities and differences between cases, the earlier case is a precedent for the later one. We are accordingly, at the end, back to where we started on the main point, namely at the material problem of defining the class (or the rule) within which equality should prevail.[29a] Rarely can there have been a more dismaying adventure in interdisciplinary helpfulness!

A further difficulty, moreover, is that lawyers also would welcome philosophers' guidance in determining when rules of law (and the classifications on which these proceed) should be changed, and when precedents should simply not be followed at all, *because they are unjust.* To tell lawyers thus hungry *for justice* to keep to the rules or to the law, or to the precedents, guides them here not a whit towards justice. It rather, indeed, seems to

---

[29] We believe that to increase the significance of his work for lawyers much closer integration of his positions on justice and on his new rhetorics is still required.

In 1959 ("*L'Idée de Justice*") Perelman was still giving an account of justice in which his theory of the role of non-stringent reasoning in relation to values played no essential part. He had, conversely, expounded the thesis that the reason applied to values is not "analytical" reason (meaning stringent reasoning or logic), but dialectical or rhetorical reasoning; yet still without any particular reference to his theory of justice. Even in 1959 he seemed still to present justice in analytical terms within the framework: *just act* (conformity to a rule); *just rule* (conformity to a more embracing rule (130), or to the ideal of justice or "juridical conscience" transcending positive law (130-132) or preordinated to positive law (133-35)); *just actor* (that is, in its historico-religious aspect, the model furnished by the divine or prophetic expositor, or the secular analogue of the free-choosing individual guided by his conscience, as to all of whom, however, distinguishing of false from true exemplars remains a problem (137-142, 144)). As to the level of the just rule, which is the most important for lawyers' purposes, he observed in 1959 on the variability of the sundry ideals of justice offered to fix the limits of the classes of "essentially similar entities", and pointed out that for a rule to be just it must not be "arbitrary". He further explained that it must have a "justifying foundation in reason". But he appears first to have squarely addressed himself to the necessary organic linkage of his justice-analysis with his theory of argumentation in *Justice et Raison* (1963), esp. c. xvi, in a paper first publ. in 1960. See *supra* n. 23.

[29a] It does not help to escape from this circle, though it does create new intractabilities, that Perelman also insists that "even justification is subject to a context", and that since the context may be destroyed, so may that justification. (See article cited *supra* n. 23, at 237.) For if the applicability of the precedent depends on the *full* context, then *no* other case will qualify as such (see Stone, *Legal System*, Ch. 7, §12); if not the full context then we still have no guide as to how much and what kind of similarity makes a precedent.

K

suggest that the justice *they* hunger for may be but an illusion. And as addressed to non-lawyers (including philosophers), this kind of answer risks building even higher walls of misunderstanding and malcommunication, on top of their excusable unfamiliarity with the nature of lawyers' problems. If, indeed, the problem of justice for lawyers were one of keeping to rules and precedents, it would be difficult to understand such views as that of Sir Patrick Devlin (as he was then) to the effect that "the just decision" always fluctuates between "the law" and the "*aequum et bonum*" of the case. Any rule of law, Lord Devlin explained, is an abstract prescription for average cases, and always more or less unjust for the particular case; and the English jury is "a unique institution . . . to enable justice to go beyond" *even the point to which the law can be stretched.*[30]

Lord Devlin's words certainly express a quite general view of lawyers that to apply a just rule to a case falling within it does not always do justice; and that this is so seems to negative much helpfulness from identifying justice with *merely* keeping to a rule. It is, indeed, surely a commonplace for lawyers that at any given time many rules of law are not even just *as rules*. So that even when we have found an indubitable rule, the conscientious lawyer may and sometimes should ask questions about the justice of it; just as, even with a rule of law indubitably agreed to be just, there may be questions to ask about the justice of applying it in a particular case apparently within it. Such questions also, *asked by lawyers about law,* cannot be answered by telling them to adhere to a rule, or to the law, or to a precedent.[31]

§3. FAIRNESS AND CONSENT AS ABSOLUTE FORMAL SPECIFICATIONS. The effort somehow to hinge justice on equality is also prominent in other strains of contemporary philosophy. "Modified utilitarianism", for example, seeks to meet the difficulties of utilitarianism by grafting onto it something resembling Kant's principle that the maxim of action should be capable of being part of a system of universal legislation.[32] In a related view of

---

30 Sir Patrick Devlin, *Trial by Jury* (1956) 153-57. For a nice contrast which brings out the point see *ex p. Herman: re Mathieson* (1960) W.N. (N.S.W.) 6, holding it improper for a small debts court magistrate, the court being also under statute a court of "equity and good conscience", to give judgment for a smaller sum than was claimed in lieu of exercising the statutory power of reopening the transaction. See esp. at 9. And see also the see-saw of courts virtually on this point in *Leeder v. Ellis* (1952) 86 C.L.R. 64, esp. the Full Court and P. C. affirming Sugerman J.'s decision at 73.

It should be unnecessary to remind the reader of Ch. 7 of our work, *Legal System*, that on the appellate level the decisive question is often what the rule of law is. On one view of what the rule is, the "justice" would be done within it, while on another view, justice could not be done because it would be outside it. The preliminary legal question, how far the law stretches, often looks uncommonly like a decision on the *justice* of the matter; not, moreover, justice under a rule, but rather the delimitation, or extension or reduction, of the class which falls within the rule, in order to allow a just decision. See for a simple recent case *Wirth* v. *W.* (1956) 98 C.L.R. 228.

In Perelman's system his notions of "equity" (*De La Justice* (1945) 44ff., esp. 48) and the conscientious "just actor" (see *supra* n. 29) are intended to leave room for these matters, as did the notion of "conscience" in the Chancellor's early activity.

31 Yet at moments it is also clear that Perelman perceives that adhering to a rule or to a rule consistent with a wider rule will not do as a description of justice even for lawyers. See "*L'Idée de Justice*", cit. *supra* n. 18, at 128, and esp. 129, 143, *Justice et Raison* (1963) c. xv, esp. 230-231.

On the treatment of Perelman's position in A. Ross, *On Law and Justice* (1958) 273ff., see J. Stone, " 'Social Engineers' and 'Rational Technologists' " (1961) 13 *Stan. L.R.* 670, 688-690; Stone and Tarello, "Justice" 347-48, n. 39

32 J. Harrison, "Utilitarianism . . ." (1952-53) 53 *Proc. Arist. Soc.* 105-134, repr. Olafson, *Social Policy* 55-79. Lamont, *Moral Judgment* 154, offers a definition of "just

justice as "fairness",[33] the ideal is thought to involve a maximum of liberty of each compatible with like liberty of all, except where inequality will work out to everyone's advantage. Thus John Rawls sees "justice" as linking liberty, equality and reward for services contributing to the common advantage in two principles, namely (1) that all participating in or affected by an institution have an equal right to the most extensive liberty compatible with a like liberty of all; and (2) that inequalities institutionally defined or fostered are arbitrary unless it is reasonable to expect them to work out to everyone's advantage and it is provided that the positions to which the inequalities pertain are open to all.[34] And he goes on to erect on this basis a third principle, that "if rational individuals have willingly and knowingly joined a cooperative scheme from an original position of equal liberty"[35] and if "they have borne equal risks in doing so, and . . . persist in their willing cooperation and have no wish to retract or no complaint to make, then that scheme is fair or at least not unfair".[36]

But other philosophers have quickly warned against the illusory elements in such egalitarian formulas, of which many lawyers have long been keenly aware. However we interpret equality, they point out, we cannot specify a limine the conditions under which we can pass from a set of "individual rights" (in terms of which equality is expressed) to a pattern of social action which does not infringe those rights. "Fairness" cannot be reduced to simple equality,[37] nor indeed adequately articulated in terms of a rule. "Experience

legislation" which is substantially that of Roscoe Pound; but it is drawn from an independent philosophical analysis with strong Benthamite and Kantian strains. See as to the latter id. 142-43. Cf. rather earlier H. Sidgwick, Methods of Ethics (5 ed. 1893) bk. iii, cc. v, xiii. For a brilliant "modified utilitarian" approach to a concrete penal problem see H.L.A. Hart, "Murder and . . . Punishment" (1957) 52 Northw. U.L.R. 433-461 passim. And see W. Friedmann, Legal Theory (4 ed. 1960) 387.

For examples of the related influence of the rather converse Kantian doctrine that every man must be treated as an end in himself, never as a means only, cf. the works of Thomson and Myers cited supra n. 17, both finally prescribing that just treatment requires that everyone be treated on the basis that he is a man. Cf. Sir Ernest Barker, Principles of Social and Political Theory (1951) bk. iv, §iii, for the view that what is involved is equality not of rights, but of legal capacity for rights; and L. T. Hobhouse, Elements of Social Justice (1922) 95. Benn and Peters, though criticising such theses (Principles 108-110, 122-24), come eventually (at 110, following E. F. Carritt, Ethical and Political Thinking (1947) 156) to the same conclusion, namely that "the only universal right . . . is the right to equal consideration". And see op. cit. 111 where the Kantian link is explicit.

[33] Which is, of course, supported by the most rudimentary intuitive notions. Cf. on notions of equality and fairness in children, A. Ross, On Law and Justice (1958) 269; Lamont, Moral Judgment 135-39, the latter tracing the gradual emergence of more abstract and flexible notions.

[34] See J. Rawls, "Justice as Fairness" (1958) 67 Phil. R. 164-194, repr. Olafson, Social Policy 80-107; id., "Constitutional Liberty . . .", in Nomos, Justice 98, esp. at 100.

[35] Rawls is naturally led by his stress on equal liberty as the basis for participation in society, to positions reminiscent of traditional "social compact" theories. But perhaps the above formulation takes him rather closer to those traditional notions than he would wish. His main use of the "consent" notion is as a hypothetical test of desirable social arrangements by reference to what "equally free" subjects would "rationally" consent to if they had the option; and he is careful to make clear that "since these persons are conceived as engaging in common practices which are already established, there is no question of our supposing them to be deciding how to set up their institutions from the start." We can only postulate that they might consider the possibilities of legitimate complaint against their institutions, and might begin by trying to settle "the principles by which complaints and thus institutions themselves are to be judged". See Nomos, Justice 104.

[36] Id. 112.

[37] R. Wollheim, "Equality" (1955-56) 56 Proc. Arist. Soc. 281-300 (repr. as "Equality and Equal Rights" in Olafson, Social Policy 111) puts the extreme hypothetical case of a community of 100 members, the first 99 of whom always give their

and knowledge of the world, and knowledge of human nature, all seem to help us, but we cannot say how."[38] Another way of saying this is that the "rights" (in the "political" or "moral" sense), equality of which between all persons is claimed to be the test of justice, turn out not to be rights *stricto sensu*, that is, rights secured by correlative legal duties of others. They are rather at most privileges, or liberties.[39] And the final outcome in distribution of goods among the holders of such "rights" is then conditioned not only by the varied capacities of the holders, but by the legally sanctioned ordering, which sets certain limits within which these privileges or liberties are (as it were) allowed to fight it out.

No one would now argue that the legal order should set no limits on the struggle between individuals of varied strengths, talents and capacities. Indeed, a major part of what we mean by justice is concerned with the question what these legal interferences should be, and when and how they should be introduced to modify the results of the struggle. We observed in 1946 that there was at least one indubitable minimum requirement of justice as sought through law. This is that society shall be so organised that men's felt wants can be freely expressed, that the law shall protect at least that expression, and provide it with the channels through which it can compete effectively for (though not necessarily attain) the support of politically organised society.[40] And this presupposition of justice which we thus stated from the lawyers' aspect seems now to have become rather centrally at issue in current philosophical and political science discussion.

Charles Fried, building on an acute critique of Rawls' positions, has stated the matter, in terms rather parallel to our above position of 1946, as requiring that we posit that the individual is always entitled in the assessment of justice to at least one "interest".[41] Only, he says, if the individual "enters the situation of justice armed with (at least) this single interest, which he could not have won for himself by his own assertion, will his position in asserting any other interest for himself be defensible". Perhaps the point is better stated in the forms that justice presupposes a man's liberty to define his own interests; that it presupposes the moral status of the individual thereby implied;[42] and that what is fundamental in this presupposition of justice is the moral nature of every human per-

---

first preferences to 99 different courses of action, while the 100th also regularly gives his preference to Course 99, preferred by the 99th member. On equality alone, Course 99 should always be preferred; yet few would accept this as the just conclusion, or even as a juster conclusion than that from merely drawing lots.

38 See *id.*, esp. repr. 124-27.

39 See Stone, *Legal System*, Ch. 4, §§6-7.

40 See *id.*, *Province* 785. *Cf.* H.L.A. Hart, "Are There Any Natural Rights?" (1955) 64 *Phil. R.* 175, 185. And *cf.* generally on "equality before the law", Benn and Peters, *Principles* 122-23; Lamont, *Moral Judgment* 134; and on the "equal consideration" which many writers arrive at as the final prescription of equality, *supra* n. 32. This "equal consideration" is clearly essential to what is meant by "fair trial" (*supra* Ch. 10, §10); but it still may not exhaust the content of "justice", or of "fairness", or even of "a fair trial".

41 See C. Fried, "Justice and Liberty", in *Nomos, Justice* 127, 141ff. As to his use of the term "liberty", adapted from Rawls, it is not necessary here to explore the terminological morass into which this and most substitute terms tend to lead. Nor need we pursue Fried's claim (*id.* 143-45) that his position amounts to "granting human liberty an ontological rather than a logical status in the concept of justice".

When, as in Buch, "*Principes Généraux*", "equality" is conceived within "a notion of equilibrium", in a dialectical relation with "liberty" as "a capacity to act to break the existing equilibrium", the indeterminacy of both concepts become commendably but also dismayingly overt.

42 See resp. *id.* 145, 143.

sonality.[43] And whatever relation we may think to be established between fairness, equality and reciprocity, and between each of these and justice,[44] we believe that this presupposition of respect for moral personality requires us to reckon not only with claims made by each individual, and with his needs insofar as these can be objectively ascertained, but also with the consequences for himself and his fellows of what disposition is made both of these claims and needs.[45]

In Rawls' latest positions, indeed, much of this is implicit. Yet they still show how vital it is, in speaking of the above indubitable minimum requirement of justice, to choose our words and speak with care. We must be careful, in particular, not to confuse "justice" with "liberty" (a confusion to which Rawls' Kantian-like position leads him rather inevitably); and *a fortiori* not to confuse it with inflated requirements as to the social structures and hierarchies within which "justice" as we see it is to be done. Rawls, perhaps by inadvertence, is led into the remote territory of "the open society", that is, one in which his two first fundamental principles of justice are observed.[46] He is concerned to show that his first principle (of maximum mutually compatible liberties of members) is the basis of constitutional liberties; and that the second principle (that inequalities must be justifiable as working to everyone's advantage and unequal positions as open to all) bases the "distinctions and hierarchies of political, economic and social forms" necessary for the desired joint activities.[47] So that, finally, for him, "the most important subject of questions of justice" is "the fundamental structure of the social system";[48] and after having warned us not to confuse "justice" with "an all-inclusive vision of a good society",[49] he ends by resolving "justice" into precisely that.[50]

Whatever the merits of this particular vision of society, the question still remains what precepts (if any) express the absolute requirements of justice in the more precise sense within such a society. As to this, we confess that we ourselves can offer only the one above stated, that social arrangements should as a minimum (even if only as a minimum) respect every man's claim to form, entertain, and articulate his own interests. And we are conscious as we do so that despite its importance as a minimum, it cannot advance us much beyond the procedural to the substantive level of the doing of justice. To say that channels must always be open for formation and articulation of interests may, indeed, carry certain implications of substance, notably as to the responsibilities of those who exercise power.[51] Yet it tells us nothing of how far and on what conditions the law should give effect to such interests. To say that the law must intervene to fix the framework for the struggle between men's interests and the extent of the support

---

[43] Cf. J. W. Chapman, "Justice and Fairness", in *Nomos, Justice* 146-169, esp. 168-69.

[44] See *id. passim* for a cogent critique from the historical, linguistic and metaphysical aspect of Rawls' efforts to reduce justice finally to fairness, and to base both on the mutual consent of "rational" beings.

[45] Cf. *id.* 149ff.

[46] *Op. cit.* 107.

[47] *Id.* 117.

[48] *Id.* 106. And cf. his "Two Concepts of Rules" (1955) 64 *Phil. R.* 3.

[49] *Op. cit.* 98-99.

[50] Nor do the critiques by Chapman and Fried cited *supra* nn. 41, 43, succeed in escaping from the misleading matrix into which the drive of Rawls' positions thus leads them. See e.g. as to the use of "liberty", *supra* n. 41. All this is apart from the unexamined identification of "the good society" with the constitutional democracy familiar to him.

[51] See Stone, *Province* 785.

given them in society does not tell us how to distinguish *interventions which are just* from those that are unjust. But then, more ambitious positions focused on equality cannot do this either. Some such modalities as are expressed in the terms "undue" or "unreasonable", or "rational" or "fair", if not in still more frankly evaluative terms,[52] always have to be introduced to handle this stage of the question. And what is required or forbidden by such evaluative terms cannot usually be determined in advance of social experience, including within this the values other than that of mere equality by which the men in the particular society are for the time being moved.[53]

This indeterminacy of equality for justice, whether or not accompanied by the above modalities, is also plain if we approach the matter through the time-dimension of present understanding.[54] When we strip from the principle of equality the prescriptions fastened upon it in course of time by the Judaeo-Christian traditions, and by the insurgency of ethical and political convictions emerging from revolutionary social movements which punctuate human history, that principle becomes very barren of guidance towards justice. The simple and ancient but still important truth is that we cannot insist on equality in all respects, of *both* treatment in law *and* positions in fact.[55] For positions in fact, independent of what the law may do, are always unequal. Equal treatment by the law operating on such factual inequalities of powers, talents and personal fortune, would often sanctify or even deepen such factual inequalities. Yet, on the other hand, to remove or reduce factual inequalities the law must itself resort to unequal treatment of the persons concerned.[56] Our choice is not between equal treatment and the making of distinctions; it is between making (or tolerating) distinctions which we can justify, and making (or tolerating) those which we cannot justify.[57] And we do not escape this reference to what men of the time and place consider justifiable, by using more "objective"-sounding words such as "arbitrary" or "not essentially similar". The gist still always is that equality may be departed from for *sufficient* reason. The crucial determinant is the *sufficiency* of the reason for making distinctions, or for saying that one case is not *essentially similar* to those coming within the rule. This same

---

[52] The evaluative nature of the rider may be very frank, as in E. F. Carritt's "some reason, other than preference, . . . to the contrary" (*op. cit. supra* n. 32, 157), and in the "good grounds" of Benn and Peters, *Principles* 110.

[53] R. Wollheim, *cit. supra* n. 37, at 127; *cf.* R. McKeon, *supra* n. 26, at 61. M. Berger, *Equality by Statute* (1952) 63, sees the line at the point when a "class" becomes a "caste", that is, a group out of or into which movement is made "virtually impossible" by sharpness of distinction in status, prestige or "style of life". And see M. Weber, "Class, Status, Party", in Gerth-Mills, *From Max Weber* 188-89; and *cf. supra* Ch. 1, §2.

[54] *Cf.* Sir Isaiah Berlin, "Equality" (1955-56) 56 *Proc. Arist. Soc.* 301-326, repr. as "Equality as an Ideal" in Olafson, *Social Policy* 128-150, esp. 129ff., 142ff.; Benn and Peters, *Principles* 114-115, 378; C. J. Friedrich, *cit. supra* n. 11, at 28-30.

[55] *Pace* the puzzling distinction in M. Jaeger, *Liberty versus Equality* (1943), when she insists that things and men must be either (absolutely) equal, or not equal, but adds that "they may be equal in some respects and not in others". See the query in Thomson, *op. cit. supra* n. 17 at 10. And see generally on this point *id.* 3ff.; Lamont, *Moral Judgment* 142-43; Brecht, *cit. supra* n. 2, at 67; Benn and Peters, *Principles* 108; A. Ross, *op. cit. supra* n. 31, at 269-274; and Myers, *op. cit. supra* n. 17 at 17ff., with which last *cf.* now the theses of J. Barzun, *The House of Intellect* (1959); J. W. Gardner, *Excellence* (1961); and Benn and Peters, *op. cit.* 118-122.

[56] For views of the equality principle as a demand for such removal, see D. D. Raphael, "Justice and Liberty" (1950-51) 51 *Proc. Arist. Soc.* 167-197; Berlin, essay cited *supra* n. 54, in Olafson, *Social Policy* 137ff. In this kind of context the word "inequality" is pejoratively used to mean one that ought to be abolished. See Benn and Peters, *Principles*, 118, and Lamont, *Moral Judgment* 139.

[57] Benn and Peters, *Principles* 115; *cf. id.* 127.

question (as we saw in the last Section) still lurks within the word "precedent" when we are told that justice means following "precedents", even when (perhaps especially when) this is offered as the lawyer's solution to the philosopher's puzzle.

Not only is some such modification of the equality principle unavoidable, but what this modification should be must spring from some other values than equality. What has still to be determined in relation to any absolute precepts of justice offered, is the justification in the given kind of situations of the value other than equality which requires us to depart from equality. There may be relevant to this any of a multitude of factors, for instance, the present environment, the capacities of individuals, their past or potential contribution to social or cultural values or good government, or even perhaps (somewhat ironically) to the achievement of equality among the rest of the community. In a sense, of course, equality remains *some part* of justice insofar as it is not to be departed from save for sufficient reasons. Yet many of the hardest problems of justice, those for which men murmur, cry out, struggle and often die, concern the question, What are sufficient reasons for departing from it? All this points to the truth that justice, far from being adequately described in terms of equality, is more usually a settlement (whose terms vary with time and place) between equality and other values.[58] This is a truth concerning *men's* efforts to give reality to justice, independently of any questions of absoluteness or universality of the ideal of justice in general. It is certainly a cardinal truth for all who are concerned with making or administering human law, or with the evaluation of their efforts. What men have in history achieved in these settlements in the course of their drive for justice, and how far we can hope to hold fast to those settlements, are vital aspects of the here-and-now of our own problem of justice. The terms of these settlements may be more informative in our search for indications of the material content of justice than any elaboration or refinement of the principle of equality itself, beyond (that is) the minimal presupposition of the title of all members of society to form and express their own interests.[58a]

§4. MATERIAL CONTENTS OF JUSTICE PERMEATE BOTH PHENOMENA OBSERVED AND OBSERVATION OF THESE BY SOCIAL SCIENTISTS. All this, of course, stresses the more the importance in the norms of justice of those material precepts which emerge in the doing of justice in concrete societies. But, also, by this very same token, such precepts cannot be offered as expressing "absolute" normative requirements of justice. To pass from

---

[58] *Cf.* Berlin, essay cited *supra* n. 54, at 148. We agree with Thomson, *op. cit. supra* n. 17 at 9, that both "equality" and "liberty" remain important criteria, even though both are hemmed in. They are hemmed in by the making of further distinctions in terms of each other or of other values, and ultimately of asserted "advantage to all concerned". *Cf.* Benn and Peters, *Principles* 111-112; Hart, *Law* 154-161; Lamont, *Moral Judgment* 160; and on the kind of argument involved *id.* 140-48 and *supra* §2. On the affiliations between "equality" and "liberty" see Thomson, *op. cit.* 20-24, 136-155, esp. at 147; and Lamont, *op. cit.* 158-161. And *cf.* the brief discussion in W. Friedmann, *Legal Theory* (4 ed. 1960) 385-89.

[58a] It is, therefore, not only unhelpful to further discussion, but also somewhat pretentious, for advocates of the Kant-like criteria "equal liberty" or "fairness" to appropriate the name "justice" to their criteria, and reduce other criteria to terms of pejoration, as is done with "utilitarianism" by J. Rawls, "Constitutional Liberty . . ." in *Nomos, Justice* 98ff., esp. 124-25. This is quite apart from the merits of the respective criteria, as to which we agree with J. W. Chapman's cutting criticisms of Rawls' position in *id.* 147ff. *Cf.* on this aspect, *supra* Ch. 4, §§22-23. And see H. A. Bedau, "Justice and Classical Utilitarianism" in *Nomos, Justice* 284-305.

acceptance of precepts in historically given societies to assertions of them as "absolute" would be to ignore the gap (or pretend to have leaped it) between facts and values, between the "is" and the "ought". But the gap cannot be ignored, nor can it really be leaped; and we have seen that attempts to bridge it have hitherto ended in defeat. The most promising attempts, we saw, proceeded from the tendency of men to assert as "facts which generate norms" what on closer examination prove to be "fact-value complexes", notions of facts with values built into them. But while this certainly brings such precepts (if they did not already and obviously enter of their own accord) into the realm of "values", they remain such only for the valuing agents who hold to them. The step from "values" of this kind, with which men of the particular society have chosen to fructify their perception of the facts of the world, to the discovery of "absolute" or "universal" or "objective" ideals, remains still unwarranted.

Despite all this, the yearning for a fusion of facts and values, which we have examined in the work of natural lawyers, and of others like Maihofer and Fuller,[59] continues to show itself, curiously enough, among sociologists. Philip Selznick has recently suggested that the modern sociological "dogma" of the separation of facts and values is due to the "drift" of sociology towards "positivism", with its demand that study of facts be free of the observer's value preferences.[60] He seems to suggest that the "dogma" is somehow discredited by the fact that whenever the social scientist studies friendship, scholarship, the family, citizenship, democracy, or other like phenomena, there is presupposed reference to some normative model of the named relation or institution. For, without this, the very subject-matter of the given social scientific inquiry cannot be identified. The point was made a generation ago, in relation to legal realist controversy, that such ideals as held by judges are indubitably a kind of facts falling for examination along with other facts within the ambit of social science. It remains correct now, even if it be dispiriting that the parallel point still needed to be made for social scientists in 1964.[61] What is wrong, however, is to suggest that this point disposes of the problem of the separateness of the spheres of "fact" and "value", or shows that "a modern version of natural law philosophy is needed for a proper understanding of the law, as well as for the fulfilment of sociology's promise".[62] And the error is scarcely neutralised by an accompanying denial that the social scientist need feel any commitment to the ideal which he uses to identify this subject-matter.[63]

Insofar as we accept the modern emphasis on "learned" as distinct from "innate" human behaviour in the formation and operation of values, and the matrix which this presupposes of transmission of values through symbol communication and social roles,[63a] we are led to positions both more and less "relativist", and in any case much more complex, than Selznick's critique would suggest. On the one hand, this matrix does not exclude the influence of biogenic and psychogenic factors in behaviour, which may well yield "natural" uniformities. Nor does it deny that *some* of the

---

59 See *supra* Ch. 7, §§11.
60 P. Selznick, "Natural Law and Sociology", in Cogley (ed.), *Natural Law* 154-194, at 157-163. *Cf.* F. H. Knight, *cit. supra* n. 12 at 15-22.
61 See Selznick, *op. cit.* 160.
62 *Id.* 156.
63 *Id.* 159-162.
63a See Stone, *Social Dimensions*, Ch. 9, §13.

interaction of individuals which shapes their valuations and conduct "is on a non-cultural or natural-sign level, so that some learned behaviour is universally human and independent of specific cultures".[63b] Arnold Rose correctly points, however, to other vital matters as militating against "cultural determinism", which (we may add) militate also against any natural-law universality of men's value postures. First, the generality of most cultural values and expectations leaves room for considerable individual choice within the limits which they prescribe, and, second, the very fact that most expectations are in terms of "roles", rather than of behaviour required of specific individuals as such, reinforces this generality. Third, for some roles, e.g., of the scientist and the prophet, it is not conformity but innovation and variation which are of the essence of the role-expectation. Fourth, the culturally transmitted materials include not only prescriptive values, but "cultural *meanings*" which "prescribe" only possible and not obligatory behaviour. Fifth, individual choice and also individual innovation may arise from the frequent internal inconsistencies in the culture, and sixth, innovation may similarly arise when the culturally-expected behaviour is "blocked". It should be added, seventh, that learned behaviour is subject to frequent and not predetermined change, since "communication of human norms is seldom precise, and what is transmitted to and internalized by the human individual or group . . . is constantly re-evaluated and modified in the light of new experience."[63c]

We need not swallow "cultural relativism" whole, moreover, to question Professor Selznick's critique of it.[64] The social sciences, he says, seek to describe "system" in personality or group structure, and assume that they know what are the "needs" or "functional requisites" for any system, be it of personality or group structure, to sustain itself. Sustention cannot be reduced, he moreover agrees, to mere survival, and as soon as we get beyond "mere survival" we are involved in kinds and levels of organisation identifiable only by reference to certain "master ideals". So that the social scientist's observation and description then have to embrace evolutionary development of the system towards increased realisation of its "implicit ideals". With all this we agree;[65] and we would add that within the field of social psychological description of values itself, there may be room not only for mere pragmatic handling of justice, for instance by reference to prevailing "aspirations in the given society", but also for explicit and systematic formulation of man's overall goals and programmes.[66] But far from this basing "a *rapprochement* between sociology and natural law" by a bridging of fact and value, its tendency is quite the opposite. For as our analysis, for instance, of John Wild's position has shown,[67] the natural law thesis that value is embedded in objectively observable facts breaks down precisely on this very same point that, *beyond mere survival*, the question what is necessary for the perfection of a creature becomes involved in clashing ideals even among the most wise. Social scientists nevertheless, we agree, deal with these ideals as facts, and should not allow any "dogma" of relativism to block inquiry concerning "what human nature consists of",[68]

[63b] See A. M. Rose, "A Systematic Summary of Symbolic Interaction Theory", in *id.*, *Social Processes* 3, at 14-15.
[63c] See Jacob-Flink, *Value Decision* 13.
[64] *Id.* 164-170.
[65] See Stone, *Social Dimensions*, Ch. 1, §2.
[66] *Cf.* I. Jenkins, *cit. supra* n. 4, esp. 201ff.
[67] *Supra* Ch. 7, §3.
[68] *Op. cit.* 170.

but rather remember that the central teaching of cultural relativism has been that of "respect for others that are human".[69] Yet it is surely wrong to **imply that objective knowledge of values** (beyond that of mere survival) is drawn by natural law from the facts of existence; for it is precisely beyond this point that natural law theorising also becomes quite problematic. What natural law has to offer as to these values (including the values of justice) is rather *the affirmation of their importance*. And if Selznick's thesis is limited to this, he should rather have framed it in terms of the need for social scientists to attend to the theory of justice in general than in terms of natural law, which is but a specific kind of such theory.

§5. MATERIAL CONTENTS OF JUSTICE ARE CONTROLLED NOT ONLY BY CONSTANT ELEMENTS IN NATURE (INCLUDING HUMAN NATURE), BUT BY CHANGING AND OFTEN UNIQUE ELEMENTS IN HUMAN EXPERIENCE. Concern with "human nature" is common to every sophisticated theory of justice and not unique to natural law. No doubt if "human nature" could be shown to include certain universal features, these might be made the basis for propositions about ethical behaviour which would be both material and absolute. This would establish at least one main plank of classical natural law positions.[70] It might also, by the same token, give us some material absolutes of justice, but only if the kind and range of behaviour involved is relevant to "justice". That men should propagate their kind, for instance, may be a "natural law", but is a comparatively remote concern of justice. And so with many of the "unities" of human nature which natural lawyers detect. Selznick, for example, lists "the search for respect . . ., for affection, and for surcease of anxiety"; and potentialities like those for "union of sex and love", for "enlargement of social insight", and for reason and aesthetic creativity.[71] The relevance of the need for respect is implied in our own minimal precept already offered;[72] but for the rest, all that *such* unities seem able to tell us about justice is that in a just society it should not be made impossible for men to realise such yearnings and potentialities.[73]

And even if this last be an important requirement, it is still rather formal than material, being equally applicable whatever be the contents of the yearnings and potentialities found among the members of the particular society.[74] The requirement that realisation of men's "natural" needs and potentialities should be fostered is finally but one aspect of the minimal

---

[69] *Id.* 169.

[70] Thus J. Cogley, Intro. to *id.* (ed.), *Natural Law*, at 20, reduces the defining assumptions of iusnaturalist positions to three: (1) a common nature of all men, distinguishing them from both beasts and angels, with rationality as the distinguishing mark allowing them (2) to learn the ends of human nature and (3) to relate their moral choices to these ends. But for other necessary hallmarks of traditional natural law, see *supra* Ch. 10, §§2-4.

[71] Selznick, essay *cit. supra* n. 60, at 169. On such grounds we must obviously agree with F. H. Knight (*cit. supra* n. 12, at 5) that Ortega y Gasset's "Man has no nature; what he has is—history", stretches truth to literary hyperbole. And see *supra* nn. 63a, 63b, 63c.

[72] *Supra* §3; and see *infra* §6, directives I, VII.

[73] *Cf.* J. W. Chapman, *cit. supra* n. 43, at 152, though the link there offered with "fairness" seems artificial.

[74] To make it absolutely valid, indeed, we should have to add that it applies only to yearnings and potentialities not too grossly inconsistent with others of the society's values: homicidal yearnings, however widespread, should plainly not be provided for. *Cf.* Blackshield, "*Pensiero Umano*" 479-480. So that even this "absolute" of justice must to this extent derive its content from material values other than justice. *Cf.* our comment on Pound, *supra* Ch. 9, §§4ff.

absolute precept we have already offered, namely that men must be free to assert their interests. Its material content is correspondingly at large.

The main difficulty remains that beyond some very limited "unities" of the above kind, and certainly as to the broader range of men's ethical demands, universal "unities" of human nature are not easily shown. Any attempt to rely complacently on the above kind of "unities" as demonstrating that men's values in general are likely to be universally held simply overlooks a capital distinction. This is between yearnings and needs which "reflect primarily the impulsive demands of the biological organism whose satisfaction is essential to the survival of the organism", and those which "have been shaped by layer upon layer of learned standards of social propriety".[74a] Obviously expectations of this latter kind are far less likely to be universally held; yet it is also in this latter area that distinctively *ethical* expectations are more likely to be found, expectations of the former kind having (as we have seen) quite a high degree of "unity" but very little relevance to "justice" or for that matter to ethical evaluation at all. Any "minimum natural law"[75] which might be built on such unities would be to morals at most rather as logic is to knowledge. It might be fundamental, irreducible, inescapable, absolute; but what it would tell us would be so scant and commonplace as to help little with actual problems.[76] Beyond any such discoverable "unities" we might, if we are sanguine, seek some kind of quasi-absolutes, by weaving together the requirements of varying "human natures" in a way which at least avoids inconsistencies among them.[77] But this would yield not any *one* natural law with material content, but as many such as there are distinctly discernible types or groupings of men. Such a "natural law", *so far as it claimed to be universal*, would have to be a formal category, into which different contents for different types of man can be poured. The matrix would be universal but merely formal; the *content* would be material, but not universal.

We must observe at this point that the assumption that to be value-significant "human nature" must be universal, is itself unwarranted. Natural law thinking may have made its own task unnecessarily difficult by assuming, in Berkeley's words,[78] that for a thing to be "natural" to the mind of man,

---

[74a] See Jacob-Flink, *Value Decision* 20, criticising the scheme of values offered by Lasswell-Kaplan, *Power*, for its obfuscation of this distinction. *Cf.* the former authors' criticism *ibid.* of value-conceptions which focus exclusively on "preferences", with no distinction between "drives and/or cathexes" and "preferences which are supported by . . . internalized sanctions"; and their own distinction (*id.* 22-23) of "values" from "beliefs" and esp. from "impulses". See on this last *supra* Ch. 10, at n. 96b.

[75] As to which see Hart, *Law* 184-195. Collected analyses of the basic beliefs of the world's main cultural traditions, such as may be found in (1951) 5 *Nat. L. Inst. Proc.*, or in P.T. Raju (ed.), *The Concept of Man* (1960), suggest indeed that there *may* be a "minimum" natural law of this kind which is universal. But despite appealing hints, nothing more is really established.

[76] See Cohen, *Ethical Systems* 105. "Not only is the value of universality limited . . . by the experimental value of diversity, but the amount of universality to be found in positive law decreases with great rapidity as we extend our view of political institutions."

[77] See, e.g., F. S. C. Northrop, *The Meeting of East and West* (1946); *id.*, "Naturalistic and Cultural Foundations for a More Effective International Law" (1950) 59 *Yale L.J.* 1430. And see Stone, *Social Dimensions*, Ch. 3, §6, Ch. 12, n. 2; and the collections cited *supra* n. 75.

[78] *Alciphron, or the Minute Philosopher* (1732) I. 14 (in A. A. Luce and T. E. Jessop (eds.), 3 *Works of George Berkeley Bishop of Cloyne* (1950) 55). The dialogue is between two Christians and two free-thinkers, the arguments quoted being offered by a free-thinker to prove that it is not "natural" to believe in God.

it must have been there at the origins,[79] and be universally and invariably[80] there. As to universality, Berkeley pointed out that just as the same plants under different conditions and cultivation may "naturally" show different features,[81] so "things may be natural to men, although they do not actually show themselves in all men, nor in equal perfection; there being as great difference of culture, and every other advantage, with respect to human nature" as there is with plants.[81a]

Berkeley addressed all this to formulations in terms of what is "natural"; so that its most obvious drive in the present context relates to theories of "natural law".[82] Its point, however, goes to all theorising about justice which regards men's actual or potential nature as relevant; and as already seen, all theories of any sophistication do regard it as relevant.[83] Moreover, it prods us to insist, with all proper caution against the revival of naive faith in the inevitability of human advances, that "variability" of men's ethical convictions in time *may be* a matter of ethical progress. Many precepts to which we currently hold, for example, even if an honest backward glance at history would not have detected them as either actually or potentially present in man's earlier exhibited "nature", may still have to be declared such that they *ought* to have been universal, and ought never again to be lost. We are entitled, in short, after confronting rather than evading the difficulties of intellectual demonstration, to affirm that such precepts are *for us at any rate* absolutes. And with this preliminary we shall venture in these concluding pages to speak of some such precepts as "quasi-absolutes of justice". We do not assert by this that these have always been present, biding their time (as it were) in the hurly-burly of social and cultural change; their appearance rather represents sometimes the product, sometimes the storm-centre, of hard-won struggles at crucial points in that change. For this reason, and because of so many unnecessary overclaims and confusions

[79] Berkeley's refutation of this supposed need for originality, that organisms develop features not there originally (as trees develop fruit), is however open to the reply that the *potentiality* for the feature claimed to be "natural" is present *ab initio*.

[80] Berkeley is of course right to see "universality" and "invariability" as distinct, but for present purposes the two ideas are thoroughly intermingled, perhaps inextricably.

[81] It is "natural for an orange-plant to produce"; but "plant it in the north end of Great Britain, and it shall with care produce, perhaps, a good salad; in the southern parts of the same island, it may, with much pains and culture, thrive and produce indifferent fruit; but in Portugal and Naples it will produce much better with little or no pains". (3 *Works* (ed. *cit.*) 56.)

[81a] *Ibid* (3 *Works* 57). The argument from plants is of course only by analogy or metaphor and not formally conclusive. A further argument showing that "a thing may be natural and yet admit of variety" is then found in the fact that while *language* is natural, there is a great variety of *languages*.

[82] Indicating that the content of natural law may vary as between different cultures and environments, yielding a kind of "natural cultural relativism". The natural lawyer's problem about "variability" from time to time would also be eased. Not so perhaps variability *between natural lawyers' pronouncements* about men and natural law of the same time and place, still prominent in contemporary efforts to state a common position. See Cogley (ed.), *Natural Law, passim*. The contributors to this effort to refurbish natural law for modern use are notably at odds as to many basic aspects of natural law. They also have to spend much time repudiating still other common "misinterpretations", without any coherent "true" interpretation of their own emerging. See, e.g., 36-47, esp. 38, where R. M. Hutchins tries to dispose of this as arising from "rhetorical difficulties", and from the mere inadequacies of "traditional natural law" for the modern scene.

[83] All the above is apart from the point that even if "universality" of a practice or belief or characteristic could be shown to exist, this might also defeat the natural lawyer's purposes. For such "universalities", once recognized, would most likely include by the same token much which the natural lawyer would not wish to sanction. See *supra* Ch. 7, §3 and *cf.* Cohen, *Ethical Systems* 103.

associated with natural law, we believe that it would be both historically wrong, and perilous to clear thought, to dub such quasi-absolutes as "natural law", even "natural law with a changing content".[83a]

§6. IDEALS WHICH MAY BE REGARDED AS QUASI-ABSOLUTE PRECEPTS OF MATERIAL JUSTICE IN OUR OWN TIME AND PLACE. It is in the terms thus carefully explained that we now make bold to say, therefore, that for men in the industrialised West at the present stage of history, there have emerged from the interplay of man's nature and potentialities with his environment, of individuals with each other and with their cultural settings, of theories of justice with "the common sense of justice", certain material precepts of justice which we regard as indubitable for our generation of men and in this sense quasi-absolute. The attempt to formulate these is momentous, even when the contents seem modest, and when they offer orientations for general concern rather than specifications for particular problems. This is so, moreover, even though by the very token that they have material content, they cannot in a Kantian sense be absolute, but only quasi-absolute— absolute so far as it is given to us, to our generation of humans, to know and act by absolutes. We formulate them thus, as a series of directives:[84]

I. Social arrangements must leave everyone free to form and assert his own interests, treating every adult sane person as morally autonomous.

II. The adjustment or shifting of advantages and burdens (including rewards and punishments) for purposes of social control through law, should proceed in terms of the goods and evils of this world only.

III. It is always incumbent on an actor to discover with maximum possible accuracy all aspects of the situation in which he acts or fails to act.

IV. Generally all action should respect the principle of reciprocity between persons.

V. Generally all action should respect the principle of equality between persons.

VI. Generally any serious invasions of the socially approved distribution of advantages should be met by the grant of appropriate remedies for the persons injured.

VII. Generally contributions to socially approved arrangements shall be acknowledged, and where appropriate shall be rewarded, by protective immunities or otherwise.

VIII. Generally any serious infringements of socially accepted values, or invasions of the socially approved distribution of advantages, shall be manifestly disapproved, where appropriate by the meting out of punishment.

IX. Punishment shall always respect the human dignity of the offender, and shall in any case not exceed reasonable proportionality to the offence. We may venture to spell out somewhat the meaning of each of these directives.

[83a] In the aspect of their limited range these precepts resemble what L. L. Fuller (*The Morality of Law* (1964), Storrs Lectures 1963 at Yale, 3ff.) calls "the morality of duty" as distinct from "the morality of aspiration". And *cf.* in some aspects C. Morris, "Law, Justice and the Public's Aspirations" in *Nomos, Justice* 170-190. We do not think that the introduction of a further and somewhat artificial refinement of the duty concept is necessarily very helpful.

[84] In this formulation I am much indebted to discussions with my colleague A. R. Blackshield after publication of his "Empiricist and Rationalist Theories of Justice" (1962) 48 *Arch. R.- und Sozialph.* 25. We have avoided the psychological form of his statement there (see esp. 89-91). And see his *"Pensiero Umano"* 482-84.

I. *Directive as to Free Assertion of Interests.*[85] This directive has already been considered in §3 above, and its wider corollary as to freedom to realise human potentialities generally has been referred to in §5. Although we have seen that its final significance may seem mostly procedural or formal, its importance as a basic presupposition places it at the very outset of any attempt to state the "quasi-absolutes of justice" for modern societies. Justice, we wrote in 1946,[86] is a function of three variables: first, the psychological facts of men's wants, demands, desires or claims, varying constantly in time and place; second, the resources of persons, commodities, environment and services available in the time and place for their satisfaction; and third, the outlets for tension between these wants, demands, desires or claims and these available resources, outlets ranging from the primitive "running amok" on the one hand, to the complex refinements of modern legal systems on the other. What is true of justice within the law is also true of the human justice which should inspire the making of law: that there should be available always orderly channels and procedures through which men can freely form and express their interests.

II. *Directive as to Earthly Justice.* Here again prime importance is attached to the recognition that in the Earthly City justice requires law, even though it cannot be wholly replaced by law.[87] This directive instructs us that we are not entitled to excuse (as many if not most earlier ages have done) the continuance of human injustice, by flourishing the blandishments of the Heavenly City. It instructs us too that justice is a function of material as well as psychological and spiritual well-being, and of concrete opportunity as well as abstract liberty.[88] John Cogley has recently affirmed, from the viewpoint of natural law, that "even its most ardent proponents do not hold that observance of natural law will produce the Kingdom of God. Natural law, rather, is directed toward making a decent place of the city of man by bringing moral order to the human communities found on earth."[89]

III. *Directive for Conscientious Discovery of the Context of Action.* The directive to consider the whole context of action requires that we obtain as full a picture as we can of all the facts and values involved in it, and

---

[85] See Stone, *Province* 785; C. Fried, in *Nomos, Justice* at 145; J. W. Chapman, in *id.* 168-69.

[86] *Op. et loc. cit.*

[87] *Cf. supra* Ch. 1, §6, Ch. 10, §10; and see Dowrick, *Justice* 28-29.

[88] No doubt a concept of Divine justice may serve as a standard or goal in the light of which to modify and improve the working of human justice, and as a source of further development of the practical ideals of human justice. But predictions of Divine justice should never be a substitute for doing human justice, as they have sometimes been in the hands of pious oppressors. G. Del Vecchio, "Divine Justice and Human Justice" (1956) 1 *Juridical R.* (N.S.) 147, seems to subordinate human justice rather too much to the Divine. When, as e.g. in his *Humanité et Unité du Droit* (1963) he affirms that Divine justice imports rendering good for evil, this is an even more unacceptable substitute for human justice. *Cf.* I. Tammelo, Book Review (1964) 50 *Arch. R.- und Sozialph.* (forthcoming), who observes that this "seems completely to destroy the concept of justice as a useful tool of thought", and that this kind of Divine Justice had better be seen as a more sublime principle which may over-ride human justice when the Divine intelligence deems this appropriate. And see Stone, *Social Dimensions*, Ch. 15, §§23-24.

[89] Cogley (ed.), *Natural Law*, Intro. 27-28; and *cf.* J. C. Murray, S.J., in *id.* 48, at 69-70. And *cf.* R. H. Cox, "Justice . . . in Locke", in *Nomos, Justice* 243-261, esp. at 253 asserting that the need, if justice is to exist, to know and respect the clear and rigid distinction between the things of this world and the things of the world to come, amounted to a central thesis of the work of John Locke. And *cf.* R. Polin in *id.* 262, at 263, and at 279-80, drawing support even from Locke's pronouncement (*Treatise of Civil Government* (1690) II, xiv, §168) that in matters of abuse of political power "there can be no *Judge on Earth*".

especially the competing values associated with the facts. Since all of these are to be affected by the action decided upon, failure to do what is possible to take them into account is a failure of justice regardless of how the decision goes. An extreme application of this directive as to the facts is that it cannot be just to penalise disobedience to a norm which commands what is in fact impossible.[90] But also generally we know the shock of discovering new relevant facts after a decision has been made.[91] The man in the street may often be found to frame judgments in disrespect of the present directive; but few of them, once their attention is directed to the matter, would deny (even in terms of a supposed "common sense of justice") that it is an essential preliminary of all just action.

The present directive does not of course mean that it is always unjust to *change* the fact-situation as found, nor does it give sacrosanctity to every value arising in the existing situation. It merely asserts the duties to assess the fact-situation diligently and honestly, and to recognise that values are only to be disturbed after conscious confrontation with other values honestly deemed superior. This directive, in short, has two main imports— respect for the true facts, and for all values involved, even though we may decide then to change some facts, or not to support some of the values.[92]

IV. *Directive of Reciprocity between Persons.* Spelled out, reciprocity here means that in any case where one element in the situation as cognised by the actor is that the situation involves a human being who has done a previous action towards the actor, the actor's response should be required generally to imitate and reciprocate that previous action. This directive is in no sense precise and self-applying but is rather a general guiding standard which should be complied with *except* where it is either obviously inappropriate, *or* in direct conflict with other values to which justice must give priority in the given situation.

V. *Directive of Equality between Persons.* Equality here means that the action taken should be such that it will affect all human beings involved,

---

[90] *Cf.* on this and some other aspects of these directives, A. Brecht, "Relative and Absolute Justice" in M. D. Forkosch (ed.), *op. cit. supra* n. 8 at 21-48. Brecht, however, esp. 33-35, is there offering "absolute" postulates of justice. And see his *Political Theory* (1959) 142ff., esp. 143-44, reducing the doctrine of "the nature of facts" to this same aspect.

[91] *Cf.* Friedrich, *cit. supra* n. 16, esp. 38-39; and on the important related point of the "epistemic interdependence of belief attributions and goal attributions", Hempel, "Rational Action" 16-18. C. Fried, *supra* n. 41, at 143n. (insofar as he is intending to deny the present point) seems rather obscure and unconvincing.

[92] Since we formulated the above we have seen the formidable thesis of H. Prosch, "The Problem of Ultimate Justification" (1961) 71 *Int. Jo. Ethics* 155-174, which in one aspect is a quasi-ontological demonstration of the central place of the context in whatever functions moral justification might be said to perform in human thought and action and feeling (161-62). An act "must issue forth into our social world . . . must agree with the relations in which we do stand to others . . .", even if it is designed to change them (161-62, 172-73). Prosch's thesis is that apart from such questions of explanation the much discussed quest for "ultimate justification" is a search for what cannot exist. There will always be such a non-justificatory explanation behind whatever justification is offered as ultimate. (See 171ff.) He also draws from the importance of the context the corollary that insofar as one's influence (and there-fore responsibility) tends to be greater in the narrower context, the priority in duties may be the very reverse of that usually reached by those who purport to find an "ultimate principle of justification" (e.g., in duty to all humanity) from which all ethical justification must spring. (See 172-73.) For a neat example of the kind of position Prosch is here questioning, see Lamont, *Moral Judgment* 9ff., esp. 10. See more generally Nelson, transl. 200; and see Greene M.R., *The Judicial Office* (1938) 10, who, however, between the wide context he attributes to "moral philosophy and psychology", and the narrow range of what "the law considers relevant", leaves "justice" rather unattached. And see *supra* §5.

in the kind of situation as cognised, equally with each other and equally with other human beings affected by previous action in "similar" situations. "Similar" here involves not merely cognition of conditions, events, acts and persons, but also a judgment of relevance which itself involves evaluation in terms of the ends of action. We have shown that claims to absoluteness of the equality principle, from the Pythagoreans onwards, must be rejected in terms of theory;[93] we add at this point that equality remains a general guiding principle, properly to be departed from where obviously inappropriate or in conflict with other values to which justice must give priority in the given situation.

VI. *Directive for Assistance to those Wronged.* Wherever the situation in which action is required arises from a serious disturbance of a socially approved distribution of advantages, the action should include redress against this disturbance. The ancient ideal of justice as restoring balance and harmony, whether or not it can be supported by theory, seems (at least in this sense) to have received continuing support and reinforcement in modern human experience with justice.

VII. *Directive for Rewarding those Contributing to Socially Approved Arrangements.* Wherever the situation in which action is required is due to a person's contribution to socially approved arrangements, the action taken *vis-à-vis* that person must be such as to express appreciation of this contribution.[94] Whether this expression should be in terms of concrete rewards, or of only deferential action, will depend on the size of the contribution and the sacrifice accompanying it, as well as on the habits and customs as to recognition in the given society, and on the positions generally of the persons involved in the particular situation.[95]

VIII. and IX. *Directives as to Punishment.* It seems correct to say that modern developments in penal theory and practice still leave intact the precept that seriously disapproved action be visited with punishment, even though drastic changes have occurred in the scope of what is "seriously disapproved".[96] As conversely with rewards, punishment may range from the infliction of concrete suffering to merely symbolic manifestation of disapproval by reprimand or the like, varying with the conduct involved, group habits and customs, and the positions of the actor and other persons involved. Modern experience, however, has come to recognise that punishment must not be disproportionate to the wrong to which it responds; and also that punishment which denies a modicum of respect to the dignity of the offender as a human being serves no worthwhile purpose in social life, but on the contrary tends to undermine the sense of common humanity on which finally social life must build.

§7. Precepts of Material Justice and Historically-Given Enclaves

---

[93] See *supra* Ch. 3, §§15-16, and this Ch., 2-3.

[94] See for the refinements and complexities involved when "desert" is sought to be graded as "personal desert", and on the relation of "desert" and "entitlement", J. Feinberg, "Justice and Personal Desert" in *Nomos, Justice* 69-97.

[95] *Cf.* generally Lamont, *Moral Judgment* 154ff.

[96] See F. H. Bradley, *Ethical Studies* (2 ed. 1927) 26-27; Lamont, *Moral Judgment* 135-36. On the more recent philosophical literature see G. Hawkins, "Freewill, Responsibility and Punishment" in *Australian Studies in Legal Philosophy* 117-137, with which *cf.* Lamont, *op. cit.* c. viii, and Stone, *Social Dimensions*, Ch. 6, §24, Ch. 12, §5. See esp. S. I. Benn, "An Approach to the Problems of Punishment" (1958) 33 *Philosophy* 332 (now rewritten as c. viii of Benn and Peters, *Principles*) for an interesting example of the blending of utilitarian and Kantian notions discussed *supra* §3.

OF JUSTICE. What are from the viewpoint of the dedications of a here-and-now society quasi-absolute precepts of justice, represent in the stream of time the ground of historically won "enclaves of justice", as we here name them. In this aspect the enclaves of justice may be seen in particular societies as embracing also, along with the quasi-absolutes, many precepts not yet clear or settled enough or not yet securely enough held, but giving promise of all this and struggled for as such. The enclaves of justice, as men struggle to seize and try to hold them, may embrace not only areas of lay consensus, but, even more, areas of partial convergence of precepts deriving from different and even divergent theorisings. Outside such enclaves, precepts may continue to conflict with each other, just as the "sense of justice" of some men may conflict with that of others; and this conflict will rarely be resolvable by stringent argument, the antagonistic positions being impervious to formal logic by dint of the diversity of their premises.

In these *outer* areas, if real communication between divergent standpoints is to continue, two things are essential. One is some such clarification of concepts as has been here attempted, not (as it were) to bind the listener's evaluative judgments, but rather to allow the evaluation of one judging subject to be presented to others. More positively stated, this involves that we recognise the importance in any case of sorting out the emotive from the intellectual components of our theories, so as to fix more precisely the points at which and from which our conflicts emerge, and sometimes even the reasons for the divergence. The other essential is to recognise that we must strive for orderly procedures of argument as between the conflicting standpoints, additionally to the stringent procedures of traditional formal logic. We must correspondingly regard these new procedures as worthwhile even though they cannot lead to full demonstration, and may not even lead to any change of conviction or growth of consensus between the listeners. In *Legal System and Lawyers' Reasonings* (Chapter 8) we have appreciated at length the claims of the so-called "new rhetorics" to provide such an orderly instrument of argument and justification. And with a forward glance to our work on *Social Dimensions of Law and Justice*, we here add that, of course, the accepted "places" from which this kind of argument must proceed, must often (if not usually) be drawn from the empirical facts of men's actual lives in actual society. The relations between law and justice and between these and society, must thus be seen as running in courses which mutually penetrate and cross each other, rather than in isolated parallels. And we intend here by the words "law" and "justice" to refer not only to what men do, but also to their theorisings about what they do.

Of the areas *within the enclaves* much more is here to be said. Any theory of justice, we have ventured to suggest, represents a more or less stable equilibrium *within its sincere proponent* between the actualities of individual and social relations as he sees them, and what it lies in him to conceive as the ideal relations of these. We may flee the tensions involved. We may accept some absolute because transcending ideal, given to us for instance by religion, or make for ourselves *a priori* idols in lieu of these. We may deny *any* meaningfulness of the ideal of justice, by scepticism towards whatever is not proven by empirical evidence. Or, accepting the tension because we must, we may seek equilibrium in some form of relativism or of "natural law with a changing content", or some degree of these.

To the holders of most (and possibly all) of these positions, their view of justice, though it looks out upon the affairs of the external world, is a matter of deeply intimate concern. Whether or not his view attains objectivity, in the sense that it appears to be held in common by many or most of his fellowmen, the stand of each is for him a personal act of combined recognition and dedication. For him and within him any theory of justice held is *normative*, binding his own being, even though for the observer what the holder recognises and is dedicated to, and how many men so hold, may be but facts to be noted and described. For the holder the theory is subjective and normative. Yet when we look at the same matter *sub specie humanitatis* and in the stream of time we can see that particular views which men have held of justice may come to have objectivity also in a very different sense. For the endless variety, change and conflict in men's views of justice down centuries and millennia have not prevented the appearance of what we have here ventured to call "enclaves of justice" in the practice of particular societies, or groups of them. And some parts of these enclave areas already yield even some precepts which we have dared to call "quasi-absolute".

In most Western societies, indeed, our very success in seizing and holding some of these enclaves may be the source of new difficulties of theorising about justice. We have seen, for example, the difficulties faced by the principle of equality of human beings as a basis of justice. In the present and indeed the general view, this principle, unless given more specific content by reference to values other than equality, leaves unavoidable choices so wide as to destroy any guidance which can be drawn from it. Yet in earlier phases of these societies where some substantial number of human beings were still excluded from the legal society, the principle of equality did *per se* seem to give guidance. No doubt in such societies some men of the time (philosophers among them) can sometimes persuade themselves that even such exclusion is justified by reference to some other principle than equality, as Aristotle, despite his belief in equality before the law, argued that some men were slaves by "nature".[97] And it has been by no means rare for societies to redefine the class of "human beings" so as to exclude from it some human beings in the empirically observable biological sense. Yet, as soon as such redefinitions lose their ephemeral self-evidence, the principle of equality itself has spoken with an unequivocal voice at any rate against the subjection of some human beings to others as if they were chattels.[98]

The equality principle holds clear directives, in short, for societies where some human beings are mere slaves to others. And to remember this helps

---

[97] And *cf.* as to the rationalisations of U.S. racial prejudice M. Berger, *op. cit. supra* n. 53 at 63ff. No doubt in Aristotle's Greece, and perhaps even in the 19th century southern U.S., the economic importance of slavery as basic to the economic and social structure would encourage rationalisations and even blindness to the whole issue. *Cf.* on John Locke's insistence on unequal property rights and on the exploitation of "natural industriousness" as both demands of and foundations for justice, the essays of R. H. Cox and R. Polin *cit. supra* n. 89, resp. at 260-61, 269.

[98] So E. N. Cahn, "Ego and Equality" (1951) 60 *Yale L.J.* 57, 65, concludes that "equality is . . . 'self-evident' " in the sense that it can become increasingly evident within the workings of the self, and that "men are created equal, not once for all, but progressively". Yet even in terms of abstract formulae for justice based on equal liberty, J. Rawls, in *Nomos, Justice* 98, 111, has shown that cases are conceivable in which slavery might be just as arising from voluntary acceptance by all of "a real and equal risk" of becoming a slave. But see *id.* 113-14 as to the unacceptability of the presuppositions necessary for this to be conceivable.

us to set off, by contrast, the point that once such gross subjection no longer exists the clarity of the equality directive also tends to fade out. Equality then raises questions of sub-classification among human beings, and therefore of what similarities and differences are "essential" for a given purpose. So, we have repeatedly seen, it then becomes often problematical what are the essential similarities and differences by reference to which the ambit of rules of law is to be decided. So far as Stammler's principles forbid the simple exclusion of some men from the legal society, for instance, they would have a clear message for a society which included slaves. But by the same token, a principle which forbad *merely that* would have no *clear* message for most of the burning problems of societies where slavery is scarcely even remembered.

The creativeness thereafter of the principle of equality, for instance in the building of guarantees of civil rights and "rights of man", or natural or fundamental rights, is not an auto-genetic creativeness. It depends on the fruitful union of equality with other values, be these conceived as the sanctity of the human soul through its reflection of the divine maker in the Judaeo-Christian tradition, or of the divinely enjoined brotherhood of man and the fatherhood of God, or man's uniqueness as a reasonable and free-willing creature. Yet, through whatever alliances of values, the enclaves held for justice in Western societies have come to include other precious territory, such as the recognition that justice in the Earthly City must be done in terms of earthly goods, and that justice requires certain general conditions and organisation to be established by the wider society if the entitlements of individuals under it are to have reality. Yet what precisely are those conditions and organisation remains an area of tensions and struggles, not yet securely held; just as within the settled enclaves the area of the mind and spirit is recognised *in principle* as not an area of legal coercion, even while tension and struggle continue as to what is the precise area of this immunity.

It is obvious that from time to time new content has entered into men's felt obligations to their fellows issuing from great acts of prophetic leadership. These, whether of secular or (more usually) religious origin, are cases of what we have elsewhere called revolution in ethical growth.[99] It is clear that they are rare. It is clear also that even when they occur, new content only slowly makes its way into the actual texture and process of group life. Not only among the ancient Israelites has the generation which receives the liberating revelation had to live out its slavish days in the desert. In any case, the present concern is not with such rare dispensations, but with the ordinary growth of men's ethical experience (especially their experience of justice) and the precepts which this experience enjoins.

In these terms it seems clear that the *theories* of justice dominant in a given time and place are usually, one way or another, emanations from what we here call the enclaves of justice occupied by the group. An enclave is, as it were, a complex of attitudes and roles and expectations, and attendant values, stably manifest in concrete segments of the group's arrangement and activities. From the standpoint of the outside observer it consists of empirically observable facts, even though within the group members it may be felt as productive of norms, and thus of obligations.[100] When

---

[99] See Stone, *Social Dimensions*, Ch. 12.

[100] I am indebted for much clarification of this and some other points to the

we say that theories of justice are emanations of the enclaves of justice held, it is to be stressed that the enclaves are not themselves theories of justice, nor substitutes to displace such theories as criteria of judgment. The theories are rather attempts (often competing attempts) to explain or justify or extend or retract or modify the ambit of the enclaves held.

Such theories remain important for themselves. They also serve, however, in the stabler Western social and legal orders, five vital functions in relation to the enclaves from which they spring. One function, on the unstable peripheries of the settled enclaves, is to aid exploration, defence or extension of the territory of the enclave at unstable points along its frontiers. The theories are (as it were) offered as maps to guide, as claims of title, and as battle-cries on the margins of areas of working consensus already gained. Marginal questions of this kind, for example, now affect the limits of the trade union's power to exclude or penalise members; but these do not bring into question our acceptance of union organisation and action as part of the requirements for justice in economic relations. A second function is to explain the inherited enclaves of consensus to on-coming generations, and to keep consensus stable and continuous in face of social change and the minor traumas which may accompany this. A third function is as a weapon against deviation by existing power-holders from expectations based upon the enclaves held. The due process of law notion as used against governmental power is, in some of its many aspects, a kind of mnemonic for certain of these more or less articulate expectations. A fourth function, closely related, is as a means of pressure on new centres of power emerging from time to time in society, to demand their acceptance of responsibilities which traditionally go with power. It is precisely in this spirit that A. A. Berle, Jr., for instance, has raised questions whether great modern corporations should not submit to due procedures in their power to hire and fire, or to remove their plant from an area whose population wholly depends on it.[101]

We should add, perhaps, before leaving the relations between enclaves and theories of justice, that these theories may be emanations from enclaves held also in the sense that they articulate a reaction (sometimes a violent reaction) to the contents or the limits of these enclaves. Such theories, like those which mark ethical revolutions sparked by charismatic leaders, bring out again the ambivalent nature of justice-theorising as between rebellious insurgency and conservative rationalising. Mostly, however, the emanation of theories of justice from the enclaves is by way of rationalising for the present generation (in a non-pejorative sense) what is held and the

discussions of a late draft of these Sections at a meeting of the Australian Society of Legal Philosophy, on April 20, 1963, and to consequential comments, esp. by Father B. Miller and Mr. R. C. L. Moffat.

In important respects Buch, "*Principes Généraux*" has sought to express what we here seek to state through the notion of enclaves. He sees such principles as a legal expression of relations "in a given stage of civilisation" (61), formulated through "enlightened individuals" but consolidated only by penetrating "to the most general knowledge of human society" (63), and concretisable only as they emerge in particular historical social situations (69). (The "general principles" notion, however, seems already too overburdened for this further task.) And *cf.* generally on the "integrative, cumulative, and evaluated" nature of men's value experience, A. M. Rose, *cit. supra* n. 64, at 16-17. "There is an *integration* of newly acquired meanings and values with existing ones, a continuing modification. . . . Man's behaviour is a product of his life history, of all his experience, both social and individual, both direct and vicarious through communication with others."

[101] See Berle, *Capitalist Revolution, passim,* esp. cc. i-iii; and *cf.* Stone, *Social Dimensions,* Ch. 7, §18.

title to hold it.[101a] And this implies the most capital point of all concerning the relation of theories of justice to the enclaves of justice. This is that the enclaves as we here conceive them are empirically-given complexes—of environment, attitudes, demands, roles, expectations, felt obligations, and other facts of biological or social endowment—all held in a certain stability within tolerable tensions. They do not therefore authenticate themselves by their mere existence as enclaves *of justice*. It must follow that recognition of them as such, and evaluation of change in them, both imply resort to some ideas about justice which are not *merely* empirically derived. The various theories of justice, as well as being emanations of the enclaves, are also bearers of these other not-merely-empirically derived ideas, including those accepted as divinely revealed. They import, at the least, rational reconstructions of phenomena which are apperceived in the enclave.

We seek here by our enclave metaphor only to lighten somewhat the obscurities of thought about justice as we have exposed them in the perspective of Western history, and to obtain a foothold from which we can approach future tasks. It is certainly not offered as any kind of *conclusion* from our examination of the millenial course of men's thinking about justice. That examination itself with the insights and perplexities, the continuities and breakdowns, the triumphs and failures which it revealed, remain the pith and substance of the present book. Still less is this metaphorical notion to be seen as a new piece of conceptual apparatus for some future justice-theorising. Had we entertained such an ambition, indeed, we would have been stopped in our tracks by the obvious imprecision of the notion.

The point of the metaphor is rather to encourage certain orientations of mood and concern in those who in future address themselves to problems of justice. It directs us, for example, to the historical struggle to achieve the gains which men now hold, as well as to the gains themselves; to the struggle of whole societies, as well as those of individuals, involved in gaining and holding such enclaves, as well as to the forces and conditions, inside and outside the particular society, which threaten what is held, or may help to defend it against such threats. It directs us, as we shall further see, to the emotional as well as intellectual commitments of these struggles. Above all, however, the metaphor serves as epilogue to this work on *Human Law and Human Justice*, and as prologue to the later work on *Social Dimensions of Law and Justice*. We saw, at the end of our study of lawyers' reasonings, that the limited potentialities of stringent reasoning urged the lawyer's concern forward to questions of policy and justice.[101b] So now the study of justice and its theories seems to compel attention to the particular human situations in time and space, to men's past as well as their present, to the actualities of their life together as well as to the theories by which they seek to reconstruct rationally these actualities. The metaphor of the enclave of justice won and held should, above all, suggest these conjunctions; and we offer it here with no purpose more ambitious than this.

§8. ENCLAVES AND THEORIES OF JUSTICE AS TENUOUSLY AND TENTATIVELY HELD. The preceding Section was written in terms apt for democratic

---

101a Of course even theories of justice seen as *mere* rationalisations are not to be discounted as such. They may rather be sensitive *indices*, showing that the rationalisers are indeed sufficiently affected by the value-standard to be led to take the trouble to attempt to justify their decisions by reference to it. *Cf.* in relation to public declarations of "interest" by policy-makers, Jacob-Flink, *Value Decision* 32.
101b See Stone, *Legal System*, Chs. 6-8, esp. Ch. 8, §§4ff.

polities of the Western type. In newly-established states, determined to transform their economies and traditional social structure and ideals, which have come to constitute the most numerous single class of states, public power is usually still struggling to stabilise itself, and the community to set limits to both public and private power. Under such conditions, often involving major individual and social traumas, theories of justice could move to the centre of the political and social stage, and the struggle to vindicate them become crucial for the whole social, political and economic future. In this kind of situation, however, theories of justice such as those examined in the present work, emerging as they do from *Western* experience, are not easy to transpose to such less developed societies. Nor are suitable indigenous theories usually either available or capable of rapid elaboration. The vindication of the abstract international principle of self-determination thus often leaves such a new state before a void of both law and justice in its internal arrangements. The expert called in to draft or improve the law of such a state may find more illumination for his problems in a study of correlations of legal and social change, such as the present writer's *Social Dimensions of Law and Justice*, than in any study of theories of justice as such.

Overall, in all kinds of societies, the deep tragedy of man's life with justice is the fragility even of the settled enclaves, even in the stabler situations. Positions which seemed securely held, and buttressed by the highest levels of intellectual and artistic achievement, disappeared in the Nazi quicksand in Germany between the two wars. Even when an enclave as a whole is firmly held, moreover, it may often be found perilously held, if held at all, as regards some social segment. The society, and its justice, as it were, are then dual and even schizophrenic, as with *apartheid* in South Africa and southern segregationism in the United States, or the legally or socially (or doubly) sanctioned anti-semitism of many societies throughout many centuries. There is the less reason, in the light of all this, for surprise in the fact that theories of justice patterned on Western experience have been short-lived in most new Asian and African states. What is transferred or adopted from the experience of other peoples is likely to be even more fragile, though occasionally, as Indian experience up to the present suggests, it may still prove viable.

This tentativeness of our gains even in the settled enclaves of justice, draws attention to another kind of tension which accompanies our hold at any one time on the enclaves of justice. We have already spoken of the tension within each of us when he seeks the *modus vivendi* which he can sustain between the facts of human relations as they face us, and the ideal of these relations as it lies in us to see them. We now notice that wherever this line of balance comes to rest for most members of a given society, it is also subjected to further stresses and tensions from the practice of justice, which embraces, of course, not only its realisation but its partial or total breakdown as well. This kind of tension, in its turn, reminds us of what we have already much observed, namely, that the *operational* value of a theory of justice, and its social influence in general, seem to be independent of the cogency with which it can be demonstrated to the intellect.

On the one hand, history presents manifold examples of inspiration and guidance to action being provided by theories which, when coldly examined, give at best only the most indeterminate indications. One explanation appears to be that determinacy towards action is a function not merely of the theory as it may be formalised in words, but also of the circumstances of time and place in which it makes its psychological impact, of the enclave of justice (as it were) from which it springs. A theory of justice which hinges on the concept of the "free-willing individual" may seem very indeterminate in a modern "free enterprise" society; it would not seem so in a feudal or caste society. Nor did it seem so in an early nineteenth century England still confronted by much of the regulated social and economic ordering of the pre-industrial-revolutionary era. Moreover, if we *had* to take one position *or* the other (which we do not), we would say that in terms of their social operation theories of justice constantly tend to become enemies of the *status quo*. And we could add that this is what should be expected from what purports to be a standard of criticism of law, law itself being necessarily more fixed and slow-moving than the phenomena it seeks to govern. Yet this would be only part of the story of the social operation of theories of justice. For theories of justice also serve, as we have suggested, to stabilise and preserve, as between the generations, the areas of consensus already achieved.

Obviously the degree of stability and assurance of continuance in the enclaves of justice varies from society to society, and from time to time within a society. A great deal of our study elsewhere of the social dimensions of law and justice bears upon the factors within each society influencing this matter of degree both for law and for theories of justice which serve to criticise its law. We need also to mention at this point, however, certain factors which transcend the experience and conditions of particular peoples, yet nevertheless bear down upon the enclaves of justice among all of them. It is, of course, a truism that the tenuousness of our hold on apparently agreed values is usually more likely to be exposed and broken in a period of shock and frustration, both for the individual and the group. Jaspers may be right in thinking that man's confrontation with the destructive power of nuclear weapons should require him to pursue reason and justice more firmly and constantly than ever before. Yet it is surely also a vast understatement to say that this is not an automatic or even the most likely result of this confrontation.[102]

We have already, indeed, begun to see the evidence which supports the latter point. The new weapons, for example, inevitably strengthen the hands of the State Leviathan against the claims of its own subjects, including claims made in title of justice. And by this we do not only mean (what is obvious enough) that inertia and fear in face of power-holders is likely to be greater as the weapons become more fearful and more exclusively controlled by the power-holders. We mean also that when the nuclear weapons of other states are poised against their own society, the importance of issues of domestic justice comes to seem (no doubt wrongly) rather less momentous to all the citizenry. Preoccupations with justice between subject and subject and government and subject tend to be subordinated to pre-occupations with national survival. This, of course, is not a new phenomenon; it is always found in war-time. The difference is that it now tends to be a phenomenon of peace-time, or (we should perhaps rather say) the no-peace-no-war-time into which peace-time has for the moment turned. These backslidings, arising from the exposed situation in which we now live, tend to be accelerated by corresponding shifts in the interests of

---

[102] K. Jaspers, *The Future of Mankind* (1961) *passim*; see e.g., *id*. 172.

theorists. While the overworked game theories of politics and military strategy are rarely offered by their exponents as a substitute for the criteria of just conduct, they are too easily mis-accepted as such. Even when they are not, the direness of the risks we face tends to demean other issues almost to the point of irrelevance. So that wherever these risks are likely to bear down, truth, and even justice itself, tend to present themselves only in national versions.

We should be aware of these fragilities and backslidings in the present generation of men, not to feed our despair, but to enable us to struggle more firmly and effectively to arrest and reverse them wherever we can, and as best we can.[103] Amid all the stress of our times there is still evidence that men of firmness and courage can protect the enclaves of consensus about justice which have already been won. No one at all familiar with the so-called "McCarthy period" of American politics in the early 1950's, and the course of judicial decisions on civil liberties from that time to this, will fail to recognise an enclave which finally held fast despite what even sober judgment might have predicted at one time. And we should surely not overlook this in the polemics which at present surround the conflicting views as to the proper limits of the functions of Justices of the Supreme Court of the United States. The same country, and to a degree the same kind of men during the same period, have begun to open up the boundary-fence which throughout American history has more or less excluded the Negro segment of American society from the American legal community.[104] Most of the other political democracies could vouch passages of recent history no less encouraging. And the epic efforts of many of the educated classes of India to carry unbroken into the new national life the enclaves of justice inherited from both the British association and the Hindu tradition, have had successes which we may still hope will be no less significant for the future of Asia.

Such undoubted grounds for keeping the human spirit high should not be mistaken for sanguineness and complacency about the future of justice among men. It is perhaps easier now than ever before in human history for all enclaves of justice in most human societies to be reduced and razed, one by one, as it is certainly easier for them all to be destroyed overnight by annihilation of their physical foundations. These very facts make it the more important that we should address ourselves more consciously than ever before to what we mean by justice, embracing in this the meanings we have inherited, but also and above all the *meaning of those meanings for ourselves in our own days*. Those inherited meanings are to be found, in part, in the theories of justice entertained by the men of past times and places in meeting the perplexities of their situations; they must be understood by us, as fully as we can ever understand the situations of

---

[103] On the value and limits of pragmatic approaches to the development of ideas of justice as seen through historical experience of changing public aspirations, see C. Morris, "Law, Justice and the Public's Aspirations" in *Nomos, Justice* 170-190; I. Jenkins, *cit. supra* n. 4, esp. 195ff. The present notion of enclaves is not intended to transcend these limits, but rather conversely to draw attention to the importance of holding on to whatever concretisation a particular society may already have achieved of whatever the justice ideal may mean. This differs too, of course, from Jenkins' own assumptions (*ibid.*) of some "grand design" "unfolding" in the relations of all things (including men) through stages (*qu.* are these historical or logical?) of "necessity", "possibility" and "purposiveness".

[104] See Berger, *op. cit. supra* n. 53, tracing the development up to 1952 in relation to U.S. minority groups generally, with many nice insights as to the limits of effective legal action in this area. And see Stone, *Social Dimensions*, Ch. 12, §6.

others, in that same spirit and context.

This returns us, significantly enough, to the relation between these areas of complex, institutionalised facts of men's stable attitudes and conduct towards each other, which we have called the enclaves of justice for the time being held in the group, and the normative power, the felt obligation for each member, which is the obverse aspect of the fact that the enclave is held. We have seen that one function of theories of justice is to help to transmit to following generations the content of what has come to be felt as obligation in the experience of those who went before. They play a vital role, along with the institutionalising of group attitudes themselves, in the recurring task of inducting oncoming generations into recognition of the values held by the group; or, in Parsons' barbaristic terms, of "internalising" the social values. Yet in another sense neither of these aids to transmission gives assurance of what Cardinal Newman called "real" assent as distinct from mere "notional" assent.[105] Both of them, as it were, are at least one place removed from the intensity of personal *engagement* which is involved for those who actually struggled to establish a particular enclave, or now struggle to extend or defend its frontiers. This, after all, is but another way of seeing why the enclaves are always in danger of being overrun; why it is important to keep this danger before all members of the society; and why it is important that a substantial number of members in each generation become *engagés* in either the defence of the enclaves or the struggle to extend them.[106]

It is precisely to express this importance that these last two Sections have been written to conclude the present book. We shall in our forthcoming work on the *Social Dimensions of Law and Justice*, especially in Chapter 12, approach the consideration of ethical convictions in human groups from the aspect of their psychological growth, structure and operation. To that enquiry the worthiness of any particular contents of men's convictions for acceptance in terms of justice is rather collateral.

In the present Sections we have in advance affirmed that the lawyer's concern with justice must go beyond the question what principles men are found to accept in their lives together, to the question what can be said about the worthiness of such principles for acceptance. We have added an expression (consistently, we believe, with what our later social psychological inquiries will reveal) of faith in the capacity of human communities to struggle towards the more worthy principles, and bear the responsibility of holding to them when they are won.

Theories of justice have been seen as mediating and retrospective, affording us a degree of access to the experience of generations in winning the enclaves of justice we inherit. And they also challenge the present generation to approve and defend, or even to extend these enclaves, and thereby to preserve the old or create new ones, from which in turn other

---

[105] J. H. Newman, *A. Grammar of Assent* (1870) 77-92, and *passim*. For a discussion of the concept of knowledge by "connaturality" or "inclination", or "experiental knowledge", as the basis on which "real" assent is generated see J. Maritain, *The Range of Reason* (1953) 22; B. Miller, "Being and the Natural Law" in *Australian Studies in Legal Philosophy* 219-235, at 223, n. 6. Father Miller has observed (letter to the writer of 22 April, 1963) that when human experience with justice is thus stressed on the positive side, and when "natural law" is understood (as Miller would understand it) as requiring that knowledge from modern social sciences be taken into account, much common ground is exposed. See *op. cit.* 232-33. And see *supra* Ch. 7, nn. 100, 122b.

[106] *Cf.* in terms of justification of values generally, the recent underlying theme of Ch. Perelman, *Justice et Raison* (1963), c. xvi (first pub. 1951).

theories will emerge. Unless enough men in their generation respond to this challenge, the assent on which the existing enclaves with their attendant theories rest is likely to fall back to mere notional assent. To sustain them, however, assent must rather be "real". It must engage not merely the cognitive but the emotive life.

This does not mean that mere knowledge of theories of justice is not itself important. It allows the ideals of past men to be brought forward, making it possible for the present generation to try to transcend them both by rational re-examination, and (above all) by subjecting them to criticism in the light of its own experience with the world. And this criticism, rational re-thinking, and transcending, must be seen as a constant need not only for previously-held and presently-received *theories* of justice, but even more vitally for the *enclaves* of justice themselves for the time being held. For, in insisting that the enclaves of justice which men hold must be ever tenaciously defended, extended and revitalised, we again stress that this is because and insofar as these enclaves are of *justice*.

The question whether an enclave occupied as an enclave of justice is such cannot ever be regarded as finally closed, certainly not by the mere fact that the enclave is for the time being held as such. If (though this would be oversimple) the normative content of the enclaves be viewed as "positive morality", then one steady function of theories of justice is that of "critical morality".[107] For we certainly cannot assume that there is any Hegelian-like inevitability in either the conquest by men of these enclaves, or in the outcomes of the continuous interactions between them and the theories of justice which arise to win the allegiance of men. An enclave held as an enclave of justice must be justified as such whenever theory arises to challenge it.

Nor, even when the critical function of theories of justice thus operates, are we to expect any inevitable Hegelian-like unfolding in men's knowledge of ethics and justice. The point is, rather, that we should be aware of the importance of this interplay and cross-checking in each generation between theories *woven by intellect* and the enclaves *experienced* in social living, and between the past and the present of both of these. And all this spells obviously the likelihood of constant change in men's knowledge of justice, including the risks of backsliding. Without the meanings of past men, to which prevailing theories of justice thus help us to penetrate, inherited enclaves again tend to degenerate into words, gestures, and technical procedures of only vestigial import. Yet unless we also go beyond those meanings, to meanings *for us* in *our* situations, we must fail at the moments of greatest challenge in the privilege and responsibility of *choice* in meeting what is before us.

This imperative forces us, still again, to emphasise that both the doing of justice, and its theorisings, challenge our powers of observing and understanding the society around us, as well as our emotive, speculative and evaluating powers. Part of the hazards which constantly threaten the enclaves of justice held, arise from the endless series of new elements which have to be grasped as we search for the meaning of justice *for us* in *our* situation. Without a rather inconceivable transformation of human powers, the stability and durability of our control over the enclaves of justice could not be assured even if we could detect substantial directives to which all men *at a given moment* would give unqualified assent. In fact,

---

[107] On which see Hart, "Law and Morals" 17-24.

as we have shown, such directives as can plausibly be offered for this purpose at any one time may often be so indeterminate as to provoke chronic disagreement, even in contemporary applications. It is possible, indeed, that the exemplifying set of directives detailed in §6 is at least consistent with most of the many and often conflicting theories of justice which this work has considered. But when theory attempts to give more conceptual precision and operational efficiency, the conflicts encased within the indeterminacies of the directives break out.

In these circumstances, even reasonable and conscientious men might be forgiven some impatience with all the efforts to understand justice. This, however, will not help us either. For however unhappy we be with the answers, the law and its officers cannot avoid being confronted day after day by the questions. Neither they nor we can rest easy with decisions based merely on fortuitous guesswork, even when buttressed by an illusory faith in self-evidence and certainty. Legislators, judges and administrators cannot suspend such decisions pending full clarification and consensus about justice, which would in effect be *sine die*. But they and we must at least do what we can to subject their decisions to reasoned examination. Towards this inescapable need studies such as the present make three contributions.

First, in this situation, they give us an orderly awareness of the intensity and many-sidedness which have characterised the making of judgments of human justice. He who has sincerely followed the strivings of his predecessors, and understood their questions and their replies within the limits of their situations, will not only avoid many pitfalls. He will also recognise the more readily a problem of justice, and be alerted to the responsibilities of choice which he bears in its solution. Second, where some personal choice cannot thus be avoided, he can be guided to the best alternatives thus far offered in human experience, so that he is not confined to what may lie casually to hand. Third, this wider awareness may equip him to preserve a certain diffidence as to the correctness of choices made, so that judgment stays open for review in future cases as insight and experience grow. Nor need this raise dismay or despair; it but reformulates that superb sense of humility and unrest which has marked the approach to their tasks of the greatest lawyers. It is for lawyers above all, and above all when they confront the judgment of justice, that "repose is not the destiny of man", and that the least they can seek is also the most they can win, "an echo of the infinite, a glimpse of its unfathomable process, a hint of the universal law".[108]

It is not given to any generation of men to complete the tasks of human improvement and redemption; but no generation is free, either, to desist from them. In meeting the challenges thus thrown up men can move forward only from where *they* stand, and it is correspondingly vital that they should note, with care and understanding, where this is and how they came to it. For human justice these wider truths bear down with great force, especially when (as too often today) justice must first be recalled to men before they can remember and recognise it. In this situation the continuity of the rich stream of Western thought to which this work has devoted itself becomes more critical than ever. A society in which the questionings of justice cease to be a constant prod and perplexity would not be human in any sense that matters.

---

[108] O. W. Holmes, Jr., "Path of the Law" 457, 466.

TABLE OF CASES

TABLE OF STATUTES

UNITED KINGDOM

STATUTES OF OTHER COUNTRIES

BIBLIOGRAPHICAL INDEX

M

INDEX OF NAMES

N

GENERAL INDEX

NOTE: Where appropriate, the TABLE OF CASES, TABLE OF STATUTES, BIBLIOGRAPHICAL INDEX and INDEX OF NAMES, should also be consulted, these items being generally included in this index only on multiplicity of reference. Cross-references, of course, refer also to any further references in rubrics indicated.